READER IN GENDER, WORK, AND ORGANIZATION

This Reader is dedicated with respect and appreciation to

RHONA RAPOPORT

A pioneer in the field,

a mentor to many, and

a dynamic contributor of insights

on gender, work, and organizations

READER IN GENDER, WORK, AND ORGANIZATION

EDITED BY

Robin J. Ely,
Erica Gabrielle Foldy, and
Maureen A. Scully

AND

The Center for Gender in
Organizations, Simmons
School of Management,
Simmons College

Blackwell
Publishing

Editorial material and organization © 2003 by the Center for Gender in Organizations, Simmons School of Management

Blackwell Publishing Ltd
350 Main Street, Malden, MA 02148-5020, USA
108 Cowley Road, Oxford OX4 1JF, UK
550 Swanston Street, Carlton, Victoria 3053, Australia

The right of the Center for Gender in Organizations, Simmons School of Management to be identified as the Author of the Editorial Material in this Work has been asserted in accordance with the UK Copyright, Designs, and Patents Act 1988.

First published 2003 by the Center for Gender in Organizations, Simmons School of Management

Library of Congress Cataloging-in-Publication Data

Ely, Robin J.
   Reader in gender, work, and organization / edited by Robin J. Ely, Erica Gabrielle Foldy, and Maureen A. Scully
      p.   cm.
Includes bibliographical references and index.
   ISBN 1-4051-0255-1 (hardcover : alk. paper) – ISBN 1-4051-0256-X
(pbk. : alk. paper)   1. Sex role in the work environment.   2. Women employees.   3. Corporate culture.   4. Organizational change   I. Scully, Maureen.   II. Foldy, Erica.   III. Title.

HD6060.6 .R425 2003
658.3/0082 21
                                                                    2002155175

A catalogue record for this title is available from the British Library.

Set in 10/12 Baskerville
by SNP Best-set Typesetter Ltd, Hong Kong
Printed and bound in the United Kingdom
by TJ International, Padstow, Cornwall

For further information on
Blackwell Publishing, visit our website:
http://www.blackwellpublishing.com

I CONTENTS

PREFACE

ROBIN J. ELY, ERICA GABRIELLE FOLDY, AND
MAUREEN A. SCULLY

What does gender have to do with work, with organizations? Everybody goes to work and everybody is involved with organizations. Shouldn't we just focus on our responsibilities and get the job done? Many people believe that thinking about gender, or race, or other dimensions of difference, is distracting at best. At worst, it actually creates problems: the more we think about gender, the more it becomes an issue. Work should be a neutral zone, untainted by politics and personal issues.

Many organizations are predicated on these assumptions. But we disagree, not only because looking at gender, work, and organizations increases our understanding of women and men in the workplace, but also because it enhances our knowledge of leadership, human resources, and other fundamental management topics. Just as one camera lens brings the foreground into focus, while another highlights the background in the distance, a gender lens illuminates facets of organizational life that previously were obscure: when we view organizational life through a gender lens, we understand more about why individuals behave the way they do, why companies are structured the way they are, and why some policies work better than other policies.

We also start from the premise that work and work organizations are not gender-neutral. Work has almost always reflected a gendered division of labor: we can all name traditional "women's work" and "men's work." In our society, organizations have been central to creating and maintaining our understanding of what is appropriate for women and what is appropriate for men. While the participation of women in the workforce, particularly in management positions, has changed dramatically over the last few decades, work organizations have not necessarily followed suit. Most were designed to complement the lifestyle of the middle-class white men who ran them. Though some changes are underway, in most cases work structures and cultures continue to reflect this orientation. But because this is the way organizations have always been, we take this orientation for granted. Only with a gender lens do these assumptions come into view and, once surfaced, become available for evaluation and revision.

But having answered our first set of questions, we immediately face another. What is "gender" anyway? In fact, scholars and practitioners have conceptualized gender in a number of different ways, which have very different implications for how we think about gender in organizations. Part I of this Reader, "Introducing Gender," describes four ways of thinking about gender and the link between gender and organizations. We call these the "four frames." Part I also presents readings that illustrate the four frames in order to differentiate them more clearly. Finally, it elaborates one frame in more detail, the fourth frame, because it illuminates previously unexplored connections among gender, work, and organization. (Because the introductory overview provides the theoretical foundations of the text, the other topic parts often refer back to it. Therefore, it is best to read the topic parts in conjunction with this introductory overview to Part 1.)

Just as a gender lens brings to light certain phenomena, a race lens or a class lens will highlight other organizational dynamics. When we look at work from the perspective of a white secretary, a lifelong clerical worker, we see aspects of organizations that we don't see from a manager's point of view. Taking the perspective of a Hispanic executive reveals other facets of how work is organized, as does the point of view of a janitor who recently emigrated from Jamaica. To understand these perspectives more fully, we not only have to add race and class lenses, we have to apply all three lenses *simultaneously*. Each of us lives many different identities at the same time, and so racial, gender, and class dynamics are thoroughly interwoven in organizations. For that reason, many of the readings we present here address not only gender, but also the intersection of gender and race, gender and class, and sometimes all three.

In this Reader, we take these varied lenses and apply them to key topics in management: negotiation, leadership, organizational change and intervention, diversity, human resource management, and globalization. In each case, we have chosen readings that not only teach us about gender and other dimensions of difference, but also expand our understanding of the topic at hand. Earlier parts focus more, though not completely, on gender dynamics, as we try to clarify what it really means to "apply a gender lens" more broadly and a "fourth frame on gender" more specifically. Later parts bring race and class more to the fore, while continuing to explore gender and the interaction of all three dimensions of difference. In these later parts, the four frames become less central to the organization of the material.

Part VII on globalization adds yet another dimension to our understanding: the world outside the organization. In the other six parts, our view is limited to life inside organizations: organizational change initiatives, compensation, mentoring, and the like. Part VII reminds us that work organizations are deeply influenced by their environment and have a profound impact in return. It continues the focus on dimensions of difference, as well, by adding the dimension of nationality to our mix. Suddenly, class, gender, and race have different meanings and different consequences when we bring in the experiences of people in different countries.

For each part, the overview describes a set of readings that compose a learning module on the topic, often including historic perspectives that have since been updated or traditional views that remain popular but to which we pose alternatives. Key readings – often excerpts from the original publications – are reproduced in this Reader. In addition, the overviews contain numerous references to the literature, which we highly recommend in order to gain a fuller understanding of the ideas. We would also like to direct readers to the website for the Center for Gender in Organizations at the Simmons School of Management, with which the editors of this volume and the authors of the part overviews are affiliated, for additional references and reading materials: www.simmons.edu/gsm/cgo.

I ACKNOWLEDGEMENTS

The Center for Gender in Organizations (CGO) at the Simmons School of Management is committed to collective learning. Crafting this Reader was an exciting adventure in collaboration, as it draws on many ideas and contributions from our community of researchers and practitioners. We appreciate having CGO as a place where we develop our work and find synergies with the work of others. We are especially grateful to the founding Codirectors of the Center, Deborah M. Kolb and Deborah Merrill-Sands, for envisioning the potential of this Reader and providing the opportunity to create it. We also appreciate the important role that Joyce K. Fletcher played in the early stages of the project. Evangelina Holvino, the current Director of CGO, as well as Associate Directors Mary Mattis and Bridgette Sheridan, have provided vital ongoing support.

We thank Simmons School of Management and Dean Patricia O'Brien for supporting this work and providing us a home and a forum for deepening and sharing our ideas about women, leadership, and organizational change. We are particularly grateful to The Ford Foundation for the generous financial and intellectual support that launched and strengthened CGO. June Zeitlin of the Ford Foundation supported the development of CGO from the outset. Jan Jaffe of the Ford Foundation worked creatively with us in developing the idea for this Reader as a way to further our mission of disseminating our ideas. We join them in our wish that this Reader will bring gender from the margins to the mainstream in business education and consultation.

Many colleagues have helped CGO in defining its mission and sharpening our ideas about gender and its relationship to how work gets done and how rewards are shared. Joan Acker, Jean Baker Miller, Ella Bell, Marta Calás, Gill Coleman, Jane Dutton, Aída Hurtado, Judith Katz, David Kelleher, Joanne Martin, Stella Nkomo, Aruna Rao, Barbara Reskin, Linda Smircich, Rieky Stuart, and David Thomas are valuable friends of CGO whose guidance shapes our projects.

This Reader is stronger for reflecting the writings and insights of members of the immediate CGO community, including Lotte Bailyn, Stacy Blake-Beard, Mark Chesler, Douglas Creed, James Cumming, Gelaye Debebe, Ruby Marks, Deborah

Merrill-Sands, Karen Proudford, Rhona Rapoport, Bridgette Sheridan, Susan Sturm, and Judy Weisinger.

We enjoyed tremendously working with the team that contributed to this Reader. Betzaluz Gutierrez-Lezama provided valuable research assistance in the early stages, and Laura Wernick stepped in with crucial assistance at the end. Jodi DeLibertis facilitated the project with superb administrative and operational support. It was a delight to work with our CGO colleagues who joined us in writing Overviews, assembling chapters, and perhaps most importantly, engaging in spirited discussions that shaped our message and our work all along the way: Joyce K. Fletcher, Evangelina Holvino, Deborah M. Kolb, and Debra Meyerson.

We thank the team at Blackwell Publishing for encouraging this project from its intellectual inception through the careful attention to all the details of publication. Rosemary Nixon inspired us to aim high in our vision for this Reader. We also appreciate the tremendous efforts of Nicola Boulton, Rhonda Pearson, Joanna Pyke, Jenny Roberts, and Karen Wilson.

Finally, we thank the countless women and men whose voices appear throughout this Reader, and throughout the research conducted by us and by our colleagues, for offering insights about their lives and work, which will ultimately help the lives and work of other women and men.

Robin J. Ely
Erica Gabrielle Foldy
Maureen A. Scully
Editors

Naming Men as Men: Implications for Work, Organization and Management (1994), David L. Collinson and Jeff Hearn, *Gender, Work and Organization*, 1 (1): 13–16. Reprinted by permission of Blackwell Publishing Ltd.

Complicating Gender: The Simultaneity of Race, Gender, and Class in Organization Change(ing) (June 2001), Evangelina Holvino, *Working paper no. 14*, Sections II and III, Boston, MA: Center for Gender in Organizations, Simmons School of Management, pp. 6–18. Reprinted by permission of Center for Gender in Organizations, Simmons School of Management.

Integrative Bargaining: Does Gender Make a Difference? (1999), Patrick S. Calhoun and William P. Smith, *International Journal of Conflict Management*, 10 (3): 203–24. Reprinted by permission of International Journal of Conflict Management.

In Theory: Gender Versus Power as a Predictor of Negotiation Behavior and Outcomes (1994), Carol Watson, *Negotiation Journal*, April 1994: 117–27. Reprinted by permission of Kluwer Academic Plenum Publishers.

Gender and the Shadow Negotiation (1998), Deborah M. Kolb, *CGO Insights, Briefing Note #3* (December 1998), Boston, MA: Center for Gender in Organizations, Simmons School of Management, pp. 1–4. Reprinted by permission of Center for Gender in Organizations, Simmons School of Management.

Rethinking Negotiation: Feminist Views of Communication and Exchange (2000), Linda L. Putnam and Deborah M. Kolb, in P. Buzzanell (ed.) (copyright © 2000), *Rethinking Organizational and Managerial Communication from Feminist Perspectives*, Thousand Oaks, CA: Sage, pp. 76–98, 102–104. Reprinted by permission of Sage Publications, Inc.

The Difference "Difference" Makes (2003), Deborah Rhode, in D. Rhode (ed.), *The Difference Difference Makes: Women and Leadership*, Stanford, CA: Stanford University Press, pp. 3–50. Reprinted by permission of ABA Publishing.

Gender, Culture, and Leadership: Toward a Culturally Distinct Model of African-American Women Executives' Leadership Strategies (copyright © 1996), Patricia S. Parker and dt ogilvie, *Leadership Quarterly*, 7 (2): 189–214, with permission from Elsevier Science.

The Greatly Exaggerated Demise of Heroic Leadership: Gender, Power and the Myth of the Female Advantage (July 2002), Joyce K. Fletcher, *CGO Insights, Briefing Note #13*, Boston, MA: Center for Gender in Organizations, Simmons School of Management, pp. 1–4. Reprinted by permission of Center for Gender in Organizations, Simmons School of Management.

When Women Lead: The Visibility–Vulnerability Spiral (1998), Kathy E. Kram and Marion McCollom Hampton, in Edward B Klein, Faith Gabelnick, and Peter Herr (eds.), *The Psychodynamics of Leadership*, Madison, CT: Psychosocial Press, pp. 193–218. Reprinted by permission of International Universities Press, Inc.

A Modest Manifesto for Shattering the Glass Ceiling (2000), Debra E. Meyerson and Joyce K. Fletcher, *Harvard Business Review*, January/February: 127–36. Copyright © 2000 by the Harvard Business School Publishing Corporation; all rights reserved.

Action Learning, Fragmentation and the Interaction of Single-, Double- and Triple-loop Change: A Case of Gay and Lesbian Workplace Advocacy (1999), Erica Gabrielle Foldy and W. E. Douglas Creed, *The Journal of Applied Behavioral Science*, 35 (2) June 1999: 207–27, copyright © 1999 NTL Institute. Reprinted by permission of Sage, Inc.

Complicating Gender: The Simultaneity of Race, Gender, and Class in Organization Change(ing) (June 2001), Evangelina Holvino, *Working paper no. 14*, Section V, Boston, MA: Center for Gender in Organizations, Simmons School of Management, pp. 3–9. Reprinted by permission of Center for Gender in Organizations, Simmons School of Management.

Tempered Radicalism (November 1999), Debra E. Meyerson and Maureen A. Scully, *CGO Insights, Briefing Note #6*, Boston, MA: Center for Gender in Organizations, Simmons School of Management, pp. 1–4. Reprinted by permission of Center for Gender in Organizations, Simmons School of Management.

The Transformation of Silence into Language and Action (1984), Audre Lorde, *Sister Out-sider*, Trumansburg, NY: Crossing Press, pp. 40–4. Copyright © 1984 by Audre Lorde, The Crossing Press, a division of Ten Speed Press, P.O. Box 7123, Berkeley, CA 94707.

Meritocracy (1997), Maureen A. Scully, in P. H. Werhane and R. E. Freeman (eds.), *Blackwell Encyclopedic Dictionary of Business Ethics*, Oxford: Blackwell Publishers, pp. 413–14. Reprinted by permission of Blackwell Publishing Ltd.

Mentoring Relationships Through the Lens of Race and Gender (October 2001), Stacy Blake-Beard, *CGO Insights, Briefing Note #10*, Boston, MA: Center for Gender in Organizations, Simmons School of Management, pp. 1–4. Reprinted by permission of Center for Gender in Organizations, Simmons School of Management.

Nickel-and-Dimed: On (Not) Getting by in America (1999), Barbara Ehrenreich, *Harpers Magazine*, January: 37–52. Reprinted by permission of International Creative Management, Inc. Copyright © 1999 by Barbara Ehrenreich. First appeared in *Harper's Magazine*.

Building Successful Multicultural Organizations: Challenges and Opportunities (1995), Marlene G. Fine, Westport, CT: Quorum Books, pp. 173–93. Copyright © 1995 by Marlene G. Fine. Reproduced with permission of Greenwood Publishing Group, Inc., Westport, CT.

Working with Diversity: A Focus on Global Organizations (November 2000), Deborah Merrill-Sands and Evangelina Holvino, with James Cumming, *Working paper no. 11*, Section III. Boston, MA: Center for Gender in Organizations, Simmons School of Management, pp. 15–26, 72–3. Reprinted with permission of Center for Gender in Organizations, Simmons School of Management.

Our Separate Ways: Barriers to Advancement (2001), Ella L. J. Edmondson Bell and Stella M. Nkomo, from *Our Separate Ways: Black and White Women and the Struggle for Professional Identity* (2001), Boston, MA: Harvard Business School Press, pp. 137–58, 296–9. Reprinted by permission of Harvard Business School Press. Copyright © 2001 by Ella L. J. Edmondson Bell and Stella M. Nkomo; all rights reserved.

Making Differences Matter: A New Paradigm for Managing Diversity (1996), David A. Thomas and Robin J. Ely, *Harvard Business Review*, September/October: 79–90. Reprinted by permission of Harvard Business Review. Copyright © 1996 by the Harvard Business School Publishing Corporation; all rights reserved.

Dangerous Liaisons: The "Feminine-in-Management" Meets "Globalization" (1993), Marta B. Calás and Linda Smircich, *Business Horizons*, 36 (2): 71–81. Reprinted with permission from *Business Horizons*. Copyright 1993 by The Trustees at Indiana University, Kelley School of Business.

The Nanny Chain (2000), Arlie R. Hochschild, *The American Prospect*, Volume 11, Number 4, January: 32–6. Reprinted with permission of The American Prospect, 5 Broad Street, Boston, MA 02019. All rights reserved.

Maquiladoras: The View from the Inside (1984), Maria Patricia Fernández Kelly, in Karen Brodkin Sacks and Dorothy Remy (eds.), *My Troubles Are Going To Have Trouble With Me*, New Brunswick, NJ: Rutgers University Press, pp. 229–46. Copyright © 1984 Rutgers, The State University. Reprinted by permission of Rutgers University Press.

It Takes Two (1992), Cynthia Enloe, in S. P. Sturdevant and B. Stolzfus (eds.), *Let the Good Times Roll: Prostitution and the U.S. Military in Asia*, New York: The New Press, pp. 22–7. Copyright © 1992 by S. P. Sturdevant. Reprinted by permission of S. P. Sturdevant.

PART I | INTRODUCING GENDER

INTRODUCING GENDER: OVERVIEW

JOYCE K. FLETCHER AND ROBIN J. ELY

For most of us, thinking about gender and management immediately brings to mind what are commonly thought of as "women's issues": sexual harassment, sex discrimination, work–family policies and, of course, the glass ceiling. In other words, thinking about gender usually gets us thinking about how doing business as usual creates problems for women. What kinds of problems, why, and what might be done to address them, has been the subject of much debate among scholars and practitioners alike. In this book, we use these debates as a way to explore conventional scholarly wisdom on the role of gender at work and for explicating an alternative point of view – one that a number of us at the Center for Gender in Organizations have been developing in collaboration with others for the past 10 years.[1] From this point of view, we move away from the notion of gender as primarily a women's issue and instead see gender as a central organizing feature of social life, with implications for women, men, and how we get work done.

In particular, we find it useful to conceptualize gender as having two interrelated parts (Ely, 1999). There is an individual component, called gender identity, which is the sense one makes of the fact that one is male or female – the story that a woman, for example, tells herself about what it means to be female, how being female shapes who she is and what happens to her. And there is a structural component, called gender relations, which is the way the social world is built, in part, by making distinctions between men and women, thus shaping differentially the material conditions of our lives – for example, the power and status women as a group have relative to men as a group, or the roles in a society that men and women play. Gender identity has no inherent content outside of gender relations: gender relations are the structural arrangements that give meaning to the categories male and female and shape people's experiences as members of those groups. They are influenced in part by all other social relations, including race, ethnicity, class, nationality, religion, and sexual identity. Although the nature of gender relations is culture-specific and has changed over time, it appears from what we know currently that they have been more or less relations of power: "gender relations have been (more) defined and (imperfectly) controlled by one of their interrelated aspects – the man" (Flax, 1990: 45). Thus power is a core element of gender as we know it. This more expansive view of gender positions organizations as central to shaping the meaning of gender, enabling us to reflect more critically on current organizational life and how it could be different.

This book is a collective effort. Different faculty at, or affiliated with, the Center have taken responsibility for moving this perspective on gender forward as it relates to their specific areas of expertise – leadership, negotiation, organizational change, diversity, human resources management, and globalization – all traditional topics in organizational behavior. In this way, we hope to broaden not only our understanding of gender, but also our understanding of these topics. We have selected readings that, to varying degrees, illustrate the range of approaches previous scholars have taken to understanding how gender relates to the topic at hand. Each of us then moves the discussion of her topic onto new terrain in some way related to the more expansive view of gender we have been developing. In Part I, we present several foundational readings on which we draw in our subsequent treatment of these topics.[2]

THE FOUR FRAMES

We capture the conventional scholarly wisdom about gender in three traditional approaches to gender in the workplace. We conceptualize each approach as a "frame" for understanding what gender is and why inequities exist between men and women at work. These three frames are rooted in the common tendency to think of gender as an individual characteristic, and gender issues as stemming primarily from differences between men and women, either in the traits and skills they possess or in the ways they are treated. Each frame implies a vision of gender equity and an approach for achieving that vision. While interventions derived from these approaches, such as training and executive development, affirmative action, and work–family policies, have achieved significant equity gains for women, their impact has been limited. We argue that this is due in large part to their limited conceptions of gender. To augment these efforts, we depart from these more traditional approaches and introduce a fourth frame for understanding and addressing the problem.

Understanding the four frames and how they differ from one another is critical to understanding many of the topics we cover in succeeding parts of this book. The first article in Part I, "Making change: A framework for promoting gender equity in organizations," authored by faculty from the Center for Gender in Organizations, summarizes the frames, their contributions, and their limitations.[3] (The four frames are also summarized in Table O1.1.) Three readings follow, each a classic treatment of gender in the workplace, representing the first three frames, respectively. According to the first frame, women have lagged behind men in their achievements because they lack the kinds of socialization experiences one needs in order to develop the traits and skills requisite for success. The route to sex equity, therefore, is to eradicate sex differences through education, exposure, and training. This perspective is represented in an excerpt from Margaret Hennig and Anne Jardim's now classic *The Managerial Woman*. Although the research on which this book is based is clearly dated, and many may balk at the stereotyped

Table O1.1 Understanding the four frames on gender

	Definition of gender	Problem definition	Vision of gender equity	Approach to change	Benefits	Limitations
Frame 1 Fix the women	Socialized sex differences	Women lack skills, know-how to "play the game"	No differences between men and women; just like men	Develop women's skills through training, mentoring, etc.	Helps individual women succeed; creates role models when they succeed	Leaves system and male standards intact; blames women as source of problem
Frame 2 Celebrate differences	Socialized sex differences; separate spheres of activity	Women's skills not valued or recognized	Differences recognized, valued, preserved	Diversity training; reward and celebrate differences, "women's ways"	Legitimates differences; "feminine" approach valued; tied to broader diversity initiatives	Reinforces stereotypes; leaves processes in place that produce differences
Frame 3 Create equal opportunities	Sex differences in treatment, access, opportunity	Differential structures of power and opportunity yield less access, fewer resources for women	Create level playing field by reducing structural barriers, biases	Policies to compensate for structural barriers, e.g., affirmative action, work–family benefits	Helps with recruiting, retaining, advancing women; eases work–family stress	Has minimal impact on organizational culture; backlash; work–family remains "woman's problem"
Frame 4 Revise work culture	A central organizing feature of social life embedded within belief systems, knowledge systems, and social practices	Social practices designed by and for white, heterosexual, class-privileged men appear neutral but uphold differences	Process of identifying and revising oppressive social practices; gender no longer an axis of power	Emergent, localized process of incremental change involving critique, new narratives, and experimentation	Exposes apparent neutrality of practices as oppressive; more likely to change organization culture; continuous process of learning	Resistance to deep change; difficult to sustain

characterizations of men and women, its perspective still pervades much of the common parlance on gender in organizational life today.

The second frame is nearly the opposite of the first. Its proponents argue that socialized differences between men and women should not be eliminated, but celebrated. In this frame, it is precisely "women's difference" from men, in particular, their "relationship orientation," that organizations need. Recognizing sex differences and the unique value women bring to the table is central to this frame's approach to achieving gender equity. We include an excerpt from Sally Helgesen's *The Female Advantage* to represent this point of view.

The third frame focuses on structural barriers to women's recruitment and advancement. From this perspective, gender is still framed as differences between men and women, but they result from differential structures of opportunity and power that block women's access and advancement, rather than from socialization processes. This frame advocates policies designed to create equal opportunities for men and women. Excerpts from Rosabeth Moss Kanter's classic book, *Men and Women of the Corporation*, represent this perspective.

The fourth frame offers a conceptual leap from thinking about gender as an individual characteristic to thinking about it as a systemic factor, influencing not only men and women, but also the very knowledge that underlies our beliefs about what makes for good workers, good work, and successful organizations (chapter 17, this volume). For example, when we think of management – an ostensibly gender-neutral activity – whose image comes to mind? Research suggests that, for most of us, it is still the image of a man – and more than likely, a white, middle- or upper-middle-class, heterosexual-appearing man. Why does this image persist even at a time when US census figures show that a full 46 percent of managers are women? One reason is that "management" evokes power, and *senior* managers – those with the real power – are still largely white men. But also at play is a far more subtle and insidious fact of organizational life, a fact that we believe lies at the heart of many of the divisions and disparities we see in the workplace today: the very model for organizing that has evolved in the Western world was created by and for a certain subset of men – white, middle-class professionals. Because these men were the architects of early industrialized efforts to systematize the workplace, the basic organizing principles that govern workplace practice – indeed, many of the implicit rules for success that influence individual and organizational action – are closely aligned with idealized masculine interests, attributes, and life situations. We believe that this history has far-reaching implications today, not only for women's ability to progress but for many men's as well (Rapoport, Rapoport, & Strelitz, 1977), and for our very sense of what organizations can be and can accomplish. We refer to our concerns for both equity and organizational functioning as the "dual agenda" (Fletcher, 1999; 2001), and devote much of this book to exploring these implications.

Thus, Frame 4 follows on Frame 3, emphasizing power as a central dimension of gender, but is grounded in a somewhat different set of theoretical and epistemological positions. From this perspective, gender is neither an individual characteristic nor simply a basis for categorization and discrimination. Rather, it is a complex set of social relations enacted across a range of social and institutional practices that exist both within and outside of formal organizations. Excerpts from the classic article by Joan Acker, "Hierarchies, jobs, bodies: A theory of gendered organizations," explore how these practices in organizations create idealized images of work, workers, and success, indirectly maintaining gender segregation and gender inequity while at the same time appearing to be gender-neutral.

The next reading, excerpts from "Doing gender," by Candace West and Don H. Zimmerman, highlights the microprocesses by which the macrogendering of organizations is achieved. It starts from the basic premise that, to some degree, we enact our identity in all of our interactions with others. Since gender is a major part of identity, we end up "doing gender" whenever we "do" anything else, including "doing business," "doing competence," or even "doing nice." Introducing this concept allows for a discussion of what it means to "do masculinity" or "do femininity" in the workplace and sets the stage for further discussions about how "doing masculinity" and "doing work" are often conflated (Fletcher, 1999; 2001). This article also introduces the notion, central to the fourth frame, that the body matters: perceptions of behavior are not gender-neutral. In perceiving and interpreting our actions and interactions, others wittingly or unwittingly take our sex into account. We all know this, of course. A man who raises his voice in a meeting to make a point is perceived quite differently from a woman who does the same thing. Nonetheless, this commonsense truism is often ignored in the management literature and, as a result, much of the managerial advice women receive is less than useful.

It is easy to see how gendered work practices and notions of ideal workers would be a problem for women who are either unable or unwilling to conform to these idealized images. More difficult to see is that relying on these images as workplace ideals is also a problem for many men who do not fit the image either, whether in personal attributes or life situations. In other words, the gendered nature of the workplace – although an especially important issue for women – also affects men. The reading by David Collinson and Jeff Hearn includes excerpts from two of their articles, "Breaking the silence: On men, masculinities, and managements," and "Naming men as men: Implications for work, organization and management." Together the excerpts contribute to an explanation of how organizations are gendered and help to broaden our view beyond the notion of gender as a "women's issue."

COMPLICATING GENDER

So far, these readings have focused on gender as a central concept for understanding organizations. But gender does not exist in isolation from other dimensions of difference, such as race, ethnicity, class, sexual identity, religion, age, and nationality. We all inhabit, enact, and respond to many different social identities simultaneously. Similarly, organizations are not only gendered, they reflect and reinforce divisions along other axes of difference as well. These divisions operate simultaneously to create interlocking systems of power; gender is only one relevant strand among many (Collins, 1995). Thinking at the individual level, most scholars and practitioners interested in gender today would agree that a focus on gender alone inappropriately masks important diversity in men's and women's experiences at work. We know, for example, that white women and women of color experience different forms of sex discrimination (Bell & Nkomo, 2001; Hurtado, 1996); that social class influences men's displays of masculinity (Fine, Weis, Addelston, & Maruza, 1997); and that the idealized images of masculinity we are often expected to emulate at work are modeled on idealized images of white, middle-class, heterosexual men (Ely & Meyerson, 2000; Rapoport, Bailyn, Fletcher, & Pruitt, 2002). Thinking at the social and institutional level, researchers increasingly recognize that a singular focus on gender occludes the role that other power relations play (Collins, 1995). For these reasons, we find that gender is incomplete as a lens for analyzing organizations: we cannot adequately understand – or challenge – gender arrangements without considering the simultaneous effects of other social and power relations as well.

Yet most research on gender in organizations ignores these effects. Race, class, and other aspects of social identity, when considered, are rarely more than add-on concerns. For example, in a survey of studies on gender and organizations published in four major academic journals between 1986 and 1995, Ely (1999) noted that only 17 percent included analyses of race or ethnicity. Without information to the contrary, it is reasonable to assume that research participants are white. Nevertheless, the results of these studies are commonly stated as if generalizable to all men and women. This practice supports the myth of men and women as monoliths. Moreover, when we describe *a* voice for women and "do not specify which women, under which specific historical circumstances, have spoken with the voice in question" (Fraser & Nicholson, 1990: 32), we invite the same charge of false generalization leveled at theories constructed by and about men. And, when we fail to specify the racial identity of white women, we obfuscate their experiences as members of the dominant racial group and position them as the norm against which other women are measured (Bell & Nkomo, 2001; Ely, 1995). To the extent that women of color deviate from this norm, they are often viewed as less effective or unfeminine, or are simply invisible altogether (Hurtado, 1989). Parallel problems exist when we ignore or leave unstated other dominant identity categories that likely influence people's experiences in significant ways. The last reading in Part I addresses this set of issues. In this excerpt from "Complicating gender: The simultaneity of race, gender, and class in organization change(ing)," Evangelina Holvino demonstrates the limitations of the liberal feminist and functionalist paradigms that dominate the literature on gender in organizations and argues instead for addressing race, gender, and class simultaneously.

NOTES

1 The original core group of collaborators included Lotte Bailyn, Gill Coleman, Robin Ely, Joyce Fletcher, Deborah Kolb, Deborah Merrill-Sands, Debra Meyerson, and Rhona Rapoport.
2 For a primer on gender and work, which summarizes much of the most up-to-date literature in the field, we recommend Padavic and Reskin (2002).
3 See Ely and Meyerson (2000) for a more extensive treatment of the four frames.

REFERENCES

Bell, E. L. J. & Nkomo, S. M. 2001. *Our separate ways: Black and white women and the struggle for professional identity.* Boston, MA: Harvard Business School Press.
Collins, P. H. 1995. Symposium on West and Fenstermaker's "Doing difference." *Gender & Society:* 9(4): 491–4.
Ely, R. J. 1995. The role of dominant identity and experience in organizational work on diver-

sity. In Susan E. Jackson & Marion N. Ruderman (eds.), *Diversity in work teams: Research paradigms for a changing workplace*. Washington, DC: American Psychological Association: 161–86.

Ely, R. J. 1999. Feminist critiques of research on gender in organizations. *Working paper #6*. Boston, MA: Center for Gender in Organizations, Simmons School of Management.

Ely, R. J. & Meyerson, D. E. 2000. Theories of gender in organizations: A new approach to organizational analysis and change. In B. Staw & R. Sutton (eds.), *Research in Organizational Behavior*: 103–52. New York: JAI Press.

Fine, M., Weis, L. Addelston, J. & Marusza, J. 1997. (In) secure times: Constructing white working-class masculinities in the late 20th century. *Gender & Society*, 11(1): 52–68.

Flax, J. 1990. Postmodernism and gender relations in feminist theory. In L. J. Nicholson (ed.), *Feminism/postmodernism*: 39–62. New York: Routledge.

Fletcher, J. K. 1999. *Disappearing acts: Gender, power, and relational practice at work*. Cambridge, MA: MIT Press.

Fletcher, J. K. 2001. Invisible work: The disappearing of relational practice at work. *CGO Insights, Briefing Note #8*: 1–4. Boston, MA: Center for Gender in Organizations, Simmons School of Management.

Fraser, N. & Nicholson, L. J. 1990. Social criticism without philosophy: An encounter between feminism and postmodernism. In Linda J. Nicholson (ed.), *Feminism/Postmodernism*: 19–38. New York: Routledge.

Hurtado, A. 1989. Relating to privilege: Seduction and rejection in the subordination of white women and women of color. *Signs*, 14(4): 833–55.

Hurtado, A. 1996. *The color of privilege: Three blasphemies on race and feminism*. Ann Arbor: University of Michigan Press.

Padavic, I. & Reskin, B. 2002. *Women and men at work*, 2nd edn. Thousand Oaks, CA: Pine Forge Press.

Rapoport, R., Bailyn, L. Fletcher, J. K., & Pruitt, B. 2002. *Beyond work family balance: Advancing gender equity and workplace performance*. San Francisco: Jossey Bass.

Rapoport, R., Rapoport, R. N., & Strelitz, Z. 1997. *Fathers, mothers and others: Towards new alliances*. London: Kegan Paul.

CHAPTER

1

MAKING CHANGE: A FRAMEWORK FOR PROMOTING GENDER EQUITY IN ORGANIZATIONS

DEBORAH KOLB, JOYCE K. FLETCHER, DEBRA E. MEYERSON, DEBORAH MERRILL-SANDS, AND ROBIN J. ELY

From CGO Insights, Briefing Note #1 (1998) Boston, MA: Center for Gender in Organizations, Simmons School of Management

Suppose your organization is committed to becoming more gender equitable. What kind of change initiative should it undertake? Recent research in the social sciences suggests that the answer to this question is far from simple. The problem is that there are many different theories about the role gender plays in organizational life and about the causes of gender inequity. Each theory has its own perspective on the problem and its own view of the appropriate remedy. Some remedies focus on eliminating overt discrimination in hiring and promotion practices, some focus on reducing the wage gap between men and women, and some focus on training and executive development. While many of these initiatives have achieved significant equity gains for women, each has its limitations, each focuses on a different definition and symptom of the problem, and none, on its own, has been able to address the issue comprehensively.

For organizations interested in addressing the issue of gender equity in a comprehensive and sustainable manner, we offer a comparative framework that illustrates why most approaches to gender equity are partial solutions and do not achieve lasting gains. Drawing on existing frameworks[1] that compare and contrast theoretical perspectives on gender in the workplace, we propose four frames through which to understand gender equity and organizational change. The first three are descriptions of traditional approaches. The fourth frame is an integrated perspective that acknowledges the complex role gender plays in organizational life. It offers a new category of organizational intervention as well as a way of recasting traditional equity initiatives.

FRAME 1: FIX THE WOMEN

The first, and probably most common approach to promoting gender equity rests on a liberal and individualistic vision of society and organizations. It assumes that individuals rise and fall on their own merits. Gender translates into biological sex, i.e., men and women. In this view, men and women are assumed to have equal access to opportunities. Women's lack of achievement in organizations relative to men's is attributed to differences in experience. A basic assumption of this approach is that women have not been socialized to the world of business and, therefore, do not know the "rules of the game." They lack the requisite training and skills to compete in the workplace or assume positions of leadership.

The goal of this approach – and thus its vision of gender equity – is to minimize these differences between women and men so that women can compete as equals. Executive development programs for women represent the hallmark of this approach. Leadership programs, assertiveness training, and workshops on presentation skills and negotiation are important interventions.

Many women have learned valuable skills from these programs. They have learned to succeed at the game as well as – or better than – many men. This has helped certain women move into positions of leadership where they serve as role models for others. However, as important as these programs are, on their own, they contribute only marginally to promoting gender equity. They may help certain women play the game, but they leave in place the structures and policies of the game itself. These programs deal with the issue on an individual level, but do little to change the systemic factors within organizations that create an uneven playing field for women.

FRAME 2: CELEBRATE DIFFERENCES

The second frame shifts the focus from eliminating difference to valuing difference. This perspective conceptualizes gender as socialized differences between men and women, embodied in different masculine and feminine styles or "ways of being." Masculine and feminine identities are seen to be shaped by different life experiences and social roles. In this frame, however, the route to equity is not to eliminate or deplore these differences, but to celebrate them. From this perspective, women are disadvantaged because work styles, skills, and attributes associated with "the feminine" are not recognized or valued in the workplace.[2]

Framing the problem of gender inequity in this way points to corrective measures that focus on acknowledging differences and valuing them. This frame often places gender equity within a broader diversity initiative, acknowledging gender as one of many important differences among workers. Intervention strategies include consciousness-raising and diversity training to promote tolerance and understanding of difference. Other initiatives focus on demonstrating how tradionally feminine activities or styles, such as listening, collaborating, nurturing, and behind-the-scenes peacemaking, are a beneficial addition to an organization's skill set. These insights can lead to important changes in cultural norms and practices – such as changes in performance evaluation criteria – that recognize talents and contributions that women often bring to the workplace.

There is no question that interventions to value gender differences have raised awareness and created workplaces that are more tolerant and flexible. While this is an important step in expanding opportunities for women, it too has its limitations. By concentrating on differences, the approach can actually reinforce gender stereotypes rather than break them down. Also, by focusing on recognition and inclusion, there is the assumption that simply naming something as valuable will make it so. It ignores the power of the masculine image that underlies most generally accepted models of success, leadership, and managerial acumen. Women who enact a feminine style, even when its contributions are recognized and applauded, find their efforts (and often themselves) rendered invisible or valued only in the most marginal sense.[3] For example, including interpersonal skills, team building, or consensus-building management styles in a performance evaluation may increase awareness that "people skills" are important in the workplace. However, it does little to challenge the way assertiveness, competition, decisiveness, and rugged individualism are assumed to be critical factors for getting organizational results. Thus, the biggest barrier to achieving gender equity in this frame is that it does not challenge the differential and hierarchical valuing of difference between the masculine and the feminine.

FRAME 3: CREATE EQUAL OPPORTUNITY

The third perspective on gender equity focuses on structural barriers. Gender in this frame is still defined in terms of differences between women and men, but it redirects attention from differences in their personal characteristics to the differential structures of opportunity that create an uneven playing field.[4] This frame points to the gender segregation of occupations and workplaces and the many ways hiring, evaluation and promotion processes are biased against women and impede their advancement – what many refer to as the "glass ceiling." The goal of this approach is to create equal opportunity by eliminating discriminatory structural and procedural barriers.

Interventions in this frame tend to be legalistic and policy-based. They include, for example, affirmative action initiatives, revised recruiting procedures, more transparent promotion policies designed to ensure fairness, sexual harassment guidelines, as well as the provision of work and family benefits such as child care, flexible arrangements, or alternative career track options. This approach can be thought of as reducing organizational constraints on women's ability to achieve or providing accommodations for what are recognized as structural disadvantages.

There is no question that these structural and policy-based interventions have contributed to improving women's opportunities. They have made it possible to recruit, retain, and promote greater numbers of women. As numbers of women increase, options for women expand and the constraints and stresses of tokenism decrease, creating an environment where women can compete on a more level playing field.[5]

These structural and policy interventions are a critical part of any gender equity initiative. Nonetheless, they too have proved insufficient in achieving lasting gains, because they have little direct effect on the informal rules and practices that govern workplace behavior. For example, applicant pools might be required to have a certain number of women candidates, but the informal selection criteria may continue to rule out those who do not fit the accepted image of the position or whose resumes have employment gaps during childbearing years. Or organizational norms may not align with the new policies. Flexible work benefits might be on the books, but using them may have negative career consequences or create backlash.[6] In the absence of cultural change in the organization, structures and policies cannot, on their own, create equitable organization.

FRAME 4: REVISE WORK CULTURE

Gender equity in the fourth frame focuses on the underlying systemic factors in organizations that lead to workplace inequity. Gender in this frame is not so much a biologic concept as it is a social construct – an organizing principle that underlies organizational life. In other words, gender in this frame is not about women or discrimination, but is about *the organization itself.*

This frame starts from the premise that organizations are inherently gendered.[7] Having been created largely by and for men, organizational systems, work practices, structures, and norms tend to reflect masculine experience, masculine values, and masculine life situations. As a result, everything we come to regard as normal and commonplace at work tends to privilege traits that are socially and culturally ascribed to men while devaluing or ignoring those ascribed to women. This includes, for example, cultural norms and assumptions in the workplace that value specific types of products and work processes, define competence and excellence of staff, and shape ideas about the best way to get work done. It also includes, for example, systems of reward and recognition that promote specific kinds of behavior as well as systems of communication and decision-making that bestow power and influence on some staff while excluding others.

The gender equity problem in the fourth frame is grounded in deeply held, and often unquestioned assumptions, that drive behavior and work practice in the organization. These assumptions appear neutral and inconsequential on the surface, but often have a differential impact on men and women. For example, a gendered assumption that undergirds much of organizational life is the informal rule that time spent at work, regardless of productivity, is a measure of commitment, loyalty, and organizational worth. The most valuable worker is one who is able, willing, and eager to put work first. This norm inherently gives privilege to those workers who do not have responsibilities in the private sphere of their lives that impede them from accepting unbounded work responsibilities.

Furthermore, in a situation where attributes and life situations that are socially ascribed to men and masculinity are perceived as normal and neutral, and those socially ascribed to women and femininity are perceived as different or deviant, not only do gender inequities arise, but the organization itself suffers from a narrow, conscripted view of its options for how to do its work. Displays of masculinity often get conflated with images of working, in a way that hurts many women, some men, *and* the work.[8] To take the example above, the image of an ideal worker as someone who has no outside responsibilities to interfere with a commitment to work can result in formal and informal work norms that make it difficult not only for women to achieve, but also many men. What is rarely recognized, however, is that it may also have significant negative consequences for organizational performance as well. This kind of assumption can lead to ineffective, costly, or inefficient work practices, such as a self-perpetuating crisis mode of operating, where working through the night or holding emergency after-hours meetings becomes the norm rather than the exception.

Gender equity interventions from the fourth frame perspective engage with basic work practices and processes, and the norms that underlie them, in order to revise them in ways that are less gendered and more effective for the organization. It is important to underscore that interventions from the fourth frame are not formulaic or procedural. Rather they are based on an ongoing process of inquiry, experimentation, and learning. This process is not a one-time fix. Instead, it is an iterative process, much like peeling an onion, where each layer reveals yet another to be explored and examined.

What are the limitations of this approach? We see two principal challenges. First, it engages the organization in a long-term process of organizational change and learning. While this can yield significant benefits both for gender equity and organizational performance, not all organizations are ready to make this level of commitment at the beginning of their work on gender equity. Secondly, we have learned that it can be difficult to keep the goal of gender equity in the forefront. It can be easily overshadowed by the more familiar – and for some, the more compelling – goal of improving organizational effectiveness. Careful and sustained attention has to be given to ensuring that staff and managers recognize and understand the gender equity implications of changes introduced.[9]

CONCLUSION

Experience has shown that promoting gender equity in organizations is a challenging task. We need to consider the unique contributions of each frame when we make interventions. It is important to recognize, however, that the first three frames can benefit from fourth frame thinking and result in more comprehensive, integrative gender equity programs. For example, executive development programs for women are still an important way to change the leadership demographics of organizations. Adding the fourth frame perspective to these initiatives can strengthen their effect. Rather than addressing women as deficient, these efforts would help women understand the larger, *systemic* effects of gender in organizations. "Fix the women" in this sense would mean supplementing training in management skills with training in the strategies to use when women find themselves in gendered situations that inhibit their ability to be effective.

Adding a fourth frame perspective to the second frame would mean that, rather than simply valuing difference, gender equity interventions would focus on how to claim space for a different model of work practice. It would, for example, focus on developing a language of competency to name alternative strategies for success and would challenge some of the unwritten and unspoken images of ideal workers, strong leaders, and exemplary managers. The interventions would not stop at identifying difference. Instead, they would challenge the way some aspects of work are overvalued simply because of their association with masculinity, while others are devalued because of their association with femininity and not because of the relative contribution they make to the final product.

It is important to continue structural and policy interventions characteristic of the third frame. Increasing the hiring, retention, and promotion of women is critical to any gender equity initiative. But adding a fourth frame perspective would mean focusing not just on policies, but on how these policies are used in practice. For example, an intervention designed to improve the recruitment of women would go beyond developing mechanisms to "cast the net widely" in distributing job announcements. It would also review the job descriptions to see how they may preclude or prejudice consideration of women, and revise them to be more inclusive.

A pure fourth frame approach builds on interventions typical of the other three frames, but it is broader and deeper and focuses on systemic changes in work culture and practices that will benefit women, men, and the organization. We believe that this level of change is essential for creating organizations that are both effective and truly gender equitable.

NOTES

1   For a comprehensive comparison of the different theoretical perspectives on gender and gender equity, see Calas, M. and L. Smircich (1996). "From 'The Women's' Point of View: Feminist Approaches to Organization Studies," *Handbook of Organization Studies*, S, Clegg, C. Hardy, and W. Nord, eds. London: Sage Publications. An earlier version of this framework is presented in Kolb, D. and D. Meyerson (forthcoming) "Moving out of the 'Armchair': Initial Attempts to Apply Feminist Organization Theory into Organizations," *Organization*.

2   See Helgessen, S. (1990). *Female Advantage: Women's Ways of Leadership*. New York: Doubleday; Rosener, J. (1990). "Ways Women Lead," *Harvard Business Review*, November–December, 68(6): 119–125

3   Fletcher, J. K. (1998). "Relational Practice: A Feminist Reconstruction of Work," *Journal of Management Inquiry*, 7(2): 163–186.

4   See Kanter, R. M. (1977). *Men and Women in the Corporation*. New York: Basic Books; Reskin, B. (1984). *Women and Men at Work*. Thousand Oaks, CA: Pine Forge Press.

5   Ely, R. (1995). "The Power of Demography: Women's Social Construction of Gender Identity at Work." *Academy of Management Journal*, 38(3): 589–634.

6   Bailyn, L, J. Fletcher, and D. Kolb (1997). "Unexpected Connections: Considering Employees' Personal Lives Can Revitalize Your Business," *Sloan Management Review*, 38(4): 11–19.

7   See Fletcher, J. and D. Merrill-Sands (1998). "Looking Below the Surface: The Gendered Nature of Organizations," *CGO Insights*, 2, December.

8   Martin, P. (1998). "Men, Masculinities, and Working from (some) Women's Standpoint." Unpublished paper presented at The Center for Gender in Organizations case conference, Simmons Institute for Leadership and Change, April, 1998.

9   Ely, R. and D. Meyerson (2000). "Holding Gender: The Challenges of Keeping the Gender Rationale Present in the Course of an Organizational Intervention." *Organization* 74(4): 589–608.

CHAPTER

2

THE MANAGERIAL WOMAN

MARGARET HENNIG AND ANNE JARDIM

From The Managerial Woman (1977) Garden City, NY: Anchor Press/Doubleday.

[. . .] From a very early age men expect to work to support at least themselves. Only a fractional minority of white women come face to face with this issue as little girls. Instead, for the individual woman the emphasis, expressed or implied, is placed on the need to find someone to support *her*. The difference in mind-set that develops from this crossroads of childhood's expectations and ambitions is enormous. Boys take one road, and most adult men cannot even remember when it was that they first understood that they would have to support themselves and what this meant. The tensions and anxieties that surround the issue are, for boys, directly related to the problems they encounter in the environment: Can they do this, can they master that, are they any good at something else? And always there is the reassurance that men do these things, and have always done them, so at worst if one can't do a particular thing very well there will be something else one *can* do. The road a girl takes conjures up different anxieties, different tensions. Will she find someone to support and look after her? Is she pretty enough, nice enough, clever enough – or too plain or too clever?

From a very early age children fantasize about their futures and the future for a little girl inescapably has a husband in it: at that point her parents are the only model she has. Fathers support wives and children and even where a mother works the father's job is usually seen as the more critical. The little girl looks at the little boys she knows and wonders – would he be a good husband, would he look after her? Would he be nice to her – nicer than her father is to her mother, or as nice? Most important of all, would he choose her? The theme of vicarious independence is very real and the anxieties associated with possible failure have to do with how one looks, with how one seems, with how one appears – *not* with what one can or cannot do.

In the light of this it hardly seems strange that the mind-set of an adult woman, even a woman with a tangible claim to career success, should still bear traces of a different reality – a reality which has far more to do with individual attributes and their effect on others and far less to do with actively engaging the environment. The difficulties which arise for women from the confrontation in a management setting of these two different realities are compounded by an unawareness on the part of both men and women that the differences even exist.

And there are still other patterns. One has to do with the ability to see one's career as an integral part of one's life. Men find it difficult to separate personal goals from career goals. They see one set as dependent on the other and they try to negotiate and to trade off between each set of goals when conflict threatens the balance. Women on the other hand actively strive for separation. They think it through and choose to make the distinction: "My personal life is quite separate from my career and that is how I want it."

While there are real reasons for the drive to maintain this separation, there are painful disadvantages to be coped with as one attempts it. The reasons for separation can range from a need to be a different person at home in order not to threaten a man because one loves or is afraid of him, to a remorseless sense of guilt unless one can simultaneously be a perfect wife, mother or lover. The latter phenomenon hinges on a complicated psychological maneuver which runs something like this: "Given that the role I *should* accept is a woman's role, then I can only justify, rationalize, explain taking on a different role if I'm so good at the woman's role that no one can question it, which then leaves me free to take on the rest."

The net outcome moving from any point on this range of motivation is intentionally the same – one lives two lives. But when one does this how is negotiation possible? How does one trade off between them, how does one balance conflict? If a woman has actively encouraged the individuals who mean a great deal to her to believe that her career life is of little significance to her, *and has consistently acted it out*, how does she get them to believe in, and help her solve, a crisis arising from a serious clash between the two? Typically she can't and in her own eyes she often fails at both. In the meantime in the absence of crisis, her life as a whole is made that much more difficult as she attempts to switch off and on from the person she is in one setting to the person she should be in the other.

Why women tend to make so explicit a separation is a much larger question whose answer lies in the society around us and both men and women explain it in very similar ways: men grow up knowing they will have to work for the rest of their lives, they are expected to, and they prepare for it. They join an organization where career advancement for men is the traditional socially sanctioned norm. However minimally, their ambitions are supported, they are seen as legitimate. A bright young man is a "comer" and even the less bright have to prove by their performance that they do not belong. In effect they have to prove failure. Women on the other hand grow up in a cloud of ambiguity: will they work or won't they? If they do, for how long? Are they expected to or aren't they and for how long? They join an organization where career advancement for women is typically the exception and where, given prior and often articulated assumptions that they don't, they have to prove by their performance that they do belong. In effect they have to prove success, and on a continuous basis. They have to prove, given prior and often articulated assumptions that they will, that their careers will not be dual, discontinuous and consequentially marked by a lack of commitment – a burden of proof to which a man is never asked to submit. They tend to feel that their lives *are* dual, that they cannot trade off between the two lives imposed upon them even though the ability to do so might well allow for optimization in both. They begin to feel that survival depends on the separation which both sides of their lives demand. [. . .]

Still another pattern of difference centers on the concept of personal strategy. Men define this as winning, as achieving a goal or reaching an objective. In discussing this issue they ask a question whose many forms bear the same meaning: What's in it for me? It is a critical question because it allows the future to be brought into consideration. What's in it for me now, attractive as it might be, might well over the long term undermine what I want ultimately to achieve. It is a question that almost inevitably evokes a "Yes, but . . ." answer if one asks it of oneself, and the "but" leads one into the attempt to predict and thus to anticipate future outcomes.

Women's definitions in contrast are definitions of process: planning, finding the best way, the best possible method. The element of time is absent from the examples they give: "In order to get a particular job done I did thus and so." But what about the implications a year from now of doing thus and so? The giver of the example suddenly realizes what she has said. She has described what was for her the best way of resolving a particular problem in the here and now with no consideration given to the way in which that resolution might or might not affect her over time.

Why this happens is again a question that reaches into the past. It focuses on an issue which though fast becoming overworked is no less valid because of that: sports – the games boys play and men follow. For example:

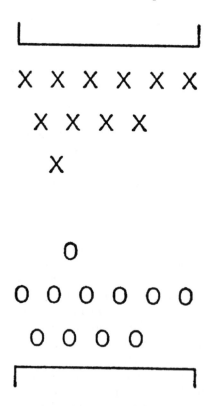

Women's comments attempt to identify what this diagram represents. Is it a game? If so, is it field hockey, football or could it be baseball? How many games need teams of eleven? Are those goal posts?

Men's comments are immediately evaluative: "It's football and it's a lousy play. Change the coach. Switch to another channel."

What lies behind this difference in response begins with small boys learning about teams, about being members of teams, about winning and losing. Their concept of strategy may at first be a very simple one: how you win may mean no more than getting the fat boys on your team so you can trample the skinny boys on the other.

But then it becomes more sophisticated and task specialization sets in. Runners *and* blockers are seen to be needed. The guys with the imagination to plan and anticipate possible outcomes achieve a value of their own. A team makes it possible to become a star and one has to learn how to manage this. A team makes it possible to share a star's luster by active association, and again one can learn how to manage this. A team can even be a place to hide, a place to learn about survival – how to stay on, how to be given another chance; "After all he's too nice a guy to drop!", or "He's not really producing yet but he's learning fast, and he's a real straight player." Over and above this, there is the drive to win and of necessity win as a team, not as a lone individual independent of everyone else.

What do men experience, learn and then internalize as working assumptions from a game like football? And does it matter that the great majority of women share neither their experience nor their assumptions?

Simply as an experience, ask a man you know to try to think back to the time when he played a team game like football. What was it like? What did he begin to learn? What did he *have* to learn if he wanted to stay on the team?

Varying only as to form, the answers we have been given – time and time again – are:

What was it like?	*What did you have to learn if you wanted*
What did you begin to learn?	*to stay on the team?*
It was boys only	Competition, you had to win
Team work	Cooperation to get a job done – you
Hard work	had to work with guys you wouldn't
Preparation and practice, practice,	choose as friends outside the team
practice	If you got swell-headed about how fast
If you were knocked down you had	you could run then the other guys
to get up again	didn't block for you any more
It gave you a sense of belonging,	Losing, what it felt like to lose
of being part of something bigger	That you win some, you lose some
than yourself	How to take criticism – from the coach,
You learned that a team needs a	your peers, the crowd
leader because motivation or lack	That you didn't get anywhere without
of it depends on the coach	planning and you had to have
You learned fast that some people	alternative plans
were better than others – but you	Once you knew the rules you could
had to have eleven	bend them – and you could
	influence the referee

Consider these answers from two points of view: the way they define an environment and the personal skills they identify as needed to survive in it. Do they describe fairly closely a management environment in a corporate setting? Do they reflect skills an effective manager must be able to rely on?

Beyond individual hard work, persistence and the ability to deal with criticism by seeing it as directed much less to the person and much more to task achievement, these answers have to do with goals and objectives; with winning and attempting to deal with loss by distancing it – you win some, you lose some; with group relationships – how to maintain and work with them; and with relationships to authority – whether it be rules or people.

These are personal skills. Boys begin to develop them in an outdoor classroom to which girls traditionally have had no access. After five to fifteen years of practice, men bring these skills with them to management jobs and they are skills critical to job performance once the dividing line between supervision and management is crossed.

Supervision typically involves responsibility for routine, predictable and specific job performance by subordinates in an area of skills with which the supervisor is extremely familiar. He or she usually "grew up" in that skill: learned it when he or she first went to work, performed it well, was promoted to supervise others to do what he or she once did.

Goals and plans to achieve them are usually set for the supervisor to follow. Problems are routine, predictable and can be solved as they arise.

Learning the more technical aspects of the job can be achieved on one's own – seminars, courses, textbooks.

The formal system of relationships required to do the job is typically vertical – up the line to one's boss, down the line to subordinates.

Crossing the line between supervision and management demands that an individual be prepared for a series of fundamental changes in the skills required to do the job, changes for which no formal training is typically available.

In management jobs, goals and plans to meet them are no longer as clearly set as they were for the supervisor. They are increasingly part of a manager's responsibility. Success at planning demands an awareness of group weaknesses and strengths and an ability to balance the one against the other without destructive conflict. "Some people are better than others but you have to have eleven."

Goal-setting. Planning. But how do you get the plan implemented?

"The team needs a leader because motivation or lack of it depends on the coach." "Knowing the rules and bending them." "Influencing the referee." "Taking criticism from (your own) coach, your peers, the crowd." "Winning *and* losing." "Winning some, losing some."

Another required shift in skills has to do with problem-solving. The supervisor deals with more or less routine day-to-day problems susceptible to more or less tried and true solutions. The manager has to *anticipate* problems and if possible be ready with alternatives. "You don't get anywhere without planning and (when problems arise) you have to have alternative plans."

Yet another shift centers on the learning system. Formal learning can teach you technical skills. Dealing with people in a task setting inevitably has to be learned informally and men have already learned the ground rules on intra-group relationships among men. "Cooperation to get a job done – if you get swell-headed about how fast you can run then the other guys don't block for you any more." "Some people are better than others but you have to have eleven."

Still another shift in skills has to do with the formal system of relationships. The simple vertical line typical of supervision – upward to a boss, downward to subordinates – becomes complicated by a network of lateral relationships with counterparts in other areas whose input or lack of it makes an impact in terms of both budget and productivity on what your own department or group can deliver. With *no* formal authority to force a desired result, one must fall back on influence – an outcome of friendship, persuasion, favors granted and owed, promises that must be kept if you want to be operative in the future, connections with people who already *have* influence, the way you yourself are seen – are you a winner, a member of "the club," or are you a potential loser?

The experience of most little girls has no parallel. The prestigious sports for girls tend to be one on one: tennis, swimming, golf, gymnastics, skating. And in the one-on-one sports, the old adage that "it's not whether you won or lost but *how* you played the game" has been so stressed that many women tennis players now in their twenties still play for "exercise" – they don't play to win. While this is changing, it is changing slowly. There cannot be many fathers with the courage to face the ridicule that must have attached to the brave man who fought the sneering insistence of the Little League coach that his daughter wear a protective cup in order to qualify for the baseball team.

Team sports. One team against another. Aiming to win, to reach an objective. It means one must develop a strategy that takes the environment into account. Who and what can help? Who and what can hinder? When? How much? How do I make use of this or counter that in order to get where I want to go? And if the objective is career advancement through the management ranks of today's corporation, who is most likely to win – the man who sees that world as it is, a world of winning and losing, of teams, of stars, of average and mediocre players, in essence *his* world, or the women struggling to find a world as it should be, as it ought to be, in search of the best possible method?

Before we are misunderstood we want to make very clear that we are placing no value judgment whatsoever on the aim to win. We are not saying it is either good or bad. What we are saying is that it is real, very real, and that far more men feel, see and act on that reality than do women. Strategy now has a bad sound, a legacy of politicians who lost sight of moral objectives and adopted without question both the tenuous ethics of the game plan and a language drawn intact form the football field; men who took the concept of winning and made it an end in itself, never questioning the meaning of what they won since winning was enough in itself. We would guess, and it is a guess, that very few women indeed could develop a mindset of this kind because so few women think of winning in personal terms. If anything, women tend to exemplify the other extreme – "Do the best you can and hope someone will notice you." For both men and women the answer to this dilemma of extremes probably lies somewhere in the middle ground – and if men need to lessen the drive to win, women as certainly need to develop it.

This does not mean that women should become more like men. It does mean that women as thinking people should assess much more concretely what's in it for them – what it is they really want, how to go about getting it and what the costs and rewards of getting it will be. If women begin to ask these questions, they must of necessity take the environment into consideration.

Yet another pattern of difference lies in the way men and women see risk. What is risk? What does it mean? The difference in response is striking. Men see risk as loss or gain; winning or losing; danger or opportunity. The responses in every group we have taught have balanced in this way – one man responds negatively, another responds positively, and they both agree that these are the two faces of risk.

Women see risk as entirely negative. It is loss, danger, injury, ruin, hurt. One avoids it as best one can. And there is yet another dimension: men see risk as affecting the future; it is risking one's potential, risking future gain, risking career advancement. A bad mistake and you may never move again. Women see risk as affecting the here and now, what they have so far managed to achieve, all that they have. One woman captured this issue in its entirety when she told us, "My husband always says to me, 'Shoot for the moon and the worst you can do is fall on a star!' And I've just realized that every time he says it I always respond, 'Sure you will. On one of the points.'"

One has only to ask oneself what this means to begin to see the behavioral answers. Risk perceived as a here-and-now danger to what one has discounts future danger; if none is perceived in the present, none is assumed in the future. For example, a recently promoted woman, a divisional product manager in an old, established consumer goods company, told us that she simply could not understand how her new boss could tolerate one of her counterparts, an incompetent fifty-seven-year-old man, his senior in age, his junior in rank and a smooth-feathered winger if ever there was one. She thought her boss was extremely competent, she liked him and she respected him, except for this.

"This guy has an even larger office than my boss. He comes in at ten o'clock and he goes to the health club at three. If you heard him in a meeting you wouldn't know he was talking about the same products. And nobody says anything!" No, she admitted, no one took him very seriously either but that wasn't the point – why was he even there? If it were up to her she would fire him, retire him early, do something, anything, but get him out of there. She felt even more strongly about it when a bright new employee whom she had interviewed for her department was hired away by his. She went to her boss. But, she said, "He laughed it off. Oh, he said things like, 'Good old Joe. You've got to get to know him. He's been here much longer than I have. He knows his way around.' Sure he knows his way around. To all the best restaurants. He does nothing all day and now they've let him have one of the brightest people we hired this year. Someone I really wanted."

We knew her boss well. He was, as she said, an extremely competent manager. A few weeks later we asked him whether things had improved. He shook his head. "She's killing herself. Joe's been around a long time. He knows a lot of people and he's beginning to hear what she's saying. She doesn't see the risk. She's going to kill herself." Why didn't he sit her down and tell her that? He looked at us. "How can I tell her that Joe is where he is because the guy he went to school with, went to college with, shares a vacation house with, and as far as I know may call every night, is marketing vice-president, corporate. She's so hell-bent on what is honest, true, right and good that all it would take is for me to say, 'You're right. He's a loser. He's only here because he's got friends,' and it would be all over the division that I said it. I can't risk that. She's got to learn. I can't help thinking that somehow a man would have picked it up. Somehow a man would have figured that somewhere Joe must have friends to have survived so long. Or at least a man might ask himself, 'Who's he? How come?' and go slowly until he found out. He wouldn't come on like a crusader because that way nobody tells you anything. I can't justify

Joe to a crusader. Why should I? I want a marketing career in this company, not a cause.

"And you know, Joe has his uses. When I want to get something to corporate without making a big thing of it – a new idea and I want to see if it'll fly – I give it to Joe and let him run. Every now and again it works. To the guy up there it looks as if good old Joe thinks sometimes and is worth the protection effort – and I get my suggestions in. Sure Joe's people do all his work. And I've got to be sure they're good. Joe will go in another five years. I've got twenty more years in this company."

Risk. For this man it was out there in the future, a risk to his potential for advancement, a risk recognized and the potential for loss to the best of his ability turned to advantage. She never even saw the career risk she was apparently so deliberately incurring. There was no risk to her current job involved, she couldn't be fired for the way she felt about Joe, so to her risk was really an irrelevant issue. And the irony was that no one was willing to accept the risk which changing her point of view involved.

Risk. A difference in response because of a difference in perception and a difference in behavior as a consequence of both. Again we are not attempting value judgments. We are not trying to identify what is right or what is wrong. We are simply saying – this is the way it happens and what happens is inevitably the reality with which one has to deal. Women see risk differently from the way men see it. As a result they act or don't act in terms of their own perception. Only the individual woman having recognized the difference can decide whether it is worth it to her to change.

There is one last pattern of difference and it has to do with style and with the role one must fill in a given setting. It is an elusive, shifting question. Different people to be dealt with, different tasks to be accomplished, require different roles and demand different styles. The role of subordinate is a universal one but it can be filled using one of a variety of behavioral styles. For example, the helper and the follower. With the helper one has a sense of someone who is active, who tries to assist, who uses his or her initiative; with the follower one has a sense of passivity, of someone who follows rules and obeys orders. But one might fill the role of subordinate equally well in the style of a junior colleague, or even of an equal or a friend.

How does one choose? What is decisive in determining the style to be adopted in a subordinate's role? Men's responses to these questions center on their bosses' expectations of them, women's on their own concept of themselves. It is a critical difference. It means that men will necessarily be more alert to cues and signals which women may neither hear nor see. And these signals may have to do with very small things – how one speaks and the language one uses, how one dresses, whether one appears quick and clever, or slow and reflective, whether one is a helper, or indeed a follower – and most important, when, and in front of whom and over what kinds of issues. The underlying question for most men is clear: what does this boss want, because the chances are he can make or break me for the next job.

Certainly there are men who resent, laugh at and even refuse to adopt the style their bosses may demand. But if they do so they either sense the price they may have to pay or they have a counterstrategy – a godfather higher up in the organization, or a clearly visible talent which will advance them in any case, or a boss who in their eyes lacks the influence to block them. In one company we know of the style demanded of junior executives is that of a loyal soldier and it is precise down to the details of the uniform – Gucci shoes. The men talk about them, laugh at them. But they buy them and wear them.

Women's responses, centering as they do on who one is, place much less weight on others' demands and expectations: "This is who I am – like it or leave it." And this means that distancing oneself from the boss, the job, the situation that may have arisen, is inevitably more difficult. There is no sense of a game being played, of a temporary adoption of a different style for reasons of self-interest. It is all for real. The investment in oneself is specific, the vulnerability to criticism and to personal hurt is consequentially greater and the ability to believe that one can do a job one does not already know, or has never done before, is that much less.

How and when does the greater flexibility that men apparently have, their larger capacity for dissembling, in the value-free sense of veiling feeling, begin to develop? We heard at least part of the answer from a twenty-eight-year-old woman, a junior officer in a large eastern bank. "There was something that used to bother me. I can remember when I was about ten, my brother was two years older, and he used to play on Saturdays with a gang of boys down the street. He'd come in for lunch and we would hear every single Saturday about two of these boys. They were just terrible. He couldn't stand them. But he'd be back out playing with them after lunch. Then at dinner we'd hear about it all over again. It got so impossible that I couldn't stand it and one day I said, 'If you don't like them why do you play with them?' He just stared at me and then he said, 'You've got to be crazy! We need eleven for the team!' I thought about it a lot and I simply couldn't understand it. I knew that if I felt like that about another girl there was no way I would have played with her."

What boys learn that girls don't: flexibility, how to develop a style, a way of behaving that makes it simpler to get what one wants. And most critical of all, how to develop that style among one's peers without even knowing that one is doing it – a far different thing from consciously attempting to win over authority figures like parents on a one-on-one basis. Boys learn how to put up with each other, to tolerate each other and to use each other to a degree that girls hardly ever find necessary. Later, against a background of shared assumptions and prior experience, men learn to sit at meetings and to put up with each other, to tolerate each other and to use each other to a degree that women often find incomprehensible. For men, friendship may be a valued outcome of interaction on the job. For women it too often tends to be a prerequisite.

Group behavior among men is in fact an issue women often raise: "How can two men who dislike each other intensely sit at a meeting pretending to be considerate and helpful to each other while everyone else knows what the situation is and still pretends to buy it? How can they be such hypocrites?"

It is a revealing question. Corporate manners tend to be the manners of a society whose members are bent on winning at one extreme and on sheer survival at the other, and one's position in relation to either extreme tends to define the status of one's membership. Until one has won, discretion is advisable. Why make enemies deliberately when making friends is a means to one's end? At the age of twelve, little boys already know that they need ten others to make a team and that they may or may not like them all.

The manners women bring with them are those of another society, a society whose members are bent on the maintenance of relationships for they are the most immediate definition of who one is. Relationships for women tend to be ends in themselves and there is little in the traditional feminine experience to contradict this. As a result, and without even knowing it, women tend to fall into the great trap of "overemotionalism": intolerance – "I don't like him or her and I can't work with either of them" – or a painful vulnerability to criticism.

If a woman assumes without thinking that the quality of relationships is her most important priority and acts on it, if she tends not to have tangible career objectives, if as a consequence she focuses her energies on job performance in the here and now, oblivious to the informal pressures and counterpressures that influence promotion, the chances are painfully small that she will be able to distance herself from the difficulties of the corporate present by making them current costs of a career future. The chances are not much greater that others, men, will even see her as acting as if she wanted one.

All of these differences in mind-set in fact add up to an image – an image that many women in management positions unconsciously convey to the men they work with. Men in management positions tend to judge other men on the basis of the assumptions they hold about themselves, about management careers in general and about the particular companies for which they work. Women's assumptions tend to be different on every level but this is hardly ever an issue that either men or women consciously deal with, and even the man who prides himself on being fair – "I try to treat everyone alike" – is inevitably applying the same standards he uses to evaluate himself and other men to the evaluation of women. As a result he tends to see someone who seems more diffident about getting ahead, someone he therefore assumes to be less "motivated," someone who may appear to be intolerant or over-reactive in comparison with the men he supervises, someone who seems to ignore the informal side of organizations. All of these perceptions come together to the lasting disadvantage of many women as middle management positions draw near.

THE FEMALE ADVANTAGE

SALLY HELGESEN

From The Female Advantage: Women's Ways of Leadership (1990)
New York: Doubleday Currency

In her classic *Toward a New Psychology of Women,* Jean Baker Miller observes that the female values of responsibility, connection, and inclusion have been devalued in our culture, which tends to celebrate the lone hero, the rugged individual. Psychologists in particular, she notes, have tended to equate a strong awareness of human interdependence with a failure to develop a strong and mature sense of self, and they have seen the desire to serve others as neurotic, something to be "worked through."[1] Yet Miller also observes that in recent years this bias has begun to diminish, as alienation, loneliness, family instability, and resulting problems of drugs and random crime have forced the recognition that a sense of human community is much needed in modern culture. In addition, the environmental consciousness that has developed is making even the most obdurate individualists admit that everyone's actions do impact on everyone else.[2]

As a result, the female view that one strengthens oneself by strengthening others is finding greater acceptance, and female values of inclusion and connection are emerging as valuable leadership qualities. As Miller notes, this kind of leadership is precisely what is needed in order to address the alienation that troubles our public sphere institutions – business, politics, medicine, and the law. Much current literature, philosophy, and social commentary focuses on the lack of human connection in these institutions, a lack which has resulted in widespread concern about this culture's inability to organize the fruits of technology to serve human ends. Miller sees this as "perhaps the central problem of the dominant male culture."[3] It amounts to the exaltation of efficiency at the expense of humane values.

What is needed, then, is leaders who can work against these feelings of alienation that affect our institutions, by bridging the gap between the demands of efficiency and the need to nurture the human spirit. Reconciling these values is particularly important in today's competitive economic landscape, where the intelligence, commitment, and enthusiasm of employees are more crucial to the success of an enterprise than they have been in the past. No longer is there a single "right way" to do things, as there was in the industrial era, when employees had simply to master a set of tasks or a predictable routine and then, making as few errors as possible, stick with that. The nature of the information economy, and the demands of the team approach, require employees who can think, participate, speak up, take initiative, and devise new ideas.

But more than just the nature of work is changing; the nature of people who work is changing too. Employees today are less likely to put up with a workplace that emphasizes efficiency at the expense of meeting human needs. According to a recent report in *The Wall Street Journal*, people entering the workplace today are more concerned with intangibles such as being happy, working in a good environment, and having opportunities for growth, than any group of people in the past.[4] A survey of college students revealed that salary ranked only sixth in importance among a list of job considerations, well behind intangibles like satisfaction and fulfillment, and that people entering today's labor-short job market are comfortable with the notion of changing companies if they experience even a well-paying job as inhumane or stifling.[5]

Given the changing nature both of work and of people who work, there emerges a need for leaders who can stimulate employees to work with zest and spirit. Such leaders must create an ambiance that reflects human values, and devise organizational structures that encourage and nurture human growth. Creating an ambiance here must be understood in the largest sense as setting a tone that expresses a unified vision of why an organization exists, and devising a style that communicates that vision.

ORGANIZING AMBIANCE

The physical space in which an organization functions gives a good indication of its values, of how well it reconciles being efficient with being humane. The organizational spaces that the women in the diary studies helped create all function as visible manifestations of their particular styles of leadership, and in very different ways give impetus to work being done with creativity and zest. [The diary studies are narratives describing the experience of four women leaders, which served as the empirical basis for the book within which this chapter appears.]

Dorothy Brunson paid deliberate attention to the physical design of the offices of her flagship station, WEBB. She says, "I collect antiques and paintings at home, but I would never surround myself with such things at the office. I believe a feeling of freshness and light is most appropriate for where people work. I get depressed just walking into most CEOs' offices. I see all that heavy expensive furniture, that dark wood and those thick carpets, and I wonder what the guy is trying to prove. Why is he trying to remove himself, create this private Oz? It's certainly inappropriate for a hands-on manager who wants to be involved. I want the style of my office to show that I'm *not* removed. I want my people to feel as if they're part of what's going on. Having lots of fancy things isolates you by proclaiming your status."

In order to facilitate the kind of constant interchange that she believes fosters spirit and fresh ideas, Dorothy Brunson has organized her suite of offices around a large glass-walled central meeting room. The informal spot works for large meetings, but also serves as a kind of "clearing," a place for people to meet and keep in touch. Brunson's own offices (both of them) have windows that open directly onto this central room, and windows cut into other offices also provide a view. In the entire suite, there are no curtains or shades on the outside windows. "I don't want anything that closes people off – from me, from each other, or from the world. Our business thrives on information, on staying in touch, and that's what I try to re-create in my offices."

The main floor of Nancy Badore's Executive Development Center is also orga-nized around a large central open room, this one circular, around which the offices fan out in a weblike structure. This meeting room, where those taking their train-ing meet with members of the staff for the kind of break time that Nancy Badore believes is so important, serves as the heart of the organization. Food, coffee, and soft drinks are set out on buffet tables in this room, to feed those in training and encourage "hanging out." Both the way the space is organized and the way it's used are reminiscent of the central piazza in an Italian town, which serves the function of knitting the populace together. "We like the place to be noisy and messy so that people will feel at ease, so we drag chairs in, do whatever we need to do," says Nancy Badore. She has also introduced the custom of scattering plates of fruit around the offices, both in order to encourage healthy eating and to provide stations for infor-mal encounters. She believes that encouraging such moments is important because "some of the most meaningful exchanges take place during those unplanned moments, when people in an organization have a chance to really get talking."

This drive to provide a way for others to keep in touch lies at the heart of the women's decisions about how to use their organizational spaces. So does their refusal to emphasize their own status. Both these impulses are manifestations of the strategy of the web, in which authority results from strengthening interconnections and drawing others close. Having this as a source of strength eliminates the need for status accoutrements, the function of which is always to define and reinforce distance. Drawing her authority from interconnections, Barbara Grogan has no need to assert her role as boss by having a separate office with a door that closes, or a lot of external space to set it apart. Instead she uses low room dividers and has no door, so that "my people can holler when they need me."

A similar focus is apparent in the way Frances Hesselbein allocates office space in the Girl Scouts' fourteen-story office building in midtown Manhattan. She decided against bunching management team members – who are the "first ring" in her orbit – together on an upper floor, as in common in so many companies as large as the Girl Scouts. "Our idea was to put management team members with the people they worked with, not to use office allocation to make a statement about who's 'on top' – who's on the highest floor, or closest to the president.

That sort of status location has no importance around here. Management team members have their offices on the same floor as their support staff so they can be in the *middle* of what's going on."

The women's spaces are not only organized in ways that foster and engage the human spirit; they are also efficient means for facilitating interaction and infor-mation flow. They contrast with the innate inefficiency of spaces organized to reflect bureaucratic divisions and hierarchical rankings, which not only discourage the spirit, but provide a physical paradigm of limited and rigid channels of access. Such spaces reveal that the exaltation of efficiency at the expense of humane values, which Jean Baker Miller describes as characteristic of our public sphere institutions, is in fact a false dichotomy. A use of space that facilitates interconnection and seeks to encourage communication will be both efficient *and* humane.

But it takes a mind that thinks beyond convention to see that these two princi-ples can be reconciled. A more prosaic and limited definition of efficiency cannot get beyond the assumption of dichotomy. I was particularly struck by the imaginativeness of Nancy Badore's policy of keeping fruit around the office in order both to encourage healthy eating and to provide spontaneous opportunities for interaction. The policy was in total contrast to one that I saw instituted in the company where I was a speechwriter at the very time our unit was charged with trying to persuade employees to take more initiative, be more creative, and think beyond the narrow confines of their job descriptions. In the midst of that campaign, even as we tried to reassure people that they mattered to the company, the head of our division abruptly ordered all the water coolers removed. Not only had he decided that providing fresh healthful water to employees was a waste of corporate profits (although extravagant perks for executives remained in place), he also believed that providing a place on every floor where people could gather spontaneously encouraged employees to fritter away time chatting with one another, rather than remaining at their desks, poring over their work. And yet it was obvious to anyone who moved around the floor that many of people's most imaginative ideas resulted from just such informal talk, from casual discussion of company policy and needs. The removal of the water coolers, a small gesture in itself, came to epitomize the company's values: sacrificing the human spirit in the interests of a narrow vision of efficiency that ended up being inefficient.

But perhaps it takes an outsider's eye to see beneath such surface dichotomies, to understand how water coolers (or bowls of fruit) could be ultimately efficient. And here is a perfect example of how women's position as historic outsiders in the corporation can provide them with an advantage in a time of rapid change. Many of the rituals of corporate life are not only deadening to the spirit, but also inefficient; ways of reinforcing status that have nothing at all to do with how the job gets done. Rather, they are ways for exemplifying what Alfred Sloan, former president of General Motors, defined as "professionalism" – that kind of autonomy and distance that become self-perpetuating. Rarely are these rituals questioned so long as insiders who share similar and established values dominate positions of leadership.

An example is a story that Marlene Sanders, the former network executive and television reporter, told at a recent media conference in Washington, D.C.[6] Sanders related how, upon being made corporate VP at her network, she was warned that she would have to learn to play one-draw poker, skill at the game being essential among the brass. She studied the game until she mastered it, imagining that it must be important, perhaps providing a useful model of corporate strategy. A few weeks later, while flying with the other New York vice presidents (all male) to Los Angeles, she spent the entire flight relieving the men of their money.

"They were *so* impressed. I had proven I could keep up with the boys who sat at the big table. I had passed their testing ritual, showed I could be as macho as them. But I realized very quickly that that was *the only purpose* the game served – it was a way of proving you were a worthy member of the club. But that worthiness had absolutely *nothing* to do with the execution of your job! Furthermore, the game provided a way to avoid discussing what was really important, preparing for our meeting, or even just getting to know one another. It was a way of distancing, not communicating, and as our plane landed in L.A. I couldn't help thinking what a colossal waste of five perfectly good hours it had been. And one thing I felt sure of: if it had been a group of women, we would never have wasted our time on such a childish game!"

The poker game provided a way for the men in the group to assert their need for status, to create definable winners and losers. In such competitive tests, a participant communicates by posing rather than by speaking and listening, which casts relationships into a purely symbolic realm. Like the isolated CEO's office with intimidatingly huge furniture and thick absorbent rugs, games that serve no purpose except to prove that you are a "winner" ultimately impede the flow of communication.

LISTENING

Communication is what defines the style of leadership that reconciles efficiency with human values. Communication involves using the voice as an instrument to disseminate vision, and also stresses the crucial role that listening plays. But in the hierarchical pyramid, being a skilled listener is not a function of leadership, since information is filtered on its way up and decisions passed down.

The women in the diary studies are all skilled listeners; it was a strong aspect of their management style. They used listening both as a tool to gather information that had bearing on managerial decisions, and as a way of making the people in their organizations feel that their ideas and beliefs were of value. Frances Hesselbein viewed listening as a discipline that lay at the very heart of her kind of leadership. In her view, a good leader was one who knew "exactly how to bring out what's best in people," and only a leader who really listened could hope to do this. Her policy of making herself personally available to hear whatever suggestions people in her company had to make – along with her refusal to look at her watch whenever anyone was talking – all evidenced her belief in the value of careful and patient listening.

For Dorothy Brunson, listening was the method she used to find the clues she needed in order to know how to handle a person. Listening told her what role she should adopt in a given situation, what aspect of herself she should play up. At Nancy Badore's Executive Development Center, which had as its mission teaching managers to "talk up the ladder," getting leaders to *listen down the ladder* was the implicit corollary. The changes in Ford's management style, in which Nancy Badore has played a part, provide an example of the role of listening in the reinvented corporation. The very crux of the company's managerial revolution has lain in requiring leaders who had previously been exclusively speakers to *listen* to what their people have to say.

Listening is perhaps the prototypical female skill. Studies on gender differences in the use of language suggest that men tend to speak far more than women, while women do more of the listening. Furthermore, the quality of women's listening is different – more intense, more thoughtful, more attentive.[7] The differences between the sexes are large and persistent in this regard, and apply both in the workplace and at home, despite many men's persistent belief that women are the "gabbers" while they are the strong, silent types.[8] But women's greater aptitude for and skill in listening hardly comes as a surprise, since listening is characteristic of subordinates, who survive by reading the emotions, discerning the desires, and anticipating the needs of those in control.

Yet, as the diary studies make clear, this propensity to listen remains with women when they have moved far beyond subordinate positions. Even when they find their voices, and start to speak assertively as leaders, women nevertheless retain a strong value and talent for listening. That this is so implies that listening is not just a consequence of subordinate status, but something women value in itself. And indeed, in *A Different Voice*, Carol Gilligan notes that the deference women exhibit in their ability and willingness to listen "is rooted not just in social subordination, but also *in the substance of their moral concern*."[9] It is a skill intrinsic to their values for responsibility, interconnection, and inclusion, not simply a result of their position, as "the second sex." Women value listening as a way of making others feel comfortable and important, and as a means of encouraging others to find their own voices and grow. Sara Ruddick, in her book *Maternal Thinking*, recognizes listening as an aspect of the "labor of care"[10] that is characteristic of how mothers nurture growth in their children. Thus a propensity and value for listening persists even when women assume leadership positions; it is an essential part of the female talent for "raising others up and drawing them forth." It is both a manifestation of moral concern that reflects women's human values, and an efficient means of stimulating the flow information.

One of the women I interviewed when preparing to write this book talked about what she called "analytic listening," an essential element of her management style. Nancy Singer is the president and CEO of Premier Banks, a six-bank division of the First of America Corporation, a holding company in the Midwest. With responsibility for 340 employees, she manages to schedule in regular time several early mornings a week so that people can come by her office just to talk.

Nancy Singer believes that most managers make the mistake of assuming that a single style of management works with everyone. "That's all wrong. Different things work with different people, but you can only know what works with who by taking the time to get to know your people. And that does not mean knowing them in broad strokes. You have to know the details, understand the fine strokes of who your people are. And that means listening to what they have to say – about themselves, about their work, about what they want from the future."[11]

As she listens, Singer is constantly analyzing. "I ask myself, what precisely motivates this person? Is it challenge? A desire to enjoy the work? Or is the motivation purely monetary? Does this person need approval from the group? How ambitious is he? What are his aspirations? Is his family and personal life a major consideration, or is his career his primary focus? When I have that kind of information I can decide how to act – who needs stroking, who needs space, who needs more mentoring. Listening helps me know when to promote, when to challenge, when to encourage, when to caution. It helps me guide the fit between a person and his or her job. To manage expectations – that's what's important! But you can't do it unless you gather detailed information, and that means listening with sensitivity to what people say."

Singer describes the process as a synthesis of intellectual power and emotional response. "What it's really all about is bringing my logical analytic skills to bear in the service of human understanding." Thus analytic listening is a skill that bridges the apparent dichotomy between a bottom-line focus and a concern for people, between ends and means, between efficient and humane.

COLLABORATIVE NEGOTIATION

Dorothy Brunson and Barbara Grogan, when asked what they viewed as their greatest strengths, both said that they were good negotiators. Dorothy Brunson's delight in the process was evident: "Let's negotiate it!" was her immediate response when anyone asked her for something. But negotiating for her was not so much a way of winning as a process that enabled her to build relationships. Her focus was both on getting a deal that served her company's interests and on keeping the other party happy, so that he or she would "keep coming back for more." Thus, by focusing on the long-term interaction, she used negotiation to bridge the gap between the efficient and the humane.

According to Leonard Greenhalgh, a professor at the Amos Tuck School of Business Administration at Dartmouth University, this approach to negotiation as a collaborate effort with long-term implications is characteristic of women. Greenhalgh has done extensive research both on what makes an effective negotiator, and on gender differences in negotiating styles. He has concluded from his studies that women's values for interdependence and mutuality make them treat negotiations within the context of continuing relationships that require contact, interaction, and agreement. By contrast, men's focus on independence, competitiveness, and autonomy makes them more likely to see negotiations as an opportunity for winning or besting an opponent than for collaborating or building a relationship.[12]

Greenhalgh points out that sports metaphors of winning, losing, and scoring points have largely governed notions of negotiations in the public realm as they have been presided over by men. He attributes this to the role that sports play in male development, and to the prevalence of competitive games among male children, which he contrasts with the relationship-oriented games played by girls. He notes that girls' games teach them the importance of preserving and enhancing relationships – a long-term focus – while boys' games teach them to preserve and enhance their own feelings of self-worth at the expense of relationships – a competitive focus that is of necessity short-term.[13] Thus Greenhalgh, in contrast to observers like Betty Harragan and the authors of *The Managerial Woman*, does not view girls' games as a pointless waste of time, but as valuable training for the task of fostering human relationships.

In addition, he cites a debilitating tendency among men to rely on rules to enforce agreements, in accord with the sports metaphor of "playing by the rules." This emphasis encourages a legalistic frame of mind that, by undermining and devaluing the importance of trust, increases a negotiator's tendency to litigate disputes. Also, Greenhalgh notes that sports norms do not permit players to let one team win this week in exchange for reciprocal leniency by the other team next week, since "the history and future of the ongoing relationship between contestants is irrelevant in sports."[14]

Because of women's gift for collaborative agreement and their concern with fostering relationships in the long term, Greenhalgh would like to see women leaders play a more active role in negotiating, for example, international treaties. He views many problems on the world stage, as well as in American business, as resulting from men's tendency to focus on winning and their eagerness to resort to legalistic resolutions.

As women's leadership qualities come to play a more dominant role in the public sphere, their particular aptitudes for long-term negotiating, analytic listening, and creating an ambiance in which people work with zest and spirit will help reconcile the split between the ideals of being efficient and being humane. This integration of female values is already producing a more collaborative kind of leadership, and changing the very ideal of what strong leadership actually is. The old lone hero leader is increasingly being recognized as not only deadening to the human spirit, but also ultimately inefficient. The Ford Motor Company, seeking a phrase to express the essence of its managerial revolution, adopted a motto that expresses this recognition: "*No more heroes!*" Thus as the values, skills, and experience of women, so long restricted to the private, domestic sphere, are integrated into the public realm, what Jean Baker Miller calls women's "much greater sense of the pleasure of close connection with physical, emotional, and mental growth than men"[15] will create an environment that meets the needs of people who work today.

NOTES

1   Miller, Jean Baker. *Toward a New Psychology of Women*. Boston: Beacon Press, 1976, pp. 24–25.
2   Ibid., pp. 40–47.
3   Ibid., p. 24.
4   *The Wall Street Journal*, October 26, 1988, p. 1.
5   Ibid., p. 1.
6   Quoted at Women and Men in the Media Conference, the National Press Club, Washington, D. C., April 10, 1989.
7   Belenky, Mary Field; Clinchy, Blythe McVicker; Goldberger, Nancy Rule; Tarule, Jill Mattuck. *Women's Ways of Knowing*. New York: Basic Books, 1989, pp. 44–45.
8   Ibid., p. 45.
9   Gilligan, Carol. *In a Different Voice*. Cambridge: Harvard University Press, 1976, p. 16.
10   Ruddick, Sara. *Maternal Thinking: Toward a Politics of Peace*. Boston: Beacon Press, 1989, pp. 82–102.
11   Interview with the author, April 27, 1989.
12   Greenhalgh, Leonard. "Effects of Sex-Role Differences on Approach to Interpersonal and Interorganizational Negotiations." Private paper, 1985.
13   Greenhalgh, Leonard. "The Case Against Winning in Negotiations," *Negotiation Journal*, April 1987, pp. 167–73.
14   Ibid., p. 171.
15   Miller, p. 40.

MEN AND WOMEN OF THE CORPORATION

ROSABETH MOSS KANTER

From Men and Women of the Corporation (1977)
New York: Basic Books

OPPORTUNITY AS A SELF-FULFILLING PROPHECY: CYCLES OF ADVANTAGE AND DISADVANTAGE

Opportunity structures shape behavior in such a way that they confirm their own prophecies. Those people set on high-mobility tracks tend to develop attitudes and values that impel them further along the track: work commitment, high aspirations, and upward orientations. Those set on low-mobility tracks tend to become indifferent, to give up, and thus to "prove" that their initial placement was correct. They develop low-risk, conservative attitudes, or become complaining critics, demonstrating how right the organization was not to let them go further. It is graphically clear how cycles of advantage and cycles of disadvantage are perpetuated in organizations and in society. What the clerical worker with low motivation to be promoted might need is a promotion; what the chronic complainer might need is a growthful challenge. But who would be likely to give it to them? [. . .]

The structure of organizations plays a powerful role in creating work behavior. Women in low-mobility organizational situations develop attitudes and orientations that are sometimes said to be characteristic of those people as individuals or "women as a group," but that can more profitably be viewed as more universal *human* responses to blocked opportunities.

Beyond sex differences

This analysis should thus lead to a reinterpretation of familiar findings about sex differences in work behavior: that men are more ambitious, task-oriented, and work-involved, and women care more about relationships at work.[1] When women seem to be less motivated or committed, it is probably because their jobs carry less opportunity. There is evidence that in general the jobs held by most women workers tend to have shorter chains of opportunity associated with them and contain fewer advancement prospects. This is true in production as well as clerical jobs. One study

Table 4.1 Percentage of Men and Women in Jobs with Long and Short Opportunity Structures in eleven Industries

	Number of non-supervisory workers	% Male	% Female	% of workers to total
1. Craft or craft type progression	1,350,000	95	5	19
2. Long, narrow pyramid progression – at least 6 steps normally	1,235,000	68	32	18
3. Moderate pyramid progression – 3 to 5 steps normally	2,045,000	39	61	29
4. Flat pyramid progression – at most, 2 steps normally	2,390,000	36	64	34
	7,020,000	54% (average)	46% (average)	100%

Source: William J. Crinker et al., *Climbing the Job Ladder*, New York: E. F. Shelley and Co., 1970, p. 13.

looked at industries employing about 17 percent of the U.S. work force (motor vehicles and parts, basic steel, communications, department and variety stores, commercial banking, insurance carriers, and hotels and motels). It was found that as the amount of progression possible in non-supervisory jobs increased (the number of steps of opportunity they contained), the proportion of women declined markedly.[2] Though women represented nearly half of all non-supervisory workers, they constituted 64 percent of workers in the "flattest" jobs (least advancement opportunities) and 5 percent of workers in the highest opportunity jobs. (See Table 4.1) A recent Canadian study examined 307 white-collar workers in twenty firms, half of them women. The women were clustered in the jobs with less control, more machine work, lower incomes, less job security, and less chance to be promoted into management. Thirty percent of the women, compared with 21 percent of the men, felt they had little or no chance of promotion; 60 percent of them, compared with 45 percent of the men, had had no promotions of any kind in the previous year. Only 5 percent of the women, versus nearly a third of the men, expected management jobs in the future. This low female expectation was confirmed by a management sample that predicted *no promotions* for 21 percent of the women (compared with 6 percent of the men).[3] Surveys have also shown that women are more likely to exhibit "normlessness": a perception that ability has little to do with getting ahead.[4]

Two sociological studies in particular bring an ironic twist to the popular picture of women as less intrinsically work-committed than men. One demonstrated that work is not a "central life interest" of factory workers by using a sample of *men*. The second showed that work is a central life interest of professionals by studying an all-women sample of nurses,[5] women who did have opportunity. Interestingly enough, these women found personal satisfaction but not necessarily personal friendships at work. In another study of teachers and nurses, the women were more committed to their organizations than the men (perhaps because the fields were defined as offering strong opportunities for women), and those with "sponsors" to aid their mobility had the highest commitment. Women can also be more committed than men at upper levels when they have had to work harder to overcome barriers; effort helps build commitment.[6] At the same time, *men with low opportu-*

nity look more like the stereotype of women in their orientations toward work, as research on blue-collar men has shown; they limit their aspirations, seek satisfaction in activities outside of work, dream of escape, interrupt their careers, emphasize leisure and consumption, and create sociable peer groups in which interpersonal relationships take precedence over other aspects of work.[7] [. . .]

> The token woman stands in the Square of the Immaculate Exception blessing pigeons from a blue pedestal. . . . The token woman is placed like a scarecrow in the long haired corn: her muscles are wooden. Why does she ride into battle on a clothes horse?
> **Marge Piercy,** *Living in the Open*

Up the ranks in Industrial Supply Corporation, one of the most consequential conditions of work for women was also among the simplest to identify: there were so few of them. On the professional and managerial levels, Industrial Supply Corporation was nearly a single-sex organization. Women held less than 10 percent of the exempt (salaried) jobs starting at the bottom grades – a 50 percent rise from a few years earlier – and there were no women at the level reporting to officers. When Indsco was asked to participate in a meeting on women in business by bringing their women executives to a civic luncheon, the corporate personnel committee had no difficulty selecting them. There were only five sufficiently senior women in the organization. [. . .]

The life of women in the corporation was influenced by the proportions in which they found themselves. Those women who were few in number among male peers and often had "only woman" status became tokens: symbols of how-women-can-do, stand-ins for all women. Sometimes they had the advantages of those who are "different" and thus were highly visible in a system where success is tied to becoming known. Sometimes they faced the loneliness of the outsider, of the stranger who intrudes upon an alien culture and may become self-estranged in the process of assimilation. In any case, their turnover and "failure rate" were known to be much higher than those of men in entry and early grade positions; in the sales function, women's turnover was twice that of men. What happened around Indsco women resembled other reports of the experiences of women in politics, law, medicine, or management who have been the few among many men.

At the same time, they also echoed the experiences of people of any kind who are rare and scarce: the lone black among whites, the lone man among women, the few foreigners among natives. Any situation where proportions of significant types of people are highly skewed can produce similar themes and processes. It was rarity and scarcity, rather than femaleness *per se*, that shaped the environment for women in the parts of Indsco mostly populated by men. . . .

THE MANY AND THE FEW: THE SIGNIFICANCE OF PROPORTIONS FOR SOCIAL LIFE

[. . .] To understand the dramas of the many and the few in the organization requires a theory and a vocabulary. Four group types can be identified on the basis of different proportional representations of kinds of people, as Figure 4.1 shows. *Uniform* groups have only one kind of person, one significant social type. The group may develop its own differentiations, of course, but groups called uniform can be

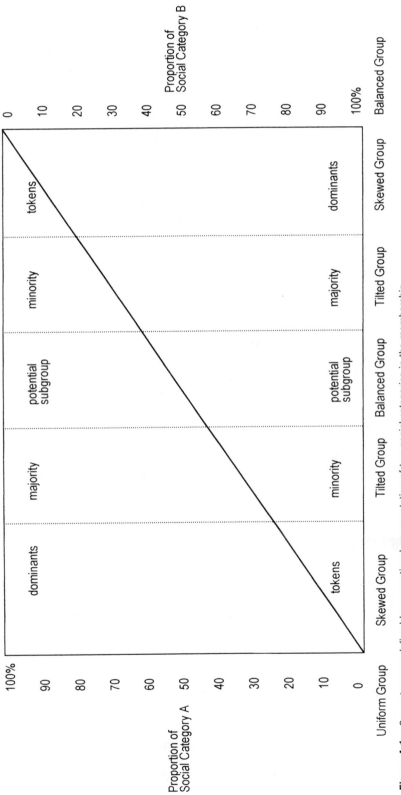

Figure 4.1 Group types as defined by proportional representation of two social categories in the membership

considered homogeneous with respect to salient external master statuses such as sex, race, or ethnicity. Uniform groups have a typological ratio of 100:0. *Skewed* groups are those in which there is a large preponderance of one type over another, up to a ratio of perhaps 85:15. The numerically dominant types also control the group and its culture in enough ways to be labeled "dominants." The few of another type in a skewed group can appropriately be called "tokens," for, like the Indsco exempt women, they are often treated as representatives of their category, as symbols rather than individuals. If the absolute size of the skewed group is small, tokens can also be solos, the only one of their kind present; but even if there are two tokens in a skewed group, it is difficult for them to generate an alliance that can become powerful in the group, as we shall see later. Next, *tilted* groups begin to move toward less extreme distributions and less exaggerated effects. In this situation, with ratios of perhaps 65:35, dominants are just a "majority" and tokens become a "minority." Minority members have potential allies among each other, can form coalitions, and can affect the culture of the group. They begin to become individuals differentiated from each other as well as a type differentiated from the majority. Finally, at about 60:40 and down to 50:50, the group becomes *balanced*. Culture and interaction reflect this balance. Majority and minority turn into potential subgroups that may or may not generate actual type-based identifications. Outcomes for individuals in such a balanced peer group, regardless of type, will depend more on other structural and personal factors, including formation of subgroups or differentiated roles and abilities.

It is the characteristics of the second type, the skewed group, that underlay the behavior and treatment of professional and managerial women observed at Indsco. If the ratio of women to men in various parts of the organization begins to shift, as affirmative action and new hiring and promotion policies promised, forms of relationships and peer culture should also change. But as of the mid-1970s, the dynamics of tokenism predominated in Indsco's exempt ranks, and women and men were in the positions of token and dominant. Tokenism, like low opportunity and low power, set in motion self-perpetuating cycles that served to reinforce the low numbers of women and, in the absence of external intervention, to keep women in the position of token.

VIEWING THE FEW: WHY TOKENS FACE SPECIAL SITUATIONS

The proportional rarity of tokens is associated with three perceptual tendencies: visibility, contrast, and assimilation. These are all derived simply from the ways any set of objects are perceived. If one sees nine X's and one 0:

$$X \quad X \quad x \quad x \quad X \quad X \quad 0 \quad X \quad x \quad X$$

the 0 will stand out. The 0 may also be overlooked, but if it is seen at all, it will get more notice than any X. Further, the X's may seem more alike than different because of their contrast with the 0. And it will be easier to assimilate the 0 to generalizations about all 0's than to do the same with the X's, which offer more examples and thus, perhaps, more variety and individuation. The same perceptual factors operate in social situations, and they generate special pressures for token women.

First, tokens get attention. One by one, they have higher visibility than dominants looked at alone; they capture a larger awareness share. A group member's awareness share, averaged over other individuals of the same social type, declines as the proportion of total membership occupied by the category increases, because each individual becomes less and less surprising, unique, or noteworthy. In Gestalt psychology terms, those who get to be common more easily become "ground" rather than "figure"; as the group moves from skewed to tilted, tokens turn into a less individually noticed minority. But for tokens, there is a "law of increasing returns": as individuals of their type represent a *smaller* numerical proportion of the overall group, they each potentially capture a *larger* share of the awareness given to that group.

Contrast – or polarization and exaggeration of differences – is the second perceptual tendency. In uniform groups, members and observers may never become self-conscious about the common culture and type, which remain taken for granted and implicit. But the presence of a person or two bearing a different set of social characteristics increases the self-consciousness of the numerically dominant population and the consciousness of observers about what makes the dominants a class. They become more aware both of their commonalities and their difference from the token, and to preserve their commonality, they try to keep the token slightly outside, to offer a boundary for the dominants. There is a tendency to exaggerate the extent of the differences between tokens and dominants, because as we see next, tokens are, by definition, too few in numbers to defeat any attempts at generalization. It is thus easier for the commonalities of dominants to be defined in contrast to the token than in tilted or balanced groups. One person can be perceptually isolated and seen as cut off from the core of the group more than many, who begin to represent too great a share of what is called the group.

Assimilation, the third perceptual tendency, involves the use of stereotypes, or familiar generalizations about a person's social type. The characteristics of a token tend to be distorted to fit the generalization. Tokens are more easily stereotyped than people found in greater proportion. If there were enough people of the token's type to let discrepant examples occur, it is eventually possible that the generalization would change to accommodate the accumulated cases. But in skewed groups, it is easier to retain the generalization and distort the perception of the token. It is also easier for tokens to find an instant identity by conforming to the preexisting stereotypes. So tokens are, ironically, both highly visible as people who are different and yet not permitted the individuality of their own unique, non-stereotypical characteristics. [. . .]

Visibility, contrast, and assimilation are each associated with particular forces and dynamics that, in turn, generate typical token responses. These dynamics are, again, similar regardless of the category from which the tokens come, although the specific kinds of people and their history of relationships with dominants provide cultural content for specific communications. Visibility tends to create *performance pressures* on the token. Contrast leads to heightening of *dominant culture boundaries*, including isolation of the token. And assimilation results in the token's *role encapsulation*.

The experiences of exempt women at Industrial Supply Corporation took their shape from these processes.

PERFORMANCE PRESSURES: LIFE IN THE LIMELIGHT

Indsco's upper-level women, especially those in sales, were highly visible, much more so than their male peers. Even those who reported they felt ignored and overlooked were known in their immediate divisions and spotted when they did something unusual. But the ones who felt ignored also seemed to be those in jobs not enmeshed in the interpersonal structure of the company: for example, a woman in public relations who had only a clerical assistant reporting to her and whose job did not occupy a space in the competitive race to the top.

In the sales force, where peer culture and informal relations were most strongly entrenched, everyone knew about the women. They were the subject of conversation, questioning, gossip, and careful scrutiny. Their placements were known and observed through the division, whereas those of most men typically were not. Their names came up at meetings, and they would easily be used as examples. Travelers to locations with women in it would bring back news of the latest about the women, along with other gossip. In other functions, too, the women developed well-known names, and their characteristics would often be broadcast through the system in anticipation of their arrival in another office to do a piece of work. A woman swore in an elevator in an Atlanta hotel while going to have drinks with colleagues, and it was known all over Chicago a few days later that she was a "radical." And some women were even told by their managers that they were watched more closely than the men. Sometimes the manager was intending to be helpful, to let the woman know that he would be right there behind her. But the net effect was the same as all of the visibility phenomena. Tokens typically performed their jobs under public and symbolic conditions different from those of dominants.

The upper-level women became public creatures. It was difficult for them to do anything in training programs, on their jobs, or even at informal social affairs that would not attract public notice. This provided the advantage of an attention-getting edge at the same time that it made privacy and anonymity impossible. A saleswoman reported: "I've been at sales meetings where all the trainees were going up to the managers – 'Hi, Mr. So-and-So' – trying to make that impression, wearing a strawberry tie, whatever, something that they could be remembered by. Whereas there were three of us [women] in a group of fifty, and all we had to do was walk in and everyone recognized us."

But their mistakes or their intimate relationships were known as readily as other information. Many felt their freedom of action was restricted, and they would have preferred to be less noticeable, as these typical comments indicated: "If it seems good to be noticed, wait until you make your first major mistake." "It's a burden for the manager who gets asked about a woman and has to answer behind-the-back stuff about her. It doesn't reach the woman unless he tells her. The manager gets it and has to deal with it." "I don't have as much freedom of behavior as men do; I can't be as independent." [. . .]

Tokens' responses to performance pressures

A manager posed the issue for scarce women this way: "Can they survive the organizational scrutiny?" The choices for those in the token position were either to over-achieve and carefully construct a public performance that minimized organizational and peer concerns, to try to turn the notoriety of publicity to advantage, or to find ways to become socially invisible. The first course means that the tokens involved are already outstanding and exceptional, able to perform well under close observation where others are ready to notice first and to attribute any problems to the characteristics that set them apart – but also able to develop skills in impressions management that permit them to retain control over the extra consequences loaded onto their acts. This choice involved creating a delicate balance between always doing well and not generating peer resentment. Such dexterity requires both job-related competence and political sensitivity that could take years to acquire. For this reason, young women just out of college had the greatest difficulty in entering male domains like the Indsco sales force and were responsible for much of the high turnover among women in sales. Women were successful, on the other hand, who were slightly older than their male peers, had strong technical backgrounds, and had already had previous experiences as token women among male peers. The success of such women was most likely to increase the prospects for hiring more women in the future; they worked for themselves and as symbols.

The second strategy, accepting notoriety and trading on it, seemed least likely to succeed in a corporate environment because of the power of peers. A few women at Indsco flaunted themselves in the public arena in which they operated and made a point out of demonstrating their "difference," as in refusing to go to certain programs, parading their high-level connections, or bypassing the routine authority structure. Such boldness was usually accompanied by top management sponsorship. But this strategy was made risky by shifting power alliances at the top; the need to secure peer cooperation in certain jobs where negotiation, bargaining, and the power of others to generate advantage or disadvantage through their use of the rules were important; and the likelihood that some current peers would eventually reach the top. Furthermore, those women who sought publicity and were getting it in part for their rarity developed a stake in not sharing the spotlight. They enjoyed their only-women status, since it gave them an advantage, and they seemed less consciously aware than the other women of the attendant dangers, pressures, psychic costs, and disadvantages. In a few instances, they operated so as to keep other women out by excessive criticism of possible new-hires or by subtly undercutting a possible woman peer (who eventually left the company), something that, we shall see later, was also pushed for by the male dominants. Thus, this second strategy eventually kept the numbers of women down both because the token herself was in danger of not succeeding and because she might keep other women out. This second strategy, then, serves to reinforce the dynamics of tokenism by ensuring that, in the absence of external pressures like affirmative action, the group remains skewed.

The third choice was more often accepted by the older generation of corporate women, who predated the women's movement and had years ago accommodated to token status. It involved attempts to limit visibility, to become "socially invisible." This strategy characterizes women who try to minimize their sexual attributes so as to blend unnoticeably into the predominant male culture, perhaps by adopting "mannish dress," as in reports by other investigators. Or it can include avoidance of public events and occasions for performance – staying away from meetings, working at home rather than in the office, keeping silent at meetings. Several of the saleswomen deliberately took such a "low profile," unlike male peers who tended to seize every opportunity to make themselves noticed. They avoided conflict, risks, or controversial situation. They were relieved or happy to step into assistant or technical staff jobs such as personnel administration or advertising, where they could quietly play background roles that kept men in the visible forefront – or they at least did not object when the corporation put them into low-visibility jobs, since for many years the company had a stake in keeping its "unusual" people hidden. . . . Women making this choice, then, did blend into the background and control their performance pressures, but at the cost of limited recognition of their competence. This choice, too, involved a psychic splitting, for rewards for such people often came with secret knowledge – knowing what they had contributed almost anonymously to an effort that made someone else look good. In general, this strategy, like the last, also reinforces the existence of tokenism and keeps the numbers of women down, because it leads the organization to conclude that women are not very effective: low risk-takers who cannot stand on their own.

The performance pressures on people in token positions generate a set of attitudes and behaviors that appear sex-linked, in the case of women, but can be understood better as situational responses, true of any person in a token role. Perhaps what has been called in the popular literature "fear of success in women," for example, is really the token woman's *fear of visibility*. . . . [This], then, is one response to performance pressures in a token's situation. The token must often choose between trying to limit visibility – and being overlooked – or taking advantage of the publicity – and being labeled a "troublemaker."

BOUNDARY HEIGHTENING AND MEMBERSHIP COSTS: TOKENS IN DOMINANTS' GROUPS

Contrast, or exaggeration of the token's differences from dominants, sets a second set of dynamics in motion. The presence of a token or two makes dominants more aware of what they have in common at the same time that it threatens that commonality. Indeed, it is often at those moments when a collectivity is threatened with change that its culture and bonds become exposed to itself; only when an obvious "outsider" appears do group members suddenly realize aspects of their common bond as insiders. The "threat" a token poses is twofold. First, the token represents the danger of challenge to the dominants' premises, either through explicit confrontation by the token or by a disaffected dominant who, through increased awareness, sees the culture for what it is and sees the possibility of alternatives. Second, the self-consciousness created by the token's presence is uncomfortable for people who prefer to operate in casual, superficial, and easygoing ways, without much psychological self-awareness and without the strain of reviewing habitual modes of action—a characteristic stance in the corporate environment. [. . .]

The token's contrast effect, then, can lead dominants to exaggerate both their commonality and the token's "difference." They move to heighten boundaries of which, previously, they might even have been aware. They erect new boundaries that at some times exclude the token or at others let her in only if she proves her loyalty.

Exaggeration of dominants' culture

Indsco men asserted group solidarity and reaffirmed shared in-group understandings in the presence of token women, first, by emphasizing and exaggerating those cultural elements they shared in contrast to the token. The token became both occasion and audience for the highlighting and dramatizing of those themes that differentiated her as the outsider. Ironically, tokens, unlike people of their type represented in greater proportion, are thus instruments for under*lining* rather than under*mining* majority culture. At Indsco, this phenomenon was most clearly in operation on occasions that brought together people from many parts of the organization who did not necessarily know each other well, as in training programs and at dinners and cocktail parties during meetings. Here the camaraderie of men, as in other work and social settings,[8] was based in part on tales of sexual adventures, ability with respect to "hunting" and capturing women, and off-color jokes. Other themes involved work prowess and sports, especially golf and fishing. The capacity for and enjoyment of drinking provided the context for displays of these themes. They were dramatized and acted out more fervently in the presence of token women than when only men were present.[9] When the men were alone, they introduced these themes in much milder form and were just as likely to share company gossip or talk of domestic matters such as a house being built. This was also in contrast to more equally mixed male–female groups in which there were a sufficient number of women to influence and change group culture and introduce a new hybrid of conversational themes based on shared male–female concerns.[10] [. . .]

Interruptions as reminders of "difference"

On more formal occasions, as in meetings, members of the numerically dominant category underscored and reinforced differences between tokens and dominants, ensuring that tokens recognized their outsider status, by making the token the occasion for "interruptions" in the flow of group events. Dominants prefaced acts with apologies or questions about appropriateness directed at the token; they then invariably went ahead with the act, having placed the token in the position of interrupter or interloper, of someone who took up the group's time. This happened often in the presence of the saleswomen. Men's questions or apologies represented a way of asking whether the old or expected cultural rules were still operative—the words and expressions permitted, the pleasures and forms of release indulged in. (Can we still swear? Toss a football? Use technical jargon? Go drinking? Tell "in" jokes?)[11] Sometimes the questions seemed motivated by a sincere desire to put the women at ease and treat them appropriately, but the net effect was the same regardless of dominants' intentions. By posing these questions overtly, dominants made the culture clear to tokens, stated the terms under which tokens enter the relationship, and reminded them that they were special people. It is a dilemma of all cross-cultural interaction that the very act of attempting to learn what to do in the presence of the different kind of person so as to integrate him can reinforce differentiation. [. . .]

Loyalty tests

At the same time that tokens may be kept on the periphery of colleague interaction, they may also be expected to demonstrate loyalty to their dominant peers. Failure to do so could result in further isolation; signs of loyalty, on the other hand, permitted the token to come closer to being included in more of the dominants' activities. Through loyalty tests, the group sought reassurance that the tokens would not turn against the dominants or use any of the information gained through their viewing of the dominants' world to do harm to the group. In the normal course of peer interactions, people learn all sorts of things about each other that could be turned against the other. Indeed, many colleague relationships are often solidified by the reciprocal knowledge of potentially damaging bits of information and the understanding that they both have an interest in preserving confidentiality. Tokens, however, pose a different problem and raise uncertainties, for their membership in a different social category could produce loyalties outside the peer cadre.

This was a quite rational concern on occasion. With government pressures and public interest mounting, Indsco women were often asked to speak to classes or women's groups or to testify before investigating committees. One woman was called in by her manager before her testimony at hearings on discrimination against women in business; he wanted to hear her testimony in advance and have censorship rights. She refused, but then made only very general and bland statements at the hearing anyway.

Peers seek reassurance about embarrassing as well as damaging disclosures. There is always the possibility that tokens will find some of what the dominants naturally do silly or ridiculous and will insult them where they feel vulnerable. Dominants also want to know that tokens will not use their inside information to make the dominants look bad or turn them into figures of fun to members of the token's category outside with whom they must interact. The joking remarks men made when seeing women colleagues occasionally eating with the secretaries (e.g., "What do you 'girls' find so interesting to talk about?") revealed some of their concerns.

Assurance could be gained by asking tokens to join with or identify with the dominants against those who represented competing loyalties; in short, dominants pressured tokens to turn against members of their own category, just as occurred in other situations where women were dominants and men tokens.[12] If tokens colluded, they made themselves psychological hostages to the majority group. For token women, the price of being "one of the boys" was a willingness to occasionally turn against "the girls." [. . .]

Responses of tokens to boundary heightening

The dilemma posed here for tokens was how to reconcile their awareness of difference generated by informal interaction with dominants with the need, in order to belong, to suppress dominants' concerns about the difference. As with performance pressures, peer group interaction around the tokens increased the effort required for a satisfactory public appearance, sometimes accompanied by distortions of private inclinations.

Of course, not all men participated in the dynamics noted. And some tokens managed to adapt very well. They used the same kind of language and expressed the same kinds of interests as many of the men. One woman loved fishing, she said, so when she came on as a manager and her office was concerned that that would end fishing trips, she could show them they had nothing to fear. Another had a boat on which she could take customers (along with her husband and their wives). A professional woman joined the men on "woman hunts," taking part in conversations in which the pro's and con's of particular targets were discussed. There were women known to be able to "drink the men under the table." It was never clear what the psychic toll of such accommodation was – whether, for example, such people would have made different choices in a balanced context – for they were also unlikely to talk about having any problems at all in their situation; they assumed they were full members.

Numerical skewing and polarized perceptions left tokens with little choice about accepting the culture of dominants. There were too few other people of the token's kind to generate a "counterculture" or to develop a shared intergroup culture. Tokens had to approach the group as single individuals. They thus had two general response possibilities. They could accept isolation, remaining only an audience for certain expressive acts of dominants. This strategy sometimes resulted in friendly but distant peer relations, with the risk of exclusion from occasions on which informal socialization and political activity took place. Or they could try to become insiders, proving their loyalty by defining themselves as exceptions and turning against their own social category.

The occurrence of the second response on the part of tokens suggests a re-examination of the popularized "women-prejudiced-against-women" hypothesis, also called the "Queen Bee syndrome," for possible structural (numerical) rather than sexual origins. Not only has this hypothesis not been confirmed in a variety of settings,[13] but the analysis offered here of the social psychological pressures on tokens to side with the majority provides a more compelling explanation for the kinds of situations most likely to produce this effect. To turn against others of one's kind (and thus risk latent self-hatred) can by a psychic cost of membership in a group dominated by another culture.

ROLE ENCAPSULATION

Tokens can never really be seen as they are, and they are always fighting stereo-types, because of a third tendency. The characteristics of tokens as individuals are often distorted to fit preexisting generaltzations about their category as a group – what I call "assimilation." Such stereotypical assumptions about what tokens "must" be like, such mistaken attributions and biased judgments, tend to force tokens into playing limited and caricatured roles. This constrains the tokens but is useful for dominant group members. Whatever ambiguity there might be around a strange person is reduced by providing a stereotyped and thus familiar place for tokens in the group, allowing dominants to make use of already-learned expectations and modes of action, like the traditional ways men expect to treat women. Familiar roles and assumptions, further, can serve to keep tokens in a bounded place and out of the mainstream of interaction where the uncertainties they arouse might be more difficult to handle. In short, tokens become encapsulated in limited roles that give them the security of a "place" but constrain their areas of permissible or rewarded action.

Status leveling

Tokens were often initially misperceived as a result of their numerical rarity. That is, an unusual woman would be treated as though she resembled women on the average – a function of what has been called "statistical discrimination" rather than outright prejudice.[14] Since people make judgments about the role being played by others on the basis of probabilistic reasoning about what a particular kind of person will be doing in a particular situation, such misperceptions are the result of statistical mistakes. Thus, women exempts at Indsco, like other tokens, encountered many instances of "mistaken identity" – first impressions that they were occupying a *usual female* position rather that their *unusual* (for a woman) job. In the office, they were often taken for secretaries; on sales trips on the road, especially when they traveled with a male colleague, they were often taken for wives or mistresses; with customers, they were first assumed to be temporarily substituting for a man who was the "real" salesperson; with a male peer at meetings, they were seen as the assistant; when entertaining customers, they were assumed to be the wife or date. (One woman sales trainee accompanied a senior salesman to call on a customer, whose initial reaction was laughter: "What won't you guys think up next? A woman!" She had the last laugh, however, for that company's chief engineer happened to be a woman with whom she had instant rapport.)

Mistaken first impressions can be corrected, although they give tokens an extra burden of spending more time untangling awkward exchanges and establishing accurate and appropriate role relations. But meanwhile, status leveling occurs. Status leveling involves making adjustments in perception of a token's professional role to fit with the expected position of the token's category – that is, bringing situational status in line with what has been called "master status," the token's social type. Even when others know that the women were not secretaries, for example, there was still a tendency to treat them like secretaries or to make secretary-like demands on them. In one blatant case, one woman was a sales trainee along with three men, all four of whom were to be given positions as summer replacements. The men were all assigned to replace salesmen; the woman was asked to replace a secretary – and only after a long and heated discussion with the manager was she given a more professional assignment. [. . .]

The woman's slot

There was also a tendency to encapsulate women and to maintain generalizations by defining special roles for women, even on the managerial and professional levels, that put them slightly apart as colleagues. Again, it was easy to do this with a small number and would have been much harder with many more women spilling over the bounds of such slots. A woman could ensure her membership by accepting a special place but then find herself confined by it. Once women began to occupy certain jobs, those jobs sometimes gradually came to be defined as "women's slots." One personnel woman at Indsco pointed this out. In her last career review, she had asked to be moved, feeling that, in another six months, she would have done and learned all she could in her present position and was ready to be upgraded. "They [the managers] told me to be patient; if I waited a year or two longer, they had just the right job for me, three grades up. I knew what they had in mind. Linda Martin [a senior woman] would be retiring by then from a benefits administration job, and they wanted to give it to me because it was considered a place to put a woman. But it had no *real* responsibilities despite its status; it was all routine work."

Affirmative action and equal employment opportunity jobs were also seen as "women's jobs." Many women, who would otherwise be interested in the growth and challenge they offered, said that they would not touch such a position: "The label makes it a dead end. It's a way of putting us out to pasture." There was no way to test the reality of such fears, given the short time the jobs had been in existence, but it could be observed that women who worked on women's personnel or training issues were finding it hard to move out into other areas. These women also found it hard to interest some other, secretly sympathetic managerial women in active advocacy of upward mobility for women because of the latter's own fears of getting too identified with a single issue. (Others, though, seized on it as a way to express their values or to get visibility.) [. . .]

Responses of tokens to role encapsulation

The dynamics of role entrapment tended to lead tokens to a variety of conservative and low-risk responses. The time and awkwardness involved in correcting mistaken impressions led some tokens to a preference for already-established relationships, for minimizing change and stranger-contact in the work situation. It was also often easier to accept stereotyped roles than to fight them, even if their acceptance meant limiting the tokens' range of expressions or demonstrations of task competence, because they offered a comfortable and certain position. The personal consequence for tokens, of course, was a measure of self-distortion. John Athanassiades, though not taking into account the effects of numerical representation, found that women in organizations tended to distort upward communication more than men, especially those with low risk-taking propensity, and argued that many observed work behaviors of women may be the result of such distortion and acceptance of organizational images. Submissiveness, frivolity, or other attributes may be feigned by people who feel they are prescribed by the dominant organizational culture.[15] This suggests that accurate conclusions about work attitudes and behavior cannot be reached by studying people in the token position, since there may always be an element of compensation or distortion involved.

The analysis also suggests another way in which tokenism can be self-perpetuating: acceptance of role encapsulation and attendant limitations on demonstration of competence may work to keep down the numbers of women in the upper ranks of the organization, thus continuing to put people in token positions. Role encapsulation confirms dominants' stereotypes and proves to them how right they were all along. On the other hand, some women try to stay away from the role traps by bending over backwards not to exhibit any characteristics that would reinforce stereotypes. This strategy, too, is an uneasy one, for it takes continual watchful effort, and it may involve unnatural self-distortion. Finally, token women must steer a course between protectiveness and abandonment. Either they allow other people to take over and fight their battles for them, staying out of the main action in stereotypical ways, or they stand much too alone. They may be unable by virtue of scarcity even to establish effective support systems of their own.

NOTES

1   There are several sets of findings purporting to show that women are more interested in relationships than in the intrinsic nature of tasks. See Keith Davis, *Human Relations at Work* (New York: McGraw-Hill, 1967), pp. 35–36; Joan E. Crowley, Teresa E. Levitan, and Robert P. Quinn, "Seven Deadly Half-Truths About Women," *Psychology Today*, 7 (1973): pp. 94–96; and an Australian study: Ruth Johnston, "Pay and Job Satisfaction:

A Survey of Some Research Findings," *International Labour Review,* 3 (May 1975): pp. 441–49. However, a laboratory experiment found that in high-opportunity situations – i.e., a competitive game with uncertainty about the outcome – the female tendency to be more relationship-oriented disappeared. The early studies were: W. Edgar Vinacke, "Sex Roles in a Three-Person Game," *Sociometry,* 22 (December 1959): pp. 343–60; Thomas K. Uesugi and W. Edgar Vinake, "Strategy in a Feminine Game," *Sociometry,* 26 (1963): pp. 35–38. The structural refutation of sex differences was: Sidney I. Lirtzman and Mahmoud A. Wahba, "Determinants of Coalitional Behavior of Men and Women: Sex Role or Situational Requirements?," *Journal of Applied Psychology,* 56 (1972): pp. 406–11.

2   William J. Grinker, Donald D. Cooke, and Arthur W. Kirsch, *Climbing the Job Ladder: A Study of Employee Advancement in Eleven Industries* (New York: Shelley and Co., 1970).

3   Patricia Marchak, "Women Workers and White Collar Unions," *Canadian Review of Sociology and Anthropology,* 10 (1973): pp. 134–147.

4   Jon Shepard, *Automation and Alienation: A Study of Office and Factory Workers* (Cambridge, Mass.: MIT Press, 1971), pp. 77–89.

5   On blue-collar men: Robert Dubin, "Industrial Workers' Worlds," *Social Problems,* 3 (January 1956): pp. 131–142. On professionals: Louis H. Orzack, "Work as a 'Central Life Interest' of Professionals," *Social Problems,* 7 (Fall 1969).

6   On teachers and nurses: J. A. Alutto, L. G. Hrebiniak, and R. C. Alonso, "On Operationalizing the Concept of Commitment," *Social Forces,* 51 (June 1973): pp. 448–54. On commitment as a function of overcoming barriers: Grusky, "Career Mobility," and Rosabeth Moss Kanter, *Commitment and Community* (Cambridge, Mass.: Harvard University Press, 1973), pp. 76–80.

7   Eli Chinoy, *Automobile Workers and the American Dream* (New York: Doubleday, 1955); Theodore V. Purcell, *Blue Collar Man: Patterns of Dual Allegiance in Industry* (Cambridge, Mass.: Harvard University Press, 1960); Chinoy, *Automobile Workers.* On "drop-outs" to small business: Kurt B. Mayer and Sidney Goldstein, "Manual Workers as Small Businessmen," in *Blue Collar World,* A. Shostak and W. Gomberg, eds. (Englewood Cliffs, New Jersey: Prentice-Hall, 1964), pp. 537–50.

8   Jeane Kirkpatrick, *Political Woman* (New York: Basic Books, 1974), p. 113; Lionel Tiger, *Men in Groups* (New York: Random House, 1969).

9   Clearly I was limited in first-hand observations of how the men acted when alone, since, by definition, if I, as a female researcher, were present, they would not have been alone. For my data here I relied on tape recordings of several meetings in which the tape was kept running even during breaks, and on informants' reports immediately after informal social events and about meetings.

10   For supportive laboratory evidence, see Elizabeth Aries, *Interaction Patterns and Themes of Male, Female, and Mixed Groups,* Unpublished Doctoral Dissertation, Harvard University, 1973.

11   For examples in another context, see Marcia Greenbaum, "Adding 'Kenntnis' to 'Kirch, Kuche, und Kinder,' " *Issues in Industrial Society,* 2 (1971): pp. 61–68.

12   Bernard E. Segal, "Male Nurses: A Study in Status Contradiction and Prestige Loss," *Social Forces,* 41 (October 1962): pp. 31–38. Personal interviews were used as a supplement.

13   Marianne Abeles Ferber and Joan Althaus Huber, "Sex of Student and Instructor: A Study of Student Bias," *American Journal of Sociology,* 80 (January 1975): pp. 949–63.

14   *Annual Report of the Council of Economic Advisers* (Washington, D.C.: U.S. Government Printing Office, 1973), p. 106.

15   John C. Athanassiades, "An Investigation of Some Communication Patterns of Female Subordinates in Hierarchical Organizations," *Human Relations,* 27 (1974): pp. 195–209.

HIERARCHIES, JOBS, BODIES: A THEORY OF GENDERED ORGANIZATIONS

JOAN ACKER

From J. L. Lorber and S. A. Farrell (eds.) (1991) *The Social Construction of Gender* (1991) Newbury Park, CA: Sage.

INVISIBLE WOMEN

Both traditional and critical approaches to organizations originate in the male, abstract intellectual domain (Smith 1988) and take as reality the world as seen from that standpoint. As a relational phenomenon, gender is difficult to see when only the masculine is present. Since men in organizations take their behavior and perspectives to represent the human, organizational structures and processes are theorized as gender-neutral. When it is acknowledged that women and men are affected differently by organizations, it is argued that gendered attitudes and behavior are brought into (and contaminate) essentially gender-neutral structures. This view of organizations separates structures from the people in them.

Current theories of organization also ignore sexuality. Certainly, a gender-neutral structure is also asexual. If sexuality is a core component of the production of gender identity, gender images, and gender inequality, organizational theory that is blind to sexuality does not immediately offer avenues into the comprehension of gender domination (Hearn and Parkin 1983, 1987). MacKinnon's (1982) compelling argument that sexual domination of women is embedded within legal organizations has not to date become part of mainstream discussions. Rather, behaviors such as sexual harassment are viewed as deviations of gendered actors, not, as MacKinnon (1979) might argue, as components of organizational structure.

FEMINIST ANALYSES OF ORGANIZATIONS

The treatment of women and gender most assimilated into the literature on organizations is Moss Kanter's *Men and Women of the Corporation* (1977). Moss Kanter sets out to show that gender differences in organizational behavior are due to structure rather than to characteristics of women and men as individuals (1977, pp. 291–2). She argues that the problems women have in large organizations are consequences of their structural placement, crowded in dead-end jobs at the bottom and exposed as tokens at the top. Gender enters the picture through organizational roles that "carry characteristic images of the kinds of people that should occupy them" (p. 250). Here, Moss Kanter recognizes the presence of gender in early models of organizations:

> A "masculine ethic" of rationality and reason can be identified in the early image of managers. This "masculine ethic" elevates the traits assumed to belong to men with educational advantages to necessities for effective organizations: a tough-minded approach to problems; analytic abilities to abstract and plan; a capacity to set aside personal, emotional considerations in the interests of task accomplishment; a cognitive superiority in problem-solving and decision making. (1974, p. 43)

Identifying the central problem of seeming gender neutrality, Moss Kanter observes: "While organizations were being defined as sex-neutral machines, masculine principles were dominating their authority structures" (1977, p. 46).

In spite of these insights, organizational structure, not gender, is the focus of Moss Kanter's analysis. In posing the argument as structure or gender, Moss Kanter also implicitly posits gender as standing outside of structure, and she fails to follow up her own observations about masculinity and organizations (1977, p. 22). Moss Kanter's analysis of the effects of organizational position applies as well to men in low-status positions. Her analysis of the effect of numbers, or the situation of the "token" worker, applies also to men as minorities in women-predominant organizations, but fails to account for gender differences in the situation of the token. In contrast to the token woman, White men in women-dominated workplaces are likely to be positively evaluated and to be rapidly promoted to positions of greater authority. The specificity of male dominance is absent in Moss Kanter's argument, even though she presents a great deal of material that illuminates gender and male dominance.

Another approach using Moss Kanter's insights but building on the theoretical work of Hartmann (1976), is the argument that organizations have a dual structure, bureaucracy and patriarchy (Ressner 1986b). Ressner argues that bureaucracy has its own dynamic, and gender enters through patriarchy, a more or less autonomous structure, that exists alongside the bureaucratic structure. The analysis of two hierarchies facilitates and clarifies the discussion of women's experiences of discrimination, exclusion, segregation, and low wages. However, this approach has all the problems of two systems theories of women's oppression (Young 1981; see also Acker 1988): the central theory of bureaucratic or organizational structure is unexamined, and patriarchy is added to allow the theorist to deal with women. Like Moss Kanter, Ressner's approach implicitly accepts the assumption of mainstream organizational theory that organizations are gender-neutral social phenomena.

Ferguson, in *The Feminist Case Against Bureaucracy* (1984), develops a radical feminist critique of bureaucracy as an organization of oppressive male power, arguing that it is both mystified and constructed through an abstract discourse on rationality, rules, and procedures. Thus, in contrast to the implicit arguments of Moss Kanter and Ressner, Ferguson views bureaucracy itself as a construction of male domination. In response to this overwhelming organization of power, bureaucrats, workers, and clients are all "feminized," as they develop ways of managing their powerlessness that at the same time perpetuate their dependence. Ferguson argues further that feminist discourse, rooted in women's experiences of caring and nurturing outside bureaucracy's control, provides a ground for opposition to bureaucracy and for the development of alternative ways of organizing society.

However, there are problems with Ferguson's theoretical formulation. Her argument that feminization is a metaphor for bureaucratization not only uses a stereotype of femininity as oppressed, weak, and passive, but also, by equating the experience of men and women clients, women workers, and men bureaucrats, obscures the specificity of women's experiences and the connections between masculinity and power (Brown 1984; see also Martin 1987; Mitchell 1986; Ressner 1986a). Ferguson builds on Foucault's (1979) analysis of power as widely diffused and constituted through discourse, and the problems in her analysis have their origin in Foucault, who also fails to place gender in his analysis of power. What results is a disembodied, and consequently gender-neutral, bureaucracy as the oppressor. That is, of course, not a new vision of bureaucracy, but it is one in which gender enters only as analogy, rather than as a complex component of processes of control and domination.

In sum, some of the best feminist attempts to theorize about gender and organizations have been trapped within the constraints of definitions of the theoretical domain that cast organizations as gender-neutral and asexual. These theories take us only part of the way to understanding how deeply embedded gender is in organizations. There is ample empirical evidence: We know now that gender segregation is an amazingly persistent pattern and that the gender identity of jobs and occupations is repeatedly reproduced, often in new forms (Bielby and Baron 1987; Reskin and Roos 1987; Strober and Arnold 1987). The reconstruction of gender segregation is an integral part of the dynamic of technological and organizational change (Cockburn 1983, 1985; Hacker 1981). Individual men and particular groups of men do not always win in these processes, but masculinity always seems to symbolize self-respect for men at the bottom and power for men at the top, while confirming for both their gender's superiority. Theories that posit organization and bureaucracy as gender-neutral cannot adequately account for this continual gendered structuring. We need different theoretical strategies that examine organizations as gendered processes in which sexuality also plays a part.

ORGANIZATIONS AS GENDERED PROCESSES

The idea that social structure and social processes are gendered has slowly emerged in diverse areas of feminist discourse. Feminists have elaborated gender as a concept to mean more than a socially constructed, binary identity and image. This turn to gender as and analytic category (Connell 1987; Harding 1986; Scott 1986) is an attempt to find new avenues into the dense and complicated problem of explaining the extraordinary persistence through history and across societies of the subordination of women. Scott, for example, defines gender as follows: "The core of the definition rests on an integral connection between two propositions; gender is a constitutive element of social relationships based on perceived differences between the sexes, and gender is a primary way of signifying relationships of power" (1986, p. 1067).

New approaches to the study of waged work, particularly studies of the labor process, see organizations as gendered, not as gender-neutral (Cockburn 1985;

Game and Pringle 1984; Knights and Willmott 1985; Phillips and Taylor 1980; Sorenson 1984) and conceptualize organizations as one of the locations of the inextricably intertwined production of both gender and class relations. Examining class and gender (Acker 1988), I have argued that class is constructed through gender and that class relations are always gendered. The structure of the labor market, relations in the workplace, the control of the work process, and the underlying wage relation are always affected by symbols of gender, processes of gender identity, and material inequalities between women and men. These processes are complexly related to, and powerfully support, the reproduction of the class structure. Here, I will focus on the interface of gender and organizations, assuming the simultaneous presence of class relations.

To say that an organization, or any other analytic unit, is gendered means that advantage and disadvantage, exploitation and control, action and emotion, meaning and identity, are patterned through and in terms of a distinction between male and female, masculine and feminine. Gender is not an addition to ongoing processes, conceived as gender-neutral. Rather, it is an integral part of those processes, which cannot be properly understood without an analysis of gender (Connell 1987). Gendering occurs in at least five interacting processes (cf. Scott 1986) that, although analytically distinct, are, in practice, parts of the same reality.

First is the construction of divisions along lines of gender – divisions of labor, of allowed behaviors, of locations in physical space, of power, including the institutionalized means of maintaining the divisions in the structures of labor markets, the family, the state. Such divisions in work organizations are well documented (e.g., Kanter 1977) as well as often obvious to casual observers. Although there are great variations in the patterns and extent of gender division, men are almost always in the highest positions of organizational power. Managers' decisions often initiate gender divisions (Cohn 1985), and organizational practices maintain them – although they also take on new forms with changes in technology and the labor process. For example, Cockburn (1983, 1985) has shown how the introduction of new technology in a number of industries was accompanied by a reorganization, but not abolition, of the gendered division of labor that left the technology in men's control and maintained the definition of skilled work as men's work and unskilled work as women's work.

Second is the construction of symbols and images that explain, express, reinforce, or sometimes oppose those divisions. These have many sources or forms in language, ideology, popular and high culture, dress, the press, and television. For example, as Moss Kanter (1975), among others, has noted, the image of the top manager or the business leader is an image of successful, forceful masculinity (see also Lipman-Blumen 1980). In Cockburn's studies, men workers' images of masculinity linked their gender with their technical skills; the possibility that women might also obtain such skills represented a threat to that masculinity.

The third set of processes that produce gendered social structures, including organizations, are interactions between women and men, women and women, men and men, including all the patterns that enact dominance and submission. For example, conversation analysis shows how gender differences in interruptions, turn taking, and setting the topic of discussion recreate gender inequality in the flow of ordinary talk (West and Zimmerman 1983). Although much of this research has used experimental groups, qualitative accounts of organizational life record the same phenomena: Men are the actors, women the emotional support (Hochschild 1983).

Fourth, these processes help to produce gendered components of individual identity, which may include consciousness of the existence of the other three aspects of gender, such as, in organizations, choice of appropriate work, language use, clothing, and presentation of self as a gendered member of an organization (Reskin and Roos 1987).

Finally, gender is implicated in the fundamental, ongoing processes of creating and conceptualizing social structures. Gender is obviously a basic constitutive element in family and kinship, but, less obviously, it helps to frame the underlying relations of other structures, including complex organizations. Gender is a consti-tutive element in organizational logic, or the underlying assumptions and practices that construct most contemporary work organizations (Clegg and Dunkerley 1980). Organizational logic appears to be gender-neutral; gender-neutral theories of bureaucracy and organizations employ and give expression to this logic. However, underlying both academic theories and practical guides for managers is a gendered substructure that is reproduced daily in practical work activities and, somewhat less frequently, in the writings of organizational theorists (cf. Smith 1988).

Organizational logic has material forms in written work rules, labor contracts, managerial directives, and other documentary tools for running large organiza-tions, including systems of job evaluation widely used in the comparable-worth strategy of feminists. Job evaluation is accomplished through the use and inter-pretation of documents that describe jobs and how they are to be evaluated. These documents contain symbolic indicators of structure; the ways that they are inter-preted and talked about in the process of job evaluation reveal the underlying orga-nizational logic. I base the following theoretical discussion on my observations of organizational logic in action in the job-evaluation component of a comparable-worth project (Acker 1987, 1989, 1990).

Job evaluation is a management tool used in every industrial country, capitalist and socialist, to rationalize the organizational hierarchy and to help in setting equi-table wages (International Labour Office 1986). Although there are many differ-ent systems of job evaluation, the underlying rationales are similar enough so that the observation of one system can provide a window into a common organizational mode of thinking and practice.

In job evaluation, the content of jobs is described and jobs are compared on cri-teria of knowledge, skill, complexity, effort, and working conditions. The particu-lar system I observed was built incrementally over many years to reflect the assessment of managers about the job components for which they were willing to pay. Thus today this system can be taken as composed of residues of these judg-ments, which are a set of decision rules that, when followed, reproduce manager-ial values. But these rules are also the imagery out of which managers construct and reconstruct their organizations. The rules of job evaluation, which help to determine pay differences between jobs, are not simply a compilation of managers' values or sets of beliefs, but are the underlying logic or organization that provides at least part of the blueprint for its structure. Every time that job evaluation is used, that structure is created or reinforced.

Job evaluation evaluates jobs, not their incumbents. The job is the basic unit in a work organization's hierarchy, a description of a set of tasks, competencies, and responsibilities represented as a position on an organizational chart. A job is separate from people. It is an empty slot, a reification that must continually be reconstructed, for positions exist only as scraps of paper until people fill them. The rationale for evaluating jobs devoid of actual workers further reveals the organizational logic: the intent is to assess the characteristics of the job, not of their incumbents who may vary in skill, industriousness, and commitment. Human beings are to be motivated, managed, and chosen to fit the job. The job exists as a thing apart.

Every job has a place in the hierarchy, another essential element in organizational logic. Hierarchies, like jobs, are devoid of actual workers and based on abstract differentiations. Hierarchy is taken for granted, only its particular form is at issue. Job evaluation is based on the assumption that workers in general see hierarchy as an acceptable principle, and the final test of the evaluation of any particular job is whether its place in the hierarchy looks reasonable. The ranking of jobs within an organization must make sense to managers, but, if the system of evaluation is to contribute to orderly working relationships, it is also important that most workers accept the ranking as just.

Organizational logic assumes a congruence between responsibility, job complexity, and hierarchical position. For example, a lower-level position, the level of most jobs, filled predominantly by women, must have equally low levels of complexity and responsibility. Complexity and responsibility are defined in terms of managerial and professional tasks. The child-care worker's responsibility for other human beings or the complexity facing the secretary who serves six different, temperamental bosses can be only minimally counted if the congruence between position level, responsibility, and complexity is to be preserved. In addition, the logic holds that two jobs at different hierarchical levels cannot be responsible for the same outcome; as a consequence, for example, tasks delegated to a secretary by a manager will not raise her hierarchical level because such tasks are still his responsibility, even though she has the practical responsibility to see that they are done. Levels of skill, complexity, and responsibility, all used in constructing hierarchy, are conceptualized as existing independently of any concrete worker.

In organizational logic, both jobs and hierarchies are abstract categories that have no occupants, no human bodies, no gender. However, an abstract job can exist, can be transformed into a concrete instance, only if there is a worker. In organizational logic, filling the abstract job is a disembodied worker who exists only for the work. Such a hypothetical worker cannot have other imperatives of existence that impinge upon the job. At the very least, outside imperatives cannot be included within the definition of the job. Too many obligations outside the boundaries of the job would make a worker unsuited for the position. The closest the disembodied worker doing the abstract job comes to a real work is the male worker whose life centers on his full-time, lifelong job, while his wife or another woman takes care of his personal needs and his children. While the realities of life in industrial capitalism never allowed all men to live out this ideal, it was the goal for labor unions and the image of the worker in social and economic theory. The woman worker, assumed to have legitimate obligations other than those required by the job, did not fit with the abstract job.

The concept "a job" is thus implicitly a gendered concept, even though organizational logic presents it as gender-neutral. A job already contains the gender-based division of labor and the separation between the public and the private sphere. The concept of a job assumes a particular gendered organization of domestic life and social production. It is an example of what Smith has called "the gender subtext of the rational and impersonal" (1988, p. 4).

Hierarchies are gendered because they also are constructed on these underlying assumptions. Those who are committed to paid employment are "naturally" more suited to responsibility and authority; those who must divide their commitments are in the lower ranks. In addition, principles of hierarchy, as exemplified in most existing job-evaluation systems, have been derived from already existing gendered structures. The best-known systems were developed by management consultants working with managers to build methods of consistently evaluating jobs and rationalizing pay and job classifications. For example, all managers with similar levels of responsibility in the firm should have similar pay. Job-evaluation systems were intended to reflect the values of managers and to produce a believable ranking of jobs based on those values. Such rankings would not deviate substantially from rankings already in place that contain gender typing and gender segregation of jobs and the clustering of women workers in the lowest and the worst-paid jobs. The concrete value judgments that constitute conventional job evaluation are designed to replicate such structures (Acker 1989). Replication is achieved in many ways; for example, skills in managing money, more often found in men's than in women's jobs, frequently receive more points than skills in dealing with clients or human relations skills, more often found in women's than in men's jobs (Steinberg and Haignere 1987).

The gender-neutral status of "a job" and of the organizational theories of which it is a part depend on the assumption that the worker is abstract, disembodied, although in actuality both the concept of "a job" and real workers are deeply gendered and "bodied." Pateman (1986), in a discussion of women and political theory, similarly points out that the most fundamental abstraction in the concept of liberal individualism is "the abstraction of the 'individual' from the body. In order for the individual to appear in liberal theory as a universal figure, who represents anyone and everyone, the individual must be disembodied" (p. 8). If the individual were not abstracted from bodily attributes, it would be clear that the individual represents one sex and one gender, not a universal being. The political fiction of the universal "individual" or "citizen," fundamental to ideas of democracy and contract, excluded women, judging them lacking in the capacities necessary for participation in civil society. Although women now have the rights of citizens in democratic states, they still stand in an ambiguous relationship to the universal individual who is "constructed from a male body so that his identity is always masculine" (Pateman 1988, p. 223). The worker with "a job" is the same universal individual who in social reality is a man. The concept of a universal worker excludes and marginalizes women who cannot, almost by definition, achieve the qualities of a real worker because to do so is to become like a man.

ORGANIZATIONAL CONTROL, GENDER, AND THE BODY

The abstract, bodiless worker, who occupies the abstract, gender-neutral job has no sexuality, no emotions, and does not procreate. The absence of sexuality, emotionality, and procreation in organizational logic and organizational theory is an additional element that both obscures and helps to reproduce the underlying gender relations.

New work on sexuality in organizations (Hearn and Parkin 1987), often indebted to Foucault (1979), suggests that this silence on sexuality may have historical roots in the development of large, all-male organizations that are the primary locations of societal power (Connell 1987). The history of modern organizations includes, among other processes, the suppression of sexuality in the interests of organization and the conceptual exclusion of the body as a concrete living whole (Burrell 1984, 1987; Hearn and Parkin 1987; Morgan 1986).

In a review of historical evidence on sexuality in early modern organizations, Burrell (1984, p. 98) suggests that "the suppression of sexuality is one of the first tasks the bureaucracy sets itself." Long before the emergence of the very large factory in the nineteenth century, other large organizations, such as armies and monasteries, which had allowed certain kinds of limited participation of women, were excluding women more and more and attempting to banish sexuality in the interests of control of members and the organization's activities (Burrell 1984, 1987; Hacker and Hacker 1987). Active sexuality was the enemy of orderly proce-dures, and excluding women from certain areas of activity may have been, at least in part, a way to control sexuality. As Burrell (1984) points out, the exclusion of women did not eliminate homosexuality, which has always been an element in the life of large all-male organizations, particularly if members spend all of their time in the organization. Insistence on heterosexuality or celibacy were ways to control homosexuality. But heterosexuality had to be practiced outside the organization, whether it was an army or a capitalist workplace. Thus the attempts to banish sexuality from the workplace were part of the wider process that differentiated the home, the location of legitimate sexual activity, from the place of capitalist pro-duction. The concept of the disembodied job symbolizes this separation of work and sexuality.

Similarly, there is no place within the disembodied job or the gender-neutral organization for other "bodied" processes, such as human reproduction (Rothman 1989) or the free expression of emotions (Hochschild 1983). Sexuality, procreation, and emotions all intrude upon and disrupt the ideal functioning of the organiza-tion, which tries to control such interferences. However, as argued above, the abstract worker is actually a man, and it is the man's body, its sexuality, minimal responsibility in procreation, and conventional control of emotions that pervades work and organizational processes. Women's bodies – female sexuality, their ability to procreate and their pregnancy, breast-feeding, and child care, menstruation, and mythic "emotionality" – are suspect, stigmatized, and used as grounds for control and exclusion.

The ranking of women's jobs is often justified on the basis of women's identifi-cation with childbearing and domestic life. Women are devalued because they are assumed to be unable to conform to the demands of the abstract job. Gender seg-regation at work is also sometimes openly justified by the necessity to control sexuality, and women may be barred from types of work, such as skilled blue-collar work or top management, where most workers are men, on the grounds that poten-tially disruptive sexual liaisons should be avoided (Lorber 1984). On the other hand, the gendered definition of some jobs "includes sexualization of the woman worker as a part of the job" (MacKinnon 1979, p. 18). These are often jobs that serve men, such as secretaries, or a largely male public (Hochschild 1983).

The maintenance of gendered hierarchy is achieved partly through such often-tacit controls based on arguments about women's reproduction, emotionality, and sexuality, helping to legitimate the organizational structures created through abstract, intellectualized techniques. More overt controls, such as sexual harassment, relegating childbearing women to lower-level mobility tracks, and penalizing (or rewarding) their emotion management, also conform to and reinforce hierarchy. MacKinnon (1979), on the basis of an extensive analysis of legal cases, argues that the willingness to tolerate sexual harassment is often a condition of the job, both a consequence and a cause of gender hierarchy.

While women's bodies are ruled out of order or sexualized and objectified, in work organizations, men's bodies are not. Indeed, male sexual imagery pervades organizational metaphors and language, helping to give form to work activities (see Hearn and Parkin 1987, for an extended discussion). For example, the military and the male world of sports are considered valuable training for organizational success and provide images for teamwork, campaigns, and tough competition. The symbolic expression of male sexuality may be used as a means of control over male workers, too, allowed or even encouraged within the bounds of the work situation to create cohesion or alleviate stress (Collinson 1988; Hearn and Parkin 1987). Management approval of pornographic pictures in the locker room or support for all-male work and play groups where casual talk is about sexual exploits or sports are examples. These symbolic expressions of male dominance also act as significant controls over women in work organizations because they are per se excluded from the informal bonding men produce with the "body talk" of sex and sports.

Symbolically, a certain kind of male heterosexual sexuality plays an important part in legitimating organizational power. Connell (1987) calls this hegemonic masculinity, emphasizing that it is formed around dominance over women and in opposition to other masculinities, although its exact content changes as historical conditions change. Currently, hegemonic masculinity is typified by the image of the strong, technically competent, authoritative leader who is sexually potent and attractive, has a family, and has his emotions under control. Images of male sexual function and patriarchal paternalism may also be embedded in notions of what the manager does when he leads his organization (Calas and Smircich 1989). Women's bodies cannot be adapted to hegemonic masculinity; to function at the top of male hierarchies requires women to render irrelevant everything that makes them women.

According to many management experts, the image of the masculine organizational leader could be expanded, without altering its basic elements, to include other qualities also needed in contemporary organizations, such as flexibility and sensitivity to the capacities and needs of subordinates. Such qualities are not necessarily the symbolic monopoly of women. For example, the wise and experienced coach is empathetic and supportive of his individual players and flexibly leads his team against devious opposition tactics to victory.

The connections between organizational power and men's sexuality may be even more deeply embedded in organizational processes. Hacker (1989) argues that eroticism and technology have common roots in human sensual pleasure and that for the engineer or the skilled worker, and probably for many other kinds of workers, there is a powerful erotic element in work processes. The pleasures of technology, Hacker continues, become harnessed to domination, and passion becomes directed toward power over nature, the machine, and other people, particularly women, in the work hierarchy. Hacker believes that men lose a great deal in this transformation of the erotic into domination, but they also win in other ways. For example, many men gain economically from the organizational gender hierarchy. As Crompton and Jones (1984) point out, men's career opportunities in white-collar work depend on the barriers that deny those opportunities to women. If the mass of female clerical workers were able to compete with men in such work, promotion probabilities for men would be drastically reduced.

Class relations as well as gender relations are reproduced in organizations. Critical, but nonfeminist, perspectives on work organizations argue that rational-technical systems for organizing work, such as job classification and evaluation systems and detailed specification of how work is to be done, are parts of pervasive systems of control that help to maintain class relations (Edwards 1979). The abstract job, devoid of a human body, is a basic unit in such systems of control. The positing of a job as an abstract category, separate from the worker, is an essential move in creating jobs as mechanisms of compulsion and control over work processes. Rational-technical (ostensibly gender-neutral) control systems are built upon and conceal a gendered substructure (Smith 1988) in which men's bodies fill the abstract jobs. Use of such abstract systems continually reproduces the underlying gender assumptions and the subordinated or excluded place of women. Gender processes, including the manipulation and management of women's and men's sexuality, procreation, and emotion, are part of the control processes of organizations, maintaining not only gender stratification but also contributing to maintaining class and, possibly, race and ethnic relations. Is the abstract worker White as well as male? Are White-male-dominated organizations also built on underlying assumptions about the proper place of people with different skin colors? Are racial differences produced by organizational practices as gender differences are?

CONCLUSION

Feminists who want to theorize about organizations face a difficult task because of the deeply embedded gendering of both organizational processes and theory. Commonsense notions, such as jobs and positions, which constitute the units managers use in making organizations and some theorists use in making theory, are posited on the prior exclusion of women. This underlying construction of a way of thinking is not simply an error, but rather a part of the processes of organization. This exclusion in turn creates fundamental inadequacies in theorizing about gender-neutral systems of positions to be filled. The creation of more adequate theory may come only as organizations are transformed in ways that dissolve the concept of the abstract job and restore the absent female body.

Such a transformation would be radical in practice because it would probably require the end of organizations as they exist today, along with a redefinition of work and work relations. The rhythm and timing of work would be adapted to the rhythms of life outside of work. Caring work would be just as important and well rewarded as other work: Having a baby or taking care of a sick mother would be as valued as making an automobile or designing computer software. Hierarchy would be abolished, and workers would run things themselves. Of course, women and men would share equally in different kinds of work. Perhaps there would be some communal or collective form of organization where work and intimate relations are closely related, children learn in places close to working adults, and workmates, lovers, and friends are all part of the same group. Utopian writers and experimenters have left us many possible models (Hacker 1989). But this brief listing begs many questions, perhaps the most important of which is how, given the present organization of economy and technology and the pervasive and powerful, impersonal, textually mediated relations of authority and hierarchy (Smith 1988), so radical a change could come about.

Feminist research and theorizing, by continuing to puzzle out how gender provides the subtext for arrangements of subordination, can make some contributions to a future in which collective action to do what needs doing – producing goods, caring for people, disposing of the garbage – is organized so that dominance, control, and subordination, particularly the subordination of women, are eradicated, or at least minimized, in our organizational life.

REFERENCES

Acker, J. 1987. "Sex Bias in Job Evaluation: A Comparable Worth Issue." Pp. 183–96 in *Ingredients for Women's Employment Policy*, edited by C. Bose and G. Spitze. Albany: SUNY Press.
——. 1988. "Class, Gender and the Relations of Distribution." *Signs: Journal of Women in Culture and Society* 13:473–97.
——. 1989. *Doing Comparable Worth: Gender, Class and Pay Equity*. Philadelphia: Temple University Press.
——. 1990. "The Oregon Case." In *State Experience with Comparable Worth*, edited by R. Steinberg. Philadelphia: Temple University Press.
Bielby, W. T., and J. N. Baron. 1987. "Undoing Discrimination: Job Integration and Comparable Worth." Pp. 211–19 in *Ingredients for Women's Employment Policy*, edited by C. Bose and G. Spitze. Albany: SUNY Press.
Brown, W. 1984. "Challenging Bureaucracy." *Women's Review of Books* 2 (November): 14–17.
Burrell, G. 1984. "Sex and Organizational Analysis." *Organization Studies* 5:97–118.
——. 1987. "No Accounting for Sexuality." *Accounting Organizations and Society* 12:89–101.
Calas, M. B., and L. Smircich. 1989. "Voicing Seduction to Silence Leadership." Paper presented to the Fourth International Conference on Organizational Symbolism and Corporate Culture, Fontainebleau, France.
Clegg, S., and D. Dunkerley. 1980. *Organization, Class and Control*. London: Routledge & Kegan Paul.
Cockburn, C. 1983. *Brothers: Male Dominance and Technological Change*. London: Pluto Press.
——. 1985. *Machinery of Dominance: Women, Men and Technical Know-How*. London: Pluto Press.
Cohn, S. 1985. *The Process of Occupational Sex-Typing*. Philadelphia: Temple University Press.
Collinson, D. L. 1988. "Engineering Honour: Masculinity, Joking and Conflict in Shop-Floor Relations." *Organizational Studies* 9:181–9.
Connell, R. W. 1987. *Gender and Power*. Stanford, CA: Stanford University Press.
Crompton, R., and G. Jones. 1984. *White-Collar Proletariate: Deskilling and Gender in Clerical Work*. Philadelphia: Temple University Press.
Edwards, R., 1979. *Contested Terrain*. New York: Basic Books.
Ferguson, K. E. 1984. *The Feminist Case Against Bureaucracy*. Philadelphia: Temple University Press.
Foucault, M. 1979. *The History of Sexuality, Vol. 1: An Introduction*. London: Allen Lane.
Game, A., and R. Pringle. 1984. *Gender at Work*. London: Pluto Press.
Hacker, S. 1981. "The Culture of Engineering: Women, Workplace, and Machine." *Women's Studies International Quarterly* 4:341–54.
——. 1989. *Pleasure, Power and Technology*. Boston: Unwin Heyman.
Hacker, B. C., and S. Hacker. 1987. "Military Institutions and the Labor Process:

Noneconomic Sources of Technological Change, Women's Subordination, and the Organization of Work." *Technology and Culture* 28:743–75.

Harding, S. 1986. *The Science Question in Feminism.* Ithaca, NY: Cornell University Press.

Hartmann, H. 1976. "Capitalism, Patriarchy, and Job Segregation by Sex." *Signs: Journal of Women in Culture and Society* 1:137–70.

Hearn, J., and P. W. Parkin. 1983. "Gender and Organizations: A Selective Review and a Critique of a Neglected Area." *Organization Studies* 4:219–42.

———. 1987. *Sex at Work.* Brighton, UK: Wheatsheaf Books.

Hochschild, A. R. 1983. *The Managed Heart.* Berkeley, CA: University of California Press.

International Labour Office. 1986. *Job Evaluation.* Geneva: ILO.

Kanter, R. Moss. 1975. "Women and the Structure of Organizations: Explorations in Theory and Behavior." Pp. 34–74 in *Another Voice,* edited by R. Moss Kanter and M. Millman. Garden City, NY: Doubleday Anchor.

———. 1977. *Men and Women of the Corporation.* New York: Basic Books.

Knights, D., and H. Willmott. 1985. *Gender and the Labour Process.* Aldershot, UK: Gower.

Lipman-Blumen, J. 1980. "Female Leadership in Formal Organization: Must the Female Leader Go Formal?" Pp. 341–62 in *Readings in Managerial Psychology,* edited by H. J. Leavitt, L. R. Pondy, and D. M. Boje. Chicago: University of Chicago Press.

Lorber, J. 1984. "Trust, Loyalty, and the Place of Women in the Organization of Work." Pp. 371–81 in *Women: A Feminist Perspective, 3rd ed.,* edited by J. Freeman. Palo Alto, CA: Mayfield.

MacKinnon, C. A. 1979. *Sexual Harassment of Working Women.* New Haven, CT: Yale University Press.

———. 1982. "Feminism, Marxism, Method and the State: An Agenda for Theory." *Signs: Journal of Women in Culture and Society* 7:515–44.

Martin, P. Yancey. 1987. "A Commentary on *The Feminist Case Against Bureaucracy.*" *Women's studies International Forum* 10:543–8.

Mitchell, D. 1986. Review of Ferguson, *The Feminist Case Against Bureaucracy.* Unpublished manuscript.

Morgan, G. 1986. *Images of Organization.* Newbury Park: Sage.

Pateman, C. 1986. "Introduction: The Theoretical Subversiveness of Feminism." Pp. 1–12 in *Feminist Challenges,* edited by C. Pateman and E. Gross. Winchester, MA: Allen & Unwin.

———. 1988. *The Sexual Contract.* Cambridge, UK: Polity Press.

Phillips, A., and B. Taylor. 1980. "Sex and Skill: Notes Towards a Feminist Economics." *Feminist Review* 6:79–88.

Reskin, B. F., and P. A. Roos. 1987. "Status Hierarchies and Sex Segregation." Pp. 3–21 in *Ingredients for Women's Employment Policy,* edited by C. Bose and G. Spitze. Albany, NY: SUNY Press.

Ressner, U. 1986a. Review of K. Ferguson, *The Feminist Case Against Bureaucracy. Economic and Industrial Democracy* 7:130–43.

———. 1986b. *The Hidden Hierarchy.* Aldershot: Gower.

Rothman, B. Katz. 1989. *Recreating Motherhood: Ideology and Technology in a Patriarchal Society.* New York: Norton.

Scott, J. 1986. "Gender: A Useful Category of Historical Analysis." *American Historical Review* 91:1053–75.

Smith, D. E. 1988. *The Everyday World as Problematic.* Boston: Northeastern University Press.

Sorenson, B. A. 1984. "The Organizational Woman and the Trojan Horse Effect." Pp. 88–105 in *Patriarchy in a Welfare Society,* edited by H. Holter. Oslo: Universitetsforlaget.

Steinberg, R., and L. Haignere. 1987. "Equitable Compensation Methodological Criteria for Comparable Worth." Pp. 157–82 in *Ingredients for Women's Employment Policy,* edited by C. Bose and G. Spitze. Albany: SUNY Press.

Strober, M. H., and C. L. Arnold. 1987. "Integrated Circuits/Segregated Labor: Women in Computer-Related Occupations and High-Tech Industries." Pp. 136–82 in *Computer Chips and Paper Clips: Technology and Women's Employment*, edited by H. Hartmann. Washington, DC: National Academy Press.

West, C., and D. H. Zimmerman. 1983. "Small Insults: A Study of Interruptions in Conversations Between Unacquainted Persons." Pp. 102–17 in *Language, Gender and Society*, edited by B. Thorne, C. Kramarae, and N. Healy. Rowley, MA: Newbury House.

Young, I. 1981. "Beyond the Unhappy Marriage: A Critique of Dual Systems Theory." Pp. 43–69 in *Women and Revolution*, edited by L. Sargent. Boston: South End Press.

CHAPTER 6 | DOING GENDER

CANDACE WEST AND DON H. ZIMMERMAN

From J. L. Lorber and S. A. Farrell (eds.) (1991) *The Social Construction of Gender* (1991) Newbury Park, CA: Sage.

In the beginning, there was sex and there was gender. Those of us who taught courses in the area in the late 1960s and early 1970s were careful to distinguish one from the other. Sex, we told students, was what was ascribed by biology: anatomy, hormones, and physiology. Gender, we said, was an achieved status: that which is constructed through psychological, cultural, and social means. To introduce the difference between the two, we drew on singular case studies of hermaphrodites (Money 1968, 1974; Money and Ehrhardt 1972) and anthropological investigations of "strange and exotic tribes" (Mead 1963, 1968).

Inevitably (and understandably), in the ensuing weeks of each term, our students became confused. Sex hardly seemed a "given" in the context of research that illustrated the sometimes ambiguous and often conflicting criteria for its ascription. And gender seemed much less an "achievement" in the context of the anthropological, psychological, and social imperatives we studied – the division of labor, the formation of gender identities, and the social subordination of women by men. Moreover, the received doctrine of gender socialization theories conveyed the strong message that while gender may be "achieved," by about age five it was certainly fixed, unvarying, and static – much like sex.

Since about 1975, the confusion has intensified and spread far beyond our individual classrooms. For one thing, we learned that the relationship between biological and cultural processes was far more complex – and reflexive – than we previously had supposed (Rossi 1984, especially pp. 10–14). For another, we discovered that certain structural arrangements, for example, between work and family, actually produce or enable some capacities, such as to mother, that we formerly associated with biology (Chodorow 1978 versus Firestone 1970). In the midst of all this, the notion of gender as a recurring achievement somehow fell by the wayside.

Our purpose in this chapter is to propose an ethnomethodologically informed, and therefore distinctively sociological, understanding of gender as a routine, methodical, and recurring accomplishment. We contend that the "doing" of gender is undertaken by women and men whose competence as members of society is hostage to its production. Doing gender involves a complex of socially guided perceptual, interactional, and micropolitical activities that cast particular pursuits as expressions of masculine and feminine "natures."

When we view gender as an accomplishment, an achieved property of situated conduct, our attention shifts from matters internal to the individual and focuses on interactional and, ultimately, institutional arenas. In one sense, of course, it is individuals who "do" gender. But it is a situated doing, carried out in the virtual or real presence of others who are presumed to be oriented to its production. Rather than as a property of individuals, we conceive of gender as an emergent feature of social situations: as both an outcome of and a rationale for various social arrangements and as a means of legitimating one of the most fundamental divisions of society.

To advance our argument, we undertake a critical examination of what sociologists have meant by *gender*, including its treatment as a role enactment in the conventional sense. . . . [*G*]*ender role* . . . focus[es] on behavioral aspects of being a woman or a man (as opposed, for example, to biological differences between the two). However, we contend that the notion of gender as a role obscures the work that is involved in producing gender in everyday activities. . . . We argue instead that participants in interactions organize their various and manifold activities to reflect or express gender, and they are disposed to perceive the behavior of others in a similar light.

To elaborate our proposal, we suggest at the outset that important but often overlooked distinctions should be observed among *sex, sex category,* and *gender*. *Sex* is a determination made through the application of socially agreed upon biological criteria for classifying persons as females or males. The criteria for classification can be genitalia at birth or chromosomal typing before birth, and they do not necessarily agree with one another. Placement in a *sex category* is achieved through application of the sex criteria, but in everyday life, categorization is established and sustained by the socially required identificatory displays that proclaim one's membership in one or the other category. In this sense, one's sex category presumes one's sex and stands as proxy for it in many situations, but sex and sex category can vary independently; that is, it is possible to claim membership in a sex category even when the sex criteria are lacking. *Gender*, in contrast, is the activity of managing situated conduct in light of normative conceptions of attitudes and activities appropriate for one's sex category. Gender activities emerge from and bolster claims to membership in a sex category.

We contend that recognition of the analytical independence of sex, sex category, and gender is essential for understanding the relationships among these elements and the interactional work involved in "being" a gendered person in society. While our primary aim is theoretical, there will be occasion to discuss fruitful directions for empirical research that follow from the formulation of gender we propose.

We begin with an assessment of the received meaning of gender, particularly in relation to the roots of this notion in presumed biological differences between women and men.

PERSPECTIVES ON SEX AND GENDER

In Western societies, the accepted cultural perspective on gender views women and men as naturally and unequivocally defined categories of being (Garfinkel 1967, pp. 116–8) with distinctive psychological and behavioral propensities that can be predicted from their reproductive functions. Competent adult members of these societies see differences between the two as fundamental and enduring, and these differences are seemingly supported by the division of labor into women's and men's work and an often elaborate differentiation of feminine and masculine attitudes and behaviors that are prominent features of social organization. Things are the way they are by virtue of the fact that men are men and women are women – a division perceived to be natural and rooted in biology, producing in turn profound psychological, behavioral, and social consequences. The structural arrangements of a society are presumed to be responsive to these differences.

Analyses of sex and gender in the social sciences, although less likely to accept uncritically the naive biological determinism of the view just presented, often retain a conception of sex-linked behaviors and traits as essential properties of individuals (for good reviews, see Hochschild 1973; Thorne 1980; Tresemer 1975; Henley 1985). The "sex differences approach" (Thorne 1980) is more commonly attributed to psychologists than to sociologists, but the survey researcher who determines the gender of respondents on the basis of the sound of their voices over the telephone is also making trait-oriented assumptions. Reducing gender to a fixed set of psychological traits or to a unitary "variable" precludes serious consideration of the ways it is used to structure distinct domains of social experience (Stacey and Thorne 1985, pp. 307–8).

Taking a different tack, role theory has attended to the social construction of gender categories, called "sex roles" or, more recently, "gender roles" and has analyzed how these are learned and enacted. Beginning with Linton (1936) and continuing through the works of Parsons (Parsons 1951; Parsons and Bales 1955) and Komarovsky (1946, 1950), role theory has emphasized the social and dynamic aspect of role construction and enactment (Connell 1983; Thorne 1980). But at the level of face-to-face interaction, the application of role theory to gender poses problems of its own (for good reviews and critiques, see Connell 1983, 1985; Kessler, Ashendon, Connell, and Dowsett 1985; Lopata and Thorne, 1978; Stacey and Thorne, 1985; Thorne 1980). Roles are *situated* identities – assumed and relinquished as the situation demands – rather than *master* identities (Hughes 1945), such as sex category, that cut across situations. Unlike most roles, such as "nurse, doctor", and "patient" or "professor" and "student", gender has no specific site or organizational context. Moreover, many roles are already gender marked, so that special qualifiers – such as "female doctor" or "male nurse" – must be added to exceptions to the rule. Thorne (1980) observes that conceptualizing gender as a role makes it difficult to assess its influence on other roles and reduces its explanatory usefulness in discussions of power and inequality. Drawing on Rubin (1975), Thorne calls for a reconceptualization of women and men as distinct social groups, constituted in "concrete, historically changing – and generally unequal – social relationships" (Thorne 1980, p. 11).

We argue that gender is not a set of traits, nor a variable, nor a role, but the product of social doings of some sort. What then is the social doing of gender? It is more than the continuous creation of the meaning of gender through human actions (Gerson and Peiss 1985). We claim that gender itself is constituted through interaction. [. . .]

SEX, SEX CATEGORY, AND GENDER

Garfinkel's (1967, pp. 118–40) case study of Agnes, a transsexual raised as a boy who adopted a female identity at age 17 and underwent a sex reassignment operation several years later, demonstrates how gender is created through interaction and at the same time structures interaction. Agnes, whom Garfinkel characterized as a "practical methodologist," developed a number of procedures for passing as a "normal, natural female" both prior to and after her surgery. She had the practical task of managing the facts that she possessed male genitalia and that she lacked the social resources a girl's biography would presumably provide in everyday interaction. In short, she needed to display herself as a woman, simultaneously learning what it was to be a woman. Of necessity, this full-time pursuit took place at a time in her life when most people's gender would be well-accredited and routinized. Agnes had to consciously contrive what the vast majority of women do without thinking. She was not faking what real women do naturally. She was obliged to analyze and figure out how to act within socially structured circumstances and conceptions of femininity that women born with appropriate biological credentials take for granted early on. As in the case of others who must "pass," such as tranvestites, Kabuki actors, or Dustin Hoffman's "Tootsie," Agnes's case makes visible what culture has made invisible – the accomplishment of gender.

Garfinkel's (1967) discussion of Agnes does not explicitly separate three analytically distinct, although empirically overlapping, concepts – sex, sex category, and gender.

Sex

Agnes did not possess the socially agreed upon biological criteria for classification as a member of the female *sex*. Still, Agnes regarded herself as a female, albeit a female with a penis, which a woman ought not to possess. The penis, she insisted, was a "mistake" in need of remedy (Garfinkel 1967, pp. 126–7, 131–2). Like other competent members of our culture, Agnes honored the notion that there are essential biological criteria that unequivocally distinguish females from males. However, if we move away from the common-sense viewpoint, we discover that the reliability of these criteria is not beyond question (Money and Brennan 1968; Money and Ehrhardt 1972; Money and Ogunro 1974; Money and Tucker 1975). Moreover, other cultures have acknowledged the existence of "cross-genders" (Blackwood 1984; Williams 1986) and the possibility of more than two sexes (Hill 1935; Martin and Voorheis 1975, pp. 84–107; but see also Cucchiari 1981, pp. 32–5).

More central to our argument is Kessler and McKenna's (1978, pp. 1–6) point that genitalia are conventionally hidden from public inspection in everyday life; yet we continue through our social rounds to "observe" a world of two naturally, normally sexed persons. It is the *presumption* that essential criteria exist, and would or should be there if looked for, that provides the basis for sex categorization. Drawing on Garfinkel, Kessler and McKenna argued that "female" and "male" are cultural events – products of what they term the "gender attribution process" – rather than some collection of traits, behaviors, or even physical attributes. Illustratively, they cite the child who, viewing a picture of someone clad in a suit and a tie, contends,

"It's a man, because he has a pee-pee" (Kessler and McKenna 1978, p. 154). Translation: "He must have a pee-pee [an essential characteristic] because I see the *insignia* of a suit and tie." Neither initial sex assignment (pronouncement at birth as a female or male) nor the actual existence of essential criteria for that assignment (possession of a clitoris and vagina or penis and testicles) has much – if anything – to do with the identification of sex category in everyday life. There, Kessler and McKenna note, we operate with a moral certainty of a world of two sexes. We do not think, "Most persons with penises are men, but some may not be" or "Most persons who dress as men have penises." Rather, we take it for granted that sex and sex category are congruent – that knowing the latter, we can deduce the rest.

Sex categorization

Agnes's claim to the categorical status of female, which she sustained by appropriate identificatory displays and other characteristics, could be discredited before her transsexual operation if her possession of a penis became known and after by her surgically constructed genitalia (see Raymond 1979, pp. 37, 138). In this regard, Agnes had to be continually alert to actual or potential threats to the security of her sex category. Her problem was not so much living up to some prototype of essential femininity but preserving her categorization as female. This task was made easy for her by a very powerful resource, namely, the process of common-sense categorization in everyday life.

The categorization of members of society into indigenous categories, such as girl or boy, or woman or man, operates in a distinctively social way. The act of categorization does not involve a positive test, in the sense of a well-defined set of criteria that must be explicitly satisfied prior to making an identification. Rather, the application of membership categories relies on an "if-can" test in everyday interaction (Sacks 1972, pp. 332–35). This test stipulates that *if* people *can be seen* as members of relevant categories, *then categorize them that way*. That is, use the category that seems appropriate, except in the presence of discrepant information or obvious features that would rule out its use. This procedure is quite in keeping with the attitude of everyday life, in which we take appearances at face value unless we have special reason to doubt them (Bernstein 1986; Garfinkel 1967, pp. 272–7; Schutz 1943). It should be added that it is precisely when we have special reason to doubt appearances that the issue of applying rigorous criteria arises, but it is rare, outside legal or bureaucratic contexts, to encounter insistence on positive tests (Garfinkel 1967, pp. 262–83; Wilson 1970).

Agnes's initial resource was the predisposition of those she encountered to take her appearance (her figure, clothing, hair style, and so on) as the undoubted appearance of a normal female. Her further resource was our cultural perspective on the properties of "natural, normally sexed persons." Garfinkel (1967, pp. 122–8) notes that in everyday life, we live in a world of two – and only two – sexes. This arrangement has a moral status in that we include ourselves and others in it as "essentially, originally, in the first place, always have been, always will be once and for all, in the final analysis, either 'male' or 'female'" (Garfinkel 1967, p. 122). [. . .]

Gender

Agnes attempted to be "120 percent female" (Garfinkel 1967, p. 129), that is, unquestionably in all ways and at all times feminine. She thought she could protect herself from disclosure before and after surgical intervention by comporting herself in a feminine manner, but she also could have given herself away by overdoing her performance. Sex categorization and the accomplishment of gender are not the same. Agnes's categorization could be secure or suspect, but did not depend on whether or not she lived up to some ideal conception of femininity. Women can be seen as unfeminine, but that does not make them "unfemale." Agnes faced an ongoing task of *being* a woman – something beyond style of dress (an identificatory display) or allowing men to light her cigarette (a gender display). Her problem was to produce configurations of behavior that would be seen by others as normative gender behavior.

Agnes's strategy of "secret apprenticeship," through which she learned expected feminine decorum by carefully attending to her fiancé's criticisms of other women, was one means of masking incompetencies and simultaneously acquiring the needed skills (Garfinkel 1967, pp. 146–7). It was through her fiancé that Agnes learned that sunbathing on the lawn in front of her apartment was "offensive" (because it put her on display to other men). She also learned from his critiques of other women that she should not insist on having things her way and that she should not offer her opinions or claim equality with men (Garfinkel 1967, pp. 147–8). (Like other women in our society Agnes learned something about power in the course of her "education.") [. . .]

[D]oing gender is not . . . easily regimented (Mithers 1982; Morris 1974). . . . To be successful, marking or displaying gender must be finely fitted to situations and modified or transformed as the occasion demands. Doing gender consists of managing such occasions so that, whatever the particulars, the outcome is seen and seeable in context as gender-appropriate or purposefully gender-inappropriate, that is, *accountable.*

GENDER AND ACCOUNTABILITY

As Heritage (1984, pp. 136–7) notes, members of society regularly engage in "descriptive accountings of states of affairs to one another," and such accounts are both serious and consequential. These descriptions name, characterize, formulate, explain, excuse, excoriate, or merely take notice of some circumstance or activity and thus place it within some social framework (locating it relative to other activities, like and unlike).

Such descriptions are themselves accountable, and societal members orient to the fact that their activities are subject to comment. Actions are often designed with an eye to their accountability, that is, how they might look and how they might be characterized. The notion of accountability also encompasses those actions undertaken so that they are specifically unremarkable and thus not worthy of more than a passing remark, because they are seen to be in accord with culturally approved standards.

Heritage (1984, p. 179) observes that the process of rendering something accountable is interactional in character:

[This] permits actors to design their actions in relation to their circumstances so as to permit others, by methodically taking account of circumstances, to recognize the action for what it is.

The key word here is *circumstances*. One circumstance that attends virtually all actions is the sex category of the actor. As Garfinkel (1967, p. 118) comments:

[T]he work and socially structured occasions of sexual passing were obstinately unyielding to [Agnes's] attempts to routinize the grounds of daily activities. This obstinacy points to the *omnirelevance* of sexual status to affairs of daily life as an invariant but unnoticed background in the texture of relevances that compose the changing actual scenes of everyday life. (emphasis added)

If sex category is omnirelevant (or even approaches being so), then a person engaged in virtually any activity may be held accountable for performance of that activity *as a woman or a man*, and their incumbency in one or the other sex category can be used to legitimate or discredit their other activities (Berger, Cohen, and Zelditch 1972; Berger, Conner, and Fisek 1974; Berger, Fisek, Norman, and Zelditch 1977; Humphreys and Berger 1981). Accordingly, virtually any activity can be assessed as to its womanly or manly nature. And note, to "do" gender is not always to live up to normative conceptions of femininity or masculinity; it is to engage in behavior *at the risk of gender assessment*. Although it is individuals who do gender, the enterprise is fundamentally interactional and institutional in character, because accountability is a feature of social relationships and its idiom is drawn from the institutional arena in which those relationships are enacted. If this is the case, can we ever *not* do gender? Insofar as a society is partitioned by "essential" differences between women and men and placement in a sex category is both relevant and enforced, doing gender is unavoidable.

RESOURCES FOR DOING GENDER

Doing gender means creating differences between girls and boys and women and men, differences that are not natural, essential, or biological. Once the differences have been constructed, they are used to reinforce the "essentialness" of gender. In a delightful account of the "arrangement between the sexes," Goffman (1977) observes the creation of a variety of institutionalized frameworks through which our "natural, normal sexedness" can be enacted. The physical features of social settings provide one obvious resource for the expression of our "essential" differences. For example, the sex segregation of North American public bathrooms distinguishes "ladies" from "gentlemen" in matters held to be fundamentally biological, even though both "are somewhat similar in the question of waste products and their elimination" (Goffman 1977, p. 135). These settings are furnished with dimorphic equipment (such as urinals for men or elaborate grooming facilities for women), even though both sexes may achieve the same ends through the same means (and apparently do so in the privacy of their own homes). To be stressed here is the fact that:

The *functioning* of sex-differentiated organs is involved, but there is nothing in this functioning that biologically recommends segregation; *that* arrangement is a totally cultural matter . . . toilet segregation is presented as a natural consequence of the difference between the sex-classes when in fact it is a means of honoring, if not producing, this difference. (Goffman 1977, p. 316)

Standardized social occasions also provide stages for evocations of the "essential female and male natures." Goffman cites organized sports as one such institutionalized framework for the expression of manliness. There, those qualities that ought "properly" to be associated with masculinity, such as endurance, strength, and competitive spirit, are celebrated by all parties concerned – participants, who may be seen to demonstrate such traits, and spectators, who applaud their demonstrations from the safety of the sidelines (1977, p. 322).

Assortative mating practices among heterosexual couples afford still further means to create and maintain differences between women and men. For example, even though size, strength, and age tend to be normally distributed among females and males (with considerable overlap between them), selective pairing ensures couples in which boys and men are visibly bigger, stronger, and older (if not "wiser") than the girls and women with whom they are paired. So, should situations emerge in which greater size, strength, or experience is called for, boys and men will be ever ready to display it and girls and women to appreciate its display (Goffman 1977, p. 321; West and Iritani 1985).

Gender may be routinely fashioned in a variety of situations that seem conventionally expressive to begin with, such as those that present "helpless" women next to heavy objects or flat tires. But, as Goffman notes, heavy, messy, and precarious concerns can be constructed from *any* social situation, "even though by standards set in other settings, this may involve something that is light, clean, and safe" (Goffman 1977, p. 324). Given these resources, it is clear that any interactional situation sets the stage for depictions of "essential" sexual natures. In sum, these situations "do not so much allow for the expression of natural differences as for the production of that difference itself" (Goffman 1977, p. 324).

Many situations are not clearly sex categorized, nor is what transpires in them obviously gender relevant. Yet any social encounter can be pressed into service in the interests of doing gender. Thus, Fishman's (1978) research on casual conversations found an asymmetrical "division of labor" in talk between heterosexual intimates. Women had to ask more questions, fill more silences, and use more attention-getting beginnings in order to be heard. Her conclusions are particularly pertinent here:

> Since interactional work is related to what constitutes being a woman, with what a woman *is*, the idea that it *is* work is obscured. The work is not seen as what women do, but as part of what they are. (Fishman 1978, p. 405)

We would argue that it is precisely such labor that helps to constitute the essential nature of women *as* women in interactional contexts (West and Zimmerman 1983, pp. 109–11; but see also Kollock, Blumstein, and Schwartz 1985).

Individuals have many social identities that may be donned or shed, muted, or made more salient, depending on the situation. One may be a friend, professional, citizen, and many other things to many different people or to the same person at different times. But we are always women or men – unless we shift into another sex category. What this means is that our identificatory displays will provide an ever-available resource for doing gender under an infinitely diverse set of circumstances.

Some occasions are organized to routinely display and celebrate behaviors that are conventionally linked to one or the other sex category. On such occasions, everyone knows his or her place in the interactional scheme of things. If an individual identified as a member of one sex category engages in behavior usually associated with the other category, this routinization is challenged. Hughes (1945, p. 356) provides an illustration of such a dilemma:

> [A] young woman . . . became part of that virile profession, engineering. The designer of an airplane is expected to go up on the maiden flight of the first plane built according to the design. He [sic] then gives a dinner to the engineers and workmen who worked on the new plane. The dinner is naturally a stag party. The young woman in question designed a plane. Her co-workers urged her not to take the risk – for which, presumably, men only are fit – of the maiden voyage. They were, in effect, asking her to be a lady instead of an engineer. She chose to be an engineer. She then gave the party and paid for it like a man. After food and the first round of toasts, she left like a lady.

On this occasion, the parties reached an accommodation that allowed a woman to engage in presumptively masculine behaviors. However, in the end, this compromise permitted demonstration of her "essential" femininity, through accountably "ladylike" behavior.

Hughes (1945, p. 357) suggests that such contradictions may be countered by managing interactions on a very narrow basis, for example, by "keeping the relationship formal and specific." But the heart of the matter is that even – perhaps, especially – if the relationship is a formal one, gender is still something one is accountable for. Thus, a woman physician (notice the special qualifier in her case) may be accorded respect for her skill and even addressed by an appropriate title. Nonetheless, she is subject to evaluation in terms of normative conceptions of appropriate attitudes and activities for her sex category and under pressure to prove that she is an "essentially" feminine being, despite appearances to the contrary (West 1984, pp. 97–101). Her sex category is used to discredit her participation in important clinical activities (Lorber 1984, pp. 52–4), while her involvement in medicine is used to discredit her commitment to her responsibilities as a wife and mother (Bourne and Wikler 1978, pp. 435–7). Simultaneously, her exclusion from the physician colleague community is maintained and her accountability *as a woman* is ensured.

In this context, "role conflict" can be viewed as a dynamic aspect of our current "arrangement between the sexes" (Goffman 1977), an arrangement that provides for occasions on which persons of a particular sex category can "see" quite clearly that they are out of place and that if they were not there, their current troubles would not exist. From the standpoint of interaction, what is at stake is the management of our "essential" natures and, from the standpoint of the individual, the continuing accomplishment of gender. If, as we have argued, sex category is omnirelevant, then any occasion, conflicted or not, offers the resources for doing gender.

We have sought to show that sex category and gender are managed properties of conduct that are contrived with respect to the fact that others will judge and respond to us in particular ways. We have claimed that a person's gender is not simply an aspect of what one is, but, more fundamentally, it is something that one *does*, and does recurrently, in interaction with others. [. . .]

GENDER, POWER, AND SOCIAL CHANGE

Let us return to the question: Can we avoid doing gender? Earlier, we proposed that, insofar as sex category is used as a fundamental criterion for differentiation, doing gender is unavoidable. It is unavoidable because of the social consequences of sex-category membership: the allocation of power and resources not only in the domestic, economic, and political domains but also in the broad arena of interpersonal relations. In virtually any situation, one's sex category can be relevant, and one's performance as an incumbent of that category (i.e., gender) can be subjected to evaluation. Maintaining such pervasive and faithful assignment of lifetime status requires legitimation.

But doing gender also renders the social arrangements based on sex category accountable as normal and natural, that is, legitimate ways of organizing social life. Differences between women and men that are created by this process can then be portrayed as fundamental and enduring dispositions. In this light, the institutional arrangements of a society can be seen as responsive to the differences, the social order being merely an accommodation to the natural order. Thus if, in doing gender, men are also doing dominance and women are doing deference (cf. Goffman 1967, pp. 47–95), the resultant social order, which supposedly reflects "natural differences," is a powerful reinforcer and legitimator of hierarchical arrangements. Frye observes:

> For efficient subordination, what's wanted is that the structure not appear to be a cultural artifact kept in place by human decision or custom, but that it appear *natural* – that it appear to be quite a direct consequence of facts about the beast which are beyond the scope of human manipulation. . . . That we are trained to behave so differently as women and men, and to behave so differently toward women and men, itself contributes mightily to the appearance of extreme dimorphism, but also, the *ways* we act as women and men, and the *ways* we act toward women and men, mold our bodies and our minds to the shape of subordination and dominance. We do become what we practice being. (Frye 1983, p. 34)

If we do gender appropriately, we simultaneously sustain, reproduce, and render legitimate the institutional arrangements that are based on sex category. If we fail to do gender appropriately, we as individuals – not the institutional arrangements – may be called to account (for our character, motives, and predispositions).

Social movements such as feminism can provide the ideology and impetus to question existing arrangements and the social support for individuals to explore alternatives to them. Legislative changes, such as those proposed by the Equal Rights Amendment, can also weaken the accountability of conduct to sex category, thereby affording the possibility of more widespread loosening of accountability in general. To be sure, equality under the law does not guarantee equality in other arenas. As Lorber points out, assurance of "scrupulous equality of categories of people considered essentially different needs constant monitoring." What such proposed changes *can* do is provide the warrant for asking why, if we wish to treat women and men as equals, there needs to be two sex categories at all (Lorber, 1986).

The sex category/gender relationship links the institutional and interactional levels, a coupling that legitimates social arrangements based on sex category and reproduces their asymmetry in face-to-face interaction. Doing gender furnishes the interactional scaffolding of social structure, along with a built-in mechanism of social control. In appreciating the institutional forces that maintain distinctions between women and men, we must not lose sight of the interactional validation of those distinctions that confers upon them their sense of "naturalness" and "rightness."

Social change, then, must be pursued at the institutional and cultural levels of sex category and at the interactional level of gender. Such a conclusion is hardly novel. Nevertheless, we suggest that it is important to recognize that the analytical distinction between institutional and interactional sphere does not pose an either/or choice when it comes to the question of effecting social change. Reconceptualizing gender not as a simple property of individuals but as an integral dynamic of social orders implies a new perspective on the entire network of gender relations:

> the social subordination of women, and the cultural practices which help sustain it; the politics of sexual object-choice, and particularly the oppression of homosexual people; the sexual division of labor, the formation of character and motive, so far as they are organized as femininity and masculinity; the role of the body in social relations, especially the politics of childbirth; and the nature of strategies of sexual liberation movements. (Connell 1985, p. 261)

Gender is a powerful ideological device, which produces, reproduces, and legitimates the choices and limits that are predicated on sex category. An understanding of how gender is produced in social situations will afford clarification of the interactional scaffolding of social structure and the social control processes that sustain it.

REFERENCES

Berger, J., B. P. Cohen, and M. Zelditch, Jr. 1972. "Status Characteristics and Social Interaction." *American Sociological Review* 37:241–55.

Berger, J., T. L. Conner, and M. Hamit Fisek, eds. 1974. *Expectation States Theory: A Theoretical Research Program.* Cambridge, MA: Winthrop.

Berger, J., M. Hamit Fisek, R. Z. Norman, and M. Zelditch, Jr. 1977. *Status Characteristics and Social Interaction: An Expectation States Approach.* New York: Elsevier.

Bernstein, R. 1986. "France Jails 2 in Odd Case of Espionage." *New York Times* (May 11).

Blackwood, E. 1984. "Sexuality and Gender in Certain Native American Tribes: The Case of Cross-Gender Females." *Signs: Journal of Women in Culture and Society* 10:27–42.

Bourne, P. G., and N. J. Wikler. 1978. "Commitment and the Cultural Mandate: Women in Medicine." *Social Problems* 25:430–40.

Chodorow, N. 1978. *The Reproduction of Mothering: Psychoanalysis and the Sociology of Gender.* Los Angeles: University of California Press.

Connell, R. W. 1983. *Which Way Is Up?* Sydney, Australia: Allen and Unwin.

———. 1985. "Theorizing Gender." *Sociology* 19:260–72.

Cucchiari, S. 1981. "The Gender Revolution and the Transition from Bisexual Horde to Patrilocal Band: The Origins of Gender Hierarchy." Pp. 31–79 in *Sexual Meanings: The Cultural Construction of Gender and Sexuality*, edited by S. B. Ortner and H. Whitehead. New York: Cambridge.

Firestone, S. 1970. *The Dialectic of Sex: The Case for Feminist Revolution*. New York: William Morrow.

Fishman, P. 1978. "Interaction: The Work Women Do." *Social Problems* 25:397–406.

Frye, M. 1983. *The Politics of Reality: Essays in Feminist Theory*. Trumansburg, NY: The Crossing Press.

Garfinkel, H. 1967. *Studies in Ethnomethodology*. Englewood Cliffs, NJ: Prentice-Hall.

Gerson, J. M., and K. Peiss. 1985. "Boundaries, Negotiation, Consciousness: Reconceptualizing Gender Relations." *Social Problems* 32:317–31.

Goffman, E. 1967 (1956). "The Nature of Deference and Demeanor." Pp. 47–95 in *Interaction Ritual*. New York: Anchor/Doubleday.

———. 1977. "The Arrangement Between the Sexes." *Theory and Society* 4:301–31.

Henley, N. M. 1985. "Psychology and Gender." *Signs: Journal of Women in Culture and Society* 11:101–19.

Heritage, J. 1984. *Garfinkel and Ethnomethodology*. Cambridge, UK: Polity Press.

Hill, W. W. 1935. "The Status of the Hermaphrodite and Transvestite in Navaho Culture." *American Anthropologist* 37:273–9.

Hochschild, A. R. 1973. "A Review of Sex Roles Research." *American Journal of Sociology* 78:1011–29.

Hughes, E. C. 1945. "Dilemmas and Contradictions of Status." *American Journal of Sociology* 50:353–9.

Humphreys, P., and J. Berger. 1981. "Theoretical Consequences of the Status Characteristics Formulation." *American Journal of Sociology* 86:953–83.

Kessler, S., D. J. Ashendon, R. W. Connell, and G. W. Dowsett. 1985. "Gender Relations in Secondary Schooling." *Sociology of Education* 58:34–48.

Kessler, S. J., and W. McKenna. 1978. *Gender: An Ethnomethodological Approach*. New York: John Wiley.

Kollock, P., P. Blumstein, and P. Schwartz. 1985. "Sex and Power in Interaction." *American Sociological Review* 50:34–46.

Komarovsky, M. 1946. "Cultural Contradictions and Sex Roles." *American Journal of Sociology* 52:184–9.

———. 1950. "Functional Analysis of Sex Roles." *American Sociological Review* 15:508–16.

Linton, R. 1936. *The Study of Man*. New York: Appleton-Century.

Lopata, H. Z., and B. Thorne. 1978. "On the Term 'Sex Roles.'" *Signs: Journal of Women in Culture and Society* 3:718–21.

Lorber, J. 1984. *Women Physicians: Careers, Status and Power*. New York: Tavistock.

———. 1986. "Dismontling Noah's Ark." *Sex Roles* 14:567–80.

Martin, M. K. and B. Voorheis. 1975. *Female of the Species*. New York: Columbia University Press.

Mead, M. 1963. *Sex and Temperament*. New York: Dell.

———. 1968. *Male and Female*. New York: Dell.

Mithers, C. L. 1982. "My Life as a Man." *Village Voice* 27 (October 5): 1ff.

Money, J. 1968. *Sex Errors of the Body*. Baltimore: Johns Hopkins University Press.

———. 1974. "Prenatal Hormones and Postnatal Sexualization in Gender Identity Differentiation." Pp. 221–95 in *Nebraska Symposium on Motivation*, Vol. 21, edited by J. K. Cole and R. Dienstbier. Lincoln: University of Nebraska Press.

———and J. G. Brennan. 1968. "Sexual Dimorphism in the Psychology of Female Transsexuals." *Journal of Nervous and Mental Disease* 147:487–99.

———and A. A. Ehrhardt. 1972. *Man and Women/Boy and Girl*. Baltimore: Johns Hopkins University Press.

——and C. Ogunro. 1974. "Behavioral Sexology: Ten Cases of Genetic Male Intersexuality with Impaired Prenatal and Pubertal Androgenization," *Archives of Sexual Behavior* 3:181–206.

——and P. Tucker. 1975. *Sexual Signatures*. Boston: Little, Brown.

Morris, J. 1974. *Conundrum*. New York: Harcourt Brace Jovanovich.

Parsons, T. 1951. *The Social System*. New York: Free Press.

——and R. F. Bales. 1955. *Family, Socialization and Interaction Process*. New York: Free Press.

Raymond, J. G. 1979. *The Transsexual Empire*. Boston: Beacon.

Rossi, A. 1984. "Gender and Parenthood." *American Sociological Review* 49:1–19.

Rubin, G. 1975. "The Traffic in Women: Notes on the 'Political Economy' of Sex." Pp. 157–210 in *Toward an Anthropology of Women*, edited by R. Reiter. New York: Monthly Review Press.

Sacks, H. 1972. "On the Analyzability of Stories by Children." Pp. 325–45 in *Directions in Sociolinguistics*, edited by J. J. Gumperz and D. Hymes. New York: Holt, Rinehart & Winston.

Schutz, A. 1943. "The Problem of Rationality in the Social World." *Economics* 10:130–49.

Stacey, J., and B. Thorne. 1985. "The Missing Feminist Revolution in Sociology." *Social Problems* 32:301–16.

Thorne, B. 1980. "Gender . . . How Is It Best Conceptualized?" Unpublished manuscript.

——. 1986. "Girls and Boys Together . . . But Mostly Apart: Gender Arrangements in Elementary Schools." Pp. 167–82 in *Relationships and Development*, edited by W. Hartup and Z. Rubin. Hillsdale, NJ: Lawrence Erlbaum.

Tresemer, D. 1975. "Assumptions Made About Gender Roles." Pp. 308–39 in *Another Voice: Feminist Perspectives on Social Life and Social Science*, edited by M. Millman and R. Moss Kanter. New York: Anchor/Doubleday.

West, C. 1984. "When the Doctor is a 'Lady': Power, Status and Gender in Physician–Patient Encounters." *Symbolic Interaction* 7:87–106.

——and B. Iritani. 1985. "Gender Politics in Mate Selection: The Male-Older Norm." Paper presented at the Annual Meeting of the American Sociological Association, August, Washington, DC.

——and D. H. Zimmerman. 1983. "Small Insults: A Study of Interruptions in Conversations Between Unacquainted Persons." Pp. 102–17 in *Language, Gender and Society*, edited by B. Thorne, C. Kramarae, and N. Henley. Rowley, MA: Newbury House.

Williams, W. L. 1986. *The Spirit and the Flesh: Sexual Diversity in American Indian Culture*. Boston: Beacon.

Wilson, T. P. 1970. "Conceptions of Interaction and Forms of Sociological Explanation." *American Sociological Review* 35:697–710.

BREAKING THE SILENCE: ON MEN, MASCULINITIES AND MANAGEMENTS

DAVID L. COLLINSON AND JEFF HEARN

From D. L. Collinson and J. Hearn (eds.) (1996) *Men as Managers, Managers as Men: Critical Perspective on Men, Masculinities, and Management*, London: Sage

Most managers in most organizations in most countries are men. Yet the conditions, processes and consequences of men's historical and contemporary domination of management have received little scrutiny. There has been a strange silence, which we believe reflects an embedded and taken-for-granted association, even conflation, of men with organizational power, authority and prestige. [. . .]

It is important to begin by examining the scale of men's "occupation" of management from the boardroom to junior levels. Women comprise less than 5 per cent of senior management in the UK and US while in Australia and many other countries, it is closer to 2 per cent (Sinclair, 1995). A Hansard Society Commission survey (Hansard Society, 1990) found that only 5 per cent of the UK Institute of Directors and less than 1 per cent of chief executives were women.[1] Despite slow but steady progress by women into more junior managerial hierarchies within UK corporations in the 1980s, recent research suggests a reversal in these trends. The 1994 National Management Survey (Institute of Management, 1995), for example, found a fall in the number of women managers from 10.2 per cent in 1993 to 9.8 per cent in 1994. While women constituted only 2.8 per cent of directors, they were: concentrated in junior managerial grades, twice as likely as their male counterparts to have resigned in the previous twelve months and paid less than their male counterparts by an average of 15.2 per cent. A 1992 survey of forty-three broadcasting organizations across the twelve member states of the European Community found that women comprised under 11 per cent of management at the top three levels (Equal Opportunities Commission, 1992).

Research in the United States suggests that those few women who reach senior managerial positions are much more likely than their male counterparts to report feeling stressed and burned out, as a result of juggling work and a disproportionate load of family obligations (*New York Times*, 1993). They are also less likely than their male counterparts either to receive training (Tharenou et al., 1994) or to be assigned tasks with high responsibility, visibility and the opportunity to demonstrate the levels of competence needed for future advancement (Ohlott et al., 1994). Moreover the few women in US corporations who become company directors are often channelled into "peripheral" committees like public affairs while their male counterparts sit on committees deemed central to corporate governance such as executive and finance committees (Bilimoria and Piderit, 1994). Hence, although not all managers are men, the male domination of most hierarchical levels within management tends to persist not only historically, but also across different societies. The development of transnational organizations, international trade, communication and world financial systems is likely to reinforce the globalized nature of these male-dominated networks and processes.

Reflecting and reinforcing this numerical dominance is a masculine or masculinist imagery that frequently pervades the managerial function and perceptions of it. This gendered imagery is reflected in the etymology of the verb to "manage" derived from the sixteenth-century Italian word *menagerie*, which meant handling things and especially horses (Williams, 1976). As Mant (1977: 20) argues, "In this derivation it was ultimately a masculine concept, to do with taking charge, directing, especially in the context of war." Indeed throughout the history of management thought and practice there has been a recurrent association between gender, hierarchy and organization on the one hand and militarism and warfare on the other. Early management writers tended to draw on military experience and language when making sense of organizational problems (Morgan, 1986; Shaw, 1990). Central to such thinking was the prioritization of the leader and manager as heroic warrior (Grint, 1995). The masculinity of this imagery is illustrated more recently by a "Heathrow management text" (Burrell, 1992) that applies to contemporary business the 2,500-year-old teaching of Sun Tzu on military strategy and the management of warfare (Krause, 1995). Its prescriptions on the "Art of War for Executives" and the ruthless "Principles of Success" regarding competitive strategy and "defeating the enemy" are deeply imbued with masculine images and assumptions.

Biographies and autobiographies of famous twentieth-century entrepreneurial male managers/owners such as Ford (Ford, 1923; Sward, 1948; Beynon, 1980), Iacocca (Iacocca, 1984), Geneen (Geneen, 1985) and Maxwell (Davies, 1992) often reveal an evangelical, personal and lifelong preoccupation with military-like efficiency, ruthless practices and autocratic control. Many of these accounts of dictatorial business leaders also demonstrate how the managerial search for efficiency can become an all-engulfing obsession. Equally, they implicitly disclose the masculine assumptions and practices that frequently predominate in management. Morgan argues that from an early age Frederick Taylor (1947) was an obsessive anal-compulsive character "driven by a relentless need to tie down and master almost every aspect of his life" (1986: 204). Scientific management, one of the most influential managerial theories of the twentieth century, is found to be the product of "a disturbed and neurotic personality" (ibid.: 205). The life history of Howard Hughes, the American innovator, entrepreneur and tycoon, is an extraordinary example of these obsessive tendencies towards control and mastery (Drosnin, 1987). Driven by a fear that his father did not respect his achievements, Hughes created a massive business empire that increasingly reflected and reinforced his concern with personal control and efficiency. He prescribed in minute detail the rules of behaviour to which his employees should adhere. Hating emotion of any kind, Hughes sought to control not only the women in his personal life, but also those who starred in his films, closely defining and monitoring their daily routines. His detachment, isolation and obsession with control grew to the point where he could no longer bear to breathe the air of other human beings because they might be germ carriers. Consequently, Hughes had his headquarters hermetically sealed and in his later years he lived totally alone in a room that was neither cleaned nor ever saw the light of day. His life history illustrates the self-defeating consequences that can ensue from an obsession with personal control through autocratic management. We would argue that the preoccupations of all these famous male entrepreneurs with work, discipline and emotional control are also indicative of highly masculine modes of thought and behaviour that prioritize "mastery" over self and other.

In the 1980s especially, journalistic profiles of male executives or "captains of industry" consistently presented "heroic", "macho"[2] images emphasizing qualities of struggle and battle, a willingness to be ruthless and brutal, a rebellious nature and an aggressive, rugged individualism (Neale, 1995).[3] Managers and senior executives were frequently depicted and portrayed themselves as "hard men", virile swashbuckling and flamboyant entrepreneurs who were reasserting a "macho" management style that insisted on the "divine right of managers to manage" (Purcell, 1982; see also Mackay, 1986; Edwards, 1987; Denham, 1991). Masculine, abrasive and highly autocratic managerial styles were widely valued and celebrated as the primary means of generating corporate success. "Man"-agement came to be defined in terms of the ability to *control* people, events, companies, environments, trade unions and new technology. In the 1990s, managers and their performance are increasingly being evaluated. One central criterion of these evaluation practices is the masculinist concern with personal power and the ability to control others and self.[4] Such masculine discourses are also embedded in conventional managerial language which is frequently gendered, for example both in terms of highly (hetero)sexualized talk about "penetrating markets" and "getting into bed with suppliers/customers/competitors", and in the extensive use of sporting metaphors and sexual joking in making sense of and rationalizing managerial decisions and practices (Scase and Goffee, 1989; Collinson et al., 1990). Designed to measure performance, annual revenue, sales and productivity figures are often treated as symbols of corporate and managerial virility (Gherardi, 1995). Equally, managerial presentational styles (especially those of management consultants) which emphasize "professional", "competent" and "rational" self-images infused with an air of total confidence, detachment and control frequently reveal masculine assumptions, particularly when presenters use sexist and racist jokes as "icebreakers" (Cockburn, 1991). Participation in male-dominated sports can significantly shape managerial interactions and indeed career progress within and between organizations, networks, labour markets and professional alliances where men seek to relate to one another as colleagues, employees, clients and customers, as well as competitors and team-mates (Jackall, 1988). A considerable amount of business is also conducted through the "entertainment" of client "guests" in male-dominated sporting spheres such as tennis and golf clubs, in "executive boxes" at football grounds and in the men-only business clubs of which many managers and executives are members (Elliott, 1959; Rogers, 1988; Allison, 1994).

Despite – possibly even because of – this frequently pervasive association between men, power and authority in organizations, the literature on management (and indeed organization theory) has consistently failed to question its gendered nature. Here again images of middle and senior management seem to be imbued with particular notions of masculinity. Whether we refer to the "ideal"[5] *prescriptive* models of management of early academic writers (for example Barnard, 1938; Fayol, 1949; Simon, 1945), *descriptive* accounts of managerial work (for example Mintzberg, 1973; Stewart, 1976; Drucker, 1979) or even more *critical* contemporary analyses (for example Willmott, 1987; Reed, 1989; Mangham and critics, 1995), the masculine imagery of management and managers seems to be taken for granted, neglected, and thereby reproduced and reinforced.[6] This neglect is illustrated by the unreflexive use of book and chapter titles such as: "The organization man" (Whyte, 1956); "Men who manage" (Dalton, 1959); "A thinking man's management", "Manager for himself" (Sampson, 1965); "The men at the top" (Elliott, 1959; Burns and Stalker, 1961); "The man and the corporation" (Guzzardi, 1966); and "The manager and his work" (Drucker, 1979). Failing to consider the gendered questions to which their titles seem to allude, all of these studies tend to say a great deal more about management than they do about men.

Yet, there is another derivation of the verb to manage, drawn from the French *ménager*, an eighteenth-century meaning which Mant (1977: 21) sees as "a more gentle, perhaps feminine usage" emphasizing careful housekeeping and domestic organization.[7] Developing this theme, Wensley (1996) has recently identified several important implications of Mrs. Beeton's (1861) *Book of Household Management* for the analysis and practice of corporate management in the 1990s. This alternative meaning makes a point which is central, namely that management, as a function, profession and practice, need not *inevitably* be dominated by masculine styles, discourses or processes generally, or by men in particular. [. . .]

> From Naming Men as Men: Implications for Work, Organization and Management (1944), Collinson and J. Hearn, *Gender Work and Organization*, 1(1): 13–16.

MULTIPLE MASCULINITIES AND MANAGEMENTS

So, how are these multiple masculinities historically embedded in organizational practices? What would a simultaneous emphasis upon unities and differences look like? We will now elaborate and illustrate our argument that various masculinities are central to the exercise of gendered power in organizations. In this section we outline several masculinities that seem to remain pervasive and privileged in organizations broadly and management more specifically, and examine their reproduction through the subjective search to identify and differentiate self. This brief account is by no means intended to be exhaustive, but rather seeks to be suggestive of new ways of analysing men and masculinities and thus power relations in contemporary organizations. It is concerned to emphasize not only how various masculinities frequently shape managerial practices, but also the way that managerial practices can impact on the emergence of various masculinities in the workplace.

In what follows we identify five discourses and practices of masculinity that appear to remain pervasive and dominant in organizations: authoritarianism; paternalism; entrepreneurialism; informalism and careerism. These are particularly interrelated with different managerial styles. Seeking to illustrate the way that power is routinely exercised in organizations, they are presented in an ideal-typical and discrete way, whereas in practice they are likely to overlap and co-exist within specific processes. We will now consider each in turn.

Authoritarianism

Authoritarianism is typically but not exclusively related to those in positions of seniority. It is characterized by an intolerance of dissent or difference, a rejection of dialogue and debate and a preference for coercive power relations based on dictatorial control and unquestioning obedience. Maddock and Parkin (1993) refer to this as the "barrack yard culture" highlighting the way in which aggressive masculinity is deeply embedded in such autocratic practices.

Based upon bullying and the creation of fear in subordinates, authoritarianism celebrates a brutal and aggressive masculinity; a criterion by which self and others are judged. It is therefore a primary source of identification with and differentiation from others. Hostility is aimed at those who fail to comply with this aggressive masculinity, e.g. women and any men as individuals or in groups that possess little institutional power and status (e.g. black people). In dismissing these groups as "weak", those who invest in authoritarianism try to differentiate and elevate their own masculine identity and power. The coercive regime of Harold Geneen at International Telephone and Telegraph is a vivid illustration of an authoritarian, highly masculine style of management (see Morgan 1986, pp. 125–6; Pascale and Athos 1982).

Paternalism

By contrast, in paternalism, men eschew coercion and seek to exercise power by emphasizing the moral basis of cooperation, the protective nature of their authority, the importance of personal trust relations and the need for employees both to invest voluntarily in their work task and to identify with the company. Highlighting the interdependent nature of hierarchical relations, paternalism engages in the "pretence of equality for the purpose of securing instrumental gain" (Kerfoot and Knights 1993, p. 670). It is also a specifically masculine discourse of control that draws on the familial metaphor of the "rule of the father" who is authoritative, benevolent, self-disciplined and wise.

A central self-justifying claim of paternalism is that power is exercised in positive ways which enhance subordinates' self-interests. Such practices are usually represented by their perpetrators as "benefitting" and "protecting" their victims (Pollert 1981; Lown 1983; Bradley 1986). "Power is exercised for the 'good' of the recipient" (Kerfoot and Knights 1993, p. 665). Paternalism frequently has the effect of reinforcing employees' compliance and legitimizing managerial prerogative both for those who are excluded (or "protected") from decision-making and for the decision-makers themselves (Collinson *et al.* 1990).

Investing in paternalism, managers seek to differentiate themselves from women and identify with other men. Older men in particular are likely to be paternalistic towards their younger male colleagues. Maddock and Parkin (1993) term this "The Gentleman's Club": a polite, "civilized" and exclusive male culture where women (and indeed younger men) are kept firmly in established roles by older male managers who are courteous and humane. So long as women conform to conventional notions of female identity, they will experience little hostility. Within these protective practices, women are treated as too "delicate" and "precious" to be involved in the so-called harsh world of business (Collinson and Knights 1986). Such practices can be traced back to a 19th century middle class conception of masculinity in which men are expected to behave in accordance with "gentlemanly principles" and where authority was ascribed on the basis of seniority, social privilege and birthright.

Entrepreneurialism

By contrast, entrepreneurialism articulates a "hard-nosed" and highly competitive approach to business and organization and is associated with more recent management styles. Prioritizing performance levels, budget targets, "penetrating new markets and territories" profits, production and costs, entrepreneurialism elevates economic efficiency and managerial control at the expense of all other criteria. Within this discourse, men as managers identify with other men who are as competitive as themselves, willing to work at a similar pace, endure long hours, be geographically mobile and meet tight production deadlines. These requirements tend to exclude some men who are not considered "man enough" or predatory enough to satisfy them and most women, whose employment, particularly in senior positions, is often seen as incompatible with entrepreneurial concerns.

Differences between men regarding entrepreneurialism are likely to be articulated along the axis of age, often with younger men being more willing to invest in this discourse than their older counterparts, many of whom may be more comfortable with a paternalistic workplace culture. This is illustrated by the selling function of many organizations where men over forty-five (approximately) find it increasingly difficult to compete for business with younger colleagues and thus to perform according to the expectations of their employer. Many older men in sales and middle management have lost their jobs in the retrenchment of the late 1980s and early 1990s. For the younger men who remain, however, their performance is likely to be increasingly monitored, evaluated and stratified. Embroiled in the struggle to be constantly productive and achieving, their masculine identities are likely to be precarious and insecure "constantly preoccupied with purposive action in the drive to be 'in control'" (Kerfoot and Knights 1993).

Equally, within this discourse of gendered entrepreneurialism, pregnancy and domestic commitments are often treated as taboo because they are perceived to challenge and even undermine everyday business practice and the taken-for-granted masculine discourse of control that separates "public" and "private" life (Martin 1990).[1] Returning to our example of selling, research suggests that a deep-seated antagonism to women's conventional domestic commitments frequently pervades this organizational function. Only those women who can comply with the male model of breadwinner employment patterns are likely to be acceptable within this dominant discourse. These women are liable to be divorced with dependent children. Hence, like young salesmen, they are perceived to bring their motivation with them, they are "needy and greedy" (Collinson and Knights 1986).

Informalism

Research has conclusively revealed the way in which men often try to build informal workplace relationships with one another on the basis of shared masculine interests and common values (e.g. Cockburn 1983; Gray 1987; Collinson 1992). Within these informal relationships men are often concerned to identify with other men within the "in-group", while simultaneously differentiating themselves from other groups of men and from women. Typically, the informal currency between men at various hierarchical levels will concentrate on humour, sport, cars, sex, women and drinking alcohol. In the worst cases, these informal and aggressive dynamics of masculinity in the workplace may also result in sexual harassment, the reduction of women in the organization to sexual objects and, where career successful, the undermining of their competence on the grounds that they must have used their sexuality to secure hierarchical advance.

The conditions, processes and consequences of informal relationships between men are not merely confined to working class employment settings such as those outlined earlier (Scase and Goffee 1989). Maddock and Parkin (1993) refer to this informalism that tends to exclude and subordinate women as "the Locker Room Culture". They argue that "It is not just junior women who are subjected to Locker Room Culture, women with power but who are isolated as chief executives or directors tell us that they have to listen to endless references to sport and sex in both formal and informal situations" (1993, p. 5). Moreover, these informal relations between men frequently transcend organizational boundaries. Relationships are developed with men working in other organizations, for example through occupational meetings (e.g. regional meetings of the Institute of Personnel Management) and through leisure/sports groups (e.g. squash, cricket, football, golf clubs).

A particularly familiar example of the influence of informal social relations on employment practices can be found in academic work. In the aforementioned article by Morgan (1981), he describes the influence of informal interactions between male academics, particularly those conducted in the faculty club, staff bar or local pub. He argues that such informal dynamics frequently counterbalance the potentially divisive tendencies of "academic machismo" (discussed earlier). Arguing that the pub is still perceived as a male dominated arena, Morgan refers to this tendency of men to feel more at ease in other men's company as "male homosociability"[2] (1981, p. 102). While the exclusion of women (and some men) from these informal interactions and relationships need not always be deliberately intended or acknowledged, he argues, they are likely to have these effects. This can be particularly important, according to Morgan, because social drinking between academics can provide an enormous amount of valuable work-related as well as personal information.

So far, we have discussed four discourses and practices of masculinity that seem to reflect and reinforce a simultaneous sense of unity and differentiation for men in organizations. Indeed these unities and differences appear to be mutually reinforcing. However, they are also quite fragile, precarious and shifting. Accordingly, they do not always establish the mutual trust, cooperation and loyalty that is claimed for them. The depth and extent of these shared unities and masculine identifications between men should therefore not be overstated. One primary reason for the fragility underpinning these unities is the extent to which more individualistic and competitive concerns also simultaneously characterize men and masculine discourses in organizations.

Careerism

Competition between men in organizations can take many symbolic and/or economic forms. In the case of middle class masculinities especially, competition is often expressed in the widespread preoccupation with hierarchical advance: careerism. The search to validate masculine identity through upward progress inevitably intensifies competition within organizations. Careerism can become a primary orientation to work characterized by an excessive concern with impression management and the differentiation and elevation of self. Such competitive strategies often reflect the way in which (middle class) men in organizations routinely define themselves and are defined as the privatized breadwinner whose primary purpose is to "provide" for their families. Competition for career progress comes to be synonymous with conventional masculinity. Upward mobility can therefore become a key objective in the search to secure a stable masculine identity. A "successful" career may be an important medium through which middle class men seek to establish masculine identities in the workplace. Yet careerism is also likely to intensify the threat to such identities in the current conditions of "delayering", widespread redundancies and extensive career bottlenecks.

Committed to upward progress, men in organizations are willing to work longer hours, meet tight deadlines, travel extensively, participate in residential training courses and move house at the behest of the company. These work demands are likely to be incompatible with domestic responsibilities. Seeking to comply with the increasingly unrealistic expectations of corporate cultures and of "total quality management", for example, men in junior and senior management frequently depend upon the support of wives to manage all domestic and familial matters. Paradoxically, attempts to create a corporate culture in the workplace can therefore distance aspiring men from their own domestic concerns and responsibilities. The search for the "happy family" in employment may be at the cost of an increasingly unhappy family in the domestic sphere. In consequence, the pressure to conform to corporate demands, combined with individuals' own concern with career progress, creates deep-seated divisions, not only between men employees, but also between their paid work and home life.

These differences, divisions and conflicts between men and multiple masculinities in organizations are particularly acute within the managerial function. Contrary to the views of earlier critical writers on management who tended to emphasize the function's unity, homogeneity and omniscience (e.g. Braverman 1974; Edwards 1979), there are a great variety of real and potential differences, divisions and/or conflicts within and between managerial groups and hierarchies. Managerial differences, for example, may be related to hierarchical position, age, industry and organization, region and country and, in particular, discipline and function. They may also be significantly shaped and reproduced through multiple masculinities.

Managerial differences can quickly turn into sources of conflict. For example young managers adhering to an "entrepreneurial" philosophy may be in conflict with older managers who prefer a more "paternalistic" style. Similarly, marketing managers may be struggling for power and influence with their managerial counterparts in production or accounting, as Armstrong (1984, 1986) has revealed in relation to the managerial professions of accountancy, engineering and personnel. A manager in sales may see a colleague in the same function as a serious threat to hierarchical progress such that career rivalry significantly shapes future behaviour.

These differences and conflicts between managers may be related to structural struggles for organizational power and influence and/or they may be shaped by the identity preoccupations of individual managers concerned with self-differentiation, self-elevation and the negation of others. In either case, we argue that multiple masculinities may well shape the motives, processes and outcomes of these intra-managerial conflicts for organizational power, status and identity. The growing critical literature on difference, division and conflict within managerial hierarchies (e.g. Child 1985; Hyman 1987; Armstrong 1984, 1986) has tended to neglect the influence of masculinities within and between managerial hierarchies despite the latter's continued dominance by men. It has also failed to address the way that these managerial alliances, differences and conflicts are likely to shift considerably over time and place.

In sum, we suggest that further research could critically examine the tensions and conflicts within these managerial hierarchies and their interrelationships with gender dynamics broadly and multiple masculinities more specifically. Further analyses might critically examine the way that multiple masculinities may be *both* a crucial basis for alliances and unities between men managers and a source of tension, division and conflict within and between managerial hierarchies. They could examine the ways in which managerial roles and identities are developed through gender relations and masculinities and indeed the ways in which particular masculinities are constructed through managerial roles and identities. Ideally these analyses would present theoretically informed case study accounts of specific organizational practices. By developing analyses of men as managers and managers as men, we may in turn produce innovative and more sophisticated accounts of the conditions, processes and consequences of power relations in contemporary organizations. In doing so we may also enhance our understanding of the management of specific gender issues in organizations, such as the extent and nature of barriers both to equal opportunity initiatives (see, for example, Buswell and Jenkins 1993) and to the management of sexual harassment cases (see, for example, Collinson and Collinson 1992).

NOTES

Breaking the silence

1   In 1976, women constituted 0.4 per cent of directors in the top 250 UK enterprises (Scott, 1989) and of these eleven women, none held more than one directorship. The "inner circle" of directors with multiple, interlocking directorships was exclusively male.
2   The term "macho", as in "macho management", could be said to carry connotations of racism, in associating certain kinds of tough aggression with Hispanic men. This is a particularly important issue in different localities and regions where Hispanic people are an oppressed group.
3   The tendency to define managers, entrepreneurs and owners as mavericks, radicals and revolutionaries in the media and in biographies is somewhat paradoxical in that they are

very much the agents of power and control within contemporary society. Comparatively, they benefit considerably from the status quo and will therefore tend to seek to conserve present arrangements. The changes they introduce are likely to be designed to reinforce rather than transform dominant power relations.

4   Even male shopfloor workers may use these masculine criteria when criticizing managers for being weak "wimps" who are not strong, authoritative and assertive managers (Collinson, 1992). Indeed it might be argued that there are some close and interesting parallels between the "tough" masculinities of both management and the shopfloor.

5   These "ideal models" of management failed to recognize the socially constructed nature of management power and practices. A primary objective of this volume is to argue that gender and masculinity are central factors in these processes of social construction. Equally, their socially constructed nature means that they are always able to change and be transformed.

6   This raises the question of to what extent such apparently diverse masculinities are predicated on similar psychosocial structures. Common themes include the assertion of independence, the denial of dependency, egocentric views of the world and an absence of nurturing of others (see Jefferson, 1994). Further related questions could include the extent to which men as managers feel compelled to achieve and how far this desire for success is fuelled by particular relationships, for example with parents (Pahl, 1995).

7   Together these two meanings of management, one related to the "public" and one to the "private" sphere, also reflect the separation between "home" and "work" that occurred in the industrial revolution and that intensified the masculinization of the paid workplace.

Naming men as men

1   In practice, of course, a similar concern to separate "business matters" from those of pregnancy and domesticity frequently characterizes authoritarianism and paternalism.

2   Here Morgan draws on Lipman-Blomen's definition of homosocial as "the seeking, enjoyment, and/or preference for the company of the same sex" (Lipman-Blumen 1976, cited in Morgan 1981, p. 102).

REFERENCES

Allison, A. (1994) *Nightwork: Sexuality, Pleasure and Corporate Masculinity in a Tokyo Hostess Club.* Chicago: University of Chicago.

Armstrong, P. (1984) "Competition between the organisational professions and the evolution of management control strategies", in K. Thompson (ed.), *Work, Employment and Unemployment.* Milton Keynes: Open University Press. pp. 97–120.

Armstrong, P. (1986) "Management control strategies and inter-professional competition: the cases of accountancy and personnel management", in D. Knights and H. Willmott (eds), *Gender and the Labour Process.* Aldershot: Gower. pp. 19–43.

Barnard, C. (1938) *The Functions of the Executive.* Cambridge, MA: Harvard University Press.

Beeton, I. (1861) *The Book of Household Management.* Facsimile 1968, London: Jonathan Cape.

Beynon, H. (1980) *Working for Ford.* Harmondsworth: Penguin.

Bilimoria, D. and Piderit, S. K. (1994) "Board committee membership: effects of sex-based bias", *Academy of Management Journal.* 37(6): 1453–77.

Burns, T. and Stalker, G. M. (1961) *The Management of Innovation.* London: Tavistock.

Burrell, G. (1992) "The organization of pleasure", in M. Alvesson and H. Willmott (eds), *Critical Management Studies.* London: Sage. pp. 66–89.

Buswell, C. and Jenkins, S. (1993) *Equal Opportunities Policies, Employment and Patriarchy.* Paper presented at the Labour Process Conference, Blackpool, UK, March.

Child, J. (1985) "Managerial strategies, new technology and the labour process", in D. Knights, H. Willmott and D. Collinson (eds), *Job Redesign*. Aldershot: Gower, pp, 107–41.

Cockburn, C. (1983) *Brothers: Male Dominance and Technological Change*. London: Pluto Press.

Cockburn, C. (1991) *In the Way of Women: Men's Resistance to Sex Equality in Organizations*. London: Macmillan/Ithaca, NY: ILR Press.

Collinson, D. L. (1992) *Managing the Shopfloor. Subjectivity, Masculinity and Workplace Culture*. Berlin: Walter de Gruyter.

Collinson, D. L. and Collinson, M. (1992) "Mismanaging sexual harassment: blaming the victim and protecting the perpetrator", *Women in Management Review*, 7(7): 11–17.

Collinson, D. L. and Knights, D. (1986) "'Men only': theories and practices of job segregation in insurance", in D. Knights and H. Willmott (eds), *Gender and the Labour Process*. Aldershot: Gower. pp. 140–78.

Collinson, D. L., Knights, D. and Collinson, M. (1990) *Managing to Discriminate*. London: Routledge.

Dalton, M. (1959) *Men Who Manage*. New York: John Wiley & Sons.

Davies, N. (1992) *The Unknown Maxwell*. London: Pan Macmillan.

Denham, D. (1991) "Research note: the 'macho' management debate and the dismissal of employees during industrial disputes", *Sociological Review*, 39(2): 349–64.

Drosnin, M. (1987) *Citizen Hughes*. New York: Henry Holt.

Drucker, P. (1979) *The Practice of Management*. London: Heinemann.

Edwards, P. K. (1987) *Managing the Factory*. Oxford: Basil Blackwell.

Edwards, R. C. (1979) *Contested Terrain: The Transformation of the Workplace in the Twentieth Century*. London: Heinemann; New York: Basic Books.

Edwards, R. (1979) *Contested Terrain: The Transformation of the Workplace in the Twentieth Century*. London: Heinemann.

Elliott, O. (1959) *Men at the Top*. London: Weidenfeld & Nicolson.

Equal Opportunities Commission (1992) *Women and Men in Britain*. London: HMSO.

Fayol, H. (1949) *General and Industrial Management*. London: Pitman.

Ford, H. (1923) *My Life and Work*. London: William Heinemann.

Geneen, H. S. (1985) *Managing*. London: Collins.

Gherardi, S. (1995) *Gender, Symbolism and Organizational Culture*. London: Sage.

Gray, S. (1987). "Sharing the shop floor," in M. Kaufman (ed.), *Beyond Patriarchy*. Toronto: Oxford University Press, pp. 216–34.

Grint, K. (1995) *Management: A Sociological Introduction*. Cambridge: Polity Press.

Guzzardi, W. (1966) *The Young Executives: How and Why Successful Managers Get Ahead*. New York: Mentor Books.

Hansard Society (1990) *Women at the Top*. London: Hansard Society.

Iacocca, L. (1984) *Iacocca: an Autobiography*. New York: Bantam.

Institute of Management (1995) *National Management Salary Survey*. Kingston upon Thames: Institute of Management.

Jackall, R. (1988) *Moral Mazes: The World of Corporate Managers*. New York: Oxford University Press.

Kerfoot, D. and Knights, D. (1993) "Management, masculinity and manipulation: from paternalism to corporate strategy in financial services in Britain", *Journal of Management Studies*, 30(4): 659–79.

Krause, D. G. (1995) *The Art of War for Executives*. London: Nicholas Brealey.

Lown, J. (1983) "Not so much a factory, more a form of patriarchy: gender and class during industrialisation", in E. Gamarnikow, D. H. J. Morgan, J. Purvis and D. E. Taylorson (eds), *Gender, Class and Work*. London: Heinemann. pp. 28–45.

Mackay, L. (1986) "The macho manager: it's no myth", *Personnel Management*, January: 25–7.

Maddock, S. and Parkin, D. (1993) "Gender cultures". *Women in Management Review*, 8(2): 3–9.

Mangham, I. L. and critics (1995) "Macintyre and the manager", *Organization*. 2(2): 181–242.

Mant, A. (1977) *The Rise and Fall of the British Manager*. London: Macmillan.

Martin, J. (1990) "Deconstructing organizational taboos: the suppression of gender conflict in organizations", *Organizational Science*, 1(4): 339–59.

Mintzberg, H. (1973) *The Nature of Managerial Work*. New York: Harper & Row.

Morgan, D. H. J. (1981) "Men, masculinity, and the process of sociological enquiry", in H. Roberts (ed.), *Doing Feminist Research*. London: Routledge & Kegan Paul. pp. 83–113.

Morgan, G. (1986) *Images of Organization*. Beverly Hills, CA: Sage.

Neale, A. (1995) "The manager as hero". Paper presented at Labor Process Conference, Blackpool, April.

New York Times (1993) "Women pay more for success", 4 July: 25.

Ohlott, P., Ruderman, M. and McCauley, C. (1994) "Gender differences in managers" developmental job experiences", *Academy of Management Journal*, 37(1): 46–67.

Pahl, R. (1995) *After Success: "Fin-de Siècle" Anxiety and Identity*. Cambridge: Polity Press.

Pascale, R. T. and Athos, A. G. (1982) *The Art of Japanese Management*. Harmondsworth, UK: Penguin.

Pollert, A. (1981) *Girls, Wives, Factory Lives*. London: Macmillan.

Purcell, J. (1982) "The rediscovery of the management prerogative: the management of labour relations in the 1980s", *Oxford Review of Economic Policy*, 7(1): 33–43.

Reed, M. (1989) *The Sociology of Management*. London: Harvester Wheatsheaf.

Rogers, B. (1988) *Men Only: An Investigation into Men's Organizations*. London: Pandora.

Sampson, R. (1965) *Managing the Managers*. New York: McGraw-Hill.

Scase, R. and Goffee, R. (1989) *Reluctant Managers*. London: Unwin Hyman.

Scott, J. (1989) "Ownership and employer control", in D. Gallie (ed.), *Employment in Britain*. Oxford: Basil Blackwell. pp. 437–64.

Shaw, M. (1990) "Strategy and social process: military context and sociological analysis", *Sociology*, 24(3): 465–73.

Simon, H. (1945) *Administrative Behaviour*. London: Macmillan.

Sinclair, A. (1995) "Sex and the MBA", *Organization*, 2(2): 295–319.

Stewart, R. (1976) *Contrasts in Management*. London: McGraw-Hill.

Sward, K. (1948) *The Legend of Henry Ford*. New York: Russell & Russell.

Taylor, F. W. (1947) *Scientific Management*. New York: Harper and Row.

Tharenou, P., Latimer, S. and Conroy, D. (1994) "How do you make it to the top? An examination of influences on women's and men's advancement', *Academy of Management Journal*, 37(4): 899–931.

Wensley, R. (1996) "Isabella Beeton: management as "everything in its place"', *London Business School Business Strategy Review*, 7(1): 37–46.

Whyte, W. H. (1956) *The Organization Man*. New York: Doubleday Anchor.

Williams, R. (1976) *Keywords*. Glasgow: Fontana.

Willmott, H. (1987) "Studying managerial work: a critique and a proposal", *Journal of Management Studies*, 24(3): 249–70.

CHAPTER

8

COMPLICATING GENDER: THE SIMULTANEITY OF RACE, GENDER, AND CLASS IN ORGANIZATION CHANGE(ING)

EVANGELINA HOLVINO

From Sections II and III of *Working Paper No. 14* (2001) Boston, MA: Center for Gender in Organizations, Simmons School of Management

WOMEN OF COLOR,[1] FEMINISMS, AND WHITE WOMEN

As early as 1974, the Combahee River Collective, a collective of Black feminists, recognized that the struggle of Black women was a "unified" struggle against race, gender, and class inequality. In "A Black Feminist Statement," they outlined their position:

> We are actively committed to struggling against racial, sexual, heterosexual, and class oppression and see as our particular task the development of integrated analysis and practice based upon the fact that the major systems of oppression are interlocking. The synthesis of these oppressions creates the conditions of our lives (Hull, Scott, and Smith, 1982: 13).

But, as Sandoval (2000: 42) documents, a hegemonic feminist theory based on the experience of white women developed, which actively suppressed the theorizing and practice of women of color and the recognition of "an original, eccentric, and coalitional cohort of U.S. feminists of color" and their contributions to feminism. The outcome of both "first wave" U.S. feminism in the mid-1800s and the "second wave" women's movement during the nineteen-seventies and eighties was that women of color were made invisible and their concerns and experiences were disappeared. For example, in discussing "how did feminism get to be 'all white'?", Barbara Smith explains that "the fears about breaking ranks in the Black community, Black lesbian leadership not getting support, the larger conservative repression, and a lack of consciousness in white women's organizations" all contributed to Black feminism not becoming as powerful as it could have (Smith and Mansbridge, 2000). In this context, Black women and Latinas developed their own separate frameworks and many today do not consider themselves feminists, meaning "white feminists" (Collins, 1989; Garcia, 1989).

Important differences between white women and women of color's theories and practices have emerged that lead to different paths when theorizing and working gender at the intersection of race and class. The scholarship documenting these differences is extensive, particularly from Black and Chicana feminists (Collins, 2000a; King, 1988; Sandoval, 2000). . . . I summarize in thematic form some of these major differences between white women and women of color, which Sandoval (2000: 46) aptly refers to as "the signs of a lived experience of difference."

"Women of color have always worked"[2]

African, African American, Latina, Asian, and other women of color have always worked and been seen as workers. "Domestic servants descended from African slaves, Chinese women sold into the U.S. prostitution market . . . and Puerto Rican feminist union organizers in the early-1900s" are just an example (Amott and Matthaei, 1991: 3). Thus, for many women of color, white feminisms' division between the public and the private spheres does not represent their reality. For example, the demands by white feminists to have the role of housewives in the private sphere recognized and to gain access to work in the public (outside the home) sphere have not been a priority for women of color. On the contrary, being able to "stay at home" and be supported by "a husband's paycheck" is considered a luxury that only white affluent women have (Glenn, 1988; Romero, 1992; Williams, 2000). Instead, women of color's demands have focused on improving their working conditions and opportunities, as they have generally been confined to positions at the bottom of the organizational hierarchy and in secondary labor markets. . . .

There are many consequences to the different relationships that white women and women of color have to their material and economic realities. One is their relationship to the community and the complex interaction between paid and unpaid work in the lives of women of color. For example, because poor and working class women do not have the same political and economic means that middle class women do, their reproductive labor frequently extends outside the boundaries of the nuclear family into the larger community – "the third shift" Romero (1997) calls it. Community work becomes, for many women of color, a way of meeting a variety of needs for the welfare and safety of their families, which they feel they "have to do"; sharing resources, improving inadequate public services, accessing networks for paid work, for example. But because conceptualizations of "community work," "volunteerism," and "activism" have been shaped by the circumstances and experience of middle class women, women of color's leadership roles, contributions, and rationale for engaging in community work are often relegated and remain unexplored (Pardo, 1997). [. . .]

"Men are not the enemy and family is not necessarily the problem"[3]

The role of the family in sustaining women of color against racism has meant that women of color do not define men as the oppressor, nor do they experience family as the most oppressive institution. While many women of color critique the nuclear family, and especially its patriarchal and heterosexual structure and ideologies, for many Black women and Latinas the family is a place where the values of the community are transmitted, and strategies to survive the racist system are taught. Family, instead of being experienced as oppressive, is experienced as a haven from the hostile environment of work and society and even a resource for upward mobility (Higginbotham and Weber, 1992; Romero, 1997).

In addition, the experience of racism leads many women of color to prioritize race as the starting point of their self-definition and social position, as white racism treats "all Blacks alike." Thus, women and men of color join in one anti-racist struggle of survival and social change. Furthermore, because race and class are frequently conflated, as when the term "Black welfare mother" is used to signify all Black women, women of color may struggle against racism, even if it means relegating issues of gender (Reynolds, 1997). As Hurtado (1996: 381) clarifies, the relationship between women and men of color is "the area in which feminists of color have made fewer inroads . . . because intergroup ethnic/racial conflict creates the need for little-questioned solidarity in order to survive." Puerto Rican, Latin American, African, and other third world women share a similar experience when liberation movements and imperialistic struggles have been framed in national/ethnic terms and women have chosen to identify first with these community struggles, joining in solidarity with men against a common oppressor, rather than seeing essentialized men as their oppressor. "We are fighting for our people; they [white women] are fighting for their individual rights," summarizes Mendez-Negrete (1999: 40). . . .

"White women are privileged too"

Many white women, especially those who are middle class or affluent, have benefited from the freedom to pursue professional opportunities because women of color look after their homes and their children. In these situations, white women have openly exploited women of color in the roles of domestic workers. They have used their racial and class privilege to sustain their social power and status and diminish the identity, social position, and options of working class women and women of color (Glenn, 1986; Reynolds, 1997; Rollins, 1985).

White women have also benefited from their whiteness in a racist system. For example, by being the only desirable mothers of the white man's progeny, a group dynamic is created where white women relate to white men through "seduction" and women of color, the undesirable ones, relate to white men through "rejection" (Hurtado, 1989). While their femininity is exalted and their virginity protected, women of color's sexuality is demonized and their femininity degraded or exoticized (Carby, 1985; Lu, 1997). Christensen (1997) explores how this positioning of white women in relation to white men also hinders their ability to engage in anti-racist and class struggles, as many white heterosexual women's middle and affluent class status is a product of the privileges derived from their relation to their fathers, husbands, lovers, and organizational male mentors. White women collude with white men in the private sphere (a dynamic of dependency) and fight the "male oppressor" in the public sphere (a dynamic of counter-dependence). White middle class and affluent women "feel so free to attack 'their' men" because of their relationship to white men in powerful social positions (Williams, 2000: 170). Working class women's demands for equality, on the other hand, are tempered by their greater fear of family instability and the potential poverty of divorce.

White women derive many benefits from this "special place for white women only" (Frost, 1980). In organizations, this dynamic translates into a tendency by white women to be complicit with white privilege and white men, while women of color confront it/them. Because of their lack of alignment with heterosexist privilege, some white lesbians and lesbians of color do not participate in the dynamics of seduction and have been able to forge alliances with women of color out of this different relation to white men (Hurtado, 1999a). Contrary to white feminisms, adds Hurtado (2000: 141), "Chicana feminisms have addressed the inclusion of men in their efforts to mobilize politically . . . [and the] recognition of difference among men helped produce complex feminisms."

"A different consciousness and a different way of knowing"

Because of the distinctive set of experiences that arise from their political and economic status and their lives in the interstices of race, class, and gender, women of color have a different view of the material reality. This unique position creates the conditions for "a different standpoint" (Collins, 1989), not white and not male. I call it "in between." Others have referred to this unique perspective of women of color as a third gender category (Sandoval, 1991); multiple consciousness (King, 1988); oppositional consciousness (Sandoval, 1991; 2000); *mestiza* and borderlands (Anzaldúa, 1987); bridge (Roshin, 1981); crossroads (Rojas, 1989); and interstitial feminisms (Pérez, 1999). [. . .]

This positionality, in turn, creates a specific relationship to knowledge and knowledge production. This positionality is informed by knowledge that expresses and validates oppression, while, at the same time, it also documents and encourages resistance to oppression (Collins, 2000b; Hurtado, 1996b). This places women of color in a unique position "to [document] the maneuvers necessary to obtain and generate knowledge . . . [a] unique knowledge that can be gleaned from the interstices of multiple and stigmatized social identities" (Hurtado, 1996: 375). [. . .]

Though this is not an exhaustive analysis, I hope to have demonstrated that there are significant differences between how women of color and white women experience, understand, and live their personal, organizational, and community lives. Mohanty (1991: 10) aptly summarizes the critique by women of color of mainstream feminism,

> Third world women's writings on feminism have consistently focused on 1) the idea of the simultaneity of oppressions . . . ; 2) the crucial role of the state in circumscribing women of color's daily lives and survival struggles; 3) the significance of memory and writing in the creation of oppositional agency; and 4) the differences, conflicts, and contradictions [in] third world women's organizations and communities . . . [and] have insisted on the complex interrelationships between feminist, antiracist, and nationalist struggles. . . . Thus, third world feminists have argued for the rewriting of history based on the *specific* locations and histories of struggle of people of color and postcolonial peoples, and on the day-to-day strategies of survival utilized by such peoples.

These differences generate important practical limitations for women working together and in working with men to change the situation of women in organizations. For example, they pose limitations to forming coalitions between working class and professional-managerial women, between white women and women of color, and between the different groups of women of color. Each group has different perceived and real needs, different agendas and priorities for change, different strategies and tactics, and different access and relation to power sources (Donleavy and Pugh 1977; Smith, 1995). The differences also underscore the importance of "complicating gender" by exploring its racialized and classed dimensions in order to get to a more complete understanding of women and their situation(s).

But, in spite of this forceful critique and the ample documentation of the different experience of women of color, the liberal feminist paradigm continues to dominate organizational research (Ely, 1999). This is a paradigm that privileges gender over race, class, and ethnicity, assumes a common oppression of all women, and seeks to provide "equal" rights and opportunities to women based on those of (white) men. And it is in the context of equal rights for individual women, usually meaning white women, that organizational issues have been framed in the United States. What it would take for the experience of women of color and their critique to enter the organizational discourse and for the dilemmas of working class women to impact how gender work is done in organizations is the concern of the rest of this paper.

RACE, GENDER, AND CLASS INTERSECTIONS: WHY DOES IT MATTER?

How can the undertanding that race, gender, and class are connected be translated into concrete interventions that seriously take into account the intersection? And what happens when we continue to intervene in organizations as if race, gender, and class were not interacting dynamics? In other words, what happens to our ability to do organizational change geared to equality and justice in the workplace when we do not have a perspective that considers and works with the intersection of class, race, and gender? I analyze the example of the glass ceiling, a well-recognized feminist contribution to organizational change, to demonstrate that in spite of its accomplishments much of what has been done so far designing change interventions to address gender equality in organizations has been constructed out of the subjectivity of white women and the theorizing of liberal/mainstream feminism.

Mainstream feminism and the glass ceiling

The "glass ceiling" is a concept popularized in the 1980s. It is used to describe a barrier so subtle that it is transparent; yet, it is so strong that it prevents women and minorities from moving up the management hierarchy (Morrison and Von Glinow, 1990). Glass ceiling studies identify organizational practices which act as barriers to managerial advancement and therefore need changing. Glass ceiling research has revealed that typical barriers to women's advancement are lack of mentoring, sex stereotypes, pipeline issues, and outmoded concepts of what it takes to be a good leader that advantage male images and devalue women's caring and people skills (Fletcher, 1992; Morrison, 1987).

But, a comparative analysis of the situation of women of color shows that their experience in organizations "is quite different from the experience of white women

... [t]he data ... show that white women and women of color differ on more items than they agree on" in glass ceiling-type surveys and interviews (White and Potts, 1999: 13). In fact, women of color have not benefited from glass ceiling interventions and from efforts to promote them. Using statistical and interview data, Martinez (2000) contradicts Nathan Glazer's contentions that Latina/os, unlike African Americans, have "made it" in the United States. For example, "[w]hile the median income for African American women who are full time workers is 86% that of white women's income, Latinas earn only 74% as much as their white counterparts. . . . [T]he median income for African American women working full time is 63% that of white men, while the median income for Latinas working full time is 54% that of white men" (Martinez, 2000: 63).

There are also marked differences in how women experience their opportunities for advancement in organizations. White women (60%) are more likely than women of color (47%) to believe that their opportunities for advancement have improved in the last five years. Women of color are more than twice as likely as white women to believe that there has been no change in advancement opportunities (38% versus 15%). They also perceive that the primary barriers to advancement are not their performance, but their lack of access to influential mentors and networking (47% versus 29%) (Giscombe, 1999). [. . .]

Limitations of mainstream feminism in addressing the intersection of race, gender and class

As the glass ceiling example suggests, the promise of and the interest in the integration of race, gender, and class talked about in mainstream feminism have not translated into concrete organizational interventions that take into account the complexity of these relations. In the few studies available, the intersection of *race and gender* is addressed by trying to understand the differences between women of color and white women in terms of their status in organizations as revealed in statistical analysis of salaries, positions, and advancement (Catalyst, 1999). Very few studies consider their unique stories and work experience as revealed in interviews, or their relationships with other groups in organizations (Bell and Nkomo, 1992; Zavella, 1987). The intersection of *class and gender*, on the other hand, is left largely unexplored, except for the focus on working class women's experience of work which in many cases are women of color (e.g., Lamphere, 1987; Mahony and Zmroczek, 1997; Sacks and Remy, 1984). I want to highlight four consequences of these limited perspectives and approaches to the intersection of race, class, and gender for understanding organizations and promoting organizational change. What they all share in common is that they "disappear"[4] an organizational dynamic that is important to understand and address in the goal of promoting gender equity and institutional change.

The women who disappear

A difficulty with mainstream feminist approaches to gender equity in organizational change efforts is that race, gender, and class are treated as independent variables and separate categories of analysis. . . . [T]hey are seen as additive – gender + race + class. For example, data on race and gender in organizational audits to monitor representation are collected and analyzed separately following the principles of statistical analysis and disaggregating data. Women of color are consistently counted twice (as women and as people of color) and at the same time disappeared, because their experience is never fully acknowledged or understood in its complexity. The differential impact of discriminatory practices on women of color and the qualitative difference of their experience is seldom documented and addressed (White and Potts, 1999).

The additive approach also makes gender the privileged dimension of difference for white feminists, as gender is the only axis of social power that blocks their way (Williams, 2000). One result of this dynamic is that the complexity of their own experience at the intersection of race, gender, and class is made invisible (Bell and Nkomo, [2001]; Ostrander, 1984). White women end up feeling and being seen as a group that does not carry race, and affluent white women are seen as a group that does not carry class; differences and diversity are "out there" in the "others" (Ely, 1995).

How class disappears

In mainstream feminist approaches to organizational change, class is eliminated from the change agenda. The intersection of gender *and* class is less figural in part because class is not seen as an unchangeable biological attribute like sex or race. For example, Loden and Rosener (1991) define race and gender as primary differences and class as a secondary difference. An essentialist[5] conception of differences prevails, which occludes the social nature of the processes and structures that construct class as an important dimension of difference and social power.

In addition, class does not become part of the change agenda because, in the liberal discourse of mainstream feminism and management, the cultural assumptions of hierarchy, meritocracy, and individualism remain unchallenged. The logic of meritocracy and capitalism posits that if women (and men) work hard, they will improve their condition and move out of their poor or working class position. Merit is presumed to be tangible and measurable, occluding the impact of structural advantages on the privileged position of dominant group members (Haney and Hurtado, 1994). Consequently, the goal of change is to provide the societal and organizational conditions for upward mobility to *individuals*. But this goal basically ignores group identity, "structural processes and class and race disadvantages" (Ferree, 1987: 326).

Organizational class hierarchies are not questioned. Instead, the differences in hierarchical positions are investigated to see whether they are so steep and rigid as to prevent those in the lower ranks from contributing. For example, some diversity interventions in organizations try to address "levelism," the impact of hierarchical levels on the performance and productivity of women and men of different races (Esty, Griffin, and Hirsch, 1995). Flatter organizations, self-managed teams, employee shares, and company sponsored day-care facilities are proposed solutions to the intersection of class and gender in organizational life (Holvino, 2000). The underlying assumption of a mainstream feminist agenda is the "well-being" of the corporation – and particularly its survival and effectiveness – rather than the alteration of its current class relations.

The dynamics of change that disappear

Marks (2001: 10) documents and analyzes how the dynamics of change in gender equity interventions in South Africa have been limited by a narrow focus on race which "ignores the way in which affirmative action policies deepen and entrench class and gender distinctions." She describes two concrete examples of how failing to take into consideration the intersection of race, gender, and class has generated dynamics that hinder moving forward in the transformation efforts towards equality in the South African context. . . .

Marks (2001: 10) documents the dynamics observed in South African organizations where "middle class white women and middle class Black women are able to form alliances across race and around class in order to preserve economic privilege, and white and Black middle class men are able to bond across race around their masculinity and around the (norm)alization of heterosexuality in the workplace." . . . The inability to understand how this dynamic across differences is playing out to hinder coordination and progress toward gender equity in the organization is based on an inability to understand how gender, class, and race divide at the same time that they connect women across dimensions of difference. Similar dynamics of fragmentation have been reported in change efforts in the United States (Proudford, 1998; Thomas and Proudford, 2000).

Another dynamic of fragmentation reported by Marks (2001: 14) is how the creation of a gender unit, charged with the responsibility of promoting gender equality, kept competing with change interventions designed by the Affirmative Action unit, charged with the responsibility for ensuring that the organization adhered to the Employment Equity Act – the racial issue. The agenda of racial equality was perceived as more important than the agenda of gender equality, enhancing efforts toward the former and hindering efforts toward the latter. Even when the officers of both units were mandated to integrate their efforts "the difficulty was in understanding the interlocking of race, gender, and class within the context of a transformation strategy." Both these examples highlight how ignoring the intersection hinders change efforts toward organizational gender equity.

Men and their differences disappear

Until recently, gender equity change efforts focused on changing women's status and opportunities by focusing solely on women's situations and experiences. [. . .]

Disappearing men from the work on gender equity is similar to disappearing "whiteness" from the work on race relations (Delgado and Stefancic, 1997; Fine, Weis, Powell, and Wong, 1997; Frankenberg, 1993). The potential for change will be limited unless the dominant side of a power dynamic is understood and theorized as well as the subordinate dimension of the relationship.

In sum, . . . the intersection of race, gender, and class cannot be fully taken up when mainstream feminism is applied to organizations. The consequence is that many organizational actors and dynamics become invisible and change options even more limited. The "field" cannot be seen in all its complexity and structured inequality. . . .

NOTES

1 While I admit to the uneasiness of using the term "women of color" because it obscures the diversity of racial-ethnic groups contained within this category, I want to focus on the commonalities among these different groups of women – Native American, Latina, Asian, and Black/African American – who share a status and an experience as racio-ethnic minorities in the United States. In this paper I have also drawn mostly from the scholarship and experience of Black women and Latinas, especially the extensive work of Chicanas. An unfortunate consequence of my choice is that the specific contributions of white and poor working class women and their differentiation from the experience and status of affluent and middle class white women has been harder to keep in focus. This is a topic which remains to be explored further. The same limitation applies to the experience of Native American and to a lesser extent, Asian women.

2 All throughout the paper, the story of race and ethnic women is closely related to the history of class and sometimes they will appear as if they were the same. Because of the prevalence of people of color in lower-echelon jobs, which restricts their economic opportunities and status, it is almost impossible to clearly separate the racial story from the class stroy in the lives of women of color. This is a dilemma that grows out of the nature of this study, because that is what working at the intersection means – class is not a separate variable, but a component of race, and gender, and vice versa. As Dubois and Ruiz (1990: xiii) remind us, "[t]he history of women cannot be studied without considering both race and class . . . [and] working-class culture cannot really be understood without reference to gender and race." One limitation of this approach is that the specific differences between white working class women and working class women of color have become difficult to explicate and explore and must remain a theme for future exploration.

3 I recognize that this argument rests on an assumption of heterosexuality and on the experience of heterosexual women, both white and of color. It is a good example of how specific attention to the intersection of sexual orientation has much to contribute to expanding our understanding of the dynamics of privilege and power among women at the intersection of race and class. This is a limitation throughout the rest of the paper, but to integrate and do justice to the complex and extensive work on gender, sexuality, and sexual orientation (Creed and Scully, 2000; Gibson-Graham, 1996; Lorber, 1999; Wishik and Pierce, 1991) is beyond the scope of this paper.

4 I am indebted to Aida Hurtado (1999b) for her work on the "disappearing dynamics of women of color" based on the cultural analysis of Latina and white women's representations in the media. In my use of this metaphor I also want to honor the powerful Latin American women's movement born out of South American mothers' and grandmothers' activism in claiming their disappeared sons and daughters who were victims of police and state brutality and violence.

5 Essentialism refers to the traditional notion that the identities of men and women, for example, are biologically, psychically and socially fixed or determined (Phoca and Wright 1999: 12). Loden and Rosener's categorization reflects, in addition, the conflation of sex and gender, where both terms seem to have the same meaning, which is based on biology and therefore essentialized. But, in feminist theory sex is seen as biologically based and gender refers to the social construction of the relation between the sexes. While the use of "gender" is not without its problems, I believe the differentiation between sex and gender is helpful.

REFERENCES

Amott, T. L. and Mattahei, J. E. 1991. *Race, Gender and Work: A Multicultural Economic History of Women in the United States.* Boston, MA: South End Press.

Anzaldúa, G. 1987. La conciencia de la mestiza: Towards a new consciousness. *Borderlands/La Frontera: The New Mestiza*, (pp. 77–98). San Francisco: Aunt Lute Foundation Books.

Bell, E. L. and Nkomo, S. M. 1992. Re-visioning women manager's lives. In A. J. Mills and P. Tancred, *Gendering Organizational Analysis*, (pp. 235–247). Newbury Park, CA: Sage.

Bell, E. L. and Nkomo, S. M. 2001. *Our Separate Ways: Black and White Women and the Struggle for Professional Identity.* Boston, MA: Harvard Business School Press.

Carby, H. 1985. "On the threshold of woman's era": Lynching, empire, and sexuality in Black feminist theory. In H. L. Gates, Jr. (Ed.), *"Race," Writing, and Difference*, (pp. 301–316). Chicago: University of Chicago Press.

Catalyst 1999. *Women of Color in Corporate Management: Opportunities and Barriers.* New York: Catalyst.

Christensen, K. 1997. With whom do you believe your lot is cast?: White feminists and racism. *Signs*, 22: 617–648.

Collins, P. H. 1989. The social construction of Black feminist thought. *Signs*, 14: 745–773.

Collins, P. H. 2000a. *Black Feminist Thought*, (2nd Edition). New York: Routledge.

Collins, P. H. 2000b. It's all in the family: Intersection of gender, race, and nation. In U. Narayan and S. Harding (Eds.), *Decentering the Center*, (pp. 156–176). Bloomington: Indiana University Press.

Creed, W. E. D. and Scully, M. 2000. Songs of ourselves. Employees' deployment of social identity in workplace encounters. *Journal of Management Inquiry*, 9: 391–412.

Delgado, R. and Stefancic, J. (Eds.). 1997. *Critical White Studies.* Philadelphia: Temple University Press.

Donleavy, M. R. and Pugh, C. A. 1977. Multi-ethnic collaboration to combat racism in educational settings. *Journal of Applied Behavioural Science*, 13 (3): 360–372.

DuBois, E. C. and Ruiz, V. 1990. *Unequal Sisters: A Multicultural Reader in U.S. Women's History.* New York: Routledge.

Ely, R. 1995. The role of dominant identity and experience in organizational work on diversity. In S. Jackson and M. Ruderman (Eds.), *Diversity in Work Teams: Research Paradigms for a Changing Workplace*, (pp. 161–186). Washington, D.C.: American Psychological Association.

Ely, R. 1999. *Feminist Critiques of Research on Gender in Organizations.* Boston, MA: Center for Gender in Organizations, Simons School of Management, Working Paper, No. 6.

Esty, K., Griffin, R., and Hirsch, M. S. 1995. *Workplace Diversity, (A Managers Guide to Solving Problems and Turning Diversity in to a Competitive Advantage).* Holbrook, MA: Adams Publishing.

Ferree, M. M. 1987. She works hard for a living: Gender and class on the job. In B. B. Hess and M. M. Ferree (Eds.), *Analyzing Gender: A Handbook of Social Science Research*, (pp. 322–347). Newbury Park: Sage.

Fine, M., Weis, L., Powell, L. C., and Wong, L. M. (Eds.). 1997. *Off White: Readings on Race, Power, and Society.* New York: Routledge.

Fletcher, J. 1992. A poststructuralist perspective on the third dimension of power. *Journal of Organizational Change Management*, 5: 31–38.

Frankenberg, R. 1993. *White Women, Race Matters: The Social Construction of Whiteness.* Minneapolis: University of Minnesota Press.

Frost, D. 1980. A special place for white women only. Unpublished manuscript. Reprinted by *WomenBridgeRace*.

Garcia, A. 1989. The development of Chicana feminist discourse, 1970–1990. In E. C. DuBois and V. L. Ruiz (Eds.), *Unequal Sisters*, (pp. 418–431). New York: Routledge.

Gibson-Graham, J. K. 1996. Reflections of postmodern feminist social research. In N. Duncan (Ed.), *Bodyspace: Destabilizing Geographies of Gender and Sexuality*, (pp. 234–44). New York: Routledge.

Giscombe, K. 1999. The experiences of women of color in corporate settings: African-American women, Latinas, and Asian American women. Boston, MA: Center for Gender in Organizations, Simmons Graduate School of Management, Seminar, April.

Glenn, E. N. 1986. *Issei, Nisei, War Bride: Three Generations of Japanese American Women in Domestic Service*. Philadelphia: Temple University Press.

Glenn, E. N. 1988. A belated industry revisited: Domestic service among Japanese-American women. In A. Stathem, E. M. Miller, and H. O. Mauksch (Eds.), *The Worth of Women's Work: A Qualitative Synthesis*, (pp. 57–75). Albany: SUNY Press.

Haney, C. and Hurtado, A. 1994. The jurisprudence of race and meritocracy: Standardized testing and "race-neutral" racism in the workplace. *Law and Human Behavior*, 18 (3): 223–248.

Higginbotham, E. and Weber, L. 1992. Moving up with kin and community: Upward social mobility for Black and white women. *Gender and Society*, 6: 416–440.

Holvino, E. 2000. Class and gender in organizatons: How do we begin to address the intersection. Boston, MA: Center for Gender in Organizations, Simmons School of Management, *CGO Insights*, No. 7

Hull, G. T., Scott, P. B., and Smith B. (Eds.). 1982. *All the Women are White, All the Blacks are Men, But Some of us are Brave: Black Women's Studies*. New York: The Feminist Press.

Hurtado, A. 1989. Relating to privilege: Seduction and rejection in the subordination and rejection of white women and women of color. *Signs*, 14: 833–855.

Hurtado, A. 1996. Strategic suspensions: Feminists of color theorize the production of knowledge. In N. Goldberger, J. Tarule, B. Clinchy, and M. Belenky (Eds.), *Knowledge, Difference, and Power: Essays Inspired by Women's Ways of Knowing*. (pp. 372–388). New York: Basic Books.

Hurtado, A. 1999a. Cross-border existence: One woman's migrant story. In M. Romero and A. J. Stewart (Eds.), *Women's Untold Stories*, (pp. 83–101). New York: Routledge.

Hurtado, A. 1999b. Disappearing dynamics of women of color. *CGO Working Papers*, No. 4. Boston, MA: Center for Gender in Organizations, Simmons School of Management.

Hurtado, A. 2000. Sitios y lenguas: Chicanas theorize feminisms. In U. Narayan and S. Harding (Eds.), *Decentering the Center*, (pp. 128–155). Bloomington: Indiana University Press.

King, D. K. 1988. Multiple jeopardy, multiple consciousness: The context of a black feminist ideology. In M. R. Malson, E. Mudimbe-Boyi, J. F. O'Barr, and M. Wyer (Eds.), *Black Women in America: Social Science Perspectives*, (pp. 265–295). Chicago: University of Chicago Press.

Lamphere, L. 1987. *From Working Daughters to Working Mothers: Immigrant Women in a New England Industrial Community*. Ithaca: Cornell University Press.

Loden, M. and Rosener, J. 1991. *Workforce America! Managing Employee Diversity as a Vital Resource*. Homewood, IL: Business One Irwin.

Lorber, J. 1999. Crossing borders and erasing boundaries: Paradoxes of identity politics. *Sociological Focus*, 32: 355–370.

Lu, L. 1997. Critical visioins: The representation and resistance of Asian women. In S. Shah (Ed.), *Dragon Ladies: Asian American Feminists Breathe Fire*, (pp. 17–28). Boston, MA: South End Press.

Mahony, P. and Zmroczek, C. 1997. *Class Matters: "Working class" Women's Perspectives on Social Class*. London: Taylor and Francis.

Marks, R. 2001. The politics and practice of institutionalizing gender equity in a post-apartheid South Africa. Boston, MA: Center for Gender in Organizations, Simmons School of Management, Working Paper, No. 12.

Martinez, T. A. 2000. Race, class, and gender in the lifestory of Chicanas: A critique of Nathan Glazer. *Race, Gender, and Class*, 7 (2): 57–75.

Mendez-Negrete, J. 1999. Awareness, consciousness, and resistance: Race, Classed, and gendered leadership interactions in Milagro County, California. *Frontiers*, 20 (1): 25–44.

Mohanty, C. T. 1991. Cartographies of struggle: Third world women and the politics of feminism. In C. T. Mohanty, A. Russo, and L. Torres (Eds.), *Third World Women and the Politics of Feminism*, (pp. 1–47). Bloomington: Indiana University Press.

Morrison, A. M. (with White, R., and Van Velsor, E.). 1987. *Breaking the Glass Ceiling*. Reading, MA: Addison-Wesley.

Morrison, A. M. and Von Glinow, M. A. 1990. Women and minorities in management. *American Psychologist*, 45: 200–208.

Ostrander, S. A. 1984. *Women of the Upper Class*. Philadelphia: Temple University Press.

Pardo, M. 1997. Working-class Mexican American women and "voluntarism": "We have to do it." In E. Higginbotham and M. Romero (Eds.), *Women and Work: Exploring Race, Ethnicity, and Class*, (pp. 197–215). Thousand Oaks, CA: Sage.

Pérez, E. 1999. *The Decolonial Imaginary: Writing Chicanas into History*. Bloomington: Indiana University Press.

Phoca, S. and Wright, R. 1999. *Introducing Postfeminism*. Cambridge, UK: Icon Books.

Proudford, K. 1998. Notes on the intra-group origins of inter-group conflict in organizations: Black-white relations as exemplar. *University of Pennsylvania Journal of Labor and Employment Law*, 1 (2): 615–637.

Reynolds, T. 1997. Class matters, "race" matters, gender matters. In P. Mahony and C. Zmroczek (Eds.), *Class Matters "Working-Class" Women's Perspectives on Social Class*, (pp. 8–17). London: Taylor and Francis.

Rojas, L. 1989. Latinas at the crossroads: An affirmation of life in Rosario Morales and Aurora Levins Morales' "Getting Home Alive." In A. Horno-Delgado, E. Ortega, N. M. Scott, and N. S. Sternback (Eds.), *Breaking Boundaries*, (pp. 166–177).

Rollins, J. 1985. *Between Women: Domestics and their Employers*. Philadelphia: Temple University Press.

Romero, M. 1992. *Maid in the USA*. New York: Routledge.

Romero, M. 1997. Epilogue. In E. Higginbotham and M. Romero (Eds.), *Women and Work: Exploring Race, Ethnicity, and Class*, (pp. 235–248). Thousand Oaks, CA: Sage.

Rushin, D. K. 1981. The bridge poem. In C. Moraga and G. Anzaldúa (Eps.), *This Bridge Called My Back*, (pp. xxi–xxii). New York: Kitchen Table, Women of Color Press.

Sacks, K. B. and Remy, D. (Eds.). 1984. *My Troubles are Going to have Trouble with Me: Everyday Trials and Triumphs of Women Workers*. New Brunswick, NJ: Rutgers University Press.

Sandoval, C. 1991. U.S. third world feminism: The theory and method of oppositional consciousness in the postmodern world. *Genders*, 10: 1–24.

Sandoval, C. 2000. *Methodology of the Oppressed*. Minneapolis: University of Minnesota Press.

Smith, B. and Mansbridge, J. 2000. How did feminism get to be all white? A conversation between Jane Mansbridge and Barbara Smith. *The American Prospect*, March 13: 32–36.

Smith, B. E. 1995. Crossing the great divides: Race, class, and gender in southern women's organizing, 1979–1991. *Gender and Society*, 9: 680–696.

Thomas, D. A. and Proudford, K. L. 2000. Making sense of race relations in organizations: Theories for practice. In R. T. Carter (Ed.), *Addressing Cultural Issues in Organizations: Beyond the Corporate Context*, (pp. 51–68). Thousand Oaks, CA: Sage.

White, M. B. and Potts, J. 1999. Just the facts: Women of color in U.S. corporations. *The Diversity Factor*, Spring: 8–15.

Williams, J. 2000. *Unbending Gender: Why Family and Work Conflict and What to do About It*. Oxford: Oxford University Press.

Wishik, H. and Pierce, C. 1991. *Sexual Orientation and Identity: Heterosexual, Lesbian, Gay and Bisexual Journeys*. Laconics, NH: New Dynamics Publications.

Zavella, P. 1987. *Women's Work and Chicano Families: Cannery Workers of the Santa Clara Valley*. Ithaca, NY: Cornell University.

NEGOTIATION: OVERVIEW

DEBORAH M. KOLB

Negotiation is a critical skill for managers today. In the not too distant past, those who negotiated did so because their jobs required them to bargain over contracts with suppliers, customers, or unions. In other words, negotiation was a skill used primarily by people who did it for a living. Now, changes in the economy and shifts in organizational structures mean that a major part of a manager's job is likely to be spent negotiating. The shifting boundaries between a firm and its suppliers, customers, employees, and even competition, require that more people than ever are likely to be both negotiating complex deals and bargaining over their implementation. Further, more often than not, managers are in roles where their responsibility exceeds their authority, which means that significant time is spent negotiating with a range of internal and external stakeholders in order to get a job done, a budget approved, or the right staff hired. In network and team structures, bargaining is a common strategy used to secure commitments and buy-in. And as people change jobs over the course of their careers, there are many opportunities to negotiate conditions and compensation or to secure funds to support new ventures.

The growing relevance of negotiation for managerial work has increased the educational demand for negotiation skills. A significant field of research has developed to meet that demand, a field that is guided by a pragmatic concern for practice. This field is marked by an interest in doing empirical research that can be easily translated into prescriptive advice that promises to make people better negotiators. Not surprisingly, with practical concerns in mind, questions about gender – specifically, are there differences between men and women in the ways they negotiate and in the outcomes they achieve – abound. Adequate answers, however, are lacking. A fourth frame perspective on gender illuminates a different set of dynamics about gender and, at the same time, expands the domain of strategic advice that can help negotiators become more effective at what they do.

DIFFERENT PERSPECTIVES ON GENDER DIFFERENCES

Gender, when equated with biological sex, is one of the most easily measured of variables, and so it is not surprising that the question "do men and women negotiate differently?" has dominated the research on gender in negotiations. Hypotheses typically posit women and men as polar opposites in their negotiation styles: women will be more cooperative and relational, whereas men will be more competitive and individualistic. Decades of research to test these hypotheses, however, have produced inconclusive results. Findings are contradictory; meta-analyses have shown a significant, but small, likelihood that women will be more cooperative (Walters, Stuhlmacher, & Meyer, 1998).

To ask questions about sex differences assumes that gender is an essential and stable attribute of individuals. Accounting for these differences requires some bio-logical, socialization, or role theory to explain why they exist. Generally, researchers argue that a woman's social development and mothering role lead her to empha-size nurturance and support in her social relations, whereas a man's social devel-opment and breadwinner role lead him to emphasize separation and individuation. These social factors are typically identified as the root causes of differences in nego-tiation styles and skills (Kolb & Coolidge, 1991). But hypotheses about sex differ-ences in development or role are not directly tested in the negotiation research; they are mobilized after the fact to explain differences found (Ely, 1999). Further-more, in accordance with a Frame 1 perspective on gender, findings that men out-perform women in negotiations, a common result in salary and compensation negotiations, are interpreted as a problem with women: they care too much about relationships, do not set their aspirations high enough, and are too emotional (Stuhlmacher & Walters, 1999). Thus, many studies of sex difference point to women's deficiencies.

In a field that prides itself on its pragmatism, the advice that comes from this stream of research can be problematic. First, it is directed only to women, telling them how they need to be "fixed" so that they might negotiate better, that is, like men. Nothing from this line of inquiry speaks to men. Second, the advice from this work may itself be gendered: to tell women to act in a more self-interested or assertive way assumes that these behaviors are gender-neutral – as if men and women behaving similarly were interchangeable. We know, however, that behaviors enacted by a woman are likely to be seen differently than when enacted by a man. This asymmetry can create double binds for women: they are damned if they do not act like men, and they are damned if they do.

A Frame 2 perspective on gender, which celebrates women's presumed differ-ence from men, is often invoked in making distinctions between two main approaches to negotiation: the integrative or mutual gains approach and the zero sum or distributive approach. Because the former approach relies on principles of relationship and cooperation, it tends to be associated with women and femininity. Reinforcing this tendency, several books (Fisher & Brown, 1987; Ury, 1990) have popularized the importance of relationships in negotiation. Thus, some negotia-tion experts advocate "feminine" attributes, such as empathy and understanding, as central to reaching desirable mutual gains outcomes (Kolb & Coolidge, 1991; Mnookin, Peppett, & Tulemello, 2000). This message is captured in the "dual concern" model of negotiation – to do well for oneself, one also has to have a high concern for the interests of the other party (Pruitt, 1981).

Research shows little support for these assumptions, however. In the first reading, "Integrative bargaining: Does gender make a difference," Patrick Calhoun and William P. Smith test whether concern for others, a presumably feminine trait, pro-duces joint gains for men and women. The findings are not encouraging. They show that it is not enough to care about the other. For women to achieve high joint gains – in this case profit – they need to be primed to pay more attention to their *own* needs. Without this priming, they too easily make concessions. For men, looking out for oneself yielded the highest joint profit; they had no need to attend to the interests of the other party. This study and others in this tradition call into question whether the appealing but simplistic idea of valuing a stereotypically feminine approach is effective. Moreover, these supposedly feminine relational skills, valorized for their presumed contribution to mutual gains, are divorced from real caring. "Empathy" has become a way to learn about the interests of the other party in order to do well for oneself (Mnookin et al., 2000), and concern for the other party translates into "enlightened self-interest" (Rubin, Pruitt, & Kim, 1994). This approach lacks any real appreciation for the relational belief system in which such attributes as empathy and caring are rooted (Fletcher, 1994, 1999). Ironically, the popularized, so-called "empathy" has become no more than an instrumental tool to achieve individual ends.

Taken together, the first and second frames on gender, which have dominated current thinking about gender and negotiations, have led to a theoretical and practical dead end. The research and pragmatic advice it suggests reinforce idealized masculine attributes – enlightened individual self-interest, analytic rationality, objectivity, and instrumentality. Attributes labeled as feminine – qualities such as empathy, concern for relationships, subjectivity, and emotional expressiveness – are valued only in the most marginal sense. They pale beside traits associated with masculinity, which are seen as intimately tied to success. Gender remains a "problem" for women, and research on gender fails to inform the theory and practice of negotiation.

A third, less developed stream of research explores how situational factors interact with gender to influence negotiation practice and outcomes. This research takes a Frame 3 approach: rather than looking only at the inherent qualities of the parties involved, it suggests that negotiators' approaches and actions will be shaped at least partly by contextual variables, such as the location and subject of the negotiation and the negotiators' relative positions of formal authority. The second reading, "Gender versus power as a predictor of negotiation behavior and outcomes," by Carol Watson, explores the importance of gender and power, where power refers to the negotiator's formal role in an organizational hierarchy as, for example, a manager or subordinate. It closely reviews eight previous studies and concludes that while both gender and power have influence on negotiation behavior and outcomes, power appears to have greater weight.

GENDER AND NEGOTIATION FROM THE PERSPECTIVE OF FRAME 4

To look at gender in negotiations from the perspective of the fourth frame is to go beyond a simple comparison between men and women and, building on Frame 3, take a deeper look at the gendered nature of the negotiation field and the role power plays in it. A fourth frame approach considers theory, research, and norms of practice and uncovers what has been silenced or ignored in the field. There are three areas that this frame illuminates: the problem of social position, the challenges of maintaining legitimacy in bargaining interactions, and the possibilities for transformative outcomes from negotiations.

Gender and the problem of social position

Several perspectives have dominated recent developments in the negotiation field: economic decision analysis (Raiffa, 1982; Lax & Sebenius, 1986), social psychology (Rubin et al., 1994; Thompson, 2001), and cognitive psychology (Neale & Bazerman, 1991). These perspectives focus on individual actors (as either principals or agents) engaged in transactional deal making. According to this view, actors achieve mutual gains through the rational analysis of issues, interests, and options and by constructing packages across differences. The problem with these rather technical models is that they neglect the very social processes that make mutual gains possible. To focus on cognitive factors, such as analytic prowess, as the major barriers to agreement minimizes how important social positioning is to one's ability to enact this approach effectively. People thus come to blame themselves and their personal deficiencies for inequities in outcomes that no amount of rationality could, in fact, correct.

A good example of this problem is the way power has been addressed. Although the role of negotiators' relative power positions has received some attention by researchers, power tends to be simplistically defined as a situational variable, most often manipulated experimentally in laboratory studies. Others have dismissed the role of power altogether, noting that powerful actors do not necessarily achieve the best outcomes (Lax & Sebenius, 1986). While that is surely true, it is also true that one's position in an organization's hierarchy, one's connection to (or exclusion from) influential networks, and one's race, class, gender, or ethnicity are all factors that can contribute to negotiators' relative power position in consequential ways. Nevertheless, bargaining power is typically seen as a function of one's alternatives – one's BATNA, or Best Alternative to a Negotiated Agreement, a concept that locates power in the choice situations of negotiators (i.e., what do they get if they walk away? For example, can they find another job?). What is missing in this analysis is an exploration of how social positioning shapes those choice situations in the first place and may impose more constraint than real choice.

Studies of women and minorities in negotiations demonstrate the importance of social positioning for how they fare (chapter 10, this volume; Kolb & Williams, 2000). In a study of salary negotiations, for example, Seidel, Polzer, and Stewart (2000) showed that lower salary outcomes for minorities could be explained by their access to social networks and not by their BATNAs. A fourth frame perspective enlarges the domain for theory and research to include the many sources of power inequities in negotiations. It brings into focus the challenges of social positioning, especially unequal status and influence, and offers strategic advice on ways to negotiate from these positions (Kolb & Williams, 2001).

Gender and the challenges of maintaining legitimacy in bargaining interactions

The fourth frame also shifts thinking about gender away from essential characteristics of men and women to the negotiation interaction itself. Gender and its enactment are quite fluid and variable; one objective from Frame 4 is to understand how and under what conditions gender is mobilized in negotiation. Understanding how people "do gender" in negotiations opens up new possibilities for strategic advice on managing the challenges that result. In the third reading, "Gender and the shadow negotiation," Deborah Kolb describes different ways that gender manifests in negotiations. One has to do with how salient, important, or relevant one's own gender identity is to oneself in a negotiation. To what degree do negotiators identify with the masculine and/or feminine sides of themselves, and how do they enact these identities in the negotiation process? For example, a man may or may not choose, either consciously or unconsciously, to act in a stereotypically masculine way – shouting, bullying, acting competitively – depending on how appropriate he thinks this behavior would be or how comfortable he would feel enacting it. By the same token, a woman may or may not take up the stereotypically feminine role of helper or creator of good relationships. Negotiators, in other words, have some choice in the degree to which they take up stereotypical gender roles in a negotiation. Recent research by Riley (in an unpublished dissertation, Harvard University, 2001) suggests that women are more likely to take up a traditional feminine role when engaged in distributive bargaining and when they are negotiating for themselves.

Expectations and stereotypes that others hold can also affect the degree to which gender is salient in a negotiation. In a series of studies, Kray, Galinsky, and Thompson (in press) show how susceptible negotiators are to positive and negative stereotypes. When masculine stereotypes are associated with negotiation effectiveness, men outperform women. Complementarily, when bargainers are primed to link negotiation effectiveness with feminine traits, women outperform men (Kray, Thompson, & Galinsky, 2001). Interestingly, the inverse framing also shapes results. When negotiators are told that masculine traits, such as self-interest, assertiveness, rationality, and limited displays of emotion, yield poor outcomes, women outperform men. And when they are told that feminine traits, such as listening well, being verbally articulate, and having insight into others' feelings, yield poor outcomes, men outperform women. This line of research shows how susceptible negotiators are to stereotypes about gender, which are even more likely to play a role in less structured, ambiguous, everyday situations than in laboratory simulations (Riley, unpublished dissertation, 2001).

The perspective of Frame 4 provokes us to consider the extent to which power complicates negotiations because gender is a relation of power. One party to a negotiation, by simply making gender salient during the process, for example, can undermine or delegitimize the other party (Kolb & Williams, 2001, 2002). Whereas such a move might simply represent a strategic shift for the initiating party, made without malice, the target of this move may nevertheless experience it as an attack that undermines the target's position and sense of self. Delegitimizing one of the parties during a negotiation reduces the likelihood of a mutually beneficial outcome, unless the delegitimized party is able to resist. Research has shown that there are a number of options in how people can resist these kinds of strategic moves and "turn" them to restore the working relationship. Unless both parties to a negotiation experience a measure of parity and legitimacy, the negotiation is likely to fail.

"Turns" are ways in which a person can respond to the discrediting or undermining actions of another by shifting the meaning of those actions (Goffman, 1967). Having a repertoire of turns – including interrupting the action, naming a challenge, reframing a question, correcting impressions, diverting attention from problems, refocusing on the underlying issue, and even moving physically – helps negotiators manage difficult negotiations (Kolb & Williams, 2000). Turns take place in the "shadow" of a negotiation. Often they are ways of resisting gender stereotypes, but they can be ways of resisting any move that puts a negotiator in a disadvantageous position (Gherardi, 1996). Viewing negotiation through a fourth frame lens reveals these shadow dynamics and thus provides insight into ways of negotiating more effectively, not only for women, but also for negotiators more generally.

Gender and the possibilities for transformative outcomes

The dominant paradigm in negotiation laboratory research (and in most teaching) is a multi-issue game, where optimal integrative outcomes are achieved by "logrolling"– making trades or packaging issues that have different relative values to bargainers. In most empirical work, there are definitively optimal outcomes, which are measurable and scoreable and achieved only through a process of trade-offs. With these criteria as the basis for assessing outcomes, other possibilities that may involve more relational concerns are defined as less than optimal. Studies of friends, dating couples, and people who have relationships with each other, for example, often emphasize fairness and equity in negotiations and so fail to achieve the kinds of optimal outcomes defined in the research (Valley, Neale, & Mannix, 1995). Thus, the design of research and the criteria by which agreements are judged forecloses other possibilities. In the fourth reading in Part II, "Rethinking negotiation: Feminist views of communication and exchange," Linda Putnam and Deborah Kolb show how the dominance of exchange in both distributive and integrative negotiations – particularly the focus on trades as the major activity of bargaining – renders invisible other ways that parties engage issues and create agreements. Negotiators can develop relationships with each other that lead to more open inquiry. More open inquiry creates new understandings about the issues in dispute, which can lead to different kinds of outcomes beyond trades.[1] Under these conditions, different combinations of skills and behavior would become more important. With this broader definition of what mutual inquiry might look like in negotiation, there are possibilities for transformative outcomes unimagined before the negotiation began.

Traditionally, the study of gender in negotiations has been narrowly conceived as one of sex differences. The results of this work are static and reinforce existing stereotypes and practices. By taking a fourth frame perspective on gender and negotiations, it becomes clear that the individualistic focus in the field misses the social and interactive dynamics that characterize negotiations in most settings. Attending to these social processes expands the strategic repertoire of what people need to know to be effective negotiators and helps us see how gendered notions permeate the negotiation field.

Note

1 Alternative models that stand in comparison to the dominant one will likely appear deficient, devalued, and inadequate, since the standards of traditional perspectives have shaped our very knowledge of a particular phenomenon. The temptation, when exposed to "difference," is to criticize it using the assumptions and criteria of the traditional

approach. Thus, relational approaches are criticized because they leave a person open to exploitation. This criticism, however, draws from and sustains the status quo. It serves to reinstate the dominant stance of the traditional model as much as it serves as a critique of its alternative.

References

Ely, R. J. 1999. Feminist critiques of research on gender in organizations. *Working paper #6*, Center for Gender in Organizations, Simmons School of Management, Boston, MA.

Fisher, R. & Brown, S. 1987. *Getting together*. New York: Penguin.

Fletcher, J. K. 1994. Castrating the feminine advantage: Feminist standpoint research and management science. *Journal of Management Inquiry*, 3: 74–8.

Fletcher, J. K. 1999. *Disappearing acts*. Cambridge, MA: MIT Press.

Gherardi, S. 1996. *Gender, symbolism, and organizational culture*. Newbury Park, CA: Sage.

Goffman, E. 1967. *Interaction ritual: Essays in face-to-face behavior*. New York: Doubleday/Anchor.

Kolb, D. M., & Coolidge, G. 1991. Her place at the table. In J. W. Breslin & J. Z. Rubin (eds.), *Negotiation theory and practice*: 261–277. Cambridge, MA: Program on Negotiation, Harvard Law School.

Kolb, D. M. & Williams, J. 2000. *The shadow negotiation: How women can master the hidden agendas that determine bargaining success*. New York: Simon and Schuster.

Kolb, D. M. & Williams, J. 2001. Breakthrough bargaining. *Harvard Business Review*, 6080, 87–107.

Kray, L., Galinsky, A., & Thompson, L. 2001. Reversing the gender gap in negotiations: An exploration of stereotype regeneration. Paper presented at the International Association for Conflict Management, 14th Annual Conference, Cergy, France.

Kray, L., Thompson, L., & Galinsky, A. Gender stereotype confirmation and reactance in negotiation. *Journal of Personality and Social Psychology*, (in press).

Lax, D. A., & Sebenius, J. K. 1986. *The manager as negotiator: Bargaining for cooperation and competitive gain*. New York, NY: The Free Press.

Mnookin, R., Peppett, S. R., & Tulemello, A. S. 2000. *Beyond winning: Negotiating to create value in deals and disputes*. Cambridge, MA: Harvard University Press.

Neale, M. A., & Bazerman, M. H. 1991. *Cognition and rationality in negotiation*. New York: The Free Press.

Pruitt, D. 1981. *Negotiation behavior*. New York: Academic Press.

Raiffa, H. 1982. *The art and science of negotiation*. Cambridge, MA: Harvard University Press.

Rubin, J. Z., Pruitt, D. & Kim, S. H. 1994. *Social conflict*. New York: McGraw-Hill.

Seidel, M.-D., Polzer, J., & Stewart, K. 2000. Friends in high places: The effects of social networks on salary negotiations. *Administrative Science Quarterly*, 45(1): 1–25.

Stuhlmacher, A. F. & Walters, A. E. 1999. Gender differences in negotiation outcomes: A meta-analysis. *Personnel Psychology*, 52(3): 653–67.

Thompson, L. 2001. *The heart and mind of the negotiator*. New Jersey: Prentice Hall.

Ury, W. 1990. *Getting past no*. New York: Bantam.

Valley, K., Neale, M. A., & Mannix, E. 1995. Friends, lovers, colleagues, strangers: The effects of relationship on the process and outcome of dyadic negotiation. In R. J. Bies, R. J. Lewicki, & B. H. Sheppard (eds.), *Research on negotiation in oganizations*, vol. V: 65–93. Greenwich, CT: JAI Press.

Walters, A. E., Stuhlmacher, A. F., & Meyer, L. L. 1998. Gender and negotiator competitiveness: A meta-analysis. *Organizational Behavior and Human Decision Processes*, 76: 1–29.

INTEGRATIVE BARGAINING: DOES GENDER MAKE A DIFFERENCE?

PATRICK S. CALHOUN AND WILLIAM P. SMITH

From *International Journal of Conflict Management* (1999)
10 (3): 203–24

As women continue to make strides in the traditionally male dominated arenas of business and politics, interest in and questions about the impact of gender on negotiation style and outcome have grown. Despite the fact that sex has been one of the most studied variables in the interpersonal gaming and negotiation literature (see e.g., Rubin & Brown, 1975; Walters, Stuhlmacher, & Meyer, 1998), there are currently few clear answers to many questions regarding the impact of gender on negotiation. Recent meta-analytic reviews examining gender differences in negotiation and choice of conflict management strategies, however, have found small but significant effects suggesting that women tend to behave less competitively and more cooperatively than men (Gayle, Preiss, & Allen, 1994; Krone, Allen, & Ludlum, 1994; Walters et al., 1998). Watson (1994) notes, however, that women's cooperativeness and lower level of competitiveness have generally been equated with weakness and ineffectiveness. And indeed some evidence from actual salary negotiations suggests something of the sort (Gerhart & Rhynes, 1991). In an examination of graduating MBA students, Gerhart and Rhynes (1991) found that while women negotiated as often as men in an effort to increase their salaries, they obtained significantly lower monetary returns from the negotiation that men. However, salary negotiations tend to be purely distributive (i.e., fixed pie) in nature, where collaborative tactics often place their users in a disadvantaged position. In fact, the clear majority of negotiation research has focused on distributive (i.e., win-lose, fixed pie) bargaining where there is an implicit assumption that winning is the desired outcome regardless of how the other party fares. Because cooperation does not necessarily help one to win, men have been credited with being more effective bargainers than women (Watson, 1994).

However, negotiations often offer the possibility of integrative agreements – agreements offering both parties more than a simple compromise could. This is true when parties' interests in various issues under negotiation differ in ways permitting trade-offs ("logrolling"), or when they can introduce new issues or options permitting both to benefit more than simply dividing fixed resources would permit (Pruitt & Rubin, 1986). Under these circumstances, it is often possible to reconcile or integrate interests and reach an agreement which produces high mutual benefit. Agreements which provide high joint benefit are preferred over other types of solutions for a number of reasons. Integrative agreements tend to be more stable and often serve to strengthen the relationship between parties. In turn, a stronger relationship increases the likelihood of developing mutually beneficial agreements in the future (Pruitt & Rubin, 1986). Thus, one goal of researchers is to identify the processes and negotiation strategies which lead to mutually beneficial integrative solutions.

Researchers have identified that cooperation is often important for the development of mutually satisfactory outcomes (Blake & Mouton, 1964; Deutsch, 1949; Pruitt & Rubin, 1986). Some have suggested that the tendency for women to approach negotiation more cooperatively may be particularly well suited for the attainment of high joint benefit (Kolb & Coolidge, 1991). Unfortunately, the impact of gender has received relatively little attention in the area of integrative bargaining. Much of the research in the integrative bargaining literature either has been done with males (e.g., Ben-Yoav & Pruitt, 1984a), or has been silent as to gender of subject (e.g., Neale, Huber, & Northcraft, 1987). When women have been included in integrative bargaining research designs (e.g., Carnevale & Lawler, 1987; Kimmel, Pruitt, Magenau, Konar-Goldband, & Carnevale, 1980; Pruitt, Carnevale, Forcey, & Van Slyck, 1986) some differences in negotiation process have been observed although there has been no evidence for differences in bargaining outcome. Stylistically, women appear to be less contentious (i.e., engaging in fewer put downs, threats, heavy commitments, and extraneous arguments) than men (Kimmel et al., 1980; cf., Pruitt et al., 1986).

While published reports reveal no evidence for gender differences in outcomes in the integrative bargaining paradigm, a number of recent studies conducted in our laboratory (Main, 1991; Marston, 1991; Pihakis, 1989), have revealed reliable differences in integrative bargaining outcomes. Surprisingly, in these studies, women consistently have obtained lower joint outcomes than men. The first study (Pihakis, 1989) used a logrolling bargaining paradigm commonly used by researchers in this area with a scenario involving a wholesaler selling small appliances to a retailer (see e.g., Kimmel et al., 1980; Pruitt & Lewis, 1975). Women obtained significantly lower joint profits ($8,428) than men ($9,222). The analysis of the interaction patterns revealed only that women made significantly larger concessions during the course of the negotiation than men.

A second experiment (Marston, 1991) was designed in order to test the hypothesis that the gender difference in joint profits was caused by differential interest in the task. Based upon Eagly's (1987) work on gender and task, it was hypothesized that the appliance task might have been particularly uninteresting for women, and this lack of interest might have accounted for the relatively low rate of integrative agreements among women. Thus, half of the same sex pairs in this experiment were given the typical appliance task, while the other half were given what both men and women rated as a more interesting task – a scenario involving a studio and agency negotiating the services of several movie performers. While the movie studio scenario did generate more integrative outcomes than the typical appliance task, there was still a significant difference between men and women in the attainment of integrative solutions. Women obtained significantly lower joint profits ($8,503) than men ($9,360). While there was some indication that the difference in outcome was smaller when the movie task was used, the interaction failed to reach statistical significance.

In a third experiment investigating somewhat different issues (Main, 1991) men and women, run in same-sex pairs, were asked by the company they represented to obtain a profit (intended to create a reservation price) somewhat larger than would be permitted by a simple compromise. High profit limits are thought to increase resistance to yielding and hence concern about own outcomes (Pruitt & Rubin, 1986). Like the previous two studies, men obtained somewhat higher joint profits ($9,541) than women ($9,199) although this difference did not reach statistical significance. An examination of the outcomes of the lower-profit members, however, indicated that the low-profit member in female pairs made significantly less than the low-profit member of male pairs. Furthermore, the lowest offers made in negotiation were lower for women than for men, suggesting that consistent with the Pihakis (1989) findings, and despite the imposed limits, women's aspirations for themselves were less resistant to the other's demands than were men's.

It is apparent that the gender difference in integrative bargaining outcomes is a reliable one in this laboratory. Process data suggested that women consistently made larger concessions than men during negotiations; this may in turn have resulted in lower joint outcomes for the women. While it is unclear why women in these studies were less resistant to yielding than men, one possible explanation concerns the motivations men and women bring into the negotiation setting. Premature yielding, which mitigates against the discovery of integrative agreements and leads to very poor joint outcomes, is likely when individuals have high concern for the other's outcomes with relatively low concern for one's own outcomes (Pruitt & Rubin, 1986). Hence, the observed tendency for women to yield in the three studies discussed above (Main, 1991; Marston, 1991; Pihakis, 1989) may reflect a relatively high level of concern for the other, which men fail to bring into the negotiation.

This hypothesis is consistent with many meta-analytic reviews of differences in social behavior (see Eagly, 1987, 1993; Eagly & Wood, 1991). In a summary of this literature, Eagly (1995) notes that in general women tend to display behaviors that can be described as concerned with the other's welfare, while men manifest more dominant and independent behaviors. In a recent meta-analytic review of much of the bargaining literature, Walters et al. (1998) found that women behaved more cooperatively than men in negotiations, suggesting that women may be relatively more concerned for the welfare of the other party than men. Indeed, a number of authors (Gray, 1994; Kolb, 1992; Kolb & Coolidge, 1991) have suggested that men and women approach negotiation from distinctly different perspectives where women are more likely to be attentive to the needs of others.

Is concern for the other (and the resultant cooperative tactics, or lack of competitive tactics) detrimental to the attainment of high mutual benefit? While concern for the other or a cooperative orientation has been identified as an important determinant of high mutual benefit (Blake & Mouton, 1964; Deutsch, 1949; Pruitt & Rubin, 1986), Ben-Yoav and Pruitt (1984a) point out that concern for the other's welfare or incentives for cooperation must be accompanied by matching levels of aspiration support if high joint benefit is to be achieved. In other words, without motivation to resist making early concessions, a tendency to cooperate or look out for the needs of others may mitigate against the discovery of the integrative potential in the conflict.

As a framework for the current investigation, we relied on Pruitt's (1983; Pruitt & Rubin, 1986) Dual Concern Model which predicts bargaining outcomes as a function of a negotiator's motivation or concern for his/her own profits in combination with his/her concern for the other's outcomes. . . . [T]he model assumes that successful integrative bargaining requires both high concern for the value of one's own outcome as well as high concern for the other's welfare. Having high concern for one's own outcomes with little or no concern for the other is likely to lead to a strategy of contentiousness as the parties rigidly maintain high aspirations for themselves, and consequently often obtain relatively low joint outcomes, as a reflection of either last-ditch compromises, or failures to reach agreement. On the other hand, having high concern for the other's outcomes with relatively low concern for one's own outcomes is likely to lead to premature yielding, mitigating against the discovery of integrative agreements and leading to very poor joint outcomes. Having low concern about either own or other's outcomes should lead to moderately poor outcomes as the parties show moderated resistance to yielding, yet little interest in benefiting the other. By contrast, having high concern for both self and other permits parties to maintain high demands for themselves while exploring possibilities for collaboration and high joint benefit.

Pruitt and his colleagues have presented consistent support for this formulation in laboratory experiments. Through externally manipulating levels of concern, Ben-Yoav and Pruitt (1984a, 1984b) have obtained precisely the pattern of results that the model predicts: higher joint profits when bargainers were highly concerned with both own and other's profits than when they were concerned with either one or the other or neither. In these studies, subjects participated in a commonly used laboratory simulation of negotiation (see Pruitt & Lewis, 1975 for a more detailed description). Concern for own outcomes was manipulated by giving subjects instructions that they must attain a certain amount of profit, i.e., a limit, or by making the subjects accountable to constituents. Concern for other's outcomes was manipulated by giving the subjects an expectation of cooperative future interaction (ECFI). Subjects were told that they would have to work together toward a common goal following the negotiation. Although it is not entirely clear how subjects interpret the ECFI manipulation, the instructions were designed to make the subjects feel dependent on each other and thus harbor concern for one another. While the results of these studies (Ben-Yoav & Pruitt, 1984a, 1984b) supported the dual concern model, women were not included as subjects.

The current experiment was designed to explore Pruitt's (1983; Pruitt & Rubin, 1986) dual concern model for men as well as for women, while using somewhat different manipulations of concern from those used in the original BenYoav and Pruitt (1984a, 1984b) studies. The study was also intended to explore any differences in reaction to externally imposed motivation on bargaining strategy and outcome in men and women in hopes that such results might permit an inference about differing motives men and women may bring into the negotiation setting.

While there is no reason to believe that the dual concern model applies only to men, there is reason to believe that men and women may differ in the concerns they bring into the negotiation situation. That is, a negotiator's concern for his/her own welfare as well as her/his concern for the other is unlikely to be simply determined by situational, i.e., experimentally manipulated factors. Based upon several discussions of sex differences in social behavior and negotiation (e.g., Eagly, 1987, 1993; Eagly & Wood, 1991; Gray, 1994; Kolb, 1992; Kolb & Coolidge, 1991) we hypothesized that women may enter the negotiation setting with a tendency toward accommodation or high concern for the other. On the other hand, we believed that men might enter the negotiation setting with no particular strong concerns for the other, as the work of Pruitt and his colleagues suggests. The high concern for other's welfare we propose is a characteristic of women that bargainers may lead them to concede quickly unless they have external reason to resist concession, especially given the tendency for all bargainers to assure at the outset that negotiations are fixed-pie in nature rather than integrative, thereby missing the opportunity for integrative agreements.

Thus, we predicted that without externally increasing resistance to yielding, i.e., concern for their own profits, women would be likely to yield and obtain poor outcomes. On the other hand, since women presumably enter the negotiation setting with high other concern, we predicted they would be inclined toward problem solving and high outcomes under any conditions where they were given incentives to resist yielding and to harbor concern for their own profits. For men, who presumably do not enter the negotiation with any particular concern for the other, we expected problem solving and high outcomes only when they were given incentives to be both concerned with their own and the other's welfare, i.e., a replication of the work of Pruitt and his colleagues. . . . [W]e expected that men would engage in contentious behavior and obtain only moderate profits when given incentives to have high self-concern with little concern for the other.

These hypotheses were tested through the use of a buyer-seller negotiation task with integrative potential. A $2 \times 2 \times 2$ design was employed, involving gender (male vs. female) and external manipulations of self-concern (high vs. low), and other concern (high vs. low). These manipulations involved, in the case of other concern, a high or low direct stake in the welfare of the other (via a share in the other's profits from the agreement, as in Krauss, 1966). This contrasts with previous research testing the dual concern hypothesis, which has used a more indirect, and hence perhaps more ambiguous, manipulation involving the expectation of future interaction (Ben-Yoav & Pruitt, 1984a, 1984b) or a positive mood induction (Pruitt, Carnevale, Ben-Yoav, Nochajski, & Van Slyck, 1983, experiment 2). For self-concern, we added an incentive manipulation to the limit manipulation used in the previous research (Ben-Yoav & Pruitt, 1984a; Pruitt et al., 1983, experiment 2) for the high self-concern condition (low self-concern had neither the limit nor the added incentive). In addition, a control group which received no external manipulations of self or other concern was run. We chose not to measure directly the motivations with which men and women entered the negotiation setting for fear of increasing demand characteristics and the likelihood of subjects artificially engaging in sex stereotyped behaviors. Thus, while the current design does not directly address whether men and women enter negotiation settings with different intrinsic motivations, inferences can be drawn about intrinsic motivations given significant differences in bargaining strategy and outcomes between men and women. Furthermore, the chosen design decreases the likelihood that any differences in bargaining strategy and outcome found between men and women would be an artifact of the experimental procedures. [. . .]

DISCUSSION

While women demonstrated the predicted pattern of results in the current experimental simulation, men did not. As expected, women engaged in problem solving and obtained high joint benefit when they were externally motivated to harbor concern for their own outcomes and resist yielding. Without this external manip-ulation of self concern, women tended to yield and obtain poor joint outcomes. This pattern of results is consistent with our hypothesis that women enter the nego-tiation setting with relatively high concern for the welfare of the other. We expected men to obtain the pattern of results demonstrated by Ben-Yoav and Pruitt (1984a, 1984b) where best outcomes were obtained only when subjects were given motiva-tion to be concerned for both their own and the other's payoffs. Men in our study, however, obtained especially high joint profits in both conditions where they were given high self concern. This is in contrast to the prediction that contentious behav-ior and non-integrative outcomes would result under the condition of high self concern in combination with little concern for the welfare of the other.

It appears that in the absence of highly contentious behavior which may miti-gate against agreement, individuals with high self concern and resistance to yield-ing can obtain high joint profits without much concern for the other. Our sample was not very contentious. In fact, only one pair out of the entire sample did not reach agreement. This is in stark contrast to the Ben-Yoav and Pruitt (1984a) study where it seems that contentious behavior was much more prevalent as 18 of 48 pairs failed to reach an agreement. Our examination of the pattern of results obtained by those individuals in the Ben-Yoav and Pruitt (1984a) study who did reach an agreement and were presumably less contentious than those pairs which failed to agree, revealed that there is little difference between the high self concern condi-tions ($10,138 versus $9,950). Thus, it appears that the pattern of results obtained by the men in our study is actually not unlike the pattern of results obtained by those pairs who reached agreement in the original Ben-Yoav and Pruitt (1984a) study.

It is currently unclear why the men in our sample failed to exhibit the level of contentious behavior shown by Ben-Yoav and Pruitt's (1984a) sample. It is possible that there are population differences between the samples or that there is some-thing particular to our laboratory setting which discourages contentious behavior, although we can not account for this. It is also possible to argue that the males in our study entered the negotiation with a high level of other concern as we assumed women did. There are several reasons we do not think this is the case. Indeed, the pattern of results in the current study lend some support to the belief that men and women may approach negotiation differently.

First, external manipulations of other concern had a significant effect on men's use of information exchange, which has been identified as a form of problem solving most likely under conditions of high trust or concern for the other (Kimmel et al., 1980). Males exchanged significantly more information when they were given incentive to harbor concern for the other's payoffs. If men entered the negotiation with a high level of concern for the other, one might expect the levels of informa-tion exchange to be roughly equal under all conditions, not simply when they were given external motivation to be concerned for the other. Presumably because women enter the negotiation setting with concern for the welfare of the other party, the external manipulation of other concern had little to no effect on their exchange of information. While this interpretation is consistent with our initial assumptions, we acknowledge that alternative explanations for this pattern are cer-tainly possible.

Further evidence is found in the condition in which subjects were given no strong incentives to be concerned for their own or the other's outcomes. In this condition, men obtained better outcomes than women. The results of this cell mirror that pattern of results obtained by an unmanipulated control group. Despite no strong external motivation to be concerned with own or other's payoffs, women tended to yield more often and obtain poorer outcomes than men. We believe that this finding reflects that women are generally more likely than men to bring a concern for the welfare of the other party into the negotiation setting.

The results of the current study support Ben-Yoav and Pruitt's (1984a) conclusion that in conflict and negotiation settings concern for the other's welfare or incentives for cooperation must be accompanied by matching levels of aspiration support if high joint benefit is to be achieved. The current results, however, raise questions regarding the dual concern model's prediction that high self concern without significant concern for the other will necessarily lead to contentious behavior and mitigate against integrative solutions. It is somewhat unclear the degree to which having little concern for the other actually encourages contentious behavior. Indeed, the men in our study and a number of men in Ben-Yoav and Pruitt's (1984a) investigation were able to reach agreements which offered high joint benefit and did so presumably with little concern for the outcomes of the other party. Further research is needed to explore the specific determinants of contentious behavior (e.g., culture of the negotiation setting, negotiator's assumptions, trust, anger) which may mitigate reaching integrative agreements. Pruitt (1983) admits that antagonistic concerns are missing in the dual concern model. Antagonism may be a particularly important determinant of contentiousness and poor outcomes.

Interestingly, women were more likely than men to perceive the other party's tactics as cooperative and view the other as friendly and trustworthy. Similarly, women were more likely than men to rate themselves as friendly and trustworthy. This finding occurred despite the fact that if anything, women tended to make more positional statements than men. Traditionally, positional commitments have been interpreted as a form of contentious behavior. Perhaps the impact of positional commitments on perceptions was softened by the use of laughter and discussion of feelings which women also displayed more often than men during the negotiation. More research is needed to determine whether the gender difference in ratings of tactics reflects differences in behavior, in perception or both.

Finally, some questions about the general strategy of this research are worth considering. First, we should note that in some sense the design of our experiment confounds gender of actor and gender of target, since we used same-sex pairs. This is in keeping with prior research on gender effects in integrative bargaining (Carnevale & Lawler, 1987; Kimmel et al., 1980; Pruitt et al., 1986). We selected this strategy on two grounds: first, most research on bargaining in general finds modest effects for gender of the actor, but not for gender of target (Walters et al., 1998). Furthermore, gender differences in mixed-sex pairs tend to be smaller than in same-sex pairs (Watson, 1994). Watson (1994) suggests that these findings are consistent with the socialization perspective on which we based our predictions of men's and women's motivations and behavior in the current study. Assuming that individuals match their behavior to that expected from a partner, men should behave more sensitively with a female partner while women should behave more competitively with a man. In turn, these astereotypical behavior patterns should minimize gender differences in mixed-sex pairs compared to same-sex pairs in which the members should exhibit high rates of gender stereotypical behavior (Watson, 1994). Consistent with this interpretation, unpublished data collected in our laboratory (Pihakis, 1989) found that in mixed sex pairs, women obtained individual profits which did not significantly differ from men ($4,347 vs. $4,521). Furthermore, male-male pairs tended to obtain higher joint outcomes ($9,222) than mixed sex pairs ($8,868) who tended to do better than all female pairs ($8,428) although the differences did not reach statistical significance. We have recently been conducting negotiation research in our laboratory with both same sex and mixed sex dyads in order to explore these issues further.

A second issue has reference to the relationship between the experimental manipulations used here and the actual motivation of participants. A major worry in experimental research of this sort, where the interest is in how motivations (in this case, concerns for own and other's welfare) influence strategy, is that the experimental manipulations may have influenced strategy directly, perhaps by cueing participants as to the tactics expected by the experimenter, or which might generally be appropriate. One reason we avoided using the expectation of cooperative future interaction used by Ben-Yoav and Pruitt (1984a, 1984b) to create concern for the other was our feeling that it may have demanded cooperative tactics via use of the term "cooperative" in the instructions to participants. Our own manipulation simply indicated to participants that they had a stake in how well the other did. It is difficult to see how this manipulation could have signaled a particular set of tactics to participants. Furthermore, the degree of overlap between our results and those of Pruitt and his colleagues using very different manipulations of other concern lends confidence to the interpretation that the manipulation in all of this research do affect the patterning of concerns in the intended way.

In summary, what do the current results say about gender differences in integrative bargaining? In the current study, results revealed a gender difference in negotiation outcome replicating previous studies conducted in our laboratory (i.e., Main, 1991; Marston, 1991; Pihakis, 1989). Female pairs obtained lower joint profits than men under conditions where bargainers received little external motivation to be particularly concerned for their own profits or the profits of the other. We believe, however, that it is misguided to conclude that men are more effective negotiators than women. There were no differences in outcome between male and female pairs when negotiators were given external reasons to be concerned for their own outcomes and resist yielding. Furthermore, post-questionnaire responses suggest that while women achieved equally high joint benefit under conditions of high resistance to yielding, they were more likely than men to perceive the other party positively. While further research is necessary to determine whether this difference in ratings of tactics reflects differences in behavior, perception or both, the quality of the relationship between negotiators is an important outcome variable which has been largely ignored in experimental simulations of negotiation. Hostility and anger between parties, whether arising from highly contentious behavior or extremely inequitable agreements, is likely to negatively affect attempts at resolving conflict in the future. Thus, the ability to resolve conflict while obtaining high outcomes and maintaining a positive relationship would seem ideal.

REFERENCES

Ben-Yoav, O., & Pruitt, D. G. (1984a). Resistance to yielding and the expectation of cooperative future interaction in negotiation. Journal of Experimental Social Psychology, 20, 325–335.

Ben-Yoav, O., & Pruitt, D. G. (1984b). Accountability to constituents: A two edged sword. Organizational Behavior and Human Performance, 34, 282–295.

Blake, R. R., & Mouton, I. S. (1964). The managerial grid. Houston, TX: Gulf.

Carnevale, P. I. D., & Lawler, E. L. (1987). Time pressure and the development of integrative agreements in bilateral negotiations. Journal of Conflict Resolution, 30, 616–659.

Deutsch, M. (1949). A theory of cooperation and competition. Human Relations, 2, 129–151.

Eagly, A. (1987). Sex differences in social behavior. A social role interpretation. Hillsdale, NJ: Erlbaum.

Eagly, A. (1993). Sex differences in human social behavior: Meta-analytic studies of social psychological research. In A. Haug, R. E. Whalen, C. Aron, & K. L. Olsen (Eds.), The development of sex differences and similarities in behaviour (pp. 421–436). London: Kluwer Academic.

Eagly, A. (1995). The science and politics of comparing women and men. American Psychologist, 50, 145–158.

Eagly, A. & Wood, W. (1991). Explaining sex differences in social behavior: A meta-analytic perspective. Personality and Social Psychology Bulletin, 100, 309–330.

Gayle, B. M., Preiss, R. W., & Allen, M. (1994). Gender differences and the use of conflict strategies. In L. H. Turner & R. M. Sterk (Eds.), Differences that make a difference (pp. 72434). Westport, CT: Bergin & Garvey.

Gerhart, B., & Rynes, S. (1991). Determinants and consequences of salary negotiations by male and female MBA graduates. Journal of Applied Psychology, 76, 256–262.

Gray, B. (1994). The gender based foundations of negotiation theory. Research on Negotiations in Organizations, 4, 3–36.

Kimmel, M. J., Pruitt, D. G., Magenau, I. M., Konar-Goldband, E., & Carnevale, P. I. D. (1980). Effects of trust, aspiration, and gender on negotiation tactics. Journal of Personality and Social Psychology, 38, 9–22.

Kolb, D. M. (1992, August). Is it her voice or her place that makes a differences? A consideration of gender issues in negotiation. Paper presented at the annual meeting of the Academy of Management, Las Vegas, NV.

Kolb, D. M. & Coolidge, G. G. (1991). Her place at the table: A consideration of gender issues in negotiation. In J. W. Breslin & J. Z. Rubin (Eds.), Negotiation theory and practice (pp. 261–277). Cambridge, MA: Program on Negotiation.

Krauss, R. M. (1966). Structural and attitudinal factors in interpersonal bargaining. Journal of Experimental Social Psychology, 2, 42–55.

Krone, K. J., Allen, M., & Ludlum, J. (1994). A meta-analysis of gender research in managerial influence. In L. H. Turner, & H. M. Sterk (Eds.), Differences that make a difference (pp. 72–84). Westport, CT Bergin & Garvey.

Main, A. (1991). Visual access and gender in interpersonal negotiation. Unpublished manuscript, Vanderbilt University.

Marston, M. (1991). Effects of gender and task on integrative bargaining. Honors thesis in psychology, Vanderbilt University.

Neale, M. A., Huber, V. L., & Northcraft, G. B. (1987). The framing of negotiations: contextual versus task frames. Organizational Behavior and Human Decision Process, 39, 228–241.

Pihakis, (1989). Couples in conflict: Effect of relationship and gender on integrative bargaining. Honors thesis in psychology, Vanderbilt University.

Pruitt, D. G. (1983). Strategic choice in negotiation. American Behavioral Scientist, 27, 162–194.

Pruitt, D. G., Carnevale, P. J. D., Ben-Yoav, O., Nochajski, T. H., & Van Slyck, M. R. (1983). Incentives for cooperation in integrative bargaining. In R. Tietz (Ed.), Aspiration levels in bargaining and economic decision making (pp. 26–52). Berlin: Springer.

Pruitt, D. G., Carnevale, P. J. D., Forcey, B., & Van Slyck, M. (1986). Gender effects in negotiation: Constituent surveillance and contentious behavior. Journal of Experimental Social Psychology, 22, 264–275.

Pruitt D. G., & Lewis, S. A. (1975). Development of integrative solutions in bilateral negotiation. Journal of Personality and Social Psychology, 31, 621–633.

Pruitt D. G., & Rubin, J. Z. (1986). Social conflict: Escalation, stalemate, and settlement. New York: Random House.

Rubin, I. Z., & Brown, (1975). The social psychology of bargaining and negotiation. New York: Academic Press.

Walters, A. E., Stuhlmacher, A. F., & Meyer, L. L. (1998). Gender and negotiator competitiveness: A meta-analysis. Organizational Behavior and Human Decision Processes, 76, 1–29.

Watson, C. (1994). Gender differences in negotiating behavior and outcomes. Fact or artifact. In A. Taylor & J. B. Miller (Eds.), Conflict and gender (pp. 191–210). Creskill, NJ: Hampton Press.

GENDER VERSUS POWER AS A PREDICTOR OF NEGOTIATION BEHAVIOR AND OUTCOMES

CAROL WATSON

From *Negotiation Journal* (1994) April: 117–27

The assumption that women are inferior simply because they are "different" from men has permeated our culture in the United States as it has many other cultures. Women's lot in life has clearly improved dramatically in this country since the 1700s, but equally clearly, there is still significant discrimination against women in our society in the 1990s.

Over the past ten to fifteen years, psychologists and sociologists have mounted a frontal assault on this long-standing "different and inferior" assumption in many domains. Their work has shown the assumption to be frequently inaccurate. Recent literature reviews show, for example, that there are not clear gender differences in verbal ability (Hyde and Linn 1988), math ability (Hyde, Fennema, and Lamon 1990), or spatial ability (Caplan, McPherson, and Tobin 1985). Nor do there appear to be gender differences in more abstract characteristics or abilities such as moral reasoning (Friedman, Robinson, and Friedman 1987) or leadership (Powell 1990). Nevertheless, the belief in significant, innate, gender differences refuses to die.

The probable reason for the durability of this belief is that, on a day-in, day-out basis, men and women *do* differ in countless ways that are apparent to each of us, researchers and members of the general public alike. One response to the dilemmas these differences have posed for women is advanced by the "cultural feminists" who have sought to fight society's inherent sexism by celebrating women as different from but superior to men (e.g., Gilligan 1982; Rosener 1990). While such theories may be appealing because they highlight women's special qualities and help women feel good about themselves (rather than inferior or deficient), the "different-but-superior" argument does not hold up to the rigorous scrutiny of careful empirical investigation any better than does the more prevalent "different-and-inferior" argument (Tavris 1992).

An alternative perspective, offered in this article, is that gender differences do exist, but that those of significance relate to contextual rather than to innate personality factors. Contextual factors consist first and most obviously of the immediate situation and its particular demands. More broadly, however, the context of an individual's life includes all aspects in the environment of that individual's life – such as work, family, class, culture, etc. (Tavris 1992).

Contextual factors have often been found to supplant personality factors in determining behavior, sometimes in highly dramatic demonstrations (e.g., Milgram 1963). Nevertheless, researchers and the general public continue to make what psychologists have dubbed the "fundamental attribution error" (Jones and Nisbett 1976). This error consists of assuming that others behave the way they do because of internal personality characteristics rather than because of external situational demands.

COOPERATIVE WOMEN, COMPETITIVE MEN?

Relatively little scholarly attention has been paid to the issue of gender differences in negotiation behavior in recent years. In fact, the question of whether such differences exist, and if so, what they are, has never been satisfactorily resolved. Early research suggested that women are "softer" negotiators than men, that they prefer an accommodating style, are generous, and are more concerned that all parties be treated fairly than they are about gaining positive substantive outcomes for themselves . . . . These early studies also showed that men are "tough" negotiators who make many demands and few concessions, and that they are more concerned about winning positive substantive outcomes for themselves than about how the other party fares (Bartos 1970). Men were also found to be more flexible negotiators than women in that they seemed to use a tit-for-tat strategy more often, and were better at finding rational strategies that allowed them to maximize gains . . . .

Although Rubin and Brown (1975) showed that these supposed gender differences in bargaining and negotiating were not consistently supported by research, there tends to be a continuing expectation that women will negotiate and bargain more cooperatively than men. Nevertheless, a few researchers have reached more negative conclusions. For instance, women have sometimes been found to lock into an unrelenting competitive stance when their partners refuse to cooperate, and this behavior has been construed by some as vindictive (Rapoport and Chammah 1965; Tedeschi, Schlenker, and Bonoma 1973). Rubin and Brown (1975) incorporated these findings into their work, but this negative view has been largely ignored by everyone else.

The fact that negotiation researchers have often depicted women as cooperative might be construed to mean that the cultural feminist perspective (i.e., that women are different but superior) has predominated in the negotiation literature. This would be an incorrect assumption, however, because women's cooperativeness has generally been equated with weakness and ineffectiveness. That is, cooperation is generally considered to be a dangerous negotiating tactic since it leaves one open to exploitation by one's opponent (e.g., Gifford 1989; Pruitt 1983). Thus, women have frequently been portrayed as "nicer" negotiators than men; and, since niceness does not help one to win, men have typically been credited with being more effective negotiators than women. In fact, some researchers have openly questioned women's negotiating competence, claiming that women's behavior in negotiations is similar to that of men who do not understand the rules of the game (Caplow 1968; Kelley 1965).

Research on leadership provides a clue as to what might account for the frequent assumption that women are overly soft, ineffective negotiators. Leadership is similar to negotiating and bargaining in that it consists of influencing others. Not surprisingly, women's leadership skills have often been doubted on grounds similar to doubts about their negotiating competence. Many studies have been devoted to examining gender differences in leadership, and the nearly universal consensus that has emerged from reviews of these studies is that, when women earn or are given the leader's role, they behave exactly the way male leaders behave (e.g., Powell 1990).

The clue this provides to our understanding of the literature on gender differences in negotiating and bargaining behavior is that the leader role typically confers power on the incumbent. Thus, one might argue that it is power rather than gender that determines how leaders behave. Power has been defined as the potential ability to influence others (Mintzberg 1983; Pfeffer 1981). It accrues from many sources. Those most commonly recognized by management scholars are legitimate, reward, coercive, expert, and charismatic power (French and Raven 1960). The number and strength of one's sources of power in a given situation will be referred to in this article as "situational power."

Similar sources of power are present in negotiating and bargaining encounters. Interestingly, the literature on disputing shows differences in the behavior of high- and low-power negotiators that mirror the most commonly assumed gender differences in negotiator behavior and outcomes (Bartos 1970). That is, high-power negotiators tend to compete whereas low-power negotiators tend to cooperate. I am suggesting, then, that because women in American society are more likely to be found in low-power positions and occupations than men, we may have been misled into assuming that observed differences in the way men and women negotiate due to gender when, in fact, they result from status and power differences.

If contextual factors such as situational power are indeed better predictors of negotiation behavior than gender, there are significant implications for both negotiation trainers and policymakers. For instance, women themselves would no longer be viewed as in need of "fixing." Instead, the practices that keep women in low-power and low-status roles in organizations and society at large would become the more legitimate focus of change. The possibility that contextual factors are more important than gender was examined by reviewing the existing literature on gender and power in negotiating and bargaining.

Scholars have offered four explanations for the origin of gender differences in negotiating behavior: gender-role socialization; situational power; gender and power combined; and "expectation states" theory.

The gender-role socialization explanation proposes that men and women will negotiate differently and be differentially successful because of the different behavioral expectations associated with their respective gender roles. The purest description of this perspective would be that, because women in U.S. society are expected to be nurturing and supportive, they should be softer, more cooperative negotiators than men. Because men are expected to be tough and task-oriented in our society, they should be harder, more competitive negotiators than women. Further, since cooperation is generally considered to be a dangerous tactic because it leaves one open to exploitation by one's opponent (e.g., Gifford 1989; Pruitt 1983), women should also be less successful negotiators than men. That is, it is assumed that cooperative women will be taken advantage of to a greater extent than competitive men.

As noted earlier, different researchers have drawn contradictory conclusions about the accuracy of the behavioral expectations associated with the gender-role socialization explanation, but most agree with the expectation concerning success.

The situational power explanation suggests that parties who have more power in a given situation, regardless of their gender, should be more competitive and successful negotiators than parties who have less power. This perspective was popularized by Rosabeth Kanter (1977) who argued that women behave the way any person in a low-power position would behave. Meeker and Weitzel-O'Neill (1977) also argued in the 1970s that women are not any more motivated to help others or to prefer harmony and equality of outcomes than men in conflict situations, but that they are forced to behave this way because of their lower status. Almost no one has examined the validity of this hypothesis for negotiation or bargaining situations.

The gender-plus-power explanation is based on the possibility that giving a person power may not eliminate the effects of his or her gender status (i.e., Fagenson 1990; Powell, Posner, and Schmidt 1984; Terborg 1977). According to this perspective, both the gender-role socialization and the situational power explanations are correct. Consequently, males who have a lot of power are expected to be extremely competitive and successful negotiators whereas women who have little power are expected to be extremely cooperative, but weak and unsuccessful. Men who have little power and women who have a lot of power are expected to be equivalent and intermediate in their competitiveness and success.

Finally, expectation states theory proposes that the effects of power and gender combine with each other, but differently under different circumstances. The specific explanation suggested by this theory is that, when men and women negotiate with each other, gender affects their power and hence, their behavior and outcomes. In particular, male gender is expected to enhance power and female gender is expected to detract from power in mixed-sex pairs.

This explanation is based on Berger's expectation states theory (Berger, Fisek, Norman, and Zelditch 1977). Expectation states theory proposes that status characteristics (i.e., gender) establish performance expectations in small group settings; thus, high-status individuals (i.e., men) are expected to be more competent than low-status individuals (i.e., women). Because of these expectations, high-status individuals do, in fact, initiate more; receive more positive reactions from others, and enjoy more influence. However, the theory argues that gender is activated as a status characteristic only in mixed-sex pairs because it is only in these pairs that gender differentiates the parties. In other words, a powerful woman who must negotiate with a man should have much more difficulty controlling the negotiation than a powerful man who negotiates with a woman. Gender is not expected to have any impact on the power of negotiators in same-sex pairs of negotiators. In other words, being a woman should not diminish your power when you face another woman nor should being a man enhance your power when you face another man.

REVIEWING THE LITERATURE

Support for these competing explanations about the origin of gender differences in negotiation behavior was examined by reviewing 34 research studies conducted since 1975 that have addressed the topic of gender differences in negotiation, conflict, or power. Only eight of these tested both gender and power and examined actual behavior rather than self-reported behavior. It is these eight studies that provided the data for this review (see Table 10.1 for a listing and brief description of the studies reviewed). Not all of these studies examined standard negotiation or bargaining situations. Nevertheless, each involved some kind of situation in which the parties had conflicting needs and desires and attempted to influence their own and their partner's outcomes.

In four of the eight studies examined, power emerged as the main explanatory variable. In one of these, gender emerged as a key explanatory variable as well. In the remaining four studies, power and gender affected each other, but in ways that are different from any of the four explanations offered earlier. No support was found for either the additive explanation or for the explanation derived from expectation states theory.

Among those studies in which power was the main explanatory factor (Dovidio, Ellyson, Keating, Heltman, and Brown 1988; Putnam and Jones 1982; Siderits, Johannsen, and Fadden 1985; Watson and Hoffman 1992), some supported the explanation as stated (i.e., that power breeds competitiveness and personally favorable outcomes), but others showed contradictory results, particularly with respect to the tactics employed by powerful parties. Among the expected results, power led to such behavior as: greater visual dominance; more expressions of overt hostility toward one's opponents; greater feelings of competitiveness, power, and control; greater expectations of cooperation from one's opponents; greater satisfaction with the outcome of negotiation; and a stronger belief that one had been successful.

However, in one of the studies (Putnam and Jones 1982), powerful parties were found to engage in more defensive than offensive strategies (retractions and accommodations as opposed to threats, rejections, or attacking arguments). In another study (Watson and Hoffman 1992), powerful parties were found to engage in problem-solving rather than competitive tactics. In this latter instance, the more powerful parties were also less successful than the less powerful parties (according to the experimenters' definition of success) although they believed they had been more successful than their less powerful opponents. Thus, while power generally led to greater dominance, competitiveness, and success, it did not necessarily always do so. Perhaps there are circumstances in which strong situational power leads parties to believe that dominant coercive strategies are unnecessary.

Very few results were found that were due strictly to gender, as mentioned earlier, and none of the gender effects concerned tactical behaviors or outcomes. However, in one study (Watson and Hoffman 1992) managerial women reported less self-confidence than managerial men before they took part in a simulated negotiation; less satisfaction with themselves after the negotiation; and the belief that they had been less successful than men, even though this was not true based on the experimenters' definition of success.

Five of the eight studies reviewed found some support for the idea that gender and power affect each other, although the results do not fit any of the explanations that could be derived from existing theory. Among these five studies, two found that having strong situational power leads men, but not women, to behave in what the researchers labeled as more competitive ways (Kravitz and Iwaniszek 1984; Scudder 1988). Competitiveness consisted of winning better payoffs for oneself in one study and of issuing bottom-line, take-it-or-leave-it statements in the other.

Table 10.1 Description of the Studies Reviewed

	Subject Population[1]	Group Composition[2]	Task	Source of Power	Dependent Variable	Hypothesis Supported[3]
Dovidio et al., 1988	U	MS	Reach agreement on three discussion questions	Expert and reward power	Visual dominance	P
Kravitz and Iwaniszek, 1984	U	SS	Coalition formation	Number of votes and alternatives	Payoff differences	G × P
Molm, 1986	U	SS & MS	Prisoner's dilemma	Control over own outcomes	Power usage	G × P
Putnam and Jones, 1982	G/U	SS & MS	Labor–management roleplay	Role	Bargainer tactics	P
Scudder, 1988	U	SS	Buyer–seller game	Role	Tactics and profit	G × P
Siderits et al., 1985	U	MS	Melian	Role	Expressions of hostility	P
Stake and Stake, 1979	U	MS	Dialogues Reach agreement on discussion task	Performance-related self-esteem	Change in opinion	G × P
Watson and Hoffman, 1992	M	SS & MS	Negotiation roleplay	Role	Feelings, behavior, and outcomes	P, G

[1] U = undergraduates   G = graduate students   M = Managers.

[2] SS = same sex   MS = mixed sex.

[3] P = situational power   G = gender   G × P = gender × power interaction.

A third study found the reverse effect (Stake and Stake 1979). That is, power in the form of performance-related self-esteem increased women's dominating behavior (i.e., number of opinions given and disagreements stated) but not men's. The results from this study are questionable, however, because to match men and women, the authors were forced to include a group of women with unusually high self-esteem and a group of men with unusually low self-esteem scores.

The remaining two studies found that powerlessness affected men differently than women (Molm 1986; Watson and Hoffman 1992). Men in low-power situations were found to adopt an approach that has been labeled "soft competition" by some researchers (i.e., Savage, Blair, and Sorenson 1989) whereas women did not. Men's approach to dealing with powerlessness consisted of stating their position and then offering logical reasons to support it.

Women's approach to powerlessness depended upon the gender of their opponents according to the results of one study (Watson and Hoffman 1992). Surprisingly, when low-power women faced a male opponent in this study, they were likely to adopt the highly competitive tactic of threatening. This result is surprising in part because it is completely contrary to the predictions of expectation states theory. The supposedly weakest participants (low-power women facing high-power men) were not expected to use the toughest tactics. Yet they did and they reported feeling somewhat more powerful and satisfied with themselves than other women in that study. Women's threatening behavior is also surprising because such an aggressive approach is generally considered dangerous and unacceptable for low-power parties. Yet it worked for the low-power women in Watson and Hoffman's (1992) study.

Another study (Molm 1986) also found that gender and power combined in ways that refuted expectation states theory. In this instance, female/female pairs of bargainers were less likely to engage in a tit-for-tat strategy than male/male pairs. Expectation-states theory predicts no gender differences in same-sex pairs. This finding is noteworthy because the tit-for-tat strategy has been found to be the best one to ensure positive, joint, long-term outcomes in mixed-motive situations. Thus, women may be less likely to settle on a cooperative pattern when they bargain with another woman than will men when they bargain with another man.

CONCLUSIONS AND IMPLICATIONS

This review yields several findings about situational power and gender that stand out as particularly noteworthy. First, and perhaps most important, situational power appears to be a better predictor of negotiator behavior and outcomes than does gender. Nevertheless, it is also clear that the impact of gender cannot be ignored. Although gender did not affect tactical behavior or outcomes in any of the studies reviewed, it did lead to differences in negotiators' confidence in one study. Further, gender interacted with situational power and other contextual factors in ways that did affect behavior and outcomes.

Power generally leads to greater dominance, competitiveness, and success for both genders. On the one hand, this indicates that women are not softer or less effective negotiators than men are, as was suggested in the 1960s and early 1970s. Given a reasonable degree of situational power, women are likely to be just as oriented toward beating their opponents as men are, and just as successful at doing so. Thus, there is no reason to mistrust women's negotiation abilities. They are capable of negotiating as competitively and successfully as men.

On the other hand, this finding also implies that women are not nicer negotiators than men are. Women are not necessarily any more fair-minded or compassionate, despite what earlier research and some current feminist writers would have us believe. Thus, if we wish to encourage more humane behavior on the part of the powerful toward the powerless, the answer is not simply to give women a chance to rule, but to change the rules governing how powerful people should behave.

The reader should not construe the assertions of the previous paragraph as an argument against empowering women, but rather as an argument against doing so because women will magically change the way those in power behave. It should not be necessary to justify women's empowerment on the grounds that they are somehow "better" people in general than are men. This is an unfair burden to place on women and an implied and equally unfair condemnation of men.

Interestingly, power did not always led to dominating, selfish behavior in the studies reviewed. In several studies, the more powerful parties to a negotiation chose less threatening approaches than their lower-power opponents. In one of these studies, the subjects were business students playing the role of management in a labor–management negotiation and in the other, the participants were practicing managers taking part in a simulated negotiation. While one might conclude that it was the simulated nature of these negotiations that led high-power parties to behave less aggressively, most of the negotiation literature has been based on simulations and role-play exercises, and this literature generally shows that power leads to dominance and aggression.

Another possibility is that being a manager or role-playing a manager leads to different uses of power than typically occur when undergraduates negotiate with other undergraduates as peers. The managerial role carries with it legitimate power which may discourage the use of coercion since subordinates are expected to know they are supposed to capitulate. In addition, in the studies that used managers or students role-playing managers (Putnam and Jones 1982; Watson and Hoffman 1992), the subjects were negotiating with parties from the same organization. Under such circumstances, they may have perceived the conflict within a more cooperative framework and may have even assumed they were responsible for creating such a cooperative framework for the good of the larger organization. These are intriguing questions that merit further research. Since much of the negotiation and conflict management literature is built on studies of undergraduates, possible limits to the generalizability of this work need to be explored.

As noted earlier, gender by itself had little impact on the behavior or outcomes of negotiators in the studies reviewed, but it did affect participants' feelings about negotiating in one of the studies. Managerial women reported significantly less confidence about negotiating than managerial men, and disparaged their success as negotiators more than men even though they had behaved no differently and had been no less successful than the men in their negotiations. This is a significant finding since women's concerns and negative self-evaluations may cause them to shy away from negotiations needlessly and inappropriately. Further, gender interacted with power and with opponent's gender in some unanticipated ways. Several studies showed that men became more aggressive when they had power and more conciliatory when they did not. Women's reactions were more variable and more likely to be dictated by additional contextual factors. In particular, women became highly aggressive when they were powerless against a male opponent. Powerful women were less willing or able to develop a cooperative tit-for-tat strategy when they negotiated with another woman than powerful men were with male opponents. This limited the ability of female/female pairs to achieve cooperative, win/win solutions.

In general, the kinds of adjustments men made to power match the recommendations of current normative models of negotiation (e.g., Savage et al. 1989). Women's adjustments to power were sometimes contradictory to the recommendation of these models though their unconventional approaches sometimes worked for them.

Although power accounted for most negotiation behavior previously thought to be gender-related, the effects found for gender alone and in combination with power suggest that women face dilemmas when negotiating that men do not. Assuming positions of power and feeling comfortable about negotiating appear to be more problematic for women than for men. Additionally, women appear to be particularly sensitive to the gender of their opponents. When their opponents are high-power males, women seem to engage in risky levels of aggressiveness. When their opponents are low-power women, they seem unable or unwilling to find a cooperative give-and-take approach. Each of these areas needs to be researched more fully so that informed recommendations can be developed for women and for men who negotiate with women.

It is important to bear in mind that the prescriptions for successful negotiating are more ambiguous for women than they are for men. The norms that guide competitive, win/lose negotiating were developed by men for men, and they are, therefore, compatible with stereotypical gender norms for men. These norms, however, are not compatible with gender norms for women. Nor can women be expected simply to adopt behaviors that are considered inappropriate for them. My own research (Korabik, Baril, and Watson 1993; Watson 1988), as well as that of others, has shown that both men and women are viewed negatively when they behave in ways that are contrary to society's gender role expectations. Thus, even when it might be appropriate for women to behave competitively to protect their own interests in a negotiation, they are likely to incur much more negative reactions for doing this than men would.

I believe the answer for women may turn out to be that they should learn the skills of principled negotiating (Fisher and Ury 1981). These authors teach negotiators how to understand and protect their own interests while maintaining a positive relationship with the other party. While both men and women would benefit from learning the skills Fisher and Ury recommend, women may need these skills more than men because of the conflicting expectations they face when negotiating. Whereas men may be able to get away with competitive tactics some of the time, women may not.

Clearly, more research on the issues raised in this review is needed. Although the hypothesis that situational power accounts for assumed gender differences was first proposed nearly twenty years ago, almost no one has sought to test it. Nevertheless, as this review shows, the hypothesis has merit. Furthermore, little thought has been given to the possible interactions between gender and contextual variables such as situational power.

It seems we have been content to restrict our research to overly simplistic hypotheses and have, therefore, failed to focus on the factors that are the more powerful determinants of negotiator behavior and outcomes. The interactive effects of gender, power, and opponent's gender that are revealed through this review, though only suggestive given the limited number of studies, point the way toward more meaningful avenues for future research concerning the role of gender in negotiation and bargaining.

REFERENCES

Bartos, O. J. 1970. Determinants and consequences of toughness. *The structure of conflict*, ed. P. Swingle. New York: Academic Press.

Berger, J., M. H. Fisek, R. Z. Norman, and M. Zelditch, Jr. 1977. *Status characteristics and social interaction: An expectation states approach.* New York: Elsevier.

Caplan, P. J., G. M. MacPherson, and P. Tobin. 1985. Do sex-related differences in spatial ability exist? *American Psychologist* 40: 786–799.

Caplow, T. 1968. *Two against one: Coalition in triads.* Englewood Cliffs, N.J.: Prentice-Hall.

Dovidio, J. F., S. L. Ellyson, C. F. Keating, K. Heltman, and C. E. Brown. 1988. The relationship of social power to visual displays of dominance between men and women. *Journal of Personality and Social Psychology* 54(2): 233–242.

Fagenson, E. A. 1990. Perceived masculine and feminine attributes examined as a function of individuals' sex and level in the organizational power hierarchy: A test of four theoretical perspectives. *Journal of applied Psychology* 75(2): 204–211.

Fisher, R. and W. L. Ury. 1981. *Getting to YES: Negotiating agreement without giving in.* Boston: Houghton Mifflin.

French, J. R. P., Jr., and B. Raven. 1960. The bases of power. In *Group dynamics*, ed. D. Cartwright and A. F. Zander. Evanston, Ill.: Row, Peterson.

Friedman, W. J., A. B. Robinson, and B. L. Friedman. 1987. Sex differences in moral judgment? *Psychology of Women Quarterly* 11: 37–46.

Gifford, D. G. 1989. *Legal negotiation: Theory and practice.* St. Paul, Minn.: West Publishing.

Gilligan, C. 1982. *In a different voice.* Cambridge, Mass.: Harvard University Press.

Hyde, J. S. and M. C. Linn. 1988. Gender differences in verbal ability: A meta-analysis. *Psychological Bulletin* 104: 53–69.

Hyde, J. S., E. Fennema, and S. Lamon. 1990. Gender differences in mathematics performance: A meta-analysis. *Psychological Bulletin* 107: 139–155.

Jones, E. E. and R. E. Nisbett. 1976. The actor and the observer: Divergent perceptions of the causes of behavior. In *Contemporary topics in social psychology*, eds. J. W. Thibaut, J. T. Spencer, and R. C. Carson. Morristown, N.J.: General Learning Press.

Kanter, R. 1977. *Men and women of the corporation.* New York: Basic Books.

Kelley, H. H. 1965. Experimental studies of threats in interpersonal negotiations. *Journal of Conflict Resolution* 9: 79–105.

Korabik, K., G. Baril, and C. Watson. 1993. Managers' conflict management style and leadership effectiveness: The moderating effects of gender. *Sex Roles* 29(5/6): 407–422.

Kravitz, D. and J. Iwaniszek. 1984. Number of coalitions and resources as sources of power in coalition bargaining. *Journal of Personality and Social Psychology* 47(3): 534–548.

Meeker, B. F. and P. A. Weitzel-O'Neill. 1977. Sex roles and interpersonal behavior in task-oriented groups. *American Sociological Review* 42: 91–105.

Milgram, S. 1963. Behavioral study of obedience. *Journal of Abnormal and Social Psychology* 67: 371–378.

Mintzberg, H. 1983. *Power in and around organizations.* Englewood Cliffs, N.J.: Prentice-Hall.

Molm, L. D. 1986. Gender, power, and legitimation: A test of three theories. *American Journal of Sociology* 91(6): 1356–1386.

Pfeffer, J. 1981. *Power in organizations.* Marshfield, Mass.: Pitman.

Powell, G. N. 1990. One more time: Do female and male managers differ? *Academy of Management Executive* 4(3): 68–76.

Powell, G. N., B. Z. Posner, and W. H. Schmidt. 1984. Sex effects in managerial value systems. *Human Relations* 37: 909–921.

Pruitt, D. 1983. Strategic choice in negotiation. *American Behavioral Scientist* 27(2): 167–194.

Putnam, L. L. and T. S. Jones. 1982. Reciprocity in negotiations: An analysis of bargaining interaction. *Communication Monographs* 49(3): 171–191.

Rosener, J. B. 1990. Ways women lead. *Harvard Business Review* November–December: 119–125.

Rapport, A. and A. M. Chammah. 1965. *Prisoner's dilemma.* Ann Arbor: University of Michigan Press.

Rubin, J. Z. and B. R. Brown. 1975. *The social psychology of bargaining and negotiation.* New York: Academic Press.

Savage, G. T., J. D. Blair, and R. L. Sorenson. 1989. Consider both relationships and substance when negotiating strategically. *Academy of Management Executive* 3(1): 37–48.

Scudder, J. N. 1988. The influence of power upon powerful speech: A social-exchange perspective. *Communication Research Reports* 5(2): 140–145.

Siderits, M. A., W. J. Johannsen, and T. F. Fadden. 1985. Gender, role, and power: A content analysis of speech. *Psychology of Women Quarterly* 9(4): 439–450.

Stake, J. E. and Stake, M. N. 1979. Performance-self-esteem and dominance behavior in mixed-sex dyads. *Journal of Personality* 47: 71–84.

Tavris, C. 1992. *The mismeasure of woman.* New York: Simon & Schuster.

Tedeschi, J. T., B. R. Schlenker, and T. W. Bonoma. 1973. *Conflict, power, and games: The experimental study of interpersonal relations.* Chicago: Aldine.

Terborg, J. 1977. Women in management: A research review. *Journal of Applied Psychology* 62: 647–664.

Watson, C. 1988. When a woman is the boss: Dilemmas in taking charge. *Group and Organization Studies* 13(2): 163–181.

Watson, C. and L. R. Hoffman. 1992. An examination of the impact of gender and power on managers' negotiation behavior and outcomes. Paper presented at the Annual Meeting of the Academy of Management, Las Vegas, Nev.

GENDER AND THE SHADOW NEGOTIATION[1]

DEBORAH M. KOLB

From C90 Insights, Briefing Note 3 # (1998) Boston, MA: Center for
Gender in Organizations, Simmons School of Management

Being able to deal with conflict and negotiate effectively is a requirement for survival in the flatter and more fluid organizations of today. Conflict is nothing new
in organizations. In the past, however, it was channeled into hierarchical structures,
formal rules and procedures, ideologies of cooperation, and into the responsibilities of certain individuals, such as senior managers. In today's organizations, where
responsibility inevitably exceeds authority to get things done, we must negotiate to
achieve our objectives. Staff are operating more in teams and collaborative partnerships, functions are increasingly networked both internally and externally, and,
with the global nature of organizations, staff are often working in culturally and
gender-diverse environments. In these more fluid systems, negotiations are constantly being carried out with managers, team members, stakeholders, colleagues,
and strategic partners over resources, authority, commitments, schedules, time,
products, and services. We negotiate to improve performance, solve problems,
strive for equity and fairness, and foster learning and innovation.

APPROACHES

Negotiation is a decision-making process involving two or more people who have
issues over which they disagree and/or resources to allocate and who have interests both in solving mutual problems and doing well for themselves. That process
can resemble the prototypical market transaction where parties exclusively pursue
their individual gain at the expense of the other. For example, I insist on a part-
time schedule to accommodate my family needs and my boss rejects my proposal.
I threaten to quit and he gives in. Or, the process can be one where parties pursue
mutual gain, looking to *expand the pie*, so that both can obtain more of what each
wants. I figure out what I need in dealing with my family issues and my boss figures
out what her needs are with respect to the organization. Together we come up with
a plan in which I go on a part-time schedule but agree to provisions that will ensure
that my project continues to achieve good progress.

Mutual gains negotiations, or collaborative problem-solving, is a creative way to negotiate in today's organizations. Mutual gains negotiations are based on the premise (and observation) that it is possible, using a certain kind of problem-solving process, to transform win/lose situations into ones where there are mutual gains. The way to do that is to focus on interests, not positions, and then to be creative in searching for options that meet these interests. The process requires some open sharing of interests and then a search for agreements that meet both parties' needs. Based on an understanding of differences in interests and concerns, it is possible to make tradeoffs and package agreements that benefit both parties.

SHADOW NEGOTIATION

In the abstract, mutual gains negotiations are easy; you can often figure out creative options. But problem-solving does not take place in a vacuum. You have to manage the social as well as the substantive part of the negotiation. At the same time as you are negotiating over the issues and considering the kinds of deals that you can make, another negotiation is taking place in tandem. It is where negotiators are really negotiating about how they will negotiate even though they do not talk about it directly. This is what we call the shadow negotiation.

The shadow negotiation is where expectations and relationships are created. If, in the substantive negotiation, we are trading proposals back and forth to make a deal, in the shadow negotiations, we are bargaining over our relationship.

We are negotiating over whose needs and interests are more important, who should count more. Working this part of the shadow negotiation requires that both negotiators feel empowered, in a good position to effectively press for their interests and needs. Something else is also going on in the shadow negotiation. To make a good deal, there needs to be mutual collaboration. To build collaboration requires the skills of connection.

It is in the shadow negotiation, where we empower ourselves and try to get connected, that gender can come into play. It can come into play at three levels:

- at the *personal* level in terms of how we see ourselves as negotiators;
- at the *expectational* level where others set the context for our action;
- at the *situational* level, where we deal with inequities of power and position.

The following story illustrates how gender enters into the shadow negotiation.

Caroline and George are physicians in a small medical center. They share weekend and evening shifts and call schedules. Recently George announced that he had planned a fishing trip and it was booked for the last week in June. Caroline tells him that it is impossible because that is the week she has promised to move her mother from her house into an apartment. George claims that he cannot change his plans as his friends are counting on him. Why, he wonders, can't Caroline change the week her mother moves. Caroline says she feels terrible, but she can't do it because her mother's apartment won't be ready until the first and she has to be out of her house by then. George suggests that Caroline's mother could stay with her for the week. Caroline rejects this idea and proposes a compromise. They could split the week. She could move her mother over the weekend, it would be hard, but then George could leave on Monday. George rejects the idea.

The two go round and round, each holding out for the week. George gets increasingly angry and beings to yell at Caroline. Upset, she starts to waiver. She hates it when George loses his temper. To cut off the growing hostility, she says she'll think about it. She not only thinks about it; she spends a sleepless night worrying. She decides that she could have her mother stay with her for the week, although it wouldn't be pleasant for either of them. But if she agrees to do it, she wants some compensation in return. Summer is coming, and she decides to trade first choice on the schedule for July and August. That seems fair to her.

The next day Caroline tells George he can have the week (he smiles). But when she tells him that in return she wants first call on the summer schedule, George stops smiling. He rejects the idea, claiming that the call schedule has nothing to do with vacation. He claims since she is willing to give up the week, she really doesn't need it. Caroline holds firm; if she can't have her choice on the schedule, he can't have the week of vacation.

GENDER DIMENSION

What's going on here? Clearly, this is a problem that could be solved in a mutual gains fashion. But that is not the issue. The essence of the problem is that Caroline can not get George to negotiate with her. Although George and Caroline are talking about how to deal with the vacation, which is the substantive issue, it is in the shadow negotiation, where gender is being enacted, that they have the problem.

Gender plays out in a number of ways in this negotiation. First, it plays out at the *personal* level. This reflects how much a negotiator identifies with the masculine or feminine view of themselves. George clearly exemplifies what we understand to be a masculine view of a negotiator. He is exclusively focused on his own interests. Caroline, on the other hand, acts in more prototypic feminine way. She cares about her own needs, but also takes responsibility for George and how he feels. It is Caroline, not George, who worries that they can not agree. It is Caroline who, as a result, takes the burden for coming up with solutions that George rejects. When negotiators, either a man or a woman, take the feminine, caring position in a negotiation, they can be at a disadvantage if the other acts only in their own interest. While caring and concern are important, in a situation like Caroline and George, they can lead to a woman's exploitation. Ironically, Caroline's efforts to accommodate George signal to him that she will not hold out for the vacation week. In a way her flexibility feeds his intransigence and makes it even more likely that she'll be the one to give in.

Gender can also play out at the level of *expectations*. Even though people behave in all kinds of ways, we have different expectations about how men and women are supposed to negotiate. We interpret their actions differently: he is aggressive and results-oriented, she is ruthless. He is rational and objective, she is calculating and manipulative. Further, we expect men to be more self-interested and women to be more caring and supportive, perhaps even to sacrifice their own interests for others. We criticize her if she does not. And, of course, that is what is happening with George and Caroline. He expects her to be the concerned one just as she expects him not to be. And these expectations are not benign. He gets angry when she does not give way. Because of these expectations, Caroline has to work harder to get George to take some responsibility for solving the problem.

Finally, the *situations* we negotiate in can also trigger gender effects. Our authority and influence in negotiations can come from many sources, but position in social structures is important. All negotiations take place in organizations that presuppose a set of hierarchical relationships that tend to be gender based. In the medical setting in which George and Caroline negotiate, men tend to hold more dominant positions. Thus, in this culture, men are deemed to be more powerful than women, even though, in this particular situation, George and Caroline are more or less equals. Several gender implications derive from this. Experience in low power positions is disempowering and can explain why people who lack power fail to recognize negotiation possibilities. Second, it suggests why Caroline may have difficulty getting George to negotiate with her – simply in this organizational culture, where he is both a physician and a man, he does not feel he has to. From a situational perspective, gender relations help us appreciate the challenge of negotiating when there are structural and/or symbolic power differentials.

What was the outcome?

George decided to bluff. He proposed a coin toss because he thought Caroline would rather talk things out than leave it to chance. But she agreed. They tossed a coin and she won. But then she felt terrible and asked him to give her a hug to show he forgave her. He did hug her, but several weeks later, when one of George's friends had a business conflict and the fishing trip was canceled, he never told her.

CHALLENGES

In the shadow negotiations, gender is enacted in the relational by-play. Although Caroline and George are talking about how to deal with the vacation, how they see each other influences how they will deal with the issues. Their problem was in the shadow negotiation.

In these shadow negotiations, there are two important challenges negotiators face. One relates to the tools you use to empower yourself so that you are in a position where you can effectively advocate for what you want and need. Caroline was not in that position. She could not get George to listen to her – she could not get him to the table. Empowering yourself involves the moves you make to enhance your situation and influence the other party.

There are three steps to empowering yourself.

- *You need to prepare yourself.* That means understanding how you get in your own way – what undermines your efficacy. Many of us focus on our own weaknesses and attribute strength and good position to our partners. When you empower yourself, you take deliberate steps to test those assumptions so that you can go into the negotiation knowing more or less where you stand. By taking sole responsibility for the problem, Caroline reinforced George's impression that she would be the accommodating one. As a result, her efforts at problem-solving are interpreted by him as signals that she will give him what he wants. Caroline must recognize the implication of her actions if she is to be more effective.
- *You need to create incentives for the other side to negotiate with you and take your interests and needs seriously.* That involves using what influence you have to

change the others' assessment of who will make concessions and how great they will be. Caroline has ceded that ground to George. She needs to exert some pressure to get him to reconsider.

- *You need to keep yourself in an empowered position.* Once into the negotiations, you may find that the other side tries to put you at a disadvantage – making light of your proposals, questioning your competence, saying something personal. To stay empowered during the negotiation requires that you recognize these moves so that you can come back from attempts to put you down.

The second challenge is to get connected to the other side so that you can work together on the problem. Caroline really wanted George to work with her in figuring out what to do. If she wants him to collaborate with her, she needs to *situate* him in such a way that he wants to participate with her to come up with solutions. So if empowering herself is meant to increase the pressure on him, connection is used to bring him into the process. Connection also has three dimensions.

- *Connection begins with a stance toward your negotiating partner.* It means being prepared to recognize that you cannot know what they are really thinking and feeling. You will need to open up a dialogue so that both parties can talk about what they want and need.
- *Connection continues with actions you take to make the other side feel that you understand and respect their interests and concerns.* If they feel appreciated and heard, they are more likely to want to work with you.
- *Connection involves what you can do to create a context for mutual problem solving.* Structuring the agenda so that people are involved, keeping the dialogue going, and working to get people to own problems together are connected actions in the shadow negotiation that make collaborative problem-solving possible.

Using her skills of connection in concert with the tools of empowerment, Caroline could bring George into the dialogue with her to find a way out of the scheduling conflict. She might increase the pressure first by suggesting that they invite the Center Director to join their discussions. An implied threat, this might create an incentive for George to reconsider his continued rejections of her offers. He does not want to be seen by the boss as a person who cannot work out a vacation schedule. But she could use this move differently. Rather than an implied threat, she could suggest it casually, but then reject it and move the conversation in a different direction. First, she might state the obvious problem – she is making all the suggestions. There has to be some reciprocity and she asks for it. But she could do more. George and Caroline need an opening so that they can talk about what is getting in the way of their dealing with the issue. She might pick up on how upset George is and give him a chance to respond. What she hopes is that by opening up the dialogue, George will start to negotiate with her about the schedule.

Collaborative problem solving is a good way to deal with conflicts in organizations. But George and Caroline's dismissive actions towards each other, actions that reflect gendered assumptions in the shadow negotiation, interfered with their ability to solve a pretty simple problem. You can only have productive problem-solving or mutual gains negotiations when all parties recognize their interdependent need to deal with each other. If we want to use negotiations to solve problems creatively, empowerment and connection need to be managed together in the shadow negotiations.

NOTE

1 The ideas in this article are based on Deborah Kolb and Judith Williams, *When Women Negotiate: Empowering Ourselves, Connecting with Others,* (New York: Simon and Schuster, 1999).

RETHINKING NEGOTIATION: FEMINIST VIEWS OF COMMUNICATION AND EXCHANGE

LINDA L. PUTNAM AND DEBORAH M. KOLB

From P. Buzzanell (ed.) (2000) *Rethinking Organizational and Managerial Communication from Feminist Perspectives*, Thousand Oaks, CA: Sage.

One type of social interaction that has become an essential skill for all walks of life is negotiation. . . . [It] is also a special type of social interaction, one that differs from group decision making (Putnam & Roloff, 1992). These differences stem from the characteristics of perceived incompatibility, interdependence between parties, and simultaneous cooperative and competitive relationships. Social interactions in traditional negotiations, then, rely on exchanges of proposals and counterproposals, making arguments for preferred outcomes, and developing strategies and tactics to obtain desired ends.

These assumptions and characteristics contribute to the conception of bargaining as a "scripted activity" (O'Connor & Adams, 1996). That is, individuals enter a negotiation with a prototype of standard actions. These scripted activities include making offers, defending and refuting positions, discussing issues, exchanging compromises, and reaching an agreement. In general, then, people share a conceptual representation that negotiation is competitive and individualistic, is defined by trades or exchanges, and often results in an impasse. Even young children learn this script and are skilled at taking positions and engaging in tradeoffs to reach a settlement (Sheldon, 1992; Sheldon & Johnson, 1994).

This chapter undertakes a revision of negotiation as a scripted social interaction. In particular, we adopt a feminist perspective to review and critique traditional models of negotiation by focusing on "exchange" as the central element of bargaining. Through an examination of the way that exchange underlies the essence of negotiation, the goals and outcomes, the nature of relationships, and the processes, we set forth an alternative model – one rooted in feminist assumptions of connectedness and co-construction of the process. We contend that, in traditional approaches to negotiation, relationship and connection disappear as the fundamental ways in which people see and define their situations. By focusing on trades, negotiation is concerned with getting to settlements rather than understanding situations. Communication within the traditional model typically serves as information exchange and the execution of bargaining tactics to foster the pursuit of a settlement.

We begin this chapter with an overview of the traditional models of negotiation and the role of exchange in these approaches. Then we present feminist critiques of exchange and position our analysis within this literature. The latter part of the chapter sets up the rudimentary elements of an alternative model by comparing the essence, goals and outcomes, relationships, and processes of this perspective with a prototype of the traditional models. We use a negotiation case to exemplify these comparisons. This chapter concludes with a summary and discussion of the situations in which this alternative might be used as a viable option to traditional approaches to negotiation.

TRADITIONAL MODELS OF NEGOTIATION

Traditional studies in negotiation fall into the arena known as negotiation analysis. This work is based on the belief that descriptions of negotiation grounded in empirical research can assist bargainers in anticipating the other side's behaviors. Negotiation analysts provide prescriptive or normative advice based on projections of how the other party is likely to behave (Sebenius, 1992).

This traditional research emanates from three general types of models: game theory, distributive and integrative bargaining, and principled negotiation. Game theory draws from economic principles and centers on maximizing gains, minimizing losses, assessing utilities of options, and reaching optimal outcomes. By applying economic rationality to decision making, this approach focuses on ascertaining alternative courses of action and shaping rational choice (Luce & Raiffa, 1957; Raiffa, 1982).

Distributive and integrative models of negotiation draw from and react to notions of economic rationality. Distributive negotiation, also called zero-sum bargaining, concentrates on maximizing individual payoffs in situations in which one person's gain is the other person's loss. Negotiators typically set target points for what each person wants and resistance points for each individual's bottom line. . . . Negotiation as a distributive process, then, is primarily a form of conflict management aimed at compromise. Successful negotiators start high, concede slowly, exaggerate the value of concessions, minimize the other party's concessions, conceal information, argue forcefully, and capture more of the bargaining zone (Lax & Sebenius, 1986).

In contrast, an integrative approach to negotiation presumes that the goals of the parties are not mutually exclusive; hence, it is possible for participants to achieve joint gains. Thus, through negotiation, individuals find ways to combine their diverse goals into a collective effort (Lewicki & Litterer, 1985). Parties start from preset positions, but through sharing information and creative problem solving, they make trades based on complementary interests that increase the size of joint gains for both individuals (Pruitt, 1981, 1983). [. . .]

Principled negotiation draws from integrative bargaining and sets forth guidelines for reaching joint gain or win-win settlements. Critical of positional bargaining that typifies the distributive process, principled negotiation urges bargainers to focus on interests, not positions; to separate people from the problem; to invent options for mutual gain; and to use objective criteria to reach settlements (Fisher, Ury, & Patton, 1991). Popular in practice, this perspective has revamped the training of negotiators and spawned major programs on mutual gains bargaining (Cutcher-Gershenfeld, 1994; Cutcher-Gershenfeld, McKersie, & Walton, 1995). However, there are barriers to reaching integrative agreements, including overconfidence about obtaining desired outcomes, framing positive and negative outcomes differently, and reliance on processes rooted in splitting the pie (Neale & Bazerman, 1991). On the prescriptive level, researchers continue to offer advice based on the management of exchanges. . . .

Each of these perspectives embraces exchange as the essence of negotiation. Gulliver (1979) even defines bargaining as "the presentation and exchange of specific proposals for terms of agreement on issues" (p. 71). In the distributive approach, the exchange of proposals is typically viewed as the vehicle or recommended strategy for settling within the bargaining zone. Exchange begins with both parties stating their asking prices or initial offers. Opening offers set the tone for trading concessions, in which the bargainers move closer to each other by exchanging incremental moves.

Exchange is also the essence of integrative and principled negotiation. In this approach, bargainers exchange information about their needs, ways of reaching a settlement, and criteria for assessing options. Exchange becomes the primary way that parties create value and discover arenas for joint gain (Lax & Sebenius, 1986). In integrative negotiation, exchange is the means through which bargainers learn and alter their perceptions about options available for joint gain (Lewicki & Litterer, 1985).

In each of these three models, exchange is the modus operandi and the very heart of negotiation (Lewicki & Litterer, 1985). It is the means by which bargainers gain a competitive edge, the way the process is enacted, the basis for reaching outcomes, and the way in which bargainers learn about the options available to them (Thompson, 1998).

EXCHANGE AND NEGOTIATION AS GENDERED ACTIVITIES

Exchange, as it functions in these three perspectives, is a gendered activity. What does it mean to say that a particular practice like exchange is gendered? A practice is seen as gendered if its attributes are more commonly associated with one gender than the other, thus making dimensions linked to the other gender less valued. Parenting, for example, entails nurturance and the giving of care, practices linked to mothering. Acts of fathering, then, often remain hidden and devalued in the process. In this chapter, we contend that both exchange and negotiation are gendered activities because of the ways that trades grow out of individualistic needs, become reduced to commodities, and emerge as instrumental activities that define the nature of outcomes.

Other feminist scholars have presented critiques of social exchange (Howard & Hollander, 1997), exchange theory (Hartsock, 1985), and utility comparisons (Ferber & Nelson, 1993; Strober, 1994). Our chapter draws from these critiques but differs from them in several important ways. First, we view exchange as the essence of the negotiation process; hence, exchange occurs within and aids in defining a particular activity, bargaining. Second, our critique of exchange in negotiations is nested in social relations rather than in the marketplace as an institution

(Hartsock, 1985). Moreover, unlike Hartsock, who adopts a feminist standpoint view, our critique and reframing of exchange does not grow out of an essentialist view of women's activity or the positioning of exchange as a materialistic phenomenon. By analyzing the taken-for-granted oppositions embedded in the traditional model of bargaining, we deconstruct negotiation as a gendered activity and set forth an alternative model, one rooted in co-construction rather than in exchange. Thus, we adopt a feminist poststructural stance to critique negotiation and offer an alternative model.

Negotiation, as we have previously argued, is also a gendered activity (Kolb & Putnam, 1997). It is gendered in that the qualities of effective bargainers (e.g., individuality and independence, competition, objectivity, analytic rationality, instrumentality, reasoning from universal principles, and strategic thinking) are linked to masculinity. Those attributes typically labeled as feminine (e.g., community, subjectivity, intuition, emotionality, expressiveness, reasoning from particular, and ad hoc thinking) are less valued. Negotiation is also gendered because of its emphasis on the framing of issues, the exercise of power in the legal system (Gray, 1994), and the way women lack voice and a sense of place at the bargaining table (Kolb & Coolidge, 1991). From a feminist standpoint, the experiences of women are typically excluded from negotiation theories and research. Furthermore, studies on gender and negotiation typically graft women onto the existing structure of bargaining (Gray, 1994).

This chapter extends this critique by focusing on the centrality of exchange in negotiation and by setting forth and alternative model – one rooted in feminist values and assumptions about social interaction. Just as economics forms the foundation for traditional perspectives, feminist thinking guides the theoretical development of an alternative model. This alternative is not simply a minor repair to existing perspectives or a change in style inserted into the dominant framework. Rather, it represents a shift in the fundamental thinking that underlies the nature and process of negotiation.

At first blush, the alternative approach may seem naive, simple, or unnatural when compared with the traditional model. However, any option that stands in comparison to the dominant discourse will likely appear deficient, devalued, and inadequate since the standards of traditional perspectives have shaped our very knowledge of a particular phenomenon. From a political stance, the traditional model surfaces as hegemonic. The temptation, when exposed to "difference," is to critique the alternative model using the assumptions and criteria of the traditional approach. Thus, a reader might criticize this alternative by arguing that "negotiators won't play by the rules or will use goals and strategies of the alternative model to exploit their opponent." This criticism, however, draws from and functions within the status quo. In many ways, it serves to reinstate the dominant stance of the traditional model rather than to critique its alternative. The alternative approach presented in this chapter must and should be critiqued, but it needs to be examined from a new set of criteria and questions, ones that develop from within and are consistent with the perspective advocated in this chapter.

This chapter, then, aims to recapture many of the features deemed absent or marginalized in traditional approaches to negotiation: namely, relationship, connection, understanding, and dialogue. We present this model as an option, not as a replacement or panacea for problems with existing approaches.

COMMODITY AS THE METAPHOR FOR EXCHANGE

Exchange, as noted previously, is the heart of negotiation. As the essence of bargaining, it not only influences the use of concessions, strategies, and tactics, but also underlies the fundamental image of the process. The dominant metaphor in understanding exchange is commodity (Howard & Hollander, 1997). Even though bargaining centers on symbolic costs and rewards, the commodity metaphor remains dominant in traditional views of negotiation. Social processes in bargaining are converted to economic language and assigned weights and measures; thus, the value of a particular offer is given a numerical weight that complies with patriarchal assumptions of objectivity (Howard & Hollander, 1997). Treating bargaining as the distribution of resources also reinforces the commodity metaphor by presuming clear divisions between costs and benefits (Hartsock, 1985). By conceiving of an exchange as a commodity, negotiators measure their achievements from the criteria of whether they made "a good deal." They simultaneously transfer aspects of their relationship such as emotional support, loyalty, and understanding to processes that can be exchanged; for example, "if you give me a good deal, I will be loyal to you" (Strober, 1994). The commodity metaphor, then, sets forth a language system of rewards, costs, resources, utilities, and trades that pervades the negotiation literature and is rooted in patriarchal values. This metaphor grounds interactions in material resources that shove identity and relationships into the shadow of negotiation (Kolb & Williams, 1999).

A feminist lens highlights elements of negotiation that are typically marginalized in or missing from exchange-based models, such as connectedness, collaboration, expressiveness, and equality. Table 12.1 contrasts the traditional and the

Table 12.1   A Comparison of Negotiation Models

Traditional Model	Alternative Model
Exchange	*Co-construction*
Trades	Mutual inquiry
Reciprocity	Integration
Goals	
Enlightened self-interest	Self-knowledge
Mutual gain	Mutual understanding
Outcomes	
Settlement	Transformation
Agreements	Jointly developed actions
Relationships	
Other as distant	Other as approachable
Interdependence through desired ends	Interdependence through connectedness
Extrinsic	Intrinsic
Instrumental	Expressive
Rational	Emotional
Process	
Proposals/counterproposals	Offering perspectives
Problem solving	Dialogue

alternative models based on four dimensions: the essence of the activity, the goals and outcomes of bargaining, the relationship of the negotiators, and the negotiation process.

A COMPARISON OF THE TRADITIONAL AND THE ALTERNATIVE PERSPECTIVES

In the traditional models, exchange and trades form the essence of the process. Both are limited by reducing the practice of bargaining to individual needs, the use of a commodity metaphor, and reliance on a language system of rewards and costs. Both of them privilege patriarchal values – namely, objectivity and materialism – as ways of depicting social processes. There is nothing inherent in the particulars of a negotiation that would suggest that one model of negotiation would dominate in a given situation. However, the processes that individuals experience in the bargaining entail vastly different approaches. The following example of a negotiation demonstrates how goals, relationships, and outcomes differ when we compare and contrast the traditional and the alternative models.

This negotiation deals with a fee arrangement between Strategic Information Technology Institute (SITI), a consulting firm, and Browne Associates. Karen Davenport, the director of programming at SITI, is in charge of the educational programs that the company offers to information technology professionals and general managers. SITI's basic 3-day educational seminar, Strategic Models in Distributive Systems, has been highly successful. On the basis of this success, Davenport has developed an advanced seminar for professionals who have completed the basic course. Since SITI does not have the resources to run these programs, the company subcontracts the marketing operations of the course to Browne Associates, a marketing and management firm.

Several years ago, Davenport's predecessor negotiated a successful contract for marketing the basic models course. Basically, Browne Associates incurs all the costs to advertise and manage the program, retains the revenues generated, and pays a guaranteed fixed fee to SITI for delivery of each course. The advanced course promises to be a good deal for both SITI and Browne Associates. SITI can use it to develop long-term relationships with companies and to enhance future consulting jobs. Having another course to market means additional revenue for Browne Associates.

Karen Davenport, SITI's programming director, and Sam Browne, the founder and president of Browne Associates, meet to negotiate the revenue-sharing arrangement for the advanced course. Although offering the advanced seminars appeals to both parties, the negotiations do not begin on an auspicious note. As Karen describes,

> We meet at our usual place for breakfast. Sam hands me his proposal. I am shocked. It is clear that the fee structure that Sam proposes is considerably less than the one that SITI receives for the basic course. SITI cannot afford to deliver the program with this loss of revenue.

The task of developing a mutually acceptable fee arrangement is the goal of the negotiation. Yet the kind of process that follows and the type of agreement reached are not predetermined. This negotiation could go in several different directions. It could follow the traditional distributive or integrative path, or it could be worked out through an alternative model of co-construction. We develop these alternatives by describing how the traditional approaches differ from the alternative model in enacting the essence of the process – exchange versus co-construction.

Exchange versus co-construction

As Table 12.1 illustrates, the traditional views of negotiation are rooted in practices of exchange, with trading, reciprocity, balance, equity, and transaction as the key characteristics. The alternative model, in contrast, is situated in co-construction, with mutual inquiry, promoting integration, blending proposals, facilitating equality, and producing collaboration as the central activities of bargaining. In traditional negotiation, progress toward a settlement is typically measured through frequent exchanges and the use of reciprocal concessions. The term *reciprocal concessions* refers to each party's response to his or her opponent's compromise with a counterproposal that concedes on issues. . . . As part of the unstated script of bargaining, reciprocity aims to equalize bargaining control. However, it often surfaces in actual negotiations as a strategy to promote one side's instrumental gain. . . .

As an alternative to exchange, co-construction occurs through connecting and creating mutual understanding. In co-construction, negotiators develop joint actions from mutual inquiry rather than trades. . . . Inquiry pushes parties to question commonly held definitions, to dispute the naming or labeling of issues, and to challenge the status quo by expanding and envisioning alternatives. Rather than using trades to generate joint gain, mutual inquiry encourages expansive thinking and envisions what might be in the future. . . . Attributes of connection and community linked to feminist thinking become central rather than marginal in the alternative model.

In the alternative mode, . . . negotiation interaction moves from deliberations about particulars (e.g., issues, positions, and facts) to discussions about the relational and organizational systems (e.g., definitions, background, lines of authority, and coherence within the system). Integration, then, becomes a way of moving negotiation "forward," not through stages or steps but through situating positions and issues within the larger context of the participants. [. . .]

Let's apply two different traditional models – distributive and exchange – and the alternative model to the example of Karen Davenport to consider how the three different routes might function differently for the same bargaining situation.

Traditional model 1: distributive exchange

In the distributive model, negotiation occurs through the exchange of a series of proposals and counterproposals. Sam claims that his costs for marketing and managing the advanced course are high and that he would be taking all the risks; therefore, he deserves a greater share of the revenues. Karen, who clearly wants this course, realizes that SITI needs Browne Associates more than it does the new course. She looks at Sam's numbers and makes a counterproposal by giving in on her initial revenue demand for SITI. Sam reinforces his position by arguing how much risk is involved and how he must cover the costs for these risks.

Karen reasons that, in the early years, no one imagined that the basic course would be so successful. The costs and the risks were equally high for both parties. Sam was getting a good deal from the basic course seminars. The new course would probably have the same life cycle, and Sam should continue to compromise on the proposed fee that he will have to pay SITI for the course delivery.

As the negotiation progresses, Karen argues that this program is going to be a real moneymaker for Browne Associates, just as the basic models course has been. She then proposes her bottom line – the same revenue arrangement that they currently have for the basic course. She implies that if SITI cannot get this arrangement, then the whole idea of an advanced course will be off the table. The negotiation proceeds with Karen and Sam going back and forth – Sam moaning about the costs and risks to Browne Associates and Karen claiming that Sam's company has minimal risks and has fared well from the original deal. In the end, both parties reach a compromise settlement. Sam pays a lower fee to SITI for the advanced course than he does for the basic seminar, but it is more than he originally proposed. Both parties feel dissatisfied with the process, and both agree to reopen the negotiation next year.

Traditional model 2: integrative exchange

In the integrative model, rather than working from positions, both parties try to decipher each other's interests and make proposals to dovetail these different interests. The integrative bargaining might proceed in this fashion. After Karen recovers from her shock regarding the low fee that Sam proposes to pay, she realizes that she needs to know more about Browne's interests in this arrangement and what is driving Sam's proposal. So Karen asks Sam why the revenue-sharing scheme for the new program is so skewed in his favor. His explanation is simple. The basic models course is a prerequisite for the advanced seminar; hence, Sam must recruit participants from the pool of applicants who have already taken the basic course, which is only about 100,000 people. His risks are high because he fears that the yield will be low, and his company will not sign on the numbers needed to make this venture profitable.

What catches Karen's attention is the risk profile that Sam presents. The new advanced program is more risky than the basic offering. If Sam's entire pool of possible attendees for the advanced course is limited, Browne Associates has no flexibility in marketing. The company could not recruit more attendees simply by sending out another direct-mail campaign. Instead, Browne Associates must target their marketing strategies to a select group.

Karen realizes that she needs an entirely different proposal and that she should not simply engage in a series of tradeoffs on the amount of revenue. She suggests that they meet later, after she has had time to develop alternatives. The next day she gives Sam an alternative proposal. Since Sam is concerned about the risk factor of the new program, Karen proposes that SITI's fee start low but ratchet up as the number of seminar participants increases. When enrollments reach the number that parallels those in the basic course, SITI will receive a higher fee per attendee than it currently does for the basic course. This prorated fee compensates for

SITI's revenue loss during the introductory period of the course when it is paid a low fee.

Although Sam responds positively to the idea, he believes that the incremental increase in fees is too steep. He prefers a slow phase-in of the higher fee. However, after tinkering with the revenues associated with the numbers, Karen and Sam reach an agreement. The settlement is a gain for both sides. By linking revenues to the number of attendees, the new course will move forward. Although the deal does not return as much revenue as Karen had hoped, particularly in the early stages, it will generate considerable cash flow in the future – for SITI and for Browne Associates.

An alternative model: mutual inquiry and co-construction

When Sam hands Karen his proposal, she is shocked. SITI is a major client for Browne, and their relationship has yielded other work for his company. It does not make sense that Sam would try to take advantage of SITI, even though the proposal looks like it. Karen says to herself, "I'm missing something here. We haven't talked enough. I don't understand what's going on. Sam is really upset and not just about the revenue. Maybe I do not fully understand his business."

Karen asks Sam to talk about his business in more detail. Sam tells Karen his situation. To recover his costs, including SITI's fixed fee, Browne needs to recruit 105 attendees for each advanced course. At the start of a mailing cycle, Sam can never predict the yield. If the numbers look low, he sends out more direct mail. Using a formula of 1 attendee per 1,000 mail announcements, Sam knows that he can fill the seminar if Browne sends out enough mail. Karen then realizes that she has never understood Sam's operations. His problems aren't just about the fee structure. In this new arrangement, he can't use a direct-mail campaign to fill the advanced course because he can approach only previous participants. If not enough people sign up for the course, then he is out of pocket. This moment serves as a turning point to pursue the relationship as a basis for negotiation.

Karen mentions to Sam that she is only beginning to see how risky the advanced program is for him. That comment opens the door for Sam to become more expressive and to approach Karen in a new light. He begins to talk about the risks of his business and that he feels he has always borne all the risks in their joint ventures. "When we started," he remarks, "nobody knew the programs would be so successful. I underwrote them. Now that the programs are successful, the institute is not only unappreciative, but you want more."

Sam's unguarded remarks raise a critical element that is driving the negotiation. Both parties consider the other company greedy, and each interprets the actions of the other through this screen. Karen shifts the negotiation away from competition to mutual recognition by affirming Sam. Karen talks about how much SITI values the work of Browne and his team, and Sam points out how much Browne Associates appreciates SITI's contributions to making the seminars successful and effective. This affirmation makes both parties more approachable and builds connectedness in goals.

As Karen inquires more deeply into Sam's business – not just about the nuts and bolts but why he has to make the decisions he does – both parties surface past resentments, renew trust, and gain a new understanding of each other. This new understanding alters the definition and direction of the conflict. It transforms theirs perceptions of past behaviors and enables them to see their relationship in a new light. Through this mode of negotiation, Karen and Sam discover their real incentives for working together. Their discussion leads them to set aside the fee arrangements and build their interdependence and connectedness by thinking of ways to fill the advanced classes and to expand the pool of recruits. Karen pursues ideas related to the sequence of the courses, and Sam questions why the courses need to be offered sequentially. Then they both develop the idea to offer the two courses simultaneously, thereby giving people the prerequisites while recruiting them into the advanced course. Thus, instead of promoting the new course as a stand-alone offering, they could couple it with the basic course; participants could remain for the 2-day advanced program after they complete the basic course. This way, Sam can approach the 10,000 existing alumni and, at the same time, prospect for new attendees for the basic course.

What is important to Karen and Sam, however, is not the outcome or solution to the problem; rather, it is the connectedness that forms in jointly developing their course of action and in building a new sense of understanding of their situation. In effect, they transform the nature of their relationship by promoting expressive-ness, appreciative inquiry, mutual recognition, and collaborative actions. Their relationship has changed because they have built a new foundation for future inter-actions, one that reduces suspicion and distrust, builds on common ground, and engages in a process of collaboration.

These three scenarios illustrate how the elements of negotiation function dif-ferently in each model. In the first two scenarios, exchange surfaces as the funda-mental activity of negotiating. In both the distributive and integrative models, Karen and Sam concentrate on their own rewards and costs and on balancing risks and revenues. Balance and reciprocity drive the way that each person weighs the other party's concessions, and they influence the basis of the integrative agreement.
. . .

In the alternative scenario, Karen engages in mutual inquiry rather than trading by asking Sam to explain his business. This inquiry, rooted in expansive thinking, allows the parties to raise issues about their relationship and to integrate the par-ticulars of the moment into the larger organizational system that connects the parties. The negotiators collaborate not only in developing a creative solution but also in surfacing their suspicions and fears about each other and in developing a sense of recognition and a new understanding of each other. As they increase their appreciation for each other and their interdependence, they voice their concerns, develop communal goals, and jointly construct an outcome. Negotiation, then, becomes a co-construction rather than an exchange. These scenarios serve as exem-plars to compare the goals and outcomes, relationships, and processes of the tra-ditional and the alternative approaches.

Goals and outcomes

Goals and outcomes in the traditional models are infused with the residue of exchange. Distributive bargainers rely on exchanges to maximize individual payoffs and to achieve settlements close to their opponents' resistance point. Mutual gains negotiators cast these goals as joint profits and strive to optimize gains for both parties. . . . Even though the goals of integrative bargaining include both self and other, the primary concern of enlightened self-interest remains for the individual whose payoffs are increased because joint gain is optimal. To return to our example, when Karen and Sam negotiate under the traditional models, their objectives are clear – to get the best deal that each person can. What differs between the distributive and integrative versions is the operation of enlightened self-interest. In the integrative version of the traditional model, Karen fashions an agreement that takes Sam's interest – in this case, risk – into account. The patriarchal value of individualism, then, remains primary in these approaches to negotiation.

The alternative view of bargaining strives for self-knowledge and mutual understanding rather than enlightened self-interest and mutual gain (see Table 12.1). Self-knowledge differs from self-interest in the way that negotiators are positioned in the process. Enlightened self-interest presumes that both parties are pursuing paths to increase their relative advantage in the situation. Self-knowledge, however, focuses on the way that co-constructing the process enlightens or informs both parties of their true needs, capabilities, and motivations. When Karen and Sam open up the negotiations and begin to hear about the experiences of the other, each learns something new about the other as well as about their own case. . . . The major goal of the alternative model is not mutual gain but, rather, mutual understanding through generating new insights, creating alternative meanings, and expanding horizons. These goals, then, embrace the feminist quality of learning through connectedness.

In the traditional model, the outcome of negotiation is closely tied to the goals of the process. . . . [But a] major limitation to treating agreement as the ultimate outcome of bargaining is the way this end drives other features of the process. Negotiation, then, as a complex process of social interaction, becomes an instrument for attaining agreement. [. . .]

Rather than striving for optimal settlements, a model of negotiation based on feminist thinking aims for outcomes rooted in jointly developed courses of action that have the potential to transform the situation. . . . A negotiation that works through the changes that occur in understandings and meanings about issues, relationships, and future actions has the potential to become different from its original conception. [. . .]

Relationships

One primary difference between the traditional and the alternative models of negotiation is the role of relationships. In the traditional model, exchange and outcomes function as the foci, while in the alternative model, relationships and process move to center stage. In the traditional model, relationships serve instrumental ends by helping bargainers reach an optimal solution. Sam Browne is a businessman, and Karen Davenport represents an important client. They have a mutual interest in continuing that lucrative relationship. Consistent with patriarchal assumptions, negotiators are distant, independent, and autonomous. The "other" person in this model constitutes a bundle of interests, needs, and goals that are discrete and distant from one's own needs. In both traditional models, Karen takes the lead in trying to figure out what Sam needs, and she proposes solutions based on her assumptions about these needs.

The alternative model, in contrast, adopts the feminist goal of connecting as the basis of relationships (Fletcher, 1998). The other person is not simply a bundle of interests, goals, and needs; this person is someone to join with, learn from, and create a unique experience with. Hence, bargainers connect with the other person to form a relationship through the process of negotiating. In the alternative scenario, Karen opens up the possibility of examining the relationship when she inquires about Sam's past experiences and frustrations in implementing the courses. Through the negotiation, they start to shape a different relationship – it is still rooted in business, but it becomes defined as a collaborative partnership rather than an instrumental connection. By attending to the relationship, bargainers become attuned to ways of nurturing each other. [. . .]

In the traditional model, individuals act independently in making decisions, but they depend on the other party to achieve their respective goals. Interdependence, then, is predetermined and instrumental, derived extrinsically from mutual efforts toward interrelated goals (Blau, 1964). In the traditional scenarios, even though Sam and Karen talk about their mutual dependence, it is a dependence based on the exigencies of the situation.

Contrary to the traditional models, interdependence forms the bond for building relationships in the alternative view. Rather than being predetermined and defined instrumentally, interdependence is co-constructed and emergent through the process of bargaining (see Table 12.1). Sam and Karen get to see how their mutual actions implicate the other company and create the conditions of distance and mistrust in their business relationship. . . . Consistent with a feminist orientation, in the alternative model, relationships are defined intrinsically as parties acquire new understandings of each other and their respective situations. Rather than being driven by instrumental goals, both parties are expressive and open to the possibilities of learning something that they do not already know. [. . .]

The traditional models also cast relationships as rational. Emotional or expressive goals are either devalued within bargaining relationships or serve instrumental ends. Bargainers are advised to remain detached from their opponent, to get beyond feelings, and to separate people from the problem (Fisher et al., 1991; Nierenberg, 1973). Emotional expressions in traditional bargaining block clear thinking and make it difficult for a negotiator to process information effectively (Daly, 1991; Fisher et al., 1991). When emotions enter into the traditional models, they often serve instrumental ends. Positive affect becomes valued in negotiation not because it grows out of relationships but because it influences creative problem solving, lowers contentious tactics, and increases cooperative behaviors (Carnevale & Isen, 1986; Isen, Daubman, & Nowicki, 1987; Thompson, 1998).

In contrast, in the alternative model, sharing feelings and experiences is an important factor that contributes to effective negotiation. A feminist lens would suggest that understanding and mutual inquiry emanate from experiential and affective dimensions of conflict (Kolb & Coolidge, 1991). Rather than being the opposite of reason, emotions are ways in which individuals know the world, reflect on and evaluate it, and change their perceptions about it (Buzzanell, 1994; Ferguson, 1984). Emotional moments in negotiation may represent turning points or shifts in the nature of a conflict. . . .

In summary, relationships in the traditional models take a backseat to instrumental goals and outcomes. Negotiators remain distant from one another and act as autonomous decision makers. They approach each other with suspicion and vacillate between competition and cooperation in their search for mutual gain. Bargaining relationships, then, are rational and defined extrinsically by the need to reach a mutually dependent end. In contrast, the alternative model, rooted in feminist thinking, places relationships at the center of the process. Bargainers enact their interdependence by connecting with each other, building trust from co-constructed meanings, and discovering new insights as a result of empathy and appreciation. Feelings and shared experiences are ways that negotiators learn about each other and their situations rather than being used instrumentally as a path to desired ends.

Negotiation process as bargaining activity

The process of negotiation has a direct influence on the relationships, goals, and outcomes of this activity. . . .

Three types of activities characterize process in traditional bargaining models: exchanging proposals and counterproposals, giving concessions, and engaging in problem solving. The exchange processes that dominate traditional models of negotiation influence how proposals are developed, initiated, accepted, and rejected. Proposals refer to the positions that parties hold on issues or their recommendations for action. . . . In the distributive scenario, Karen and Sam confine their negotiation to trading offers and counteroffers of the fee that SITI will receive from the advanced course. [. . .]

Disputants in the alternative model offer perspectives or alternative understandings rather than proposals and counterproposals (see Table 12.1). Rooted in feminist thinking, the giving of perspectives treats ideas as the expression of viewpoints (Foss & Griffin, 1995). Unlike proposals, perspectives are tentative notions that represent works in progress. A perspective is one of many legitimate viewpoints expressed; it is the offering of an idea, which is different from advocating or seeking support for it. The offering of a personal experience or story, then, is not used as evidence to support a position – it is simply the giving of a perspective. The sharing of stories in the alternative scenario reveals different information than that exchanged in the monetary proposals and justifications for them. Sam's story about his relationship with SITI reveals to Karen how and why he is approaching the negotiation in this manner and the issues that form the roots of his concerns. Likewise, Sam is able to understand Karen's perspective and why SITI needs to explore proposals that look beyond the short run. Both parties come to understand that any deal has to recognize the life cycle of the seminars, the way that both companies do business, and their mutual goals of filling the classes. [. . .]

Another difference between the traditional and alternative models is the notion of problem solving (see Table 12.1). As the fundamental activity of integrative bargaining, problem solving fosters brainstorming and bridging solutions, addresses the needs of both sides, and facilitates creative solutions (Lewicki & Litterer, 1985). . . . Critics contend that, by isolating components into parts, problem solving ignores the systemic and interactive nature of issues, consequently distancing problems from their context in time and space (Baruch Bush & Folger, 1994). [. . .]

The alternative model of negotiation relies on dialogue rather than problem solving for generating options. Dialogue aims to join with the other person in connective thinking and envisioning alternative courses of action (Bohm, 1996). . . .

[It also] aims to transform the conversation by focusing on presumptions that people bring to situations and by creating something additive that never existed before (Isaacs, 1993; Johannesen, 1971). [. . .]

CONCLUSION AND DISCUSSION

Negotiation is not simply the process of making trades. It is an activity in which conflicting ideas form the basis for questioning, integrating issues into the larger system, representing multiple voices, and producing joint action. This alternative for thinking about negotiation stands in contrast to traditional approaches. Exchange forms the foundation that underlies traditional bargaining – the goals and outcomes, relationships, activity, and social interaction.

We contend that exchange and negotiation are gendered activities in that both processes privilege attributes typically identified with patriarchal values. Specifically, exchange casts commodity, cost-benefit ratios, and utilities as rational, materialistic, and objective approaches to decision making. The principles that underlie exchange such as reciprocity, balance, equity, and transaction also reflect a gender bias by relying on agentic goals and reasoning from universal principles. The goals and outcomes of bargaining highlight the instrumentality of a continual drive to reach a mutually satisfactory settlement.

Relationships in the traditional models reaffirm this gender bias through an emphasis on distance, instrumentality, and rationality. Bargainers are treated as autonomous decision makers who develop interdependence extrinsically by vacillating between competition and cooperation. Emotions and feeling are either overpowered by rational processes or coopted to serve instrumental ends. Exchanging proposals and concessions functions from the principles of reciprocity and balance. Problem solving in integrative negotiation privilege rationality and the separation of interrelated issues into isolated segments.

The alternative model of negotiation, influenced by feminist thinking accentuates those features that are marginalized in traditional models. Treating negotiation as co-construction elevates relationships to the center stage. Employing dialogue as primary grounds negotiation interaction in community, mutual understanding, and connectedness. The alternative model operates from the principle of equality to strive for integration, collaboration and mutual inquiry among diverse voices. Negotiation becomes the process of building a relationship, one that strives for mutual recognition and empathy. The types of interactions that characterize the alternative model are sharing experiences, offering perspectives, deliberating about ideas, telling personal narratives, engaging in circular questioning, and envisioning through resourcement and reframing. These forms of social interaction support the feminist practices of intuition, expressiveness, and shared feelings that are typically absent in traditional approaches.

This comparison of traditional and alternative models stems from prototypes, that is, from coherent and isomorphic views of each category. Deviations from these prototypes are more likely the rule rather than the exception. The dichotomous representation of each exaggerates the differences between them. This analysis, however, uncovers marginalized and unappreciated aspects of negotiation, ones that are often ignored in the traditional literature. Thus, the traditional and alternative models are presented as extremes to differentiate between the two approaches, even though the traditional models vary in form and function across types of bargaining. [. . .]

Co-construction as an alternative view of negotiation is not an approach that replaces traditional models; it also cannot be used in every bargaining encounter. . . . In any negotiation, parties can begin from a point of mutuality. In some and perhaps many cases, the other person will connect by pursuing goals, strategies, and processes that differ from traditional models. However, if the other person refuses to engage, to pursue mutual inquiry, and to share mutual recognition, a negotiator can resort to traditional options. Mutual inquiry means that both parties must take risks to engage in a relational orientation to negotiation. [. . .]

This critique of traditional models of negotiation adds to a growing body of literature aimed at developing options and possibilities that are not easily coopted into the dominant orientation. The development of a truly alternative model of negotiation, one that is rooted in nonpatriarchal values, is essential to enhancing the discipline's ability to explain communication in conflict management. This chapter takes another step forward in advancing this goal by presenting an alternative to the dominant theories of negotiation, one rooted in feminist thinking and principles.

REFERENCES

Baruch Bush, R. A., & Folger, J. P. 1994. *The Promise of Mediation: Responding to Conflict through Empowerment and Recognition.* San Francisco, CA: Jossey Bass.

Blau, P. M. 1964. *Exchange and Power in Social Life.* New York: John Wiley.

Bohm, D. 1996. *On Dialogue.* London: Routledge.

Buzzanell, P. M. 1994. Gaining a voice: Feminist perspectives in organizational communication. *Management Communication Quarterly,* 7:339–383.

Carnevale, P. J. D., & Isen, A. M. 1986. The influence of positive affect and visual access on the discovery of integrative solutions in bilateral negotiation. *Organizational Behavior and Human Decision Process,* 37:1–13.

Cutcher-Gershenfeld, J. E. 1994. Bargaining over how to bargain in labor-management negotiations. *Negotiation Journal,* 10(4):323–335.

Cutcher-Gershenfeld, J. McKersie, R. B., & Walton, R. E. 1995. *Pathways to Change: Case Studies of Strategic Negotiations.* Kalamazoo, MI: W. E. Upjohn Institute for Employment Research.

Daly, J. P. 1991. The effects of anger on negotiations over mergers and acquisitions. *Negotiation Journal,* 7:31–39.

Ferber, M. A., & Nelson, J. A. 1993. *Beyond Economic Man: Feminist Theory and Economics.* Chicago: University of Chicago Press.

Ferguson, K. E. 1984. *The Feminist Case against Bureaucracy.* Philadelphia: Temple University Press.

Fisher, R., Ury, W., & Patton, B. 1991. *Getting to Yes.* (2nd ed.). Boston, MA: Houghton Mifflin.

Fletcher, J. K. 1998. Relational practice: A feminist reconstruction of work. *Journal of Management Inquiry,* 7(2):164–186.

Foss, S. K., & Griffin, C. L. 1995. Beyond persuasion: A proposal for an invitational rhetoric. *Communication Monographs,* 62:2–18.

Gray, B. 1994. The gender-based foundations of negotiation theory. In R. J. Lewicki, B. H. Sheppard, & R. Bies (Eds.), *Research on Negotiation in Organizations,* 4:3–36. Greenwich, CT: JAI Press.

Gulliver, P. H. 1979. *Disputes and Negotiations: A Cross-Cultural Perspective.* New York: Academic Press.

Hartsock, N. C. M. 1985. Exchange theory: Critique from a feminist standpoint. *Current Perspectives in Social Theory*, 6:57–70. Greenwich, CT: JAI Press.

Howard, J. A., & Hollander, J. A. 1997. *Gendered Situations, Gendered Selves: A Gender Lens on Social Psychology*. Thousand Oaks, CA: Sage.

Isaacs, W. N. 1993. Taking flight: Dialogue, collective thinking, and organizational learning. *Organizational Dynamics*, 22:24–39.

Isen, A. M., Daubman, K. A., & Nowicki, G. P. 1987. Positive affect facilitates creative problem solving. *Journal of Personality and Social Psychology*, 52:1122–1131.

Johannesen, R. L. 1971. The emerging concept of communication as dialogue. *Quarterly Journal of Speech*, 57:373–382.

Kolb, D. M., & Coolidge, G. 1991. Her place at the table. In J. W. Breslin & J. Z. Rubin (Eds.), *Negotiation Theory and Practice*, (pp. 261–277). Cambridge, MA: Program on Negotiation, Harvard Law School.

Kolb, & Putnam, L. L. 1997. Through the looking glass: Negotiation theory refracted through the lens of gender. In S. E. Gleason (Ed.), *Workplace Dispute Resolution: Directions for the Twenty-First Century*, (pp. 231–257). East Lansing, MI: Michigan state University Press.

Kolb, & Williams, J. 1999. *Tough Enough: Gender in the Shadow of Negotiations*. New York: Simon and Schuster.

Lax, D. A., & Sebenius, J. K. 1986. *The Manager as Negotiator: Bargaining for Cooperation and Competitive Gain*. New York, NY: The Free Press.

Lewicki, R. L., & Litterer, J. A. 1985. *Negotiation*. Homewood, IL: Richard D. Irwin.

Luce, R. D., & Raiffa, H. 1957. *Games and Decisions*. New York, NY: John Wiley.

Neale, M. A., & Bazerman, M. H. 1991. *Cognition and Rationality in Negotiation*. New York: The Free Press.

Nierenberg, G. 1973. *Fundamentals of Negotiating*. New York: Hawthorn Books.

O'Connor, K. M., & Adams, A. A. 1996. June. *Scripts in bilateral negotiation*. Paper presented at the International Association for Conflict Management, Cornell University, Ithaca, NY.

Pruitt, D. G. 1981. *Negotiation Behavior*. New York: Academic Press.

Pruitt, D. G. 1983. Integrative agreements: Nature and antecedents. In M. H. Bazerman & R. J. Lewicki (Eds.), *Negotiating in Organizations*, (pp. 35–50). Beverly Hills, CA: Sage.

Putnam, L. L., & Roloff, M. E. 1992. Communication perspectives on negotiation. In L. L. Putnam & M. E. Roloff (Ed.), *Communication and Negotiation*, (pp. 1–17). Newbury Park, CA: Sage Publications.

Raiffa, H. 1982. *The Art and Science of Negotiation*. Cambridge: Harvard University Press.

Sebenius, J. K. 1992. Negotiation analysis: A characterization and review. *Management Science*, 38:18–39.

Sheldon, A. 1992. Preschool girls' discourse competence: Managing conflict and negotiation power. In K. Hall, M. Bucholtz, & B. Moonwomon (Eds.), *Locating Power*, 2:528–539. Berkeley, CA: Berkeley Linguistic Society.

Sheldon, A., & Johnson, D. 1994. Preschool negotiators: Linguistic differences in how girls and boys regulate the expression of dissent in same-sex groups. In R. Lewicki, B. H. Sheppard, & R. Bies (Eds.), *Research on Negotiation in Organizations*, 4:37–67. Greenwich, CT: JAI Press.

Strober, M. H. 1994. Can feminist thought improve economics? *American Economic Association Papers and Proceedings*, 84(2):143–147.

Thompson, L. 1998. *The Mind and Heart of the Negotiator*. Upper Saddle River, NJ: Prentice Hall.

PART III | LEADERSHIP

LEADERSHIP: OVERVIEW

ROBIN J. ELY

Leadership is perhaps the most prized activity in Western organizations today and thus occupies a central place in the curricula of most Western business schools and schools of management. In organizations and in the management cases we study, we routinely evaluate managers for their "leadership," by which we typically mean a particular constellation of valued abilities, including the ability to provide a vision and influence others to realize it (Heifetz, 1994). Accordingly, questions about who leaders are and what makes for effective leadership have long preoccupied Western scholars. To the early proponents of "great man" theories of leadership, which posited that the rise to power is rooted in a "heroic" set of personal talents, skills, and physical attributes, the notion of women as candidates for greatness was inconceivable (Heifetz, 1994). Until relatively recently, scholars assumed without reflection that these valued traits were gender-neutral, though manifested predominantly in men. Women, and thus gender, were simply irrelevant. In recent years, however, EEO legislation and the press for equality in the workplace have brought unprecedented numbers of women into organizations' professional and managerial ranks, making this notion no longer tenable. As women began moving into these roles, questions about "women in leadership" rose to the fore among both scholars and practitioners. "Women in leadership" is now among the main themes in contemporary leadership research (Calás & Smircich, 1988). Nevertheless, this topic remains elusive, sometimes even taboo, in the classrooms of many business schools and schools of management.

Part III is intended to offer a way into the topic that will stimulate critical discussion of important themes relevant not only to gender but to leadership as well. Taking this approach involves seeing leadership through a gender lens to illuminate many of the assumptions we normally take for granted about what leadership is and who leaders are. Using this lens, we can see how these assumptions may handicap not only women and others traditionally underrepresented in leadership roles, but organizations as well.

A large portion of research addressing this topic has centered on questions about whether or not men's and women's leadership styles are different in ways that are consistent with cultural stereotypes (Eagly & Johnson, 1990). Do men leaders pay more attention to task? Are women leaders more concerned with people's feelings? Despite the fact that most reviews of quantitative research show no support in organizational studies and minimal support in laboratory studies for sex differences in leadership style, stereotypes of men and women leaders pervade cultural images and assumptions, and questions about sex differences in leadership style continue to spark the interest of practitioners and scholars alike.

Most feminists would agree that the perception of sex differences in leader behavior, grounded in reality or not, has reinforced inequality between men and women. Yet they differ in their perspectives on why this is so and what to do about it. The four frames on gender again offer a useful way to understand these different perspectives. The readings in Part III present concepts, theory, and research that illustrate or test ideas within each frame and thus, taken together, should stimulate a rich discussion of the range of issues and debates this topic has generated.

DIFFERENT PERSPECTIVES ON GENDER DIFFERENCES

According to Frame 1, sex-role socialization has rendered women less skilled than men to compete in the world of business. If women are to reach parity with men in leadership roles they must gain the requisite leadership skills, which they currently lack. Thus, any differences in leadership style should be repudiated and, in an ideal world, eradicated. The way to do this is to "fix the women" so that they can compete more effectively with men for these roles. The change agenda of organizations that adopt this frame is therefore to minimize sex differences, primarily through education and training. This perspective is well captured in the reading by Hennig and Jardim in Part I.

Critics of this perspective have argued that it reinforces an asymmetric view of the role gender plays in leadership: it implicitly casts men's leadership as generic leadership uninfluenced by masculine gender and male experience. As such, men's leadership constitutes the presumed gender-neutral norm against which women's leadership is measured and evaluated. To the extent that women deviate from this norm their leadership is viewed as less effective or absent altogether. Hence, the comparative approach to leadership espoused in Frame 1 has tended not only to devalue women but in so doing to narrow our understanding of what might constitute the full range of effective leader behavior.

This criticism has led some feminist scholars to take a Frame 2 perspective on gender and leadership, which seeks to celebrate rather than devalue women's presumed differences from men. In this frame, the meaning of leadership is reconceived to include the relational and emotional competencies that women are perceived to have developed as leaders in the domestic sphere of home and family, competencies that, according to this view, men tend to lack. Hence, rather than seeking to overcome traditional feminine experience, these scholars exalt it, urging organizations to celebrate women and the usefulness of their feminized differences. Evidence for the validity of this perspective has been largely descriptive, based on interviews with women leaders (see, e.g., Rosener, 1990).

Proponents of a third approach argue that these frames focus too heavily on the characteristics of women and inappropriately disregard situational factors that may more accurately explain women's underrepresentation in leadership roles. According to Frame 3, the relative dearth of women leaders results, not from socialization processes, but from differential structures of opportunity, reward, and power that block women's access and advancement. These include hiring, evaluation, and promotion processes that reflect sexist attitudes toward and expectations of women (Kanter, 1977; Reskin, 1988; Ridgeway, 1993; Strober, 1984, 1994); social and professional networks that give men greater access to information and support (Burt 1992; Ibarra, 1992; Kram, 1985; Morrison, White & Velsor, 1987; Podolny & Baron, 1997); and professional and managerial women's token status, which subjects them to increased performance pressures, isolation from informal social and professional networks, and stereotyped role encapsulation (for reviews, see Konrad & Gutek, 1987; Konrad, Winter & Gutek, 1992; Martin, 1985). Interventions designed within this frame are often legislative or policy-based. Their goal is to eliminate or compensate for structural barriers that have limited women's access to leadership roles by changing structures of power that have become codified in organizational processes and procedures.

The first reading by Deborah Rhode, "The difference 'difference' makes," provides a compelling and thorough review of the literature bearing on many of the questions and concerns raised in these three perspectives on gender and leadership: are there sex differences in leader behavior, making women either worse (Frame 1) or better (Frame 2) candidates for leadership roles? According to Rhode's review, probably not. There is little empirical support for the notion that sex differences in leader attitudes and behaviors – of which there seem to be few – explain sex differences in who has managed to achieve leadership positions. Alternatively, are there sex differences in opportunity that make a difference in women's attainment of leadership roles (Frame 3)? Rhode's review points to a resounding "yes." Gender stereotypes, limited access to mentors, and workplace practices that fail to accommodate family commitments have clearly made it more difficult for women to achieve and succeed in leadership roles.

The second reading, "Gender, culture, and leadership: Toward a culturally distinct model of African-American women executives' leadership strategies," by Patricia Parker and dt ogilvie, draws from all three frames to address a similar set of questions about leadership and African American women. Parker and ogilvie differentiate between the socialization experiences of African American and white women (Frames 1 and 2), describing many of the strengths African American women executives consequently bring to leadership roles (Frame 2). They also identify discriminatory practices in organizations that create barriers for African American women (Frame 3), many of which result from particular forms of sexism, which they face because they are black, and particular forms of racism, which they face because they are women. These create a distinct social experience for African American women executives, they argue, based on which these women develop unique strategies to ensure leadership success – strategies that can be informative for all leaders.

GENDER AND LEADERSHIP FROM THE PERSPECTIVE OF FRAME 4

Although interventions from each of the three frames reviewed here have clearly made important differences in women's ability to achieve and succeed in leadership roles, their impact has been limited. Thus we build on these more traditional approaches with a fourth frame. Like earlier critics, proponents of this frame begin with the recognition that leadership, as we know it, is steeped in idealized masculine images – the heroic individual, who is "big, colorful, fast, assertive" (Heifetz, 1994: 15) – under the guise of gender neutrality. Teddy Roosevelt's image of a leader as "the man . . . whose face is marred by dust and sweat and blood" is particularly vivid in this regard. As others have noted, linking the highly exalted practice we call "leadership" to traits that have been culturally ascribed to men, such as individualism, assertiveness, and courage, implicitly devalues those ascribed to women, such as collaboration, caring, and support. However, this insight leads proponents of Frame 4, unlike earlier critics, neither to repudiate nor to celebrate feminine traits in order to increase women's representation in leadership roles. Indeed, they reject the assumption of sex-linked traits and skills and move away from women's underrepresentation as the focal problem. Rather, they use the occasion of women's underrepresentation to ask the more critical questions: "Who else is missing from these roles? What else is missing from the activity we call leadership? What new possibilities open up for people and organizations when the gendered aspects of leadership come to light?"

As we have seen in Parts I and II, the answers to these questions have implications for both equity and organizational effectiveness. According to a Frame 4 perspective, masculine images of leadership make it difficult for women to play these roles, not because they in fact *are* any less individualistic, assertive, or courageous than their male counterparts, nor any more collaborative, caring, and supportive – indeed, there is little empirical support for either of these beliefs – but because they *are expected to be*, and thus are placed in a double bind. If they enact the stereotypically masculine role of a leader, they are insufficiently feminine, but if they enact the stereotypically feminine role of a woman they are insufficiently leader-like (i.e., masculine). Men who enact too stereotypically feminine a role at work may also come up short. Moreover, the idealized masculinity of the prototypical leader is also the idealized masculinity of men who are white, middle-class or upper-middle-class, and heterosexual; the stereotypical gender images on which leadership is based are not neutral with respect to race, class, or sexual orientation. Therefore, a person's "fit" for leadership roles depends on other aspects of social identity as well. By recognizing the complex relationships among bodies, stereotypes, and expectations, a Frame 4 perspective broadens concerns about equity beyond women and beyond gender as well. What happens when people, including men, deviate from the idealized image of the leader? How can we understand the experiences of women of color in leadership roles? (The reading by Parker and ogilvie addresses this second question.)

But the problem runs deeper still than the limits that gender and other stereotypes place on some people's ability to achieve and succeed in leadership roles. It lies in the limits this conception of leadership places upon the leader's ability to connect deeply with the people around him or her, to transform the self from isolated entity to "self-in-relation" (Surrey, 1985), where intellect, emotion, spirit, and will converge in social interactions (Palmer, 1998). Some have called this ability "emotional intelligence" (Goleman, 1998); others have called it the basis for adaptive learning (Senge, 1990). Across these areas of work, scholars are recognizing these limits and appreciating the merits of a more relational approach and are beginning to formulate a new model of leadership, commonly called "postheroic" leadership. This new model ostensibly rejects much of the traditional masculine model in favor of a more dynamic, multidirectional, relational activity aimed at collective learning. Despite the increasing popularity of this notion in sophisticated management circles (see Badaracco, 2001), postheroic models of leadership have not really taken hold in practice. The last two readings in Part III provide some insight into why.

In "The greatly exaggerated demise of heroic leadership: Gender, power, and the myth of the female advantage," Joyce Fletcher takes a Frame 4 perspective on this new model and considers its implications for gender equity and organizational effectiveness. She argues that although the traits associated with postheroic leadership are ostensibly consistent with images of idealized femininity, this shift neither gives women an advantage in today's business environment nor delivers on its transformational promise. Truly shifting to postheroic leadership, she argues, requires not simply a shift in sex-linked images of leaders, but a thoroughgoing break with the notion of leadership as an individual actor's engaging the world from a position of power and control. This shift has not happened and, Fletcher argues, will not happen until we examine – and break apart – the deep connections between gender and power that underlie this conception of leadership. The challenge posed for us in this paper is: can we use women's disproportionate under-representation in leadership roles as the opportunity for rethinking leadership altogether?

The last reading in Part III, "When women lead: The visibility–vulnerability spiral," by Kathy Kram and Marion McCollom Hampton, describes how such an opportunity arises. Exploring the psychodynamics of leadership, Kram and McCollom Hampton argue that followers unconsciously reinforce these heroic images to the detriment of themselves, the leader, and the organization. Women leaders' token status heightens their visibility in these roles, and so they are especially vulnerable to these problematic expectations. But women's presence in these roles may also make these limiting dynamics of leadership more salient, and their effective response to them may provide an important opportunity for organization members to learn – about themselves, about others, and about their organization.

Indeed, seeing leadership through a gender lens suggests that learning may be one of the central functions of leadership. A Frame 4 perspective submits that differences of all kinds can become a resource for individual and organizational change (Bailyn, 1993), and learning is one mechanism by which this happens (Ely & Thomas, 2001). Learning from differences requires that people truly engage each other – and themselves – and become transformed in the process. What is the role of leadership in this process? Perhaps to lead effectively requires being in an active state of learning – about self and other, about work and the organization. Leaders in this context are constantly vigilant for opportunities to test old assumptions and new ideas. They create opportunities for people to speak their minds and to bring their whole selves to their work and to their interactions with others at work. In the course of these interactions, the organization's norms, values, and practices are opened to scrutiny, providing the necessary impetus to question and change traditional beliefs, including those that legitimate inequalities (Ely & Meyerson, 2000). These kinds of changes in turn drive and support structural changes in the organization that enable a more diverse group of people to achieve and succeed in leadership roles. In this way, this approach builds directly on the structural approach of Frame 3, further challenging existing power relations and the social interactions and belief systems that reinforce and maintain them. The premise of Frame 4 is that women, men, organizations, and the surrounding social system all stand to benefit.

REFERENCES

Badaracco, J. 2001. We don't need another hero. *Harvard Business Review*, 79(8):120–6.

Bailyn, L. 1993. *Breaking the mold: Women, men and time in the new corporate world.* New York: Free Press.

Burt, R. 1992. *Structural holes.* Cambridge, MA: Harvard University Press.

Calás, M. B. & Smircich, L. 1988. Reading leadership as a form of cultural analysis. In J. G. Hunt, R. Baliga, P. Dachler, & C. Schreisheim (eds.), *Emerging leadership vistas*: 201–26. Lexington, MA: Lexington Books.

Eagly, A. H. & Johnson, B. T. 1990. Gender and leadership style: A meta-analysis. *Psychological Bulletin*, 108: 233–56.

Ely, R. J. & Meyerson, D. E. 2000. Theories of gender in organizations: A new approach to organizational analysis and change. In B. Staw & R. Sutton (eds.), *Research in Organizational Behavior*: 103–52. New York: JAI Press.

Ely, R. J. & Thomas, D. A. 2001. Cultural diversity at work: The effects of diversity perspectives on work group processes and outcomes. *Administrative Science Quarterly*, 46: 229–73.

Goleman, D. 1998. *Working with emotional intelligence.* NY: Bantam Books.

Heifetz, R. A. 1994. *Leadership without easy answers.* Cambridge, MA: Harvard University Press.

Ibarra, H. 1992. Homophily and differential returns: Sex differences in network structure and access in an advertising firm. *Administrative Science Quarterly*, 37: 422–47.

Kanter, R. M. 1977. *Men and women of the corporation.* New York: Basic Books.

Konrad, A. & Gutek, B. A. 1987. Theory and research on group composition: Applications to the status of women and ethnic minorities. In S. Oskamp & S. Spacapan (eds.), *Interpersonal processes*: 85–121. Newbury Park, CA: Sage.

Konrad, A. M., Winter, S. & Gutek, B. A. 1992. Diversity in work group sex composition: Implications for majority and minority members. *Research in the Sociology of Organizations*, 10: 115–40.

Kram, K. E. 1985. *Mentoring at work: Developmental relationships in organizational life.* Glenview, IL: Scott, Foresman.

Martin, P. Y. 1985. Group sex composition in work organizations: A structural-normative model. *Research in the Sociology of Organizations*, 4: 311–49.

Morrison, A. M., White, R. P., & Van Velsor, E. 1987. *Breaking the glass ceiling: Can women reach the top of America's largest corporations?* Reading, MA: Addison-Wesley.

Palmer, P. J. 1998. *The courage to teach.* San Francisco: Jossey Bass.

Podolny, J. & Baron, J. 1997. Resources and relationships: Social networks, mobility and satisfaction in the workplace. *American Sociological Review*, 62(5): 673–93.

Reskin, B. F. 1988. Bringing the men back in: Sex differentiation and the devaluation of women's work. *Gender and Society*, 2: 58–81.

Ridgeway, C. L. 1993. Gender, status, and the social psychology of expectations. In P. England (ed.), *Theory on gender/feminism on theory*: 175–98. New York: Aldine.

Rosener, J. B. 1990. Ways women lead. *Harvard Business Review*, November-December: 3–10.

Senge, Peter. 1990. *The fifth discipline.* New York: Doubleday.

Strober, M. 1984. Toward a general theory of occupational sex segregation: The case of public school teaching. In B. Reskin (ed.), *Sex segregation in the workplace*: 144–56. Washington, DC: National Academy Press.

Strober, M. 1994. Gender and occupational segregation. In T. Husén & T. N. Postlethwaite (eds.), *The International Encyclopedia of Education*: 248–52. Oxford: Pergamon Press.

Surrey, J. 1985. *The self in relation.* Stone Center Work in Progress #13, Wellesley College Centers for Women, Wellesley, MA.

THE DIFFERENCE "DIFFERENCE" MAKES

DEBORAH RHODE

From D. Rhode (ed.) (2003) *The Difference Difference Makes: Women and Leadership*, Stanford, CA: Stanford University Press

INTRODUCTION

For most of recorded history, women were largely excluded from formal leadership positions. A comprehensive review of encyclopedia entries published just after the turn of the last century identified only about 850 eminent women, famous or infamous, throughout the preceding 2000 years. In rank order, they included queens, politicians, mothers, mistresses, wives, beauties, religious figures, and "women of tragic fate."[1] Few of these women had acquired leadership positions in their own right. Most exercised influence through relationships with men.

Since that publication, we have witnessed a transformation in gender roles. As Charlotte Bunch of the Women's Global Leadership Institute notes, "over the last three decades, women have taken a leadership role in redefining fundamental aspects of our lives – work, family, sexuality, equality, and justice."[2] Yet our progress is incomplete. Women remain dramatically underrepresented in formal leadership positions. . . . [This chapter] examines "the difference difference makes" both in access to leadership and in its exercise. . . .

Summarizing the relevant research is a daunting task. The last quarter century has witnessed a rapidly expanding volume of commentary on leadership, gender difference, and the relationship between the two. Surveys in the early 1990s identified over five thousand scholarly works on leadership and some five hundred programs in colleges and universities.[3] The market for leadership training, self-help publications, and popular commentary has expanded as well, with a growing segment focused on women.[4] Part of this attention is directed to gender differences in opportunities, to the glass ceilings that exclude many women from leadership positions, and to the subtle biases that confront women who attain such positions. A second area of emphasis involves gender differences in the exercise of leadership differences in the styles, effectiveness, and priorities of men and women.

Yet despite this cottage industry of commentary, key concepts remain elusive. To begin with, there is no consensus on what accounts for effective leadership. At its core, leadership is generally viewed as the ability to influence and inspire others to act beyond what their jobs or roles require.[5] The traditional assumption was that leaders had distinctive personal traits. However, most contemporary research suggests that effectiveness also depends heavily on context, and on the relationship between the characteristics of leaders and the needs, goals, and circumstances of their followers.[6] Researchers have identified a broad range of qualities, behaviors, and processes that are conducive to effective leadership, but have not provided widely accepted theories about the leadership techniques or training that are most successful in practice.[7]

The literature on gender difference is similarly expansive, and the concept is similarly elusive. No issue is more central, or more contested, among those concerned with equality for women. There is widespread agreement that gender difference does make a difference in virtually all aspects of social experience. But there is no corresponding consensus on the origins or implications of difference in many contexts, including leadership. Nor is there agreement on the extent to which gender differences are experienced differently by different groups in different contexts. As researchers have increasingly noted, there is no "generic woman," and too little work has explored the interrelationship between gender and situational forces or other characteristics such as race, class, ethnicity, age, and sexual orientation.[8]

Yet despite these limitations, recent research casts considerable light on the opportunities and obstacles for women leaders. This chapter explores key findings concerning the difference "difference" makes in leadership. The focus is on formal, high-level positions in law, politics, and business, because these are the contexts where the greatest public influence is exercised and the most systematic information is available.

This focus is not meant to understate the importance of women's leadership in other contexts or to assume that formal positions always carry the most power. For example, many women have had enormous influence through their roles in workplace committees, community organizations, professional associations, and social reform movements. Yet although such contributions should not be undervalued, neither should we overlook the effects of exclusion from formal policy positions. By gaining a better sense of what we know and what we only think we know about women's leadership opportunities, we may also find ways to expand their roles and responsibilities in the pursuit of public interests.

GENDER DIFFERENCES IN LEADERSHIP OPPORTUNITIES

A central problem for American women is the lack of consensus that there is a significant problem.[9] Gender inequalities in leadership opportunities are pervasive; perceptions of inequality are not. A widespread assumption is that barriers have been coming down, women have been moving up, and equal treatment is an accomplished fact in public life. Two-thirds of surveyed men and three-quarters of male business leaders do not believe that women encounter significant discrimination for top positions in business, the professions, or government.[10] In the most recent poll by the *Journal of the American Bar Association* (*JABA*), over half of lawyers of both sexes agreed that women are treated equally in the profession. Only a quarter of female lawyers and 3 percent of male lawyers thought that prospects for advancement were greater for men than for women.[11] Although other surveys paint a somewhat less optimistic picture, many Americans agree with the statement by Hewlett

Packard's CEO at the time of her appointment: "the accomplishments of women across industry demonstrate that there is not a glass ceiling."[12]

Such views are hard to square with the facts. Although women have made enormous progress over the last several decades, they remain underrepresented at the top and overrepresented at the bottom in both the public and private sectors. Women now account for about half of managerial and professional positions but only 12 percent of corporate officers, 4 percent of top corporate earners, and about 1 percent of the Fortune 500 CEOs.[13] Almost 30 percent of lawyers are women, but they represent only about 15 percent of federal judges and law firm partners, 10 percent of law school deans and general counsel positions at Fortune 500 companies, and 5 percent of managing partners at major law firms.[14] Women constitute over half of American voters but only 25 percent of senior executive branch officials, 22 percent of state legislators, 16 percent of the mayors of large cities, 13 percent of congressional representatives, 6 percent of state governors, and no congressional committee chairs.[15] The United States ranks fiftieth in the percentage of women elected to legislative offices.[16] The underrepresentation of women of color is even greater. They account for only about 3 percent of state legislators, 3 percent of congressional representatives, 1 percent of corporate officers, and under 1 percent of law firm partners. Only two women of color serve as mayors of large cities; and only one as general counsel of a Fortune 500 corporation. None serve as chief executives or state governors.[17]

What explains these disparities is a matter of dispute. One common assumption is that they are the product of cultural lag; current inequalities are the legacy of discriminatory practices that are no longer legal, and it is only a matter of time until women catch up. About two-thirds of male chief executive officers attribute women's low representation in leadership positions to the fact that they have not been in the pipeline long enough.[18] Such assumptions are an equally common theme in gender bias studies on the legal profession.[19] However, this pipeline theory cannot explain the underrepresentation of women leaders in fields such as law or management, where they have long constituted between a third and half of new entrants.[20] Nor can cultural lag explain the disparities in advancement among male and female candidates with comparable qualifications.[21] For example, studies involving thousands of lawyers with similar entry-level credentials have found that men are at least twice as likely as women to obtain partnership.[22] As discussion below indicates, many female professionals still do not receive the same opportunities to develop leadership qualifications as their male colleagues. In short, the pipeline leaks, and if we wait for time to correct the problem, we will be waiting a very long time. At current rates of change, it will be almost three centuries before women are as likely as men to become top managers in major corporations, or to achieve equal representation in Congress.[23]

In accounting for gender disparities, a wide array of research reveals certain persistent and pervasive patterns. Women's opportunities for leadership are constrained by traditional gender stereotypes, inadequate access to mentors and informal networks of support, and inflexible workplace structures.

Gender stereotypes

In order to make sense of a complex social world, individuals rely on a variety of techniques to categorize information. One strategy involves stereotypes, which

associate certain socially defined characteristics with identifiable groups. In virtually every society, gender is a fundamental aspect of human identity, and gender
stereotypes influence beliefs, behaviors, and self-concepts at both conscious and
unconscious levels.[24] Perceptions of leadership ability are inescapably affected by
these stereotypes, which work against women's advancement in several respects.

First, and most fundamentally, the characteristics traditionally associated with
women are at odds with the characteristics traditionally associated with leadership.[25]
It is scarcely surprising that positions of greatest power should be identified with
men, since those positions have historically been dominated by men. The "great
man" theories of leadership that once dominated the field were not using the term
generically.[26] Most qualities traditionally linked with leaders have been masculine:
forceful, assertive decisions, authoritative, and so forth.

Although recent theories of leadership have stressed the need for interpersonal
qualities more commonly associated with women, such as cooperation and collaboration, women aspiring to leadership still face double standards and double
binds. They risk appearing too "soft" or too "strident," too aggressive or not aggressive enough.[27] And what is assertive in a man often seems abrasive in a woman. An
overview of more than a hundred studies involving evaluations of leaders indicates
that women are rated lower when they adopt "masculine," authoritative styles, particularly when the evaluators are men or the role is one typically occupied by men.[28]
Since other research suggests that individuals with masculine styles are more likely
to emerge as leaders than those with feminine styles, women face tradeoffs that
men do not.[29] The dilemma is not, of course, insolvable. As discussion below notes,
many women leaders have found approaches that effectively combine masculine
and feminine traits. But most researchers agree that the range of appropriate behavior is narrower for women than for men, especially in traditionally male-dominated
fields such as law, management, and politics. Women who take strong positions
risk being stereotyped as "bitchy," "difficult," or "manly."[30] Women who try to avoid
those assessments risk losing ground to men who are less accommodating.

A related obstacle for female leaders is that they often lack the presumption of
competence accorded to their male counterparts. Despite a broad array of evidence
summarized below finding that women perform at least as effectively as men in
leadership roles, an equally substantial body of research indicates that women face
greater difficulty in establishing their qualifications and credibility.[31] Surveys of
women professionals find that the vast majority believe that they are held to higher
standards than their male counterparts.[32] . . . Where the number of women is small,
as is often the case in leadership contexts, their performance is subject to special
scrutiny and more demanding requirements.[33] The devaluation of women and the
influence of gender stereotypes is especially likely in organizations that have few
women in leadership positions.[34] Even in experimental situations where male and
female performance is objectively equal, women are held to higher standards, and
their competence is rated lower.[35]

A wide array of research similarly finds that many women internalize these stereotypes. They see themselves as less deserving of rewards for the same performance
and often lack confidence to take the risks or seek the challenges that would equip
them for leadership roles.[36] Preconceptions about women's lesser competence or
experience then become self-fulfilling prophesies. Such pattens also help explain
why women are less likely to be viewed as leaders as similarly situated men.[37] For
example, when individuals see a man seated at the head of a table for a meeting,

they typically assume that he is the leader; they do not make the same assumption about a woman.[38] Nor do they accord her the same deference. And when women do seek to exercise control or authority, they have more difficulty than men in doing so effectively. Behavior that is acceptable for male leaders is often considered "bossy" and "domineering" in their female counterparts.[39] Indeed, executive training programs are now available to reeducate "bully broads" whose "toughness" is perceived to be a liability.[40]

Autobiographical accounts and opinion polls reveal repeated patterns of such double standards and demeaning stereotypes. Accomplished attorneys still face questions such as whether they can "really understand all the economics involved in this case."[41] Women seeking public office are still considered less able to manage conflict or financial affairs.[42] Only half of surveyed Americans believe that people are comfortable with the idea of a woman president.[43] Traditional gender biases are particularly common when evaluators have little accountability for their assessments and when those evaluated are women of color.[44] Disfavored groups find that their mistakes are more readily noticed and their achievements more often attributed to luck or special treatment.[45] Adverse stereotypes are most problematic for women of color who are frequently assumed to owe their positions to affirmative action rather than professional qualifications.[46]

Women with children face additional double standards and double binds. Working mothers are held to higher standards than working fathers and are often criticized for being insufficiently committed, either as parents or professionals. Those who seem willing to sacrifice family needs to workplace demands appear lacking as mothers. Those who take extended leaves or reduced schedules appear lacking as lawyers. These mixed messages leave many women with the uncomfortable sense that whatever they are doing, they should be doing something else.[47] Assumptions about the inadequate commitment of working mothers adversely influence performance evaluations, promotion decisions, and opportunities for challenging assignments that are prerequisites for leadership roles.[48] After maternity leaves, some women lawyers report being given such routine work that they are tempted to offer responses such as, "Look, I had a baby not a lobotomy."[49] Former Congresswoman Pat Schroeder encountered so many questions about her ability to balance family and work responsibilities that she finally pointed out that she had both a "brain and a uterus, and they both work."[50] [. . .]

Any resolution of these challenges is problematic. Many women who wait to seek leadership positions until their children are grown never catch up with male competitors. Other women who attempt to juggle demanding work and family obligations simultaneously may lack sufficient "face time" to allay colleagues' or voters' concerns. Politicians who miss "too many pancake breakfasts" have been thought "insufficiently committed" to justify party support for higher office.[51] And women lawyers who "cook and tell," by acknowledging the need to be home for dinner, frequently find themselves off the track for advancement.[52] The irony is that it generally takes exceptional career commitment for women to juggle competing work and family responsibilities in unsupportive working environments. As one lawyer told a Boston Bar Association task force: "On most days I am taking care of children or commuting or working from the moment I get up until I fall in bed at night. No one would choose this if they weren't very committed."[53]

The force of traditional stereotypes is compounded by other biases. People are more likely to notice and recall information that confirms prior assumptions than information that contradicts them.[54] Since many lawyers assume that a working mother is unlikely to be fully committed to her career, they more easily remember the times when she left early than the times when she stayed late. So too, attorneys who assume that women of color are beneficiaries of preferential treatment, not meritocratic selection, will recall their errors more readily than their insights. A related problem is that people share what psychologists label a "just world" bias.[55] They want to believe that, in the absence of special treatment, individuals generally get what they deserve and deserve what they get. Perceptions of performance frequently are adjusted to match observed outcomes. If women, particularly women of color, are underrepresented in positions of greatest prominence, the most psychologically convenient explanation is that they lack the necessary qualifications or commitment.

These assumptions can again become self-fulfilling prophesies. Expectations affect evaluations, work assignments, and other career development opportunities. In effect, biased assumptions adversely affect performance, which reinforces the initial assumptions. Those in leadership positions are less likely to support and mentor women who appear unlikely to succeed. Women who are not supported are less likely to succeed and are more likely to leave. Their disproportionate attrition then reduces the pool of women mentors and role models and perpetuates the assumptions that perpetuate the problem.[56]

The problem is compounded by the disincentives to raise it. A common response is to "shoot the messenger." Women who express concerns learn that they are "overreacting" or exercising "bad judgment."[57] For example, one African-American attorney serving on her corporate employer's equal opportunity task force made the mistake of candidly reporting problems in her own department. As she learned, many colleagues are "not really comfortable" with complaints about discrimination and they don't want to work with people "who make [them] uncomfortable."[58] The result is to stifle candid discussions of diversity-related issues. Targets of bias are reluctant to appear confrontational, and decision-makers are reluctant to air concerns about performance that could make them appear biased.[59] Moreover, because stereotypes operate at unconscious levels and selections for leadership positions involve subjective and confidential judgements, the extent of bias is hard to assess. It is, however, instructive that in large scale surveys of senior executive women, the most frequently cited obstacle to advancement is "male stereotyping and preconceptions."[60] The problem is not only that women are unprepared for leadership positions, but also that some men are unprepared to have them in such positions or to provide the career development opportunities that would get them there.

Unconscious bias is a problem not only for the individual women who encounter leadership barriers, but also for their employers, who are failing to take full advantage of the talent pool available. Limited opportunities for career development adversely affect female employees' morale, performance, and retention. . . . For many employers, women's high rates of attrition impose substantial costs in recruitment, training, and disruption of working relationships.[61]

Mentoring and support networks

Another common obstacle for women leaders is the difficulty in obtaining mentors and access to informal networks of advice, contacts, and support. In surveys of upper-level management, almost half of women of color and close to a third of white women cite the lack of influential mentors as a major barrier to advancement.[62] Women lawyers and politicians experience similar problems.[63] Many men who endorse equal opportunity in principle fall short in practice; their efforts focus on other men who seem most similar in backgrounds, experiences, and values.[64] As one participant in the Department of Labor's Glass Ceiling survey explained, "What's important [in organizations] is comfort, chemistry . . . and collaborations," which are harder to sustain among those who seem "different."[65] Concerns about sexual harassment or the appearance of impropriety can heighten that discomfort. Some men are reluctant to mentor or be seen alone with female colleagues because of "how it might be perceived."[66] Others enjoy the bonding that occurs in all-male social or sporting events.

Surveys of professional women offer repeated refrains of exclusion from "boys clubs" or "old boys' networks."[67] Participation in informal networks is particularly difficult for women with demanding family commitments, who lack time for the social activities that could generate collegial support and client contacts. As Catalyst President Sheila Wellington notes, at the end of the day, many "men head for drinks. Women for the dry cleaners."[68] Men pick up tips; women pick up kids, laundry, dinner, and the house.

The result is that many women remain out of the loop of career development. They are not adequately educated in their organization's unstated practices and politics. They are not given enough challenging, high-visibility assignments. They are not included in social and marketing events that yield professional opportunities. And they aren't helped to plan a career progression that will groom them for leadership. Even when they obtain senior positions, many women often lack the support from influential clients and colleagues that would confer significant power.[69]

Problems of exclusion are greatest for those who appear "different" on other grounds as well as gender, such as race, ethnicity, disability, or sexual orientation. Many women of color report being treated as outsiders by white colleagues, and as potential competitors by minority men.[70] In one recent ABA survey, less than 10 percent of black attorneys believed that law firms had a genuine commitment to diversity, and other studies reflect similar skepticism about corporate legal departments.[71] Despite growing tolerance toward gay and lesbian attorneys, those who are open about their sexual orientation too often risk isolation and denial of access to clients who might be "uncomfortable" working closely with them.[72] Even in jurisdictions that prohibit discrimination on the basis of sexual orientation, some professionals are quite explicit about their prejudices. As one anonymous participant in a Los Angeles bar survey described his firm's attitude: "Don't have any, don't want any."[73]

Men are, of course, not the only group responsible for these patterns of exclusion. Recent research chronicles lingering difficulties with what sociologists once labeled "Queen Bees": women who believe that they managed without special help, so why can't everyone else?[74] These women enjoy the special status that comes with being one of the few females at the top of the pecking order and are willing to serve as proof that gender is no barrier to those who are qualified. Although the vast majority of women leaders are more sensitive to gender-related problems, they are not always actively involved in the solution. Some women are hesitant to become "typed as a woman" by frequently raising "women's issues," by appearing to favor other women, or by participating in women's networking groups.[75] Other senior women, particularly women of color, do what they can but are too overcommitted to provide sufficient mentoring for all the junior colleagues who need assistance.[76] Given the demographics of upper-level positions, women will remain at a disadvantage unless and until adequate support networks are seen as both individual and institutional priorities.

Workplace structures

A similar point can be made about workplace practices that fail to accommodate family commitments. A wide gap persists between formal policies and actual practices. Although most women in law and upper-level management are in businesses or partnerships that offer part-time work and/or flexible schedules, few of these women feel able to take advantage of such options. For example, over 90 percent of surveyed law firms report policies permitting part-time schedules, yet only about 3 percent of lawyers actually use them.[77] Most women surveyed believe, with good reason, that any reduction in hours or availability would jeopardize their prospects for advancement and could put them "permanently out to pasture."[78] They doubt, as do senior women in other contexts, that their organizations truly support workplace flexibility.[79] That doubt is reinforced by a wide variety of research, which finds that even short-term adjustments in working schedules, such as leaves or part-term status for under a year, results in long-term reductions in earnings and advancement.[80]

The problem is compounded by the sweatshop schedules routinely expected of those who seek or occupy leadership positions. Hourly requirements have increased dramatically over the last two decades, and what has not changed is the number of hours in the day.[81] For senior executives, top government officials, and partners in law firms, all work and no play is fast becoming the norm rather than the exception; fifty to seventy hour work weeks are typical.[82] Unsurprisingly, most surveyed female executives and lawyers feel that they do not have sufficient time for themselves or their families.[83] Few supervisors are as blunt as the partner who informed one junior colleague, "Law is no place for a woman with a child."[84] But surveys on work and family issues consistently report that leadership positions are incompatible with involved parenting.[85] That same message is sent by resistance to "special" treatment for women seeking to accommodate family obligations without compromising opportunities for advancement. As one observer wryly put it, "Can a woman have a high-powered professional career and still have children? Sure, just as long as she doesn't plan on ever seeing them."[86] And women who do not have a family, often lack time for relationships that might lead to one. Unmarried law firm associates routinely end up with disproportionate work because they have no acceptable reason for refusing it.[87]

Although the inadequacy of family-friendly policies is not just a "women's issue," women pay a disproportionate price. Part of the problem involves women's biological clock. The demands of bearing and caring for young children generally are most intense during the same period in which the foundations for career development are laid. Moreover, despite a significant increase in men's domestic work over the last two decades, women continue to shoulder the major burden.[88] Most male leaders in business and professional positions have spouses who are full-time homemakers or who are working part-time. The same is not true of female leaders, who, with few exceptions, are either single or have partners with full-time jobs.[89]

Underlying these inequalities are long-standing socialization patterns and workplace practices. Only about 13 percent of Fortune 1000 companies and 10 percent of surveyed law firms offer the same paid parental leave to fathers as well as mothers, and few men actually take them.[90] Although involved fathers are receiving somewhat greater support, most research suggests that the special leeway extends only so far. As a male lawyer explained to a Boston Bar Association work–family task force, it may be "okay [for men] to say that they would like to spend more time with the kids, but it is not okay to do it, except once in a while."[91]

In short, many workplace structures leave both men and women feeling unfairly treated. Men feel that they have fewer acceptable justifications than women for seeking reduced schedules. Women feel that their justifications will never be seen as truly acceptable as long as they are viewed as "women's issues." In short, men cannot readily get on the "mommy track." Women cannot readily get off it.

The resistance to flexible or reduced schedules stems from multiple causes. Part of the problem involves the long-standing devaluation of "women's work" in the home and many decision-makers' failure to appreciate the conflicts it presents in workplaces designed by and for men. The problems are exacerbated by recent increases in competition and technological innovations, which have accelerated the pace of commercial life and created expectations of instant responsiveness.[92] . . . In some fields, unpredictable deadlines, uneven workloads, or frequent travel pose particular difficulties. In other contexts, a willingness to work long hours often is viewed as a proxy for harder to measure qualities such as commitment, ambition, and reliability under pressure.[93] The result is a "rat race equilibrium" in which most individuals feel that they would be better off with shorter or more flexible schedules but find themselves in workplaces that offer no such alternatives.[94]

The result is that those with substantial family commitments often drop off the promotion track, leaving behind a decision-making structure insulated from their concerns. Many professional and business leaders who have made substantial personal sacrifices to reach their positions resent the burdens imposed by colleagues with different priorities. Law firm surveys repeatedly find senior women as well as men whose attitude is, "I had to give up a lot. You [should] too."[95] If women want to be "players," the message is that they have to play by the existing rules.[96]

Yet these rules make little sense, even from a narrow economic calculus. A wide array of research from both professional and business settings indicates that part-time employees are more efficient than their full-time counterparts, particularly those working sweatshop schedules.[97] Bleary burned-out lawyers on the midnight shift seldom provide cost-effective services and they are more susceptible to stress-related health disorders.[98] Nor are these full-time employees necessarily more accessible than those on reduced or flexible schedules. An attorney at a deposition for another client is less available than an attorney with a cell phone on the playground. What little research is available finds no negative impact on client relations from reduced or flexible schedules.[99] And considerable data indicate that such arrangements save money in the long run by reducing absenteeism, attrition, and corresponding recruitment and training costs.[100] [. . .]

The effect of unequal opportunities

Law has been of limited effectiveness in addressing these dynamics of gender dis-advantages. Unlike previous, more overt, forms of discrimination, current inequal-ities are typically a function of unconscious bias, patterns of interaction, and workplace structures. These consequences are often difficult to trace to discrete intentional actions of identifiable individuals.[101] Legal claims of discrimination are therefore hard to prove and expensive to pursue, financially and psychologically. Plaintiffs are putting their performance on trial and the portraits that emerge are seldom entirely flattering. Even the rare complainant who wins in court may lose in life. Backlash, blackballing, and informal retaliation are common problems.[102] Moreover, the risk of discrimination claims often discourages employers from collecting data that would reveal systemic problems.[103]

This absence of information masks the true costs of gender inequality in leadership. Most obviously, the barriers to women's advancement compromise fundamental principles of equal opportunity and social justice. These barriers carry an organizational price as well. Workplaces that are preoccupied with short-term measures of productivity and bottom-line costs of family policies may fail to calculate the longer-term costs in recruitment and retention. As management experts have increasingly recognized, the "business case for diversity" is clear. A wide array of research indicates that the representation of women in leadership positions has a positive correlation with organizational performance, measured in tangible terms such as organizational growth, increased market share, and return on investment.[104] Although correlation does not always imply causation, there are strong reasons to believe that greater diversity in fact promotes effective leadership.

The most obvious reason is demographic. Women represent a substantial share of the pool of talent available for leadership. Organizations that create a culture of equal opportunity are better able to attract, retain, and motivate the most qualified individuals.[105] . . .

A second rationale for ensuring equal access to leadership positions is that women have distinct perspectives to contribute. In order to perform effectively in an increasingly competitive and multicultural environment, organizations need advisors with diverse backgrounds, experiences, and styles of leadership.[106] The point is not that there is some single "woman's point of view." But as the following discussion indicates, gender differences do make some difference, and they need to be registered in leadership positions.

GENDER DIFFERENCES IN LEADERSHIP STYLES AND PRIORITIES

Leadership styles

The last two decades have witnessed the growth of a cottage industry of commen-tary on gender differences in leadership. Over two hundred empirical studies and a still greater volume of journalistic and pop psychological accounts have attempted to assess such differences in leadership styles and effectiveness.[107] These analyses reflect quite different views of women's "different voice," in part because their methodologies and quality vary considerably. [...] Taken together, these studies challenge some conventional assumptions about women's leadership.

First, perceptions of gender differences in style or effectiveness remain common, although the evidence for such differences is weaker than commonly supposed. For example, a survey of senior executives by the Economic Group and Korn Ferry International identified five top traits in female managers that reflect widely accepted stereotypes: effective women leaders were thought to be empathetic, supportive, nurturing, relation-building, and sharing.[108] ...

The factual basis for such assumptions is thin. It comes largely from self-reports and laboratory studies, which often indicate that women leaders display greater interpersonal skills and adopt more participatory, democratic styles, while men rely on more directive and task-oriented approaches.[109] Yet other large-scale studies based on self-reports find no such gender differences.[110] Nor do these differences emerge in most research involving evaluations of leaders by supervisors, subordinates, and peers in real-world settings.[111] Most of these studies also fail to reveal significant gender differences in the effectiveness of leaders although, as noted earlier, there are some contexts in which women are rated more poorly than men.[112] These tend to involve predominantly male evaluators and male-dominated roles, such as military service. But in some contexts, women are rated as more effective. One recent study by the Foundation for Future Leadership involving some six thousand evaluations of nine hundred managers found that women scored better than men on all but three of thirty-one measures; female managers did worse only in coping with pressure and their own frustrations, and scored the same in delegating authority.[113] Three other recent large-scale studies involving a total of over sixty-five thousand managers similarly found that women outperformed men on all but few measures.[114]

In accounting for these divergent results, authorities on leadership offer several explanations. One involves socialization. Conventional gender roles encourage women to develop interpersonal skills and sensitivities, which increase their comfort level with participatory styles.[115] A second explanation involves sex stereotypes, which are particularly likely to influence lab studies and self-reports. In experimental situations, where participants have relatively little information about each other, they are more likely to fall back on conventional assumptions about appropriate masculine and feminine behavior. Such stereotypical assumptions may also discourage individuals from behaving or describing their behavior in ways that deviate from traditional norms.[116] Since women do not enjoy the same presumption of competence or the same latitude for assertiveness as their male colleagues, a less autocratic leadership style may seem necessary.[117] A third explanation is that few studies on effectiveness adequately control for variations in perceived power, so some gender-linked differences also may have more to do with variations in authority than in performance.[118]

... Women who have achieved leadership positions generally have been selected and socialized to conform to accepted organizational norms.[119] It stands to reason that their styles are similar to those of male counterparts, particularly since recent trends in leadership education have encouraged both sexes to adopt more collaborative, interpersonally sensitive approaches.[120] Nor is it surprising that some studies find superior performance by women leaders, given the hurdles that they have had to surmount to reach upper-level positions and the pressures that they have faced to exceed expectations.

Leadership priorities

A more important, but far less studied, cluster of issues involves the extent to which women use their leadership differently than men, the reasons for such differences, and conditions under which they emerge. Of particular interest are the circumstances and motivations that encourage women leaders to support women's issues.

On the relatively infrequent occasions when researchers ask whether women have different leadership priorities than men, the answer generally is "some women some of the time." The most systematic studies involve judges and politicians. With respect to judicial behavior, the findings are mixed, and their reliability is sometimes limited by small sample sizes and inadequate controls for factors other than gender. Early studies tended not to find significant gender differences in judges' voting behavior, even in cases involving women's rights.[121] By contrast, some of the more recent studies have found differences at least on certain issues, although not always on women's rights or on sentencing matters traditionally thought to inspire feminine compassion.[122] [. . .]

What limited information is available about women lawyers and senior managers provides a similarly mixed record. Many of these women have made a crucial difference in promoting women's issues and in creating institutional structures that will do the same. The ABA's Commission on Women in the Profession is a reflection of those efforts, as are women's bar associations, women's management and leadership organizations, and women's networks in law firms and corporations. These institutions have both provided support for individual members and pressed for fundamental changes on issues such as family leaves, sexual harassment, flexible or reduced schedules, performance evaluations, mentoring programs, and other diversity initiatives.[123]

Yet surveys of law firms and corporations also reveal large numbers of senior women who do not actively advocate women's interests. One of the most common complaints by female associates is that some powerful female partners have not "played a role in promoting the opportunities and quality of life" for junior colleagues.[124] Studies of corporate managers find similar reluctance by many female leaders to press gender issues openly.[125] Underlying these different priorities are differences in personal experience and commitments, personal rewards and risks, and personal influence and self-confidence.

Personal experience and commitment

The most obvious factor accounting for different levels of support for women's issues among women leaders is their personal investment in those issues. For some women, their own experiences of discrimination, marginalization, or work/family conflicts leave them with a desire to make life better for their successors.[126] Other women, who do not initially see themselves as advocates for women's issues, take on that identity when they realize that others are unwilling to do so.[127] . . . Many senior women in business and professional contexts . . . end up representing the "woman's point of view" partly by default. They are often asked to serve as the "token woman" to ensure the fact (or at least the appearance) of diversity, or are enlisted by other female colleagues to raise their concerns. In these circumstances, many women leaders feel a responsibility to speak out on gender issues that would otherwise remain unacknowledged and unaddressed.[128]

However, as noted earlier, not all women who experience gender bias or who occupy positions where women are underrepresented become committed to reform. Some of these leaders have internalized the values of the culture in which they have succeeded. As their colleagues note, these women have "gotten there the hard way," "given up a lot," and "have conformed to the system."[129] Their assumption is that if they managed, so can anyone else.

Rewards and risks

What lessons women draw from their own struggle may in part depend on what consequences they anticipate from continuing the struggle on behalf of other women.

The costs and benefits of raising gender-related concerns vary considerably across contexts. For some women, the rewards from pressing such concerns outweigh the risks. Either they are "not high enough" in leadership circles to worry that their advocacy will seem threatening, or they are high enough that their own career will not be threatened.[130] So too, some women work in organizations or represent political constituencies that make it safe to raise women's issues, and to "stand up for what [they] believe."[131] Other, more tangible benefits can also result from becoming a "squeaky wheel."[132] For lawyers or senior managers, these benefits may include more equitable compensation structures, greater flexibility in workplace schedules, increased career or client development opportunities, and a larger critical mass of supportive female colleagues.[133] . . . Even where career-related rewards are absent, many women take substantial personal satisfaction from helping to ensure that the next generation has opportunities that they did not.

Yet for other women, any such benefits come at too great a cost. Surveys of female lawyers, politicians, and corporate executives reflect common concerns. The first involves becoming "pigeon-holed" as a "feminist" or "women's libber."[134] In most leadership settings, these labels are not meant as compliments. . . . [W]omen working within conservative organizations similarly worry about taking positions that will brand them as "extremist," "militant," "strident," "oversensitive," "abrasive," "disruptive," or "difficult to work with."[135] Even when they express gender-related concerns in gentle, nonconfrontational terms, women may risk being dismissed as "self-serving" "whiners" "who are unable to compete without special treatment."[136]

Such reputational risks leave women leaders in a double bind. Those who "rock the boat" on women's issues may lose the collegial support and career development opportunities that would provide a power base within their organizations and make their advocacy effective.[137] But those who obtain influence by becoming one of the "good old boys" cannot easily defect when gender-related issues arise.[138] So too, women who sacrificed a satisfying family life to obtain leadership positions have difficulty supporting junior colleagues who want similar status without making similar sacrifices. As one of those colleagues put it, the attitude is "I don't have what you have and therefore you can't have what I have."[139]

Personal influence

How women leaders balance the rewards and risks of pressing women's issues also depends on their position within an organization. Most obviously, as former New York Times columnist Anna Quindlin notes, women who feel confident that they are "not going to get busted down to private any time soon" have the greatest opportunity to help other women who lack that security.[140] Judges with life appointments, elected officials with "safe seats," law firm partners with a large client base, or senior executives with outstanding profit records often can afford to deliver unwelcome tidings without serious risks.

Whether they are willing to do so may depend in part on their confidence that such advocacy will prove effective. Can they convince senior colleagues that there *is* a serious "woman problem" in their workplace? Can they make a persuasive business case for reform? Can they minimize the backlash that claims of "special treatment" often generate? And can they avoid the "battle fatigue" that comes from persistently raising concerns that others find inconvenient to acknowledge, let alone address?[141] Helping more women leaders reach better answers to these questions must be part of any reform agenda.

Notes

1   Karin Klenke, *Women and Leadership, A Contextual Perspective* 27 (1996).
2   Charlotte Bunch, quoted in Helen S. Astin and Carole Leland, *Women of Influence, Women of Vision: A Cross-Generational Study of Leaders and Social Change* xi (1991).
3   Klenke, *Women and Leadership*, at 12, 241; *Talking Leadership: Conversations with Powerful Women* 7–8 (Mary S. Hartmen ed., 1995).
4   Barbara Kellerman, *Reinventing Leadership: Making the Connection between Politics and Business* 177 (1999).
5   Jeanette N. Cleveland, Margaret Stockdale, & Kevin R. Murphy, *Women and Men in Organizations: Sex and Gender Issues at Work* 287, 319 (2000); Sumru Erkut, *Inside Women's Power: Learning from Leaders* 2 (2001).
6   Klenke, *Women and Leadership*, at 61; Cleveland, Stockdale & Murphy, *Women and Men in Organizations*, at 288–292.
7   Klenke, *Women and Leadership*, at 12; Kellerman, *Reinventing Leadership*, at 149, 175–179.
8   Elizabeth V. Spelman, *Inessential Woman: Problems of Exclusion in Feminist Thought* 114–117 (1988); Deborah L. Rhode, *Speaking of Sex* 22, 41 (1997).
9   Rhode, *Speaking of Sex*, at 1–19.
10 Federal Glass Ceiling Commission, *Good for Business: Making Full Use of the Nation's Human Capital*, 145 (1995).
11 Hope Viner Samborn, "Higher Hurdles for Women," *ABA J.*, September, 2000, at 30, 33.
12 John Markoff, 'Hewlett-Packard Picks Rising Star at Lucent as Its Chief Executive," *N.Y. Times*, July 20, 1999, at C1 (Quoting Fiorina); for more pessimistic assessments see text at note 32 infra; *Catalyst, Women in Law: Making the Case* 22 (2000); Abbie F. Willard & Paula A. Patton, National Association for Law Placement, *Perceptions of Partnership: The Allure and Accessibility of the Brass Ring* (1999).
13 Catalyst, *Catalyst Facts: Women in Business* (2000), and *2000 Census of Women Corporate Officers and Top Earners* (2000). See also Tamar Lewin, "Women Profit Less Than Men in the Nonprofit World, Too," *N.Y. Times*, June 3, 2001 at A26 (reporting gender disparities in the nonprofit sector).
14 *ABA Commission on Women in the Profession: A Snapshot of Women in the Law in the Year 2000*; ABA Commission on Women in the Profession, *The Unfinished Agenda: Women and the Legal Profession* 14 (2001).
15 Marjorie E. Kornhauser , "A Legislator named Sue: Re-Imagining the Income Tax," 5 *Journal of Gender, Race, and Justice* 289, n. 2 (2002); Marie Tessier, "Washington Lookout: Women's Appointments Plummet Under Bush," *Women's ENews*, July 1, 2001 at women's enews.org.; Center for American Women in Politics, *Women in Elected Office*, 2000 Fact Sheet Summaries (May, 2000); Ruth B. Mandel, "Women's Leadership in

American Politics: The Legacy and the Promise," in *The American Woman 2001–2002: Getting to the Top* 43, 45 (Cynthia B. Costello & Ann J. Stone, eds. 2001); Associated Press, "No Women Chair House Panels," *Houston Chronicle*, Jan 6, 2001, at A1; Mary Hawkesworth, "Gender Gap: American Women Still Trail in Elected Office," *Dallas Morning News*, March 8, 2000, at 17A.

16 Kornhauser, "A Legislator Named Sue," at 289 n. 2.

17 Catalyst, 2000 *Census of Women Corporate Officers and Top Earners*; ABA Commission on Opportunities for Minorities in the Profession, *Miles to Go; Progress of Minorities in the Legal Profession*, 3–5 (2000).

18 Catalyst, *Women in Corporate Leadership: Progress and Prospects* 37 (1996).

19 Rhode, *Speaking of Sex*, at 3–4; Report of the Ninth Circuit Gender Bias Task Force, The Effects of Gender in the Federal Courts, 60 (Discussion draft, 1992) (quoting male attorney's suggestion that women should "relax and let time take care of the problem").

20 ABA Commission on Women in the Profession, *Unfinished Agenda*, at 14.

21 Virginia Valian, *Why So Slow?: The Advancement of Women* 214–16 (1998); Rhode, *Speaking of Sex*, at 141–146; Virginia Valian, "The Cognitive Basis of Gender Bias," 65 *Brook. L. Rev.* 1037 (1999); Cherryl Simrell King, "Sex Role Identity and Decision Styles: How Gender Helps Explain the Paucity of Women at the Top," in *Gender Power, Leadership and Governance* 67, 71 (Georgia Duerst-Lahti, Rita Mae Kelly, eds., 1995).

22 ABA, Young Lawyers Division, *The State of the Legal Profession* (1991). See also Cynthia Fuchs Epstein et al., "Glass Ceilings and Open Doors: Women's Advancement in the Legal Profession," 64 *Fordham L. Rev.* 291 (1995) (noting that in the period of study, men's chances of making partnership were 17 percent and women's 5 percent); Cynthia Grant Bowman, "Bibliographical Essay: Women and the Legal Profession," 7 *Am. U. J. Gender, Soc, Pol'y & L.* 149, 164 (1999) (citing studies).

23 Gail Collins, "A Social Glacier Roars," *N.Y. Times Magazine*, May 16, 1999, at 77; Eleanor Clift and Tom Brazaitis, *Madame President: Shattering the Last Glass Ceiling*, 18 (2000); Marcia Lynn Whicker and Lois Duke Whitaker, "Women in Congress," in *Women in Politics: Outsiders or Insiders?* 171 (Lois Duke Whitaker, ed. 1999).

24 For general discussion of gender stereotypes and schema, see Valian, *Why So Slow*, at 16–17; Rhode, *Speaking of Sex*, at 145–47 Mark R. Poirier, "Gender Stereotypes at Work," 65 *Brook. L. Rev.* 1073, 1086–89 (1999).

25 International Labour Organization, *Breaking the Glass Ceiling: Women in Management*, 4 (1997). See sources cited in Marilyn J. Davidson and Ronald J. Burke, *Women in Management: Current Research Issues* 3 (1994); Georgia Duerst-Lahti and Rita Mae Kelly, "On Governance, Leadership and Gender," in *Gender Power, Leadership, and Governance*, at 12, 24–26; Mary Anne C. Case, "Disaggregating Gender From Sex and Sexual Orientation: The Effeminate Man in the Law and Feminist Jurisprudence," 105 *Yale L. J.* 1, 72–73 (1995); Judith A. Kolb, "The Effect of Gender Role, Attitude Toward Leadership, and Self-Confidence on Leader Emergence: Implications for Leadership Development," 4 *Hum. Resource Dev. Q.* 305, 307 (1999); Richard F. Martell, "Sex Stereotyping in the Executive Suite: 'Much Ado About Something,'" 13 *J. Soc. Behav. and Personality* 127 (1998).

26 Lahti and Kelly, "On Governance," at 24. For a compilation of great man approaches, see *Political Leadership: A Source Book* (Barbara Kellmrman, ed. 1986).

27 See Joan Brockman, *Gender in the Legal Profession* 154–158 (2001); Kathleen Hall Jamieson, *Beyond the Double Bind: Women and Leadership* 4, 129 (1995) (quoting Barbara Boxer and Jean Kirkpatrick); Joyce K. Fletcher, *Disappearing Acts: Gender, Power, and Relational Practice at Work* 118 (1999); Peggy Ornstein, *Flux: Women, Sex, Work, Kids, Love, and Life in a Half Changed World* 51 (2000); *Nine and Counting: The Women of the Senate* 181 (Barbara Mikulski et al., eds., 2000); Ann M. Morrison et al., *Breaking the Glass Ceiling: Can Women Reach the Top of America's Largest Corporations?* 54, 61–62 (1994); Deborah L. Rhode, "Gender and Professional Roles," 63 *Fordham L. Rev.* 39, 67 (1994);

Alice H. Eagly, Mona G. Makhijani, Bruce G. Klonsky, "Gender and the Evaluation of Leaders: A Meta-Analysis," 111 *Psychological Bulletin* 3, 17 (1992).

28 Eagly, Makhijani, & Klonsky, "Gender and The Evaluation of Leaders," at 17; Cleveland, Stockdale, & Murphy, *Women and Men in Organizations*, at 106, 307; Rochelle Sharpe, "New Studies Find that Female Managers Outshine Their Male Counterparts in Almost Every Measure," *Businessweek Online*, Nov. 20, 2000, http/www.businessweek.com.

29 Judith A. Kolb, "Are We Still Stereotyping Leadership?: Look at Gender and Other Predictors of Leader Emergence," 28 *Small Group Research* 370 (1997): Russell L. Kent and Sherry E. Moss, "Effects of Sex and Gender Role on Leader Emergence," 37 *Acad. of Mgmt. J.* 1335 (1994).

30 Suzanne Nossel and Elizabeth Westfall, *Presumed Equal: What America's Top Lawyers Really Think About Their Firms*, xii, 214, 222, 269, 279 (2d ed. 1998); Maureen Dowd, "A Man and A Woman," *N.Y. Times* Sept. 20, 2000, at A27; Barbara Lee Family Foundation, *Keys to the Governor's Office* 24 (2001); Judy Percy Martinez, "Professionalism: One and Only One Woman's Perspective," 75 *Tulane L. Rev.* 11713, 1724 (2001). See also International Labour Organiation, *Breaking the Glass Ceiling* 59 (discussing narrower range of acceptable behavior for women than men).

31 See studies cited in Kay Deaux & Marianne La France, "Gender," in *The Handbook of Social Psychology* 788 (Daniel T. Gilbert et al., 4th ed., 1998). Rhode, *Speaking of Sex*, at 145; Federal Glass Ceiling Commission, *Good for Business*, at 26–28, 64–72, 93–96, 104–106; Valian, "Cognitive Basis," 1046–49; Cecilia J. Ridgeway and Shelly J. Correl, "Limiting Inequality Through Interaction: The End(s) of Gender," 29 *Contemp. Sociol.* 110, 113 (2000); Diana L. Bridge, "The Glass Ceiling and Sexual Stereotyping: Historical and Legal Perspectives of Women in the Workplace," 4 *Va. J. of Soc. Pol'y & L.* 581, 605–606 (1997).

32 Catalyst. *Women in Financial Services: The Word on the Street* (New York: Catalyst, 2001); Catalyst, Center for the Education of Women, University of Michigan and University of Michigan Business School, *Women and the MBA: Gateway to Opportunity* 22–29 (New York: Catalyst, 2000); ABA Commission on Women in the Profession, *Fair Measure: Toward Effective Attorney Evaluations* 14 (1997).

33 Susan Estrich "The Gender Trap," *San Jose Mercury News*, Dec. 9, 2001, at D1; Thomas F. Pettigrew and Joanne Martin, "Shaping the Organizational Context for Black American Inclusion," 43 *J. Soc, Issues* 41, 36–57 (1987). For the classic description of the problem, see Rosabeth Moss Kanter, *Men and Women of the Corporation* (1977).

34 Robin J. Ely, "The Power in Demography: Women's Social Construction of Gender Identity at Work," 38 *Acad, Management J.* 589, 614, 619 (1995).

35 Martha Foschi, "Double Standards in the Evaluation of Men and Women," 59 *Soc. Psych.* 237 (1996); Jacqueline Landau, "The Relationship of Race and Gender to Managers' Rating Of Promotion Potential," 16 *J. Organizational Behav.* 391 (1995).

36 See studies cited in Rhode, *Speaking of Sex*, at 145; Valian, "Cognitive Basis," at 1050.

37 Ridgeway and Correl, "Limiting Inequality," at 116.

38 Valian, "Cognitive Basis," at 1048–49.

39 Valian, *Why So Slow*, at 131.

40 Viela Banerjee, "Some 'Bullies' Seek Ways to Soften Up; Toughness Has Risks For Women Executives," *N.Y. Times*, Aug. 10, 2001, at C1.

41 Rhode, "Gender and Professional Roles," at 66.

42 Barbara Lee Family Foundation, *Keys to the Governor's Office*, at 13; Maria Braden, *Women Politicians and the Media* 131 (1996).

43 National Women's Leadership Summit, Roper ASW Poll, Apr., 2002.

44 Catalyst, *Women of Color in Corporate Management: Three Years Later*, 27–29 (2002); Sheila Wellington & Katherine Giscombe, "Women and Leadership in Corporate America," in *The American Woman*, at 90; Foschi, "Double Standards;" Federal Glass Ceiling

Commission, *Good for Business*, 26–28, 64–72, 93–96, 104–106; ABA Commission on Opportunities for Minorities in the Profession, *Miles to Go*, at 3–5; Multicultural Women Attorneys' Network of the ABA, *The Burdens of Both, The Privileges of Neither: A Report*, 23–24 (1994).

45 See sources cited in Rhode, *Speaking of Sex*, at 145; Bridge, "The Glass Ceiling," 605–606. Jacob Herring, "The Everyday Realities of Minority Professional Life in the Majority Workplace," discussed in Bar Association of San Francisco Committee on Minority Employment, *Interim Report: Goals and Timetables for Minority Hiring and Recruitment*, 28 (2000).

46 See Paul M. Barrett, *The Good Black: A True Story of Race in America*, 55–56, 279–80 (1999); Orenstein, *Flux*, at 76; Rhode, *Speaking of Sex*, at 163–171; Ridgeway and Correl, "Limiting Inequality," at 114; Wellington & Giscombe, "Women and Leadership in Corporate America," at 87, 102; T. Shawn Taylor, "Executive Strategies: Women of Color Must Confront Unique Obstacles," *Chi. Tribune*, June 24, 2001, at 3C.

47 Cameron Stracher, "All Aboard The Mommy Track," *Am. Law.*, March 1999, at 126; Deborah L. Rhode, "Myths of Meritocracy," 65 *Fordham L. Rev.* 585, 592–93 (1996); Meredith K. Wadman, "Family and Work," *Washington Lawyer*, November, December, 1998, 33; Willard & Patton, *Perceptions of Partnership*, at 99; Cynthia Fuchs Epstein et al., "Glass Ceilings and Open Doors," at 391–399.

48 Epstein et al., "Glass Ceilings and Open Doors," at 298; Harvard Women's Law Association, *Presumed Equal: What America's Top Lawyers Really Think About Their Firms* 72 (1995); Rhode, "Myths of Meritocracy," at 588; International Labour Organization, *Breaking the Glass Ceiling*, at 61.

49 Harvard Women's Law Association. *Presumed Equal*, at 72.

50 Pat Schroeder, *24 Years of House Work . . . and the Place is Still a Mess* 128 (1998).

51 Amy H. Handlin, *Whatever Happened to the Year of the Woman?: Why Women Still Aren't Making It to the Top in Politics* 29 (1998). See also Mikulski et al., *Nine and Counting*, at 181; Catherine Cowan, "Women Find a Home in State Government," *State Government News*, March 2001, at 10, 11.

52 Rhode, "Gender and Professional Roles," at 62–63; Deborah L Rhode, "Balanced Lives for Lawyers," 70 *Fordham Law Review* 2207, 2213 (2002).

53 Boston Bar Ass'n Task Force on Professional Challenges and Family Needs, *Facing the Grail: Confronting the Cost of Work-Family Imbalance* 25 (1999); Laura Gatland, "The Top 5 Myths About Part-Time Partners," *Perspectives*, Spring, 1997, at 11.

54 Linda Hamilton Krieger, "The Content of our Categories: A Cognitive Bias Approach to Discrimination and Equal Employment Opportunity," 47 *Stan. L. Rev.* 1161, 1207–09 (1995); Federal Glass Ceiling Commission, *Good for Business*, 26–28, 64–72, 93–96, 104–06, 123–25.

55 Melvin J. Lerner, *The Belief in a Just World*, vii–viii (1980); Valian, "Cognitive Basis," at 1059.

56 Epstein et al., "Glass Ceilings and Open Doors," at 28; ABA Commission, *Miles to Go*, at 6–7, 14–15; Bar Ass'n of San Francisco, *Goals '95 Report: Goals and Timetables for Minority Hiring and Advancement* 17, 25 (1996); David B. Wilkins and G. Mitu Gulati, "Why Are There So Few Black Lawyers in Corporate Law Firms? An Institutional Analysis," 84 *Calif. L. Rev.* 493, 570 (1996); David A. Thomas and Karen L. Proudford, "Making Sense of Race Relations in Organizations," in *Addressing Cultural Issues in Organizations: Theory for Practice* (Robert T. Carter, ed. 2000).

57 "Green Pastures," *Perspectives*, Summer 1995, at 3; Barrett, *The Good Black*, at 59; Martinez, "Professionalism," at 1724.

58 "Green Pastures," at 3.

59 Thomas and Proudford, "Making Sense of Race."

60 Catalyst, *Women in Corporate Leadership: Progress and Prospects* 37 (1996). See also International Labour Organization, *Breaking the Glass Ceiling*, at 4 (discussing role of stereotypes).

61   National Association for Law Placement (NALP) Foundation, *Keeping the Keepers: Strategies for Associate Retention in Times of Attrition* (1998); Rhode, "Balanced Life for Lawyers," at 2209, 2218.

62   Catalyst, *Women of Color*, at 13; Catalyst, *Women in Corporate Leadership*, at 37. See also Catalyst, *Women and the MBA*, at 53; Catalyst, *Women in Financial Services*.

63   Cowan, "Women in State Government," at 11; Rhode, "Myths of Meritocracy," at 589; Nossel and Westfall, *Presumed Equal*; Ida O. Abbott, *The Lawyer's Guide to Mentoring* (2000); Catalyst, *Women in Law*, at 4–6; and NALP Foundation, *The Lateral Lawyer* (finding that 40% of surveyed women wanted better training and mentoring).

64   Mats Alvesson and Yvonne Due Billing, *Understanding Gender and Organizations* 194 (1997); Michael Roper, "'Seduction and Succession': Circuits of Homosocial Desire in Management" in *Men as Managers, Managers as Men: Critical Perspectives on Men, Masculinities, and Managements* 210 (David L. Collinson and Jeff Hearn, eds. 1996); Judith Lorber, *Paradoxes of Gender* 237–38 (1994).

65   Federal Glass Ceiling Commission, *Good for Business*, at 28; Wellington & Giscombe, "Women and Leadership in Corporate America," at 92.

66   Epstein et al., "Glass Ceilings and Open Doors," at 356; Klenke, *Women in Leadership*, at 185.

67   A striking number of women volunteered these descriptions in a recent survey of large law firms. Nossel and Westfall, *Presumed Equal*, 68, 99, 113, 129, 144, 173, 179, 187, 194, 200, 203, 204, 224, 228, 259, 264, 274; 356, 361, 366, 374, 379. See also Catalyst, *Women in Corporate Leadership*, at 37; Orenstein, *Flux*, at 21; Milculski et al., *Nine and Counting*; Whicker and Whitaker, "Women in Congress"; Linda Witt, *Running as a Woman: Gender and Power in American Politics* (1994).

68   Sheila Wellington & Catalyst, *Be Your Own Mentor* 110 (2001).

69   Nossel and Westfall, *Presumed Equal*, at 9, 45, 101, 176, 211–12, 291.

70   Report of the Ninth Circuit Gender Bias Task Force, at 171. See also Catalyst, *Women of Color in Corporate Management: Dynamics of Career Advancement* 15 (1999); Ella L. Bell, Toni Denton and Stella Nicomo, "Women of Color in Management: Toward an Inclusive Approach," in *Women in Management: Trends, Issues, and Challenges in Managerial Diversity*, 114 (Ellen A. Fagenson, ed. 1993).

71   Wendell LaGrand, "Getting There, Staying There," *ABA J.*, Feb. 1999, at 54; Cliff Hacker, "Making the Majors," *ABA J.* Feb. 1997, at 58.

72   Los Angeles County Bar Ass'n Ad Hoc Committee on Sexual Orientation Bias, "The Los Angeles County Bar Ass'n Report on Sexual Orientation Bias," reprinted in 4 *S. Cal. L. & Women's Stud.* 295, 444–49, 471 (1995). See also Nossel and Westfall, *Presumed Equal*, at 256, 266, 297; William B. Rubenstein, "Queer Studies II: Some Reflections on the Study of Sexual Orientation Bias in the Legal Profession," 8 *UCLA Women's L. J.* 379, 394 (1998). Some evidence suggests that these patterns are changing, especially in the large firms. For comments suggesting supportive attitudes toward gay and lesbian attorneys, see Nossel and Westfall, *Presumed Equal*, at 76, 90–91, 138, 144, 168, 175, 251, 288–91, 319.

73   "Los Angeles Report on Sexual Orientation Bias," at 312.

74   Klenke, *Women in Management*, at 185; Epstein, et al., "Glass Ceilings and Open Doors," at 408; Harvard Women's Law Association, *Presumed Equal*, at 18; Orenstein, *Flux*, at 52; Rhode, "Myths of Meritocracy," at 590; Nossel and Westfall, *Presumed Equal*, at 126, 187, 266, 277, 297.

75   *Talking Leadership: Conversations with Powerful Women*, at 128; Nossel and Westfall, *Presumed Equal*, at 50, 59, 176; Handlin, *Whatever Happened to the Year of the Woman*, at 52–58; Amy Saltzman, "Woman versus Woman: Why Aren't More Female Executives Mentoring Their Junior Counterparts?," *U.S. News & World Rep.*, March 25, 1996 (citing survey findings that women are less likely than men to mentor).

76   Saltzman, "Women versus Women;" Catalyst, *Women of Color*, 13, 22; Nossel and West-
     fall, *Presumed Equal*, at xii, 131, 266, 299; Cynthia Fuchs Epstein, Carroll Seron, Bonnie
     Oglensky, and Robert Saute, *The Part-Time Paradox: Time Norms, Professional Lives, Family,
     and Gender*, 5 (1999); Handlin, *Whatever Happened to the Year of the Woman*, at 49–50.
77   Epstein et al., *The Part-Time Paradox*, at 5; Willard and Patton, *Perceptions of Partnership*,
     at 99; Catalyst, *A New Approach to Flexibility: Managing the Work Time Equation* 16, 25–27
     (1997).
78   Nossel and Westfall, *Presumed Equal*, at 168; see also 3, 14, 59, 71, 180–81, 194, 199, 255,
     358, 362, 366, 375; Women's Bar Association of Massachusetts, *More Than Part Time*
     (2000); Michael D. Goldhaber, "'Part Time Never Works' Discuss," *Nat'l L. J.* Dec. 4,
     200, at A 51. In a recent study of part-time lawyers, only 1% had become partners.
     Epstein et al., *The Part-Time Paradox*, at 56.
79   Catalyst, *A New Approach*, at 37–38.
80   Ann Crittendon, *The Price of Motherhood* 96 (2000). See also Epstein et al., *Part-Time
     Paradox*.
81   Juliet B. Schor, *The Overworked American: The Unexpected Decline of Leisure* 1–5, 79–82
     (1993).
82   Joan Williams, *Unbending Gender: Why Family and Work Conflict and What to Do About It*,
     671 (2000); Arlie Russell Hochschild, *The Time Bind: When Work Becomes Home and Home
     Becomes Work* 70 (1997); Carl T. Bogus, "The Death of an Honorable Profession." 71
     Ind. L. J. 911, 925–926 (1996).
83   Betsy Morris, "Executive Women Confront Midlife Crisis," *Fortune*, Sept. 18, 1995; Carl
     T. Bogus, "The Death of an Honorable Profession," 71 *Ind. L. J.* 911, 926 (1996).
84   Marilyn Tucker, "Will Women Lawyers Ever Be Happy?," *Law Practice Management*, Jan.,
     Feb. 1998, at 45.
85   Williams, *Unbending Gender*, at 71; See Catalyst, *A New Approach to Flexibility*, at 33.
86   Lorraine T. Zappert, "Getting It Right," 85 (2000).
87   Nossel and Westfall, *Presumed Equal*, at 90, 259, 270.
88   The extent of the inequality is estimated differently by researchers using different
     methodologies. Compare studies cited in Williams, *Unbending Gender*, at 71 (citing
     studies suggesting that women perform about 70 percent of the tasks); Rhode, *Speak-
     ing of Sex*, at 7–8, 149 (citing studies suggesting that employed women spend about
     twice as much time on family matters as employed men); with Tamar Lewin, "Men
     Assuming Bigger Role at Home," citing James T. Bond, et al., *The 1997 National Study
     of the Changing Workforce* (1998); Mark Williams Walsh, "So Where are the Corporate
     Husbands?" *N. Y. Times*, June 24, 2001, at 1, 13; Deborah L. Rhode, "Balanced Lives,"
     102 *Columbia University Law Review* 834, 841–42 (2002).
89   Williams, *Unbending Gender*, at 71; Rhode, "Balanced Lives for Lawyers," at 2213.
90   Families and Work Institute, *Business Work-Life Study* (1998); John Turrettini, "Mommie
     Dearest," *Am. Law.*, April 2000, at 19; *Final Report and Recommendations of the Eighth
     Circuit Gender Fairness Task Force*, 31 *Creighton L. Rev.* 7, 54 (1997); Linda Chavez, *Results
     of Lawyers Work And Family Study of Alternative Schedules at Law Firms in the District of
     Columbia* (May, 2000).
91   Boston Bar Association, *Facing the Grail*, at 17. See also Catalyst, *A New Approach To Flex-
     ibility*, at 25–26; Catalyst, *Women and the MBA*, at 63.
92   Epstein et al., *The Part Time Paradox*, at 5; Deborah L. Rhode, *In the Interests of Justice:
     Reframing the Legal Profession* 41 (2000); ABA Commission on Women in the Profession,
     Balanced Lives: Changing the Culture of Legal Practice (prepared for the Commission by
     Deborah L. Rhode, 2001).
93   Renee M. Landers, James B. Rebitzer, and Lowell J. Taylor, "Rat Race Redux: Adverse
     Selection in the Determination of Work Hours In Law Firms," 86 *Am. Econ. Rev.*, 329
     (1996); Epstein et al., *The Part-Time Paradox*, at 56; Rhode, "Balanced Life for Lawyers,"
     at 2211.

94 Landers, Rebitzer, and Taylor, "Rat Race Redux."

95 Nossel and Westfall, *Presumed Equal*, at 126 (quoting lawyer at Fried Frank). See id., at 9, 44, 187, 266, 277, 297.

96 Nossel and Westfall, *Presumed Equal*, at 21, 24, 261, 277.

97 ABA Commission on Women, *Balanced Lives*, at 23.

98 Rapoport, Bailyn, Fletches, and Pruitt, *Beyond Work-Family Balance*, at 7; Rhode, *Balanced Lives*, at 840; Rhode, *Balanced Lives for Lawyers*, at 2218.

99 "Firm Feedback on Part-Time Lawyering," *Mass. Lawyers Weekly*, April 22, 1996, at B4 (reporting findings of Boston Bar Association study indicating little impact on client relations); *New Models for Part-Time or Flex-Time Partnerships, Compensation and Benefits for Law Offices*, Jan., 1997, at 12; "Part Time Partners," *Am. Law.*, April 1997, at 82.

100 Williams, *Unbending Gender*, 71–73; Boston Bar Assoc. *Facing the Grail*, at 39; Catalyst, *A New Approach to Flexibility*, at 20–21; Rhode, "Balanced Lives for Lawyers," at 2217–2219.

101 Susan Sturm, "Second Generation Employment Disctrimination: A Structural Approach." 101 *Colum. L. Rev.* 458 (2001).

102 Id., Rhode, *Speaking of Sex*, at 161–62. Patrick McGeehan, "Wall Street Highflier to Outcast: A Woman's Story," *N. Y. Times*, Feb. 10, 2002, Section 3 at 1.

103 Sturm, "Second Generation," at 476.

104 Cleveland, Stockdale, & Murphy, *Women and Men in Organizations*, at 363; Business and Professional Women Foundation and American Management Association, *Compensation and Benefits: A Focus on Gender* (1999); Theresa M. Welbourne, Wall Street Susan Stites-Doe and James J. Cordiro, "The Impact of Women Managers on Firm Performance: Evidence from large U.S. Firms," *Int'l Rev. of Women and Leadership*, July, 1997.

105 Catalyst, *Women in Corporate Leadership*, at 70 (reporting survey in which 98 percent of senior executive women cited demographic reasons to support initiatives aimed at women's advancement). National Association of Law Placement Foundation, *Beyond the Bidding Wars: A Survey of Associate Attrition, Departure, Destinations, and Workplace Initiatives* (2000); Catalyst, *Women in Corporate Management*; Robin Ely and David Thomas, "Making Differences Matter: A New Paradigm for Managing Diversity," *Harvard Business Review*, Sept.–Oct. 1996, at 79.

106 Catalyst, *Women in Corporate Management*; Thomas & Ely, "Making Differences Matter," at 79.

107 See Robert I. Kabacoff, *Management Research Group, Gender Differences in Organizational Leadership: A Large Sample Study 1* (1998).

108 Betsy Wangensteen, "Managing Style: What's Gender Got to Do With It?," *Crain's N.Y. Bus.*, Sept. 29, 1997, at 23. See also Judy Wajcman, *Managing Like A Man: Men and Women in Corporate Management 66* (1998).

109 Cleveland, Stockdale & Murphy, "Gender and Leadership," at 307; Eagly and Johnson, "Gender and Leadership Style," at 233–256; Eagly, Karau, and Makhijani, "Gender and the Effectiveness of Leaders," at 125–145: Kabacoff, "Gender Differences in Organizational Leadership." See also Jean Lipman-Blumen, "Connective Leadership: Female Leadership Styles in the 21st Century Workplace," 35 *Soc. Perspectives* 183, 200–01 (1992).

110 Radcliffe Public Policy Institute and The Boston Club, *Suiting Themselves: Women's Leadership Styles in Today's Workplace* (1999).

111 Gary N. Power, *Women and Men in Management* 45–49, 105–109 (1988); Klenke, *Women and Leadership*, at 160; Rosalind Chait Barnett and Janet Chibley Hyde, "Women, Men, Work, and Family: An Expansionist Theory," 56 *American Psychologist* 781, 790–91 (2001); Gary N. Powell, "One More Time: Do Female and Male Managers Differ?," 4 *Acad. of Mgmt. Executive* 68 (1990); Eagly and Johnson, "Gender and Leadership Style," at 246–47; King, "Sex Role Identity and Decision Style," at 66. See Alvesonn and Due Billing, *Understanding Gender in Organizations*, at 146, 151; Linda Molm and Mark Hedley, "Gender, Power and Social Exchange," in *Gender, Interaction and Inequality 8* (Cecilia L. Ridgeway, ed. 1992); Burke and Davidson, "Women in Management."

112 For studies finding no difference, see S. B. Shimanoff and M. M. Jenkins, "Leadership and Gender: Challenging Assumptions and Recognizing Resources," in *Small Group Communication* (R. S. Cathcart and L. A. Samovar, eds. 504); Barnett and Hyde, *Women, Men, Work, and Family*, at 791; Sue Platz, "Sex Differences in Leadership: How Real Are They," *Acad. of Mgmt. Rev.* 118 (1986). For studies finding some differences. Eagly, Karau, & Makhijani, "Gender and the Effectiveness of Leaders," at 126–40; Eagly, Makhijani, & Klonsky, "Gender and the Evaluation of Leaders," at 16–18.

113 Brian S. Moskal, "Women Make Better Managers," *Industry Wk.*, Feb. 3, 1997, at 17.

114 Sharpe, "New Studies."

115 Eagly and Wood, "Explaining Sex Differences," at 314; Eagly, Makhijani, & Klonsky, "Gender and the Evaluation of Leaders," at 18.

116 Klenke, *Women and Leadership*, at 151; Cleveland, Stockdale & Murphy, *Gender and Leadership*, at 307; Eagly, Makhijani, & Klonsky, "Gender and the Evaluation of Leaders," at 18; Eagly & Wood, "Explaining Sex Differences," at 314 (1991).

117 Eagly & Johnson, "Gender and Leadership Style," at 247–48.

118 Klenke, *Women and Leadership*, at 154; Deaux & La France, "Gender."

119 Joanne Martin & Debra Meyerson, "Women and Power: Confronting Resistance and Disorganized Action," in *Power and Influence in Organizations* 311, 313 (Roderick M. Kramer & Margaret A. Neale, eds. 1998); Cynthia Fuchs Epstein, *Deceptive Distinctions: Sex, Gender, and the Social Order* 173–84 (1988). See also Brockman, *Gender in the Legal Profession*, at 158 (describing some women's felt need to prove themselves.)

120 Cleveland, Stockdale, & Murphy, *Women and Men in Organizations*, at 293–99; Kellerman, *Reinventing Leadership*, at 149. See also Lipman-Blumen, "Connective Leadership," at 183–201.

121 Michael E. Solimine and Susan E. Wheatley, "Rethinking Feminist Judging," 70 *Ind. L. J.* 891 (1995); Thomas G. Walker & Deborah J. Barrow, "Diversification of the Federal Bench: Policy and Process Ramifications," 47 *J. Pol.* 596, 607 (1985); John Gruhl et al., "Women as Policymakers: The Case of Trial Judges," 25 *Am. J. Pol. Science* 308, 319–20 (1981).

122 Daniel R. Pinello, *Gay Rights and American Law* Table 6.2 (forthcoming 2003) (finding women judges substantially more likely to rule in favor of gay rights but not controlling for other potentially relevant characteristics); Theresa M. Beiner, "What Will Diversity on the Bench Mean for Justice?," 6 *Mich. J. Gender and L.* 113 (1999) (suggesting some differences on civil rights suits); Sue Davis, Susan Haire, & Donald R. Songer, Voting Behavior and Gender on the U.S. Court of Appeals 77 *Judicature* 129 (1993) (finding some differences in employment discrimination and search and seizure cases but not obscenity cases); Jennifer A. Segal, "The Decision Making of Clinton's Nontraditional Judicial Appointees," 80 *Judicature* 279 (1997) (finding differences on individual liberties and criminal procedure but not on women's issues); Jeffrey Toobin, "Women in Black," *New Yorker*, Oct. 30, 2000, at 48 (finding greater severity in enforcement of the criminal laws in general and the death penalty in particular by Texas's female judges than male judges).

123 Catalyst, *Creating Women's Networks* (1999); ABA Commission on Women, *Unfinished Agenda*; ABA Commission on Women, *Balanced Lives*.

124 Nossel & Westfall, *Presumed Equal*, at 349. See also id., at 30, 187, 261, 266–67, 365.

125 Martin & Meyerson, "Women and Power," at 340; Susan J. Ashford, "Championing Charged Issues: The Case of Gender Equity Within Organizations," in *Power and Influence in Organizations*, at 349, 375–76.

126 Tamerius, "Sex, Gender, and Leadership," at 99 (recounting politicians' lack of maternity leave); Hartmann, *Talking Leadership*, at 229–30 (quoting Patricia Schroeder).

127 Susan J. Carroll, Center for American Women in Politics, *Representing Women: Congresswomen's Perceptions of Their Representational Roles*, 4 (2000) (quoting Leslie Byrne).

128 See Ashford, "Championing Charged Issues," at 366; *Dear Sisters Dear Daughters: Words of Wisdom from Multicultural Women Attorneys Who've Been There and Done That* (Karen

Clanton, ed. 2000); Deborah L. Rhode, "The 'Woman's Point of View,' " 38 *J. Leg. Educ.* 39 (1988).

129   Nossel and Westfall, *Presumed Equal,* at 277, 126, 261. See also id. at 187, 251, 266, 277.
130   Ashford, "Championing Charged Issues," at 365.
131   Id., at 365–66, 370.
132   Id., at 365.
133   Id., at 365–66.
134   Id., at 369–70; Carroll, *Representing Women,* at 9–10; see also Carroll, "The Politics of Difference," 18 (noting that less than half of surveyed politicians identify as feminists).
135   Id., at 369–70, 375. See also Nossel and Westfall, *Presumed Equal,* at 105, 108; Handlin, *Whatever Happened to the Year of the Woman,* at 52.
136   Id., at 370, 375; see also Jennifer L. Pierce, *Gender Trials: Emotional Lives in Contemporary Law Firms,* 176–77 (1995); Nossel and Westfall, *Presumed Equal,* at 50, 59, 105; Peter Glick and Susan T. Fiske, "Hostile and benevolent Sexism," 21 *Psychol. of Women,* 119, 129 (1997).
137   Nossel and Westfall, *Presumed Equal,* at 50; Catalyst, *Advancing Women in Business,* at 23.
138   The terms come from Carroll, *Representing Women,* at 9 (Quoting Cynthia McKinney).
139   Epstein et al., *The Part-Time Paradox,* at 67.
140   Hartman, *Talking Leadership,* at 186 (quoting Quindlin).
141   Nossel and Westfall, *Presumed Equal,* at 180. See also Debra E. Meyerson & Maureen A. Scully "Tempered Radicalism and the Politics of Ambivalence and Change," 6 *Org. Science* 585, 598 (1995).

GENDER, CULTURE, AND LEADERSHIP: TOWARD A CULTURALLY DISTINCT MODEL OF AFRICAN-AMERICAN WOMEN EXECUTIVES' LEADERSHIP STRATEGIES

PATRICIA S. PARKER AND dt ogilvie

From Leadership Quarterly (1996) 7(2): 189–214

INTRODUCTION

Power and authority are not terms usually associated with African-American women in the leadership literature. Yet, a growing number of African-American women have broken through the "glass ceiling" (Morrison et al., 1987) and climbed over the "concrete wall" (Bell & Nkomo, 1992) to assume positions of power and authority in dominant culture organizations (see Baskerville, Tucker, & Whittingham-Barnes, 1991).

Although rarely acknowledged as such, there are currently two culturally distinct models of leadership in the literature. The predominant model is based on an Anglo-male hierarchical approach (Loden, 1985). In contrast, a "distinctly female" model (Grossman & Chester, 1990; Helgesen, 1990; Loden, 1985) has developed in recent years. Both leadership models can be defined as culturally distinct because they are formulated from a middle-class Anglo-American perspective (Betters-Reed & Moore, 1992) and reflect the socialized traits, behaviors, styles, and culture of members of that group. This paper challenges the practice of universally applying culture-specific leadership models. We develop and advance the idea of a culturally distinct leadership model as revealed in the experiences of African-American women managers and executives. We submit that rather than forcing other models on African-American women's experiences, researchers should make a systematic study of leadership by African-American women from *their* cultural point of view (Parker, 1994).

We argue that African-American women's unique cultural experiences (Collins, 1986; Harding, 1991; Ruddick, 1989) should inform theoretical explanations of their leadership approach. We argue further, following Bell and Nkomo (1992), that the gender-centered focus of the women in management literature fails to provide a complete framework for examining the interactive effects of racism and sexism that may impact the exercise of leadership by African-American women executives (AAWEs) in majority White (dominant culture) organizations.

Although all leadership behavior is complex, we assert that the *nature* of the complexity of AAWEs is different in ways that are organizationally relevant (McDaniel, 1995). We argue that AAWEs' leadership strategies reflect and are shaped by their socialization as Black women,[1] and by their unique social location within dominant culture organizations. This is reflected in their behavioral complexity (Hooijberg, 1992), which allows them to maintain self-efficacy in spite of problems they may have in one role (Linville, 1985, 1987). Living in a racially divided society, we argue, causes AAWEs to use divergent thinking, creativity, risk-taking, and boundary spanning to develop effective strategies of leadership that allow them to adapt to their bicultural world (Bell, 1989, 1990).

BACKGROUND AND SIGNIFICANCE

Over the past 20 years, an extensive literature on "women in management" has developed (Bass, 1990) which focuses on the leadership traits, styles, behaviors and experiences of women managers (see Deaux, 1984; Eagly, 1991; Riger & Galligan, 1980) and attempts to identify and account for gender differences in leadership.

The traditional model of leadership arose from the study of White men.[2] It is a Paramilitary model of control and competitive behavior based on White men (Loden, 1985) because they were the ones who managed successfully and women/Blacks were not considered – they were invisible. With the influx of women into management in the 1960s and 70s, it was widely postulated that women, who were viewed in terms of social category stereotypes, must adapt (Kanter, 1977).

Eventually, however, research findings began to reflect a "distinctly female" model of leadership (Grossman & Chester, 1990; Helgesen, 1990; Lunneborg, 1990) characterized by expression of feelings, greater use of intuition in problem solving (e.g., Agor, 1984), and an increased emphasis on managing personal relationships. Cooperation, teamwork, empathy, and collaboration were emphasized (Loden, 1985; Rosener, 1990). This model, based on the experiences of Anglo women, argues that women tend to place leadership at the center of a network or web (Helgesen, 1990).

We discuss two problematic assumptions that underlie the Anglo-dominated gender and leadership research. Namely, that gender operates similarly across all racial and cultural groups, and that racism and sexism are parallel processes that produce similar effects across race and gender groups (Grossman & Chester, 1990; Helgesen, 1990; Lunneborg, 1990; however, cf. Ely, 1991). The assumption that gender operates similarly across all racial and cultural groups ignores the cultural traditions to which African-American women are socialized, and which Anglo women do not share (e.g., Burgess & Horton, 1993; Dugger, 1991; King, 1988; Ladner, 1972; Malson, 1983).

The assumption that racism and sexism are parallel processes has led researchers to focus on the commonalities that exist across race and gender groups. For example, Ibarra (1993) cites three commonalities between women and racial minorities: numerical minority status, lower social status, and being subject to negative stereotypes and attributions about work-related competencies, aptitudes, and fitness for managerial responsibilities (Ibarra, 1993, p. 66).

This focus on commonalities has made it possible to identify important processes related to institutionalized racism and sexism (e.g., Kanter, 1977) and some general effects of such processes on minorities and women (e.g., internalized feelings of inferiority and powerlessness). However, as Smith and Stewart (1983) argue, the assumption of parallelism led to research that masks substantive qualitative differences that exist among different race and gender groups (Chafe, 1977; Morrison & Von Glinow, 1990) and that can best be understood by looking at the interaction of race and gender, rather than treating these as separate, but parallel constructs. "It has become increasingly clear . . . that racism and sexism must be understood not merely as independent parallel processes, but as processes standing in a dynamic relation to each other . . . [R]acism and sexism really do not exist as 'pure' processes, independent of each other" (Smith & Stewart, 1983, pp. 1–2). These researchers point to key theoretical questions, such as whether the effects of racism for Black women are different from those of Black men, as well as whether sexism is experienced differently by Black and White women (Smith & Stewart, 1983, p. 5).

We argue that the race-sex analogy is theoretically inadequate for examining the leadership strategies of AAWEs and call for an examination of "the constructive nature of difference" that AAWEs offer (Calas & Jacques, 1988, quoted in Ely, 1991, p. 366). Cox and Nkomo (1990, p. 428) argue that "theory construction . . . should give more attention to the intersection of race and gender," which is seldom done, despite evidence that suggests that the organizational experiences of White women differ from those of Black women (Alderfer, Alderfer, Tucker, & Tucker, 1980) and those of minority men differ from those of minority women (Cox & Nkomo, 1990; Fernandez, 1981). They call for theory and research that address race-gender and cross-race combinations and that use race or ethnicity as a moderator of attributions (e.g., Deaux & Emswiller, 1974) about skills and abilities (Cox & Nkomo, 1990). This paper is in that spirit. Research on leadership should benefit if we get away from "White researchers studying White people and acting as if the findings apply to all racial groups" (Alderfer, 1990, p. 494).

THEORETICAL FRAMEWORK

African-American women executives' leadership strategies and tactics may be conceptualized as a function of (a) their socialized traits, behaviors, and styles, and (b) their distinct social location within dominant culture organizations (see Figure 14.1). We use a "contextual interactive" (Smith & Stewart, 1983) cross-cultural model (see Triandis & Albert, 1987) to develop an understanding of AAWEs' leadership strategies as being in many ways distinct from those of other cultural groups.[3] Preliminary insights on the cultural variations that exist between Anglo-American and African-American socialization processes are discussed next.

Cross-cultural comparisons of socialized leadership traits, behaviors, and styles

The socialized traits associated with effective leadership in American society are intelligence, independence, autonomy, aggressiveness, and self-confidence (Bass, 1981, 1990). Such traits are thought to be correlated with specific leadership behaviors. The behavioral traits associated with effective leadership are task-orientation

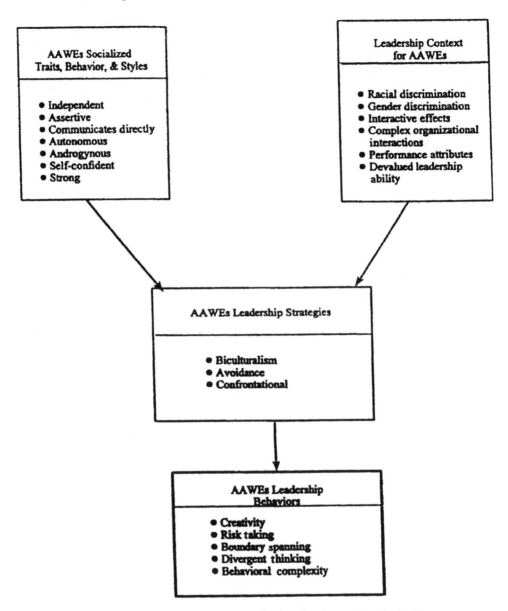

Figure 14.1 A culturally distinct model of African-American female executives' leadership

(i.e., concern with organizing activities to perform tasks), operationalized as "initiating structure" (see Stogdill & Coons, 1957), and interpersonal-orientation (i.e., concern with the morale and welfare of the people in the setting), operationalized as "consideration" (see Stogdill & Coons, 1957). More recently, leader behavior has been conceptualized as transformational versus transactional, which goes beyond leadership transactions based on initiation of structure and consideration (see Bass, 1985).

Gender and leadership style often address two aspects of leadership: (a) the extent to which leaders are democratic or autocratic in their decision-making orientation (e.g., participative vs. nonparticipative); and (b) communication strategies

Table 14.1 Conceptualizing leadership traits, behavior and styles cross-culturally: A socialization perspective

	Anglo-Americans		African-Americans	
	Females	Males	Females	Males
Traits	Supportive	Self-confident	Self-confident	NC
	Cooperative	Independent	Independent	NC
	Nurturing	Autonomous	Autonomous	NC
			Nurturing	NC
Behavior	Collaborative	Instrumental	Androgynous	NC
	Interdependent	Assertive	Communicate directly	NC
Styles	Democratic	Autocratic	Democratic	NC
	Participative	Directing	Directing/ participative	NC
	"Weak" influence strategies	"Strong" influence strategies	"Strong" influence strategies	NC
	Altruism-based strategies	Punishment-based strategies		NC
	Transformational	Transactional	Transformational	NC

NC = not considered.

used to influence subordinates, superiors, and other coworkers. Yet, there are differences in the cultural traditions into which specific groups are socialized that arguably can produce some differences in leadership. Such differences are discussed above (see Table 14.1).

Socialized leadership traits, behaviors, and styles of Anglo-American women and men

Early gender-role socialization theories (Chodorow, 1978; Kohlberg, 1969; Money & Ehrhardt, 1972), based on studies of Anglo-Americans boys and girls, argue that Anglo-American girls are socialized to be dependent and nurturing, whereas Anglo-American boys learn to be independent and aggressive. More recent theoretical positions on Anglo-American gender role socialization (cf. Dugger, 1991; Wood, 1994) reflect the changing attitudes and values about sexual identity among American cultural groups. These later theorists argue that women's increased independence in the systems of social relations (i.e., work and family) makes them more likely to challenge traditional views of gender.

Yet there remains strong evidence of the effects of traditional socialization on Anglo female and male leadership behavior. For example, Tannen traces gendered communication behavior patterns to differences in girls' and boys' communication with parents and peers. She argues that women and men typically engage in distinctive styles of communication with different purposes, rules, and understandings of how to interpret talk (Tannen 1990, 1994). The goal of men's talk is to exert control, preserve independence, and enhance status; the goal of women's talk is to establish and maintain relationships with others. Tannen's work seems to support the view of gender-role identity for Anglo women and men (also see Maltz & Borker, 1982, for similar findings regarding girls' and boys' play).

The socialized traits associated with the Anglo female model of leadership are supportive, conforming, and nurturing, which emphasize the leadership behaviors of consideration and participation (interpersonal orientation), while the traits associated with the traditional male model of leadership are autonomy, strength, and self-confidence in ability (Petty & Miles, 1976), which emphasize the leadership behaviors of structuring and directing (task orientation) (Stogdill & Coons, 1957). Further, Anglo-American women tend to be more transformational in their leadership approach, while Anglo men tend to be more transactional (Rosener, 1990).

In regard to the leadership styles of Anglo-American women and men, a meta-analytical study of the traditional gender and leadership literature (Eagly & Johnson, 1990) found gender differences in measures of democratic and participative tendencies among leaders: women are more democratic and participative, and men are more autocratic and directive. A second aspect of leadership style relates to the use of power and influence. Several studies have compared the influence strategies used by female and male managers (Ayers-Nachamkin et al., 1982; Harper & Hirokawa, 1988; Mainiero, 1986). Mainiero's (1986) field study of 98 upper and lower level male and female managers from two companies found that women tended to rely more on the strategy of acquiescence (i.e., submissiveness) than do men, even when both had the same level of perceived position power.

The findings on the use of power by Anglo-American men and women suggest that men tend to use direct, rational, and confrontational influence strategies, and are confident in their leadership abilities. Women, however, are reported to use more need-based and learned helplessness strategies, and are less confident in their leadership abilities (see, e.g., Conrad, 1985; Harper and Hirokawa, 1988; Instone, Major, and Bunker, 1983; Kanter, 1977).

African-American women's socialization experiences differ form those of Anglo-American women and men. As a result, we argue, leadership traits, behaviors, and styles vary cross-culturally.

Socialized leadership traits, behaviors, and styles of African-American women

Research on African-American families (Bardwell, Cochran, & Walker, 1986; Hale-Benson, 1986) demonstrates that both sexes are socialized toward autonomy and nurturing of children. Further, compared to other groups, African-American families tend to emphasize egalitarian relationships between men and women (Bell, 1971; Davis, 1977; McAdoo, 1987; Rutledge, 1980; Scott-Jones & Nelson-LeGall, 1986; Willie, 1985). That is, African-American family structures tend to have flexible gender roles (Scott-Jones & Clark, 1986). This may stem from African cultural traditions in which behavioral standards for males and females are the same (Lewis, 1975), or from the history of African men and women in both the family and the labor force (Murray, 1975).

Research specifically focused on African-American girls (Epstein, 1973; Gilligan, et al., 1992; Jones, 1992; Ladner, 1972; Malson, 1983) reveals socialization experiences that emphasize possessing a degree of autonomy, strength, independence, and self-confidence in ability (Epstein, 1973; Ladner, 1972). For example, a study by Ladner (1972) suggests that African-American adolescent girls are encouraged to be more independent than Anglo-American girls, irrespective of social class. Thus, whereas assertiveness, independence, and self-confidence have more often been associated with Anglo men than Anglo women, for African-American families these characteristics have always been valued in girls as well as boys (Scott-Jones & Nelson-LeGall, 1986).

African-American mothers (often described as strong disciplinarians and overly protective) manage to raise daughters who are self-reliant and assertive (Collins, 1990). African-American girls are not socialized to be "passive" or "irrational." Rather, their mothers socialize them to be independent, strong, and self-confident, "because they are determined to mold their daughters into whole and self-actualizing persons in a society that devalues Black women" (Wade-Gayles, 1984, p. 12; Gilligan et al., 1992, p. 28).

African-American adolescent girls are socialized by their mothers to become bicultural and resist standards of the dominant culture, including internalizing the ideology about race (Collins, 1990; Greene, 1990a, 1990b; hooks, 1984). The risk of resisting conventions of femininity and racial position could be costly in a society that demands conformity (Taylor, 1991, p. 11). However, contrary to expectations, African-American adolescents have been found to have better self-images, higher self-esteem, greater emotional stability, and less self-consciousness than comparable Anglo adolescents (Gibbs, 1985, p. 29; Root, 1990, p. 257). Although African-American girls and women tend to be devalued by both White and Black society in favor of Anglo women, they "have been able to maintain a positive sense of self against what appears to be overwhelming odds" (Smith, 1982, p. 281).

Smith's (1982) review of the literature found that African-American female adolescents tend to have equal or higher educational and career aspirations than Anglo female adolescents (see Moore, Simms, & Betsy, 1986). Their aspirations were also higher than those of African-American adolescent males, and they had greater expectations of reaching their career goals (Gilligan et al., 1992, p. 31).

Since African-American women do not define themselves in terms of the traditional cultural prescriptions for gender (Dugger, 1991), it follows, then, that their leadership traits and behaviors would not correspond to such prescriptions. Some of the socialized traits identified in the literature as being associated with African-American women – autonomy, strength, independence and self-confidence in ability – are traits that are also associated with the traditional male model of leadership (Petty & Miles, 1976). However, African-American women are also socialized to be nurturing – supportive, caring, and considerate – traits often associated with the traditional female model of leadership (Petty & Miles, 1976).

In gender role theory, the task and interpersonal style orientations are respectively labeled "masculine" and "feminine" (Bem, 1974; Eagly, 1987). Masculine characteristics are those related to instrumentality and agency, whereas feminine traits are those in the interpersonal and expressive domains. That African-American women tend to have traits and behaviors corresponding to both the Anglo male and female leadership models indicates they are likely to be androgynous (Bem, 1974) in their leadership approach, with "androgyny" representing a combination of masculine and feminine traits.

In a study of the sex role attitudes and socialization antecedents among a sample of 123 Black women and 45 White women, Binion (1990) found that the majority of the Black subjects reported androgynous sexual identities but had traditional beliefs about the female role in the family. Black women have a mixed set of gender roles (Wilson, 1986) because they need to be androgynous or masculine to succeed in the work world, "but they must also maintain traditional beliefs about the female role in order to sustain meaningful relationships within their domestic network;

especially with men" (Binion, 1990, p. 505; Gilligan et al., 1992, p. 19). And, "for Black women masculine traits are not antithetical to beliefs about the desirability or legitimacy of certain stereotypic feminine role expectations . . . [especially the] mothering role" (Binion, 1990, p. 503).

Jones (1992), in one of the few studies on African-American women's actual leadership behavior, administered the Multifactor Leadership Questionnaire (MLQ) (Bass, 1985) to 17 African-American women college presidents and found that their leadership was more transformational than transactional. Follow up interviews confirmed this finding. Indeed, the college presidents described their leadership approach in terms of participative management, empowerment, team building, vision creation, and hands-on, roll-up-your-sleeves supervision (Jones, 1992, p. 120), a mix of masculine and feminine leadership approaches.

Very little empirical research focuses on the leadership styles of African-American women. Although there is a dearth of research on whether African-American women's leadership style is democratic or autocratic, the conflict literature discusses African-American women's influence strategies. Ting-Toomey (1986) found that Black female college students tended to engage in more direct controlling conflict strategies than White female college students. Shuter and Turner (1992) found that Black female managers described their approach to conflict resolution as reduction-oriented.

The leadership traits, behaviors, and styles of African-Americans appear to reflect a mix of traits, behaviors, and styles that are associated with both Anglo-American genders. It seems reasonable to suggest that these characteristics could translate into a distinctly African-American leadership style. Clearly, the need for further research of racial-gender differences is warranted.

Despite the evidence that socialized leadership traits, behaviors and styles, and leadership context differ by race and gender, what leadership means from the perspective of Black women remains unclear. For example, how are the socialized traits of independence and autonomy enacted from the standpoint of women who have inherited a legacy of resistance to racial oppression and of creative struggle to ensure the survival of the Black family? How are the leadership behaviors of control and structuring defined from the perspective of resistance to oppression and creative struggle, rather than from the perspective of assumed White male privilege?

The leadership context for African-American women executives

Situation-centered (Deaux, 1984; Riger & Galligan, 1980) explanations of gender and leadership attempt to identify characteristics of the societal and organizational contexts that account for gender differences in leadership. Perhaps based on the assumption that women share a common gender identity, much of this research assumes that race and sex are analogous social categories, implicitly or explicitly drawing parallels between the social processes of racism and sexism.

However, situational factors within dominant culture organizations combine to create a distinct social location for AAWEs within such organizations. Smith and Stewart (1983, p. 8) make this point elegantly:

> [Among the four groups of Black women, Black men, White women, and White men,] the group we know least about is the group most consistently excluded from our

research on racism and sexism: Black women. We have begun to learn from a few vocal and articulate individuals that for Black women sexism is experienced on two levels: in the context of White men's racism, and in the context of their shared oppression with Black men (see hooks, [sic] 1981, and Hood, 1978). Similarly, Black women's friendship and sisterhood with White women is affected by White women's implicit and explicit endorsement of racist practices and attitudes directed at Black women and men (see Hood, 1978). Black women's relationships with each other must surely be intensified by their shared experience of complex power relations with Black men and White men and women (see Higgenbotham, 1982; Meyers, 1975).

The context of gender and racial discrimination and their interactive effects are examined below. Further, we look beyond discrimination to issues related to racial and gender privilege that may create differences in the leadership situations in which members of various cultural groups find themselves.

Racial discrimination

African-American women report that racism, rather than sexism, is the greater barrier to opportunity in dominant culture organizations (Parker, 1994; Talley-Ross, 1992). Bessie Delany (Delany & Delany, 1993) states this rather eloquently,

> I was torn between two issues – colored rights and women's rights. But it seemed to me that no matter how much I had to put up with as a woman, the bigger problem was being colored. People looked at me, and the first thing they saw was *Nigger*, not *woman*.

Only a few studies have examined how race impacts leadership in dominant culture organizations, but it remains unclear whether both African-American men and women are included in the study samples (e.g., King & Bass, 1974; Mayhand & Grusky, 1972; Miner, 1977; O'Reilly & Roberts, 1973; Richards & Jaffee, 1972; Shull & Anthony, 1978). Like all socially created phenomena, racism is complex (Giddens, 1979; Weick, 1979a). However, these studies generally treat race as a demographic variable, without exploring the complexities of race that are deeply ingrained in the social fabric of our society and its organizations (Cox & Nkomo, 1990). More importantly, the studies ignore the possibility of interactive race and gender effects, even when both African-American men and women are included in study samples (e.g., Thomas, 1982).

Gender discrimination

There is evidence that Anglo women and African-American women experience gender oppression differently (Bell & Nkomo, 1992; Betters-Reed & Moore, 1992; Fernandez, 1975, 1981; hooks, 1981). Fernandez (1981) found that the African-American female managers in his study were more critical about the treatment of female managers than were White and other minority women managers in the study, indicating that AAWEs may be more sensitive to gender discrimination than other women.

African-American women are often excluded from important organizational networks, forcing them to create other strategies for gaining access to information. Thus, AAWEs may engage in boundary spanning (Bell, 1990) and develop a broad base of mentors to assist them in their career development efforts (Thomas, 1990).

Table 14.2 Chi-square analysis for race and gender of mentor/sponsor by race and gender protégé

Sponsors/Mentors	Protégés				
	Black Men	White Men	Black Women	White Women	Totals
1. Black men	14	1	23	3	41
	(22%)	(1%)	(16%)	(2%)	(8%)
2. White men	36	109	55	105	305
	(56%)	(91%)	(38%)	(67%)	(63%)
3. Black women	4	0	38	2	44
	(6%)		(26%)	(1%)	(9%)
4. White women	11	10	28	47	96
	(16%)	(8%)	(19%)	(30%)	(20%)
Totals	65	120	144	157	486
	(13%)	(25%)	(30%)	(32%)	

Chi-square = 156.63; $p < 0.0001$; $df = 9$. Relationships for which there were incomplete data were included in the analysis. Adapted from Thomas, 1990, p. 485.

Thomas' study of mentor-protégé relationships by race and gender points up an interesting observation (see Table 14.2). Thomas studied 487 mentor-protégé relationships in the WRL Corporation, a major public utility company in the Northeast, which is 10% Black and 30% female (Thomas, 1990). Although White men formed the largest group of mentors for all races and genders, and disproportionately so for White men and women, only Black women had a fairly even distribution of mentors by race and gender. White men were mentored primarily by White men with a smattering of them being mentored by White women; White women were mentored primarily by White men and White women; Black men were primarily mentored by White and Black men and Black women; but Black women were mentored by White men, Black women, White women, and Black men, in that order. These data indicate that Black women cross gender and race boundaries to create resource relationships.

Thomas (1990) found that Black protégés' relationships with Black mentors were significantly more often skip-level relationships, with peers, or localized outside of the departmental context, than were their cross-race relationships. This may be due to the distribution of positions held by Black managers; they would probably be more dispersed across departments and across levels, so that the likelihood of finding a concentration of Black managers above one in one's department would be low. Black managers in this company seemed to develop relationships that crossed traditional boundaries of hierarchy and area specialization (Thomas, 1990, p. 488; also see Ibarra, 1995). It may also be that Black women were less observant of traditional organizational boundaries in their relationships with both Whites and Blacks.

Research by hooks (1981) suggests that some Black women view sexual harassment as motivated only by racism in White men, and do not recognize it as sexist in Black men (hooks, 1981). Such distinctions are likely influenced by cultural norms. Researchers (Bell, 1992; hooks, 1981) have observed that Black men often view unsolicited sexual advances toward Black women as appropriate behavior. Further, by speaking out about such behavior Black women run the risk of being accused of adding yet another attack against the already besieged Black man. Thus, while Anglo women may experience anxiety about reporting sexual harassment for fear of jeopardizing their jobs, Black women may also experience anxiety about job security, but with the added anxiety of feeling they are betraying their race if Black men are involved (Bell, 1992).

Interactive effects of racial and gender discrimination

There is some preliminary evidence of the interactive effects of racism and sexism on African-American women's organizational behavior. For African-American women, racism and sexism should be viewed as combining in such a way that they create a "distinct social location" (Dugger, 1991) rather than an additive form of "double disadvantage" (Dugger, 1991; King, 1988; Smith & Stewart, 1983). At the societal level, the distinct social status of African-American women is painfully clear. African-American women are the most disadvantaged group in American society in terms of economic and social status (DiTomaso & Smith, 1996). For example, African-American women's median income is 87%, 36%, and 60% of the median income of Anglo females, Anglo males and African-American males, respectively (Hymowitz, 1992, p. 116). Further, the number of African-American women heading households in 1990 was 56% compared to 17% for Anglo women (Bell, 1992). Thus, relative to other groups, African-American women earn less, but are more likely to manage alone, the dual responsibilities of work and family.

Despite this awareness that racism and sexism combine to impact African-American women's status in the larger society, we do not yet fully understand how these processes interact to affect the context for leadership in dominant culture organizations. We use an interactive approach to understand how the experiences of African-American women leaders in organizations are culturally distinct from other groups (Smith & Stewart, 1983, p. 7), and the ways in which African-American women perceive the interactive effects of race and gender.

Recent research (Bell & Nkomo, 1992; Dugger, 1991) confirms that African-American women have a heightened sensitivity to gender discrimination. Bell and Nkomo (1992) surveyed a national sample of 238 African-American and 477 Anglo women in middle and upper levels of management. Theirs is one of the few studies that asked respondents directly about the influence of race and gender on their career perceptions, and that explicitly includes race and racial identity as analytical variables rather than using race as a mere demographic variable. Results showed that the African-American women in the study perceived a higher frequency of sex discrimination than the Anglo women.

Dugger's (1991) survey of 296 Black women and 2,607 White women in the United States found that Black women were more likely than White women to believe that women are victims of discrimination ($b = .084$). Some research suggests that AAWEs in dominant culture organizations not only experience sexism differently from Anglo and other women, they also view racism differently from African-American men in such organizations.

Research by Fernandez reported comments by an upper-level African-American female employee about discrimination faced in corporate America:

> . . . throughout my entire life and career, I have had to deal with comments, innuendos and prejudices as a woman first and also as a Black. As a woman the questions

have been: Does she have the strength of will and character to do the job? Will she get pregnant at a time when we need her most? Will she be emotional in a bad situation? Is she going to be a liability to the organization? Then there is the thought that "we don't need to pay her as much as we would pay a man." As a Black the questions have been: Is she dependable? Is she intelligent enough to really do the job? You know how loud angry Blacks can be, will she be able to carry herself in such a manner that makes the organization look good? Is she able to speak well, without a lot of slang? (Fernandez, 1993, pp. 259–260).

Complex organizational interactions

Within dominant culture organizations, African-American women often must negotiate organizational interactions constrained by the effects of centuries-old, stereotypical images of Black women that pervade Western society (Dumas, 1979; Morton, 1991) and that influence perceptions of Black women's roles and status in the workplace (Bell & Nkomo, 1992). Such negative stereotyping is likely to produce complex interactional dilemmas (Dumas, 1979) for AAWEs in dominant culture organizations. Bell and Nkomo's (1992) research on the career perceptions of Anglo and African-American women provides evidence that AAWEs may frequently experience interpersonal conflict within dominant culture organizations. Compared to other groups, the African-American women in their study perceived greater interpersonal conflicts with Anglo women, African-American men, and Anglo men. Bell and Nkomo (1992) interpret their findings within the context of the racial and sexual tensions (including stereotyping of Black women) underlying interactions among African-American women and the other groups.

One example of negative stereotyping relates to perceptions of African-American women's communication style. Weitz and Gordon's (1993) survey of 256 White undergraduates about their perceptions of images of Black women showed that their images of Black women differed substantially from those of American (presumably White) women in general. Black women were characterized as loud, talkative, aggressive, intelligent, straightforward, and argumentative.

Because of such characterizations in the workplace, AAWEs may find themselves responding to organizational members who hold negative perceptions about Black women's interaction style. Because open emotional expressiveness is highly valued in the African-American culture, when conflicted relationships do exist, Black women tend to communicate negative feelings in a direct fashion (McGoldrick et al., 1988). But, in a study of the perceptions, attitudes, and behaviors of 17 African-American and 42 Anglo-American working women concerning workplace conflict, Shuter and Turner (1992) found that the White women saw themselves as more conflict-avoidant than Black women and perceived that Black women maintain conflict more than the Black women thought they maintained. Indeed, the African-American women reported using conflict-reducing strategies more than Anglo-American women thought they did. The researchers interpret their findings as a function of stereotypic thinking, noting that African-Americans may perceive themselves as using more socially appropriate approaches to conflict than Anglo-Americans think they do (Shuter & Turner, 1992, p. 15).

Devalued leadership ability

Black women are not praised for their adaptability, courage, and resilience in the face of grim odds (Pettman, 1991, p. 195) – attributes that might inform a culturally distinct leadership model. Instead, they are often portrayed as "Black matri-archs," represented as dominant, pathological, deviant, and a threat to Black family life (Lubiano, 1992). This construction is accomplished within a context of racist assumptions about womanhood (Morton, 1991; Palmer, 1983), in which the ideal-ized attributes of "true womanhood" are assigned to White women. Black women do not see the image of White womanhood as applicable to them. Therefore, they are stigmatized for failing to conform to conventional feminine stereotypes, which contributes to the devaluation of their leadership ability.

In Weitz and Gordon's (1993) study, White subjects rated positive traits less positive and negative traits less negative when exhibited by Black women than by American women in general. What is seen as negative in White women (very religious, loud, asexual, having too many children, and weak) is considered less negative (and more appropriate?) for Black women. These traits may have fit into an overall negative impression of Black women and were, therefore, in regard to Black women, not viewed as negative. These results point to the possibility that even though White women report negative attributions about their performance relative to White men, Black women are negatively differentiated from White women, creating an even wider performance attribution gap between White men and Black women.

The above findings suggest that situational factors within dominant culture orga-nizations combine to create a distinct social location for AAWEs within such orga-nizations. African-American women executives are more likely to suffer from the interactive effects of racial and gender discrimination, while Anglo men and women enjoy the benefits of racial privilege. Although Anglo women do face gender dis-crimination, the effect of race on gender discrimination makes gender discrimi-nation even more pernicious for African-American women. The leadership literature fails to look at racial privilege as a distinct social location that has impact on leadership style.

A large body of literature addresses the effect of situational constraints on White women; less research[4] addresses the unique constraints that AAWEs face, which are very different from those that White women face. We know from the extensive women in leadership literature what meaning Anglo women create from their social location, but we do not know what meaning African-American women create or what interpretations they make of their unique social location. Furthermore, we do not have any research that shows how this affects AAWEs' leadership – what types of adjustments or what types of strategic behaviors they develop to manage their unique social location.

TOWARD A CULTURALLY DISTINCT MODEL OF AAWEs' LEADERSHIP

We submit that there is sufficient evidence that socialized leadership traits, behav-iors, and styles, and leadership context differ by race and gender. It therefore becomes important to understand what leadership means from the perspective of African-American women. Forcing one culture's models on African-American women's experiences deprives scholars of potentially rich data that can increase our understanding of leadership. Instead, we argue, culture-specific models should be developed and investigated. Thus, we assert, the enactment of leadership by African-American women must be viewed from the unique vantage point of African-American women.

bell hooks (1984) observed that African-American women are the only group that cannot be seen as oppressors to another race and/or gender group. These unique circumstances are likely to produce strategic responses that may be unique to that group. African-American women's leadership ability should take into account the strategies for adaptability and transformation that African-American women have developed through generations of labor force participation in the United States (Scott, 1991).

Strategic responses to constraints on leadership

Leadership strategies

There is preliminary evidence of African-American women's strategic behavior in dominant culture organizations. Indeed, there is evidence that AAWEs' success in dominant culture organizations may vary as a function of the choice of strategies used to negotiate the dual impacts of racism and sexism. Research by Evans and Herr (1991) on the influence of racism and sexism in the career development of African-American women shows that African-American women use two coping strategies to survive the effects of discrimination in the workplace: (a) avoid potentially harmful working environments, and (b) alter or lower career goals, (Bell and Nkomo's [1992] research suggests that despite the significant negative influence of race on their career progress, African-American women managers are not less satisfied with their progress than are Anglo-American women, perhaps due to their lower expectation of advancement because of their awareness of the negative effects of race on their careers.)

Conversely, White's (1990) interview study of African-American women managers' interaction with dominant corporate culture revealed three strategies for success: risk taking, campaigning, and networking/mentoring. Based on this preliminary evidence, it appears that there are two competing models of strategies African-American women use for survival in dominant culture organizations: an avoidance model and a confrontation model.[5] It is also possible that they use a flexible strategy in which they choose avoidance and confrontation as their assessment of their situation warrants. We argue that successful Black leaders use a variety of strategies to ensure their success in even the most adverse dominant culture situations. We further theorize that such strategies inform a culturally distinct model of leadership by AAWEs.

Leadership behaviors

What resistance/adaptive strategies do African-American women leaders use in response to their unique social location within dominant culture organizations? In a study of 21 African-American women professionals who have careers in predominantly White organizations, Bell (1989, 1990) used a developmental framework to examine the women's bicultural life experiences. Bell (1989, 1990) defines biculturalism as the challenge of managing the tensions between two cultural worlds (one Black, the other White), each of which is shaped by vastly different socio-historical conditions, including racism and sexism. She argues that in response to living in a racially divided society, the African-American woman must "create dynamic, fluid life structures that shape the patterns of their social interactions, relationships, and mobility, both within and between the two cultural contexts" (p. 462).

Bell's research (1989, 1990) provides preliminary evidence that AAWEs are active in reshaping interactional contexts constrained by race and gender bias. Her work found that African-American women used divergent thinking, creativity, risk-taking, and boundary spanning as adaptive responses to biculturalism. These responses are widely considered to be desirable leadership behaviors (e.g., Mintzberg, 1973; Quinn, 1988). Below, we discuss these behaviors from the cultural perspective of AAWEs.

Behavioral complexity

Behavioral complexity theory (Hooijberg, 1992) offers a useful framework to examine AAWEs' leadership styles. Behavioral complexity refers to the ability to successfully manage multiple, diverse roles and skills (Hooijberg & Quinn, 1992). Behavioral complexity requires cognitive complexity as well as a complex set of performance skills that allow one to play multiple, competing roles in highly integrated and complementary fashion (Hooijberg & Quinn, 1992, p. 164). A person who is behaviorally complex can manage successfully more roles and skills than one who is behaviorally simple.

Biculturalism leads to complex life structures. African-American women must bridge multiple realities and manage complex multiple contexts (environmental, social, and cultural). They hold multiple gender roles including those of workers, heads of households, mothers, and lovers (Hyde, 1985). In fact, the AAWE finds herself "caught up in a possible conflicting web of expectations which are far more complex than those of simply being a professional, being a woman, or being Black" (Gilkes, 1982, p. 290; quoted in Bell, 1990, p. 460).

One's environment triggers changes in behavioral complexity. Hooijberg and Quinn (1992) propose "that having to deal with challenges to the work role will elicit the enactment of new leadership roles and/or the rebalancing of leadership roles. This change, in turn, we propose, will lead to more behavioral complexity. It is the interaction between the individual and his or her environment that stimulates development" (p. 169). Racism, sexism, racial and gender discrimination, and racial and gender prejudice create a changing environment full of contradiction and inconsistencies for women of color. These societal forces, and societal expectations of Blacks defined primarily by White men, result in an uncertain and unstable position that causes a lot of stress (Herbert, 1990). "Black women . . . must consider whether an incident was motivated by their race, their sex, or both (Smith & Stewart, 1983)" (Denton, 1990, p. 448). The experience of being Black is significantly different from that of being White. "Blacks have been forced to make adaptive and defensive adjustments that are quite different from those of their White counterparts" (Herbert, 1990, p. 434).

In 1903, W.E.B. DuBois discussed the "double consciousness" that Black people must possess to survive. To be bicultural means to be able to successfully manage the beliefs, values, standards, and expectations of both the dominant culture and one's own culture, even though one's culture is devalued by that dominant culture (Bell, 1990; Gilligan et al., 1992; Root, 1990; Soctt-Jones & Nelson-LeGalll, 1986). Boykin and Toms (1985) expanded the concept of biculturalism with "a triple quandary conceptual framework" (p. 47) within which socialization takes place: (a) in the mainstream of American society, (b) being a member of an oppressed minority group, and (c) the Black culture. They argue that a "triple consciousness" is necessary to successfully manage these three distinct and competing domains. If we add gender to this model, we can argue that AAWEs may have "quadruple consciousness." Race, ethnicity, society, and gender add layers of complexity to the world in which AAWEs operate.

The cognitive and behavioral complexity of AAWEs must match the complexity of their environment (Ashby, 1956). "Effective leaders are those who have the cognitive and behavioral complexity to recognize and react to paradox, contradiction, and complexity in their environments" (Denison, Hooijberg, & Quinn, 1993, p. 1). African-American women possess a "well-documented facility to encompass seemingly contradictory role expectations of worker, homemaker, and mother" (King, 1988, pp. 50–51). In order to manage the complexity of their multiple roles and their bicultural environment, AAWEs use highly flexible behavioral strategies that allow them to maintain their Black cultural identity (Bell, 1990). A key strategy is to compartmentalize their various roles and contexts by maintaining sharp boundaries among them (Bell, 1990). This way of organizing their world helps these women to maintain their self-esteem, since it is not dependent on just one role. Having multiple, compartmentalized roles gives them perspective on a setback or problem in one role because it is only one part of their identity (Linville, 1985, 1987). In fact, findings from a longitudinal study by Barnett, Marshall, and Singer (1992), in which they obtained data from a two-year, three-wave study of a stratified random sample of 403 working women in various occupations, support previous cross-sectional research which showed that "the more roles a woman occupies, the better her mental and physical health" (Barnett, Marshall, & Singer, 1992, p. 641) and self-efficacy (Linville, 1985, 1987).

Other researchers have found that . . .

> biculturalism presents advantages to overall mental health (Szapocznik et al., 1988; Szapocznik & Kurtines, 1980; Fernandez-Barillas & Morrison, 1984). As one example of the research evidence on this, Fernandez-Barillas and Morrison found that bicultural Mexican-American students at a predominantly Anglo university experienced significantly less stress and displayed significantly better adjustment to the college environment than students with monocultural identities . . . [R]esearch with Latinos and Southeast Asian immigrants has shown that biculturals have higher work satisfaction than persons with monominority identities (Wong-Rieger & Quintana, 1987) (Cox, 1993, p. 55).

Creativity

There is a strong relationship between leader performance and creative capacities (Bass, 1981) in the leadership literature. African-American women executives must exercise creativity as they meet "the dual challenge of transforming stereotypical images and simultaneously creating new professional roles" (Bell, 1990, p. 460). In fact, biculturalism, perhaps because it spurs divergent thinking, "for many Afro-American female[s] . . . has been an excitement to creativity" (Collins, 1986, p. 51; Gilligan et al., 1992, p. 25). Nemeth (1986), in an experiment that examined nonracial minority groups' versus nonracial majority groups' word formation strategies, found that minority groups used multiple strategies, developed more solutions than did majority groups, and "that persistent exposure to minority viewpoints stimulates creative thought processes" (Cox, 1993, p. 32).

Creativity may be evidenced in leadership performance by using new approaches, considering multiple features of the problem situation, and applying a variety of different experiences to the problem (Mumford & Connelly, 1991, p. 303). In fact, ogilvie's (1994) research found that applying creative approaches in changing environments characterized by stochastic and nontautological information can result in new and effective solutions to problems.

Boundary spanning

Boundary roles often emerge or are created to help individuals manage the uncertainty of open systems (Mumford & Connelly, 1991, p. 292). Because of their bicultural life structure, AAWEs live on the boundaries of two distinctly different cultures (Bell, 1990). Although their "careers anchor them in the dominant culture, they straddle the Black and White worlds. More than most Black women, career-oriented African-American women are thrust into White society" (Bell, 1990, p. 468).

Leadership is a property of boundary role positions, which lead to and are affected by interpersonal influence (Mumford & Connelly, 1991). Because of their complex bicultural life structures and ability to cross cultural boundaries, career-oriented African-American women have a high degree of resources such as having access to information, knowledge, and different kinds of life experiences available to them (Bell, 1990). They have large complex networks which tend to grow based on the level of their involvement with the people in their networks (Bell, 1990).

While these studies do not examine the exercise of leadership by AAWEs, the findings do suggest that because of race and gender-related constraints operating in dominant culture organizations, and influenced by racial and sexual dynamics in society at large, African-American women behave strategically to restructure potentially constraining situations to ensure success – including, most likely, leadership success. [. . .]

NOTES

1   We use the term "Black" when we refer to people of African descent who may or may not define themselves as African-American. In other instances, we use the terms "Black" or "White" when we discuss research findings in which the authors delineated racial groups under study as "Black" or "White." The terms "African-American" and "Anglo-American" or "Anglo" are used to represent the corresponding racial and ethnic groups in the United States. (We use the terms "Anglo-American" and "Anglo" interchangeably to represent Anglo-American women and men.)

2   When we refer to Anglo or White men, we refer to those men who fit the traditional American male image. Men who exhibit more "feminine" characteristics and men with physical disabilities may find their experiences to be different. This study focuses on the comparison of AAWEs with the traditional male model. It is hoped that other researchers will begin exploring leadership issues of these other groups.

3   We do not mean to imply that the African-American, or any other, culture is a monolith. We feel that to begin to talk about intragroup differences at this stage is not helpful and will do little to advance scholarship. Once a general model of leadership strategies of AAWEs is articulated, scholars can then begin to address differences from the model within that group, as well as compare it to other groups, such as Asian-American, Hispanic-American, or Native-American women and men, or to models in other parts of the world.

4   Few researchers have taken the opportunity to look at leadership styles of African-American women in an historical and literary context as evidenced in narrative and

autobiographical work to inform their understanding of leadership ability. Works such as Patrice Gains' book, *Laughing in the Dark,* Ella Baker's book on Sojourner Truth, *This little light of mine,* are only a few examples of these types of works.

5 The Delany sisters (1993) show how they used these strategies growing up in the South in the late 1800s and early 1900s.

REFERENCES

Agor, W. H. (1984). *Intuitive management: Integrating left and right brain management skills.* Englewood Cliffs, NJ: Prentice-Hall.

Alderfer, C. P. (1990). Reflections on race relations and organizations. *Journal of Organizational Behavior, 11,* 493–495.

Alderfer, C. P., Alderfer, C., Tucker, L., & Tucker, R. (1980). Diagnosing race relations in management. *Journal of Applied Behavioral Science, 16,* 135–166.

Ashby, W. R. (1956). *An introduction to cybernetics.* London: Chapman Hall, Ltd.

Ayers-Nachamkin, B., Cann, C. H., Reed, R., & Horne, A. (1982). Sex and ethnic differences in the use of power. *Journal of Applied Psychology, 667,* 464–471.

Bardwell, J. R., Cochran, S. W., & Walker, S. (1986). Relationship of parental education, race, and gender to sex role stereotyping in 5-year-old kindergartners. *Sex Roles, 15,* 275–281.

Barnett, R. C., Marshall, N. L., & Singer, J. D. (1992). Job experiences over time, multiple roles, and women's mental health: A longitudinal study. *Journal of Personality and Social Psychology, 62,* 634–644.

Baskerville, D. M., Tucker, S. H., & Whittingham-Barnes, D. (1991). Women of power and influence in corporate America. *Black Enterprise Magazine, August,* 39–58.

Bass, B. M. (1981). *Stogdill's handbook of leadership: A survey of theory, research.* New York: Free Press.

Bass, B. M. (1985). *Leadership and performance beyond expectations.* New York: Free Press.

Bass, B. M. (1990). *Bass and Stogdill's handbook of leadership: Theory, research, and managerial applications.* New York: Free Press.

Bell, E. L. (1989). *The power within: Bicultural life structures and stress among Black women.* Unpublished doctoral dissertation, Case Western Reserve University.

Bell, E. L. (1990). The bicultural life experience of career-oriented Black women. *Journal of Organizational Behavior, 11,* 459–477.

Bell, E. L. (1992). Myths, stereotypes, and realities of Black women: A personal reflection. *Journal of Applied Behavioral Science, 28,* 363–376.

Bell, E. L., & Nkomo, S. (1992). *The glass ceiling vs. the concrete wall: Career perceptions of white and African-American women managers.* Working paper no. 3470-92, Massachusetts Institute of Technology.

Bell, R. (1971). The related importance of mother and wife roles among Black lower class women. In R. Staples (Ed.), *The Black family: Essays and studies* (pp. 248–255). Belmont, CA: Wadsworth.

Bem, S. (1974). The measurement of psychological androgyny. *Journal of Consulting and Clinical Psychology, 42,* 155–162.

Betters-Reed, B., & Moore, L. (1992). Managing diversity: Focusing on women and the white wash dilemma. In U. Sekaran & F. T. L. Leong (Eds.), *Womanpower: Managing in times of demographic turbulence* (pp. 31–58). Newbury Park, CA: Sage.

Binion, V. (1990). Psychological androgyny: A black female perspective. *Sex Roles, 22,* 487–507.

Boykin, W., & Toms, F. (1985). Black child socialization: A conceptual framework. In H. McAdoo & J. McAdoo (Eds.), *Black children: Social, educational, and parental environments* (pp. 33–52). Beverly Hills, CA: Sage.

Burgess, N. J., & Horton, H. D. (1993). African-American women and work: A socio-historical perspective. *Journal of Family History, 18,* 53–63.

Chafe, W. (1977). *Women and equality: Changing patterns in American culture.* University Park, PA: Pennsylvania State University Press.

Chodorow, N. J. (1978). *The reproduction of mothering: Psychoanalysis and the sociology of gender.* Berkeley, CA: University of California Press.

Collins, H. P. (1986). Learning from the outsider within. *Social Problems, 33,* 514–532.

Collins, H. P. (1990). *Black feminist thought: Knowledge, consciousness, and the politics of empowerment.* Boston, MA: Unwin Hyman.

Conrad, C. (1985). *Strategic organizational communication: Cultures, situations, and adaptation.* New York: Holt Rinehart and Winston.

Cox, T., Jr. (1993). *Cultural diversity in organizations: Theory, research and practice.* San Francisco, CA: Berrett-Koehler Publishers.

Cox, T., Jr., & Nkomo, S. M. (1990). Invisible men and women: A status report on race as a variable in organization behavior research: *Journal of Organizational Behavior, 11,* 419–431.

Davis, M. S. (1977). Sex-risk factors in career development of 61 female high school students. *Dissertation Abstracts International, 38,* 1847B. [University Microfilms No. 77–21, 704.]

Deaux, K. (1984). From individual differences to social categories: Analysis of a decade's research on gender. *American Psychologist, 39,* 105–116.

Deaux, K., & Emswiller, T. (1974). Explanations of successful performance in sex-linked tasks: What is skill for the male is luck for the female. *Journal of Personality and Social Psychology, 29,* 80–85.

Delany, S, & Delany, A. E. (1993). *Having our say: The Delany sisters' first 100 years.* New York: Kodansha America, Inc.

Denison, D. R., Hooijberg, R., & Quinn, R. E. (1993). Paradox and performance: a theory of behavioral complexity in managerial leadership. *Organization Science, 6,* 524–540.

Denton, T. C. (1990). Bonding and supportive relationships among Black professional women: Rituals of restoration. *Journal of Organizational Behavior, 11,* 447–457.

DiTomaso, N., & Smith, S. A. (1996). Race, ethnic minorities and white women in management: Changes and challenges. In J. Tang & E. Smith (Eds.), *Minorities and women in American professions.* Albany, NY: SUNY Press.

DuBois, W. E. B. (1903). *Souls of black folk.* New York: New American Library.

Dugger, K. (1991). Social location and gender role attitudes: A comparison of black and white women. In B. Lorber & S. Farrell (Eds.), *The social construction of gender* (pp. 38–55). Newbury Park, CA: Sage.

Dumas, R. G. (1979). Dilemmas of black females in leadership. *Journal of Personality and Social Systems, 2(1),* 3–14.

Eagly, A. (1987). *Sex differences in social behavior: A social-role interpretation.* Hillsdale, NJ: Lawrence Erlbaum.

Eagly, A. H. (1991, August). Gender and leadership. Presented at the annual meeting of the American Psychological Association, San Francisco, CA.

Eagly, A. H., & Johnson, B. T. (1990). Gender and leadership style: A meta-analysis. *Psychological Bulletin, 108,* 233–256.

Ely, R. (1991). Gender difference: What difference does it make? In J. L. Wall & L. R. Jauch, (Eds.), *Academy of Management Best Paper Proceedings* (pp. 363–367). Academy of Management.

Epstein, C. (1973). Black and female: the double whammy. *Psychology Today, August,* 57.

Evans, K. M., & Herr, E. L. (1991). The influence of racism and sexism in the career development of African-American women. *Journal of Multicultural Counseling and Development, 19,* 130–125.

Fernandez, J. P. (1975). *Black managers in white corporations.* New York: John Wiley and Sons.

Fernandez, J. P. (1981). *Racism and sexism in corporate life.* Lexington, MA: Lexington Books.

Fernandez, J. P. (1993). *The diversity advantage: How American business can outperform Japanese and European companies in the global marketplace.* New York: Lexington Books.

Fernandez-Barillas, H. J., & Morrison, T. L. (1984). Cultural affiliation and adjustment among male Mexican-American college students. *Psychological Reports, 55,* 855–860.

Gibbs, J. T. (1985). City girls: Psychosocial adjustment of urban black adolescent females. *Sage, 2,* 28–36.

Giddens, A. (1979). *Central problems in social theory.* London, Macmillian.

Gilkes, C. T. (1982). Successful rebellious professionals: The Black woman's professional identity and community commitment. *Psychology of Women Quarterly, 6,* 289–311.

Gilligan, C., Taylor, J. M., Tolman, D., Sullivan, A., Pleasants, P., & Dorney, J. (1992). *The relational world of adolescent girls considered to be at risk.* Final report to the Boston Foundation "Understanding adolescents: A study of urban teens considered to be at risk and a project to strengthen connections between girls and women." Harvard Graduate School of Education, Cambridge, MA.

Greene, B. (1990a). Sturdy bridges: The role of African-American mothers in the socialization of African-American children. *Women and Therapy, 10,* 205–225.

Greene, B. (1990b). What has gone on before: The legacy of racism and sexism in the lives of black mothers and daughters. *Women and Therapy, 9,* 207–230.

Greenhaus, J., & Parasuraman, S. (1993). Job performance attributions and career advancement prospects: An examination of gender and race effects. *Organizational Behavior and Human Decision Processes, 55(2),* 273–297.

Grossman, H., & Chester, N. (1990). *The experience and meaning of work in women's lives.* Hillsdale, NJ: Lawrence Erlbaum.

Hale-Benson, J. E. (1986). *Black children: Their roots, culture, and learning styles* (rev. ed.). Provo, UT: Brigham Young University Press.

Harding, S. (1991). *Whose science? Whose knowledge? Thinking from women's lives.* Ithaca, NY: Cornell University Press.

Harper, N. L., & Hirokawa, R. Y. (1988). A comparison of the persuasive strategies used by female and male managers I: An examination of downward influence. *Communication Quarterly, 36,* 157–168.

Helgesen, S. (1990). *The female advantage: Women's ways of leadership.* New York: Doubleday.

Herbert, J. I. (1990). Integrating race and adult psychosocial development. *Journal of Organizational Behavior, 11,* 433–446.

Higginbotham, E. (1982). Two representative issues in contemporary sociological work on black women. In G. T. Hull, P. B. Scott, and B. Smith (Eds.), *All the women are white; all the blacks are men, but some of us are brave.* Old Westbury, NY: Feminist Press.

Hood, E. F. (1978). Black women, white women: Separate paths to liberation. *The Black Scholar, April,* 45–56.

Hooijberg, R. (1992). *Behavioral complexity and managerial effectiveness: A new perspective on managerial leadership.* Unpublished doctoral dissertation, University of Michigan, Ann Arbor, MI.

Hooijberg, R., & Quinn, R. E. (1992). Behavioral complexity and the development of effective managers. In R. L. Philips & J. G. Hunt (Eds.), *Strategic leadership: A multiorganizational-level perspective* (pp. 161–175). Westport, CT: Quorum.

hooks, B. (1981). *Ain't I a woman: Black women and feminism.* Boston, MA: South End Press.

hooks, B. (1984). *Feminist theory from margin to center.* Boston, MA: South End Press.

Hyde, J. (1985). *Half the human experience.* Lexington, MA: DC Heath.

Hymowitz, C. (1992). Who earns what? *Smart Money, October,* 110–116.

Ibarra, H. (1993). Personal networks of women and minorities in management: A conceptual framework. *Academy of Management Review, 18(1),* 56–87.

Ibarra, H. (1995). Race, opportunity, and diversity of social circles in managerial networks. *Academy of Management Journal, 38,* 673–703.

Instone, D., Major, B., & Bunker, B. B. (1983). Gender, self confidence, and social influence strategies: An organizational simulation. *Journal of Personality and Social Psychology*, *44*, 322–333.

Jones, M. C. (1992). *Learning to lead: A study of the developmental paths of African-American women college presidents*. Unpublished dissertation, The George Washington University.

Kanter, R. M. (1977). *Men and women of the corporation*. New York: Basic Books.

King, D. C., & Bass, B. M. (1974). Leadership, power, and influence. In H. L. Fromkin & J. J. Sherwood (Eds.), *Integrating the organization* (pp. 247–268). New York: Free Press.

King, D. K. (1988). Multiple jeopardy, multiple consciousness: The context of a black feminist ideology. *Signs*, *14(1)*, 42–72.

Kohlberg, L. (1969). Stage and sequence: The cognitive developmental approach to socialization. In D. Goslin (Ed.), *The handbook of socialization theory and research* (pp. 347–480). Chicago, IL: Rand McNally.

Ladner, J. (1972). *Tomorrow's tomorrow: The black woman*. New York: Anchor Books.

Lewis, D. K. (1975). The Black family: Socialization and sex roles. *Phylon*, *36*, 221–237.

Linville, P. W. (1985). Self-complexity and affective extremity: Don't put all of your eggs in one cognitive basket. *Social cognition*, *3*, 94–120.

Linville, P. W. (1987). Self-complexity as a cognitive buffer against stress-related illness and depression. *Journal of Personality and Social Psychology*, *52*, 663–676.

Loden, M. (1985). *Feminine leadership or how to succeed in business without being one of the boys*. New York: Times Books.

Lubiano, W. (1992). Black ladies, welfare queens, and state minstrels: Ideological war by narrative means. In Toni Morrison (Ed.), *Race-ing justice, en-gendering power: Essays on Anita Hill, Clarence Thomas, and the construction of social reality* (pp. 323–361). New York: Pantheon Books.

Lunneborg, P. W. (1990). *Women changing work*. New York: Greenwood Press.

Mainiero, L. A. (1986). Coping with powerlessness: The relationship of gender and job dependency to empowerment strategy-usage. *Administrative Science Quarterly*, *31*, 633–653.

Malson, M. R. (1983). Black women's sex roles: The social context for a new ideology. *Journal of Social Issues*, *39*, 101–113.

Maltz, D. N., & Borker, R. (1982). A cultural approach to male-female miscommunication. In J. J. Gumpertz (Ed.), *Language and social identity* (pp. 196–216). Cambridge, MA: Cambridge University Press.

Mayhand, E., & Grusky, O. (1972). A preliminary experiment on the effects of Black supervisors on White and Black subordinates. *Journal of Black Studies*, *2*, 461–470.

McAdoo, H. (Ed.). (1987). *Black families*. Beverly Hills, CA: Sage.

McDaniel, R. R., Jr. (1995, April 7). Personal correspondence.

McGoldrick, M., Garcia-Preto, N., Hines, P. M., & Lee, E. (1988). Ethnicity and women. In McGoldrick, C. M. Anderson, and F. Walsh (Eds.), *Women in families*, (pp. 169–199). New York: Norton.

Meyers, L. W. (1975). Black women and self esteem. In M. Milman and R. Kantor (Eds.), *Another voice* (pp. 240–250). New York: Anchor.

Miner, J. B. (1977). Motivational potential for upgrading among minority and female managers. *Journal of Applied Psychology*, *31*, 739–760.

Mintzberg, H. (1973). *The nature of managerial work*. New York: Harper Row.

Money, J., & Ehrhardt, A. (1972). *Man and woman: Boy and girl*. Baltimore, MD: Johns Hopkins University Press.

Moore, K., Simms, M., & Betsy, C. (1986). *Choice and circumstance: Racial differences in adolescent sexuality and fertility*. New Brunswick, NJ: Transaction Books.

Morrison, A. M., & Von Glinow, M. A. (1990). Women and minorities in management. *American Psychologist*, *45*, 200–208.

Morrison, A. M., White, R. P., Van Velsor, E., & the Center for Creative Leadership. (1987). *Breaking the glass ceiling: Can women reach the top of America's largest corporations?* Reading, MA: Addison-Wesley.

Morton, P. (1991). *Disfigured images: The historical assault on Afro-American women*. Westport, CT: Greenwood Press.

Mumford, M. D., & Connelly, M. S. (1991). Leaders as creators: Leader performance and problem solving in ill-defined domains. *Leadership Quarterly, 2,* 289–315.

Murray, P. S. (1975). The liberation of the black woman. In J. Freeman (Ed.), *Women: A feminist perspective* (pp. 177–193). Palo Alto, CA: Mayfield.

Nelson, J. (1993). *Volunteer slavery: My authentic Negro experience.* New York: Penguin Books.

Nemeth, C. J. (1986). Differential contributions of majority and minority influence. *Psychological Review, 93,* 23–32.

Nkomo, S., & Cox, T. (1989). Gender differences in the upward mobility of black managers: Double whammy or double advantage. *Sex Roles, 21,* 828–839.

ogilvie, d. (1994). *The strategic decision making process: Using imagination to improve solutions in unstable environments.* Unpublished Ph.D. dissertation, The University of Texas at Austin.

O'Reilly, C. A., III, & Roberts, K. H. (1973). Job satisfaction among whites and nonwhites: A cross-cultural approach. *Journal of Applied Psychology, 57,* 295–299.

Palmer, P. M. (1983). White women/black women: The dualism of female identity and experience in the United States. *Feminist Studies, 9,* 153–155.

Parker, P. S. (1994, November). The usefulness of a cross-cultural model for examining the impact of African-American women executives on dominant organizational culture. Paper presented at the annual meeting of the Speech Communication Association, New Orleans, LA.

Pettman, J. (1991). Racis, sexism, and sociology. In G. Bottomley, M. de Lepervanche, and J. Martin (Eds.), *Intersexions: Gender, class, culture, ethnicity* (pp. 197–202). Sydney: Allen and Unwin.

Petty. M. M., & Miles, R. (1976). Leader sex-role stereotyping in a female dominated work culture. *Personnel Psychology, 29,* 393–404.

Quinn, R. E. (1988). *Beyond rational management: Mastering the paradoxes and competing demands of high performance.* San Francisco, CA: Jossey-Bass.

Richards, S. A., & Jaffee, C. L. (1972). Blacks supervising whites: A study of interracial difficulties in working together in a simulated organization. *Journal of Applied Psychology, 56,* 234–240.

Riger, S., & Galligan, P. (1980). Women in management: An exploration of competing paradigms. *American Psychologist, 35,* 902–910.

Root, M. (1990). Disordered eating in women of color. *Sex Roles, 22,* 7–8.

Rosener, J. B. (1990). Ways women lead. *Harvard Business Review, 68(6),* 119–125.

Ruddick, S. (1989). *Maternal thinking: Towards a politics of peace.* Boston, MA: Beacon Press.

Rutledge, E. (1980). Marital interaction goals of black women: Strengths and effects. In L. Rose (Ed.), *The black woman.* Beverly Hills, CA: Sage.

Scott, K. Y. (1991). *The habit of surviving: Black women's strategies for life.* New Brunswick, NJ: Rutgers University Press.

Scott-Jones, D., & Clark, M. (1986). The school experiences of black girls: The interaction of gender, race, and socioeconomic status. *Phi Delta Kappan, 67,* 520–526.

Scott-Jones, D., & Nelson-LeGall, S. (1986). Defining black families, past and present. In E. Seidman & J. Rappaport (Eds.), *Redefining social problems* (pp. 83–100). New York: Plenum Press.

Shull, F., & Anthony, W. P. (1978). Do black and white supervisory problem solving styles differ? *Personnel Psychology, 31,* 761–782.

Shuter, R., & Turner, L. H. (1992, May). African-American and white women in the workplace: Perceptions of conflict communication. Paper presented at the annual conference of the International Communication Association, Miami, FL.

Smith, E. (1982). The Black female adolescent: A review of the literature. *Psychology of Women Quarterly, 6,* 261–288.

Smith, A., & Stewart, A. J. (1983). Approaches to studying racism and sexism in black women's lives. *Journal of Social Issues, 39,* 1–15.

Stogdill, R. M., & Coons, A. E. (1957) Leader behavior: Its description and measurement. Columbus, OH: Ohio State University, Bureau of Business Research.

Szapocznik, J., & Kurtines, W. (1980). Acculturation, biculturalism and adjustment among Cuban Americans. In A. Padilla (Ed.), *Psychological dimensions on the acculturation process: Theories, models, and some new findings* (pp. 139–159). Boulder, CO: Westview.

Szapocznik, J., Santisteban, D., Kurtines, W., Perez-Vidal, A., & Herdis, O. (1988). Bicultural effectiveness training: A treatment intervention for enhancing intercultural adjustment in Cuban American families. *Hispanic Journal of Behavioral Sciences, 6,* 317–344.

Talley-Ross, N. C. (1992). The African-American woman practicing in nontraditional professions: A life history approach. *Dissertation Abstracts International, 52/11,* 3986A.

Tannen, D. (1990). *You just don't understand: Women and men in conversation.* New York: William Morrow.

Tannen, D. (1994). *Talking 9 to 5: How women's and men's conversational styles affect who gets heard, who gets credit, and what gets done at work.* New York: William Morrow.

Taylor, J. M. (1991, August). *Breaking the silence: Questions about race.* Presented at the annual meeting of the American Psychological Association, San Francisco.

Thomas, D. A. (1990). The impact of race on managers' experiences of developmental relationships (mentoring and sponsorship): An intra-organizational study. *Journal of Organizational Behavior, 11,* 479–492.

Thomas, V. G. (1982). The relationship of race and gender of supervisor, subordinates, and organization to estimated stress and supervisory style in a simulated organization: A study of business administration and management students. *Dissertation Abstracts International, 44(12B),* 3970.

Ting-Toomey, S. (1986). Conflict communication styles in Black and White subjective cultures. In W. Gudykunst & Y. Kim (Eds.), *Interethnic Communication* (pp. 7–88). Newbury Park, CA: Sage.

Triandis, H. C., & Albert, R. D. (1987). Cross-cultural perspectives. In F. M. Jablin, L. L. Putnam, K. H. Roberts, & L. W. Porter (Eds.), *Handbook of organizational communication, an interdisciplinary perspective.* Newbury Park, CA: Sage.

Wade-Gayles, G. (1984). The truths of our mothers' lives: Mother-daughter relationships in black women's fiction. *Sage, 1,* 8–12.

Weick, K. E. (1979a). Cognitive processes in organizations. *Research in Organizational Behavior, 1,* 41–74.

Weick, K. E. (1979b). *The social psychology of organizing,* 2nd. ed. Reading, MA: Addison-Wesley.

Weitz, R., & Gordon, L. (1993). Images of black women among Anglo college students. *Sex Roles, 28,* 19–34.

White, Y. S. (1990). Understanding the black woman manager's interaction with the corporate culture. *Western Journal of Black Studies, 14,* 182–186.

Willie, C. (1985). *Black and white families: A study in complementarity.* Dix Hills, NY: General Hall.

Wilson, P. M. (1986). Black culture and sexuality. Special issue: Human sexuality, ethnoculture and social work. *Journal of Social work and Human Sexuality, 4(3),* 29–46.

Wood, J. T. (1994). *Gendered lives: Communication, gender and culture.* Belmont, CA: Wadsworth.

Wong-Rieger, D., & Quintana, D. (1987). Comparative acculturation of Southeast Asian and Hispanic immigrants and sojourners. *Journal of Cross-Cultural Psychology, 18,* 345–362.

THE GREATLY EXAGGERATED DEMISE OF HEROIC LEADERSHIP: GENDER, POWER, AND THE MYTH OF THE FEMALE ADVANTAGE

JOYCE K. FLETCHER

From *CGO Insights, Briefing Note #* 13 (2002) Boston, MA: Center for Gender in Organizations, Simmons School of Management

NEW LEADERSHIP PRACTICES

New models of leadership recognize that workplace effectiveness depends less on individual, heroic action and more on collaborative practices distributed throughout an organization. The belief that "we don't need another hero" has ushered in an era of what is often called "post-heroic" or shared leadership. This new, more relational approach is intended to transform stodgy, top-down organizational structures into flexible, knowledge-based entities able to meet the demands of the information age and global economy.[1]

Despite the rhetoric calling for a new approach, there is ample evidence that people – and organizations – find it difficult to put this new leadership model into practice. Here, I argue that the difficulties result not only from the fact that new models challenge old ways of thinking, but that these challenges are linked in subtle ways to gender and power.

POST-HEROIC LEADERSHIP: WHAT IS IT?

Embedded in new models of leadership are three significant challenges to the heroic paradigm. First, new models of leadership question the very concept of an autonomous self and individual achievement. Peggy McIntosh, for example, notes that while we may focus on leaders as heroes, they are but the tip of the iceberg. In reality, their "individual achievement" is enabled by a vast network of collaboration and support. Wilfred Draft uses another, equally compelling image from the sea. He notes that while we might see the white caps in the water as leading, it is actually the deep blue sea that determines the direction and power of the ocean.[2]

Second, new models challenge static, command-and-control images of leadership. Instead, leadership is envisioned as a collaborative social process, one that is more mutual and relies on egalitarian, less hierarchical interactions between leaders and followers. There are many popularized images such as servant leadership, connective leadership or bottom-up leadership that convey this challenge to the old paradigm.[3]

Third, new models challenge the goal of good leadership and the skills it requires. It is no longer assumed that leaders will have all the solutions and the charisma to get others to implement them. Instead, leaders are expected to create conditions under which collective learning and continuous improvement can occur. Achieving these knowledge-based outcomes depends not so much on technical expertise but on what is commonly called emotional or relational intelligence. This includes skills such as self-awareness, listening, and empathy, as well as the ability to relate to, learn from, and empower others.

In summary, post-heroic leadership is a paradigm shift in what it means to be a leader. It re-envisions the *who* of leadership by challenging the primacy of individual achievement, the *what* of leadership by focusing on collective learning and mutual influence, and the *how* of leadership by noting the more egalitarian relational skills and emotional intelligence needed to practice it.

WHAT DO GENDER AND POWER HAVE TO DO WITH IT?

Many have noted that this paradigm shift in what it means to be a good leader is gendered. That is, the traits commonly associated with traditional, heroic leadership are closely aligned with stereotypical images of masculinity. Men or women can display them, but the traits themselves – such as individualism, assertiveness, and dominance – are socially ascribed to men in our culture and generally understood as masculine. In contrast, traits associated with post-heroic leadership – empathy, capacity for listening, relational ability – are socially ascribed to women and generally understood as feminine. The popular interpretation of this phenomenon is to predict that the shift to new leadership practices will create a "female advantage" giving women a leg up in today's business environment.[4]

But the implications of the gendered nature of the shift to new models of leadership are far more complex – and interesting – than this popular interpretation suggests. More complex because the shift is related to a gendered power dynamic, not just to gender. And more interesting because it is not about sex differences per se, but about a gender-linked shift in the very understanding of how to achieve business success. To explore these deeper implications we need to understand *why* we associate certain characteristics with masculinity and femininity and what that has to do with the rules for business success.

The reason we sex-type certain attributes lies in something commonly called the "separate spheres" phenomenon. This refers to the way we tend to view the social world as being separated into two spheres of activity: the public sphere of paid work where we "produce things" and the private sphere of family and community where we "grow people." This way of seeing the world is so "natural" that we rarely think of it or question its influence. But if we do look more closely, there are three influential characteristics embedded in this world view: The spheres are seen as *separate* (i.e., there are different definitions of what it takes to be effective in each of them); *unequally valued* (i.e., labor in the work sphere is assumed to be skilled, complex, and dependent on training, whereas labor in the domestic sphere is assumed to be unskilled, innate, and dependent on personal characteristics) and *sex-linked* (i.e., men and images of idealized masculinity are associated with the first and women and images of idealized femininity are associated with the second). The leadership implications of this sex-linked separation of the two spheres of life are significant. Not only does it help explain why we so readily attribute the label "feminine" and "masculine" to certain characteristics, it also calls attention to the fact that most of us carry a sex-linked set of principles – an underlying logic of effectiveness – about how to do good work in each sphere that is assumed to be appropriate for that sphere alone.

It is important to note that *in practice*, the separation and sex-linked nature of the two spheres is more myth than reality. Men are active participants in the domestic family sphere and women are active participants in the work sphere. Nonetheless, although they do not match reality, these idealized images of sex-linked attributes and inclinations have a powerful effect on how men and women act – and are expected to act – in each sphere and what types of behavior are considered appropriate – or tainted as inappropriate – in each.

The notion of separate spheres helps us see that new models of leadership violate some basic principles and beliefs – about gender, power, individual achievement, and even work and family – that we, as a society, hold dear. Engaging this shift is neither trivial nor benign. As our understanding of organizations changes and we begin to acknowledge the relational aspects of good practice and the collaborative nature of achievement, the very logic underlying organizational practice – a logic supported by a number of broader societal norms and beliefs – is being challenged.

The gender and power dynamics associated with this challenge are significant and can help answer three paradoxical questions related to the implementation of new leadership practices: Why, if there is general agreement on the need for new leadership practices, are the practices themselves not more visible in the workplace? Why, if these new models are aligned with the feminine, are not more women being propelled to the top? And why, if there is transformational potential in these new models of leadership, are organizations not being transformed?

WHY ARE NEW LEADERSHIP PRACTICES NOT MORE VISIBLE?

While the new rhetoric about leadership has been around for several years, the reality in most organizations has lagged far behind. In fact, the everyday narratives about leadership – the stories people tell about business successes, the legends that are passed on as exemplars of leadership behavior – remain stuck in the language of heroic individualism.

Ron Heifetz and Donald Laurie, for example, note that despite all the data supporting the need to facilitate collective learning "managers and leaders rarely receive promotions for providing the leadership required to do (this) adaptive work."[5] Michael Beer notes that in recounting the story of their success, leaders themselves tend to ignore the relational practices and social networks of influence that accounted for that success and focus almost exclusively on individual actions and decisions. What accounts for this phenomenon? Conventional wisdom holds that it is due to the nature of identity and ego, whereby once we have achieved a goal and gained some prominence for having achieved it, we naturally downplay the help we have been given and reconstruct our behavior – in our own minds as well as in the perception of others – as individual action.

A gender and power perspective suggests that something additional might be going on. Western society conflates images of "doing work" with displays of idealized masculinity rooted in heroic images of individualism. As the definition of doing work changes, reflecting beliefs about the importance of egalitarian relationships and the collaborative nature of achievement, the behavioral displays signaling competence need to change. But there are two problems with this shift. One, it requires a set of relational actions that have long been associated – incorrectly but surely – with displays of femininity and unconsciously coded as inappropriate to the work sphere. Two, because these relational actions are associated with the domestic sphere they are not likely to be seen as requiring skill of any sort, but instead, are likely to be attributed to one's natural inclination or personality. This makes it difficult to acknowledge them as leadership competence.

The difficulty is complicated by another power dynamic, related to gender but also to other aspects of identity. New leadership requires relational skills such as mutuality, an openness to influence, and a willingness to acknowledge the collaborative nature of achievement. But, because of our strong, societal beliefs about individual achievement and meritocracy, this stance of "needing others" is tainted. In addition, in any system of unequal power (inequities based on race, class, sex, or organizational level, for example), it falls on those with less power to be ultra-sensitive and attuned to the perceptions, desires and implicit requests of the more powerful.[6] Because this attunement to others requires relational skills, most of us unconsciously associate the use of these skills with a *lack* of power.

The unconscious association of relational skills with femininity and powerlessness helps explain why heroic images of leadership and individual business success are so resilient. Leadership, like all social processes, is an occasion to enact one's identity. Although new models implicitly acknowledge that relational wisdom is critical to business success, they do not take into account that acting on this wisdom requires displaying characteristics that subtly mark us as "feminine" and "powerless."

Is it any wonder then, that leaders avoid describing these relational leadership practices when speaking of their own successes, and instead focus on other, more individualistic actions? The rhetoric may be "we don't need another hero," but practicing new leadership engages significant identity issues and is antithetical to how we have been taught to express ourselves at work. Attempts to change behavior without a recognition of these deeper identity issues is unlikely to have much effect because these issues exert potent – albeit invisible – influence on leader and follower behavior, expectations, and experience.

WHAT HAS HAPPENED TO THE "FEMALE ADVANTAGE?

We might expect that women would stand to benefit from the move to newer, more relational models of leadership. Yet, if we look at today's top leaders, we find few women among them. Why, if there is a female advantage, are women not rising more quickly? One explanation can be found by exploring some additional gender dynamics and the double binds they create for women at work.

The principles of new leadership are generally presented as if the social identity of the actor is irrelevant. At a practical level, we all know this is untrue. Our interpretation of events is always contextual and is influenced by many factors, including the social identity (sex, race, class, etc.) of the actor. A boss saying "drop by my office" is interpreted quite differently from a peer saying the same thing. A white man slamming his fist on the table during a meeting is perceived quite differently from a man of color – or any woman – doing the same thing. We filter behavior through schema that influence and determine what we see, what we expect to see, and how we interpret it.

Gender schema are particularly powerful, which means that the experience and consequences of practicing new leadership will be different for women and men. Men, while they risk being labeled wimps when they engage in new leadership behaviors, may have an easier time proclaiming what they do as "new." Women, on the other hand, may have a harder time distinguishing what they do as something new, because it looks like they are just doing what women do.

But there is another, even thornier problem women encounter. The femininity associated with the domestic sphere of family and community is that of *mothering*, a labor of love that entails selfless giving. Mothers are people we expect to nurture and support us, to be the wind beneath our wings, wanting nothing in return but our success. This confusion of new leadership with selfless giving and mothering creates special problems for women.[7] People who put post-heroic leadership into practice have a right to expect that others will join them in creating the kind of environment where collective learning and mutual empowerment can exist. Indeed, to be effective, post-heroic leadership must have embedded within it an expectation of reciprocity. But gender expectations constrain this possibility for women. When attempts to lead are misunderstood as mothering, the expectation of reciprocity embedded in the practice is rendered invisible. As a result, women are often expected to nurture selflessly, to enable others while expecting nothing in return, to work mutually in non-mutual situations, and to practice less hierarchical forms of interacting even in hierarchical contexts. Thus, many women experience the so-called female advantage as a form of exploitation, where their behavior benefits the bottom line but does not mark them as leadership potential.

IS THE WORKPLACE BEING TRANSFORMED?

The transformational call of the new leadership is to create learning organizations that are able to manage dynamic processes, leverage the learning from diverse perspectives, and accommodate the interests of multiple stakeholders. This potential will be unleashed by tapping into the expertise of the collective, establishing more fluid patterns of influence and power, and using difference – including difference that comes from social identity – to challenge assumptions, learn, grow, and innovate.[8]

However, this transformation is not living up to its promise. Not only are new leadership practices rarely enacted, but those brave enough to try often fall victim to the gender and power dynamics noted above. The result is that the transformative potential of new leadership practices is being co-opted, silencing its most radical challenges to workplace norms about power, individual achievement, meritocracy, and the privileging of managerial and hierarchical knowledge.[9] For example, in the wake of September 11th, a plethora of articles in the business press written by popular advocates of post-heroic leadership evoke yearnings for the old heroic leadership with an interesting sleight of hand. Although post-heroic principles are touted, it is individual leaders who are highlighted and personal characteristics such as integrity, charisma, and vision that are described. Reading it, one would assume that the way to create less hierarchical, more adaptive leadership paradigms depends on simply hiring *better hierarchical leaders* who have "emotional intelligence" or who "value relationships."[10]

The challenge of post-heroic leadership goes well beyond these important interpersonal skills, however. Being a post-heroic leader requires not only relational skills, but also a set of beliefs and principles, indeed a different mental model of how to exercise power and how to achieve workplace success. When this alternative logic of effectiveness is dropped, the essence of post-heroic leadership is in danger because its transformational aspects are undermined. The skills and behaviors may be noted, but the basic principles of human growth and interdependence that would present the most serious challenge to old leadership models are cut off. In other words, the new leadership is being incorporated into the mainstream discourse according to the rules of the old paradigm. The result is yet another idealized image of heroic leadership – post-heroic heroes.

The death of heroic leadership cannot be accomplished by simply reconstituting old models with new language. Capturing the transformational promise of new models of leadership will require recognizing and naming the radical nature of its challenge and the gender and power dynamics inherent in it. It will require acknowledging the way post-heroic leadership challenges current power dynamics, the way it threatens the myth of individual achievement and related beliefs about meritocracy, the way it highlights the collaborative subtext of life that we have all been taught to ignore, and the way it engages displays of one's gender identity. Without explicit recognition of these complicated dynamics, the transformational potential of this new model of leadership is unlikely to be realized.

NOTES

1 See Badarraco, J. 2001. We don't need another hero. *Harvard Business Review*, 79 (8), 120–126. For an overview of new models of leadership, see Pearce, C. & H. Sims. 2000. Shared leadership: Toward a multi-level theory of leadership. In M. Beyerlein, D. Johnson & S. Beyerlein (Eds.), *Advances in the Interdisciplinary Studies of Work Teams*, Vol 7. New York: JAI Press.

2 See Draft, W. 2001. *The Deep Blue Sea*. San Francisco: Jossey Bass; McIntosh, P. 1989. *Feeling Like a Fraud, Part 2*. Working Paper #37, Wellesley Centers for Women. Wellesley, MA: Wellesley College.

3 See Greenleaf, R. 1977. *Servant Leadership*. San Francisco: Jossey Bass; Lipman Blumen, J. 1996. *The Connective Edge*. San Francisco: Jossey Bass; Bradford, D. & A. Cohen. 1998. *Power Up*. NY: Wiley; Block, P. 1993. *Stewardship: Choosing Service Over Self-Interest*. San Francisco: Berrett-Koehler.

4 The perspective on the gendered nature of organizational norms has its roots in Joan Acker's (1990) ground breaking work: Hierarchies, jobs, bodies: A theory of gendered organizations. *Gender & Society* 4: 139–158. The idea that gendered norms would translate into an advantage for women came much later and was popularized in works such as Helgeson, S. 1990. *The Female Advantage*. NY: Doubleday; and Rosener, J. 1995. *America's Competitive Secret*. NY: Oxford University Press.

5 Conger, J., G. Spreitzer & E. Lawler (Eds.) 1999. *The Leader's Change Handbook*. San Francisco: Jossey Bass, p. 65. See also for the following and other perspectives on the challenges of new models of leadership.

6 Miller, J. B. 1976. *Toward a New Psychology of Women*. Boston: Beacon Press.

7 Fletcher, J. K. 2001. *CGO Insights, No. 8 Invisible Work: The Disappearing of Relational Practice at Work*. Boston: Center for Gender in Oragnizations.

8 For a discussion of learning from diversity, see Bailyn, L. 1993. *Breaking the Mold*. New York: The Free Press; and Thomas, D. & R. Ely. 1996. Making differences matter: A new paradigm for managing diversity. *Harvard Business Review*. September–October: 79–90. For an understanding of how individuals can use difference to create change, see Meyerson, D. & M. A. Scully. 1999. *CGO Insights, No. 6: Tempered Radicalism: Changing the Workplace from Within*. Boston: Center for Gender in Organizations.

9 For a deeper discussion of the process and effects of co-optation, see Fletcher, J. K. 1994. Castrating the female advantage. *Journal of Management Inquiry*. 3 (1) 74–82.

10 See Fletcher, J. K. & K. Kaeufer. (Forthcoming). Shared leadership: Paradox and possibility. In C. Pearce and J. Conger (Eds.), *Shared Leadership: Current Thinking, Future Trends*. Thousand Oaks, CA: Sage.

WHEN WOMEN LEAD: THE VISIBILITY – VULNERABILITY SPIRAL

KATHY E. KRAM AND MARION MCCOLLOM HAMPTON

From E. Klein, F. Gabelnick, & P. Herr (eds.) (1998) *The Psychodynamics of Leadership*, Madison, CT: Psychosocial Press.

"New Kinds of Leadership Required" say the headlines in management journals and the business press. Practitioners and scholars alike are recognizing that organizations struggling to survive in an increasingly complex and changing environment need leadership that is transformational, collaborative, and relationship-oriented (Bennis & Nanus, 1986; Hammer & Champy, 1993; Handy, 1990). Writers agree that if organizations are to become more adaptive and responsive to tumultuous and competitive environments, they will have to become flatter and more flexible and to rely more on teams as critical integrating structures. The consensus is, organizations need leaders who offer a new vision of the effective organization and who can model the skills and attitudes necessary to enact that vision.

It is easy to notice that the leadership traits that are extolled in this contemporary discourse generally match those that have been described as the characteristically "female" approach to management, an approach that is theorized to spring from sex-role socialization and contemporary sex-role expectations (Baker Miller, 1991; Gilligan, 1982; Hegelson, 1990; Huff, 1990). The capacity to care for others, listen, empathize, and search for collaborative solutions regularly surface in studies of women managers as the qualities that enable women to be effective in organizational roles (Belenky, Clinchy, Goldberger, & Tarule, 1986; Marshall, 1984; Rosener, 1990). Indeed, it has been noted frequently that the operative approach women typically adopt in relation to their work is distinct from the agency approach typically found among traditional male leaders – and this is now considered good news for organizations and for women (Bakan, 1966; Marshall, 1984; Urch Druskat, 1993).

Why, then, is it still so difficult for women to move into and succeed in leadership roles in organizations? The need for new forms of leadership has been consistently espoused, yet women continue to encounter obstacles as they ascend organizations. The purpose of this chapter is to lift up for examination the unique challenges posed to women leaders by the combined and interacting effect of (1) the heightened visibility women experience in leadership roles, and (2) a perceived and actual vulnerability they accept when they occupy these roles. While it is true that the differentiation, and resulting visibility, that attaches to *all* leaders makes them vulnerable to criticism and attack (Slater, 1966), we offer here a theoretically based argument for how these conditions may be exacerbated for women.

We begin by drawing on theory to propose an explanation for the mostly invisible processes that pose a critical challenge to women in leadership roles. Using object relations theories from the psychodynamic literature (Wells, 1995), we explore the kinds of projective processes that are stirred when women are placed in formal organizational leadership roles. These dynamics almost guarantee (and research has shown) that women leaders will be experienced as violating traditional role expectations, either of leaders or of women or both. These dynamics result in role overload, role confusion, threats to the leader's self-esteem, and strained relationships, all of which can undermine effectiveness in a leadership role.

To illustrate these dynamics, we have drawn on our own experiences in assuming leadership roles in an academic setting. Not only have we personally experienced the substantial challenges that come with heightened visibility in this setting, but it is also true that in academia – as in many contemporary organizations – women have difficulty surviving the climb from junior to senior levels. Women are underrepresented among tenured faculty, and the culture is dominated by traditionally male values. [. . .]

Our analysis suggests that women must find ways to leverage the experience of vulnerability that comes with our heightened visibility, by seizing the opportunity to learn about self and to diagnose organizational dynamics while keeping our integrity and self-esteem intact. We will illustrate how women (and men as well) may treat the experience of vulnerability, and how some responses to vulnerability can undermine effectiveness. Finally, we pose a scenario in which vulnerability can actually enhance leadership capacity and turn threats to leadership into growth, learning, and greater efficacy in the role.

THE DYNAMICS OF VISIBILITY AND VULNERABILITY: A THEORETICAL MODEL

While both men and women assume risk when they take on leadership roles in organizations, a wide range of organizational forces – including minority–majority group dynamics, sex-role stereotypes, ethnocentric intergroup relations, and unconscious fantasies about organizational leaders – combine to heighten the risk for women leaders by compounding the inevitable threats to their effectiveness as leaders (Cox, 1993; Kanter, 1977; Morrison, White, & Van Velsor, 1987). Here we propose an explanation for these complex processes; the argument is based on Kleinian object relations theory, which we summarize below.

The theory base: Object relations

Object relations theory is a psychodynamic theory of early childhood emotional development expounded most prominently by Melanie Klein (Segal, 1992; Wells, 1995). Essentially, Klein proposed that humans at a very early age utilize two psychological mechanisms to cope with unpleasant emotions: splitting and projection. In order to "preserve" the experience of a caring, attentive mother in the (inevitable) situations in which the mother is not fulfilling all the infant's needs (to eat or to feel dry, for example), the infant mentally creates two mothers: a bad one, at whom to be rageful, and a good mother, to be the all-caring protector and comforter that the infant needs. This psychological mechanism is called splitting, "an action undertaken in fantasy that can be used to separate things that belong together" (Segal, 1992, p. 36). This mechanism allows the infant and, later, the adult in stressful situations, to cope with anxiety by separating the "self" from painful feelings.

Projection, or projective identification, the second mechanism, is closely related. Klein proposed that infants learn to distance themselves from destructive feelings by disowning them and actively "placing" those feelings in someone else. [. . .]

In this paper, we propose that fantasies (unconscious wishes and fears) and projections about leadership combine with fantasies and projections about women to produce a spiraling effect in the anxiety-laden organizational environment. The spiral, which we will describe in more detail, is roughly as follows: the more visible a woman becomes as a leader, the more she is subject to scrutiny and criticism. This enhances her vulnerability to the collective dynamics of splitting and projective identification. Once these dynamics have been set in motion, her behavior and person become even more visible as people, with a variety of motives, find it necessary to keep close tabs on her. The challenges that come with this scrutiny can either undermine her success or, if overcome, allow her to climb higher in the organization, where she is even more in the minority and, therefore, more visible and vulnerable to the next round of the spiral.

Visibility

The minority status of women in organizations, and particularly in leadership positions, creates the first step in what we have called the visibility–vulnerability spiral. In many areas of management, women are still a novelty, particularly at senior levels in organizations. We know primarily from Kanter's (1977) work, that skewed numbers among organizational groups of any type produce subtle yet potent dynamics that undermine the group that is represented at the "token" or "minority" level. With minority status comes a documented set of experiences, including heightened visibility, intense scrutiny of performance, and pressure to assimilate into the majority culture (Kanter, 1977).

Kanter developed a simple but eloquent "case" using X's and O's to illustrate her point about minority–majority dynamics. Looking at an O in a group of X's tells the story: the O becomes the object of attention because it is different; the O's performance is closely scrutinized because the X's have never worked with an O before; the O feels isolated but finds it futile to try to fit in with the X's; the O feels its performance reflects on the capabilities of other O's and theirs on it. Research supports this story; the simple fact of being demographically "different" from the majority of others is correlated with a variety of negative outcomes, including low social integration in the work unit and greater turnover (Tsui, Egan, & O'Reilly, 1992).

In this chapter, we focus our analysis in particular on the dynamic impact of one of these experiences – visibility – as it seems to drive many of the other processes Kanter identifies. And organizational literature confirms that women leaders regularly experience heightened visibility, especially at senior positions, where their numbers are fewer (Morrison et al., 1987; Owen & Todor, 1993).

The experience of visibility by itself is not necessarily negative. All leaders depend on it for recognition and influence. Visibility ensures that a leader's performance gets noticed; if the role is performed well, this recognition can propel an individual into positions of greater status and authority. We argue, however, that women leaders are likely to experience visibility more negatively than their male counterparts, in part because they face a far more complex array of conscious and unconscious expectations for their behavior

For example, while male leaders are expected to be strong, aggressive, and competitive, women who display similar characteristics are criticized for being "too aggressive" and "too masculine" (Morrison et al., 1987; O'Leary & Ickovics, 1992; Powell, 1993). At the same time, women in masculine environments who bring more "feminine" qualities to their leadership roles – a caring, nurturing, collaborative style – may be labeled as "wishy-washy" and not fit for the leadership task (Harragan, 1977; Lindsay & Pasquali, 1993).

To understand these competing role expectations, we need to look more carefully at the projections carried, first by women, and then by organizational leaders. This helps us understand the confusion when women take organizational leadership roles.

Vulnerability

It is necessary to restate an obvious but unpalatable fact of contemporary society in order to make this argument: women are still perceived to be the weaker sex. While this "fact" is true along some dimensions (women are physically weaker and more frequently victims of violence), it has recently been understood as a stereotype, a cultural perception reinforced by, and reinforcing, historical social structures and norms (for example, about appropriate sex role behavior) (Bayes & Newton, 1985). Much of the change in thinking about gender roles since the 1970s has been a broader recognition that women are not as weak as the culture has painted them: women are now seen as capable of taking care of themselves financially, for example, and able to represent others' interests in professional roles. However, despite these changes, women are still likely to be perceived as vulnerable, perhaps easily victimized and therefore in need of protection.

As vulnerability is an unpleasant emotion, under stressful conditions, individuals will tend to split their own feelings of vulnerability off and project them onto others; this allows us to feel that others, rather than ourselves, are vulnerable. Sexrole socialization prepares women to experience and handle this difficult emotion (Jordan, Kaplan, Baker Miller, Stiver, & Surrey, 1991). Indeed, women are generally quite familiar with the experience of vulnerability; typically, they can describe the discomfort and have learned how to manage it (usually via relationships with others).

In contrast, men are far more likely to disown a sense of vulnerability. Object relations theory suggests that these gender-distinctive orientations toward vulnerability will produce a collusive dynamic in intergroup settings, in which men project their vulnerability and women all too easily absorb it. Smith and his colleagues have described this dynamic in detail (Smith, Simmons, & Thames, 1989).

Work organizations provide exactly the kind of setting in which feelings of vulnerability are likely to provoke a splitting and projective process. Contemporary work organizations derive historically from military organizations and retain aspects of the military culture (for example, in the ideas of hierarchy, chain of command, and discipline in carrying out orders). Vestiges of this history are evident in metaphors and imagery in use by managers when organizations face major changes (Hirsch & Andrews, 1983). This suggests that organizational conflict, whether it is among groups inside the organization or across the organizational boundary, is experienced as competition ranging in intensity from sports competition to warfare. From this perspective, the prospect of defeat is the equivalent of humiliation (at best) or extermination (at worst).

Research confirms that organization members hold powerful unconscious expectations of the leaders to defend their groups, to carry the flag for their group, and to win on these conscious and unconscious battlefields (Smith & Berg, 1987). To the extent that leaders lose the various struggles they undertake (for resources, market share, reputation) they are likely to be criticized, scapegoated, and/or unseated. When organizational or group survival is at stake, the intensity of the attack rises with the level of anxiety experienced by group members (Hirschhorn & Young, 1991).

What happens then when women take on leadership roles in organizational settings? In overly simplified terms, unconscious stereotypes about women collide with unconscious expectations of the leader role (Bayes & Newton, 1985; Eagly, Karan, & Makhijani, 1995). The appointment of a female leader, by this logic, must inevitably raise the anxiety of group members: if she is a woman, she is vulnerable; if she is vulnerable, then the survival of our group is in jeopardy.

What is particularly complex about the dynamics of vulnerability for women leaders is that it is both real and projected. On the one hand, all leaders take a real risk (to career, to reputation) by virtue of the role they occupy. On the other hand, women leaders are far more likely than their male peers to be the target of projected vulnerability, given the social roles they carry and the splitting and projection process, which requires that the object of the projections is to be seen as either all powerful or completely vulnerable. This means, we argue, that the real vulnerability of women leaders in role is greater than the vulnerability experienced by most men in those same roles, due to what we call the visibility–vulnerability spiral.

The spiral: Real vulnerability

The spiral starts, as we have said, because women are in the minority, and therefore visible. Assuming unconsciously that she is vulnerable, and perhaps projecting their own vulnerability onto her, followers will watch their female leader closely to make sure she can withstand attack from other groups (which probably have male leaders). Peers will scrutinize her to see how strong an opponent she will be, if things heat up. Even well-meaning superiors will watch her closely if they feel guilty about putting her in jeopardy by giving her a leadership role.

This intense scrutiny – some of it well-intentioned – creates what we are calling real vulnerability, or risk of failure in role, for the female leader for several reasons. Under such intense scrutiny, small errors – that male leaders might be able to cover or repair – will be noticed sooner, examined more closely, and criticized more often

(Aker, 1983). In addition, Kleinian theory would predict that men are more likely to notice errors or question the judgment of women than of other men, because splitting dynamics tend to lead people to locate fault in the "other" group rather than in their own. Finally, and paradoxically, behaviors that are not sex-role appropriate (i.e., too aggressive or competitive) will be noticed immediately and criticized. Such gender-specific expectations are likely to result in negative attributions of women leaders, particularly in highly prescriptive organizational cultures in which appropriate sex-role behavior is clearly – and narrowly – delineated (Cox, 1993). This combination of dynamics means that, in general, a woman's performance in a role is more likely to be negatively evaluated than a man's, especially in male-dominated organizations where the evaluators are likely to be male (Eagly, Makhijani, & Klonsky, 1992).

Under these circumstances, women leaders may experience substantial risk in acting on personal authority in their role, narrowing their repertoire of leadership styles, and thus limiting their effectiveness. Ultimately, such close scrutiny is likely to undermine self-confidence, a critical psychological state for any leader undertaking a new challenge. And, because women characteristically derive their sense of identity and self-esteem from relationships with others (Baker Miller, 1976; Jordan et al., 1991), criticism increases their internal experience of real vulnerability as well (Eagly et al., 1995).

These real sources of vulnerability combine with projected vulnerability – particularly from those who are anxious about their female leader – to produce a spiraling dynamic. As a leader's vulnerability (real and projected) increases, people watch them even more carefully.

The visibility–vulnerability spiral in action

. . . /[T]he spiral is set into motion as women are disproportionately asked to "represent" their gender by taking on a variety of visible, formal roles as well as relatively invisible, informal roles (Baker Miller, 1976; Fletcher, 1996).

Ironically, these opportunities to take on new roles are just what women and people of color have been seeking. Yet unless the visibility – vulnerability spiral is understood and effectively managed, individual self-esteem, well-being, and performance will suffer. In particular, the opportunity for women to flourish in a leadership capacity is often undermined by substantial role overload, close scrutiny of leadership style, and increasingly strained relationships, all the products of the visibility–vulnerability spiral. We draw on our own experiences as women in academic settings to illustrate each of these typical dilemmas.

Role overload

The range of roles that we have been invited, selected, and/or subtly pressured to assume have created opportunities for leadership *and* made us highly visible. In reflecting on our personal experiences we discovered that both of us are "on display" regularly – in program catalogs, in orientation sessions for new students and alumni, in facilitating and presenting at critical events such as faculty retreats.

While some of these require little effort, others require considerable involvement. All of them combined make us highly visible.

Additionally, in a setting such as ours, where women are underrepresented in senior ranks, we are regularly asked to take on a variety of formal roles: to chair particular committees, to join a committee in order to create more diversity in membership, and/or to take on substantial administrative roles (e.g., Marion to be MBA faculty director and Kathy to be department chair). These leadership opportunities have allowed us to create vision, to mobilize resources, and to have an impact within the school. . . .

Less obvious, but equally potent in their effects, are the informal roles we are tacitly expected to fulfill. We find ourselves, like other "scarce" professional women, fully immersed in mentoring, counseling, and nurturing faculty colleagues and students (Sekaran & Kassner, 1992). Examples of such relational practice (Fletcher, 1996) abound: an undergraduate student invites us to coffee to talk about his relationship with his father; a faculty member calls us to talk at length about his personal development plan; or, individual faculty members stop by to process difficult meetings with us, seeking advice and comfort.

While we view this work as important, it drains us of personal and professional time and energy. And, as Ann Huff (1990) describes, we are all too willing to collude with others who expect us to always be available to fulfill these critical emotional needs. Indeed, we tend to want to meet others' needs, and we have the relationship skills to do so (Fletcher, 1996).

The visibility–vulnerability spiral is set into motion when we assert our boundaries and become temporarily unavailable for counsel (i.e., close the office door, screen telephone calls, or say no to a lunch invitation). While necessary for professional survival, these actions paradoxically invoke disappointment, criticism, and/or anger as we violate unconscious, ingrained gender expectations (Gutek & Cohen, 1987). Department colleagues, for example, at first could not understand Kathy's decision not to attend a department retreat during her sabbatical year. [. . .]

Close scrutiny of leadership style

In listening to other women reflect on their experiences, we have noted that many of us feel closely scrutinized during most of our efforts to lead. The visibility–vulnerability spiral starts working when we sense the scrutiny and internalize the discomfort and criticism as a reflection on our competence. The opportunities for this dynamic abound in the department chair role, where there is little formal authority but wide-ranging expectations about what is to be accomplished, particularly during periods of organizational transition. What is noteworthy about Kathy's experience in this role is that considerable discomfort seemed to surface regardless of the style she chose. An entry from her personal journal illustrates this clearly: "When I chose a participative style to complete the business plan for the department, some thought I should take charge more. When I acted more decisively regarding several resource allocation issues I was viewed as too autocratic."

When one is new to a role, it is all too easy to internalize criticism as data that one is not competent. Yet discussions with male department chairs at other universities, combined with written accounts of other women's experiences in university administration (Sekaran & Kassner, 1992), suggest that male department chairs receive less criticism of lesser intensity in response to the same styles of influence and decision making. While all leaders are likely to be criticized as they attempt to influence others (regardless of their styles), the nature of these reactions are shaped and fueled by unconsciously held gender expectations (Morrison et al., 1987; Owen & Todor, 1993). That is, the same behavior (e.g., an autocratic style) coming from a female leader will be more highly criticized. This, combined with women's tendency to "take in" the criticism, heighten our experience of vulnerability. [. . .]

It appears that whatever style is enacted, we are either not feminine enough (not sufficiently nurturant when wielding authority) or not masculine enough ("wishy-washy" or "touchy-feely" when using a participative style). It is possible that our own tendency to be open, to sense others' reactions, and to encourage others to talk about their experience make discomfort with our styles discussible, while discomfort with our male colleagues remains unspoken. However, the actual discomfort with women's leadership styles, combined with a greater willingness to make them public, ultimately heighten our visibility and vulnerability.

Strained relationships

It appears to us that as we have assumed leadership roles, historically supportive relationships have become strained. Mentors, peers, and junior colleagues have had a variety of reactions to our attempts to lead, many of which are discomforting. These strains seem to affect not only us and those that we deal with regularly, but also relationships between men and women in the larger system.

For example, as we have moved into leadership positions, we have begun to outgrow the need for the kind of coaching and protection that our mentors provided earlier. Not only is change experienced as a loss (for both parties), but there is increasing discomfort as we necessarily enact styles and strategies that are different from those used by our male mentors. While all protégés experience this (Kram, 1988), our hunch is that women in minority leadership roles – and our male mentors – experience this separation more intensely.

There are several forces that may combine to make this a more intense and difficult transition than in male–male mentorships. Most importantly, it seems to us, is the extent to which the father–daughter alliance is familiar and satisfying to both parties. And, since women protégées are, in fact, increasingly vulnerable as they advance in their organizations, continued paternal concern about our welfare is not unwarranted. Second, while male protégés can find success in emulating their mentors' styles, this strategy doesn't work for us because of the sex-role expectations previously outlined. We have repeatedly discovered that if we try to use our position and authority as our male mentors do – for example, by declining a request to take on another committee assignment – we are viewed as harsh, arrogant, or aggressive.

From our perspective, we are profoundly disappointed at the realization that the alliance with senior males does not make our leadership style acceptable (we are still not X's). In the end, the transition to a more peerlike relationship is difficult, in part, because the visibility–vulnerability spiral undermines both parties' sense that the relationship has successfully prepared us for leadership. While all mentor relationships experience difficulty as they transition to more peerlike alliances, the texture of the transition is likely to be of a different quality when the mentor is male and protégée is female. Indeed, sons are expected to act increasingly independently and to succeed at doing so, while daughters are expected to need protection – and actually do – even as they become more independent, since the organizational world is less hospitable to them.

Other senior colleagues also seemed more comfortable with us when we were in the apprentice stage; we have both experienced strain in relationships with senior colleagues as we became more independent and outspoken. As long as we are asking questions and seeking advice and support, these relationships flourish. When we begin to offer differing views or to turn down offers of "help" (Marion turned down a junior role on a research team in order to focus on her own research), we sense discomfort. All junior faculty sense such discomfort as they embrace their own authority, but the increased autonomy and assertiveness of junior men may be greeted with less ambivalence than ours.

Similarly, our junior faculty colleagues and students seem to react with ambivalence to our increasing status and authority. While they may be pleased that competent women are ascending in the organization, they notice that, as we advance, our perspective changes to reflect our more senior status. We necessarily become less accessible as our responsibilities increase and the challenges mount. [. . .]

These relationship strains enhance the vulnerability women feel, particularly since our development and self-concept is nurtured primarily through connection with others (Baker Miller, 1991; Gilligan, 1982). Paradoxically, the challenges posed by increasing visibility and vulnerability so consume our energy that we can lose touch with our female and male peers who might empathize and act as a sounding board. [. . .]

The discomforts described here absorb lots of energy, and generally go undiscussed. Perhaps we would feel less vulnerable if somehow these relationship strains were made discussible and all of us could learn through joint inquiry about the complexities posed in heretofore satisfying relationships when we ascend organizations and begin to lead.

RESPONSES THAT STRENGTHEN AND RESPONSES THAT DERAIL

The dynamics we have described here require women in leadership roles to attend to a number of challenges – including role overload, close scrutiny, and strained relationships – that threaten to undermine our self-esteem and personal effectiveness. Whether the subtle yet potent visibility–vulnerability spiral actually derails our leadership potential is a function of how we choose to respond. Our analysis suggests that there are three basic responses to heightened visibility and vulnerability, each with its own consequences (see Table 16.1).

The internalizing response

Research suggests that women are socialized to respond to excessive scrutiny and criticism by devaluing, or splitting and denying, the parts of themselves that produce discomfort for others (Baker Miller, 1976, 1991; Jordan et al., 1991;

Table 16.1 Responses to heightened visibility and vulnerability

	Internalizing	Externalizing	Integrating
Basic Stance	Looking inward	Looking outward	Looking inward and outward
	Blaming the self	Blaming the system	Using interpretive skills for complex understanding
	Accommodating	Confronting	Listening, empathizing, empowering self and others
Consequences for the individual	Suppression of valued parts of self	Limited personal learning	Enhanced personal learning
	Loss of self-esteem	Self-esteem maintained	Self-esteem enhanced
	Pressure to conform	Personal beliefs and style are maintained	Adaptability
Consequences for the organization	Risk of derailment	Risk of derailment	Better assessment of organization dynamics
	Loss of a valuable resource	Loss of a valuable resource	Better leadership
	Diversity in leadership is discouraged	Adaptability in leadership is minimal	Organizational learning from a variety of sources

Lindsay & Pasquali, 1993). We intuitively respond by looking inward at what we may have done to evoke such negative responses to our actions. This reflexive response – based on a desire to meet others' needs and expectations – results in attempts to accommodate by altering our fundamental style, by devaluing important aspects of our self-identity, and ultimately by leaving the organization. This response, as we have experienced it, represents a substantial threat to our self-esteem. [. . .]

This pattern of response is costly for both the individual and the organization. Internalizing criticism not only enhances vulnerability, but also discourages women from enacting their own individual styles. Self-doubt leads us to accommodate more, to follow a "safe" path, rather than asserting a different perspective. The organization thus loses a valuable leadership resource.

The externalizing response

An alternative response to heightened visibility and criticism involves shifting blame outside the self to explain why one's actions seem unacceptable to others. This appears to be a more common response among men who, as a result of their socialization, have been taught to respond with a "thick skin" (Kimmel, 1987; Pleck, 1981). Frequently, this response is angry and narcissistic, motivated more by a fundamental desire to win or be right than by connection and collaboration (Baker Miller, 1991; Gilligan, 1982). The externalizing response is protective of self-esteem but also can enable leaders to stay with unpopular (and often correct) decisions.

Rather than look inward for explanations or blame, those with this response look for forces in the system that are responsible for criticism or attack. Thus, for example, resistance to one's ideas or style, criticism of one's lack of accessibility, or discomfort with one's bold actions will be interpreted as others' limitations rather than as a reflection on one's personal effectiveness (Sheppard, 1992).

This pattern of response – typified by externalizing blame and criticism – minimizes vulnerability, both real and projected. However, this response also limits the opportunity to learn about self, about one's impact on others, or about the system one is attempting to influence. Those who use the externalizing response generally do not invite more data from others through active listening, empathy, and sensitivity to others' affect. They are unlikely to better understand the assumptions, values, and/or needs underlying negative responses to their actions. [. . .]

The integrating response

Questioning one's actions, as in the internalizing response, is not necessarily self-undermining. Indeed, it is through such self-reflection and sensitivity to the impact of one's behavior that personal learning and growth can occur. In order to understand how women have been successful as leaders – despite the dilemmas outlined here – we have tried to describe a response, which we have observed occasionally in ourselves and in others, in which vulnerability actually becomes a source of strength. In this response, the experience of heightened visibility and vulnerability is leveraged for learning: about self, about others, and about the system one is attempting to lead. Those who enact this response have the capacity to sense and empathize with others' reactions, to empower others to voice their concerns, and to develop personal and organizational insight from others' criticism and attack. Rather than allowing vulnerability to derail self-esteem and competence, those who take an integrating approach turn this capacity to absorb others' reactions into a strength.

In practice, the integrating response assumes there is a third kind of vulnerability (we have discussed real and projected): proactive vulnerability, or openness, to others' reactions. Individuals examine reactions to leadership attempts for what might be learned about the impact of one's actions, others' needs and values, and systemic forces such as cultural imperatives and other sources of resistance that might be shaping them. Relationship strains and close scrutiny by others are viewed as opportunities to learn rather than (or, more realistically, in addition to) threats to self-esteem and effectiveness. [. . .]

This response has much in common with what others have described as essential to effective leadership in contemporary organizations. The ability to seize opportunities to learn about self – one's strengths and weaknesses – and then to effectively alter one's strategy is a competence that is shared by successful leaders (Bennis & Nanus, 1986). And, as Argyris (1982, 1985) clearly articulates, double loop learning – the capacity to modify basic assumptions and frameworks in response to feedback – is what enables individuals to effectively adapt to complex organizational environments. [. . .]

CONCLUSIONS

The integrating response is essential if women (and men) are to understand and effectively manage the visibility–vulnerability spiral. Yet, it is not easily enacted. Far too often, we react to the anxiety and difficulty of our situation by internalizing or externalizing. Neither of these promotes much learning, and the internalizing response – most often observed in women – is likely to undermine self-esteem and, ultimately, derail us from leadership tracks.

Our analysis leads to the conviction that the capacity to be vulnerable in a pro-active sense – that is, open to others' responses – is actually a critical leadership competence. Vulnerability is a strength when it enables personal and organizational learning. Only when men and women develop and effectively utilize this competence will a broader range of much needed leadership styles emerge in organizations. [. . .]

REFERENCES

Aker, S. (1983). Women, the other academics. *Women's Studies International Forum, 6*(2), 191–202.
Argyris, C. (1982). *Reasoning, learning, and action: Individual and organizational.* San Francisco: Jossey-Bass.
Argyris, C. (1985). *Strategy, change, and defensive routines.* Boston: Pitman.
Bakan, D. (1966). *The duality of human experience.* Boston: Beacon.
Baker Miller, J. (1976). *Towards a new psychology of women.* Boston: Beacon.
Baker Miller, J. (1991). The development of women's sense of self. In J. V. Jordan, A. G. Kaplan, J. Baker Miller, I. P. Stiver, & J. L. Surray (Eds.), *Women's growth in connection* (pp. 11–26). New York: Guilford.
Bayes, M., & Newton, P. (1985). Women in authority: A sociopsychological analysis. In A. Colman & M. Geller (Eds.), *Group relations reader* (Vol. 2, pp. 309–322). Jupiter, FL: A. K. Rice Institute.
Belenky, M., Clinchy, B., Goldberger, N., & Tarule, J. (1986). *Women's Ways of Knowing.* New York: Basic.
Bennis, W., & Nanus, B. (1986). *Leaders.* New York: Harper & Row.
Cox, T., Jr. (1993). *Cultural diversity in organizations.* San Francisco: Berrett-Koehler.
Eagly, A., Karan, S., & Makhijani, M. (1995). Gender and the effectiveness of leaders: A meta-analysis. *Psychological Bulletin, 117*(1), 125–145.
Eagly, A., Makhijani, M., & Klonsky, B. (1992). Gender and the evaluation of leaders: A meta-analysis. *Psychological Bulletin, 111*(1), 3–22.
Fletcher, J. (1996). Relational theory in the workplace. Work in Progress Series #77, Wellesley College Centers for Research on Women, Wellesley, MA.
Gilligan, C. (1982). *In a different voice: Psychological, theory and women's development.* Cambridge, MA: Harvard University Press.
Gutek, B., & Cohen, A. (1987). Sex roles, sex role spillover, and sex at work: A comparison of men's and women's experiences. *Human Relations, 40*(2), 97–115.
Hammer, M., & Champy, J. (1993). *Reengineering the corporation.* New York: HarperCollins.
Handy, C. (1990). *The age of unreason.* Boston: Harvard Business School Press.
Harragan, B. (1977). *Games mother never taught you.* New York: Warner.
Helgesen, S. (1990). *The female advantage: Women's ways of leadership.* New York: Doubleday Currency.
Hirsch, P., & Andrews, J. (1983). Ambushes, shootouts, and knights of the roundtable: The language of corporate takeovers. In L. Pondy (Ed.), *Organizational symbolism* (pp. 145–156). Greenwich, CT: JAI Press.

Hirschhorn, L., & Young, D. (1991). Dealing with the anxiety of working: Social defenses as coping strategy. In M. F. R. Kets de Vries, et al. (Eds.), *Organizations on the Couch* (pp. 215–240). San Francisco: Jossey-Bass.

Huff, A. (1990). *Wives of the organization.* Working paper presented at the Women and Work Conference, Arlington, TX.

Jordan, J., Kaplan, A., Baker Miller, J., Stiver, I., & Surrey, J. (1991). *Women's growth in connection.* New York: Guilford.

Kanter, R. (1977). *Men and women of the corporation.* New York: Basic.

Kimmel, M. (Ed.), (1987). *Changing men: New directions in research on men and masculinity.* Newbury Park, CA: Sage.

Kram, K. (1988). *Mentoring at work: Developmental relationships in organizational life.* Lanham, MD: University Press of America.

Lindsay, C., & Pasquali, J. (1993). The wounded feminine: From organizational abuse to personal healing. *Business Horizons, 36*(2), 35–41.

Marshall, J. (1984). *Women managers: Travelers in a male world.* New York: Wiley.

Morrison, A., White, R, & Van Velsor, E. (1987). *Breaking the glass ceiling: Can women reach the top of America's largest corporations?* Reading, MA: Addison-Wesley.

Owen, C., & Todor, W. (1993). Attitudes toward women as managers: Still the same. *Business Horizons 36*(2), 12–26.

O'Leary, V., & Ickovics, J. (1992). Cracking the glass ceiling: Overcoming isolation and alienation. In U. Sekaran & F. Leong (Eds.), *Womenpower: Managing in times of demographic turbulence* (pp. 7–31). Newbury Park, CA: Sage.

Pleck, J. (1981). *The myth of masculinity.* Cambridge, MA: MIT Press.

Powell, G. (1993). *Women and men in management* (2nd ed.). Newbury Park, CA: Sage.

Rosener, J. (1990, November–December). Ways women lead. *Harvard Business Review, 68*(6), 119–125.

Segal, J. (1992). *Mslanis Klsin.* Newbury Park, CA: Sage.

Sekaran, U., & Kassner, M. (1992). University systems for the 21st century: Proactive adaptation. In U. Sekaran & F. Leong (Eds.), *Women-power: Managing in times of demographic turbulence* (pp. 163–191). Newbury Park, CA: Sage.

Sheppard, D. (1992). Women managers' perceptions of gender and organizational life. In A. Mills & P. Tancred (Eds.), *Gendering organizational analysis* (pp. 151–166). Newbury Park, CA: Sage.

Slater, P. (1966). *Microcosm: Structural, psychological and religious evolution in groups.* New York: Wiley.

Smith, K., & Berg, D. (1987). Intergroup influences: The paradoxes of scarcity, perception, and power. In D. Berg & K. Smith (Eds.), *The paradoxes of group life* (pp. 182–204). San Francisco: Jossey-Bass.

Smith, K., Simmons, V., & Thames, T. (1989). Fix the women: An intervention into an organizational conflict based on parallel process thinking. *Journal of Applied Behavioral Science, 25*(1), 11–29.

Tsui, A., Egan, T., & O'Reilly, C. (1992). Being different: Relational demography and organizational attachment. *Administrative Sciences Quarterly 37*, 549–579.

Urch Druskat, V. (1993). Gender and leadership style: Transformational and transactional leadership in the Roman Catholic church. *Leadership Quarterly, 5*(2), 99–119.

Wells, I., (1995). The Group-as-a-whole. In J. Gillette and M. McCollom (Eds.), *Groups in Context* (pp. 49–85). Lanham, MD: University Press of America.

PART IV | ORGANIZATIONAL CHANGE AND INTERVENTION

ORGANIZATIONAL CHANGE AND INTERVENTION: OVERVIEW

DEBRA E. MEYERSON AND ROBIN J. ELY

Different ways of understanding gender suggest different explanations for the persistence of gender inequities. And each explanation recommends a different approach to change, including appropriate targets of change and methods to initiate and diffuse change. The first reading in Part IV, "A modest manifesto for shattering the glass ceiling," by Debra E. Meyerson and Joyce K. Fletcher (2000), summarizes the four approaches to gender to which we refer throughout this book and contrasts the methods of change that each advocates. It argues that interventions derived from the first three frames, though responsible for important changes in organizations, have not been sufficient. Not only has women's progress been slow and restricted primarily to white women, but those who have progressed have often done so by assimilating, however uncomfortably, into predominantly male organizations (Ely, 1995). Organizations themselves have changed little, and women who ascend to top positions tend to be relatively disempowered (Martin & Meyerson, 1998). Moreover, sex roles and relations between men and women in the home have changed little since early depictions of work/family integration (Rapoport & Rapoport, 1965) and alternatives remain difficult to realize (Rapoport, 1976), which limits the changes possible in the workplace.

What explains the tenacity of these disparities? Why has the large number of organizational efforts to recruit and advance women failed to result in substantial gains for women? Why have women, as a group, remained relatively powerless at work? In this book, we have argued that the answers to these questions lie in organizations' failure to question – and change – prevailing notions about what constitutes the most appropriate and effective ways to define and accomplish work, recognize and reward competence, understand and interpret behavior. These unquestioned work practices support deeply entrenched divisions and disparities between men and women, often in subtle and insidious ways.

To address this problem, we turn to a fourth frame for understanding gender. In this frame, we begin with the premise that organizations are "gendered." By this, we mean that many work practices reflect and support men's experiences and life situations, because they have been created largely by and for men. Now taken as the *sine qua non* of organizational life, these practices appear to be gender-neutral. Despite a lack of discriminatory intent, however, such practices frequently have a differential impact on different groups of people, placing women and others who do not "fit" at a relative disadvantage. In addition, standard practice may not always be best practice. Thus women's presence in positions traditionally held by white men can act as a catalyst for organization members to reflect, experiment, learn, and change their work practices in ways that enhance both gender equity and work effectiveness.

The intervention strategy implied in this approach to gender is an emergent, localized process of incremental change in work practices – changes that, taken together, have the power to transform organizations in ways that benefit women, men, and the work. Meyerson and Fletcher introduce this approach to change under the rubric "small wins" (Weick, 1984) and demonstrate the power of small wins to amplify when they are used to challenge prevailing understandings.

There are numerous methods for advancing organization change in a manner consistent with a Frame 4 perspective on gender. (See Merrill-Sands, Holvino, and Cumming, 2000, for a review.) One commonly used method is collaborative action research, which combines research with organizational change and involves organization members across the hierarchy directly in a diagnosis and change process. (See Rapoport, Bailyn, Fletcher, & Pruitt, 2002; Meyerson & Kolb, 2000; Coleman & Rippon, 2000; and Ely & Meyerson, 2000, for applications of this method to gender initiatives in organizations.) This approach has several advantages over other, more traditional, top-down approaches, including generating involvement and commitment, stimulating dialogue through action experiments, and building the knowledge and skills of many change agents. Action research projects also tend to generate less resistance than top-down approaches because they involve those people directly affected by changes. The next reading, by Erica Gabrielle Foldy and Douglas Creed, "Action learning, fragmentation, and the interaction of single-, double-, and triple-loop change: A case of gay and lesbian workplace advocacy," provides a detailed illustration of the action learning approach. This article distinguishes between change processes that engage "single-loop" learning, in which actors change work practices without addressing underlying values or understandings, and those that engage "double-loop" or "triple-loop" learning, in which actors change their values and understandings as they transform the work environment. This article also shows how these different learning processes can build on each other to disrupt traditional power arrangements, thereby advancing broader transformational goals consistent with a Frame 4 approach.

In the next reading, an excerpt from "Complicating gender: The simultaneity of race, gender, and class in organization change(ing)," Evangelina Holvino develops a set of "simple rules" for guiding organizational change efforts, together with specific strategies for implementing them. These rules and strategies recognize the deep connections among race, gender, class, and ethnicity and help to ensure that change strategies in organizations address them.

With the next paper, "Tempered radicalism," by Debra Meyerson and Maureen Scully, we shift gears and turn to the individuals who take up a change agenda in organizations. These change agents can be thought of as "tempered radicals," a term these authors coined to describe people who seek to advance change while remaining legitimate within their professions or organizations. Tempered radicals "identify with and are committed to their organizations, and are also committed to a cause, community, or ideology that is fundamentally different from, and possibly at odds with, the dominant culture of their organization" (Meyerson & Scully, 1995: 586). This paper introduces the notion of tempered radicalism and explores different motivations for acting as a tempered radical. Debra Meyerson's (2001) book, *Tempered Radicals*, expands on this concept and introduces a spectrum of action strategies people use to advance their values and catalyze learning and change. It illustrates how the actions of tempered radicals constitute a form of leadership that is neither dramatic nor heroic, but is nonetheless essential to an organization's capacity to learn and adapt. Tempered radicals subscribe to an approach to change that is consistent with the fourth frame. They aim to advance an agenda that is revolutionary in nature – that challenges something fundamental about the dominant culture; yet they recognize the value of changing small, seemingly inconsequential work practices as a way to disrupt the status quo in potentially consequential ways.

This part concludes with an inspirational piece by Audre Lorde, "The transformation of silence into language and action." Lorde's paper is a poetic call to individuals to act as tempered radicals – to speak out against injustices and challenge practices, assumptions, and images that systematically constrain and disadvantage marginalized groups of people.

REFERENCES

Coleman, G. & Rippin, 2000. Putting feminist theory to work: Collaboration as a means towards organizational change. *Organization*, 7: 573–87.

Ely, R. J. 1995. The power in demography: Women's social constructions of gender identity at work. *Academy of Management Journal*, 38: 589–634.

Ely, R. J. & Meyerson, D. E. 2000. Advancing gender equity in organizations: The challenge and importance of maintaining a gender narrative. *Organization*, 7: 589–608.

Martin, J. & Meyerson, D. E. 1998. Women and power: Conformity, resistance, and disorganized coaction. In R. Kramer and M. Neale (eds.), *Power and influence in organizations*: 311–48. Thousand Oaks, CA: Sage.

Meyerson, D. E. 2001. *Tempered radicals: How people use difference to inspire change at work.* Boston, MA: Harvard Business School Press.

Meyerson, D. E. & Kolb, D. 2000. Moving out of the armchair: Developing a framework to bridge the gap between feminist theory and practice. *Organization*, 7: 553–71.

Meyerson, D. E. & Scully, M. A. 1995. Tempered radicalism and the politics of ambivalence and change. *Organization Science*, 6(5): 585–600.

Merrill-Sands, D. & Holvino, E. with Cumming, J. (2000). Working with diversity: A focus on global organizations, *Working paper # 11*, Boston, MA: Center for Gender in Organizations, Simmons School of Management.

Rapoport, R. Bailyn, L. Fletcher, J. K., & Pruitt, B. 2002. *Beyond work family balance: Advancing gender equity and workplace performance.* San Francisco: Jossey Bass.

Rapoport, R. 1976. *Dual-career families re-examined: New integrations of work and family.* New York: Harper Collins.

Rapoport, R. & Rapoport, R. N. 1965. Work and family in contemporary society. *Sociological Review*, 30: 381–94.

Weick, K. E. 1984. Small wins: Redefining the scale of social problems. *American Psychologist*: 40–9.

17 | A MODEST MANIFESTO FOR SHATTERING THE GLASS CEILING[1]

DEBRA E. MEYERSON AND JOYCE K. FLETCHER

From Harvard Business Review (2000) Jan/Feb: 127–36

The new millennium provides an occasion to celebrate the remarkable progress made by women. That women now hold seats on corporate boards, run major companies, and are regularly featured on the covers of business magazines as prominent leaders and power brokers would have been unimaginable even a half century ago.

But the truth is, women at the highest levels of business are still rare. They comprise only 10% of senior managers in *Fortune* 500 companies; less than 4% of the uppermost ranks of CEO, president, executive vice president, and COO; and less than 3% of top corporate earners.[2] Statistics also suggest that as women approach the top of the corporate ladder, many jump off, frustrated or disillusioned with the business world. Clearly, there have been gains, but as we enter the year 2000, the glass ceiling remains. What will it take to finally shatter it?

> It took a revolution to get women where they are in business today. But now, to push hard-won gains wider and deeper, a different approach is necessary. It is a strategy based on small wins – incremental changes that have the power to transform organizations positively for both men and women.

Not a revolution. Not this time. In 1962, 1977, and even 1985, the women's movement used radical rhetoric and legal action to drive out overt discrimination, but most of the barriers that persist today are insidious – a revolution couldn't find them to blast away. Rather, gender discrimination now is so deeply embedded in organizational life as to be virtually indiscernible. Even the women who feel its impact are often hard-pressed to know what hit them.

That is why we believe that the glass ceiling will be shattered in the new millennium only through a strategy that uses *small wins*[3] – incremental changes aimed at biases so entrenched in the system that they're not even noticed until they're gone. Our research shows that the small-wins strategy is a powerful way of chipping away the barriers that hold women back without sparking the kind of sound and fury that scares people into resistance. And because the small-wins strategy creates change through diagnosis, dialogue, and experimentation, it usually improves overall efficiency and performance. The strategy benefits not just women but also men and the organization as a whole.

THE PROBLEM WITH NO NAME

Time was, it was easy to spot gender discrimination in the corporate world. A respected female executive would lose a promotion to a male colleague with less experience, for instance, or a talented female manager would find herself demoted after her maternity leave. Today such blatant cases are rare; they've been wiped out by laws and by organizations' increased awareness that they have nothing to gain, and much to lose, by keeping women out of positions of authority.

That doesn't mean, however, that gender inequity has vanished. It has just gone underground. Today discrimination against women lingers in a plethora of work practices and cultural norms that only appear unbiased. They are common and mundane – and woven into the fabric of an organization's status quo – which is why most people don't notice them, let alone question them. But they create a subtle pattern of *systemic* disadvantage, which blocks all but a few women from career advancement.

For an example of this modern-day gender inequity, take the case of a global retail company based in Europe that couldn't figure out why it had so few women in senior positions and such high turnover among women in its middle-manager ranks. The problem was particularly vexing because the company's executives publicly touted their respect for women and insisted they wanted the company to be "a great place for women to work."

Despite its size, the company had a strong entrepreneurial culture. Rules and authority were informal; people were as casual about their schedules as they were about the dress code. Meetings were routinely canceled and regularly ran late. Deadlines were ignored because they constantly shifted, and new initiatives arose so frequently that people thought nothing of interrupting one another or declaring crises that demanded immediate attention.

The company's cultural norms grew from its manner of conducting business. For instance, managers were expected to be available at all times to attend delayed or emergency meetings. And these meetings themselves followed certain norms. Because roles and authority at the company were ambiguous, people felt free to make suggestions – even decisions – about any area of the company that interested them. A manager in charge of window displays, for example, might very well recommend a change in merchandising, or vice versa. To prevent changes in their own area from being made without their input, managers scrambled to attend as many meetings as possible. They had to in order to protect their turf.

The company's norms made it extraordinarily difficult for everyone – women and men – to work effectively. But they were particularly pernicious for women for two reasons. First, women typically bear a disproportionate amount of responsibility for home and family and thus have more demands on their time outside the office. Women who worked set hours – even if they spanned ten hours a day – ended up missing essential conversations and important plans for new products. Their circumscribed schedules also made them appear less committed than their male counterparts. In most instances, that was not the case, but the way the company operated day to day – its very system – made it impossible to prove otherwise.

The meetings themselves were run in a way that put women in a double bind. People often had to speak up to defend their turf, but when women did so, they were vilified. They were labeled "control freaks"; men acting the same way were called "passionate." As one female executive told us, "If you stick your neck out, you're dead."

A major investment firm provides another example of how invisible – even unintentional – gender discrimination thrives in today's companies. The firm sincerely wanted to increase the number of women it was hiring from business schools. It reasoned it would be able to hire more women if it screened more women, so it increased the number of women interviewed during recruiting visits to business school campuses. The change, however, had no impact. Why? Because, the 30 minutes allotted for each interview – the standard practice at most business schools – was not long enough for middle-aged male managers, who were conducting the vast majority of the interviews, to connect with young female candidates sufficiently to see beyond their directly relevant technical abilities. Therefore, most women were disqualified from the running. They hadn't had enough time to impress their interviewer.

THE ROOTS OF INEQUITY

The barriers to women's advancement in organizations today have a relatively straightforward cause. Most organizations have been created by and for men and are based on male experiences. Even though women have entered the workforce in droves in the past generation, and it is generally agreed that they add enormous value, organizational definitions of competence and leadership are still predicated on traits stereotypically associated with men: tough, aggressive, decisive. And even though many households today have working fathers and mothers, most organizations act as if the historical division of household labor still holds – with women primarily responsible for matters of the hearth. Outdated or not, those realities drive organizational life. Therefore, the global retail company was able to develop a practice of late and last-minute meetings because most men can be available 15 hours a day. The investment firm developed a practice of screening out women candidates because men, who were doing most of the interviewing, *naturally* bond with other men. In other words, organizational practices mirror societal norms.

That the "problem with no name" arises from a male-based culture does not mean that men are to blame. In fact, our perspective on gender discrimination does not presume intent, and it certainly does not assume that all men benefit from the way work is currently organized. Lots of companies run by men are working hard to create a fair environment for both sexes. And many men do not embrace the traditional division of labor; some men surely wish the conventions of a *Father Knows Best* world would vanish.

Men, then, are not to blame for the pervasive gender inequity in organizations today – but neither are women. And yet our research shows that ever since gender inequity came onto the scene as one of business's big problems, women have blamed themselves. That feeling has been reinforced by managers who have tried to solve the problem by fixing women. Indeed, over the past 30-odd years, organizations have used three approaches to rout gender discrimination, each one implying that women are somehow to blame because they "just don't fit in."

TALL PEOPLE IN A SHORT WORLD

To describe the three approaches, we like to use a metaphor that replaces gender with height. Imagine, therefore, a world made by and for short people. In this world, everyone in power is under five-foot-five, and the most powerful are rarely taller than five-foot-three. Now imagine that after years of discrimination, tall people finally call for change – and short people agree that the current world is unfair and amends should be made.

Short people first try to right things by teaching tall people to act like short people – to minimize their differences by stooping to fit in the doorways, for example, or by hunching over to fit in the small chairs in the conference room. Once tall people learn these behaviors, short people insist, they will fit right in.

Some short people take another approach to routing discrimination: they make their world more accommodating to tall people by fixing some of the structural barriers that get in their way. They build six-foot-high doors in the back of the building and purchase desks that don't knock tall people's knees. They even go so far as to create some less demanding career paths – tall-people tracks – for those who are unwilling or unable to put up with the many realities of the short world that just can't be changed.

Other short people take a third approach: they celebrate the differences of their tall associates. Tall people stand out in a crowd, short people say, and they can reach things on high shelves. Let's recognize the worth of those skills and put them to good use! And so the short people "create equity" by putting tall people in jobs where their height is an advantage, like working in a warehouse or designing brand extensions targeted to tall people.

Those three approaches should sound familiar to anyone who has been involved in the many gender initiatives proliferating in the corporate world. Companies that take the first approach encourage women to assimilate – to adopt more masculine attributes and learn the "games their mothers never taught them." Thus, HR departments train women in assertive leadership, decision making, and even golf. Male colleagues take women to their lunch clubs, coach them on speaking up more in meetings, and suggest they take "tough guy" assignments in factories or abroad.

Companies that take the second approach accommodate the unique needs and situations of women. Many offer formal mentoring programs to compensate for women's exclusion from informal networks. Others add alternative career tracks or an extra year on the tenure clock to help women in their childbearing years. Still others offer extended maternity leave, flexible work arrangements, even rooms for nursing infants.

In the third approach, companies forgo assimilation and accommodation and instead emphasize the differences that women bring to the workplace. They institute sensitivity training to help male managers appreciate traditionally "feminine" activities or styles, such as listening and collaborating. And they eagerly put women's assumed differences to work by channeling them into jobs where they market products to women or head up HR initiatives.

All of these approaches have helped advance women's equity in the corporate world. But by now they have gone about as far as they can. Why? Because they proffer solutions that deal with the *symptoms* of gender inequity rather than the sources of inequity itself. Take the first approach. While many female executives can now play golf and have used relationships formed on the fairways to move into positions of greater power, these new skills will never eradicate the deeply entrenched, systemic factors within corporations that hold many women back.

The same is true of the second approach of accommodation through special policies and benefits. It gives women stilts to play on an uneven playing field, but it doesn't flatten out the field itself. So, for example, mentoring programs may help women meet key people in a company's hierarchy, but they don't change the fact that informal networks, to which few women are privy, determine who really gets resources, information, and opportunities. Launching family-friendly programs doesn't challenge the belief that balancing home and work is fundamentally a woman's problem. And adding time to a tenure clock or providing alternative career tracks does little to change the expectation that truly committed employees put work first – they need no accommodation.

The limits of the third approach are also clear. Telling people to "value differences" doesn't mean they will. That is why so many women who are encouraged to use "feminine" skills and styles find their efforts valued only in the most marginal sense. For example, women are applauded for holding teams together and are even told, "we couldn't have succeeded without you," but when promotions and rewards are distributed, they are awarded to the "rugged individuals" who assertively promoted their own ideas or came up with a onetime technical fix. Ultimately, the celebration approach may actually channel women into dead-end jobs and reinforce unhelpful stereotypes.

A FOURTH APPROACH: LINKING EQUITY AND EFFECTIVENESS

Since 1992, we have helped organizations implement a fourth approach to eradicating gender inequity. This approach starts with the premise – to continue the metaphor – that the world of short people cannot be repaired with piecemeal fixes aimed at how tall people act and what work they do. Because the short world has been in the making for hundreds, if not thousands, of years, its assumptions, and practices – such as job descriptions that conflate the physical characteristics of short people with the requirements of the job – will not be undone by assimilation or accommodation or even celebration. It will be undone by a persistent campaign of incremental changes that discover and destroy the deeply embedded roots of discrimination. These changes will be driven by short and tall people together – because both will ultimately benefit from a world where height is irrelevant to the way work is designed and distributed.

Returning to the real world of men and women, the fourth approach starts with the belief that gender inequity is rooted in our cultural patterns and therefore in our organizational systems. Although its goals are revolutionary, it doesn't advocate revolution. Instead, it emphasizes that existing systems can be reinvented by altering the raw materials of organizing – concrete, everyday practices in which biases are expressed.

The fourth approach begins when someone, somewhere in the organization realizes that the business is grappling with a gender inequity problem. Usually, the problem makes itself known through several traditional indicators. For example, recruiting efforts fail to get women to join the company in meaningful numbers; many women are stalled just before they reach leadership positions or are not rising at the same rate as their male colleagues; women tend to hold low-visibility jobs or jobs in classic "women's" departments, such as HR; senior women are waiting longer or opting to have fewer (or no) children; women have fewer resources to accomplish comparable tasks; women's pay and pay raises are not on par with men's; and women are leaving the organization at above average rates.

After recognizing that there is a problem, the next step is diagnosis. (For a description of the diagnosis stage of the small-wins strategy, see Box 17.1 "How to Begin Small Wins.") Then people must get together to talk about the work culture and determine which everyday practices are undermining effectiveness. Next, experimentation begins. Managers can launch a small initiative – or several at one time – to try to eradicate the practices that produce inequity and replace them with practices that work better for everyone. Often the experiment works – and more quickly than people would suspect. Sometimes it fixes only the symptom and loses its link to the underlying cause. When that happens, other incremental changes must be tried before a real win occurs.

Box 17.1 How to Begin Small Wins

Once an organization determines that it has a problem – female employees won't join the company, say, or women are leaving in alarming numbers – it is time to start searching for causes. Such diagnosis involves senior managers probing an organization's practices and beliefs to uncover its deeply embedded sources of inequity. But how?

An effective first step is often one-on-one interviews with employees to uncover practices and beliefs in the company's culture – how work gets done, for instance, what activities are valued, and what the assumptions are about competence. After that, focus groups can more closely examine questionable practices. Some companies have found it useful to have women and men meet separately for these initial discussions, as long as the outcomes of these meetings are shared.

Diagnosis isn't always straightforward. After all, the group is looking for the source of a relatively invisible problem. Yet we have found a collection of questions that help keep the process on track:

- How do people in this organization accomplish their work? What, if anything, gets in the way?
- Who succeeds in this organization? Who doesn't?
- How and when do we interact with one another? Who participates? Who doesn't?
- What kinds of work and work styles are valued in this organization? What kinds are invisible?

- What is expected of leaders in this company?
- What are the norms about time in this organization?
- What aspects of individual performance are discussed the most in evaluations?
- How is competence identified during hiring and performance evaluations?

After the initial diagnosis, managers should identify cultural patterns and their consequences. For example, Which practices affect men differently than women, and why? Which ones have unintended consequences for the business? Following this analysis, change agents can discuss these patterns with different people. We call this stage "holding up the mirror," and it represents the first part of developing a new shared narrative in the organization.

The next step, of course, is designing the small wins. We have found that by this point in the process, groups usually have little trouble identifying ways to make concrete changes. It is critical, however, that the managers guiding the process keep the number and scope of initiatives relatively limited and strategically targeted. Managers and other change agents should remind the organization that a single experiment should not be seen as an end in itself. Each small win is a trial intervention and a probe for learning, intended not to overturn the system but to slowly and surely make it better.

Small wins are not formulaic. Each organization is unique, and its expressions of gender inequity are, too. Consider, then, how the following companies used incremental change to bring about systemic change.

Let's begin with the European retail company that was having trouble keeping its women employees. When the problem finally became impossible to ignore, the president invited us to help the organization understand what was going on. The answer wasn't immediately obvious, of course, but as we began talking to people, it became clear that it had something to do with the lack of clarity and discipline around time. Then the question was raised, Did that lack of clarity affect men and women differently? The answer was a resounding yes.

After discussing and testing the idea further, executives started using the phrase "unbounded time" to refer to meeting overruns, last-minute schedule changes, and tardiness. The term struck a chord; it quickly circulated throughout the company and sparked widespread conversation about how meeting overload and lax scheduling damaged everyone's productivity and creativity.

Because the small-wins strategy creates changes through diagnosis, dialogue, and experimentation, it benefits not just women but also men and the organization as a whole.

At that point, the president could have asked the company's female managers to become more available (assimilation). He could have mandated that all meetings take place between nine and five (accommodation). Or he could have suggested that female employees work together in projects and at times that played to their unique strengths (celebration). Instead, he and a few other senior managers quietly began to model a more disciplined use of time, and even discouraged people who suggested last-minute or late-night meetings.

Soon people began to catch on, and a new narrative started to spread through the company. The phrase "unbounded time" was used more and more often when people wanted to signal that they thought others were contributing to ineffectiveness and inequity by being late or allowing meetings to run overtime. People realized that the lack of clarity and discipline in the company had negative consequences not just for people but also for the quality of work. Over a nine-month period, norms began to shift, and as new people were hired, senior managers made sure that they understood the company was "informal *and* disciplined." To this day, the concept of "unboundedness" pops up whenever people feel the organization is slipping back into norms that silently support gender inequity.

The small-wins strategy also worked at the investment firm that tried – unsuccessfully – to hire more women by increasing the number of interviews. After executives realized that their 30-minute interviewing approach was backfiring, they began to investigate their entire recruiting practice. They examined how the questions they asked candidates, their interview procedures, and even the places in which they were recruiting might be giving traditional people – that is, male MBAs – an advantage.

And so a series of small initiatives was launched. First, the firm lengthened its interviews to 45 minutes. Partners acknowledged that shorter interviews might have been forcing them to rely on first impressions, which are so often a function of perceived similarity. Although comfort level may make an interview go smoothly, it doesn't tell you if a candidate has valuable skills, ideas, and experience. Second, and perhaps more important, the firm revised its interviewing protocol. In the past, partners questioned candidates primarily about their previous "deal experience," which allowed only those who had worked on Wall Street to shine. Again, that practice favored men, as most investment bank associates are men. In their new approach, managers followed a set protocol and began asking candidates to talk about how they would contribute to the firm's mission. The interviews shifted radically in tone and substance. Instead of boasting from former Wall Street stars, they heard many nontraditional candidates – both women and men – describe a panoply of managerial skills, creative experiences, and diverse work styles. And indeed, these people are bringing new energy and talent into the firm. (As an added bonus, the following year the firm arrived at one prominent business school to find it was earning a reputation as a great place to work, making its recruiting efforts even more fruitful.)

Both the retail company and investment firm saw their equity and performance improve after implementing changes in their systems that could hardly be called radical. The same kind of success story can be told about an international scientific research institute. The institute, which produces new agricultural technologies for farmers, had a strong cultural norm of rewarding individual achievement. When a breakthrough was reached, a new product was developed, or a grant was won, individual scientists usually got the credit and rewards. The norm meant that support work by secretaries and technicians, as well as by scientists and professionals in departments like biotechnology and economics, was often ignored.

Paradoxically, top-level managers at the institute spoke enthusiastically about the value of teamwork and asserted that success was a group, not an individual, product. In fact, the organization planned to move to a team-based structure because senior managers considered it an imperative for addressing complex cross-functional challenges. But in the everyday workings of the organization, no one paid much heed to supporting contributors. The stars were individual "heroes."

The undervaluation of support work was an issue that affected many women because they were more likely to be in staff positions or scientific roles that were perceived as support disciplines. In addition, women more often took on support work because they were expected to do so or because they felt it was critical to a project's success. They connected people with one another, for instance, smoothed disagreements, facilitated teamwork, and taught employees new skills.

Many women expressed frustration with this type of work because it simply wasn't recognized or rewarded. Yet they were reluctant to stop because the costs of not doing it were clear to them. Without it, information would flow less easily, people would miss deadlines, more crises would erupt, and teams would break down. As we talked with them, women began to recognize the value of their efforts, and they gave them a name: "invisible work."

As in the European retail company, naming the problem had a striking effect. It turned out that invisible work wasn't just a problem for women. Men and women started talking about how the lack of value placed on invisible work was related to much larger systemic patterns. For example, people noted that the company tended to give sole credit for projects to the lead scientists, even when others had contributed or had helped spare the projects from major crises. People, especially women, admitted that mentors and bosses had advised them – and they had often advised one another – to avoid taking on invisible work to focus on work that would afford more recognition. Stemming from these informal discussions, a narrative about the importance of invisible work began to spread throughout the organization.

For senior managers who saw the link between invisible work and their goal of moving to a team-based structure, the challenge was to find ways to make invisible work visible – and to ensure it was valued and more widely shared by men and women. A task force on the topic proposed a new organization wide evaluation system that would gather input from peers and direct reports – people to whom an employee's invisible work is visible. Although that step seemed insignificant to many, it was approved and launched.

Several years later, people say that the institute is a different place. The first small win – the new evaluation process – gave way to others, such as a new process to increase information flow up, down, and sideways; new criteria for team leaders that emphasize facilitation rather than direction; and new norms about tapping expertise, no matter where it resides in the hierarchy. Implicitly, these changes challenged the prevailing masculine, individualist image of competence and leadership and opened the way for alternatives more conducive to teamwork. Today both men and women say there is a stronger sense of fairness. And senior managers say that the systemic changes brought about by the small-wins strategy were central to the institute's successful move to a team-based structure.

SMALL WINS CAN MAKE BIG GAINS

It's surprising how quickly people can come up with ideas for small wins – and how quickly they can be put into action. Take, for example, the case of the finance department at a large manufacturing company. The department had a strong norm of *overdoing* work. Whenever senior managers asked for information, the department's analysts would generate multiple scenarios complete with sophisticated graphs and charts.

The fact was, however, senior managers often only wanted an analyst's back-of-the-envelope estimates. People in the finance department even suspected as much, but there was an unspoken policy of never asking the question. The reasons? First, they worried that questions would indicate that they couldn't figure out the scope of the request themselves and hence were not competent. Second, many of the requests came in at the end of the day. Analysts feared that asking, "How much detail do you want?" might look like a way to avoid working late. To show their commitment, they felt they had to stay and give every request the full treatment.

The norm of devoting hours on end to each request hit women in the department especially hard. As women in an industry dominated by men, they felt they had to work extra hard to demonstrate their competence and commitment, especially when commitment was measured, at least in part, by time spent at work. However, the norm negatively affected men, too. The extra work, simply put, was a waste of time; it lowered productivity and dampened enthusiasm. The organization suffered: talented people avoided the department because of its reputation for overtime.

The small-wins process at this company began when we met with a group of analysts and managers in the finance department. We presented our diagnosis of the root causes of the overwork problem and asked if they could come up with small, concrete solutions to counteract it. It didn't take them long. Within an hour, the analysts had designed a one-page form that asked senior managers to describe the parameters of each request. How much detail was required? What was the desired output? The form very simply took the onus off individuals to ask taboo questions, relieving women of the fear that they might appear less than committed and allowing all analysts – not just women – to use their time more productively.

Interestingly, after only a short time, the form was dropped. Analysts reported that simply having a conversation with their managers about the company's norms and taboos changed the department's dynamics. By establishing an open dialogue, analysts could now ask clarifying questions without fearing that they were signaling incompetence or lack of commitment.

Small wins make sense even at companies that already have programs designed to combat gender inequity. Consider the case of a New York advertising agency that was particularly proud of its mentoring program aimed at developing high-potential female leaders. Although that program got women's names into the mix, the jobs that women were ultimately offered tended to be in human resource-type positions – positions women were thought to be particularly well suited for. These jobs often required a high level of skill, but their lack of rainmaking potential resulted in career disadvantages that accumulated over time.

The situation was compounded by an unspoken rule at the company of never saying no to developmental opportunities. This norm, like so many others, seems gender neutral. It appears to be a risk for both men and women to pass up opportunities, particularly those offered in the name of developing leadership potential. Yet because of the different types of opportunities offered, women stood to lose whether they said yes or no. Saying no signaled lack of commitment. But saying yes meant they would spend valuable time and energy doing a job that was unlikely to yield the same career benefits that men were deriving from the opportunities offered to them. What made the situation particularly problematic for the organization was that the HR-type jobs that women were reluctant to accept were often critical to overall functioning.

The women in the mentoring programs were the first to realize the negative impact of the company's informal policy of channeling women into these critical HR positions. So they got together to brainstorm about ways to extricate themselves from their double bind. . . . The women coached one another on how to respond to the HR-type job offers in ways that would do minimal damage to their careers. For instance, they came up with the solution of accepting the job with the stipulation that senior managers assign its year-end objectives a "rainmaking equivalency quotient." The group pushed senior managers to think about the underlying assumptions of putting women in HR jobs. Did they really believe men could not manage people? If so, didn't that mean that men should be given the developmental opportunities in HR? These questions led senior managers to several revelations, which were especially important since the organization had recently decided to sell itself to potential clients as the relationship-oriented alternative to other agencies. The full effect of this small-win effort, launched recently, will likely be seen over the course of the next few years.

THE POWER OF SMALL WINS

Small wins are not silver bullets; anyone familiar with real organizational change knows that there is no such thing. Rather, the reason small wins work so effectively is that they are not random efforts. They unearth and upend systemic barriers to women's progress. Consider how:

First, small wins tied to the fourth approach help organizations give a name to practices and assumptions that are so subtle they are rarely questioned, let alone seen as the root of organizational ineffectiveness. When the retail company started using the phrase "unbounded time," people began developing a shared understanding of how the lack of discipline around time affected men and women differently and how the lack of boundaries in the culture contributed to people's inability to get work accomplished. The act of naming the "problem with no name" opens up the possibility of change.

Second, small wins combine changes in behavior with changes in understanding. When a small win works – when it makes even a minor difference in systemic practices – it helps to verify a larger theory. It says that something bigger is going on.

Third, and related, small wins tie the local to the global. That is, people involved in small wins see how their efforts affect larger, systemic change, in much the same way as people taking part in small-town recycling campaigns come to understand their impact in decreasing global warming. This big-picture outlook is both energizing and self-reinforcing, and it links seemingly unrelated small wins together.

Fourth, small wins have a way of snowballing. One small change begets another, and eventually these small changes add up to a whole new system. Consider again the investment firm that revised its recruiting processes. It realized that something as simple as lengthening interview time could begin to address its recruitment problem. But if it had stopped there, it is unlikely that fundamental changes would have occurred. Recognizing why the length of an interview was an issue – how "feeling comfortable" and "fitting the mold" had been implicit selection criteria – helped the firm make additional, more substantial changes in, for instance, the questions asked. This change is encouraging the executives to look into initiatives to revise other practices, ranging from publicity to training, that also held hidden biases, not just for women but also for other underrepresented groups.

The fifth and final source of power in the small-wins approach is that it routs discrimination by fixing the organization, not the women who work for it. In that way, it frees women from feelings of self-blame and anger that can come with invisible inequity. And it removes the label of troublemaker from women who complain that something is not right. Small wins say, "Yes, something is wrong. It is the organization itself, and when it is fixed, all will benefit."

As we enter the new millennium, we believe that it is time for new metaphors to capture the subtle, systemic forms of discrimination that still linger. It's not the ceiling that's holding women back; it's the whole structure of the organizations in which we work: the foundation, the beams, the walls, the very air. The barriers to advancement are not just above women, they are all around them. But dismantling our organizations isn't the solution. We must ferret out the hidden barriers to equity and effectiveness one by one. The fourth approach asks leaders to act as thoughtful architects and to reconstruct buildings beam by beam, room by room, rebuilding with practices that are stronger and more equitable, not just for women but for all people.

NOTES

1   The research for this article began in 1992 and is ongoing. Our work – including interviews, surveys, archival data, focus groups, and observations – has taken place at 11 organizations. They included three *Fortune* 500 companies, two international research organizations, two public agencies, a global retail organization, an investment firm, a school, and a private foundation. The goal of each project was to create the kind of small wins and learning reported in this article.

   The ideas presented in this article were developed in collaboration with three colleagues: Robin Ely, an associate professor at Columbia University's School of International and Public Affairs in New York City and an affiliated faculty member at the Center for Gender in Organizations, Simmons Graduate School of Management, in Boston; Deborah Kolb, a codirector of the Center for Gender in Organizations, a professor of management at Simmons Graduate School of Management, and a senior fellow at the Program on Negotiation at Harvard Law School; and anthropologist Deborah Merrill-Sands, a codirector of the Center for Gender in Organizations and an expert in conducting research on gender in organizations.

   The research in this article builds directly on the foundational work of Lotte Bailyn, the T. Wilson Professor of Management at the MIT Sloan School of Management in Cambridge, Massachusetts, and Rhona Rapoport, director of the Institute of Family and Environmental Research in London. They also collaborated on many of the projects mentioned in this article.

2.   Statistics on women of color are even more drastic. Although women of color make up 23% of the U.S. women's workforce, they account for only 14% of women in managerial roles. African-American women comprise only 6% of the women in managerial roles.

   The small-wins approach to change was developed by Karl Weick. See "Small Wins: Redefining the Scale of Social Problems," *American Psychologist*, 1984.

ACTION LEARNING, FRAGMENTATION, AND THE INTERACTION OF SINGLE-, DOUBLE-, AND TRIPLE-LOOP CHANGE: A CASE OF GAY AND LESBIAN WORKPLACE ADVOCACY[1]

ERICA GABRIELLE FOLDY AND W. E. DOUGLAS CREED

From *Journal of Applied Behavioral Science* (1999) 35(2): 207–27

Despite a rich and diverse history of research (e.g., Gersick, 1991; Sutton, 1987; Tushman & Romanelli, 1985; Van de Ven & Poole, 1995), organizational change continues to captivate and challenge management scholars. Understanding change means understanding the fundamental nature of today's organizations as they strive to adapt to an ever more complex environment. Capturing the change process requires attention to three levels: the individuals and groups within organizations, the organizations themselves, and the societal contexts within which they operate. It also requires attention to how those levels interact – reinforcing, modifying, and opposing each other, often simultaneously. In this article, we propose a framework for understanding variegated, contradictory change processes, building on the substantial literature on action learning. By applying this framework to a case study of a change that challenged individuals, their organization, and the larger society, we illustrate both how change permeates all three levels and how that change can be dissected and then reconstructed.

Action learning, or the concept of single-, double-, and triple-loop learning (Argyris & Schön, 1978, 1996; Nielsen, 1993b), is a very powerful tool for understanding change. Briefly, single-loop learning changes an actor's strategies, or the assumptions behind those strategies, without addressing the actor's driving values. Here, actors (individual or collective) change their approach to more effectively or efficiently reach existing goals. In double-loop learning, actors question and ultimately transform their driving values. Triple-loop learning goes beyond the actors' values, addressing the values of the actors' societal environments or tradition systems.

Most efforts to apply the action-learning framework (e.g., Argyris, Putnam, & Smith, 1985; Nielsen, 1993a, 1993b, 1996a, 1996b; Nielsen & Bartunek, 1996; Torbert, 1994; Torbert & Fisher, 1992) have shared a similar unitary approach, equating method with outcome, and understanding a change process as a single method or level of action learning, either single loop, double loop, or triple loop. For example, a particular company's decision to include ethical criteria as part of its decision making might be characterized simply as double-lop learning because it may require a change in the values underlying that company's decision-making framework. In contrast, a company's decision to launch a new product line might be seen as single loop because it simply suggests a change that largely conforms to the organization's current strategy.

The action-learning framework enables relatively neat distinctions between tinkering with current conceptions about how things should be done (single-loop learning), thinking outside the box of the actor (double-loop learning), and questioning society's more encompassing box. The latter, questioning the nature of the tradition system itself, is an example of triple-loop learning. It provides a useful shorthand for both researchers and practitioners. But the power of action learning is diminished if variation along this continuum is reduced to a trichotomous global characterization. Can a radical change effort that takes on the current framework succeed without appealing to some of that framework's traditional values? Can a change effort bold enough to challenge societal norms happen without challenging organizational or individual values? In other words, can single-loop, double-loop, and triple-loop methods of change happen entirely autonomously? Or is it their *interaction* that ultimately determines the nature and extent of organizational change?

We argue that the interaction of single-loop, double-loop, and triple-loop methods (rather than their independence) should be the focus of analysis. Influenced by postmodern approaches to the study of organizations (e.g., Boje, 1993, 1995; Cooper & Burrell, 1988), we treat change efforts as multilayered and fragmented. Although the traditional use of action learning focuses on single, dominant understandings, we create an action-learning framework that goes beyond the simple trichotomous approach by attending to the contradictory facets of a single change effort. We then provide an illustration of this new framework with the case of a company's decision to dramatically change its attitude toward its gay and lesbian employees. A shorthand characterization of this change effort might depict it as a story of remarkably successful triple-loop change. Our framework instead untangles the strands of single-, double-, and triple-loop learning, showing how they interacted to create a rough, unfinished change impossible to encapsulate with a simple triple-loop label. We offer this framework as a contribution to the action-learning lexicon, useful for analyzing other change efforts.

We start with the story of the change effort, followed by an analysis of the case. As part of the analysis, we summarize and apply the traditional approach of action learning to the case. We then argue for an approach influenced by postmodern perspectives. We then suggest and apply a new action-learning framework that facilitates such an approach by allowing the analysis of multiple methods within a single change effort.

THE FINANCIAL SERVICES COMPANY: INSURING ACCEPTANCE

Methodology

In early 1996, our research team approached the Minnesota Work Place Alliance (WPA), an alliance of gay, lesbian, bisexual, and transgender (GLBT)[2] employee groups in the Twin Cities and at the time one of the most advanced GLBT "group of groups" in America. Through the WPA, we were able to interview 65 individuals at 24 Twin Cities employers, including GLBT employee advocates, their allies, corporate diversity managers, and in some cases, key executive decision makers. Our focus was on the dynamics behind the adoption and diffusion of inclusive practices, particularly domestic partner benefits (DPBs), the role of key advocates or idea champions, and the nature of the debate surrounding GLBT-friendly policies.

In the vast majority of these interviews, the Financial Services Company (FSC), a *Fortune* 500 insurance company, was pointed to as the region's leader in the area of GLBT-inclusive policies and programming. We therefore focus on FSC, where we interviewed seven people, including the chief executive officer (CEO), the executive vice president of human resources (VP of HR), the corporate diversity officer, the leaders of the GLBT network, and two of its members. Our case also draws on insights from other WPA members who had witnessed events at FSC and from media coverage of the GLBT network and events at FSC.[3]

Our initial impression, fueled by the accounts of WPA activists from outside the company, was that FSC's move to the cutting edge had been relatively easy and straightforward. This was especially surprising when juxtaposed with the experiences of many other companies represented in the WPA. Therefore, in our interviews with FSC insiders, we raised questions about the relative ease of the change process. These inquiries revealed that change at FSC was by no means smooth sailing.

The advocacy effort at FSC

In October 1994, FSC hosted the second WPA Executive Forum, bringing together representatives of Twin Cities employers to discuss GLBT employment issues. The CEO of FSC, Paul Lennox, opened the forum with an unexpected announcement: FSC would be offering DPBs to both the opposite- and same-sex unmarried partners of its employees. This is a frequently retold success story for GLBT advocates in the Twin Cities. The people behind it, especially Alison Guzman, are role models for Twin Cities GLBT employee advocates. But Alison and her allies all indicate that their successes must be understood within the context of FSC's ongoing diversity initiative that laid the groundwork for what came later.

FSC's diversity initiative began in the early 1990s when CEO Paul Lennox determined that to avoid becoming a "Hartford dinosaur" FSC needed to realize the potential of all its employees in responding to its diverse markets. In 1991, as part of this strategic change, FSC engaged diversity consultants and began a process of self-assessment that included culture audits, a look at its history and values, an all-employee survey, and employee focus groups formed along such lines as race and gender.

In 1992, two GLBT leaders from different areas of FSC emerged. Alison Guzman, a mid-level payables accountant with 14 years of service at FSC and a lesbian, was one of the few people HR had been able to enlist in a lesbian focus group. At this time, Guzman was neither fully out of nor entirely in the closet at FSC. Her participation was triggered by watching Pat Buchanan at the 1992 Republican National Convention on television. She wondered, "Why are not regular business people . . . coming out? . . . Why aren't people stopping the hate that Pat Buchanan is talking about?" Following the lesbian focus group, Guzman began working with HR on the diversity initiative. According to the current corporate diversity officer, Alison's firsthand account of GLBT experience at FSC was pivotal in shaping FSC's definition of the dimensions of diversity and laying a foundation for what came later: "We included sexual orientation in our definition . . . a major thing . . . that made things that we did downstream a lot easier . . . [because then] we were continuing to manage against what we said we're about."

At about this time, a gay actuarial analyst, Kent Rosener, was mobilized by what he saw as FSC's hypocritical behavior regarding diversity. FSC was, by early 1992, already outspoken about its ever stronger commitment to diversity and, he says, did have a good record on other diversity issues. Yet Rosener also encountered insensitivity and sometimes outright homophobia in the workplace. In one team training session, the facilitator asked people to write the name of a celebrity dream date on a card. After they had come to know each other as a team, they would match participants to their cards. "Either I had to come out to the class in order to play the game, or I would have had to pretend I was straight. . . . I kind of withdrew." Rosener turned in a blank card and was chastised for not being a team player.

Finally, in the fall of 1992, Rosener read in a company newsletter an executive's comment that FSC had not yet begun to deal with GLBT issues. Rosener took this as a cue that the company was ready for input. He joined his division's diversity committee. During a planning meeting, Kent decided to out himself when proposing that the division take up GLBT issues. To committee members' shock, the chair cut him off. The next day, the chair apologized, saying that Kent's proposals were too controversial for a divisional initiative and that he would have to work with people at the corporate level.

Kent approached two women in corporate HR who recognized an opportunity to bring together a group whose members are often as hidden from each other as they are from management. The HR staffers, Rose Smith and Jan White, introduced Alison and Kent. Though this may come as a surprise to those not familiar with the power of the corporate closet, despite 5 years with FSC, Kent had not known a single GLBT employee. Alison relates, "We got together and met, all of a sudden it grew to like four of us. Then the next step was forming the network, which was the idea of FSC." Smith and White, acting in the name of FSC, strategized with Rosener and Guzman that a systematic education program would have to pave the way for policy changes. They created an informal task force to design and implement these grassroots educational programs.

To launch the informal network, Smith and White obtained Alison's permission to name her as the contact person for this new network. For Alison, it was a major hurdle.

> I knew of high-level people at FSC who were gay or lesbian and I wished that they would've come out. I did not want to come out. I had lots of fears, but [the higher level people] weren't [coming out] and . . . I don't believe in outing people, so . . . I just finally said, "I gotta do it myself."

She did it via an e-mail to FSC's 10,000 domestic employees on January 1, 1993.

The network was named the Gay, Lesbian and Friends, or GLF, Network. *Friends* was meant to be a cover for bisexuals and transgender people; Kent and Alison reasoned that explicitly including those constituencies by name would make their job of educating and gaining acceptance even more difficult. Supportive heterosexuals understood the word *friends* to refer to them, however, and quickly signed up in large numbers.

The network's next step was to contact John Stanton, the VP of HR, with a letter requesting DPBs. His terse, "homophobic" denial was very dispiriting for the GLF Network, according to Guzman, but in her e-mail response she said that they understood that there were difficult issues and that "we felt very strongly that this is something we should have, and we wanted to work with him. Anything that we could do, any information that we could provide, we would be there for him." She then invited Stanton to lunch for a conversation both see as pivotal. Free to ask any question about a domain many people are afraid to talk about, Stanton came to recognize he had to deal with "my own biases, my own background, set of experiences and my own baggage."

Quite quickly, Stanton made a dramatic shift and became a powerful advocate for GLBT employees inside FSC and the Twin Cities. Stanton took the issue to Paul Lennox, the CEO, who saw it was the right thing to do. But, as Craig Williams, corporate diversity officer, explains, "We didn't go all the way to bright on this thing; we just didn't say, 'Oh sexual orientation, we got everybody.' It was . . . evolutionary. . . . You have to start to build some relationships . . . start to understand the things you're being exposed to."

In October 1993, about 10 months after its emergence as an informal network, the GLF Network, along with networks for African Americans, Native Americans, women, and Latinos, was officially recognized. Rosener acknowledges that this might sound quick, but to him, at the time, it seemed like a difficult 10 months of hard work, significant personal risk, and exposure to scrutiny. For example, prior to recognition, the content of all the GLF Network's communications had been screened by senior executives. Executive support continued to grow, but the request for DPBs was yet to be granted.

Through many retellings, one story of CEO Lennox's public support has gained almost mythic status, both with GLF Network members and members of the WPA. In June of 1994, in FSC's daily broadcast e-mail to employees, the GLF Network announced a meeting in the headquarters cafeteria to plan for Gay Pride Week. To Lennox, such announcements were not unusual: "The day before, the garden club had been on." It sparked a furious reaction from two regional offices in particular: Dallas and Atlanta. In Dallas, half of the employees signed a petition excoriating Lennox for allowing such a meeting and saying he was unfit to lead the company. Lennox flew to Dallas the next week and met with all 400 employees in groups of about 50. "I would not let them get away with this. I challenged people. . . . I don't care if you are brown or if you're black, you're going to have this kind of opportunity and would you deny that [to others]?" The next week, in Atlanta, he told employees,

> "This is the way this company is going to run and if you are really uncomfortable with that then maybe you might be happier working some place else." I laid it right on the line, and in one week the whole issue was gone.

If by "the whole issue," Lennox meant open insurrection, yes, it was gone. But as Stanton and Lennox both related, the cultural challenges posed by any proposed changes in HR policy still would require extensive coalition building within FSC senior ranks and attitude change at all levels.

In October 1994 – less than 2 years after Guzman's "huge outing" by e-mail but 2 long years of careful behind-the-scenes advocacy, extensive educational programming, extramural work on launching the WPA Executive Forum and cementing the infrastructure of a regional GLBT employee network, and extensive research on other companies' experiences with instituting DPBs – FSC announced the offering of DPBs to both GLBT and straight employees, effective January 1995. All involved describe these 2 years as a long journey. No one at FSC believes that the problem of homophobia is solved, a fact that Rosener, Guzman, Stanton, and Lennox all pointed to as a continuing challenge in FSC's culture change effort.

RESHAPING ACTION LEARNING AS AN ANALYTIC TOOL: A POSTMODERN APPROACH

How can action learning help us analyze the events at FSC? We begin by briefly summarizing the traditional approach to action learning and applying it to this case. Then, we argue for understanding the change from a postmodern perspective, one that highlights complexity and discrepancy rather than integrated totality. Using the FSC case, we then suggest a new action-learning framework.

The concept of action learning comes originally from the work of Argyris and Schön (1978). They suggest that change efforts can be characterized as either single loop or double loop. In single-loop action learning, actors (whether individuals, groups, or organizations) consider more effective methods or strategies for achieving their guiding principles (which may be manifested as goals, policies, or values), but these actors are not open to questioning those principles. Actors modify their approach to better implement current policies or reach current objectives. These policies or objectives are closed to scrutiny. Double-loop action learning, on the other hand, results when actors do evaluate and change their guiding principles. Actors alter their approach by modifying driving values. The concept of triple-loop action learning, which places action learning in a larger social context, was suggested by Nielsen (1993a, 1993b). In triple-loop action learning, actors go beyond questioning their own values and consider the values of the societal tradition system in which their actions are taking place.

What kind of action learning took place at FSC? The traditional, unitary approach to action learning would suggest that triple-loop learning took place. Triple-loop learning occurs when actors change not only their own guiding principles but challenge the values of the larger tradition system. FSC adopted new rules and norms for behavior that both transformed the company's posture toward its GLBT employees and implicitly challenged society's norms about homosexuality as well. . . .

Using the lens of the traditional unitary approach to action learning, we agree with this assessment. However, we believe that this totalizing approach glosses over aspects of this change effort that are subtler, more varied, and in many cases, more interesting. Taking a closer look reveals an intertwining of single-, double-, and triple-loop approaches, a maze that resists simplification. [. . .]

To hone or sharpen action learning as a tool able to make finer distinctions, we break it down into component parts. As Table 18.1 illustrates, the term *action-learning method* actually refers to three different components of a change effort: the arguments (or justifications) given for change, the practices used to bring about

Table 18.1 The components of the action-learning method

Action-learning method		
Argument for change	Practice to create change	Outcome of change effort

Table 18.2 Action-learning arguments at Financial Services Company

Argument	Summary	Action-Learning Level
"The business case."	Welcoming gay, lesbian, bisexual, and transgender (GLBT) employees could increase their commitment to the company and open new markets, thus increasing the company's profitability.	Single loop
"Helping us move in the direction we needed to move."	Company leaders wanted to change their conservative corporate culture into one that embraced risk taking and initiative. Welcoming GLBT employees modeled this approach.	Double loop
"A company . . . that's always been family friendly."	Financial Services Company prided itself on its forward-thinking work/family practices such as on-site day care. Although the company interpreted the addition of gay families as within their current approach, such an addition challenged both company and societal norms about what constitutes a family.	Triple loop

change, and the outcomes of the change. In most action-learning literature, method and outcome are assumed to be one and the same (e.g., Nielsen, 1993b. 1996b). A single-loop learning method will lead to a single-loop learning outcome: The method is in fact inferred from its outcome. Nor has method been broken down into constituent parts such as argument and practice. At most, there has been some effort to distinguish outcome from critique of the learning process. We suggest changing this approach. These three separate components – argument, practice, and outcome – can be decoupled and analyzed in isolation from each other, rather than treating the action-learning method as an indissoluble whole. To illustrate how this can work, we will describe each component in turn and illustrate its analysis with examples from the case of FSC. Tables 18.2 and 3 summarize this analysis.

Action-learning arguments

Single-, double-, and triple-loop arguments all refer to the actor's justifications for creating change. A single-loop argument would appeal to the actor's governing values or framework. An action would be justified on the basis that it conformed to the actor's current beliefs. This justification is often automatic and unconscious. For example, a manager might decide to hire a white candidate over a black candidate because no positions at that level have ever been filled by a nonwhite employee or because the manager believes that a black candidate, by definition, could not possibly be qualified for such a position. The manager is simply applying her current understanding of the world to her decision making. A double-loop reason for action, on the other hand, would involve an actor changing his or her values. In this case, the manager might change her governing framework and decide that adding diversity to her work group would benefit the company, or that, although the black candidate does not have the same qualifications as other people who have held the position, he brings another kind of expertise that could be helpful. A triple-loop reason for action shifts attention to higher levels of influence. Now, the actor sees him- or herself as part of the larger society and addresses larger societal dynamics or objectives. Perhaps the manager decides that changing her own thinking is not enough; challenging institutional racism as a societal issue is the only way to really level the playing field for African Americans. The manager is engaging in triple-loop learning.

The case of FSC provides a more complex illustration. The change agents at FSC gave a number of reasons for taking action regarding their GLBT employees. As Table 18.2 illustrates, these arguments and their implications for single-, double-, or triple-loop learning were quite varied.

1. "The business case" (Paul Lennox)

All of the key players at FSC argued that a strong business case for creating a GLBT-friendly workplace was essential if change was to happen. One such argument is to point to market demographics. According to VP of HR Stanton, "If you care about market share, if you care about growing your business, if you care about profitability, you better be paying attention to segments of your markets that represent significant opportunity for you." The logic: Only companies that treat their GLBT employees fairly will be able to tap the GLBT market.

But both Stanton and CEO Lennox also pointed to the competitive advantage of a committed workforce. According to Lennox,

> Our markets were changing. The nature of the employee/employer relationship was changing. People who were working here were going to be changing. . . . I get paid to think about where we are 5 years from now and we have got to make these changes.

For Lennox, this meant building a more culturally diverse workforce with everyone able to realize his or her potential. Lennox argued that if FSC did well by its employees, they would respond in turn. As an insurance company, FSC does not have significant assets in patents, machinery, or products; according to Lennox, "It's not trite to say that people are our most valuable asset." [. . .]

[Both] respondents are saying that openly welcoming FSC's GLBT employees would further the company's mission and enhance its profitability. [They] agreed that making this bottom-line argument was crucial to the effort's success. These arguments are all single loop: They justify taking action within the already established goals and values of the company. In reality, it is that very limitation that made them so potent and that allowed other, more far-reaching justifications as well (cf. Austin, 1997).

2. "Helping us move in the direction we needed to move" (John Stanton)

Both Lennox and Stanton positioned their taking on GLBT issues as part of a larger cultural shift the company had to make. According to Stanton,

> My challenge was a huge organization culture and business culture challenge. . . . [The GLBT advocacy effort] fit very nicely into helping us move into the direction that we needed to move. Culturally, we were . . . a standard, top-down, command and control, very paternalistic culture. . . . You can't go from pretty good to great with that kind of a culture, with employees that were afraid to take risks, wouldn't take initiative.

How could top management model the kind of risk-taking behavior it expected from its employees? Taking bold action regarding their GLBT employees was an unmistakable example, particularly action that was a response to grassroots initiative. Lennox used the gay advocacy effort to signal his new approach. "I knew that I had to drive this company into a much more international sphere. . . . [FSC] was incredibly parochial and narrow in its views."

In this case, the company's top management team attempted double-loop learning – a transformational change – in the company's belief systems. They identified a bold move on GLBT issues as significant leverage for this larger goal. This reason for action, then, would be double loop.

3. "A company . . . that has always been family friendly" (John Stanton)

Stanton pointed out that the FSC culture

> has always been family friendly and open to things like a child care center . . . [and] flexible work schedules, long before this stuff was in vogue. So you bring the best of the culture forward and try to apply it with the needs of the company.

Interestingly, Stanton seems to be arguing that expanding benefits to GLBT families was a within-culture change, a change within the boundaries of the best the culture had to offer. Lennox offered a kindred argument when responding to board criticism by depicting the adoption of DPBs as a "modest change . . . because in terms of cost, it is not a major, significant cost item." Although the experience of many companies suggests that DPBs do not add significantly to costs, to evaluate the change only in terms of costs is to diminish the moral and cultural issues at stake. Both Stanton and Lennox defend their decision using single-loop arguments, suggesting that DPBs represented a small change in current personnel policies.

From another standpoint, however, including GLBT families in the FSC family album was a radical departure from the current practice of both the company and the country. As noted earlier, taking the step of providing benefits to the partners of gay employees was hardly status quo. We would argue that the inclusion of GLBT families into FSC's family album is more than double loop, more than just a challenge to the company's norms. It is a challenge to the prevailing conservative norms of much of American society and therefore would constitute triple-loop change. [. . .]

This reinforces our doubts about simple labels to summarize complex events. Key players at FSC used single-, double-, and despite their more cautious inclinations, triple-loop arguments, providing them access to different audiences. The

Table 18.3 Action-learning practices at Financial Services Company

Practice	Summary	Action-learning level
"We knew the atmosphere, we knew the culture."	Gay, lesbian, bisexual, and transgender advocates were careful to work within corporate norms as much as possible.	Single loop
"The reason we're called the Gay, Lesbian and Friends Network is because we were a very conservative company."	The name for the employee network was initially meant as a cover for bisexual and transgender employees because advocates thought explicit mention would decrease support. Other employees interpreted the name as an invitation for straight employees to join, a manifestation of the company's current, inclusive culture.	Single loop
"Try to do some personal work."	Both gay advocates and key corporate leaders emphasized the need for individuals to work through the issue on their own so they could achieve their own sense of comfort about gay issues.	Double loop

narrow, single-loop arguments allowed them to reach and unite more conservative constituencies. The broader, more challenging double-loop arguments are part of a larger cultural change program, an effective justification for company leaders. The triple-loop arguments put the company on record about a controversial social issue and gained the company a supportive constituency of GLBT workplace activists in the Twin Cities area. A simple single-loop, double-loop, or triple-loop label for what happened at FSC would erase these distinctions.

Action-learning practices

Single-, double-, and triple-loop practices follow a framework similar to that of reasons for action. Single-loop actions operate within the actor's current framework of what is acceptable practice. For example, let's take a centralized and hierarchical company with strict norms about employees approaching managers other than their own direct supervisors. The company, in the interests of better communication, might modify its practice so that employees can address their supervisors' direct superiors if there is some reason why approaching one's own supervisor is problematic. As opposed to that single-loop change in practice, the company might decide instead to decentralize the company, creating project teams that cut across divisions and hierarchical levels – a double-loop change in practice. A triple-loop change, however, would challenge societal norms about authority and control in business. The company could decide instead to become an employee-owned and -managed business, with employees holding the majority of the seats on the board of directors. As Table 18.3 illustrates, the actions at FSC provide a good example of how individuals used different action-learning practices.

1. "We knew the atmosphere, we knew the culture" (Alison Guzman)

Informants, both activists and company leaders, agreed that the GLBT advocates' actions were careful, measured, and sensitive to FSC culture. "We didn't want to burn any bridges and to be in people's faces because we didn't think it was the way to go," noted Guzman. From his perspective as VP of HR, Stanton agreed. In response to a query about why it seemed easier to institute GLBT-friendly policies at FSC, Stanton said, "I don't think it was easy. I think that it was a group of dedicated people who understood the culture here and who understood the way that we needed to do things." This is single-loop practice, actions that operate within the clear boundaries of the acceptable in a given situation.

The gay advocacy effort was also within-culture in a different way: The company had already made a commitment to diversity issues. It had well-functioning diversity structures in place as well as an ideological investment in valuing and realizing the potential of individual differences. Guzman stated that the foundation for their success was built "6 or 7 years ago with the diversity initiative. . . . If it was not there we wouldn't be where we are right now." CEO Lennox also made this clear, noting, "I wasn't driving this because it was a gay/lesbian issue. I was driving this because I considered it an integral part of our diversity efforts."

In this case, GLBT advocates were able to take advantage of a double-loop change – the commitment to diversity – that had started years earlier and that made their own efforts justifiable with a single-loop argument congruent with that change. Diversity had now been institutionalized, opening up options for single-loop change. This example suggests that action-learning actions may be variable and relative. Whether actions or arguments are single, double, or triple loop may not be inherent but a function of other factors, such as the analyst, the context, or the audience.

2. "The reason we're called the Gay, Lesbian and Friends Network is because we were a very conservative company" (Alison Guzman)

A hallmark of GLBT advocacy at FSC is its inclusiveness, with its employee network as both a symbolic and concrete manifestation of that. The main network, called the Gay, Lesbian and Friends Network, includes both homosexual and heterosexual employees. This inclusiveness, as Guzman's quotation suggests, was a way of staying within the company's norms of inclusivity and friendliness; in other words, a single-loop, nonthreatening practice. [. . .]

3. "Try to do some personal work" (John Stanton)

Embedded in this change effort was a fundamental belief that individuals needed to work through the issue on their own, to achieve their own sense of comfort with GLBT issues in the workplace. Stanton's own personal transformation on the issue has been very influential.

> It's just like anything, as you [go] through this personal exploration the light bulb tends to go on. . . . My wife will tell you it was like this personal transformation took place, and I said I just dealt with the fear. . . . It's really why I believe, and I still have a hard time in influencing and persuading even our own executives around this notion of personal work. . . . Try to understand . . . your own biases and your own prejudices and your own baggage.

The GLBT advocates also had a similar framework. "We understood that they had a lot of learning to go through just like we did" (Guzman). Rosener noted,

> We've always had the argument that we're not getting equal pay because we're not getting the same benefits, but that was always really aside. . . . It's never where we really pushed it as far as education. It has always been the acceptance of who I am.

Although policy changes are crucial, for Rosener the fundamental issue is people's ability to accept individuals different from themselves.

This emphasis on individual reflection and change is, really, an emphasis on double-loop practice, which requires actors' willingness to reevaluate their own driving values. Both advocates and organizational leaders went beyond simply suggesting single-loop changes in behavior; they very explicitly encouraged individual transformations as essential to the open inclusion of the company's GLBT employees.

In this case, key actors used both single-loop and double-loop practices: single loop to carefully stay within company norms and double loop to encourage individuals to evaluate and possibly change their beliefs. Triple-loop actions that would have directly challenged overarching societal norms (e.g., an action in the vein of ACT-UP, with overt challenges such as, "We're here. We're queer. Get used to it.") were rejected as too risky. Indeed, using more confrontational methods might have undermined the actors' double-loop strategy of emphasizing personal change. In this setting, at least, the patient, understanding attitude of key GLBT advocates perhaps fostered a safer climate in which individuals felt more comfortable thinking through their own issues.

Action-learning outcomes

Having now analyzed reasons for action and the practices themselves, we turn to outcomes. In line with our previous analyses, we suggest that outcomes can also be characterized as single loop, double loop, and triple loop. This departs from previous use of the action-learning framework, which did not distinguish between action-learning method and action-learning outcome. In most action-learning literature, method and outcome are assumed to be one and the same. If a single-loop change has resulted, then a single-loop method must have been used. We believe it would be helpful to disentangle action-learning method and action-learning outcome and consider them as two separate concepts.

The outcomes of the GLBT advocacy effort at FSC are complex and not easily summed up with a unitary action-learning label. The clearest outcomes are that FSC has created a formal network that encourages GLBT people to come out of the corporate closet – freely and openly associating with one another and affirming their traditionally stigmatized identities – and that FSC has made its HR policies more inclusive. GLBT employees and their partners in committed relationships (and unmarried heterosexual employees) have access to the same array of partner benefits as their married colleagues. Given that FSC has traditionally been a conservative company, that represents a transformation of the company's earlier framework. Of course, these changes also challenge the prevailing societal norms regarding public acceptance of GLBT orientations and what constitutes a legitimate family. FSC has also enabled the GLF Network's participation in regional advocacy networks and supported its leaders' teaching workshops on workplace organizing at such events as the National Gay and Lesbian Task Force's annual Creating Change Conference. The events at FSC have spread ripples across the Twin Cities, the Midwest, and the country, an indication of triple-loop change.

But tracking the change effort in more detail reveals a muddier picture. Many of the informants agreed that change has been incomplete. CEO Lennox noted, "We know that we still got lots of barriers around here." VP of HR Stanton suggested there was still work to be done "in the execution and . . . development in our policies to make them as open and inclusive as we can."

Concerns focus on whether employees' values, their attitudes, have changed along with the rules. Many agreed that behavior has changed. "We've been successful at turning over the set of rules that we've had here around diversity. You get a lot of people lined up, because that is just what we do around here," said Stanton. In many cases, language has changed. "I would challenge you to find anybody, somebody who cannot repeat the litany [about diversity]," Lennox said, but he then added, "They may not always agree with it." Clearly, deeper attitudinal change, double-loop learning, has not necessarily followed suit, though it certainly has occurred. Stanton noted,

> In some ways I see true sensitivity within our population, but in other pockets it's more acceptance that this is the way it is but I don't really – on a personal level, "I'll do what you tell me here at work, but when I go home I'm kind of going back to my home."

A number of people expressed concern about "the field," the vast network of FSC offices around the country. Lennox notes, "We only have 25% of our employees in the United States who live here in Minnesota. The rest of them are all over the rest of the country. How do we reach them?" Stanton was quite clear:

> I hope you come away from your interviews here with the notion that there's been a breakthrough and we're at a certain level with this here at [FSC]. It is not equal across the entire organization. We have places in the organization where we have a lot more work to do.

One HR professional noted, "Most of our field offices don't have any gay employees who are out," because employees perceive these environments as less safe. [. . .]

ACTION LEARNING, FRAGMENTATION, AND THE INTERACTION OF SINGLE-, DOUBLE-, AND TRIPLE-LOOP CHANGE

What happened at FSC? A once hidebound company placed itself at the cutting edge of HR policy, a change that has inspired GLBT employee advocates in and beyond the Twin Cities, that has triggered discussions among senior management at other major companies, and that represents another step in the diffusion and institutionalization of DPBs as an HR policy. And yet, many of FSC's employees and offices lag behind. Most gay employees apparently do not feel safe in the field, and many do not even feel safe in corporate headquarters. Public actions and language may conform, but private attitudes often rebel. Simply naming this process as triple-loop learning ignores the niches and pockets, fragments and factions of resistance and inertia that accompany any substantial change effort.

Simple, unitary labels also have another consequence: They imply a separation between single-, double-, and triple-loop methods of change. Using only one method – single-loop, double-loop, or triple-loop – to summarize a change effort implies that only one method has been used. Sometimes there is an implication that the three methods are mutually exclusive: Triple-loop change happens when single- and double-loop change are not present. [. . .]

The FSC case suggests that, far from action-learning methods being mutually exclusive, higher change levels – double- or triple-loop – cannot happen without lower level changes happening concurrently. That is, triple-loop change cannot occur without simultaneous double- and single-loop change, while double-loop change cannot happen without single-loop change. This notion is at the heart of the change effort at FSC.

To begin with, single-loop arguments and practices were central to the success of the FSC effort. All the key players agreed that creating new markets and fostering employee commitment were their most persuasive justifications. In fact, it was those single-loop arguments that laid the foundation for the use of double- and triple-loop arguments. Without that foundation, those more challenging reasons would have been ignored. If at least some of the behaviors of key actors had not remained congruent with prevailing company culture, the effort would likely have stalled immediately. This suggests a powerful linkage: that single-loop justifications and actions must accompany any transformational change – whether double or triple loop – for it to succeed. After all, the organization has been unified on the basis of the current framework and practice; it must be moved, at least partially, on the basis of them as well.

Furthermore, change that takes on societal norms cannot happen unless organizations and individuals within that society challenge their own value systems. To arrive at the point where one is ready to challenge the tradition system, one has to have undergone some kind of transformation oneself. Both FSC and many of its members transformed their thinking on GLBT issues. Once this had happened, they could not help but question the traditional way American society has viewed homosexuality.

In other words, triple-loop change cannot happen without single-loop and double-loop change. Single- and double-loop change are embedded in and are constitutive of triple-loop change. Smilarly, single-loop change is embedded in double-loop change. They happen concurrently, sometimes cross-fertilizing and sometimes at cross-purposes, but ultimately, it is that continuous interaction out of which change efforts grow. But although higher levels of action learning are constituted by lower levels, the reverse is not true. Single-loop learning, by definition, is learning that is not influenced by double-loop considerations. Single-loop learning stays within the actor's governing values. Similarly, double-loop learning is learning that does not consider larger societal values but transforms only the actor's framework. [. . .]

Acknowledging this connection also holds two important lessons, both seemingly contradictory, for change strategists. To foster frame-breaking change, one must begin within the frame. To foster company-wide change, one must highlight individual work. But our analysis brings up other lessons as well. Most important, given that change is fragmentary, multilayered, and contradictory, in a sense change strategy must be as well. Change strategists must be protean strategists, able to speak to multiple audiences with multiple justifications as part of a multiplicity of practices. [...]

Although these strategic insights are very preliminary, they suggest that our framework enhances the larger strategic potential of the action-learning literature. Decoupling argument, action, and outcome allows change strategists to consider each component separately, design multiple approaches, tailor these to different constituencies, and weave them back together to create a coherent whole. By leveraging multiplicity and flexibility, this tool provides a vehicle for more nuanced methods.

Acknowledging the connection between single-, double-, and triple-loop methods of change is important in another respect. If scholars are to look at organizational change from the postmodern perspective, then localized accounts become much more salient. One cannot understand a broader organizational change without attention to individual sites of struggle: how individual employees have participated or resisted, how different work groups have adapted or rebelled, and how different subcultures have modified the effort. Scholars cannot understand organizational change without detailed attention to the broad and shifting range of reactions and effects it creates.

Our framework of action-learning arguments, practices, and outcomes facilitates a postmodern approach because it allows a more variegated, more contextual understanding of the multiple elements of organizational change. By adding this ingredient to the already robust action-learning brew, we hope to give it even greater power as a force for understanding organizations.

NOTES

1   Both authors contributed equally to this article. Many thanks to Jean Bartunek, Richard Nielsen, Jenny Rudolph, Steve Taylor, and Bill Torbert for their comments and suggestions. Special thanks to Maureen Scully and John Austin for their guidance and contributions as fellow members of our research team.
2   *Transgender* refers to individuals whose self-concept and/or social presentation is inconsistent with social norms based on their biological sex. It is not necessarily related to sexual orientation.
3   Financial Services Company is a pseudonym, as are all of the names used. All interviews were transcribed, and transcript copies are available from the authors. To preserve the integrity of the pseudonyms, citations for media coverage are available only on request.

REFERENCES

Argyris, C., Putnam, R., & Smith, D. M. (1985). *Action science.* San Francisco: Jossey-Bass.
Argyris, C., & Schön, D. A. (1978). *Organizational learning: A theory of action perspective.* Reading, MA: Addison-Wesley.
Argyris, C., & Schön, D. A. (1996). *Organizational learning II: Theory method and practice.* Reading, MA: Addison-Wesley.
Austin, J. R. (1997). A method for facilitating controversial change in organizations. Branch Rickey and the Brooklyn Dodgers. *Journal of Applied Behavioral Science, 33*(1), 101–118.
Boje, D. M. (1993). On being postmodern in the academy: An interview with Stewart Clegg. *Journal of Management Inquiry, 2*(2), 191–200.
Boje, D. M. (1995). Stories of the storytelling organization: A postmodern analysis of Disney as "Tamara-Land." *Academy of Management Journal, 38*(4), 997–1035.

Cooper, R., & Burrell, G. (1988). Modernism, postmodernism and organizational analysis: An introduction. *Organization Studies, 9*(1), 91–112.

Gersick, C. J. G. (1991). Revolutionary change theories: A multilevel exploration of the punctuated equilibrium paradigm. *Academy of Management Review, 16*, 10–36.

Nielsen, R. P. (1993a). Varieties of postmodernism as moments in ethics action-learning. *Business Ethics Quarterly, 3*(3), 251–269.

Nielsen, R. P. (1993b). Woolman's "I am we" triple-loop action-learning: Origin and application in organization ethics. *Journal of Applied Behavioral Science, 29*(1), 117–138.

Nielsen, R. P. (1996a). *The politics of ethics: Methods for acting, learning and sometimes fighting with others in addressing ethics problems in organizational life.* New York: Oxford University Press.

Nielsen, R. P. (1996b). Varieties of dialectic change processes. *Journal of Management Inquiry, 5*(3), 276–292.

Nielsen, R. P., & Bartunek, J. M. (1996). Opening narrow, routinized schemata to ethical stakeholder consciousness and action. *Business and Society, 35*(4), 483–519.

Sutton, R. J. (1987). The process of organizational death: Disbanding and reconnecting. *Administrative Science Quarterly, 32*, 542–569.

Torbert, W. (1994). Managerial learning, organizational learning: A potentially powerful redundancy. *Management Learning, 25*(1), 57–70.

Torbert, W., & Fisher, D. (1992). Autobiographical awareness as a catalyst for managerial and organizational development. *Management Education and Development, 23*(3), 182–198.

Tushman, M. L., & Romanelli, E. (1985). Organizational evolution: A metamorphosis model of convergence and reorientation. In L. L. Cummings & B. M. Staw (Eds.), *Research in organizational behavior* (7, pp. 171–222). Greenwich, CT: JAI.

Van de Ven, A. H., & Poole, M. S. (1995). Explaining development and change in organizations. *Academy of Management Review, 20*, 510–540.

COMPLICATING GENDER: THE SIMULTANEITY OF RACE, GENDER, AND CLASS IN ORGANIZATION CHANGE(ING)

EVANGELINA HOLVINO

From Section V of *Working Paper No. 14* (2001) Boston, MA: Center for Gender in Organizations, Simmons School of Management

MOVING FORWARD TO ADDRESS THE SIMULTANEITY OF RACE, GENDER, AND CLASS IN ORGANIZATIONS

[...] How do we create organizational change that addresses the simultaneity of race, class and gender in origins. I begin by providing "a short list of simple rules." While the "rules" serve as the general framing, I propose five specific guidelines or moves that help translate them into a lens that works at the intersection of gender, class, and race. [...]

"Simple rules" and a standpoint to work the simultaneity of race, class, and gender in organizations

Charlotte Bunch (1980: 194), a radical feminist, identified five criteria to evaluate specific feminist reforms, where "reform is not a solution but . . . a strategy toward [the] larger goal [of radical change to end the oppression of all]." . . . I have modified Bunch's criteria into six guidelines that can function as a set of simple rules for developing concrete change interventions or research agendas that address the simultaneity of race, gender, and class in organizations. Like Bunch (1980: 199), I suggest that while "every reform will not necessarily advance all five criteria," no intervention should be undertaken that is in opposition to any one of these guidelines.

- The intervention materially improves the condition of [all] women. . . .
- The intervention builds self-respect, strength, and confidence in the organizational actors. . . .
- The intervention gives those involved a sense of collective power and helps them build structures for further change. . . .
- The intervention educates and enhances the ability of organizational actors to be critical and challenging of the system. . . .

- The intervention weakens, or at least helps question, patriarchal, capitalist, ethnocentric, racist, neo-colonial, and heterosexist control of institutions and helps shift structures of power over these. . . .
- The intervention challenges current modes of representation and dominant ideologies at the same time that it acknowledges contradiction and reflects on its own deployment of power. . . .

I propose that to translate these guidelines into more practical ways to work the simultaneity of race, gender, and class in organizations requires the following five moves. These moves constitute the multiple lenses that make for a standpoint at the intersection and which in turn, provide guidelines for action.

- Pay attention to different axes of power and domination – class, race, gender, sexuality and nation – without prioritizing one or the other. This means paying attention to the many ways in which difference and the social processes of race, gender, and class intertwine and "move around," as opposed to being localized in "the oppressed" or "the oppressor." Whiteness, affluence, masculinities, and the myriad of ways in which women are positioned differently along dimensions of difference and power become targets of study and change.

  For example, how does my own positionality as a heterosexual, professional, Western, woman of color in my organization silence non-Western, lesbian, working class women at the same time that my own woman of color voice is silenced by the dominant white feminist academic discourse of a research center in a management school, which like most institutions in the Eastern region of the U.S. "elevates" Black women as the representatives of all women of color?
- Pay attention to the material and the symbolic and discursive practices; one without the other will not do. As Russo (1991: 306) reminds us, "It is not simply a matter of ideology, ideas, stereotypes, images, and/or misguided perceptions. It is about power and control, be it in terms of money, construction of ideology, or control over organizational agenda."

  For example, how is the silencing accomplished in everyday organizational practices, such as: Who gets invited to a major program event? Who gets remunerated for participating in it and how much? Who determines the theme and title of the event? How is the event structured so that some participants will be able to speak and others will remain silent?
- Attend to the socially constructed nature of identity, power relations, and difference, at the same time that these constructions are always seen in relation to and linked to the material social processes and institutional practices that create advantages and disadvantages for different groups (West and Fenstermaker, 1995).

  For example, how is my "Latinaness" constructed in the organization and how does my behavior, style, and contributions fit or not fit the dominant behaviors, styles, and accepted institutional practices? How is my identity and status, constructed at the intersection of race, class, gender, and nation different and similar to the identity of the school's Latina cleaning woman? And what does that have to do with the situation of Latinas in society and the labor market, where by far the majority are service workers and less than one percent have a doctorate degree?

- Encourage and sustain critical dialogues that acknowledge complexity and contradiction – the contradiction of multiple identities and the complexity of the overlay of class, gender, and ethnicity as they occur in social reality (Kalantzis, 1990).

  For example, my academic white Western training demands that I write in the third person, use lots of citations, and construct a rational argument in written form in a language that is not my own while the Latina longs for stories and metaphors, the magical, and the Spanish language. How do I negotiate with myself my own ambitions for success within the white feminist academy and with my colleagues who want me to be a successful Latina academic writer, an oxymoron of sorts? And are these contradictions and complexities silenced, talked about, or regulated through organizational norms about appropriate ways of writing without a dialogue that problematizes writing and knowledge-making?

- Attend to the social and historical context and the ways in which context and history show in everyday practices (Britton, 2000: 423; Marks, 1999).

  For example, in the context of a research center in a prestigious private college, how is the intersection of race, gender, and class already overdetermined by class? In the context of the profession of organization development, with its top-driven commitment to organizational change, what can be said about organizational justice or health? In the aftermath of the recent elections and current conservative political climate, what support is there for changing the social relations of race, class, and gender?

While these lenses may provide some guidance, they are still too general and complex. Today, what can be done differently to work the simultaneity of gender, class, and race in an organization?

Methods and ways of working with the simultaneity

Three concrete activities or interventions for how to enter organizations with a lens that acknowledges the *simultaneity* of race, gender, and class as processes of identity, institutional, and social practice are proposed: 1) researching and publicizing the hidden stories at the intersection of race, gender, and class to help change dominant organizational narratives; 2) identifying, untangling, and changing the differential impact of everyday practices in organizations; and 3) identifying and linking internal organizational processes with external societal processes to understand organizational dynamics within a broader social context. In other words, working at the boundary of organization and society. I will expand on each of these and offer an organizational inquiry and/or consulting example.

1. Researching and publicizing the hidden stories at the intersection of race, gender, and class

"Legitimate knowledge can only be written in small stories or modest narratives, mindful of their locality in space and time and capable of disappearing as needed"

(Calás and Smircich, 1999: 664). Telling the stories and articulating the narratives of organizational actors across different axes of power and identity is an important contribution to changing the dominant organizational discourse because it brings to light alternative narratives that seldom find their way into mainstream accounts and organizational mythologies (Ely and Meyerson, 2000).

One purpose of this type of intervention is to help change dominant organizational narratives that privilege the experience of white men and white women and that construct organizations within the liberal paradigm of maleness, heterosexism, whiteness, and Westerness. These are narratives that construct and reproduce particular kinds of identities with particular relations and access to power. For example, Bell and Nkomo's [2001] in-depth stories of white and Black women's narratives in corporations reveal important differences in how the two groups learn and experience race. The researchers found that while white women learn to keep their distance from Blacks, to be "color blind," and to exhibit the appropriate etiquette when in the presence of Blacks, Black women learn to "armor" themselves psychologically in order to be respectable, to buffer themselves from racism, and to develop courage. These different attitudes are brought to the organization as these women advance into management positions impacting every aspect of their work, from who they confide in and talk to, to the judgments they make about others' competence, and to how they negotiate their own careers and leadership roles.

Reynolds (1997), on the other hand, calls for Black women researchers to stop inquiring about the differences between white and Black women and to start addressing the differences and diversity among Black women. Proudford's (1998) research suggests that this may be indeed a very good move. Until intra-group dynamics are understood and have a legitimate place to be explored, relations between groups of women may very well continue to be superficial and/or contentious. Hurtado (2001) engages in exactly this type of differentiated life-story-telling by exploring the lives of young Latinas in higher education. Managers and organizational change consultants seeking new ideas to reduce the dropout rates of Latinas in higher education would benefit from reading these narratives through a lens that attends to the intersection.

Considering another axis of power, Ostrander (1984) provides us with rich narratives of upper class women. These narratives have much to contribute to understanding race, class, and gender relations in the experience of dominance as white and affluent (Ely, 1995). They remind us that the intersection of class, race, and gender lives also in white women (DuCille, 1994). But this requires that accounts of women managers make visible their class position and background, instead of just presenting them as "women managers" (Marshall, 1989; Morrison, 1987).

A second purpose of telling the stories at the intersection of race, class, and gender is to change the experience that organizational members have of each other across dimensions of difference from that of a "generalized other" to the "concrete other" (Benhabib, 1992; Hurtado, 1999). "Women's first place of identity and political awareness is the body," says Harcourt (2001: 204). But, as long as women are experienced and presented in organizations and organizational literature as if they did not have race, ethnicity, class, sexuality – in other words, as disembodied human beings – women will only be seen and interacted with in terms of abstract and stereotypical images that "the dominant" (men, white, heterosexual, Anglo) have of "the other." Seeing and working at the intersection of gender, class, race, ethnicity, and nation, for example, allows for the specificity of concrete bodies and histories to enter and begin to shape organizational dynamics. It is only in the context of concrete actors that real interactions that produce change can take place. As Benhabib (1992: 159) proposes, moving from the generalized other to the concrete other shifts the dynamics from "formal equality and reciprocity [where] each is entitled to expect and to assume from us what we can expect and assume from him or her . . . to norms of equity and complementary reciprocity [where] each is entitled to expect and to assume from the other behaviors through which the other feels recognized and confirmed as an individual with specific needs, talents and capacities."

Hegemonic identities produced and reproduced through organizational and social practices can be disrupted by the collection and dissemination of these differentiated stories and narratives that work at the level of identity practices.

2. Identifying, untangling, and changing the differential and material impact of everyday practices in organizations

If we understand that "women" is not a universal experience or category, then it is imperative that we identify, untangle, and change the differential impact that everyday practices have for different women in different types of organizations. An "even more focused and differentiated analysis" is needed, argues Smith (1995), so that the specificity of the experience of the simultaneity of race, ethnicity, and class can be understood and taken up. This type of analysis focuses on institutional practices.

Catalyst's (1999) study shows that white women are likely to be promoted more rapidly than women of color. Women of color report the lack of access to mentors and sponsors and the lack of networking with influential colleagues as the primary barriers to their advancement. White women, on the other hand, are more likely to attribute their advancement to exceeding performance expectations. Studying these different situations and perceptions reveals a different organizational picture and suggests different change interventions for different groups of women. For example, given what we know of the challenges involved in cross-racial mentoring (Thomas, 1993) and give that we also know that white women relate to white men through seduction and women of color relate to white men through rejection, are we to continue to design mentoring programs that are the same for white women and for women of color? Are we to continue to provide the same advice for white women as for women of color about how to advance their careers?

Barber (1992) provides another example of studying the differential impact on different women at the intersection of gender and class. She explored how class impacted gender consciousness in a group of working class women on the production floor by causing them to deal with "sexual harassment" through joking and not reporting their harassment to their supervisors. This is a very different approach than the one recommended by human resource staff and the dominant literature on sexual harassment. Were there women less interested and committed to ending their oppression? No, but the way they managed their harassment was shaped by their different experience of the simultaneity of gender and race as working class women. Should we continue to do sexual harassment training by asking all women to report incidents of sexual harassment to their supervisor and the human resource manager? Should human resource managers begin to collect and report statistics about sexual harassment that differentiate among the responses of white and women of color across different levels in the organizational hierarchy? Coalitions and alliances between women are highly unlikely until the specificity of the experience of different women is articulated and reflected upon by each other and by the organization.

Acker suggests that we study regimes of inequality, that is, "the precise patterns of inequality" and their "historical and present manifestations in the organization" through case studies that shed light on the differential impact that class and race have on men and women (personal communication, June 30, 1999). She enumerates various forms in which these patterns could be made visible through detailed descriptions of the characteristics of the inequality regimes in a specific organization, for example: 1) What constitutes the dimension(s) of inequality that form the basis of the regime; 2) How are the patterns of inequality visible or not and to whom; 3) What is the legitimacy of these forms of inequality and how is this legitimacy accomplished; and 4) What are the practices and the organizational structures by which inequality is sustained, including methods of control and compliance (Acker, 1999)? It is my experience that organizational members can engage in this kind of analysis across race, gender, and class differences if the appropriate conditions for safety and inquiry are created.

3. Identifying and connecting internal organizational processes with external and seemingly unrelated societal processes to understand organizational dynamics within a broader social context and social change agenda

The third suggested intervention is based on paying more than lip service to the boundary of organization and its environment (Miller and Rice, 1967; Trist, 1977), taking the environment to mean the societal context, in order to identify and connect internal organizational processes with external societal processes. This in turn will help locate organizational dynamics within a broader social context and develop change interventions within a larger social justice agenda. This focuses the analyses at the level of social practices.

For example, to understand the changing roles of Latinos and Latinas, who make up the majority of the workforce in the *maquiladora* industry along the U.S.-Mexican border, it is important that a larger analysis of globalization, gender, and the distribution of power and resources in the global economy be incorporated. Fernández Kelly (1994) notes that as the workforce reconfigures because of globalization few men make gains as technicians and professionals, while many more jobs previously associated with female employment at lower levels in the hierarchy go to both men and women. These changing roles between men and women create dilemmas that show up both within the workplace and in the communities to which these workers belong (Hondagneu-Sotelo, 1992; Williams, 1988). Attempting an organizational change intervention without an analysis of this social context – the relationship between the "outside and the inside" – and how those interactions support and hinder organizational change produces very limited change strategies.

Another outcome of this type of intervention is to specifically locate organizations and their actors in their particular social context. Much can be learned from the experience in other countries, and especially the experience in so-called "third world" countries, where more comprehensive analyses of the interaction between the social/societal context and the internal organizational dynamics of change are demanded by the societal context itself (Marks, 1999, 2001; Seidman, 1999).

REFERENCES

Acker, J. 1999. Rewriting class, race, and gender: Problems in feminist rethinking. In M. M. Ferree, J. Lorber, and B. B. Hess (Eds.), *Revisioning Gender*, (pp. 44–69). Thousand Oaks, CA: Sage.

Barber, P. G. 1992. Conflicting loyalties: Gender, class and equity politics in working class culture. *Canadian Women Studies*, 12 (3): 80–83.

Bell, E. L. and Nkomo, S. M. 2001. *Our Separate Ways: Black and White Women Forging Paths in Corporate America.* Cambridge, MA: Harvard Business School Press.

Benhabib, S. 1992. *Situating the Self: Gender, Community and Postmodernism in Contemporary Ethics.* New York: Routledge.

Britton, D. M. 2000. The epistemology of the gendered organization. *Gender and Society*, 14 (3): 418–434.

Bunch, C. 1980. The reform tool kit. In C. Bunch (Ed.), *Building Feminist Theory: Essays from Quest*, (pp. 189–201). London: Longman.

Calás, M. B. and Smircich, L. 1999. Past postmodernism? Reflections and tentative directions. *Academy of Management Review*, 24: 649–671.

Catalyst 1999. *Women of Color in Corporate Management: Opportunities and Barriers.* New York: Catalyst.

DuCille, A. 1994. The occult of true Black womanhood: Critical demeanor and Black feminist studies. *Signs*, 19: 591–629.

Ely, R. 1995. The role of dominant identity and experience in organizational work on diversity. In S. Jackson and M. Ruderman (Eds.), *Diversity in Work Teams: Research Paradigms for a Changing Workplace*, (pp. 161–186). Washington, D.C.: American Psychological Association.

Ely, R. and Meyerson, D. 2000. *Theories of Gender in Organizations: A New Approach to Organizational Analysis and Change.* Boston, MA: Center for Gender in Organizations, Simmons Graduate School of Management, Working Paper, No. 8.

Fernández Kelly, M. P. 1994. Making sense of gender in the world economy. *Focus on Latin America Organization* 1 (2): 249–275.

Harcourt, W. 2001. The politics of place and racism in Australia: A personal exploration. *Meridians*, 1: 194–207.

Hondagneu-Sotelo, P. 1992. Overcoming patriarchal constraints: The reconstruction of gender relations among Mexican immigrant women and men. *Gender and Society*, 6: 393–415.

Hurtado, A. 1990a. Cross-border existence: One woman's migrant story. In M. Romero and A. J. Stewart (Eds.), *Women's Untold Stories*, (pp. 83–101). New York: Routledge.

Hurtado, A. 2001. *Voicing Feminisms: Young Chicanas Speak out on Identity and Sexuality.* New York: New York University Press.

Kalantzis, M. 1990. Ethnicity meets gender meets class in Australia. In S. Watson (Ed.), *Playing the State: Australian Feminist Interventions*, (pp. 39–59). London: Verso.

Marks, R. 1990. Gender, race, and class dynamics in post apartheid South Africa. Boston, MA: Center for Gender in Organizations, Simmons Graduate School of Management. Working Paper, No. 9.

Marshall, J. 1989. Revisioning career concepts: A feminist invitation. In M. B. Arthur, D. T. Hall, and B. S. Lawrence (Eds.), *Handbook of Career Theory*, (pp. 275–291). Cambridge, UK: Cambridge University Press.

Miller, E. and Rice, A. K. 1967. *Systems of Organization.* London: Tavistock.

Morrison, A. M. (with White, R., and Van Velsor, E.). 1987. *Breaking the Glass Ceiling.* Reading, MA: Addison-Wesley.

Ostrander, S. A. 1984. *Women of the Upper Class.* Philadelphia: Temple University Press.

Proudford, K. 1998. Notes on the intra-group origins of inter-group conflict in organizations:

Black-white relations as exemplar. *University of Pennsylvania Journal of Labor and Employment Law*, 1 (2): 615–637.

Reynolds, T. 1997. Class matters, "race" matters, gender matters. In P. Mahony and C. Zmroczek (Eds.), *Class Matters: "Working-Class" Women's Perspectives on Social Class*, (pp. 8–17). London: Taylor and Francis.

Russo, A. 1991. "We cannot live without our lives": White women, antiracism, and feminism. In C. T. Mohanty, A. Russo and L. Torres, *Third World Women and the Politics of Feminism*, (pp. 297–313). Bloomington: Indiana University Press.

Seidman, G. W. 1999. Gendered citizenship: South Africa's democratic transition and the construction of a gendered state. *Gender and Society*, 13 (3): 287–307.

Smith, B. E. 1995. Crossing the great divides: Race, class, and gender in southern women's organizing, 1979–1991. *Gender and Society*, 9: 680–696.

Thomas, D. A. 1993. Racial dynamics in cross-race developmental relationships. *Administrative Science Quarterly*, 38: 169–194.

Trist, E. 1977. Collaboration in work settings: A personal perspective. *Journal of Applied Behavioral Science*, 13 (3): 268–278.

West, C. and Fenstermaker, S. 1995. Doing difference. *Gender and Society*, 9: 8–37.

Williams, N. 1988. Role making among married Mexican American women: Issues of class and ethnicity. *Journal of Applied Behavioral Science*, 24: 203–217.

CHAPTER

20 TEMPERED RADICALISM: CHANGING THE WORKPLACE FROM WITHIN

DEBRA E. MEYERSON AND MAUREEN A. SCULLY

From *CGO Insights, Briefing Note #6* (1999) Boston, MA: Center for Gender in Organizations, Simmons School of Management

Tempered radicalism is a proactive approach to surviving in an organization while keeping one's sense of self intact and pursuing changes to make the workplace more equitable and inclusive. Women and men whose identities or ideals do not fit with the dominant culture where they work can relate to this delicate balancing act: fitting in just enough to stay in the game while using an insider's leverage to change the game. Tempered radicals are "individuals who identify with and are committed to their organizations and also to a cause, community, or ideology that is fundamentally different from, and possibly at odds with, the dominant culture of their organization."[1]

The dominant culture often reflects norms that make sense to and derive from the historical experiences of white, middle class, fairly conformist, male employees, implicitly assuming that identity to be typical. Tempered radicals, who differ in any or all of these respects, feel nonetheless that it is worthwhile to make the effort to belong fully to their organization, in part because being an insider lets them pursue work they love and/or earn a livelihood. They do not want to become so captivated by fitting in that they forget who they are and why they want to make changes. Nor do they want to rock the boat so hard that they risk not being heard or taken seriously, or even being shown the door.

Women and men from different backgrounds, races, ethnicities, sexual orientations, ages, professions, and political persuasions have resonated to the concept of tempered radicalism as they try, in their own ways, to maintain legitimacy within traditional contexts, while they assert themselves and their hopes for social change.

Some examples of tempered radicalism in its simplest form give a sense of how it plays out in a range of issues from personal style to professional agendas. At a professional women's networking dinner, one woman wondered if she should wear a pant suit to an interview, being true to her informal style from the start, or wear a more traditional skirt suit and wait to be more herself until she was onboard for awhile. Each choice had its costs and benefits. Tempered radicalism seeks a midway course, such as wearing a traditionally tailored suit with some idiosyncratic accessories. Another woman wondered whether she should begin to lobby for on-site child care or wait until she attained a more senior position. She feared she would not get a promotion if she became known as a strident women's rights advocate, but also feared that waiting to make a difference would defer her concerns too long.

Such dilemmas preoccupy many employees who do not readily fit the mold. Many leave the mainstream or move from job to job, hoping to find a more comfortable fit. Some surrender to silence, feeling victimized and disempowered. Others try assimilation, with all its little privileges and nagging costs. The losses for individuals are both obvious and subtle, and organizations lose the energy and perspective of valuable contributors.

Exit, surrender, and assimilation are not the only options. Navigating between conformity and marginalization, tempered radicals preserve their distinctive identities and engage productively in change efforts. The hazards of tempered radicalism include feeling ambivalent much of the time. Ambivalence can be a discomforting state that people often want to escape. To restore a sense of consistency they may either leave the organization or assimilate. However, a creatively maintained ambivalence keeps tempered radicals going: assimilating to some degree in adroit ways, breaking into bursts of spontaneity as small local opportunities arise, standing up for cherished beliefs when the moment is right, finding unexpected allies among those who also sometimes hide their commitments, or burrowing into the organization to make quiet and selective changes.

Tempered radicalism arises from a desire for authenticity or from a conviction that change is needed. These two motives[2] are experienced differently and are illustrated with women's examples in the next two sections.

WOMEN'S DESIRE FOR AUTHENTICITY

For women in predominantly male organizations, the tension between personal and professional commitments is palpable. Some women move sequentially between dual identities, attending to one at a time. Others want to have the dual aspects of their identity in play simultaneously.

This struggle often leaves them in a double bind. "The aggressiveness, dedication, and emotional detachment traditionally presumed necessary for advancement in the most prestigious and well-paid occupations are incompatible with the traits commonly viewed as attractive in women: deference, sensitivity, and self-sacrifice. . . . Females aspiring to high-status positions remain subject to a familiar double bind. Those conforming to traditional characteristics of femininity are often thought lacking in the requisite assertiveness and initiative, yet those conforming to a masculine model of success may be ostracized in work settings as bitchy, aggressive, and uncooperative."[3]

Although this double bind can be maddening, women are beginning to improvise a sustainable mix of authenticity and legitimacy. Co-workers may subtly test a woman's "fit" with the group, expecting her to prove she is "one of the guys" and not likely to "raise a fuss" about how things are done. Women may resist these seemingly mundane tests, for example, by not laughing at a sexist joke. Tempered radicals raise their objections cautiously and selectively, so they are rarely seen for what they are – challengers of the established culture.[4]

For example, Jennifer Donaldson,[5] a senior manager of a technical division of a fast growing medical equipment company, had been steadily promoted and was the only woman at her level. Because her male peers were loud and aggressive, meetings were like shouting contests. At one meeting, a top executive asked Donaldson for her opinion. After she began to speak, the men interrupted and argued among themselves. Donaldson stepped in and said, "Excuse me, if we want to get some work done, we can start to listen to each other, or else I'm not going to waste my time here."

Silence followed her comment, which she had cleverly couched in the accepted terms of using time well. She went on calmly to outline her thoughts on the topic at hand. Though worried about the risk she had taken, she was pleasantly surprised afterwards when the president thanked her for her courage and convictions. He promised that he would take personal responsibility for running better meetings with more effective norms for interacting. To her further surprise, many of the men at the meeting thanked her and admitted that they too hated these shouting matches; one man said he found them to be a waste of time, all about showmanship and "testosterone in action."

Donaldson's steady refusal to participate and her carefully chosen statement reflected who she was without compromise. She enabled her colleagues to reflect on their behavior and its implications. In doing so, she cracked the door open just wide enough for new norms to be ushered in. She might have been just different enough from the group that she could safely say "the emperor has no clothes" and have this exposé be welcomed by those who had been uncomfortably complicit with the status quo.

Women often experience pressures to conform as undermining, personal affronts. They may go along with them nonetheless, because women are strongly socialized into the individualistic culture of the contemporary organization. With their eyes on their careers, they try to fit in, perhaps with the faith that personal achievement is the best victory. They may miss the broader ramification that, each time they pass a conformity test, the very norms that make organizational life difficult for women are reinforced. White women might be given more frequent invitations and temptations to become insiders. Ironically, as they learn to be insiders, they may become less likely to use their hard won insider privilege to lobby for broadly beneficial organizational changes.[6]

Important as career concerns may be, the struggles of women in organizations are part of a broader societal concern about equality and fairness, cherished ideals to which many organizations and communities aspire. Missed opportunities are costly. Because being political in an organization is discouraged and risky, some women who propel changes will deny that they are change agents. For others, it is the explicit commitment to broader change that gives them courage despite personal risks.

WOMEN'S COMMITMENT TO CHANGE

Some women wrestle with how to use their savvy insider knowledge to advance the changes they envision, such as hiring and promoting more women and members of underrepresented groups, reducing pay inequities, managing participatively, or creating programs to help women and men integrate work and life responsibilities. They balance boldness and caution, sometimes focusing on just getting issues onto the agenda, so others can weigh in and share the heat. They test ideas before taking them public.

For example, Elsa Jackson, a Jamaican marketing executive for a large cosmetics company, had been worried that her company's advertising campaigns were alienating Caribbean women by portraying them as housekeepers and nannies. She did not want to make a big deal of it and be seen as over-sensitive, but she was offended and saw an opportunity to address the societal issue of harmful stereotypes. She turned to some trusted colleagues in another department, with whom she could rehearse how to voice her concerns and see how she would be received. Jackson was surprised at how much they welcomed her comments. When she raised her concerns to the advertising group, the company quickly withdrew a number of campaigns. Moreover, the advertising group recruited a woman of color to add to the team. From then on, Elsa found it less difficult to voice her concerns on a range of issues, a gain both for her and the company.

As another example, a group of women engineers at a software company had begun meeting to discover and address their shared concerns as women. It came to their attention that administrative assistants were not getting a share of the generous group bonus for meeting a deadline, even though they had worked late and made essential contributions. Professional women do not always join ranks with administrative support personnel to advocate change for women in lower positions. In this case, however, the engineers recognized the political significance of the larger, shared issue that women's work becomes invisible. As group member Amy Wong explained, "I think we all felt this kinship there, because for women – and it just so happens that 95% of the people in the administrative assistant job are women – it's that whole cycle of being underpaid, in jobs that are less well paid. We all recognized how that occurs, and we wanted to see that stopped. Women's work was not being valued. I think we realized that a group with more power needs to help the ones with less power."[7] Proposed changes that threaten deeply held ideas about what is fair or images of who is a valuable contributor are likely to generate resistance and backlash. In this case, senior managers agreed that support staff were eligible for the bonus, and even asserted that it had been their intention all along, perhaps, as Wong speculated, to save face when her group framed the issue as one of basic fairness. She saw it as a success that top managers took ownership of the new policy.

TEMPERED RADICALS' STRATEGIES FOR AUTHENTICITY AND CHANGE

Our research has surfaced some strategies that tempered radicals use to find a viable middle course between conformity and stridency.

Experiment with "small wins"

First, tempered radicals should recognize the significance of a small win, "a concrete, complete, implemented outcome of moderate importance. By itself, one small win may seem unimportant. A series of wins at small but significant tasks, however, may reveal a pattern that attracts allies, deters opponents, and lowers resistance to subsequent proposals. Small wins are controllable opportunities that produce visible results."[8]

For example, Diane Morris was the only woman on the professional staff at a research institute in The Netherlands. She was asked for two years in a row to serve as rapporteur for the annual meeting, an onerous job with little professional visibility or benefit. She realized when she was asked again in the third year that none of the professional men in her cohort had been asked to assume this role and that it was hurting her career to be trapped in a stereotypically female support role. She went to the head of the institute and pointed out that, while she had been pleased to help out in the past, the demands of her research meant that she could not be rapporteur this year, but she would be delighted to help out by chairing a session on the program. She suggested that one of the newly recruited men might learn more about the institute by taking on the rapporteur role. Moreover, she proposed that the effort to recruit more women might be advanced by having a woman in a visible chair role. This intervention was a valuable "small win" in that it changed a taken-for-granted practice and introduced gender equity into both behind-the-scenes and visible roles. Younger women research associates, as well as senior men, noticed the affirming message sent by having a woman chair a session.

> *Between conformity and marginalization, tempered radicals find room to be authentic and make "small wins"*

Keep the momentum going even when wins are small

It is tempting to minimize small wins. They can seem insignificant or distracting in light of the magnitude of pressing issues. For example, at a high tech company, a diversity committee designed a T-shirt to proclaim their values with a clever logo. A T-shirt may sound trivial in the face of deeply rooted inequalities. However, it was a small win in a casual culture where people designed T-shirts for all sorts of events and products and often wore them to work. Seeing diversity T-shirts in the daily mix next to more mainstream T-shirts made committee members proud. Moreover, as Maria Rosario explained, she found that when she wore the T-shirt, people began to ask her questions about diversity, providing occasions for serious discussions where previously it had felt too abrupt, awkward, or preachy to raise these topics. Recognizing small wins for what they are – little but meaningful incursions into a culture – can provide the basis for subsequent and cumulative small wins, as well as the periodic large win. Change agents, who can easily become tired or overwhelmed, can build confidence and sustain momentum.

Engage in local, spontaneous, authentic action

Sometimes just being one's self pushes a different idea of who "we" are in this organization and models an alternative way to work. For example, the quest for authenticity and change came together for Jessica Kohn, a lesbian woman in a middle management position at a bank. She explained that the simple act of talking about her personal life in everyday conversation at work was also a political act for her, challenging the assumptions of heterosexuality. "I had to make some one-on-one decisions, and I just decided, I'm not going to hide. I'm not going to wear my lavender L [for lesbian] or whatever, but when appropriate, the conversation just naturally slips to one's personal life, and I just make it clear that I have a partner. Her name is Jean." While a broader campaign for domestic partner benefits was already underway at the bank, her local actions were an equally important piece of the effort to make a more inclusive workplace.[9]

Build relationships and form alliances for support

Tempered radicalism can be lonely. Individuals may look around and suspect that they are alone in grappling with alignment and wishing for change. It is crucial to find allies and to nurture connections. For example, Shataya Washington explained how she felt less alone after joining an email discussion group for women and finding some like-minded people elsewhere in her organization. She explained, "For me, and the other participants, it made me feel that I was not alone, because I could go to lunch or hang around with my friends who belonged and hear very similar stories to mine. So it normalized and validated our experiences."

Group meetings can be the crucible for small wins. For example, Susan Rogers, a partner in a management consulting firm, wanted to help junior women. She arranged a firm-sponsored monthly luncheon for the women consultants in her office. Rogers did not revolutionize her firm's hiring or evaluation policies. Instead, she achieved a small win by creating a network in which these ideas could be discussed and gradually broached. This forum enabled Rogers to find sympathetic colleagues and place her ideas in the context of networking and learning, an approach valued by the firm. The new terminology and framing used in her monthly lunches gradually permeated other conversations. By bringing challenging ideas into the organizational dialogue, Rogers nudged the boundaries of accepted practice.

CONCLUSION

While the specifics may vary, tempered radicals all face challenges related to the maintenance of personal authenticity and the management of change. The tactics that tempered radicals employ will be influenced by their motives for tempered radicalism and by the details of their local setting. Indeed, it is their insiders' knowledge of the local nuances, language, and norms that can make them versatile and effective change agents. Tempered radicals can sustain their engagement, despite discomforting ambivalence and potential risks, by joining with others. Since publishing our first article on tempered radicalism, we have often heard the reaction: "Oh, there's a name for what I'm doing. And others must be doing it, too." There is power in having a named identity, rather than a vague sense of misalignment, and in knowing that one's change efforts, which might feel fragmented and sporadic in themselves, can connect meaningfully with the efforts of others and produce significant changes for the collective good.

Encouraging and responding to the strategies of tempered radicalism fortifies individuals and also provides resources – in the form of empowered and energetic employees – for organizations to be creative and adaptive in a world of diversity and continuous change.

NOTES

1 This note is based on our article: Meyerson, D. and Scully, M. (1995). "Tempered radicalism and the politics of ambivalence and change," *Organization Science*, Vol. 6, No. 5, pp. 585–600. We chose the term "tempered radicalism" because it plays on layers of meaning. Tempered means moderated, but for radicals who fear "selling out," it recalls having a "temper" that fuels passionate engagement. In physics, to temper a metal means to heat it up then cool it down to make it stronger, analogous to the process that makes insider change agents effective.

2 This distinction is elaborated in D. Meyerson's book (2001), *Tempered Radicals: How People use Difference to Inspire Change at Work*. Boston: Harvard Business School Press.

3 Rhode, D. (1988). "Perspectives on professional women," *Stanford Law Rev.*, 40, p. 1163.

4 Adapted from Meyerson, D. and Merrill, K. (2000). "Professional women as change agents: The choice of 'tempered radicalism.' In D. Smith (ed.), *Women at Work: Leadership for the Next Century*. Upper Saddle River, NJ: Prentice Hall.

5 All names have been changed to respect confidentiality.

6 The role of race in black and white women's different approaches to tempered radicalism and the prospects for alliances between them is discussed in Bell, E., Meyerson, D., Nkomo, S., and Scully, M. (2001). "Tempered radicalism revisited: Black and white women making sense of black women's enactments and white women's silences." *CGO Working paper*, no. 13. Boston: Center for Gender in Organizations, Simmons School of Management.

7 Several examples are drawn from Scully, M. and Segal, A. (2002). "Passion with an umbrella: Grassroots activists in organizations." *Research in the Sociology of Organizations*, 19, pp. 125–66.

8 Weick, K. (1984). "Small wins: Redefining the scale of social problems," *American Psychologist*, Vol. 39, pp. 40–49.

9 Creed, W.E.D. and Scully, M. (2000). "Songs of ourselves: Employees' enactment of identity in everyday workplace encounters," *Journal of Management Inquiry*, 9(4), pp. 391–412.

THE TRANSFORMATION OF SILENCE INTO LANGUAGE AND ACTION

AUDRE LORDE

From *Sister Outsider*: 40–4 (1984) Trumansburg, NY: Crossing Press
Paper first delivered at the Modern Language Association's "Lesbian
and Literature Panel," Chicago, December 28, 1977

I HAVE COME to believe over and over again that what is most important to me must be spoken, made verbal and shared, even at the risk of having it bruised or mis-understood. That the speaking profits me, beyond any other effect. I am standing here as a Black lesbian poet, and the meaning of all that waits upon the fact that I am still alive, and might not have been. Less than two months ago I was told by two doctors, one female and one male, that I would have to have breast surgery, and that there was a 60 to 80 percent chance that the tumor was malignant. Between that telling and the actual surgery, there was a three-week period of the agony of an involuntary reorganization of my entire life. The surgery was completed, and the growth was benign.

But within those three weeks, I was forced to look upon myself and my living with a harsh and urgent clarity that has left me still shaken but much stronger. This is a situation faced by many women, by some of you here today. Some of what I experienced during that time has helped elucidate for me much of what I feel con-cerning the transformation of silence into language and action.

In becoming forcibly and essentially aware of my mortality, and of what I wished and wanted for my life, however short it might be, priorities and omissions became strongly etched in a merciless light, and what I most regretted were my silences. Of what had I *ever* been afraid? To question or to speak as I believed could have meant pain, or death. But we all hurt in so many different ways, all the time, and pain will either change or end. Death, on the other hand, is the final silence. And that might be coming quickly, now, without regard for whether I had ever spoken what needed to be said, or had only betrayed myself into small silences, while I planned someday to speak, or waited for someone else's words. And I began to recognize a source of power within myself that comes from the knowledge that while it is most desirable not to be afraid, learning to put fear into a perspective gave me great strength.

I was going to die, if not sooner then later, whether or not I had ever spoken myself. My silences had not protected me. Your silence will not protect you. But for every real word spoken, for every attempt I had ever made to speak those truths for which I am still seeking, I had made contact with other women while we examined the words to fit a world in which we all believed, bridging our differences. And it was the concern and caring of all those women which gave me strength and enabled me to scrutinize the essentials of my living.

The women who sustained me through that period were Black and white, old and young, lesbian, bisexual, and heterosexual, and we all shared a war against the tyrannies of silence. They all gave me a strength and concern without which I could not have survived intact. Within those weeks of acute fear came the knowledge – within the war we are all waging with the forces of death, subtle and otherwise, conscious or not – I am not only a casualty, I am also a warrior.

What are the words you do not yet have? What do you need to say? What are the tyrannies you swallow day by day and attempt to make your own, until you will sicken and die of them, still in silence? Perhaps for some of you here today, I am the face of one of your fears. Because I am woman, because I am Black, because I am lesbian, because I am myself – a Black woman warrior poet doing my work – come to ask you, are you doing yours?

And of course I am afraid, because the transformation of silence into language and action is an act of self-revelation, and that always seems fraught with danger. But my daughter, when I told her of our topic and my difficulty with it, said, "Tell them about how you're never really a whole person if you remain silent, because there's always that one little piece inside you that wants to be spoken out, and if you keep ignoring it, it gets madder and madder and hotter and hotter, and if you don't speak it out one day it will just up and punch you in the mouth from the inside."

In the cause of silence, each of us draws the face of her own fear – fear of contempt, of censure, or some judgment, or recognition, of challenge, of annihilation. But most of all, I think, we fear the visibility without which we cannot truly live. Within this country where racial difference creates a constant, if unspoken, distortion of vision, Black women have on one hand always been highly visible, and so, on the other hand, have been rendered invisible through the depersonalization of racism. Even within the women's movement, we have had to fight, and still do, for that very visibility which also renders us most vulnerable, our Blackness. For to survive in the mouth of this dragon we call america, we have had to learn this first and most vital lesson – that we were never meant to survive. Not as human beings. And neither were most of you here today, Black or not. And that visibility which makes us most vulnerable is that which also is the source of our greatest strength. Because the machine will try to grind you into dust anyway, whether or not we speak. We can sit in our corners mute forever while our sisters and our selves are wasted, while our children are distorted and destroyed, while our earth is poisoned; we can sit in our safe corners mute as bottles, and we will still be no less afraid.

In my house this year we are celebrating the feast of Kwanza, the African-american festival of harvest which begins the day after Christmas and lasts for seven days. There are seven principles of Kwanza, one for each day. The first principle is Umoja, which means unity, the decision to strive for and maintain unity in self and community. The principle for yesterday, the second day, was Kujichagulia – self-determination – the decision to define ourselves, name ourselves, and speak for ourselves, instead of being defined and spoken for by others. Today is the third day of Kwanza, and the principle for today is Ujima – collective work and responsibility – the decision to build and maintain ourselves and our communities together and to recognize and solve our problems together.

Each of us is here now because in one way or another we share a commitment to language and to the power of language, and to the reclaiming of that language which has been made to work against us. In the transformation of silence into language and action, it is vitally necessary for each one of us to establish or examine her function in that transformation and to recognize her role as vital within that transformation.

For those of us who write, it is necessary to scrutinize not only the truth of what we speak, but the truth of that language by which we speak it. For others, it is to share and spread also those words that are meaningful to us. But primarily for us all, it is necessary to teach by living and speaking those truths which we believe and know beyond understanding. Because in this way alone we can survive, by taking part in a process of life that is creative and continuing, that is growth.

And it is never without fear – of visibility, of the harsh light of scrutiny and perhaps judgment, of pain, of death. But we have lived through all of those already, in silence, except death. And I remind myself all the time now that if I were to have been born mute, or had maintained an oath of silence my whole life long for safety, I would still have suffered, and I would still die. It is very good for establishing perspective.

And where the words of women are crying to be heard, we must each of us recognize our responsibility to seek those words out, to read them and share them and examine them in their pertinence to our lives. That we not hide behind the mockeries of separations that have been imposed upon us and which so often we accept as our own. For instance, "I can't possibly teach Black women's writing – their experience is so different from mine." Yet how many years have you spent teaching Plato and Shakespeare and Proust? Or another, "She's a white woman and what could she possibly have to say to me?" Or, "She's a lesbian, what would my husband say, or my chairman?" Or again, "This woman writes of her sons and I have no children." And all the other endless ways in which we rob ourselves of ourselves and each other.

We can learn to work and speak when we are afraid in the same way we have learned to work and speak when we are tired. For we have been socialized to respect fear more than our own needs for language and definition, and while we wait in silence for that final luxury of fearlessness, the weight of that silence will choke us.

The fact that we are here and that I speak these words is an attempt to break that silence and bridge some of those differences between us, for it is not difference which immobilizes us, but silence. And there are so many silences to be broken.

PART V | HUMAN RESOURCE MANAGEMENT

HUMAN RESOURCE MANAGEMENT: OVERVIEW

MAUREEN A. SCULLY

Many of the issues addressed in this reader share an underlying question about whether women have the same opportunities as men in organizations – opportunities to make a living, to do meaningful work, to contribute and excel, to be recognized and rewarded. Broadening the scope of opportunities for a wider range of employees can achieve two valued ends: social justice and organizational effectiveness. Part V focuses on the opportunity structure in organizations. It explores more fully the concerns of Frame 3 about access and power, adding Frame 4 concerns about uncovering deep assumptions about how work gets done and who is a meritorious worker as well as keeping the commitment to "complicating gender" by considering race and class. The issues herein are often addressed in the human resource function in organizations and are covered variously in courses on human resource management (HRM), organizational behavior, and career development, which examine practices such as performance evaluation, advancement, mentoring, and pay. But the opportunity structure can also be an underlying factor in issues to do with entrepreneurship (who has the opportunity to get venture capital?), strategy (whose business plans are taken seriously?), and technology (for whom does technology open new opportunities?).

The term "opportunity structure" is used by sociologists and has the advantage of conveying that opportunities are part of a structure or a pattern of practices, assumptions, and relationships that affect how people fare in organizations. The emphasis on structure removes the focus from individual traits as the sole determinant of opportunities. There is a robust belief in the West – increasingly imposed on global organizations – that the workplace is a meritocracy. The first brief reading, "Meritocracy," which comes from a dictionary of social science terms, introduces the idea of meritocracy and its popular appeal in the USA. The strong belief in meritocracy tends to focus attention on individuals' efforts, abilities, and strategies for advancement, and causes people to overlook long-standing and deeply entrenched aspects of the structure of the workplace. While talents and motivations matter, they are developed and realized within a structure. There is a well-developed research literature on how similar skills are seen and rewarded differently depending on the gender, race, and class of the individuals who possess them and how the sorting of people into "gendered" jobs creates inequalities that affect opportunities (e.g., Baron & Bielby, 1985; Cohen, Broschak, & Haveman, 1998; Reskin & Cassirer, 1996; Reskin, McBrier, & Kmec, 1999). The shift from a focus on individuals' skills to the structures in which they develop and deploy their skills is in keeping with a move from Frames 1 and 2, with their emphasis on individuals' assimilation or uniqueness, to Frames 3 and 4, with their emphasis on structures and a deeply systemic approach to transformation.

The idea of an "opportunity structure," while a useful starting place, poses a problem as well as a possibility. The problem is that seeing organizations as places of "opportunity" has been the perspective and interpretation of white and middle- and upper-class men and women. A focus on the opportunity structure trains our gaze on advancement opportunities, the glass ceiling, and women's entrée into senior management. Of course, these issues are important and relevant to other groups as well; they deserve consideration, as long as we recognize that they do not affect all women – even those who are professionals and managers – in the same way or to the same extent (Bell & Nkomo, 2001; Catalyst, 1998). But the plight of women managers – even women from different racial groups – is merely one aspect of the opportunity structure. The possibility that arises in using the term "opportunity structure" is that of expanding the idea of opportunity to include the concerns of women and men whose wages hover near or below a living wage, who are struggling to keep a job and feed their families, and for whom the promised "opportunities" of work have been elusive. Using a lens of gender, race, and class simultaneously – rather than a gender lens alone – enables us to see aspects of the opportunity structure that we would otherwise miss. In doing so, we can then diagnose where opportunities are absent and need to be created, to the benefit of a wider range of organizational stakeholders and often to the benefit of the organization. From this perspective, low wage work is a problem at the center of HRM concerns: low wage jobs are created by corporations, and the dilemmas of surviving on low wage jobs in turn affect how work gets done in organizations.

The second reading, "Mentoring relationships through the lens of race and gender," by Stacy Blake-Beard, considers mentoring programs, a popular remedy for inequalities; it views them through the lens of race and gender simultaneously for a critical re-examination of their premises. Many companies realize that their formal evaluation and promotion system, left to run by itself, will systematically select people who already represent the "in group" in the organization, typically white men. Mentoring programs are intended to provide the informal advice, access, and networking opportunities that white men have typically enjoyed to white women and men and women of color. This reading shows how the experience of mentoring – from finding a mentor to sorting through the advice from a mentor – is different depending on one's gender and race, particularly for women of color. While mentoring advice often emphasizes assimilation, taking into account the perspective of women of color reminds us that there must be alternative approaches for employees who may want to get ahead in their organization without sacrificing their identities and without narrowing the full range of contributions they have to offer.

If a fresh approach to mentoring helps a more diverse range of employees to advance, what will be their rewards? The gender wage gap – or the problem of equal pay for equal work – has been studied extensively over the past 30 years. For years, economists have tracked the gap in base pay as it has slowly narrowed (and sometimes widened again), but this gap in base pay tells only part of the story. Recent research by Elvira and Graham (2002) considers the new and increasingly popular methods of pay, such as variable pay and bonuses. Informally, women have reported that their base pay keeps apace, but that when it comes to discretionary rewards like stock options, they feel they fall behind their male counterparts. Such a gap has not been documented empirically until now. Forms of pay that allow managers more discretion, such as bonuses, result in larger gender gaps than forms of pay that are more formalized and governed by rules, such as base pay.

Why might women be rewarded differently? Are there biases in the perception of who has merit in the meritocracy? Zimmer (1987) explored this issue in a study of male and female prison guards. Women have increasingly entered the role of prison guard as this sector of the service economy has grown and now provides some of the better paying lower level jobs, particularly in rural areas. The prison system has traditionally rewarded male guards for keeping a tough demeanor and breaking up fights. Women's approach to the guard role, in contrast, involves preventing rather than breaking up fights by using negotiation skills and developing concern for the prisoners, who reciprocate with better behavior for small favors or kindnesses. Where a tough demeanor and breaking up fights are considered hallmarks of meritorious job performance, however, it is harder for women to be rewarded for their contributions to the job. A different lens on what the nature of merit and contribution are in this system is necessary. In valuing women's contributions, the prison as an organization stands to gain as well, as the prevention rather than the breaking up of fights is a valuable organizational end. This example from the prison setting can be extended to other types of workplaces.

To understand the opportunity structure, it is clearly important to keep class in the mix of simultaneously considered identities, along with gender and race (Holvino, 2001). The USA is characterized by a growing skew between the highest and lowest paid workers. The belief that the USA is a meritocracy is invoked to rationalize this difference: jobs at the top are worth more than jobs at the bottom, and people at the top do work that is more essential and are therefore more deserving. A close look at the work of people in the lowest levels of the economy, however, shows just how essential it is to the operation of many organizations. For example, in a large multinational hotel chain, hourly workers constitute some 75 percent of the total workforce. Hotel guests interact almost entirely with hourly workers, from porters to those who make the beds, and form their impression of the hotel from them. Hotels depend on guests' decisions to return, which are formed from the labor of front-line service workers. Thus, their work is just as essential to the operation of the business, but their rewards are far fewer, often not even meeting the living wage standard of their region. From the bottom line perspective of the organization, Heskett and colleagues (1994) demonstrate that the satisfaction of service employees is linked in an overall system to customer satisfaction. From a justice perspective, the promise of the meritocracy will only be delivered if hard work is rewarded by a sustainable livelihood; otherwise, the meritocratic ideal is revealed to be a myth. In the third reading, "Nickeled and dimed: On (not) getting by in America," by Barbara Ehrenreich, the everyday experiences of trying to make ends meet while occupying a service job are documented with details that are usually hidden from the view of more privileged workers.

The typical concerns of human resource professionals are to locate and document inequalities in opportunities, including access to mentoring, fair performance evaluations, and rewards. The legal system has intervened in organizations to support and enforce change, through affirmative action and equal employment opportunity measures. Gradually, this legalistic approach, begun in the 1970s, has evolved into "diversity management" and an emphasis on copying best practices (Kelly & Dobbin, 1998). A more progressive and less reactive approach to HRM involves actively seeking ways to address inequalities – rather than simply documenting them or moving only when prompted externally by laws – and ways to create and benefit from a more inclusive workplace. In the final reading in this part, an excerpt from the book, *Building Successful Multicultural Organizations*, Marlene Fine gives us some sense of what this more progressive, less reactive approach could look like. Rather than developing new policies, Fine reviews basic organizational processes, like recruitment, promotion, evaluation, and career development, and suggests how they should look in organizations that have made a commitment to addressing diversity. While progressive HR managers can play an important role in addressing structures of opportunity, as emphasized in a Frame 3 approach, there is also room for other managers and employees to use their everyday knowledge of the organization. They can use their vantage point to tackle undermining assumptions, in the spirit of Frame 4, such that the impetus for organizational change is widely dispersed. Employee network and activist groups (Friedman, 1996; Scully and Segal, 2002) can be one mechanism for pushing such deep organizational change.[1]

NOTE

1 This approach to change is more fully explored in Part IV on Organizational Change and Intervention.

REFERENCES

Baron, J. N. & Bielby, W. T. 1985. Organizational barriers to gender equality: Sex segregation of jobs and opportunities. In Alice Rossi (ed.), *Gender and the Life Course*. 233–51. New York: Aldine.

Catalyst. 1998. *Women of color in corporate management: Dynamics of career advancement*. New York: Catalyst: 1–41.

Cohen, L. E., Broschak, J. P., & Haveman, H. A. 1998. And then there were more? The effects of organizational sex composition on the hiring and promotion of managers. *American Sociological Review*, 63(5): 711–27.

Elvira, M. & Graham, M. 2002. Not just a formality: Pay system formalization and gender earnings effects. *Organization Science*, 13(6): 601–17.

Friedman, R. A. 1996. Defining the scope and logic of minority and female network groups: Can separation enhance integration? *Research in Personnel and Human Resources Management*, 14: 307–49.

Heskett, J. L., Jones, T. O., Loveman, G., Sasser, W. E., & Schlesinger, L. A. 1994. Putting the service–profit chain to work. *Harvard Business Review*, 72(2): 164–174.

Holvino, Evangelina. 2001. Complicating gender: The simultaneity of race, gender, and class in organization change(ing). *Working Paper No. 14*. Boston, MA: Center for Gender in Organizations, Simmons School of Management.

Kelly, E. & Dobbin, F. 1998. How affirmative action became diversity management. *American Behavioral Scientist*, 41(7): 960–84.

Reskin, B. F. & Cassirer, N. 1996. Occupational segregation by gender, race and ethnicity. *Sociological Focus*, 29(3): 231–43.

Reskin, B. F., McBrier, D. B., & Kmec, J. A. 1999. The determinants and consequences of workplace sex and race composition. *Annual Review of Sociology*, 25: 335–61.

Scully, M. & Segal, A. 2002. Passion with an umbrella: Grassroots activists in the workplace. *Research in the Sociology of Organizations*, 19: 125–68.

Zimmer, L. 1987. How women shape the prison guard role. *Gender & Society*: 1(4): 415–31.

MERITOCRACY

MAUREEN A. SCULLY

From R. E. Freeman & P. H. Werhane (eds.) 1997 *Blackwell Encyclopedic Dictionary of Business Ethics*: 413–14.

meritocracy a social system in which merit or talent is the basis for sorting people into positions and distributing rewards, such that the positions of highest authority are occupied by those of greatest merit. The term "meritocracy" is a satirical invention of Young (1958), who wrote a fable about a future society that could not abide the perfect meritocracy it created. The term is now applied, without the irony, to advanced capitalist systems of status attainment and reward allocation, usually to distinguish them favorably from aristocratic or class-based systems, where birth or family privileges determine an individual's status (Bell, 1972). A meritocracy relies on three principles (Daniels, 1978): 1) merit is a well-defined and measurable basis for selecting individuals for positions, 2) individuals have equal opportunity to develop and display their merits and to advance, and 3) the positions into which individuals are sorted are mapped to stratified levels of rewards (such as income or status). An organization or an entire society might espouse and try to operate on meritocratic principles.

Proponents of meritocracy highlight several advantages. A meritocracy is fair in that everyone has an opportunity to advance and rewards are proportional to meritorious contributions; merit is distinguished from equality or need, other fair bases of reward. Meritocracy motivates people. Functional sociologists argue that meritocracy directs the most talented people into the most functionally important positions and thereby enhances a society's survival and efficiency.

The idea of meritocracy enters into ethical discussion about social systems – whether societies or organizations – in two ways, which are addressed in the following sections. First, a social system can be evaluated for the extent to which it lives up to meritocratic promises. Second, the moral basis of meritocracy as a distributive system can be assessed. This critical stance is less common, because meritocracy is accepted as a fair and legitimate principle and deeply woven into the culture and political rhetoric in many advanced capitalist societies and organizations.

THE PURSUIT OF MERITOCRACY AS FAIRNESS

In societies, debate rages over whether equal opportunity and meritocracy have been achieved. One position is that class and privilege, not talent, determine who gets ahead, so the society is not a true meritocracy. It follows that programs should be created to improve opportunities for the disadvantaged, redistribute wealth, and assist the undeservingly poor. An opposing position is that talent and hard work drive advancement and that the society is a meritocracy or a close enough approximation. It follows that no redress is needed and people in the lowest positions should work harder. At stake in this debate is the question of whether a society is just.

In organizations, reward systems that are variations on meritocracy, such as pay-for-skills or pay-for-performance, are assessed from the standpoint of the three principles of meritocracy. There are discussions about whether chosen measures of merit are appropriate and measurable, whether biases compromise equality of opportunity, and how steeply and how high the reward curve should rise. . . . At the societal and organizational levels, the focus is often fine-tuning a meritocracy.

THE MORAL TENOR OF LIFE IN A MERITOCRACY

A second ethical approach to meritocracy probes whether a perfectly fine-tuned meritocracy has undesirable implications, three of which are considered here – privileging a dominant class while denigrating the poor, amplifying unearned differences in merit, and potentially compromising cooperation. First, meritocratic ideology legitimates inequality, by painting a picture where "success comes to those whose energies and abilities deserve it, failures have only themselves to blame" (Mann, 1970, p. 427). Meritocracy is a "ruling ideology" (Marx & Engels, 1978, p. 64) that may serve the privileged by justifying their status and curbing resistance. Weber (1978, p. 953) writes that "every highly privileged group develops the myth of its natural superiority." The concomitant feelings of inferiority among those in lower positions have been called "the hidden injuries of class" (Sennett & Cobb, 1972). However, empirical evidence suggests that people in the lowest positions are not necessarily overcome by belief in meritocracy and have ways of making sense of their position other than blaming themselves (Scully, 1993). While meritocratic ideology may not fully legitimate inequality, it may raise enough uncertainties about distributive justice that resistance is not mobilized.

Second, the links between merit and reward may be difficult to justify on the grounds of moral desert inasmuch as merit may be unearned or a weak basis for special treatment. Historically, the Protestant ethic justified the link between hard work (as an indictor of moral rectitude) and wealth (as a possible indicator of salvation). . . . However, merit, whether ability (such as I.Q.) or the capacity to exert effort and achieve goals, may be inherited or beyond an individual's control (Sher, 1979). If so, it becomes difficult to argue that a person's very "life chances" (income, housing, education) should be linked to their merits. For example, a society where people with mental handicaps routinely receive fewer resources seems cruel. Moreover, a meritocracy seems to assume that performance must be coaxed from the talented, which suggests they are more petulant than morally deserving. An alternative system, which may be more idealistic than practical, might be designed around the talented sharing their gifts without extra rewards; meaningful work can be its own reward.

Third, merit-based differences are divisive. They can create a climate where cooperation and concern for others are mitigated and where smug success and embarrassing failure charge the tenor of social life. For example, organizations are discovering that the individualistic and competitive spirit of merit-based rewards can undermine teamwork. Because meritocracy is such a taken-for-granted ideal, the search for alternative reward systems for societies and organizations has been difficult (Donnellon & Scully, 1994). A less competitively individualistic society, perhaps based on communitarianism, might distribute occupations and tasks by merit but not skew rewards in other domains by merit (Walzer, 1983). The inclusion of meritocracy in the lexicon of business ethics is a reminder to evaluate the very assumptions about fairness and the social contract that guide the everyday operations of individuals and organizations.

REFERENCES

Bell, D. (1972). On meritocracy and equality. *Public Interest*, 29, 29–68.

Daniels, N. (1978). Merit and meritocracy. *Philosophy and Public Affairs*, 3, 206–23.

Donnellon, A. & Scully, M. (1994). Teams, merit, and rewards: Will the post-bureaucratic organization be a post-meritocratic organization? In A. Donnellon & C. Hecksher (eds), *The Post-Bureaucratic Organization*. Thousand Oaks, Calif.: Sage Publications.

Mann, M. (1970). The social cohesion of liberal democracy. *American Sociological Review*, 35, 423–39.

Marx, K. & Engels, F. (1978). *The German Ideology*. (ed.), C. J. Arthur. New York: International Publishers.

Scully, M. (1993). *The Imperfect Legitimation of Inequality in Internal Labor Markets*. Working Paper 3520–93. Sloan School of Management, MIT, Cambridge, Mass.

Sennett, R. & Cobb, J. (1972). *The Hidden Injuries of Class*. New York: Vintage Books.

Sher, G. (1979). Effort, ability and personal desert. *Philosophy and Public Affairs*, 8, 361–76.

Walzer, M. (1983). *Spheres of Justice: A Defense of Pluralism and Equality*. New York: Basic Books.

Weber, M. (1978). *Economy and Society: An Outline of Interpretive Sociology*, vol. 2, (eds), G. Roth & C. Wittich. Berkeley, Calif.: University of California Press.

Young, M. (1958). *The Rise of the Meritocracy*. New York: Penguin Books.

MENTORING RELATIONSHIPS THROUGH THE LENS OF RACE AND GENDER

STACY BLAKE-BEARD

CGO Insights, Briefing Note # 10 (2001) Boston, MA: Center for Gender in Organizations, Simmons School of Management

> *Mentors are guides. They lead us along the journey of our lives. We trust them because they have been there before. They embody our hopes, cast light on the way ahead, interpret arcane signs, warn us of lurking dangers and point out unexpected delights along the way.* (Daloz, 1987)

As Daloz's[1] description implies, mentoring holds a special place in the pantheon of developmental relationships used by employees in organization. A mentor has been defined as a senior person emotionally invested in the development of a junior person. She offers both career guidance and socioemotional support to her protégé.[2] The benefits of mentoring, which have been widely touted in both the popular and scholarly literatures include: greater career satisfaction, promotions, compensation, self-esteem at work, and job involvement.[3] Individuals in mentoring relationships are clearly at an advantage when compared to those who do not have access to such relationships. Although these relationships are not without their challenges,[4] when mentoring is enacted between colleagues in the manner described by Daloz, there is not a more potent and critical relationship available to guide a protégé's career development.

THE IMPORTANCE OF MENTORING FOR WOMEN: A GUIDE THROUGH THE MINEFIELD

Mentoring relationships have been suggested as particularly crucial to the career development and advancement of women. A recent book from Sheila Wellington and Catalyst, a not-for-profit research organization focusing on issues of women's advancement in corporations, suggests that access to mentoring is "the single most important reason why men tend to rise higher than women."[5] In a recent survey of 1,251 executive women, four out of five senior women executives indicated that a mentor had been significant to their success.[6]

Mentoring may be particularly important to women, because despite a number of advances, women are still hitting the glass ceiling, an invisible barrier to advancement based on gender biases.[7] These biases are readily evident when you consider the relative progress, or lack thereof, of women into the upper levels of business, government, academia, and the professions. Although women make up 50% of managerial and specialized professional positions in U.S. organizations, there is still a disconcerting dearth of women in top leadership roles.[8] Mentoring has been suggested as one effective tool to address this dearth.

Anecdotal accounts and empirical research suggest that mentoring is a powerful mechanism in aiding women in their journey to the executive suite.[9] Contrary to expectations, the research shows that women are as likely to have a mentor as men. Women are also as likely as men to act as mentors. Ragins's review of the mentoring literature suggests that male and female protégés also experience similar outcomes from mentoring relationships. In terms of career outcomes, career mobility, job satisfaction, and promotions resulting from mentoring are not moderated by gender.[10]

But there are critical gender differences in men's and women's *experiences* of mentoring. While access to mentoring for women and men may be comparable, women often have to work harder to establish relationships that cross lines of gender, hierarchy and, for women of color, race. Women are also more likely to be involved in a cross-gender relationship; most mentors are still men by virtue of their position at the top of organizations. These male mentors may serve a different purpose for female protégés than they do for their male charges; they act in several roles that help women navigate the minefield they face in moving up the corporate hierarchy.[11] Mentors provide legitimacy to their female protégés, challenge gender-based stereotypes, offer reflected power, and share information that is generally only gained with admission to the "old boys' network." Each one of these functions is critical for women in a way that is not necessarily so for men. The mentors are in fact vouching for their female protégés; the message that their mentoring relationships send is, "My female protégé is okay. We can let her in." This explicit recognition of men's and women's differential experiences of mentoring suggests that the power dynamics and relationship building are more complicated in cross-gender mentoring relationships and that they may demand more from both the mentors and the protégés.

Not surprisingly, the picture becomes more complex when we look at mentoring relationships through the lens of *both* gender and race. When we look more closely at the research on gender and mentoring, a number of questions about which group of women is being given entrée arise. In fact, samples for much of the research on mentoring are predominantly white. Based on the research conducted in the past two decades, we know virtually nothing about the mentoring experiences of women of color.[12] Do women of color gain similar benefits to those reported by white women in their mentoring relationships? What benefits and challenges are raised by cultivating mentoring relationships at the crossroads of race and gender? Why don't we have more information about the experiences of women of color; where are their voices in the mentoring literature?

WHERE ARE THE VOICES OF WOMEN OF COLOR?

In fact, the voices of women of color have been absent from the mentoring literature for several reasons. In 1990, Cox and Nkomo[13] wrote about the relative absence of published research on race and ethnicity. They posited that for a number of reasons, research on race is not published to the same extent as other important organizational topics. While the 1990s have seen a promising increase in the number of articles published that focus on race and ethnicity, scholars doing research in this arena still face questions about the legitimacy and validity of their work.

Second, there is an assumption that the experiences of all women are explained by looking at white women.[14] This tendency has been labeled the "prefix error" – that which does not carry a prefix is assumed to be universal. Thus although mentoring has been clearly linked to the advancement of women in general (white women inferred), its role in the career development of women of color has not been clearly defined. This pattern of assumptions is not new. The early empirical research on mentoring was done using predominantly male samples. In the early 1980s, there was a realization that the mentoring experiences of men may not fully explain the experiences of women. Just as the research that focused solely on men and their mentoring relationships was insufficient to fully illustrate women's mentoring experiences, it is also not enough to study white women and suggest that their experiences are universally descriptive of women of color.

A third reason for the lack of information on the mentoring experiences of women of color is the challenge of recruiting sufficient numbers of study participants to participate in research efforts. Of 2.9 million women holding managerial and administrative jobs in the private sector (the population traditionally studied in the management literature), only 14 percent are women of color.[15] Standard methods of sampling have not yielded data sets that include women of color in sufficient numbers to speak to their experience. Each of these three reasons bears some culpability for the dearth of research on women of color's mentoring experiences. It is only through consciously and proactively working to overcome the barriers that I've discussed that we will give voice to women of color and their mentoring experiences.

MENTORING EXPERIENCES OF WOMEN OF COLOR: WHAT WE KNOW

As noted above, there have been few empirical efforts to examine the mentoring experiences of women of color in the management literature. In the past five years, there has been an emergence of research exploring the career experiences of women across the continuum of ethnicity. Catalyst conducted a three-year, multiphase study of women of color in corporate management, surveying 1,735 women of color from 30 companies.[16] Bell and Nkomo's comparative study focuses on the life and career experiences of successful black and white women in the corporate sector, based on life history interviews of 120 women and an in-depth survey of 825 women.[17] Based on findings from both Catalyst and Bell and Nkomo, a picture of the mentoring experiences of women of color is beginning to emerge.

A number of commonalities regarding career advancement emanated from the two studies. Results from both studies indicate that in comparison to white women, women of color are underrepresented in senior management positions and are promoted more slowly. Women of color were also less satisfied with their career progress than white women. These results are parallel to findings from my research. In a study of the mentoring experiences of 195 professional black and white women,

I found that black women reported lower levels of satisfaction with their careers than white women.[18] Women of color agree that a critical resource for their successful career advancement is having an influential mentor or sponsor. Research from Catalyst found that 44% of women of color rated access to a mentor among the top four success criteria in comparison to 37% of white women.[19] Yet, one of the most striking findings from the Catalyst study is that 47% of women of color reported that lack of access to a mentor was a barrier to their advancement, in contrast to 29% of white women. This particular comparison suggests that lack of access to a mentor is more salient to women of color than it is to their white counterparts.

While there are a number of similarities across the mentoring experiences of women of color, there are also some differences; the mentoring experiences of women of color are not monolithic. The Catalyst study presents a number of interesting contrasts among the three groups of women of color respondents. For example, Asian-American women were significantly less likely than either African-American or Hispanic women to report that they received advice on career strategies from their mentors. African-American women were more likely to report a relationship characterized by mutual respect and trust with mentors of color.

Results from studies on the experiences of women of color have yielded other differences, highlighting tensions and raising new questions. For example, how do the experiences of women of color vary along the dimension of organizational rank? Results from the Catalyst study indicate that mentoring was more prevalent for senior-level women of color than women at lower levels. Generational differences may be yet another dimension that yields important distinctions among women of color. Bell and Nkomo noted that few of the African-American women managers in their study had mentors. Their study participants were pioneers, members of the first significant wave of women to enter managerial positions in the workplace. Do the mentoring experiences of those trailblazers represent those of more recent arrivals to the corporate arena? In my study of black and white alumnae from several top-tier MBA programs, black women reported as much access to mentoring as their white counterparts.[20] But there are significant differences in the black women in my study and those in the Bell and Nkomo study. The women in my study were younger and had less work experience. How are these contrary results explained? Are they the result of changing organizational dynamics or can they be attributed to something unique about the samples that were used? These findings reveal fruitful areas for further inquiry; more research on the effects of variation in organizational rank and generational differences among women of color is needed.

The areas of convergence and divergence found in the small but growing body of research at the intersection of race and gender suggests that there are a number of areas where further exploration and deeper analysis can lead to an enhanced understanding of the collective and unique mentoring experiences of women of color.

THE PROMISE OF PRAXIS: SUGGESTIONS TO RESEARCHERS AND PRACTITIONERS

The research and ideas presented here suggest that there is work to be done on two fronts, both research and practice. I offer suggestions to researchers seeking to explore and understand the effects of the interaction of race and gender on mentoring relationships. I also have suggestions for practitioners, who are on the front line working with white women and women of color and strategizing about how to use this information to affect change in organizations.

Researchers should consider:

Being open to using different methodologies.

The intersection of race and gender is a relatively new area of inquiry in the management literature. Kram (1985) discusses the need to utilize a flexible data collection method when studying a novel topic.[21] As such, researchers should be open to using a variety of methodological approaches, including in-depth qualitative interviews as well as large-scale quantitative surveys. Of course, these decisions about methodology are accompanied by tradeoffs; large-scale quantitative studies offer some measure of generalizability while in-depth qualitative studies may provide rich descriptive accounts. We will need inquiry from both perspectives to build our knowledge on the effects of race and gender on mentoring relationships.

Being purposeful about obtaining diverse samples.

With careful consideration and proactive strategizing, researchers can find ways to reach out to diverse populations such that the resulting samples are inclusive. These efforts will not necessarily be convenient or cost effective; researchers may have to partner with associations or other groups dedicated to serving the diverse constituents that they would like to include in their research efforts. Once researchers get diverse samples, every effort should be made not to lump together groups across ethnicities. The experiences of each group are rooted in their own particular socio-historical journey to the 21st century; this unique perspective affects their lives in organizations today and should be taken into consideration.

Exploring other literatures and theoretical frameworks.

Because the women in management literature has focused primarily on white women's experiences, researchers will need to reach across to alternative literatures and theoretical frameworks. Holvino suggests that there is value to looking at other theoretical frameworks as they "influence the questions we ask, the questions that remain hidden and the outcomes and methods sought."[22] She explores the possible contribution of four feminist frameworks to the development of organizational interventions that address the intersection of race and gender. Another example can be found in the work of Helen Muller.[23] In her exploration of American Indian women managers, Muller draws on the literature of anthropologists and American Indian women. In my own research, I draw on the writing of black feminists and from theoretical frameworks grounded in the fields of psychology and sociology.[24] Only by reaching across disciplines and frameworks will we gain access to theories and empirical support to build a foundation from which we can explicate women of color's mentoring experiences.

Practitioners should consider:

Providing support to women of color employees.

Results from the recent research on women of color in corporate management suggest that their managers may play a particularly crucial role in their development and advancement. Because women of color have less access to mentors, managers should be equipped to both mentor and manage their women of color employees. Survey data indicate that the majority of mentors of women of color will be white men. Thus, women of color face a greater probability of having to develop mentoring relationships that cross both gender and race lines. All of the research on cross-race and cross-gender mentoring suggests that these relationships are challenging to develop and maintain. Catalyst suggests that managers should be trained, evaluated, and rewarded on their ability to support and advance their direct-reports, including women of color.

Being judicious users of formal mentoring programs.

Formal mentoring programs are a popular organizational intervention; recent statistics suggest that one-third of the nation's major corporations are implementing formal mentoring programs.[25] Many companies are using formal mentoring programs as a way to reach out to those who may have less access to mentoring relationships. But, an emerging body of research on formal versus informal mentoring indicates that these initiatives should be developed with some caution. In my review of the formal mentoring research, I note several internal and external challenges women should consider as they participate in formal mentoring programs.[26] Results from research on formal mentoring suggest that participants in formal initiatives do not gain the same benefits as protégés engaged in informal mentoring relationships. Ragins and Cotton warn that organizations may not be aiding their female employees if women turn towards ineffective, formal mentors rather than developing relationships with informal mentors.[27]

Examining organizational practices and systems.

Is the organization mentoring-friendly? There are a number of questions that organizational leaders should ask to assess the readiness of their environment to support a culture of mentoring. Are there opportunities for communication and interaction across organizational levels? Is the development of employees a valued function? Do the reward and evaluation systems reflect the importance of mentoring and developmental support for all employees? Supportive and effective interpersonal interactions do not develop in a vacuum; women of color have a greater chance of developing mentoring relationships in an environment that is supportive of mentoring.

CONCLUSION

Mentoring relationships provide a critical source of support for the professional development of women. Until very recently, a common and unspoken assumption was held that if we learned about the mentoring experiences and outcomes for white women, we would be able to speak to the experiences of all women. But the nascent body of research by scholars examining the mentoring experiences of women of color clearly debunks this assumption. We need to be far more proactive and thoughtful about how mentoring relationships may be differentially accessed based on the intersection of race and gender. We must contemplate how our research paradigms and frameworks should be adjusted to accommodate hypotheses and samples that are inclusive of the mentoring experiences of women along the spectrum of ethnic diversity. The challenges of mentoring, particularly across lines of race and gender, are not insignificant. But the promise of mentoring, that women of all ethnicities are supported in reaching their fullest potential, is a goal for which it is worthy to strive.

NOTES

1 Daloz, L. A. (1987). *Effective Teaching and Mentoring: Realizing the Transformational Power of Adult Learning Experiences.* San Francisco, CA: Jossey Bass.
2 Crosby, F. J. (1999). The developmental literature on developmental relationships. In A. J. Murrell, F. J. Crosby & R. J. Ely (Eds.), *Mentoring Dilemmas: Developmental Relationships Within Multicultural Organizations.* Mahwah, NJ: Lawrence Erlbaum.
3 Ragins, B. R. (1999). Gender and mentoring relationships: A review and research agenda for the next decade. In G. N. Powell (Ed.), *Handbook of Gender & Work.* Thousand Oaks, CA: Sage Publications.
4 O'Neill, R. M. & Sankowsky, D. (forthcoming). The Caligula phenomenon: Mentoring relationships and theoretical abuse. *Journal of Management Inquiry.*
5 Wellington, S. & Catalyst. (2001). *Be Your Own Mentor: Strategies from Top Women on the Secrets of Success.* New York: Random House.
6 Catalyst. (1996). *Women in Corporate Leadership: Progress and Prospects.* New York: Catalyst.
7 Morrison, A., White, R., Velsor, E. and the Center for Creative Leadership. (1994). *Breaking the Glass Ceiling: Can Women Reach the Top of America's Largest Corporation?* Reading, MA: Addison-Wesley.
8 Merrill-Sands, D. & Kolb, D. M. (2001). *Women as Leaders: The Paradox of Success. CGO Insights, No. 9.* Boston, MA: CGO, Simmons School of Management.
9 O'Neill, R. M., Horton, S. & Crosby, F. J. (1999). Gender issues in developmental relationships. In A. J. Murrell, F. J. Crosby & R. J. Ely (Eds.), *Mentoring Dilemmas: Developmental Relationships Within Multicultural Organizations.* Mahwah, NJ: Lawrence Erlbaum.
10 Ragins, B. R. (1999).
11 Ragins, B. R. (1999).
12 Blake-Beard, S. D. (1999). The costs of living as an outsider within: An analysis of the mentoring relationships and career success of black and white women in the corporate sector. *Journal of Career Development,* 26(1), 21–36.
13 Cox, T. & Nkomo, S. M. (1990). Invisible men and women: A status report on race as a variable in organizational behavior research. *Journal of Organizational Behavior,* 11, 419–431.
14 Bell, E. L., Denton, T. C. & Nkomo, S. (1993). Women of color in management: Toward an inclusive analysis. In E. Fagenson (Ed.), *Women in Management: Vol. 4. Trends, Issues, and Challenges in Managerial Diversity* (pp. 105–130). Newbury Park, CA: Sage.
15 Wellington, S. & Catalyst. (2001).
16 Catalyst. (1999). *Women of Color in Corporate Management: Opportunities and Barriers* (p. 5). New York, NY: Catalyst.
17 Bell, E. & Nkomo, S. (2001). *Our Separate Ways: Black and White Women and the Struggle for Professional Identity.* Boston, MA: Harvard Business School press.
18 Blake-Beard, S. D. (1999).

19 These statistics are from a comparison of data from the Catalyst (1999) study of women of color in the corporate sector with data from a Catalyst (1996) study of comparable white women.

20 Blake-Beard, S. D. (1999).

21 Kram, K. E. (1985). *Mentoring at Work: Developmental Relationships in Organizational Life.* Glenville, IL: Scott, Foresman & Co.

22 Holvino, E. (2001). *Complicating Gender: The Simultaneity of Race, Gender and Class in Organization Change(ing). CGO Working Paper No. 14.* Boston, MA: CGO, Simmons School of Management.

23 Muller, H. J. (1998). American Indian women managers: Living in two worlds. *Journal of Management Inquiry,* 7(1), 4–28.

24 Blake, S. (1999). At the crossroads of race and gender: Lessons from the mentoring experiences of professional black women. In A. J. Murrell, F. J. Crosby & R. J. Ely (Eds.), *Mentoring Dilemmas: Developmental Relationships Within Multicultural Organizations.* Mahwah, NJ: Lawrence Erlbaum.

25 Ragins, B. R. & Cotton, J. L. (1999). Mentor functions and outcomes: A comparison of men and women in formal and informal mentoring relationships. *Journal of Applied Psychology,* 84(4), 529–550.

26 Blake-Beard, S. D. (2001). Taking a hard look at formal mentoring programs: A consideration of potential challenges facing women. *Journal of Management Development,* 20(4), 331–345.

27 Ragins & Cotton. (1999).

CHAPTER

24

NICKEL-AND-DIMED: ON (NOT) GETTING BY IN AMERICA

BARBARA EHRENREICH

From Harper's Magazine (1999) January: 37–52

At the beginning of June 1998 I leave behind everything that normally soothes the ego and sustains the body – home, career, companion, reputation, ATM card – for a plunge into the low-wage workforce. There, I become another, occupationally much diminished "Barbara Ehrenreich" – depicted on job-application forms as a divorced homemaker whose sole work experience consists of housekeeping in a few private homes. I am terrified, at the beginning, of being unmasked for what I am: a middle-class journalist setting out to explore the world that welfare mothers are entering, at the rate of approximately 50,000 a month, as welfare reform kicks in. Happily, though, my fears turn out to be entirely unwarranted: during a month of poverty and toil, my name goes unnoticed and for the most part unuttered. In this parallel universe where my father never got out of the mines and I never got through college, I am "baby," "honey," "blondie," and, most commonly, "girl."

My first task is to find a place to live. I figure that if I can earn $7 an hour – which, from the want ads, seems doable – I can afford to spend $500 on rent, or maybe, with severe economies, $600. In the Key West area, where I live, this pretty much confines me to flophouses and trailer homes – like the one, a pleasing fifteen-minute drive from town, that has no air-conditioning, no screens, no fans, no television, . . . The big problem with this place, though, is the rent, which at $675 a month is well beyond my reach. All right, Key West is expensive. But so is New York City, or the Bay Area, or Jackson Hole, or Telluride, or Boston, or any other place where tourists and the wealthy compete for living space with the people who clean their toilets and fry their hash browns.[1] Still, it is a shock to realize that "trailer trash" has become, for me, a demographic category to aspire to.

So I decide to make the common trade-off between affordability and convenience, and go for a $500-a-month efficiency thirty miles up a two-lane highway from the employment opportunities of Key West, meaning forty-five minutes if there's no road construction. [. . .]

My aim is nothing so mistily subjective as to "experience poverty" or find out how it "really feels" to be a long-term low-wage worker. I've had enough unchosen encounters with poverty and the world of low-wage work to know it's not a place you want to visit for touristic purposes; it just smells too much like fear. And with all my real-life assets – bank account, IRA, health insurance, multiroom home – waiting indulgently in the background, I am, of course, thoroughly insulated from the terrors that afflict the genuinely poor.

No, this is a purely objective, scientific sort of mission. The humanitarian rationale for welfare reform – as opposed to the more punitive and stingy impulses that may actually have motivated it – is that work will lift poor women out of poverty while simultaneously inflating their self-esteem and hence their future value in the labor market. Thus, whatever the hassles involved in finding child care, transportation, etc., the transition from welfare to work will end happily, in greater prosperity for all. Now there are many problems with this comforting prediction, such as the fact that the economy will inevitably undergo a downturn, eliminating many jobs. Even without a downturn, the influx of a million former welfare recipients into the low-wage labor market could depress wages by as much as 11.9 percent according to the Economic Policy Institute (EPI) in Washington, D.C.

But is it really possible to make a living on the kinds of jobs currently available to unskilled people? Mathematically, the answer is no, as can be shown by taking $6 to $7 an hour, perhaps subtracting a dollar or two an hour for child care, multiplying by 160 hours a month, and comparing the result to the prevailing rents. According to the National Coalition for the Homeless, for example, in 1998 it took, on average nationwide, an hourly wage of $8.89 to afford a one-bedroom apartment, and the Preamble Center for Public Policy estimates that the odds against a typical welfare recipient's landing a job at such a "living wage" are about 97 to 1. If these numbers are right, low-wage work is not a solution to poverty and possibly not even to homelessness.

It may seem excessive to put this proposition to an experimental test. . . . But I am an experimental scientist by training. In that business, you don't just sit at a desk and theorize; you plunge into the everyday chaos of nature, where surprises lurk in the most mundane measurements. Maybe, when I got into it, I would discover some hidden economies in the world of the low-wage worker. After all, if 30 percent of the workforce toils for less than $8 an hour, according to the EPI, they may have found some tricks as yet unknown to me. Maybe – who knows? – I would even be able to detect in myself the bracing psychological effects of getting out of the house, as promised by the welfare wonks at places like the Heritage Foundation. Or, on the other hand, maybe there would be unexpected costs – physical, mental, or financial – to throw off all my calculations. Ideally, I should do this with two small children in tow, that being the welfare average, but mine are grown and no one is willing to lend me theirs for a month-long vacation in penury. So this is not the perfect experiment, just a test of the best possible case: an unencumbered woman, smart and even strong, attempting to live more or less off the land. [. . .]

I decide on two rules: One, I cannot use any skills derived from my education or usual work – not that there are a lot of want ads for satirical essayists anyway. Two, I have to take the best-paid job that is offered me and of course do my best to hold it [. . .]

My career [begins] at the Hearthside, I shall call it, one small profit center within a global discount hotel chain, where for two weeks I work from 2:00 till 10:00 P.M. for $2.43 an hour plus tips.[2] . . .

For the next eight hours, I run after the agile Gail, the wiry middle-aged waitress who is assigned to train me, absorbing bits of instruction along with fragments of personal tragedy. All food must be trayed, and the reason she's so tired today is that she woke up in a cold sweat thinking of her boyfriend, who killed himself recently in an upstate prison. No refills on lemonade. And the reason he was in prison is that a few DUIs caught up with him, that's all, could have happened to anyone. Carry the creamers to the table in a monkey bowl, never in your hand. And after he was gone she spent several months living in her truck, peeing in a plastic pee bottle and reading by candlelight at night, but you can't live in a truck in the summer, since you need to have the windows down, which means anything can get in, from mosquitoes on up.

At least Gail puts to rest any fears I had of appearing overqualified. From the first day on, I find that of all the things I have left behind, such as home and identity, what I miss the most is competence. Not that I have ever felt utterly competent in the writing business, in which one day's success augurs nothing at all for the next. But in my writing life, I at least have some notion of procedure: do the research, make the outline, rough out a draft, etc. As a server, though, I am beset by requests like bees: more iced tea here, ketchup over there, a to-go box for table fourteen, and where are the high chairs, anyway? Of the twenty-seven tables, up to six are usually mine at any time, though on slow afternoons or if Gail is off, I sometimes have the whole place to myself. There is the touch-screen computer-ordering system to master, which is, I suppose, meant to minimize server-cook contact, but in practice requires constant verbal fine-tuning: "That's gravy on the mashed, okay? None on the meatloaf," and so forth – while the cook scowls as if I were inventing these refinements just to torment him. Plus, something I had forgotten in the years since I was eighteen: about a third of a server's job is "side work" that's invisible to customers – sweeping, scrubbing, slicing, refilling, and restocking. If it isn't all done, every little bit of it, you're going to face the 6:00 P.M. dinner rush defenseless and probably go down in flames. I screw up dozens of times at the beginning, sustained in my shame entirely by Gail's support – "It's okay, baby, everyone does that sometime" – because, to my total surprise and despite the scientific detachment I am doing my best to maintain, I care. [. . .]

Still, when I wake up at 4:00 A.M. in my own cold sweat, I am not thinking about the writing deadlines I'm neglecting; I'm thinking about the table whose order I screwed up so that one of the boys didn't get his kiddie meal until the rest of the family had moved on to their Key Lime pies. That's the other powerful motivation I hadn't expected – the customers, or "patients," as I can't help thinking of them on account of the mysterious vulnerability that seems to have left them temporarily unable to feed themselves. After a few days at the Hearthside, I feel the service ethic kick in like a shot of oxytocin, the nurturance hormone. The plurality of my customers are hard-working locals – truck drivers, construction workers, even house-keepers from the attached hotel – and I want them to have the closest to a "fine dining" experience that the grubby circumstances will allow. No "you guys" for me; everyone over twelve is "sir" or "ma'am." I ply them with iced tea and coffee refills; I return, mid-meal, to inquire how everything is; I doll up their salads with chopped raw mushrooms, summer squash slices, or whatever bits of produce I can find that have survived their sojourn in the cold-storage room mold-free. [. . .]

Sometimes I play with the fantasy that I am a princess who, in penance for some tiny transgression, has undertaken to feed each of her subjects by hand. But the non-princesses working with me are just as indulgent, even when this means flouting management rules – concerning, for example, the number of croutons that can go on a salad (six). "Put on all you want," Gail whispers, "as long as Stu isn't looking." She dips into her own tip money to buy biscuits and gravy for an out-of-work mechanic who's used up all his money on dental surgery, inspiring me to pick up the tab for his milk and pie. Maybe the same high levels of agape can be found throughout the "hospitality industry." . . .

At the Hearthside, we utilize whatever bits of autonomy we have to ply our customers with the illicit calories that signal our love. It is our job as servers to assemble the salads and desserts, pouring the dressings and squirting the whipped cream. We also control the number of butter patties out customers get and the amount of sour cream on their baked potatoes. So if you wonder why Americans are so obese, consider the fact that waitresses both express their humanity and earn their tips through the covert distribution of fats.

Ten days into it, this is beginning to look like a livable lifestyle. [. . .]

I could drift along like this, in some dreamy proletarian idyll, except for two things. One is management. If I have kept this subject on the margins thus far it is because I still flinch to think that I spent all those weeks under the surveillance of men (and later women) whose job it was to monitor my behavior for signs of sloth, theft, drug abuse, of worse. Not that managers and especially "assistant managers" in low-wage settings like this are exactly the class enemy. In the restaurant business, they are mostly former cooks or servers, still capable of pinch-hitting in the kitchen or on the floor, just as in hotels they are likely to be former clerks, and paid a salary of only about $400 a week. But everyone knows they have crossed over to the other side, which is, crudely put, corporate as opposed to human. Cooks want to prepare tasty meals; servers want to serve them graciously; but managers are there for only one reason – to make sure that money is made for some theoretical entity that exists far away in Chicago or New York, if a corporation can be said to have a physical existence at all. Reflecting on her career, Gail tells me ruefully that she had sworn, years ago, never to work for a corporation again. "They don't cut you no slack. You give and you give, and they take."

Managers can sit – for hours at a time if they want – but it's their job to see that no one else ever does, even when there's nothing to do, and this is why, for servers, slow times can be as exhausting as rushes. You start dragging out each little chore, because if the manager on duty catches you in an idle moment, he will give you something far nastier to do. So I wipe, I clean, I consolidate ketchup bottles and recheck the cheesecake supply, even tour the tables to make sure the customer evaluation forms are all standing perkily in their places – wondering all the time how many calories I burn in these strictly theatrical exercises. When, on a particularly dead afternoon, Stu finds me glancing at a *USA Today* a customer has left behind, he assigns me to vacuum the entire floor with the broken vacuum cleaner that has a handle only two feet long, and the only way to do that without incurring orthopedic damage is to proceed from spot to spot on your knees.

On my first Friday at the Hearthside there is a "mandatory meeting for all restaurant employees," which I attend, eager for insight into our overall marketing strategy and the niche (your basic Ohio cuisine with a tropical twist?) we aim to inhabit. But there is no "we" at this meeting. Phillip, our top manager except for an occasional "consultant" sent out by corporate headquarters, opens it with a sneer: "The break room – it's disgusting. Butts in the ashtrays, newspapers lying around, crumbs." This windowless little room, which also houses the time clock for the entire hotel, is where we stash our bags and civilian clothes and take our half-hour meal breaks. But a break room is not a right, he tells us. It can be taken away. [. . .]

The other problem, in addition to the less-than-nurturing management style, is that this job shows no sign of being financially viable. You might imagine, from a comfortable distance, that people who live, year in and year out, on $6 to $10 an hour have discovered some survival stratagems unknown to the middle class. But no. It's not hard to get my co-workers to talk about their living situations, because housing, in almost every case, is the principal source of disruption in their lives, the first thing they fill you in on when they arrive for their shifts. After a week, I have compiled the following survey:

- Gail is sharing a room in a well-known downtown flophouse for which she and a roommate pay about $250 a week. Her roommate, a male friend, has begun hitting on her, driving her nuts, but the rent would be impossible alone.
- Claude, the Haitian cook, is desperate to get out of the two-room apartment he shares with his girlfriend and two other, unrelated, people. As far as I can determine, the other Haitian men (most of whom only speak Creole) live in similarly crowded situations.
- Annette, a twenty-year-old server who is six months pregnant and has been abandoned by her boyfriend, lives with her mother, a postal clerk.
- Marianne and her boyfriend are paying $170 a week for a one-person trailer.
- Jack, who is, at $10 an hour, the wealthiest of us, lives in the trailer he owns, paying only the $400-a-month lot fee.
- The other white cook, Andy, lives on his dry-docked boat, which as far as I can tell from his loving descriptions, can't be more than twenty feet long. He offers to take me out on it, once it's repaired, but the offer comes with inquiries as to my marital status, so I do not follow up on it.
- Tina and her husband are paying $60 a night for a double room in Days Inn. This is because they have no car and the Days Inn is within walking distance of the Hearthside. When Marianne, one of the breakfast servers, is tossed out of her trailer for subletting (which is against the trailer-park rules), she leaves her boyfriend and moves in with Tina and her husband.
- Joan, who had fooled me with her numerous and tasteful outfits (hostesses wear their own clothes), lives in a van she parks behind a shopping center at night and showers in Tina's motel room. The clothes are from thrift shops.[3]

It strikes me, in my middle-class solipsism, that there is gross improvidence in some of these arrangements. When Gail and I are wrapping silverware in napkins – the only task for which we are permitted to sit – she tells me she is thinking of escaping from her roommate by moving into the Days Inn herself. I am astounded: How can she even think of paying between $40 and $60 a day? But if I was afraid of sounding like a social worker, I come out just sounding like a fool. She squints at me in disbelief, "And where am I supposed to get a month's rent and a month's deposit for an apartment?" I'd been feeling pretty smug about my $500 efficiency, but of course it was made possible only by the $1,300 I had allotted myself for start-up costs when I began my low-wage life: $1,000 for the first month's rent and deposit, $100 for initial groceries and cash in my pocket, $200 stuffed away for emergencies. In poverty, as in certain propositions in physics, starting conditions are everything.

There are no secret economies that nourish the poor, on the contrary, there are a host of special costs. If you can't put up the two months' rent you need to secure an apartment, you end up paying through the nose for a room by the week. If you have only a room, with a hot plate at best, you can't save by cooking up huge lentil stews that can be frozen for the week ahead. You eat fast food, or the hot dogs and styrofoam cups of soup that can be microwaved in a convenience store. If you have no money for health insurance – and the Hearthside's niggardly plan kicks in only after three months – you go without routine care or prescription drugs and end up paying the price. [. . .]

My own situation, when I sit down to assess it after two weeks of work, would not be much better if this were my actual life. The seductive thing about waitressing is that you don't have to wait for payday to feel a few bills in your pocket, and my tips usually cover meals and gas, plus something left over to stuff into the kitchen drawer I use as a bank. But as the tourist business slows in the summer heat, I sometimes leave work with only $20 in tips (the gross is higher, but servers share about 15 percent of their tips with the busboys and bartenders). With wages included, this amounts to about the minimum wage of $5.15 an hour. Although the sum in the drawer is piling up, at the present rate of accumulation it will be more than a hundred dollars short of my rent when the end of the month comes around. Nor can I see any expenses to cut. True, I haven't gone the lentil-stew route yet, but that's because I don't have a large cooking pot, pot holders, or a ladle to stir with (which cost about $30 at Kmart, less at thrift stores), not to mention onions, carrots, and the indispensable bay leaf. I do make my lunch almost every day – usually some slow-burning, high-protein combo like frozen chicken patties with melted cheese on top and canned pinto beans on the side. Dinner is at the Hearthside, which offers its employees a choice of BLT, fish sandwich, or hamburger for only $2. The burger lasts longest, especially if it's heaped with gut-puckering jalapeños, but by midnight my stomach is growling again.

So unless I want to start using my car as a residence, I have to find a second, or alternative, job. [. . .] Jerry's, which is part of a well-known national family restaurant chain and physically attached here to another budget hotel chain, is ready to use me at once. The prospect is both exciting and terrifying, because, with about the same number of tables and counter seats, Jerry's attracts three or four times the volume of customers as the gloomy old Hearthside. [. . .]

Now, the Industrial Revolution is not an easy transition, especially when you have to zip through it in just a couple of days. I have gone from craft work straight into the factory, from the air-conditioned morgue of the Hearthside directly into the flames. Customers arrive in human waves, sometimes disgorged fifty at a time from their tour buses, peckish and whiny. Instead of two "girls" on the floor at once, there can be as many as six of us running around in our brilliant pink-and-orange Hawaiian shirts. Conversations, either with customers or fellow employees, seldom last more than twenty seconds at a time. [. . .]

I start out with the beautiful, heroic idea of handling the two jobs at once, and for two days I almost do it: the breakfast/lunch shift at Jerry's, which goes till 2:00, arriving at the Hearthside at 2:10, and attempting to hold out until 10:00. In the ten minutes between jobs, I pick up a spicy chicken sandwich at the Wendy's drive-through window, gobble it down in the car, and change from khaki slacks to black, from Hawaiian to rust polo. There is a problem, though. When during the 3:00 to 4:00 P.M. dead time I finally sit down to wrap silver, my flesh seems to bond to the seat. I try to refuel with a purloined cup of soup, as I've seen Gail and Joan do dozens of times, but a manager catches me and hisses "No eating!" though there's not a customer around to be offended by the sight of food making contact with a server's lips. So I tell Gail I'm going to quit, and she hugs me and says she might just follow me to Jerry's herself.

But the chances of this are minuscule. She has left the flophouse and her annoying roommate and is back to living in her beat-up old truck. But guess what? she reports to me excitedly later that evening: Phillip has given her permission to park overnight in the hotel parking lot, as long as she keeps out of sight, and the parking lot should be totally safe, since it's patrolled by a hotel security guard! With the Hearthside offering benefits like that, how could anyone think of leaving?

Gail would have triumphed at Jerry's, I'm sure, but for me it's a crash course in exhaustion management. Years ago, the kindly fry cook who trained me to waitress at a Los Angeles truck stop used to say: Never make an unnecessary trip; if you don't have to walk fast, walk slow; if you don't have to walk, stand. But at Jerry's the effort of distinguishing necessary from unnecessary and urgent from whenever would itself be too much of an energy drain. The only thing to do is to treat each shift as a one-time-only emergency: you've got fifty starving people out there, lying scattered on the battlefield, so get out there and feed them! Forget that you will have to do this again tomorrow, forget that you will have to be alert enough to dodge the drunks on the drive home tonight – just burn, burn, burn! Ideally, at some point you enter what servers call "a rhythm" and psychologists term a "flow state," in which signals pass from the sense organs directly to the muscles, bypassing the cerebral cortex, and a Zen-like emptiness sets in. . . .

But there's another capacity of the neuromuscular system, which is pain. I start tossing back drugstore-brand ibuprofen pills as if they were vitamin C, four before each shift, because an old mouse-related repetitive-stress injury in my upper back has come back to full-spasm strength, thanks to the tray carrying. In my ordinary life, this level of disability might justify a day of ice packs and stretching. Here I comfort myself with the Aleve commercial in which the cute blue-collar guy asks: If you quit after working four hours, what would your boss say? And the not-so-cute blue-collar guy, who's lugging a metal beam on his back, answers: He'd fire me, that's what. But fortunately, the commercial tells us, we workers can exert the same kind of authority over our painkillers that our bosses exert over us. If Tylenol doesn't want to work for more than four hours, you just fire its ass and switch to Aleve. [. . .]

[A]s the days go by, my old life is beginning to look exceedingly strange. The e-mails and phone messages addressed to my former self come from a distant race of people with exotic concerns and far too much time on their hands. The neighborly market I used to cruise for produce now looks forbiddingly like a Manhattan yuppie emporium. And when I sit down one morning in my real home to pay bills from my past life, I am dazzled at the two- and three-figure sums owed to outfits like Club Body Tech and Amazon.com. [. . .]

On my third night, [B.J., one of the managers,] pulls me aside abruptly and brings her face so close that it looks as if she's planning to butt me with her forehead. But instead of saying, "You're fired," she says, "You're doing fine." The only trouble is I'm spending time chatting with customers: "That's how they're getting you." Furthermore I am letting them "run me," which means harassment by sequential demands: you bring the ketchup and they decide they want extra Thousand Island; you bring that and they announce they now need a side of fries; and so on into distraction. . . .

I mumble thanks for the advice, feeling like I've just been stripped naked by the crazed enforcer of some ancient sumptuary law: No chatting for you, girl. No fancy service ethic allowed for the serfs. Chatting with customers is for the beautiful young college-educated servers in the downtown carpaccio joints, the kids who can make $70 to $100 a night. What had I been thinking? My job is to move orders from tables to kitchen and then trays from kitchen to tables. Customers are, in fact, the major obstacle to the smooth transformation of information into food and food into money – they are, in short, the enemy. And the painful thing is that I'm beginning to see it this way myself. . . . The worst, for some reason, are the Visible Christians – like the ten-person table, all jolly and sanctified after Sunday-night service, who run me mercilessly and then leave me $1 on a $92 bill. . . .

I make friends, over time, with the other "girls" who work my shift: Nita, the tattooed twenty-something who taunts us by going around saying brightly, "Have we started making money yet?" Ellen, whose teenage son cooks on the graveyard shift and who once managed a restaurant in Massachusetts but won't try out for management here because she prefers being a "common worker" and not "ordering people around." Easy-going fiftyish Lucy, with the raucous laugh, who limps toward the end of the shift because of something that has gone wrong with her leg, the exact nature of which cannot be determined without health insurance. We talk about the usual girl things – men, children, and the sinister allure of Jerry's chocolate peanut-butter cream pie – though no one, I notice, ever brings up anything potentially expensive, like shopping or movies. As at the Hearthside, the only recreation ever referred to is partying, which requires little more than some beer, a joint, and a few close friends. Still, no one here is homeless, or cops to it anyway, thanks usually to a working husband or boyfriend. All in all, we form a reliable mutual-support group: If one of us is feeling sick or overwhelmed, another one will "bev" a table or even carry trays for her. If one of us is off sneaking a cigarette or a pee,[4] the others will do their best to conceal her absence from the enforcers of corporate rationality.

But my saving human connection – my oxytocin receptor, as it were – is George, the nineteen-year-old, fresh-off-the-boat Czech dishwasher. We get to talking when he asks me, tortuously, how much cigarettes cost at Jerry's. I do my best to explain that they cost over a dollar more here than at a regular store and suggest that he just take one from the half-filled packs that are always lying around on the break table. But that would be unthinkable. Except for the one tiny earring signaling his allegiance to some vaguely alternative point of view, George is a perfect straight arrow – crew-cut, hardworking, and hungry for eye contact. "Czech Republic," I ask, "or Slovakia?" and he seems delighted that I know the difference. . . .

My project is to teach George English. "How are you today, George?" I say at the start of each shift. "I am good, and how are you today, Barbara?" I learn that he is not paid by Jerry's but by the "agent" who shipped him over – $5 an hour, with the agent getting the dollar or so difference between that and what Jerry's pays dishwashers. I learn also that he shares an apartment with a crowd of other Czech "dishers" as he calls them, and that he cannot sleep until one of them goes off for his shift, leaving a vacant bed. [. . .]

I make the decision to move closer to Key West. First, because of the drive. Second and third, also because of the drive: gas is eating up $4 to $5 a day, and although Jerry's is as high-volume as you can get, the tips average only 10 percent, and not just for a newbie like me. Between the base pay of $2.15 an hour and the obligation to share tips with the busboys and dishwashers, we're averaging only about $7.50 an hour. Then there is the $30 I had to spend on the regulation tan slacks worn by Jerry's servers – a setback it could take weeks to absorb. (I had combed the town's two downscale department stores hoping for something cheaper but decided in the end that these marked-down Dockers, originally $49, were more likely to survive a daily washing.) Of my fellow servers, everyone who lacks a working husband or boyfriend seems to have a second job: Nita does something at a computer eight hours a day; another welds. Without the forty-five-minute commute, I can picture myself working two jobs and having the time to shower between them.

So I take the $500 deposit I have coming from my landlord, the $400 I have earned toward the next month's rent, plus the $200 reserved for emergencies, and use the $1,100 to pay the rent and deposit on trailer number 46 in the Overseas Trailer Park, a mile from the cluster of budget hotels that constitute Key West's version of an industrial park. Number 46 is about eight feet in width and shaped like a barbell inside, with a narrow region – because of the sink and the stove – separating the bedroom from what might optimistically be called the "living" area, with its two-person table and half-sized couch. The bathroom is so small my knees rub against the shower stall when I sit on the toilet, and you can't just leap out of the bed, you have to climb down to the foot of it in order to find a patch of floor space to stand on. Outside, I am within a few yards of a liquor store, a bar that advertises "free beer tomorrow," a convenience store, and a Burger King – but no supermarket or, alas, laundromat. By reputation, the Overseas park is a nest of crime and crack, and I am hoping at least for some vibrant, multicultural street life. But desolation rules night and day, except for a thin stream of pedestrian traffic heading for their jobs at the Sheraton or 7-Eleven. There are not exactly people here but what amounts to canned labor, being preserved from the heat between shifts.

In line with my reduced living conditions, a new form of ugliness arises at Jerry's. [. . .] [T]he next day, when I go for straws, for the first time I find the dry-storage room locked. Ted, the portly assistant manager who opens it for me, explains that he caught one of the dishwashers attempting to steal something, and, unfortunately, the miscreant will be with us until a replacement can be found – hence the locked door. I neglect to ask what he had been trying to steal, but Ted tells me who he is – the kid with the buzz cut and the earring. You know, he's back there right now.

I wish I could say I rushed back and confronted George to get his side of the story. I wish I could say I stood up to Ted and insisted that George be given a translator and allowed to defend himself, or announced that I'd find a lawyer who'd handle the case pro bono. The mystery to me is that there's not much worth stealing in the dry-storage room, at least not in any fenceable quantity: "Is Gyorgi here, and am having 200 – maybe 250 – ketchup packets. What do you say?" My guess is that he had taken – if he had taken anything at all – some Saltines or a can of cherry-pie mix, and that the motive for taking it was hunger.

So why didn't I intervene? Certainly not because I was held back by the kind of moral paralysis that can pass as journalistic objectivity. On the contrary, something new – something loathsome and servile – had infected me, along with the kitchen odors that I could still sniff on my bra when I finally undressed at night. In real life I am moderately brave, but plenty of brave people shed their courage in concentration camps, and maybe something similar goes on in the infinitely more congenial milieu of the low-wage American workplace. Maybe, in a month or two more at Jerry's, I might have regained my crusading spirit. Then again, in a month or two I might have turned into a different person altogether – say, the kind of person who would have turned George in.

But this is not something I am slated to find out. When my month-long plunge into poverty is almost over, I finally land my dream job – housekeeping . . . [at] the hotel attached to Jerry's [. . .]

I can do this two-job thing, is my theory, if I can drink enough caffeine and avoid getting distracted by George's ever more obvious suffering.[5] The first few days after being caught he seemed not to understand the trouble he was in, and our chirpy little conversations had continued. But the last couple of shifts he's been listless and unshaven, and tonight he looks like the ghost we all know him to be, with dark half-moons hanging from his eyes. At one point, when I am briefly immobilized by the task of filling little paper cups with sour cream for baked potatoes, he comes over and looks as if he'd like to explore the limits of our shared vocabulary, but I am called to the floor for a table. I resolve to give him all my tips that night and to hell with the experiment in low-wage money management. At eight, Ellen and I grab a snack together standing at the mephitic end of the kitchen counter, but I can only manage two or three mozzarella sticks and lunch had been a mere handful of McNuggets. I am not tired at all, I assure myself, though it may be that there is simply no more "I" left to do the tiredness monitoring. What I would see, if I were more alert to the situation, is that the forces of destruction are already massing against me. There is only one cook on duty, a young man named Jesus ("Hay-Sue," that is) and he is new to the job. And there is Joy, who shows up to take over in the middle of the shift, wearing high heels and a long, clingy white dress and fuming as if she'd just been stood up in some cocktail bar.

Then it comes, the perfect storm. Four of my tables fill up at once. Four tables is nothing for me now, but only so long as they are obligingly staggered. As I bev table 27, tables 25, 28, and 24 are watching enviously. As I bev 25, 24 glowers because their bevs haven't even been ordered. Twenty-eight is four yuppyish types, meaning everything on the side and agonizing instructions as to the chicken Caesars. Twenty-five is a middle-aged black couple, who complain, with some justice, that the iced tea isn't fresh and the tabletop is sticky. But table 24 is the meteorological event of the century: ten British tourists who seem to have made the decision to absorb the American experience entirely by mouth. Here everyone has at least two drinks – iced tea and milk shake, Michelob and water (with lemon slice, please) – and a huge promiscuous orgy of breakfast specials, mozz sticks, chicken strips, quesadillas, burgers with cheese and without, sides of hash browns with cheddar, with onions, with gravy, seasoned fries, plain fries, banana splits. Poor Jesus! Poor me! Because when I arrive with their first tray of food – after three prior trips just to refill bevs – Princess Di refuses to eat her chicken strips with her pancake-and-sausage special, since, as she now reveals, the strips were meant to be an appetizer. Maybe the others would have accepted their meals, but Di, who is deep into her third Michelob, insists that everything else go back while they work on their "starters." Meanwhile, the yuppies are waving me down for more decaf and the black couple looks ready to summon the NAACP.

   Much of what happened next is lost in the fog of war. Jesus starts going under. The little printer on the counter in front of him is spewing out orders faster than he can rip them off, much less produce the meals. Even the invincible Ellen is ashen from stress. I bring table 24 their reheated main courses, which they immediately reject as either too cold or fossilized by the microwave. When I return to the kitchen with their trays (three trays in three trips), Joy confronts me with arms akimbo: "What is this?" She means the food – the plates of rejected pancakes, hash browns in assorted flavors, toasts, burgers, sausages, eggs. "Uh, scrambled with cheddar," I try, "and that's . . ." "NO," she screams in my face. "Is it a traditional, a super-scramble, an eye-opener?" I pretend to study my check for a clue, but entropy has been up to its tricks, not only on the plates but in my head, and I have to admit that the original order is beyond reconstruction. "You don't know an eye-opener from a traditional?" she demands in outrage. All I know, in fact, is that my legs have lost interest in the current venture and have announced their intention to fold. I am saved by a yuppie (mercifully not one of mine) who chooses this moment to charge into the kitchen to bellow that his food is twenty-five minutes late. Joy screams at him to get the hell out of her kitchen, please, and then turns on Jesus in a fury, hurling an empty tray across the room for emphasis.

   I leave. I don't walk out, I just leave. I don't finish my side work or pick up my credit-card tips, if any, at the cash register or, of course, ask Joy's permission to go. And the surprising thing is that you *can* walk out without permission, that the door opens, that the thick tropical night air parts to let me pass, that my car is still parked where I left it. There is no vindication in this exit, no fuck-you surge of relief, just an overwhelming, dank sense of failure pressing down on me and the entire parking lot. I had gone into this venture in the spirit of science, to test a mathematical proposition, but somewhere along the line, in the tunnel vision imposed by long shifts and relentless concentration, it became a test of myself, and clearly I have failed. Not only had I flamed out as a housekeeper/server, I had even forgotten to give George my tips, and, for reasons perhaps best known to hard-working, generous people like Gail and Ellen, this hurts. I don't cry, but I am in a position to realize, for the first time in many years, that the tear ducts are still there, and still capable of doing their job.

   When I moved out of the trailer park, I gave the key to number 46 to Gail and arranged for my deposit to be transferred to her. She told me that Joan is still living in her van and that Stu had been fired from the Hearthside. I never found out what happened to George.

   In one month, I had earned approximately $1,040 and spent $517 on food, gas, toiletries, laundry, phone, and utilities. If I had remained in my $500 efficiency, I would have been able to pay the rent and have $22 left over (which is $78 less than the cash I had in my pocket at the start of the month). During this time I bought no clothing except for the required slacks and no prescription drugs or medical care (I did finally buy some vitamin B to compensate for the lack of vegetables in my diet). Perhaps I could have saved a little on food if I had gotten to a super-market more often, instead of convenience stores, but it should be noted that I lost almost four pounds in four weeks, on a diet weighted heavily toward burgers and fries.

   How former welfare recipients and single mothers will (and do) survive in the low-wage workforce, I cannot imagine. Maybe they will figure out how to condense their lives – including child-raising, laundry, romance, and meals – into the couple of hours between full-time jobs. Maybe they will take up residence in their vehicles, if they have one. All I know is that I couldn't hold two jobs and I couldn't make enough money to live on with one. And I had advantages unthinkable to many of the long-term poor – health, stamina, a working car, and no children to care for and support. Certainly nothing in my experience contradicts the conclusion of Kathryn Edin and Laura Lein, in their recent book *Making Ends Meet: How Single Mothers Survive Welfare and Low-Wage Work*, that low-wage work actually involves more hardship and deprivation than life at the mercy of the welfare state. In the coming months and years, economic conditions for the working poor are bound to worsen, even without the almost inevitable recession. As mentioned earlier, the influx of former welfare recipients into the low-skilled workforce will have a depressing effect on both wages and the number of jobs available. A general economic downturn will only enhance these effects, and the working poor will of course be facing it without the slight, but nonetheless often saving, protection of welfare as a backup.

The thinking behind welfare reform was that even the humblest jobs are morally uplifting and psychologically buoying. In reality they are likely to be fraught with insult and stress. But I did discover one redeeming feature of the most abject low-wage work – the camaraderie of people who are, in almost all cases, far too smart and funny and caring for the work they do and the wages they're paid. The hope, of course, is that someday these people will come to know what they're worth, and take appropriate action.

NOTES

1 According to the Department of Housing and Urban Development, the "fair-market rent" for an efficiency is $551 here in Monroe County, Florida. A comparable rent in the five boroughs of New York City is $704; in San Francisco, $713; and in the heart of Silicon Valley, $808. The fair-market rent for an area is defined as the amount that would be needed to pay rent plus utilities for "privately owned, decent, safe, and sanitary rental housing of a modest (non-luxury) nature with suitable amenities."

2 According to the Fair Labor Standards Act, employers are not required to pay "tipped employees," such as restaurant servers, more than $2.13 an hour in direct wages. However, if the sum of tips plus $2.13 an hour falls below the minimum wage, or $5.15 an hour, the employer is required to make up the difference. This fact was not mentioned by managers or otherwise publicized at either of the restaurants where I worked.

3 I could find no statistics on the number of employed people living in cars or vans, but according to the National Coalition for the Homeless's 1997 report "Myths and Facts About Homelessness," nearly one in five homeless people (in twenty-nine cities across the nation) is employed in a full- or part-time job.

4 Until April 1998, there was no federally mandated right to bathroom breaks. According to Marc Linder and Ingrid Nygaard, authors of *Void Where Prohibited: Rest Breaks and the Right to Urinate on Company Time* (Cornell University Press, 1997), "The right to rest and void at work is not high on the list of social or political causes supported by professional or executive employees, who enjoy personal workplace liberties that millions of factory workers can only daydream about. . . . While we were dismayed to discover that workers lacked an acknowledged legal right to void at work, [the workers] were amazed by outsiders' naive belief that their employers would permit them to perform this basic bodily function when necessary. . . . A factory worker, not allowed a break for six-hour stretches, voided into pads worn inside her uniform; and a kindergarten teacher in a school without aides had to take all twenty children with her to the bathroom and line them up outside the stall door when she voided."

5   In 1996, the number of persons holding two or more jobs averaged 7.8 million, or 6.2 percent of the workforce. It was about the same rate for men and for women (6.1 versus 6.2), though the kinds of jobs differ by gender. About two thirds of multiple jobholders work one job full-time and the other part-time. Only a heroic minority – 4 percent of men and 2 percent of women – work two full-time jobs simultaneously. (From John F. Stinson Jr., "New Data on Multiple Jobholding Available from the CPS," in the Monthly Labor Review, March 1997.)

BUILDING SUCCESSFUL MULTICULTURAL ORGANIZATIONS: CHALLENGES AND OPPORTUNITIES

MARLENE G. FINE

MULTICULTURAL POLICIES AND PRACTICES

An organizational culture that is open, supportive, and flexible should give rise to organizational policies and practices that also are open, supportive, and flexible. Multicultural policies and practices are open to new people and their cultures are supportive and nurturing to all employees, and are sufficiently flexible to accommodate the needs of all employees. Multicultural policies and practices should pervade all aspects of the organization, from marketing through operations, not just human resource management. Human resources must be the starting point, however, in developing multicultural policies and practices because a multicultural work force that is multiculturally literate provides the foundation for multicultural organizational policies and practices.

Recruiting and hiring a multicultural work force

Proactive recruiting

Organizations that want to develop a multicultural work force should continue (or implement, if they have not already done so) their proactive recruiting efforts. Although issues of cultural diversity have supplanted affirmative action concerns in organizations, the concept of proactive recruiting, which is inherent in affirmative action, is still very important. [. . .]

Proactive recruiting can take a variety of forms. Companies can expand their employment advertising beyond traditional outlets. In many areas of the country, for example, minority communities have their own newspapers and television stations. In Boston, many companies routinely advertise employment opportunities in the *Bay State Banner*, a local newspaper that has wide readership in communities of color. Organizations can also recruit through the networks that are most influential in particular minority communities. Organizations that are serious about recruiting African Americans, for example, need to make connections in local African American churches and community youth programs. In some instances, companies need to recruit out of their geographical location. GrandMet, for example, expanded its recruiting out of its primarily white midwestern location in order to create a pool of applicants of color.

Printing advertisements in traditional newspapers or professional journals that say "EEO/Equal Opportunity Employer" or "Women and Minorities Invited to Apply" is not enough. Proactive recruiting involves positive action, going to others rather than waiting for them to come to you. [. . .]

Often the lack of representation of particular cultural groups within a profession or industry is the result of that group's lack of representation in educational programs that provide the necessary training or credentials for positions in the profession or industry. For example, colleges and universities have difficulty hiring minority faculty in many disciplines. Although the reasons for the difficulty are varied and generally complex, one fundamental reason is that there is not a sufficiently large pool of minority candidates with Ph.D.s from which to recruit. To eliminate that problem, institutions of higher education need to find ways to place more minority candidates in the academic pipeline. They could, for example, hire talented minority students who have a Master's degree, sponsor their doctoral work, and guarantee them a tenure-track position if they satisfactorily complete their doctoral degrees. Some universities have formed consortia to offer scholarships to women and/or students of color that want to pursue doctoral degrees in academic fields in which women or people of color are underrepresented. Although these programs do not provide a guarantee to the sponsoring institutions that the students will join their faculties when their degrees are completed, they do increase the pool of available candidates, thus improving recruiting efforts at all colleges and universities.

Several years ago, the Boston hotels developed an innovative program for developing minority managers, in which each member hotel identified employees of color who it believed had management potential. These employees came from the ranks of chambermaids and other jobs that are generally not considered for management positions because they lack the necessary education and training. The employees were offered management training, paid for by all the participating hotels. When they completed the training, they could be hired by any hotel in the group that had an appropriate management position available.

An important cultural issue is embedded in proactive recruiting. Members of minority cultures that have been historically excluded from traditionally white institutions are understandably suspicious of the genuineness of the invitation to apply for employment. Simply telling them that they are welcome to apply is insufficient to overcome their suspicions. In fact, the verbal invitation, whether written or oral, is often viewed as just another lie, given to meet the letter but not the spirit of the law. Companies that do not back up their words with actions to match them often find themselves having difficulty recruiting people of color. [. . .]

Successful recruiting involves knowing and understanding the cultural expectations of the communities in which you plan to recruit. Several years ago, I attended a senior level meeting at a federal agency in which senior managers were reporting that they were not having any success recruiting young African American college graduates to the agency. They said that they were losing the young graduates to industry, where they could command significantly higher salaries than they could working for the government. The Equal Employment Opportunity officer, an older African American male, listened to the conversation for a while, then told the managers that they were using the wrong strategy. He suggested that recruiters stress the agency's mission and the contribution that the agency makes to the public good, rather than apologizing for the lower salary. African Americans have a long history of government employment, both because government positions were open to blacks long before corporate America opened its doors, and because African American culture highly values community service. [. . .]

Redefining qualifications

Redefining job qualifications can take a variety of forms, from recognizing the organizational skills inherent in raising a family and maintaining a household to reconceptualizing the job itself. Whatever form it takes, however, redefining job qualifications does not mean hiring less qualified employees; it means, instead, hiring differently qualified employees.

The most common form of redefining qualifications is recognizing nontraditional ways of acquiring particular skills. Most positions in organizations require a particular set of skills, and individual organizations and professions tend to have a fixed idea about how people acquire those skills. [. . .]

Fixed concepts of appropriate education, training, or experience can both severely limit the pool of qualified applicants and exclude women and people of color. For example, companies based in one part of the country often recruit heavily at colleges and universities in their region, and, in some instances, firms show a marked preference for graduates of local schools. In Boston, for example, where higher education is one of the city's biggest businesses, firms have a tendency to recruit locally because so many college graduates are available. And given the New England elitism that favors private over public schools, graduates of private schools are generally preferred. Statistically, however, limiting recruiting to people who have degrees from Boston, or even New England, schools severely restricts the number of African Americans, Hispanics, and American Indians who will be hired. If Boston companies want to increase the pool of applicants, they need to recruit and be willing to hire people with degrees from schools outside of New England. . . .

Expanding the definition of the education and experience that fit a particular job also should include a willingness to consider unusual qualifications. Many women who are returning to or just entering the work force after spending a number of years at home raising children argue quite convincingly that their experience at home has given them excellent organizational and interpersonal skills. Historically, women have also filled the vast majority of volunteer positions in the United States, and have been active in community, school, and religious activities. In these positions, they have acquired numerous business skills, such as fundraising, organizing events, developing and overseeing large budgets, mobilizing resources, and negotiating with different constituencies. [. . .]

This tendency to adhere to rigid definitions of appropriate qualifications also restricts employees' mobility within an organization. For example, human resource departments are known as female-friendly departments, and they are often staffed by women. Most senior women in organizations, in fact, are from the human resource function. Because human resources is a support function, however, and one that is often considered less central than other support areas in organizations, women are rarely able to make a lateral move to a central area. The typical line of succession promotes people with experience in operations, who have line authority, or people in staff positions in the financial end of the business. The conventional wisdom is that experience in human resources does not give managers a sufficient background in understanding the company and what it does. That conventional wisdom frequently limits women's promotional opportunities.

African Americans face similar promotional barriers. For example, African American males are often tapped to be the Equal Employment Opportunity or affirmative action officers in organizations, positions that carry important titles and admission to senior management meetings, but rarely include any line authority. As are positions in human resources, these positions are often an organizational deadend for the people in them.

To find senior women and people of color to appoint, organizations need to look beyond traditional career paths, ignore conventional wisdom, and promote people based on unconventional aspects of their experience, education, or training. Organizations can look at employees' activities and achievements in the community; at the skills required to do the work in their current positions, even if the work itself is not similar to the work in the position for which they are being considered; or at personal characteristics that suggest the person will be able to learn new concepts and take on new responsibilities. These individuals are no less qualified – they are just differently qualified. And, in some cases, people with different qualifications can bring new visions of how to accomplish work creatively and productively.

Redefining qualifications, however, can go well beyond recognizing nontraditional ways of acquiring the requisite skills. For some positions, organizations need to reconceptualize the qualifications and skills that are actually needed to accomplish the work. Often such reconceptualizations are based on reorganizing departments or functions; sometimes they are based on redefining or refocusing the organization's mission, objectives, or strategies. For example, if a manufacturing firm seeks to increase its market share by developing a new market among Hispanic consumers, it will need employees working in new product development and marketing who are knowledgeable about Hispanic culture. Once that strategy has been set by the company, the qualifications for some positions in product management or marketing must change. I am not suggesting that certain positions be reserved for members of particular cultural groups, or that, in this example, a non-Hispanic would be incapable of doing the work. I am suggesting, rather, that knowledge of Hispanic culture is necessary to accomplish the work. All things being equal, an Hispanic applicant may be more qualified for the position than a non-Hispanic. [. . .]

Supervision and evaluation

As I stated previously, having a culturally diverse work force does not guarantee that an organization will have a multicultural culture. Creating that culture also requires supervision and evaluation practices and policies that accommodate and nurture cultural differences.

Culturally appropriate supervision

All employees need supervision, but the degree and kind of attention they need varies by individual. Supervisors who provide culturally appropriate supervision are able to both motivate individual employees by using culturally specific incentives, and create cohesive and productive teamwork among culturally diverse employees.

Culturally appropriate supervision bears little resemblance to the traditional concept of supervision, which is defined as directing and inspecting the work of employees. In culturally appropriate supervision, the supervisor's role is neither to ensure rigid conformance to established modes of doing work nor to create employees in the supervisor's image. Instead, the supervisor's task is to provide the environment and resources that all of his or her employees need to be fully productive members of the organization. Culturally appropriate supervision empowers employees, enlarging instead of constraining their modes of working. Managers serve rather than supervise their employees: They are used by or are of use to their employees rather than vice versa.

Providing culturally appropriate supervision requires training in both multicultural literacy and management as service. To create culturally diverse work teams, managers must recognize and value diverse work styles, problem-solving strategies, ways of learning and knowing, and opinions about problems and solutions. To learn how to recognize and value diversity, managers need to learn about different cultures and how to ask questions when they encounter new cultures or behaviors they do not know how to interpret. They also need to explore the implications of viewing supervision as service rather than direction.

Asking questions, serving others, and being sensitive to nuances of difference in the behavior and demeanor of others are all part of a process of decentering the self and making others the central focus. That process dramatically alters the task of managing, and suggests a new and very different picture of the skills and personal characteristics of good managers. Traditionally, organizations have valued and rewarded individual initiative and individual achievement. Individuals who are identified as "comers" in the organization are promoted to managerial positions; they stand out because they combine technical expertise with personal drive and motivation. Those qualities, however, make them self-centered and focused on their own achievements, characteristics that undermine their ability to manage a culturally diverse work force. Managers, therefore, need to learn how to readjust their lenses and focus on others rather than themselves.

In addition to ensuring that managers receive appropriate training, organizations also need to develop reward systems that reward managers for their new roles. Performance appraisals should include an evaluation of a manager's ability to create culturally diverse teams and to motivate culturally diverse employees. In making that evaluation, evaluators need to gather information from team members. The productivity of the team as a whole and the job satisfaction of individual team members are important indicators of how well a manager is serving the team.

Culturally specific assessments of behavior

Successful reward systems in organizations depend, to a large extent, on fair and appropriate assessments of behavior. In a culturally diverse organization, fair assessments of an employee's behavior must be culturally specific; in other words, the assessments should be based on interpretations of the behavior that are within the employee's cultural frame. For example, an Asian worker who speaks softly should not be identified as shy or lacking in leadership qualities. Asians are usually soft spoken, but that vocal quality reflects their cultural upbringing rather than their sociability or leadership abilities.

Culturally specific assessments of behavior are not only based on identifying the appropriate cultural frame for interpreting the behavior, they also depend on identifying and defining the required behaviors. Managers need to define clearly the attributes they value in workers, and to question their tacit assumptions about those attributes. For example, good communication skills are almost always at the top of the list of requisite skills for managers. When I ask managers what they mean by good communication skills, they usually say they mean the ability to speak or write well, or to talk to other people one-on-one. Those definitions, however, are circular; they do not specify the particular communicative behaviors that make up good communication. Without a clear definition of the specific behaviors involved in good communication, the assessment category can become an excuse to screen out people who are different.

Several years ago, in an organizational training session with managers on communicating across gender and race, I asked the participants to describe the communication skills of good managers. Later in the session, participants were asked to describe how men and women communicate. When the individual lists were combined to create a composite sketch of male and female communication characteristics, the participants were surprised to discover that the list of female characteristics was virtually identical to the earlier list they had created describing the communication skills of good managers. The group was quiet for a moment, until a male manager asked, "If women have better communication skills, then why do we promote so few women to management positions?"

One part of the answer to that question is that managers often do not specify the behavioral characteristics of good communicators. Instead, evaluation forms usually include the global category, "communication skills," and the assessment of "good" communication skills generally gets attached to white males. Having evaluators deconstruct the global category and define clearly the specific behaviors that compose the category often causes them to question tacit assumptions about who performs well and who does not.

Another way to raise questions about tacit assumptions about job performance is to ask a wider range of people to evaluate an individual's performance. A multicultural team is likely to bring together different understandings of an employee's performance, creating a fuller and more accurate assessment. [. . .]

Development and support

Organizations need to develop and support a multicultural work force, providing both career development opportunities and social and emotional support for employees. I have put career development and social/emotional support together because they are interdependent activities. The psychological well-being of employees is often affected by whether they believe that they can develop professionally in the organization. Employees who believe that they are at a professional deadend in an organization generally lose interest in and commitment to their jobs. Conversely, their professional success depends on their ability to cope with the social and emotional stresses of organizational life.

While this interdependence of professional development and social/emotional support is true for all employees, it is especially significant for employees who have historically been excluded from organizational life. Traditional professional development opportunities in organizations favor white males, and women and people of color face additional stress in the workplace based on their cultural differences. The combination of the lack of professional opportunities and the additional job stress intensifies the pressures on women and people of color, often deadening their creativity and diminishing their productivity, and sometimes driving them out of organizational life.

Career development

Most organizations provide little support in the area of career development for any employees. Career development opportunities usually comprise a few management training courses and some general or technical skills courses (e.g., public speaking, writing, computer applications, sales, new accounting procedures). A few large organizations have succession planning programs in place, but these provide opportunities for only a few senior personnel in the organization. A full range of career development offerings might include providing information about careers in general and specific jobs that are available in the company, offering employees different career tracks and opportunities to move to new jobs, access to mentoring relationships, support for education and training generally, and special training programs.

Although all employees, regardless of gender or race, should have access to career development programs and can benefit significantly from them, women and people of color have particular needs and can reap particular benefits from them.

Support for career development begins with providing information about careers, both generically and more specifically within the organization. Most people have a fairly narrow range of vision about the career opportunities they have, and they rarely think beyond their next move, which is usually seen as a step up the organizational ladder from their current position. All employees need to be able to expand their vision, and to think more broadly about the possibilities they have based on their skills and interests.

Being able to envision one's self in a different job or a new career path depends in large part on an individual's knowledge of the new job. Many people gain that knowledge through the people we know personally: through families, friends, communities, and work. Women and people of color often lack access to that knowledge because either they encounter few professionals or business people in their families and communities, or they have been socialized into particular career and job expectations. Organizations can expand the opportunities available to women and people of color simply by developing a resource library with information about particular jobs and careers. Having human resource staff available who can provide advice about preparation for particular jobs or careers, resume writing, interviewing, and other career skills would be even more helpful.

In addition to providing information and advice, organizations can expand the career opportunities of women and people of color by developing new career paths within the organization that include lateral moves and different career tracks. Traditional career paths in organizations tend to mirror the hierarchical assumptions of male patterns of thinking and organizing. Success is defined in terms of moving up the organizational ladder. The next step on the ladder is usually occupied by the person above you on the organizational chart, and at some point in the ascent, the steps shift from technical to managerial.

Other organizational moves are necessary, however, to ensure that women and people of color have adequate opportunities for professional growth and personal success. Just as women are often socialized into particular careers (e.g., teaching, social work, and nursing), women and people of color are often pigeonholed into particular places in organizations. Human resources, as was mentioned, is sometimes characterized as an organizational ghetto for women. Breaking out of the ghetto requires that women develop expertise in other areas of the organization, especially functional rather than support areas. A lateral move to a different department could be helpful in gaining the necessary knowledge and experience to fashion a new and more rewarding career path.

Other alternative career paths are also helpful in attracting and retaining diverse workers. [. . .] [O]rganizations might consider offering employees a variety of career tracks as options. For example, women or men could choose more flexible job configurations that would give them more time at home with young children or ill family members or to devote to community service. Although assuming that women should be responsible for raising children is sexist, recognizing the reality that women usually take on that responsibility (along with the responsibility of caring for elderly parents) is pragmatic. Organizations that offer women options such as flextime, job sharing, and shorter work weeks enhance their ability to attract and retain women employees.

[This] concept also opens the door to other career tracks. For example, not all employees who have technical expertise in their professional fields (e.g., accounting, engineering, science, information systems) want to move into managerial positions. Yet unless they do, their careers tend to stall out, leaving them with no opportunities to receive organizational rewards and no incentives to improve their skills. Professional/technical career tracks would give employees who want to continue to specialize in their technical areas the opportunity to advance their careers without taking on managerial responsibilities.

I am not suggesting that all women and people of color need or want alternative career tracks, nor am I suggesting that employees who choose these options will always have the same opportunities to showcase their talents that employees in more conventional positions generally have. I am only saying that organizations that offer a variety of career tracks will be better able to support a diverse work force, including white males. [. . .]

Mentoring is another aspect of career development that is important for the success of women and people of color. A mentor is an experienced manager who relates well to a less experienced employee and facilitates the personal development of that employee (Kram, 1985). Mentoring relationships usually develop informally in organizations, most often between individuals who are drawn together because they share a common background or interests. Mentors serve a variety of functions for their protégés, both aiding them in their career development and supporting them interpersonally (Noe, 1988). Mentors may sponsor their protégés for new positions or assignments, give them visibility in the organization, coach them on their managerial skills, protect them from organizational politics, or just be available for informal discussions about their work or personal lives. Mentors also serve as role models, helping less experienced employees learn how to negotiate organizational life.

Although all employees benefit from mentoring, women and people of color often need mentoring to a greater extent than do white men. They especially need mentors who can serve as role models. Some women, for example, need mentors who will help them overcome sex-role stereotypes. People of color, particularly African Americans, need mentors who can show them how to deal with the subtle (and sometimes not so subtle) racism that pervades most organizations in the United States.

Despite their greater need, women and people of color often have difficulty finding mentors. Organizational studies show that people generally feel most comfortable with members of their own sex and/or race. Since most mentoring relationships develop spontaneously between people who feel a natural affinity toward each other, they are usually same-sex or same-race relationships. The paucity of women and people of color in senior positions substantially decreases the likelihood that women and people of color will informally find mentors.

Even when women and people of color try to cross gender and racial boundaries in establishing mentoring relationships, several other factors decrease the chances that they will be mentored. First, they tend to be outside of the informal organizational networks where mentors are available. They are not likely to be playing golf, tennis, or squash at the same clubs as more senior white males, nor are they likely to be asked to have drinks with a group of senior managers after working hours. Second, women and people of color are less likely to be identified as a "rising star" in the organization. Just as protégés seek mentors who have access to power and organizational resources, mentors look for protégés who have the potential to make the mentor's star shine even brighter. [. . .]

Organizations can create opportunities for women and people of color to find mentors through formal mentoring programs. Although the concept of a *formal* mentoring program is somewhat of an oxymoron (since mentoring relationships are usually spontaneous and informal), formal mentoring programs can work. For such programs to be successful, however, organizations must adequately prepare participants and must create structural changes that encourage mentoring (Burke & McKeen, 1988). First, both mentors and their protégés need to participate in training programs that allow them to learn about mentoring and to explore their respective roles as mentors and protégés. Second, the reward system needs to be changed to include rewards for successfully mentoring less experienced employees; concomitantly, the performance appraisal system should be revised to include evaluations of an employee's performance as either (or both) mentor and protégé. Third, organizations need to create new job designs that encourage more frequent and meaningful interaction among junior and senior employees. In addition to these structural changes, companies need to develop a pool of qualified and trained mentors and to match mentors and protégés carefully. In some cases, organizations may need to look externally for suitable mentors.

Social/emotional support

Having a social support network is fundamental to the psychological health of most individuals. Although our closest interpersonal relationships are usually with family members or friends outside of the workplace, most of us enjoy personal friendships with at least a few coworkers and friendly acquaintanceships with others. These relationships give us places to go at work where we can be ourselves without being afraid that a moment of vulnerability, or a comment made in anger or jest, will be used against us.

Many women and people of color either do not have the opportunity to establish such friendships or cannot afford the luxury of trusting others in the organization, although the stress created by their numerical isolation and cultural differences heightens their need for interpersonal support. Women and people of color need to have opportunities at work to be with others who are like themselves and who will allow them to be themselves. They need to talk with other people who can help them do some reality testing so that they can distinguish discrimination and racism from the ordinary hurdles everyone in an organization encounters and endures.

Organizations can help women and people of color cope with the stress of being different by encouraging and supporting both informal and formal social networking. Networks can range from informal lunchtime groups to more structured, formal bodies, such as a women's caucus that carries the imprimatur of the company. Both kinds of network provide needed social and emotional support for women and people of color. More formal structures can also give them a voice in the organization and provide management a way to gather information about their needs and concerns. [. . .]

REFERENCES

Burke, R. J. & McKeen, C. (1988). Work and family: What we know and what we need to know. *Canadian Journal of Administrative Sciences*, 5: 30–40.

Kram, K. E. (1985). *Mentoring at work: Developmental relationships in organizational life.* Glenview, IL: Scott Foresman.

Noe, R. A. (1988). Women and mentoring: A review and research agenda. *Academy of Management Review*, 13 (1): 65–78.

DIVERSITY: OVERVIEW

ROBIN J. ELY AND ERICA GABRIELLE FOLDY

"Diversity" hit the radar screen of American managers in the late 1980s when the Hudson Institute released its now widely cited report about the changing demographics of the American labor force (Johnston & Packer, 1987). By the year 2000, it projected, 85 percent of new entrants to the workforce would be women, people of color, and new immigrants. The report was a godsend for those in search of corporate attention to their concerns about inequality in the workplace, and many used these projections to create a sense of urgency among managers and educators alike. In the face of such broad demographic change, they argued, organizations that do not cultivate and use the talents of their entire staff risk losing their competitive edge (Morrison, White, & Van Velsor, 1992). This message has launched thousands of diversity initiatives in large and small organizations, across industries, economic sectors, and geographic areas.

Since then, the term "diversity" has been used to capture all manner of differences in the workplace including differences in social identities, such as gender, race, ethnicity, sexual orientation, class, nationality, and religion; differences in organizational groups, such as functional or educational background and tenure; and differences in individual characteristics, such as idiosyncratic attitudes, values, cognitive styles, and preferences. In Part VI we are concerned with differences in social identities, how they shape the kinds of experiences people have at work, and the effect they have on the way work groups function.

We begin with an excerpt from Deborah Merrill-Sands, Evangelina Holvino, and James Cumming's, "Working with diversity: A focus on global organizations," which explains what we mean by social identity, or a "social differences lens" on diversity. This reading illustrates why something we may take for granted, like our gender or racial identity, is actually far more complex than we might imagine. Even more importantly, it illustrates how social identity group memberships are associated in the larger society with certain power positions, such that some social identity groups have greater power, prestige, and status than others. In Western society, men, as a group, are more powerful – have higher status and hold more positions of formal organizational and political power – than women, as a group. Similarly whites are more powerful than people of color; presumed heterosexuals are more powerful than lesbian, gay, bisexual, or transgendered people; and the middle, upper-middle, and upper classes are more powerful than the working or lower classes. To understand the impact of social diversity in work groups, one must consider the history of social relations among social identity groups, especially the relative power positions of these groups both in the work organization and the societal context in which it is embedded.

WORKPLACE EXPERIENCES

Social identity groups' relative power positions shape members' workplace experiences and outcomes in important ways. A great deal of research has documented the difficulties encountered in the workplace by those in the lower power position, including white women, immigrants, people of color, gays and lesbians, and people with disabilities (Creed & Scully, 2000; Greenhaus, Parasuraman, & Wormley, 1990; Ibarra, 1993; Kanter, 1977; Mighty, 1997; Powell & Butterfield, 1997; Stone & Colella, 1996). Such difficulties range from lower salaries and fewer promotions, to weaker social networks and fewer mentoring opportunities, to feelings of marginality and isolation, to the suffering of outright and explicit discrimination.[1]

In Part VI, we delve more deeply into the subjective experiences of some of these groups. For background, we recommend a report from Catalyst (1999), a research and consulting firm on women in the for-profit sector, that summarizes the results of a survey of women managers and professionals of Asian, Hispanic, and African descent in Fortune 1000 companies. Focusing specifically on career advancement, it reports that women from these three groups feel that they face significant obstacles to advancement, such as fewer ties to influential colleagues and fewer high-visibility assignments. The report also indicates that women of color are promoted less rapidly than white women.

The second reading is a chapter from Ella Bell and Stella Nkomo's book, *Our Separate Ways: Black and White Women and the Struggle for Professional Identity*, an extensive study of black and white women executives. In this reading, Bell and Nkomo explore differences in how these two groups of women view the barriers to their advancement. Most simply, whereas white women may face a "glass ceiling," African American women encounter "a concrete wall topped by a glass ceiling" (p. 343). Both groups are often held to a higher standard and excluded from informal networks, but these problems manifest differently for black and white women. In addition, black women face "daily doses of racism" at work (p. 345).

DIVERSITY INITIATIVES IN ORGANIZATIONS

Part VI closes by examining organizational diversity initiatives – both what they look like and what they accomplish. While organizations have always managed diversity – women, people of color, and immigrants have long constituted a significant portion of the US labor market – the Hudson Institute's projections came at a time when ongoing societal and ideological shifts were forcing managers to revamp the strategies they had traditionally employed. The USA had moved from a system of legal segregation, where blacks and whites were legally isolated from each other, to the abolition of legal racism. Likewise, the women's movement, along with broad economic and demographic changes, was responsible for a host of legal and social reforms, which transformed significantly the nature of sex roles in our society. Prior to these changes, racial segregation of work and the importation of rigidly prescribed sex roles from the home and family constituted the organizational mechanisms by which diversity was "managed." These mechanisms served to obfuscate the reality of a diverse workforce, and to support, from the perspective of the dominant culture, the myth of a homogeneous workplace. But changes in societal paradigms for dealing with inequality changed work roles for many white women and minorities. With members of these groups moving into managerial and professional positions traditionally reserved for white men, the assumption of homogeneity became less easy to sustain. Organizations found themselves, for the first time, needing to respond more competitively to the employment demands and requirements of these workers.

At the same time, a growing emphasis on quality as the key to success in a competitive and global marketplace prompted management to rely increasingly on better teamwork, more flexibility, and an organizational culture that encourages people to contribute their full range of abilities to the work at hand. These efforts reinforce for people that it is not only what they do, but also who they are, that matters. Identity thus came to the fore as a potential source of relevant experience, knowledge, and insight. It seemed reasonable to assume, at least in theory, that a more diverse workforce would be better equipped to bring a broader range of perspectives to increasingly complex problems.

The result was a proliferation of books, articles, and courses on managing diversity (see, e.g., Esty, Griffin & Hirsch, 1995; Kossek & Lobel, 1996; Loden & Rosener, 1991). It is fair to say that we have learned a significant amount from this work. Nevertheless, diversity initiatives have not, for the most part, delivered on their promise. They are controversial in many workplaces among members of all social identity groups, and they rarely catalyze the fundamental changes that are necessary in organizations for them to be effective. Prasad and Mills (1997) offer a critical perspective on the managing diversity "movement" for its "upbeat naivete" (1997: 5) and general ignorance of "the multitude of political interactions between dominant and non-dominant groups within organizations" (1997: 18). These authors argue that without very direct attention to the power differentials among different groups in organizations, diversity initiatives will achieve little.

Another approach to diversity programs acknowledges their limitations, but suggests practical, if challenging, ways to overcome them. The last reading, "Making differences matter: A new paradigm for managing diversity," by David Thomas and Robin Ely, addresses an important puzzle: heterogeneity brings with it both difficulties and opportunities. Mixed groups tend to be more creative and make better decisions (Watson, Kumar, & Michaelson, 1993; Cox, Lobel, & McLeod, 1991); however, they also are likely to experience greater conflict and miscommunication (Shaw, 1981; Tsui, Egan, & Xin, 1995). This reading addresses the crucial question: what can managers do to eliminate the negative effects of diversity and, at the same time, turn diversity into an asset? It suggests that an organization's "diversity perspective" is what makes the difference. A diversity perspective is the set of normative beliefs and expectations about social identity diversity and its role in a work group. It includes the rationale that guides people's efforts to create and respond to social identity diversity in a work group; normative beliefs about the value of social identity at work; expectations about the kind of impact, if any, social identity differences can and should have on the group and its work; and beliefs about what constitutes progress toward the ideal multicultural work group (Ely & Thomas, 2001). Thomas and Ely identified three such perspectives: the discrimination-and-fairness perspective, the access-and-legitimacy perspective, and the learning-and-effectiveness perspective.[2] Their research suggests that, whereas all three have been successful in motivating managers to diversify their staffs, only the learning-and-effectiveness perspective provides the rationale and guidance needed to achieve sustained benefits from diversity.

DIVERSITY PERSPECTIVES AND GENDER FRAMES

Not surprisingly, there are some parallels between these diversity perspectives and the gender frames described in this book – after all, gender is often a central focus of many diversity initiatives, so the logic surrounding gender equity becomes intertwined with diversity more broadly. Most importantly, we see the fourth frame and the learning-and-effectiveness perspective as mutually reinforcing. According to the learning-and-effectiveness perspective, the insights, skills, and experiences employees have developed as members of various social identity groups are potentially valuable resources that the organization can use to rethink its primary tasks and redefine its markets, products, and business practices in ways that will advance its mission. Hence, just as Frame 4 uses women's entry into the workplace as an occasion for critically examining traditional beliefs about work and organizations, so too the learning-and-effectiveness perspective links diversity to work processes – the way people do and experience the work – in a manner that makes diversity a resource for learning and adaptive change.

An access-and-legitimacy perspective on diversity is based in a recognition that the organization's markets and constituencies are culturally diverse. It therefore behooves the organization to match that diversity in parts of its own workforce as a way of gaining access to and legitimacy with those markets and constituent groups. This perspective constitutes the rationale behind the now popularly touted "business case for diversity" (Cox & Blake, 1991). Frame 2, or the "celebrate differences" frame, takes a similarly instrumental view of gender, suggesting that women bring to the organization a set of traits and skills that the organization can use to its advantage. In both cases, however, organizations typically fail to incorporate the cultural competencies of target groups into their core functions. As a result, these groups remain marginalized in roles that are often devalued. Devaluing, dismissing, or making invisible important aspects of work limits organizational knowledge, learning, and adaptability (Fletcher, 1999).

Finally, the discrimination-and-fairness perspective is characterized by a belief in a culturally diverse workforce as a moral imperative to ensure justice and the fair treatment of all members of society. It focuses diversification efforts on providing equal opportunities in hiring and promotion, suppressing prejudicial attitudes, and eliminating discrimination. In contrast to the previous two perspectives, in the discrimination-and-fairness perspective there is no instrumental link between diversity and the group's work. According to this perspective, one measures progress in diversity by how well a work group achieves its recruitment and retention goals. Numbers are a key indicator of success. Hence, its advocates often use the assimilative and legislative tactics of Frames 1 and 3, respectively. In this perspective, with no instrumental link between these efforts and the organization's work, however, and with people's attention narrowly focused on questions about fair treatment, social identity differences are a sensitive topic, and people are easily defensive. This uneasiness limits people's ability to bring all relevant skills and insights to bear on their work, thus compromising their ability to be maximally effective.

These readings were chosen to convey something of the complexity of what it means to address diversity and difference in organizations. When a work organization chooses this path, it chooses to challenge deeply embedded ways of thinking, working, and organizing. In fact, when organizations do this work, they go beyond their own boundaries to become social change agents.

NOTES

1   We address a number of these problems in Part V, where we consider how opportunities are structured differently for different groups.
2   This perspective is labeled the "integration-and-learning" perspective in Ely and Thomas (2001).

REFERENCES

Catalyst 1999. *Women of Color in Corporate Management: Opportunities and Barriers.* New York: Catalyst.

Cox, T. & Blake, S. 1991. Managing cultural diversity: Implications for organizational effectiveness. *The Executive,* 5(3): 45–56.

Cox, T., Lobel, S. & McLeod, P. 1991. Effects of ethnic group cultural differences on competitive and cooperative behavior on a group task. *Academy of Management Journal,* 34(4): 827–47.

Creed, W. E. D. & Scully, M. A. 2000. Songs of ourselves: Employees' deployment of social identity in workplace encounters. *Journal of Management Inquiry,* 9(4): 391–412.

Ely, R. J. & Thomas, D. A. 2001. Cultural diversity at work: The effects of diversity perspectives on work group processes and outcomes. *Administrative Science Quarterly,* 46: 229–73.

Esty, K., Griffin, R. & Hirsch, M. S. 1995. *Workplace diversity: A manager's guide to solving problems and turning diversity into a competitive advantage.* Holbrook, MA: Adams Media Corporation.

Fletcher, J. K. 1999. *Disappearing acts: Gender, power, and relational practice at work.* Cambridge, MA: MIT Press.

Greenhaus, J. H., Parasuraman, S. & Wormley, W. M. 1990. Effects of race on organizational experiences, job performance evaluations, and career outcomes. *Academy of Management Journal,* 33(1): 64–86.

Ibarra, H. 1993. Personal networks of women and minorities in management: A conceptual framework. *Academy of Management* Review, 18(1): 56–87.

Johnton, W. B. & Packer, A. E. 1987. *Workforce 2000: Work and Workers for the Twenty-First Century.* Indianapolis, IN: Hudson Institute.

Kanter, R. M. 1977/1993. *Men and women of the corporation.* New York: Basic Books.

Kossek, E. E. & Lobel, S. A. 1996. *Managing diversity: Human resource strategies for transforming the workplace.* Cambridge, MA: Blackwell.

Loden, M. & Rosener, J. B. 1991. *Workforce America! Managing employee diversity as a vital resource.* Burr Ridge, IL: Irwin Professional Publishing.

Mighty, E. J. 1997. Triple jeopardy: Immigrant women of color in the labor force. In P. Prasad, A. J. Mills, M. Elmes, and A. Prasad (eds.), *Managing the organizational melting pot: Dilemmas of workplace diversity:* 312–39. Thousand Oaks, CA: Sage.

Morrison, A. M., White, R. & Van Velsor, E. 1992. *The new leaders.* San Francisco: Jossey-Bass.

Powell, G. N. & Butterfield, D. A. 1997. Effect of race on promotions to top management in a federal department. *Academy of Management Journal,* 40(1): 112–28.

Prasad, P. & Mills, A. J. 1997. From showcase to shadow: Understanding the dilemmas of managing workplace diversity. In P. Prasad, A. J. Mills, M. Elmes, and A. Prasad (eds.), *Managing the organizational melting pot: Dilemmas of workplace diversity:* 3–18. Thousand Oaks, CA: Sage.

Shaw, M. 1981. *Group behavior: The psychology of group behavior.* New York: McGraw-Hill.

Stone, D. L. & Colella, A. 1996. A model of factors affecting the treatment of disabled individuals in organizations. *Academy of Management Review,* 21(2): 352–401.

Tsui, A., Egan, T. & Xin, K. 1995. Diversity in organizations: Lessons from demography research. In M. Chemers, S. Okampo, S. and Costanzo, *Diversity in organizations: New perspectives from a changing workplace:* 191–219. Thousand Oaks, CA: Sage.

Watson, W., Kumar, K. & Michaelson, L. 1993. Cultural diversity's impact on interaction process and performance. *Academy of Management Journal,* 36(3): 590–610.

WORKING WITH DIVERSITY: A FOCUS ON GLOBAL ORGANIZATIONS

DEBORAH MERRILL-SANDS AND EVANGELINA HOLVINO
WITH JAMES CUMMING

From Working Paper #11 (2000) Boston, MA: Center for Gender in Organizations, Simmons School of Management

LENSES ON DIVERSITY

. . . While there are many aspects of diversity, we believe it is important for an organization to focus on those aspects that are most salient for its mission, its strategic organizational objectives, its work, its historical context and its operational objectives for working with diversity. For example, an organization with a largely western, Caucasian, male professional workforce may elect to focus on working with gender diversity or functional diversity during the initial stages of a diversity initiative. Alternatively, an organization that has recently had a significant change in the composition of its staff by race and ethnicity may elect to focus on that aspect of diversity first. Diversity in international organizations is among the most complex. Staff members are diverse along multiple dimensions of identity. Stakeholders, partners, clients, and beneficiaries represent a wide range of cultural, social, economic, and political systems. And the organizations' work is targeted to a plurality of regions and countries with diverse political, agro-ecological, and socio-economic conditions. This is why it is so important to tailor a diversity initiative to a specific context.

To assist organizations in developing an operational definition of diversity and selecting an approach that is most relevant, we have synthesized the literature and experience on diversity into three primary approaches, or lenses.

- *Social differences lens* – focuses on differences shaped by membership in identity groups that reflect salient social categories.
- *Cultural differences lens* – focuses on cultural differences of diverse nationalities or ethnic groups.
- *Cognitive-functional lens* – focuses on diversity in task-related knowledge, skills and experiences as well as differences in styles by which individuals access information and acquire knowledge.

These lenses represent distinct and major streams of work on diversity. When focused on organizations, all of these lenses help to shine light on how differences in group affiliation affect the organization's work culture, systems, and work practices, as well as its social relations. They also reveal the effect on the behavior, and work and career outcomes, of individual staff members. The lenses differ primarily in the types of group differences treated. Each lens illuminates specific dimensions of diversity and occludes others, as in a figure ground in which one image is predominant over another depending on the angle of viewing. The variations in emphasis of the three lenses can be seen through definitions of diversity employed (see Box 26.1). . . .

Box 26.1 Definition of Diversity Using Different Lenses

Social differences lens

- "Diversity refers to diversity in identities based on membership in social and demographic groups and how differences in identities affect social relations in organizations. We define diversity as a mixture of people with different group identities within the same social system" (Nkomo and Cox, 1996: 338).
- "Diversity focuses on issues of racism, sexism, heterosexism, classism, ableism and other forms of discrimination at the individual, identity group and system levels" (Cross et al., 1994).
- "Diversity should be understood as the varied perspectives and approaches to work that members of different identity groups bring" (Thomas and Ely, 1996: 80).
- "The concept of diversity . . . can encompass a broad range of differences. . . . But it is those features that make us like some specified group of people and different than other groups that constitute the principal thrust of much [of the] current work on diversity in organizations. Thus, diversity in organizations is typically seen to be composed of variations in race, gender, ethnicity, nationality, sexual orientation, physical abilities, social class, age and other socially meaningful categorizations, *together with the additional differences caused by or signified by these markers*" [emphasis added] (Ferdman, 1995: 37).

Cultural differences lens

- "Diversity exists both within and among cultures; however, within a single culture certain behaviors are favored and others repressed. The norm for a society is the most common and generally acceptable pattern of values, attitudes and behavior. . . . A cultural orientation describes the attitudes of most of the people most of the time, not all of the people all of the time. Accurate stereotypes reflect societal or cultural norms" (Adler, 1986: 17).
- "The term multicultural diversity competence refers to the ability to demonstrate respect and understanding, to communicate effectively and to work collaboratively with people from different cultural backgrounds" (Garcia, 1995).

Cognitive-functional lens

- "Cognitive diversity focuses on the way people take in information, the way they internalize the information and analyze it, and the way they apply the information. Cognitive diversity embraces the spectrum of styles by which individuals acquire knowledge. At the heart of cognitive diversity is the appreciation and acceptance of differences in perceiving, reasoning and problem solving" (Idea Connections, training materials, copyright protected).

- "New sources of diversity from within the organization [include] employees from nontraditional lines of business, functions that have an historically subordinate role, or a newly acquired subsidiary with a distinctive culture" (Kossek and Lobel, 1996: 2).

Broad definitions

- "Diversity among people reflects the many characteristics that make us who we are, including nationality, race, culture, ethnic background, gender, age, religion, native language, physical ability, sexual orientation, education and profession" (International Monetary Fund, 1999).
- "Diverstiy refers to any mixture of items characterized by differences *and* similarities. . . . Diversity refers to the collective [all-inclusive] mixture of differences and similarities along a given dimension" (Thomas, 1995: 246).

SOCIAL DIFFERENCES LENS

The social differences lens focuses on identities, specifically identities that are based on membership in groups that reflect salient social categories, such as race, gender, ethnicity, class, age or sexual orientation. These are categories that can be viewed as socially marked or valenced, meaning that they are significant in shaping how societies are organized and how individuals within societies categorize themselves and others.[1] Often these categories shape the distribution of roles, power, opportunities, and resources in societies. As a result, in many societies, these identity categories are "legislated" to prevent discrimination and ensure equal opportunities.[2]

The social differences lens draws primarily on the fields of sociology and organizational behavior. It reflects three primary streams of research and practice: 1) social identity theory; 2) race and gender research and practice; and 3) organizational demography.[3] This lens focuses on how differences among group identities affect social relations, work behaviors, distribution of opportunities, and work outcomes in organizations. The lens recognizes that "individuals do not leave their racial, gender or ethnic identities at the door when they enter an organization" (Nkomo and Cox, 1996: 342).

A clear concept of identity is fundamental to this lens. Two useful definitions follow:

. . . an [identity] group [is a group] whose members . . . have participated in equivalent historical experiences, are currently subjected to similar social forces, and as a result have consonant world views.

(Alderfer, 1987)

Social identity includes those aspects of the individual's self-identity that derive from the "individual's knowledge of his or her memberships in social groups together with the emotional significance of that knowledge".

(Turner and Giles, 1981: 24)

Social identity theorists emphasize that identity is partially defined through the relationships among diverse groups. They see social identity as shaped by both social categorization and social comparison in which characteristics of one group (e.g., status or power) achieve significance in relation to perceived differences from other groups (Hurtado, 1997; Tajfel, 1982; Turner and Giles, 1981).

Drawing on the various streams of theory and practice that inform the social identity lens, we have distilled five elements that are critical when using this lens to work with diversity in organizations.

- Identities are socially constructed.
- Identity is multidimensional.
- Identity is defined by self-identification as well as categorization by others.
- Social categories and identities embody differences in power and privilege.
- Identities shape cognition, experiences, worldviews, and perspectives.

The following sections offer an expanded explanation of these five elements.

Identities are socially constructed

Identity is not innate or essential, but socially constructed.[4] Identity is defined by the cultural, historical, social, and political context in which an individual or a group is operating. It is this context that shapes the meaning and import of different social categories and the experiences of members who identify with specific groups. For example, the identity of being black in South Africa is constructed very differently from that of being black in Ethiopia where there has not been a potent legacy of colonial oppression and apartheid. The differences in social construction of black identity in these two contexts will result in different identity experiences for individuals and have different impacts on the opportunities available to them. As Cock and Bernstein (1988: 23) argue, "Considering differences in an ahistorical, sociopolitical vacuum lacks any explanatory power, and renders 'diversity' an empty concept".

The socially constructed nature of group identities can result in structural differences in societies and organizations that create privilege for some and disadvantage for others.[5] Gender, race, ethnicity, sexual orientation, class, religion, and age are all identity categories that have operated in this way across different social and historical contexts. Applying this lens in an organizational context helps to illuminate the source and impact of both overt and subtle structural differences on work and career outcomes of members of different identity groups. Historically, this has been the dominant focus of scholars and practitioners using this lens. However, it is important to stress that social construction of identity also shapes the cognitions, experiences, perspectives, values, and worldviews of people belonging to specific identity groups.[6] In this way, this lens also illuminates "the varied perspectives and approaches to work that members of different identity groups bring by virtue of their different life experiences" (Thomas and Ely, 1996: 80). This variety in perspectives and experiences is a knowledge asset that organizations are increasingly trying to optimize.

Identities are multidimensional

Identity is multifaceted and fluid. Individuals have multiple identities and "identities intersect to create an amalgamated identity" (Nkomo and Cox, 1996).[7] How identities interact and which aspects of identity are salient depend on the organizational context in which the person or group is functioning. Hence, being a foreign national might become a salient dimension of one's identity in a work group or organization where the majority of members represent a single nationality. But in a multicultural work group of professionals from similar fields, the individual's age or gender identity might be a more profound marker of difference or similarity. Similarly, individuals within social groups and across different contexts differ in the relative importance they assign to any particular social identity based on their self-concept.[8]

Attention to the multifaceted nature of identity has important implications for working with diversity in organizations. It focuses attention on the variability of experiences among people sharing one common dimension of identity such as gender, but differing in other dimensions such as ethnicity or race. It also underscores the complexity and challenge of working with diversity in organizations. Research in the United States and South Africa, for example, shows how women of color and working-class women tend to be "disappeared" in organizationl change efforts aimed at promoting gender equity (see Box 26.2).[9] Issues, experiences, and concerns of white, middle-class, heterosexual, and professional women as the dominant identity group, have tended to capture the change agenda. Even among professional women as a group, the experiences of white women have overshadowed those of women of color.[10] The lesson is that when multiple identities are not attended to, the experiences of some groups inevitably become marginalized and silenced.

Box 26.2 Implications of Multiple Dimensions of Identity for Fostering Gender Equity in Organizations – Case Examples

The following two examples focus on issues of work–personal life integration. They illustrate the challenges and importance of working with multiple dimensions of identity in diversity initiatives. Organizational interventions aimed at fostering gender equity can have varied impacts on different groups of women depending, for example, on their race or class.

Case example – Race and gender intersections, USA

Ely and Meyerson (1998: 3) illustrate how aspects of identity, such as race and ethnicity, shape some women's experiences in the organization differently from others: "although women of all ethnicities had difficulty moving ahead, the patterns of derailment were different for white women than for women of color. In particular, stereotypes about white women – that they are organized, efficient and productive – kept them in front-office, nine-to-five, staff jobs. In contrast, stereotypes about women of color – that they are less productive but more willing to work nontraditional hours – kept them in equally low-level staff jobs, but doing the kinds of behind-the-scenes, around-the-clock work that the organization ostensibly required to keep it running smoothly. Needless-to-say, these two forms of "ghettoization" had different impacts on the two groups of women. Although both groups were essentially sealed in dead-end jobs, these placements created more childcare problems for women of color than for white women, whose nine-to-five jobs made it easier for them to rely on traditional childcare arrangements. Women of color were absent from work more often than their white counterparts because of the difficulties they had finding reliable, affordable childcare during their work hours, which further reinforced the perception of them as less efficient and less productive."

Case example – Race and gender intersections, South Africa

Marks (2001) illustrates the impact of multiple dimensions of identity on a gender equity initiative in a parastatal in South Africa. As a part of its organizational transformation process after the dismantling of apartheid, the organization reviewed its internal structures and operating systems. In response to equity concerns raised by a women's forum, management created two positions: a gender coordinator for the Gender Unit and an officer for the Affirmative Action Unit. The two units were expected to integrate their work as far as possible. Over time, however, the racial differences among women in the organization became more visible and explicit. The work of the Gender Unit and the women's forum became associated with the issue of white women, who were generally at higher levels of the organization. Black secretaries, for example, did not feel that "real issues" of career advancement, salaries and work schedules that they found most pressing were being addressed by the Gender Unit. At the same time, the work of the Affirmative Action Unit focused on issues of black staff, but here women were a less privileged constituency than men. Again, their priority issues were not at the top of the change agenda. Because both these "disappearing" processes focused on gender as white and race as masculine, women of color and the issues that concerned them most remained marginal in the organization.

Recognizing multiple dimensions of identity also helps us understand why it is often difficult to form alliances among members of diverse identity groups along a single dimension of identity, such as gender or race.[11] For example, focusing again on gender, the experiences and priority concerns of women at upper and lower levels of the hierarchy in organizations are usually very different. Women at senior levels may focus on "glass ceiling" issues of advancement, opportunities for mentoring and access to informal networks. Women at the lower levels may focus on issues of support for childcare, work schedule flexibility, sexual harassment, and salary parity. Blindness to these differences sets up false expectations of shared interests as the basis for forming coalitions for change (see Box 26.2).

Identity is defined by self and others

Identity is defined relationally. It is a category with which individuals identify and a category to which others assign the individual.[12] It is important to recognize that not all individuals within a group view a specific dimension of identity in the same way or as equally important. Regarding categorization by others, it is important to understand that even when people do not self-identify with particular identity groups, others often categorize them as belonging to those groups, especially when physical or other markers are visible.[13] This, in turn, can affect others' expectations of an individual's values, work practices, or interpersonal styles (whether or not these are justified). These dynamics can be thought of in terms of stereotyping, schemas, and dominant group identities.

Stereotyping

Stereotyping is the most blatant result of identity defined by others. Stereotyping is the process of making generalizations about a person or a group based on a perceived difference and little information about them. But it is important to remember that the process of categorizing is often subtle and unconscious, based on an individual's past experiences with members of a specific identity group or cultural and familial learning that have been part of their socialization process. The more competitive the relationship between the in-group and out-group, the more negative the stereotypes that each group has about the other.[14]

Schemas

Valian (1998), in her concept of schemas, stresses that we all carry a set of implicit, or unconscious, hypotheses about different social groups. We draw on these hypotheses, or cognitive frameworks, to categorize new individuals. These schemas also shape our expectations of people of different identity groups, our evaluation of their work and our interpretations of their behaviors. Schemas are natural ways of organizing the world. However, as long as they operate at the unconscious and unarticulated level, they inadvertently influence our interpretation and evaluation of others' behaviors in either an overly positive or negative manner. For example, Ferrari (1972), studying international teams in an intergovernmental organization, found that schemas about people from developed or developing countries defined perceptions of competence. At the formation of new teams, individuals *a priori* assessed those members who were from developed countries as more competent and qualified. Once people had worked together in team context, these implicit rankings disappeared.[15] Alderfer (1992), in a long-term study on race relations in a major corporation in the United States, shows how race schemas shape staff perceptions of equity of opportunities in advancement. He found, for example, that the vast majority of white women and men agreed with the statement that "Qualified blacks are promoted more rapidly than equally qualified whites," while the vast majority of black women and men agreed with the statement that "Qualified whites are promoted more rapidly than equally qualified blacks." These examples illustrate the importance of understanding the schemas that are shaping individual's categorization and expectations of others in any given organizational context as a critical first step in working with diversity.

Dominant identities

One of the most interesting dynamics in self-identification and categorization by others is the tendency for those who belong to traditionally dominant groups in organizations (such as white professional men in organizations of Western industrialized countries) *not* to identify consciously with their identity group. They perceive their identity group implicitly as "the norm" by which every other group is categorized as "the other" (see Box 26.3).[16]

A recurrent finding in the study of whiteness is the fact that white respondents do not consider their "whiteness" as an identity or marker of group membership per se. That is, whiteness is a "natural identity" because it has not been problematic and therefore salient to most respondents in these studies. In fact, most white respondents are hard pressed to define whiteness and the privileges that it brings to those who own it. Interestingly enough, whiteness becomes much more definable when the privilege it accords its owners is lost.

(Hurtado and Stewart, 1996: 299)

Yet, the experience of members of dominant identity groups in organizations is very much shaped by their own and others' schemas, or expectations, of the opportunities, power, and status that accrue to members of such groups. There is a significant body of research on diversity in work groups in Western countries and international teams, for example, that shows that members of dominant and higher status identity groups typically display more aggressive nonverbal behaviors, speak more often, interrupt others more often, state more commands and have more opportunity to influence.[17]

The implications for work on diversity is that attention should not be restricted solely to seeking to understand the schemas that shape expectations and interpretations of behaviors of people in identity groups with minority representation or "newcomer" status. It is equally important to understand and try to make more explicit the schemas that define norms and expectations of members of dominant or established groups.[18] This type of analysis deepens understanding of the subtle processes that can lead to accrued privilege and status for some while disadvantaging others (see Box 26.3). It can also help to identify areas of shared interest, so that members of dominant groups can ally with other groups in promoting organizational change aimed at supporting diversity.[19]

Box 26.3 Making White Privilege Visible

"White Privilege: Unpacking the Invisible Knapsack" is a powerful reflective essay by Peggy McIntosh (1990). As a feminist scholar and practitioner seeking to understand the invisibility of male privilege, she adopted the viewpoint of a white person and undertook a reflective examination of her own unearned privilege, as a white person in the United States. She recognized that as a white person she had been taught about racism as something that puts others at a *dis*advantage. She had not been taught to see the corollary that white privilege is something that put her at an advantage. She concludes that whites are carefully taught not to recognize white privilege, just as men are taught not to recognize male privilege. "For me white privilege has turned out to be an elusive and fugitive subject. The pressure to avoid it is great, for in facing it I must give up the myth of meritocracy."

To make privilege visible and tangible, she constructed a list of 50 advantages that she experiences on a daily basis as a white person in the United States, including the following:

- I can open the front page of the paper and see people of my race widely represented.
- I can be pretty sure of having my voice heard in a group in which I am the only member of my race.

- I can be casual about whether or not to listen to another person's voice in a group in which s/he is the only member of his/her race.
- I can do well in a challenging situation without being called a credit to my race.
- I am never asked to speak for all the people of my racial group.
- I can be pretty sure that if I ask to talk to the "person in charge," I will be facing a person of my race.
- If I have low credibility as a leader, I can be sure that my race is not the problem.
- I can take a job with an affirmative action employer without having co-workers on the job suspect that I got it because of my race.

McIntosh and other scholars argue that white privilege and other forms of dominance, such as male privilege or the privilege conferred to nationals of countries in the North, are embedded in the social and organizational systems that we take for granted. "I was taught to see racism only in individual acts of meanness, not in invisible systems conferring dominance on my group." These systems appear neutral and natural, yet they inevitably and systematically reproduce advantage for some and disadvantage for others.

Diverse social categories and identities embody differences in power and in status

The social categories that flow from social differences are rarely neutral. These categories often mark differences in status and social power among groups and determine specific groups' relative access to resources and power within organizations and the broader social system. In this way, not all dimensions of diversity have equal import for shaping social relations and work outcomes in organizations. To understand diversity dynamics and work effectively with differences in organizations, it is important to give explicit attention to the nexus between social differences and power relationships within organizations and the larger society(ies) in which they are embedded. These status and power differences get reproduced in organizations and are embedded in organizational structures, policies, norms, and work practices. In this way, they subtly confer privilege to some groups and disadvantage to others. As a result, different identity groups have very different experiences and opportunities within organizations and these differences tend to accumulate and expand over time.[20] Nkomo (1996: 245) argues:

> Diversity [in organizations] has its effects exactly because distinctions made on the basis of identity are not benign. . . . It is important to be aware of the "relational" dimension of diversity. Dichotomies are created (black versus white, men versus women). However dichotomies are not symmetric. Someone or some group becomes the "other," and otherness has a very unique meaning for the socio-historically embedded categories of race, ethnicity, and gender. Differences between people based on these categories are grounded within structures of power inequalities and unequal access to resources.

Voiced in another way by an organizational practitioner, Dawn Cross, the Director of Diversity at Corning, Inc. in the United States, observes:

> Because images of success in many organization are based on traits [considered as norms for] white men, even the best-intentioned people try to get people of color and white women to fit the old image rather than creating new images of success.

> *(in Morrison et al., 1993: 13)*

Identities shape cognitions, experiences, worldviews,
and perspectives

Historically, the social differences lens has been used to illuminate and address
inequalities in organizations and to ensure equal opportunities for people of
diverse identity groups. However, while not diminishing the importance of equality and justice in organizations, it is also important to view social identity differences
as an asset, rather than solely as a problem to be fixed. Social identity shapes the
way individuals are socialized and their experiences in families, communities, and
the larger society. In this way, it influences their worldview, perspectives, values, and
cognition. . . . [T]his plurality of ways of viewing, experiencing, and knowing the
world is a valuable asset to organizations seeking to be flexible, innovative, and
responsive to diverse clientele or stakeholders.

Considerable research has explored the link between specific traits and identities, as, for example, in the field of women in management. Yet, results have been
inconclusive.[21] This ambiguity in findings most likely derives from lack of attention
to the influence of social and organizational context (see Box 26.4) and to the
impact of multiple identity group affiliation (see "Identities are multidimensional"
[above]). Moreover, traits, such as collaboration, performed by members of different identity groups, are perceived and interpreted differently, depending on
the context of the organization and larger society. For example, Fletcher (1999)
observed in her study of software engineers in the United States that collaborative
or supportive work behaviors demonstrated by women were invisible and generally
construed as "natural and nice." These were expected behaviors for women under
the gender schemas operating in the organization and larger society. When men
presented these same behaviors, they were more visible and recognized as contributing to effectiveness. They were labeled with terms such as "fostering team
work," "anticipating problems," and "coaching."

Box 26.4 Changing Culture to Harness the Benefits of Diversity

Cox et al. (1991), drawing on Hofstede's (1990) work on cultural differences, examined whether members of ethnic minorities in the United States (African Americans,
Hispanics, and Asians) with collaborative-cooperative cultural norms would opt more
often for cooperative behavior in group settings than Anglos who operate from more
individualistic-competitive norms. In a laboratory setting, they found that members
of minority ethic groups had significantly stronger cooperative orientations. They also
found that the ethnically diverse groups made significantly more cooperative choices
than groups comprised solely of Anglos. Importantly, however, they found that the
difference was much more marked in contexts where the groups expected the other
group to cooperate. The authors conclude that organizations cannot strengthen cooperative behavior and work practices in the workplace by simply hiring more members
of ethnic groups with cooperative-collective norms as is sometimes assumed.
Organizations will only benefit from this if the organizational culture changes and
provides signals that cooperation can lead to mutual gain and will be reciprocated by
cooperation.

Given the analytic complexities of associating specific traits with specific identity groups, we believe it is more useful to recognize that identity shapes experiences and to focus on how organizations can learn from the different perspectives, sources of knowledge, professional networks, or ways of working that members of different identity groups bring to the organization. From this perspective, for example, Thomas and Ely (1996: 80) argue the importance of linking social identity differences directly to the work of the organization (see Box 26.5):

(Diverse staff) bring different, important, and competitively relevant knowledge and perspectives about how to actually do work – how to design processes, reach goals, frame tasks, create effective teams, communicate ideas, and lead. When allowed to, members of these groups can help companies grow and improve by challenging basic assumptions about an organization's functions, strategies, operations, practices, and procedures. And in doing so, they are able to bring more of their whole selves to the workplace and identify more fully with the work that they do, setting in motion a virtuous circle. . . . Only when companies start thinking about diversity holistically – as providing fresh and meaningful approaches to work . . . will they be able to reap its full rewards.

Relative emphasis on dimensions of identity

Age, sexual orientation, and class are identity dimensions that have not received as much attention in research or practice on diversity. They are all clearly important and valenced categories influencing individuals' experiences in organizations and career and work outcomes. Social class and sexual orientation are more challenging to work with since visible makers are usually less salient.[22] In many cases, individuals have to make explicit choices about whether to identify themselves as homosexual or heterosexual, or as affluent or working class, and, thus, open themselves up to categorization by others.

Inclusivity is a challenge when visible identities trigger potentially judgmental or divisible reactions. . . . A distinct set of challenges arises when employees bring invisible, marginalized, or even stigmatized aspects of their identity into the workplace.

(Creed and Scully, 2000: 391)

Box 26.5 Connecting Diversity and Work Practices

Thomas and Ely (1996) stress the importance of working with diversity in the context of the actual work to be done. They illustrate this point with an example of a financial services firm where the widely held assumption, or norm, was that the only way to develop successful sales was through aggressive, rapid, cold calls. On this assumption, the company rewarded sales staff based on the number of calls made. An internal review of their diversity initiatives, however, challenged this assumption about effectiveness. It revealed that the first and third most profitable employees were women who used a very different sales technique. Rather than cold calls, they slowly but surely built up long-term relationships with clients. The review concluded that "the company's top management has now made the link between different identity groups and different approaches and has come to see that there is more than one right way to get positive results."

Working with class differences in organizations is also challenging because acceptance of class inequities is so embedded in organizational concepts and norms of hierarchy, meritocracy, and wage labor.[23] Acker (1999), for example, is calling for researchers and practitioners to give renewed attention to class as a critical dimension of organization. In other cultural contexts where class differences are socially recognized, such as Latin America, it may be important and easier to include class as a significant dimension of organizational diversity as it is already part and parcel of the social structure in which the organization is operating. In spite of the difficulty in addressing these other dimensions of identity, they are critical dimensions of diversity that need to be incorporated more fully into working with social differences in organizations. [. . .]

NOTES

1 Kirkham (1996); Nkomo and Cox (1996); Whartot (1992).
2 Cross and Blackburn White (1996); Ely and Thomas (2001); Kirkham (1996); Thomas and Ely (1996).
3 Nkomo and Cox (1996).
4 Essed (1990, 1996); Nkomo and Cox (1996); Wharton (1992).
5 This is what Cross et al. (1994) have referred to as the "isms": classism, racism, sexism, heterosexism, and ethnocentrism.
6 Alderfer (1992); Cox and Blake (1991); Ely and Meyerson (1998); Ely and Thomas (Forthcoming); Nkomo and Cox (1996); Thomas and Ely (1996).
7 Alderfer (1992); Bell, Denton and Nkomo (1993); Bell and Nkomo (1992); Holvino (1994); Hurtado (1989); Mama (1995).
8 Nkomo and Cox (1996); Ferdman and Gallegos (Forthcoming); Foldy (1999); Wharton (1992).
9 Catalyst (1999); Centre for Gender in Organizations (2000); Crenshaw (1993); Ely and Meyerson (1998); Holvinon (1999); Hurtado (1999); Hurtado and Stewart (1996); marks (2001); Proudford (1998).
10 Catalyst (1999).
11 Center for Gender in Organizations (2000); Hurtado (1989, 1999); Marks (2001); Proudford (1998).
12 Ferdman (1995); Foldy (1999); Nkomo and Cox (1996); Ragins (1997); Wharton (1992).
13 Jackson et al. (1995); Kirkham (1996); McGrath et al. (1995).
14 Avigor (1953) cited in Triandis (1995).
15 Cited in Canney Davison and Ward (1999: 59).
16 Acker (1990); Collinson and Hearn (1994); Crenshaw (1993, 1992); Crowfoot and Chesler (1996), Ely (1996); Essed (1990); Fine (1996); Fletcher and Merrill-Sands (1998); Guinier (1998); Hurtado (1989, 1997, 1999); Hurtado and Stewart (1996); Jacques (1999); Kirkham (1996); Kolb et al. (1998); Martin (1996); McIntosh (1990); Tajfel (1982).
17 Canney Davison and Ward (1999); Sessa and Jackson (1995).
18 Crowfoot and Chesler (1996); Ely (1996); Fine (1996); Hurtado and Stewart (1996); Kossed and Zonia (1993); McIntosh (1990); Nkomo and Cox (1996); Tsui et al. (1992); Valian (1998).
19 Crowfoot and Chesler (1996); Proudford (1998); Scully and Creed (1999).
20 Acker (1990); Alderfer (1992); Bond and Pyle (1998); Cole and Singer (1991); Cross and Blackburn White (1996); Ely and Meyerson (1998); Fletcher and Merrill-Sands (1998); Greenhaus et al. (1990); Kirkham (1996); Kolb et al. (1998); Meyerson and

Fletcher (2000); Morrison et al. (1993); Sessa and Jackson (1995); Nkomo (1992); Nkomo and Cox (1996); Ragins (1995); Valian (1998).
21 Gilligan (1982); Kabacoff (1998); Powell (1993); Rosener (1990).
22 Greed and Scully (2000).
23 Holvino (1999); Holvino (2000); Mahony and Zmroczek (1997).

References

Acker, J. 1990. Hierarchies, jobs, bodies: A theory of gendered organizations. *Gender and Society*, 4: 139–158.

Acker, J. 1999. *Revisiting Class: Lessons from Theorizing Race and Gender in Organizations.* Boston, MA: Center for Gender in Organizations, Simmons School of Management, Working Paper, No. 5.

Adler, N. J. 1986. *International Dimensions of Organizational Behavior.* Boston, MA: Kent.

Alderfer, C. 1987. An intergroup perspective on group dynamics. In J. Lorsch (Eds.), *Handbook of Organizational Behavior*, (pp. 190–222). Englewood Cliffs, NJ: Prentice Hall.

Alderfer, C. 1992. Changing race relations embedded in organizations: Report on a long-term project with the XYC Corporation. In S. Jackson and Associates (Eds.), *Diversity in the Workplace: Human Resources Initiatives*, (pp. 138–166). New York: The Guilford Press.

Avigor, R. 1953. Études experimentales de la genèse des stéréotypes. *Cahiers International de Sociologie*, 5: 154–168.

Bell, E. L., Denton, T. C., and Nkomo, S. M. 1993. Women of color in management: Toward an inclusive analysis. In E. A. Fagenson (Ed.), *Women in Management: Trends, Issues and Challenges in Managerial Diversity*, (pp. 105–30). Newbury Park, CA: Sage.

Bell, E. L. and Nkomo, S. M. 1992. Re-visioning women manager's lives. In A. J. Mills and P. Tancred (Eds.), *Gendering Organizational Analysis*, (pp. 235–247). Newbury Park, CA: Sage.

Bond, M. and Pyle, J. 1998. Diversity dilemmas at work. *Journal of Management Inquiry*, 7 (3): 252–269.

Canney Davison, S. and Ward, K. 1999. *Leading International Teams*. London: McGraw Hill.

Catalyst 1999. *Women of Color in Corporate Management: Opportunities and Barriers.* New York: Catalyst.

Center for Gender in Organizations 2000. *Conference Report. Gender at Work: Beyond White, Western, Middle-Class, Heterosexual, Professional Women.* Boston, MA: Center for Gender in Organizations, Simmons School of Management.

Cock, J. and Bernstein, A. 1988. Diversity and disadvantage: Feminist perspectives from the USA and South Africa. *Politikon*, 25 (2): 17–29.

Cole, J. R. and Singer, B. 1991. A theoretical explanation. In H. Zuckerman, J. Cole, and J. Bruer (Eds.), *The Outer Circle: Women in the Scientiific Community*, (pp. 277–310). New York: W. W. Norton.

Collinson, D. and Hearn, J. 1994. Naming men as men: Implications for work, organization, and management. *Gender, Work, and Organization*, 1 (1): 2–22.

Cox, T. 1993. *Cultural Diversity in Organizations: Theory, Research, and Practice.* San Franciso: Berrett-Koehler.

Cox, T. and Blake, S. 1991. Managing Cultural diversity: Implications for organizations. *Academy of Management Executive* 5 (3): 34–47.

Cox, T., Lobel, S., and McLeod, P. 1991. Effects of ethnic group cultural differences on cooperative and competitive behavior on a group task. *Academy of Management Journal*, 34 (4): 827–847.

Creed, D. and Scully, M. (2000). Songs of ourselves: Employees' deployment of social identity in everyday workplace environments. *Journal of Management Inquiry*, 9: 391–412.

Crenshaw, K. 1992. Race, gender, and sexual harassment. *Southern California Law Review*, 65: 1467–1467.

Crenshaw, K. 1993. Demarginalizing the intersection of race and sex: A black feminist critique of antidiscrimination doctrine, feminist theory, and antiracist policies. In D. Kelly Weisberg (Ed.), *Feminist Legal Theory: Foundations*, (pp. 383–395). Philadelphia: Temple University Press.

Cross, E. and Blackburn White, M. (Eds.) 1996. *The Diversity Factor: Capturing the Competitive Advantage of a Changing Work force*. Chicago: Irwin Professional Publishing.

Cross, E., Katz, J., Miller, F. and Seashore, E. 1994. *The Promise of Diversity: Over 40 Voices Discuss Strategies for Eliminating Discrimination in Organizations*. Burr Ridge, IL: Irwin Professional Publishing.

Crowfoot, J. and Chesler, M. 1996. White men's roles in multicultural coalitions. In B. Bowser and R. Hunt (Eds.), *Impacts of Racism on White American*, (pp. 202–229). Thousand Oaks, CA and London: Sage.

Ely, R. 1996. The role of dominant identity and experience in organizational work on diversity. In S. Jackson and M. Ruderman (Eds.), *Diversity in Work Teams: Research Paradigms for a Changing Workplace*, (pp. 161–186). Washington, D.C.: American Psychological Association.

Ely, R. and Meyerson, D. 1998. Reflections on moving from a gender to a broader diversity lens. *CG Gender Lens*, a newsletter of the CGIAR Gender Program. Washington, D.C.: CGIAR Gender Staffing Program, 3(2): 5–6. Also printed as *CGO Insights*. Boston, MA: Center for Gender in Organizations, Simmons School of Management, March 1999, No. 4.

Ely, R. and Thomas, D. A. 2001. Cultural diversity at work: The moderating effects of work group perspectives on diversity. *Administrative Science Quarterly*, 46: 229–273.

Essed, P. 1990. *Understanding Everyday Racism*. Alameda, CA: Hunter House.

Essed, P. 1996. *Diversity: Gender, Color, and Culture*. Amherst, MA: University of Massachusetts.

Ferarri, S. 1972. Human behaviour in international groups. *Management International Review*, XII (6): 31–35.

Ferdman, B. 1995. Cultural identity and diversity in organizations: Bridging the gap between group differences and individual uniqueness. In M. Chemers, S. Oskamp, and M. Costanzo (Eds.), *Diversity in Organizations: New Perspectives for a Changing Workplace*, (pp. 37–61). Thousand Oaks, CA: Sage.

Ferdman, B. and Gallegos, P. forthcoming. Racial identity development and Latinos in the United States. In C. Wijeyesinghe and B. Jackson (Eds.), *Reflections on Racial Identity Development: Essays in Theory, Practice, and Discourse*. New York: University Press.

Fine, M. 1996. Witnessing whiteness. In M. Fine, L. Poweel, L. Weis, and M. Wong (Eds.), *Off White: Readings on Society, Race, and Culture*, (pp. 297–311). New York: Routledge.

Fletcher, J. 1999. *Disappearing Acts: Gender, Power, and Relational Practice at Work*. Cambridge, MA: The MIT Press.

Fletcher, J. and Merrill-Sands, D. 1998. Looking below the surface: The gendered nature of Organizations. *CG Gender Lens*. Washington, DC: CGIAR Gender Program, 3 (1): 3. Also printed as *CGO Insights*, No. 2, Boston, MA: Center for Gender in Organizations, Simmons School of Management, November, 1998.

Foldy, E. 1999. Managing diversity: Identity and power in organizations. Proposal for Dissertation Research, Carroll School of Management, Boston College, August 5, 1999. Manuscript.

Garcia, M. H. 1995. An anthropological approach to multicultural diversity training. *Journal of Applied Behavioral Science*, 31 (4): 490–504.

Gilligan, C. 1982. *In a Different Voice: Psychological Theory and Women's Development*. Cambridge, MA: Harvard University Press.

Greenhaus, J., Parasuraman, S. and Wormley, W. 1990. Effects of race on organizational experiences, job performance evaluations and career outcomes. *Academy of Management Journal*, 33 (1): 64–86.

Guinier, L. 1998. Lessons and challenges of becoming gentlemen. *New York University Review of Law and Social Change*, 24 (1): 1–16.

Hofstede, G., et al., 1990. Measuring organizational cultures: A qualitative and quantitative study across twenty cases. *Administrative Science Quarterly*, 35: 286–316.

Holvino, E. 1994. Women of color in organizations: Revising our models of gender at work. In E. Y. Cross, J. H. Katz, F. A. Miller, and E. W. Seashore (Eds.), *The Promise of Diversity*, (pp. 52–59). New York: Irwin/NTL.

Holvino, E. 1999. Class: The unmentionable difference in T-groups. In *Reading Book for Human Relations Training*, (pp. 117–119). Alexandria, VA: NTL Institute.

Holvino, E. 2000. Social diversity in social change organizations: Standpoint learnings for organizational consulting. In R. T. Carter (Ed.), *Addressing Cultural Issues in Organizations: Beyond the Corporate Context.* Thousand Oaks, CA: Sage.

Hurtado, A. 1989. Relating to privilege: Seduction and rejection in the subordination and rejection of white women and woman of color. *Signs*, 14: 833–855.

Hurtado, A. 1997. Understanding multiple group identities: Inserting women into cultural transformations. *Journal of Social Issues*, 53 (2): 292–329.

Hurtado, A. 1999. *Disappearing Dynamics of Women of Color.* CGO Working Paper, No. 4. Boston, MA: Center for Gender in Organizations, Simmons School of Management.

Hurtado, A. and Stewart, A. 1996. Through the looking glass: Implications of studying white-ness for feminist methods. in M. Fine. L. Powell, L. Weis, and M. Wong (Eds.), *Off White: Readings on Society, Race, and Culture*, (pp. 297–311). New York: Routledge.

Idea Connections. 2000. Copyrighted training materials. Rochester, NY. Permission to quote granted September 2000.

International Monetary Fund. 1999. *What is Diversity?* Washington, D.C.: International Monetary Fund, Brochure.

Jackson, S., May, K. and Whitney, K. 1995. Understanding the dynamics of diversity in decision-making teams. In R. Guzzo, E. Salas and Associates (Eds.), *Team Effectiveness and Decision-Making in Organizations*, (pp. 204–262). San Francisco: Jossey-Bass.

Jacques, R. 1999. What about us? The challenge of diversity. *CG Gender Lens.* Washington, D.C.: CGIAR Gender Program, 4 (1).

Kabacoff, R. 1998. *Gender Differences in Organizational Leadership: A Large Sample Study.* Portland, ME: Management Research Group.

Kirkham, K. 1996. Managing in a diverse work force: From incident to "ism." In E. Cross and M. Blackburn White, *The Diversity Factor*, (pp. 24–46). Chicago: Irwin Professional Publishing.

Kolb, D., Fletcher, J., Meyerson, D., Merrill-Sands, D. and Ely, R. 1998. Making change: A framework for promoting gender equity in organizations. CGO *Insights*, No. 1. Boston, MA: Center for Gender in Organizations, Simmons School of Management.

Kossek, E. and Lobel, S. 1996. Introduction: Transforming human resource systems to manage diversity – an introduction and orienting framework. In E. Kossek and S. Lobel (Eds.), *Managing Diversity: Human Resource Strategies for Transforming the Workplace*, (pp. 1–19). Cambridge, MA: Blackwell.

Kossek, E. and Zonia, S. 1993. Assessing diversity climate: A field study of reactions to employer efforts to promote diversity. *Journal of Organizational Behavior*, 14: 61–81.

Mahony, P. and Zmroczek, C. 1997. *Class Matters: "Working-Class" Women's Perspectives on Social Class.* London: Taylor and Francis.

Mama, A. 1995. *Beyond the Masks: Race, Gender, and Subjectivity (Critical Psychology).* London: Routledge.

Marks, R. 2001. *The Politics and Practice of Institutionalizing Gender Equity in a Post Apartheid South Africa.* Boston, MA: Gender in Organizations, Simmons School of Management. Working Paper No. 12.

Martin, Patricia Yancey. 1996. Gendering and evaluating dynamics: Men, masculinities, and managements. In D. Collinson and J. Hearn (Eds.), *Men as Managers, Managers as Men*, (pp. 186–209). London: Sage.

McGrath, J., Berdahl, L. and Arrow, H. 1995. Traits, expectations, culture, and clout: The dynamics of diversity in groups. In S. Jackson and M. Ruderman (Eds.), *Diversity in Work Teams: Research Paradigms for a Changing* Workplace, (pp. 17–46). Washington, D.C.: American Psychological Association.

McIntosh, P. 1990. White privilege: unpacking the invisible knapsack. *Independent School*, Winter Issue: 31–34. (http://www. seamonkey.ed.asu.edu/~mcisaac/emc598ge).

Meyerson, D. E. and Fletcher, J. K. 2000. A modest manifesto for shattering the shattering the glass ceiling. *Harvard Business Review*, January/February: 127–36.

Morrison, A., Ruderman, M., and Hughes-James, M. 1993. *Making Diversity Happen: Controversies and Solutions*. Greensboro, NC: The Center for Creative Leadership.

Nkomo, S. 1992. The emperor has no clothes: Rewriting "race in organizations". *Academy of Management Review*, 17 (3):487–513.

Nkomo, S. 1996. Identities and the complexity of diversity. In S. Jackson and M. Ruderman (Eds.), *Diversity in Work Teams: Research Paradigms for a Changing Workplace*, (pp. 247–253). Washington, D.C.: American Psychological Association.

Nkomo, S. and Cox, T. 1996. Diverse identities in organizations. In S. Clegg, C. Hardy and W. Nord (Eds.), *Handbook of Organization Studies*, (pp. 338–356). London and Thousand Oaks: Sage Publications.

Powell, G. 1993. *Women and Men in Management*. Newbury Park, CA: Sage.

Proudford, K. 1998. Notes on the intra-group origins of inter-group conflict in organizations: Black-white relations as an exemplar. *University of Pennsylvania Journal of Labor and Employment Law*, 1, (2).

Ragins, B. 1997. Diversified mentoring relationships in organizations: A power perspective. *The Academy of Management Review*, 22 (2): 482–521.

Rosener, J. 1990. Ways women lead. *Harvard Business Review*, November–December: 119–125.

Scully, M. and Creed, D. 1999. Restructured families: Issues of equality and need. *The Annals of the American Academy*, 562: 45–65.

Sessa, V. and Jackson, S. 1995. Diversity in decision-making teams: All differences are not created equal. In M. Chemers, S. Oskamp and M. Costanzo (Eds.), *Diversity in Organizations: New perspectives for a Changing Workplace*, (pp. 133–156). London: Sage.

Tajfel, H. 1982. *Social Identity and Intergroup Relations*. New York: Cambridge University Press.

Thomas, D. and Ely, R. 1996. Making differences matter: A new paradigm for managing diversity. *Harvard Business Review*. September–October: 79–90.

Thomas, R. 1995. A diversity framework. In M. Chemers, S. Oskamp and M. A. Costanzo (Eds.), *Diversity in Organizations: New Perspectives for a Changing Workplace*, (pp. 245–263). Thousand Oaks, CA: Sage.

Triandis, H. 1995. The importance of contexts in studies of diversity. In S. Jackson and M. Ruderman (Eds.), *Diversity in Work Teams: Research Paradigms for a Changing Workplace*, (pp. 225–233). Washington, D.C.: American Psychological Association.

Tsui, A. S., Egan, T. D., and O'Reilly, C. A. 1992. Being different: Relational demography and organizational attachment. *Administrative Science Quarterly*, 37: 549–579.

Turner, J. C. and Giles, H. 1981. *Intergroup Behavior*. New York: Basil Blackwell.

Valian, V. 1998. *Why so Slow? The Advancement of Women*. Cambridge, MA: MIT Press.

Wharton, A. 1992. The social construction of gender and race in organizations: A social identity and group mobilization perspective. *Research in the Sociology of Organizations*, 10: 55–84.

OUR SEPARATE WAYS: BARRIERS TO ADVANCEMENT

ELLA L. J. EDMONDSON BELL AND STELLA M. NKOMO

From Our Separate Ways: Black and White Women and the Struggle for Professional Identity (2001), Boston, MA: Harvard Business School Press

MUCH HAS BEEN WRITTEN both in the popular press and in academic circles about the glass ceiling blocking women's advancement to top-level positions in corporate America.[1] The metaphor aptly captures the dilemma of women managers trying to rise to the top.[2] However, when the effects of race and gender are taken into account, the metaphor is insufficient.

The obstacles to advancement perceived by the black women managers were different both in degree and kind from the obstacles perceived by white women managers. As black women, they were subjected to a particular form of sexism shaped by racism and racial stereotyping.[3] The theoretical concept of *racialized sexism* also captures the idea that the experience of gender discrimination in the workplace depends on a woman's race.[4] For black women managers, sexism is entwined with racism. To understand the perceptions of black women managers regarding the barriers they encountered, we must imagine a two-dimensional structure: a concrete wall topped by a glass ceiling.

NATIONAL SURVEY RESULTS

Our survey data offers a quantitative picture of the differences we found. First and foremost, the white women managers in our national survey made greater progress in reaching upper-level management positions. Thirty-two percent of the white women managers were in top-level management positions compared to 14 percent of the African-American women managers surveyed. When we analyzed the respondents' employment histories, we found important differences. The proportion of jobs held that were demotions for black women was considerably greater than for white women. Similarly, black women tended to make more lateral moves in their companies than white women. The difference in managerial levels is also reflected in salary level differences. Twenty-seven percent of the white women were earning $100,000 or more, compared to 10 percent of the African-American women. A larger percentage of the white women managers (67 percent) were satisfied with their career progress; only 58 percent of African-American women managers were satisfied. One of the important keys to career advancement is proving one's ability in "line positions" – jobs that have direct impact on a company's bottom line. The white women surveyed had an edge over the black women in gaining experience in line positions (70 percent versus 61 percent).

As a consequence, we found less satisfaction among the African-American women with their present positions. Sixty-two percent of the African American women managers surveyed agreed with the statement, "I am satisfied with my current position," compared to 75 percent of the white women. While 74 percent of the white women agreed with the statement, "I have considerable decision-making power in my position," only 59 percent of the African-American women agreed. White women managers perceived their current responsibilities to be more significant than African-American women did, and they also believed to a much greater degree that their jobs allowed them to use their skills and knowledge. These differences existed even though there were no differences in the educational levels of the black and white women managers in our sample.

There were also significant differences in perceptions of relationships with colleagues. The African-American women managers were more inclined to feel that they had to outperform their white colleagues – both male and female – to succeed. African-American women had less positive perceptions of their relationships with their bosses and colleagues. Consequently, they reported receiving less collegial support than did the white women managers in the survey. Generally, the white women surveyed were more positive than African-American women about their organizations' overall management of race and gender relations and commitment to the advancement of women and people of color. African-American women did not feel their companies were implementing policies that would advance people of color.

PERCEPTIONS OF THE CONCRETE WALL

Our interviews supported much of what we found in our national survey. We asked women about obstacles to their career advancement, about how they saw the road to the top in their corporations, and about how they felt about the progress of their careers. While there were some similarities between how black and white women perceived obstacles to career advancement, there were also a number of striking differences in their perceptions. Our goal here is not to suggest that one group of women experienced greater or lesser challenges in the workplace, but rather to illuminate the specific nature of the barriers as perceived by the women themselves. The stories of Karen Brown and Jean Hendrick give depth to the responses we heard during our interviews.

Karen Brown's career moved smoothly upward for the first eight years after college. She had advanced well beyond her initial position as a management trainee with a large retailer, and her career showed steady progress, with promotions every two years like clockwork. But she hit a wall in her fourth position as sales manager, a position "reserved only for men" where "there certainly weren't any blacks." The white men she worked with, in her words, "treated me with such disrespect." She faced constant challenges to her authority and almost daily incidents of racism. Her boss ignored her but constantly complained about her poor performance to the personnel department. "He never even came to my office. He never talked to me – never said one word to me. There was one incident where I had a lot of work to prepare for something and did all of it but two things. I had arranged for two of the guys I worked with to do these two things while I was away, but they didn't do them." Karen was blamed for the incomplete work. Then she was asked to return to her old position as an assistant sales manager. It was a demotion. To advance her career, Karen had to leave the company.

The day she arrived at the company where she has spent nineteen years, Jean Hendrick knew she wanted to become one of the few female officers. "There was no question in my mind that's what I wanted. I was positive I was capable of doing it. To me it was only a matter of time before *they* realized that's what I should be doing." But her climb up the corporate ladder wasn't that simple. She became an officer after eight years, which she describes as "a big deal, especially for women." Less than two years later, she was promoted to vice president. At the time she had her baby, she was the first female officer to have a child. Then the promotions slowed, and she languished between lateral moves. Finally, seven years later, she was promoted to a group vice president position. Jean has been told by more than one male colleague to dress less colorfully and to talk less about her children. "I've been criticized for being too dramatic, too emotional, whatever. In other words, I was asked to be more like them, more like the men." She wonders if she will be able to move higher, into the very top echelon of the company. "The company has become suddenly chauvinistic. In the past they were, and then they weren't. Maybe it's just a little bit of a growing pain. I'm trying to be optimistic. A lot of women are feeling it now."

While the glass ceiling represents the inability of women like Jean Hendrick to rise above a certain level in the corporate hierarchy, the concrete wall facing African-American women managers is more persistent and more pernicious. It manifests itself in six ways: daily doses of racism, being held to a higher standard, the invisibility vise, exclusion from informal networks, challenges to authority, and hollow company commitment to the advancement of minorities.

Daily doses of racism

One of the most distinctive elements of the concrete wall is what we call "daily doses of racism." The everyday occurrence of such incidents almost renders them mundane.[5] Any one dose, taken alone, might be viewed as inconsequential. But cumulatively they take their toll, marginalizing and humiliating black women managers. White colleagues, both male and female, often downplayed the racial element of the incidents, offering race-neutral explanations. Black women managers were invariably admonished by dominant group colleagues that the incidents were a "joke," a "mistake," not important," or an occurrence that "had nothing to do with their race" that "could have happened to anyone."

Our interviews with African-American women were full of vivid descriptions of daily doses of racism. Deborah Jones, a senior-level human resources executive, remembers an episode that still angers her today: "At the consulting company I worked for, we held an annual partners meeting. I was a principal by then, and we had the meeting at our office. We were having a very big reception and then a dinner. We were all there, including partners from all over the world. Besides me, the only other blacks present were a black guy, Kenneth, who was also a principal, and the receptionist. Everybody was having a very wonderful time. The partner who ran one of the European offices and I were talking. He told me they had lunch every day in his office. I said, "That's a really nice perk." He asked, "Do you serve lunch here?" I said, "No, we don't do that." He said, "No, I mean do you serve the lunch to the consultants every day?" Again, I said, "No, we don't do that," and he asked me again. Then I realized that this man was asking me if I personally made lunch for the consultants. So when it dawned on me, when the lightbulb went on, I said, "No. However, should we ever require that consultants serve lunch to each other every day, I'll be delighted to take my turn." He kind of looked at me, turned red as a beet, and didn't know what else to say. Two other principals heard the exchange. One said, "Deborah, I'm so sorry." I just left the room. Later, I spoke with the head of our office, who wanted to tell me that's not what the partner meant. I said, "Oh yes, that's what he meant." Then he said, 'Oh, well he must have been joking." I said "No, he wasn't joking." Then he said, 'Oh, I bet you he would have said that to my wife.' I said, 'I seriously doubt that he would have said that to your wife.' " Deborah's experience is not unusual. The partner assumed she was not a consultant despite the setting and the purpose of the event. We heard similar stories from other interviewees who were mistaken by whites as secretaries, as assistants, or as anyone other than the manager in charge.

Sometimes the dose of racism was more blatant. Anna Smalls, who at the time of the interview was the highest ranking African-American woman manager in her investment-banking company, remembered being stunned by an incident. "We were at an off-site business meeting. I was the only black woman present. It was evening. The formal portion of the meeting for the day was over. After the meeting, a small group from my work team went to the bar for drinks. There were four white males, all managers. They asked me if I wanted to join them. I thought it would be best to go to my room and not get involved in socializing, but then I figured it was important for me to act like I was part of the team. So I went. Everybody gathered around the bar for drinks. The five of us were standing in a circle. One of the guys said to me, "My, this was a good year for you, you did like 187 percent for the year." I said, "Yes, I had a good year." Then one of the other guys looks me right in the face and jokingly says, "You little black bitch." I couldn't believe it was coming out of his mouth. It was very insulting. The other guys dropped their jaws. I mean, they looked at him as if they couldn't believe what he'd said. I'd been called a black bitch before, but not in my work environment. It's been on the streets with a cab driver, that kind of thing. But this was a peer. This was a business environment. This was where people were supposed to be professional." When we asked Anna, "What did the other men say or do?" she answered, "Nothing."

An African-American woman can be undercut by white men either because of her race or because of her gender. The two are so often fused that it is difficult for African-American women to determine whether they are experiencing racism or sexism or both. In this incident the words of the white male colleague are significant. He did not simply say "bitch" but "black bitch." U.S. courts have held that the use of "bitch" is a form of sex discrimination as it is a derogatory word used to denigrate women. In a 1977 sex-discrimination case on the question of whether the word "bitch" used by a male in reference to a woman constitutes prejudice, the court agreed with the plaintiff's argument that "a bitch is a female dog, which when in heat, actively seeks insemination; judged by the cultural standards of the time, such a dog is considered lewd – one of the meanings of bitch when applied to women."[6] Historically, the sexuality of black women has been portrayed as wanton.[7] When the word "black" is combined with "bitch," it relegates a black woman to a profoundly inferior position, grounded in the devalued status of being both black and female. It is a poignant reminder of her societal status, despite outstanding performance.

The women spoke as well of racial incidents that cropped up in everyday business interactions. They were not so much directed at the women personally but directed at black people as a group. Mamie Jefferson, the only African-American among the top management of her retail company, notices such slips in everyday conversations or at meetings. "We were having a buyers' meeting – me and the other senior-level vice presidents – and the candy buyer, an older white woman who was in charge of candy, cookies, and things like that, had brought in some cookies for the meeting and had put them on a side table. One of the cookies was a vanilla wafer. People were standing around the table and someone made a comment about vanilla wafers, whether or not they should eat one. I'm sure she didn't know I was in the room; her back was to me. And she turned to the other white managers and said something to the effect, "Well, you'd better be careful or people will think you're black." There's a notion that the primary consumers of vanilla wafers are black people. It was just like somebody making a statement about black people eating watermelon. The whole thing was just one of those ill-thought, ill-spoken phrases that happen in conversations in a company." Mamie told us the woman making the comment was oblivious to her presence. Sometimes the comments were more harsh and direct. Brenda Boyd, now a mid-level communications executive, remembered the head of corporate communications saying during a meeting discussing advertising budgets that "he didn't know why we advertise in black newspapers because black people don't read."

We detected a sense of bewilderment from the women as they spoke about these doses of racism. But what was most striking to us were the reactions of the women. As one woman told us, "I've had some tough situations in my company because of racism, not blatant, but the normal kind." Racism described as "normal" was a theme pervading many of our interviews. Sometimes it was perceived as so "normal" that several women responded "No" when directly asked, "Have you ever experienced discrimination because of your race?" Yet during the course of their interviews they recounted personal, overt, and negative racial experiences. Perhaps their perceptions reflect the extent to which African-American women face racism in their everyday work lives. Daily doses of racism are so common that women become inured to them; they become almost a backdrop to their daily work environment. Additionally, African-American women often sublimate such experiences in order to cope with the frustration, humiliation, and anger caused by being targets of racial incidents, thereby lessening their sting. Other researchers have found that often members of minority groups minimize personal discrimination as a form of self-protection.[8]

Nonetheless, the women were not devoid of feelings about these episodes. Patricia Triggs said she just "carries it." "I come home some days and I'm real unhappy because of somebody's ignorance. I remember at one site there was a guy who had an office right beside mine, separated only by glass. This white man could not part his lips. He walked by me every morning and afternoon to get coffee but he never spoke. The first couple of times I said, "Good morning." He said nothing. After a while I knew this man could not speak to me. I really knew it when I was walking down the hall with a white woman colleague, and he spoke to her but not me. It's stuff like that I carry with me, and it's hard to get rid of how it makes me feel."

Held to a higher standard

Often the discriminatory barriers the African-American women managers experienced manifested themselves more subtly. Being stereotyped as incompetent and unqualified for the jobs they held is one example. Julia Smith, recounting her early experiences at a Fortune 500 manufacturing company, told us that she "clawed" her way to vice president in the financial division of her company. "During my first year at the company they apparently thought I was God's gift. I had this fabulous background academically. I had an Ivy League M.B.A. I worked for this guy who was a comer in the organization. We worked well together. He was nice and gave me a lot of visibility because I was sort of his favorite. I worked my ass off. I did great work. I made him look good. I really worked hard because I thought that at last they were ready not to let race be a factor. They had gone to great lengths to bring in people who were well qualified and black. I was going to give it my best shot. This is my career and reputation, I thought. I got my first review, which was very high. I had been identified as high potential in absolute terms."

"But when it came to the next job, I ended up in a staff position in the chairman's office supporting the board of directors and the executive committees, including the strategic planning groups, both national and international. But it wasn't crunching numbers in the strictest sense. I complained that I wasn't crunching numbers and wanted to know what was happening. They said not to worry because the job had visibility with the chairman and it was important work. But when it came time to move to the next level, they said, "She's unproven with the numbers." I said, "Wait, you guys put me here. You told me it was important, and I believed you and worked my tail off." They said, "Well you know we need to put you in another numbers job before we can move you to the next level." I said, "I asked you for that originally. At the very least I'm sitting here with a degree from a prestigious women's college, a master's degree in economics, an M.B.A. from an Ivy League school, and a great track record. Don't I deserve the presumption that I can crunch a few numbers?"

Many of the African-American women we interviewed believed they were held to higher and often different standards that their white colleagues, even when their credentials were extraordinary. Sixty-five percent of the African-American women managers who participated in our national survey believed they had to outperform their white colleagues for the same rewards. Said Julia, "You have to be 1,000 percent on top of stuff to move ahead at the same level."

Whitney Hamilton remembered a similar challenge at her newspaper. "I saw, when I was coming along, white guys go from reporters to editors overnight – literally overnight. One even went from reporter to being an assistant managing editor overnight. But when it came time for me to become an editor, I was told there were things I needed to do first." As a result, the women often felt they were in the spotlight where they could not dare underperform. "Black women need to do work that is sterling – not good work, but sterling work – on a consistent basis," Patricia Triggs told us. "Because I was black and female I always felt like there was a judge out there. There was a lot of weight on me. I thought, "If I don't do this, will they never let anybody else [black] come and do it?"

The African-American women felt they were held to higher standard because they were always fighting the stereotype of being incompetent, despite having the right educational and experience credentials. On one hand they are held to a higher standard, having to jump additional hurdles to advance in their jobs. On the other hand, when they display competence, their colleagues often express surprise. Deborah Jones recalled one of her white male colleagues asking her, "Where did you learn to speak like that?" Even though she expressed confusion about the question, her colleague persisted in wanting to know if she had taken a special speech course to learn how to speak. Psychologists refer to this as the "flower blooming in winter" effect.[9] When majority group members set lower standards for a black woman and she exceeds the standards, then the black woman's performance becomes remarkable. Or they treat the woman as an exception to her race and gender, leaving intact the general stereotype of black women as incompetent and unqualified. "They were surprised that I was smart, competent, and capable because they didn't expect that," said Whitney Hamilton. "People have preconceived notions about black women. I get high praise sometimes because I think they didn't expect anything. When I can speak English and do whatever I am supposed to do, people are just overwhelmed. I then become the exception."

Patricia Triggs found it was often difficult for some of the white male managers whom she encountered to accept that she could do things as well as they could. "I do not fault them for their ignorance, but it just offends their egos if you can do it and are black. They don't know it offends their ego. They sit there making objective decisions like you're not quite ready, you have to work on this, or you have to work on that.'

Psychologists suggest that stereotyping occurs as a way of filling information voids about people. Again, at the time these women entered corporate America, there were few if any models or examples of successful African-American women managers. In a decade when male-dominated corporations openly questioned whether women could even be managers, African-American women presented an altogether different challenge. There were no reference points, no models of them in authority positions for white colleagues to draw upon. Rather, the most pervasive images of African-American women ingrained into society were either negative images or images of African-American women in subservient roles.[10] The language and actions of white colleagues suggest they define black women first as black and female before seeing them as managers and executives.[11] The women we interviewed were faced with the dual challenge of transforming negative stereotypical images and simultaneously creating new professional roles.

Julia Smith's story is instructive about another dimension of the issues black women managers face. She was placed in a highly visible position in her company that was not a position that would lead to a higher level of responsibility. African-American women managers often find themselves in this predicament – placed in highly visible positions that benefit the company but not necessarily their careers. They can be unwittingly used as "affirmative action cover girls." Sociologist Sharon Collins found in her study of black mobility in white corporations that black executives are sometimes placed in positions that present an image of diversity to external audiences to serve race-related purposes.[12] Instead of Julia advancing to the next level of management, she ended up having to prove her ability once again in a position with the same level of responsibility. Our national survey data indicated that black women managers experienced a higher level of lateral moves and demotions within their organizations than did white women managers. Thomas and Gabarro, in their recent study of minority executive career paths, reported a similar pattern. Minorities had longer proving periods compared to the dominant group executives in the sample.[13]

We need to point out here that the white women we interviewed also talked about stereotyping as the major obstacle to their corporate mobility.[14] However, the stereotyping they describe centered on gender differences: male colleagues believing they could not have a career and a family, for example, or male colleagues criticizing "feminine style of behavior." Gender stereotyping, not surprisingly, was perceived to be more prevalent among older men – the men at the highest ranks of the organization. Gina Davidson, who today manages a large power plant, a rare position for a woman, stated "White guys over fifty-five are the biggest pain in life. For whatever reasons, as a group they are just Neanderthals."

Not only did the women have to confront negative stereotypes, they also came up against resistance to the very idea of women in the corporate suite. Gloria Goldberg, who has reached a senior level in investment banking, talked about how foreign the idea of a woman at the officer level was at the time of her promotion. "It took me probably a year to make vice president, a year and a half longer than the other guys. I know I was bringing in more business than half of them. It was not overt sexism you were fighting but something else. It was the decision by an old-line investment company to move a woman up. The question wasn't can she do the work as well as a guy, but do we really want a female officer? You were fighting a different battle than any of the guys who just had to do the work well."

Sylvia Whitaker, who is the most senior woman executive at the southern corporate headquarters of the insurance company she works for, told us: "I just wish someone could wave their magic wand and put away all this Southern male traditional mind-set that they're born with. They can't help it. I wish that I could take the environment I was in and the years that I've spent and project it twenty years down the road where it would all fit together nicely. It's just that women are before their time in the South. It's just the way it is. And it's not out of badness. I haven't really run into what I call pure male chauvinism in the ugliest form. It's just there."

Gender stereotyping made the women fear they would be seen as too emotional, too unassertive, and not committed enough to their careers; in addition, they feel viewed as helpers and not as primary breadwinners. Such stereotyping becomes justification for differential treatment. Sylvia Whitaker was taken aback when she encountered such stereotyping in her boss. "I was trying to tell him about an agreement we had made when I started working for him. I was giving him some feedback about how he wasn't meeting that agreement. He wasn't being defensive about the feedback, but what he said to me as he looked me in the eye was, "You know what you just sounded like don't you?" I said, "No." He said, "A jealous female." Something in my head went "Warning, warning. You've worked for this guy for a year now and you had no clue. When you least expected it, that ugly thing showed its face." I've been accused of a lot of things in my life, but this was the first time anyone had ever called me a jealous female." Earlier in her career when she revealed that she was pregnant, another boss told her "You will never be successful doing both. You cannot be a good parent and be a successful manager here."

Sometimes the gender stereotyping goes beyond words. Jean Hendrick recounted being told several times by male colleagues not to use her hands when she spoke; they said she was too demonstrative. "I remember going into a meeting with a senior-level white male. Two of my assistants were also in the meeting. We had met to discuss a pretty significant problem that would require action. We were in discussion, and I was animatedly describing a solution to a problem that he had presented. I was using my hands as I spoke. He went over to the drapes on the window and removed the tieback. He came over to me and tied my hands together. Then he said, "Jean, let's see if you can talk now." I was a senior officer and my subordinates were in that room. I immediately locked my jaw and pretended that I wasn't able to pronounce my words with my hands tied together in order to make everyone laugh. I was making a joke to protect him from being embarrassed for being so dumb."

Jean's story underscores the nature of the gender stereotyping white women faced entering male-dominated environments. Research has demonstrated that women managers are expected to adopt masculine personality traits rather than maintaining feminine qualities in order to be accepted and to succeed in the corporate environment.[15] Additionally, research has shown that women are more likely to be verbally interrupted than men.[16] But Jean's story illustrates more than the denigrating effect of gender stereotypes. The behavior of the senior white male reflects the ways in which some white men resist gender equality in the workplace. According to Cynthia Cockburn, one way men resisted women's invasion into spaces of male domination was through the reassertion of male supremacy. She further suggests that male opposition can range from the administrative to the physical.[17] It is hard to imagine a man who speaks in an animated manner having his hands tied by a colleague. Jean was not just a victim of stereotyping but also of harassment. The tying of her hands demonstrates how a potentially powerful woman can be cut down to size by sexual means. Tying her hands can be viewed as a controlling gesture designed to diminish any power Jean may have had in the meeting and even in the organization. His comment, "Let's see if you can talk now," can be taken as a direct challenge to her power and a reminder that she was not conforming to proper managerial behavior.

Another rationale used to block promotion opportunities and justify lower wages was that these women were not the primary wage earners in their families. A number of women told stories of pay discrimination based on such reasoning. As one interviewee remembered, "Six years ago I had a peer, we both worked for the same boss. He had five people reporting to him, I had twenty-five. He was paid $15,000 more a year than I was. When I confronted my manager about it, he said, "Well, he's got a family to support.'"

Gender stereotyping was also perceived to affect the types of work assignments and positions available to women. Investment banker Gloria Goldberg remembered, "When they handed out the random walk-in-the-door assignments, the women were always given the absolute garbage deals. There were never real deals assigned to them. The men were given the sure things." She went on to point out that "the key to promotion in investment banking is making big deals." Women were often excluded from jobs that led most directly to the senior ranks. They were usually assigned to human resources or communications, positions of far less status and rank. Ann Gilbert, who is now a vice president in her investment-banking firm, observed, "I think women still tend to be viewed as being technically incompetent. Or as adding value in more of a staff support role, more than in a line position."

The invisibility vise

Another barrier that surfaced in the black women's narratives is what we label the "invisibility vise." Black women perceive that their white colleagues feel more comfortable with blacks whose racial identity is suppressed, yet African-American women managers often want to maintain a strong, "visible" racial identity at work. This clash catches African-American women in a vise. Karen Brown, one of the highest level African-American women managers in corporate America today, talked eloquently about certain objects she keeps in her office: "See that book sitting over there," she said, pointing to a table. "A colleague looked at the book a couple months ago and he said, "Why do you have that book here?" I said, "I want to remind people that the person in this office is a black woman." I want no doubt about that because, guess what? They forget sometimes. You ought to hear the stuff that comes out of their mouths. They forget I'm a black woman. It's like I'm invisible. It's amazing to me. When they get comfortable with you, you become invisible." She continued to explain how her boss had compared her to another black employee. "He said 'Karen, you know Kent just wears his blackness.' I said, "What about me?" And he said, "You don't wear your blackness." I told him this enrages me because it means two things have happened. One is that I have made him awfully comfortable with me because I am black. Second, there's something wrong here if I have to be seen as nonblack. I was really upset. . . . I mean I was shut down for weeks behind that."

Deborah Jones had a similar experience as the only black woman in her company. "I found out that my boss used to tell people that I was black, but if you didn't know that I was black, you didn't think about it. What bothered me was that Jim had to create a rationale in his mind for my blackness. That's what he had to do to make me acceptable to clients. There is no way that I could ever walk around thinking that I'm not black."

To be accepted, African-American women are expected to assimilate. They have to literally lose their blackness for white colleagues to feel comfortable with them. White-dominated organizations often make cultural assimilation the price of acceptability for racial minorities.[18] This, of course, is a condition impossible for the African-American women to fulfill. They take this as an affront to their identity, but it is also a threat to their ambition, as maintaining a strong racial identity at work is an important grounding and coping mechanism. Most of the African-American women we interviewed were not willing to leave that part of themselves, learned from their family and educational experiences outside of the corporation. This makes sense, since armoring – the socialization from family early in life – helped these women withstand the racism and sexism they encountered in their later years. This armoring is indeed one of the major reasons why the black women in our study have been successful in corporate America despite the challenges they face daily.

It may seem puzzling that the black women had such a negative response to being made raceless by their white colleagues. Isn't this a positive result, as it meant they were viewed simply as individuals? It may appear black women want it both ways. On the one hand they are upset because their colleagues cannot get beyond race and gender and accept them as managers, yet at the same time they do not want colleagues to ignore their racial identity. How can these apparently contradictory perceptions be reconciled? Without question, having a clear sense of their racial identity helped them to maintain self-esteem and confidence in the face of racism and sexism in their work environments. But the implication that they acted in a way to conceal their racial identity (i.e., "acting white") or that they were focused on making white people comfortable was disturbing to the black women we interviewed.

This notion of comfort also surfaced in the narratives of the white women. They talked of what we refer to as sexual tension – men feeling "uncomfortable" working with women. Although not explicitly stated, it was clear these women were talking about white men working with white women as their equals. "All it boils down to is being comfortable," Sylvia Whitakers said. "Men and women, side by side working together. For some reason low in the ranks, that's very comfortable and no one has a problem with it. There's something that happens on that top floor. Something about it is not comfortable. Up to this point all of their life experiences with top people have been with all men.' Judy Rosener refers to this phenomenon as sexual static.[19]

A significant part of this sexual tension arises from the newness of women in nontraditional roles. When women leave the home and enter the public sphere, they violate the original, if tacit, sexual contract. In the original terms of this contract, a woman's place was in the home, not the boardroom. Jean Hendrick offered this observation, "I think there are men who are very easily intimidated by smart, strong women because in their experience women are not like that; plus, they're not attracted to women like that. So they don't know how to handle them. . . . Men who are used to thinking of women as sexual partners or as potential relationships don't really know how to deal when they're presented with an intelligent, opinionated, forceful woman. It is very awkward."

Again, we point to the historical period during which these women entered their corporate careers. The introduction of women into jobs traditionally reserved for men changed social relations in organizations. Noted organizational scholars Hearn and Parkin argue that the presence of women in nontraditional places in organizations creates charged sexualized social relations.[20] "For a lot of men," Jean Hendrick observed, "their first thought about women is sexual, and that makes them uncomfortable. And men don't like to be uncomfortable. They're under enough pressure and so they'll find all kinds of other things to say that are negative about this gal. She's too this, she doesn't understand finance – never mind they hired her for a creative position – or she waves her hand around too much when she talks, or I heard she went out with one of the guys. What they're really saying is, 'She makes me uncomfortable and I don't know how to deal with it. Therefore, I don't want her around.' "

On the outside: exclusion from informal networks

Another barrier experienced by the black women is limited access to informal and social networks in their organizations. The African-American women we interviewed felt they had less access to these networks in their organizations than white men and white women. As a result, they felt cut off from important organizational information, and less accepted as full members of the organization. Many of the women spoke of the critical importance of informal networks in career advancement. In most corporations, excellent performance is necessary for advancement but is not the sole criterion. Getting ahead also depends on access to informal networks and the relationships those networks can foster – mentorships, sponsorships, and help from colleagues. Building these relationships requires that the women be part of the social networks within the company. In our national survey, we found that having white men in their network and being accepted by white men on the job helped African-American women managers attain higher management levels. Yet, only 59 percent of the African-American women reported having white men in their networks, compared to 91 percent of the white women managers.[21] As we pointed out in the previous chapter, African-American women often feel as if they are outsiders in their own organizations.

Julia Smith told us how networks affect job opportunities in her Fortune 100 company, "When you network, you find a new job much as you would if you were out in the world looking. Once you have good results in one place, you have visibility; you will be hired away. When someone in your network gets a new set of responsibilities, he or she usually brings people along that he knows, trusts, or has worked with in the past." Black folks, Julia Smith says, just don't have the kind of extensive networks that allow for repeated quid pro quos. "It means that black folks who do not have those relationships don't move." Anna Smalls, a vice president in a Wall Street investment-banking firm, confirmed that view. "The firm is just like a fraternity. That's how it's run. My white male colleagues are very socially connected. It's a great big kind of brotherly thing. They like to deal with certain clients. They have the old boy network and the old lines of communication. That's how they do business." Formal and informal networks can serve to reinforce the dominance of white men, thereby institutionalizing inequality.

Similarly, the white women managers also believed that exclusion from the "old boy network" was one of the barriers to women's advancement. Sylvia Whitaker calls it the armpit phenomenon: "They put you under their armpit and say come fly with me up to the executive suite. They (the men) are earmarked from day one. I truly believe that unless you have been lucky enough to get into the 'armpit' track, your chances of advancing may still be real but it's going to take a lot longer." Likewise, Ann Gilbert told us, "I think women are still coming of age in the business world. Some men don't quite know how to deal with it. Some men still resent women being there. There's kind of an intrinsic good old boy system or network in place that you have to work around. If you don't go golfing with the guys on Saturday or you don't shoot a few hoops with the guys after work, you don't ever get to be a full-fledged member of the team. And men relate very differently to women than they do to men. Men are still the primary power force in businesses."

Informal social functions and networks, on and off the job, are said to foster collegiality and strengthen working relationships. But for many of our black interviewees, such events served as a source of anxiety. First, many of the black women we interviewed rejected the idea of using informal networks to advance because such settings could engender negative experiences, like Anna Small's experience when she joined colleagues at a bar only to be called a "black bitch." Other black women shared stories of painful rejection when they tried to participated in social activities. One interviewee explained her reluctance to socialize outside of work. "One of my colleagues invited me to a party, but she apparently didn't let her in-laws know that a black couple was coming. When we walked up to the door, we could hear everybody having a good time. I rang the doorbell, but nobody came. The door was open so my husband and I walked in and everybody stopped, just froze. I guess they were saying to themselves, "These black people are at the wrong party." But the woman who invited me said, "Oh, come on in." My husband said, "Let's get out of here." I said, "No, we're going to stay." We go in there and sure enough the first thing someone asks my husband is "What do you do?" He tells them he's supervisor with the public transit system. They walk off to another couple. My husband said, "Don't you ever ask me to go to another one of these functions." I didn't even pressure him after that experience. But it's just hard. In order to move up you've got to participate in all those things. My marriage is important to me and my family is important. But I'm not going to allow a job make him uncomfortable in order for me to move. I'd rather not have it if I have to go through all that just to get the title of vice president."

Challenges to authority

African-American women managers – but not their white counterparts – expressed frustration over the lack of control and authority in their managerial roles. The African-American women in our national survey sample reported challenges to their authority from bosses, subordinates, and colleagues.[22] These challenges may well emanate from a lack of acceptance of black women in authority positions. Consequently, these challenges created an obstacle to their ability to demonstrate competence.

After having tough but supportive bosses in the early part of her career, Karen Brown was almost devastated when a new boss "appointed this guy who worked for him and who was my peer to be over me and to check up on the work I was doing. He never told me that but I found out about it. I just remember it was awful. I'll never forget it because my friend came to town and she sat in my office and said I looked like I was in a lot of pain. I didn't understand it. I was being watched. I was being set up."

Colleen Powell, an upper-level executive in corporate treasury, recounted how a white female supervisor at a much lower level challenged her authority by attempting to take away her secretarial support. She believed this would never have happened to another officer at her level. "Without consulting with me, she calls my secretary and tells her to report to human resources to interview for another job in the company. She also told my secretary not to tell anybody that she was going to human resources. Well, my secretary calls me. I tell her to do what she says, and we will deal with it. I had put a lot of time and effort in training my secretary. When I checked with human resources, they said this supervisor had told them she had cleared this action with me. I said, "I assure you, she did not clear it with me." The situation escalated and there was a meeting of this supervisor, a human resources representative, my boss, and myself. During the meeting, the supervisor tells me she doesn't think I need anybody with the skills I had outlined. I said, "Wait a minute." She had the unmitigated gall to tell me what I need, when she is there not to tell me what I need but to accommodate my needs. After the meeting was over, I stayed to talk with my boss. I told him I considered it deceitful, disrespectful, and unprofessional. I said to him, "Well, what do you think?" He then says, "Well, I have never known her to be deceitful or disrespectful." He then goes on to say, "She may have told me and I may have forgotten to tell you." I realized then the situation was graver than I had thought. The two of them had conspired. It made me angry. I don't think she would have done this to a man or to a white woman. Perhaps she felt she could get away with it with me for some reason."

Hollow commitment to the advancement of women and minorities

The final barrier the black women perceived was hollow company commitment to advancing women and minorities in companies. Our survey data echo what we heard from women we interviewed: skepticism about their companies' efforts to affect real change. Patricia Triggs was of the opinion that top management in her company wants diversity and multiculturalism, and yet fears it. "The classic mind-set preventing progress is, 'Power is a zero-sum game, and right now I own it and those I parcel it out to are like me and do what I say, so I know I will always own the power. If I have to share the power with people who are not like me and do not do what I say, I may have to give up some of it.'" Dawn Stanley told us that black men and women in her manufacturing company feel there's "no corporate commitment to supporting or promoting them. There is no commitment in terms of getting managers to promote blacks who work with them." Another interviewee was even more explicit in talking about her experience: "If you don't have a senior management person who says this is the approach we're going to take, you're never going to get there. It will be the same ten white men on the staff going around to all the plants saying we're getting serious about our diversity this year. It'll be the same ten white men who have been here for the last ten years. They do the same dog-and-pony show. But it doesn't change." We found that only 21 percent of the African-American women who completed our national survey felt their companies were committed to the advancement of people of color in management. In contrast, white women were much more positive about the efforts of their companies to advance women and minorities. The women's perceptions point to the fact that African-American women need a commitment beyond mere words issued by top management. Careers can be blocked at lower levels of an organization when managers are not held accountable for the advancement of African-American women.

PERCEPTIONS OF CAREER PROGRESS

An obvious questions remains: How did the women feel about their overall career progress in corporate America? A large percentage of the black women felt they were *behind* where they should be while about the same percentage of white women felt they were *ahead* of where they expected to be. (See Table 27.1) When we analyzed the black women's reasons for feeling they were behind in their career progress, we found that the majority attributed the lack of progress to being stalled in their companies. Karen Brown, a senior human resource executive, told us bluntly, "I am blocked here. Right now it doesn't trouble me. . . . But in two years it will." Deborah Jones, a production executive, told us, "I think I'm a little bit behind in two ways. First, I think I should be making more money. I make a lot of

Table 27.1 Interviewees' perceptions of career progress

Level of Progress	Black Women	White Women
Ahead of expectations	23 percent	38 percent
Where expected	28	21
Behind	39	25
No opinion or did not answer	10	16

money, but I think I should be making more for somebody who has my years of experience at my age with the kind of exposure that I've had and with my ability. Second, I think I should be at a different level and have a different title. That's where I see the glass ceiling, by the way." Brenda Boyd too, expected to have made better progress in her company, which she had thought was more receptive to women. "Well, I'm behind where I expected to be in my career. I would have thought I'd be vice president by now. I thought this company would be a very likely place to be a vice president. There's a receptivity to women and there are black officers, whereas at my last company it was inconceivable for a woman or for a black person."

White women explained their lack of progress differently. Few attributed their slow progress to gender discrimination or company failure. A majority of the women offered explanations related to the nature of the work, cited things they had not done to assure their promotion, or suggested they were not "really behind." For example, Ann Gilbert attributed her slow career progress to changes in the banking industry. "The job I'm in now is a less management-oriented and more project-oriented position. I probably would have imagined more management responsibility now although this change has been very positive in terms of broadening my perspective on banking and in general." Marketing director Joyce Canton said of her feeling of being behind, "I'm not particularly impatient about the fact that I am overdue for a promotion to vice president. This assignment, while it's lateral, feels like a completely different job." Jean Hendrick assessed her career progress in this way: "I'm a little behind where I should be. I don't mean I'm behind in my accomplishments. But I should have gotten myself to one of the top positions. I don't know that I ever will, for two reasons. First, I don't know what's going to happen to the company. Second, I just still don't know if I am willing to come across in the way that will get me there. So while I feel that I should really be at the top, there's a step that I haven't taken. It may be that I'm just not perceived as enough of a business person – a real, real business person."

The white women who felt they were ahead of their expectations for their careers expressed surprise and amazement at how far they had progressed. For the most part, they were not comparing themselves to white men but to their early lives. This was true of women from both humble and privileged backgrounds. Sandra Martin told us, "I'm ahead and I don't really know what to do about it. I told my boss when I got promoted to senior vice president, 'I don't know what to ask for next. I'm stunned.' And he grinned and said, 'Don't worry about it. Tomorrow you'll think of something.'" Cecilia Monroe said, "I am so much ahead of wherever I thought I would be career wise and money wise that I'm just in awe sometimes." Gloria Goldberg, who grew up in an elite suburb of Westchester County, was no less exuberant in describing her progress: "I'm not just ahead. I think I'm beyond anything I ever imagined other than in daydreams."

We heard some of this sentiment in the voices of the black women. Many made it clear that they had achieved far more than what they thought their early backgrounds and race would allow. Yet, most were careful to distinguish that from where they should be compared to the white men in their companies. Typical of this expression is what we heard from Colleen Powell. Being a mid-level executive in a Fortune 500 company far exceeds what Colleen Powell expected in terms of career or professional prospects. As a young girl, she had to grow up incredibly fast after her mother left home to escape an abusive relationship. "But it does not mean I am where I should be. I cannot complain. I live a very good life. I can take care of myself. I am relatively independent . . . I have been very fortunate in comparison to many other people, in comparison to most people in this country. Look, I can get on a plane and ride first class. If I get tired of the situation here, I can make a reservation on a plane and fly first class to our international sites. Not many people can do that. I am extremely appreciative of all this because, except by the grace of God, I could be some place else." But when it comes to measuring her progress against white men in her company, Colleen made it clear that she is behind. "Based on what I contribute in comparison to what others contribute I deserve something else."

The women in our study encountered formidable barriers to their careers. If the barriers described by the white women seem less daunting, it may be because they have indeed made greater progress in attaining high-level management positions. Yet, despite these barriers, all of the women in our study have attained a measure of career success. How did these women crack the glass ceilings and scale the concrete walls they encountered? How do they make sense of their mobility? . . . [H]ow they perceived these barriers resulted in very different strategies for overcoming them.

NOTES

1 There are a number of studies of the glass ceiling. In fact the term first appeared in an article by Carol Hymowitz and Timothy Schellhardt, "The Glass Ceiling," in "The Corporate Woman: A Special Report," *Wall Street Journal*, 24 March 1986. Also see Ann Morrison et al., *Breaking the Glass Ceiling: Can Women Make It to the Top of America's Largest Corporations?* (Reading, MA: Addison-Wesley, 1988, 1992); Lisa Mainero et al., "Gender Gap in the Executive Suite: CEOs and Female Executives Report on Breaking the Glass Ceiling," *Academy of Management Executive* 12 (1998): 28–42; Gary N. Powell, "The Glass Ceiling: Explaining the Good and Bad News," in *Women in Management: Current Research Issues*, vol. 2, ed. Marilyn J. Davidson and Ronald J. Burke (London: Sage Publications, 2000), 236–249; and Catalyst, *Census of Women Corporate Officers and Top Earners* (New York: Catalyst, 1997). There are also several studies completed by the U.S. Department of Labor through its Glass Ceiling Commission. See *Good for Business: Making Full Use of the Nation's Human Capital: A Fact-Finding Report of the Federal Glass Ceiling Commission* (Washington, DC: GPO, 1995).

2 Again we want to point out that much of the glass ceiling research has been done on white populations.

3 Other studies point out that minority women feel they are at greater disadvantage than white women, white men, or male members of minority groups. See, for example, Mor

Barak, David A. Cherin, and Sherry Berkman, "Organizational and Personal Dimensions in Diversity Climate: Ethnic and Gender Differences in Employee Perceptions," *Journal of Applied Behavioral Science* 34, no. 1 (1998): 82–104; and Ellen E. Kossek and S. C. Zonia, "Assessing Diversity Climate: A Field Study of Reactions to Employer Efforts to Promote Diversity," *Journal of Organizational Behavior* 14 (1993): 61–81.

4 A budding body of research demonstrates that different combinations of gender and race can produce distinctive work experiences. See, for example, Darlyne Bailey, Donald Wolfe, and C. R. Wolfe, "The Contextual Impact of Social Support Across Race and Gender: Implications for African-American Women in the Workplace," *Journal of Black Studies* 26, no. 3 (1996): 297–307; Stella Nkomo and Taylor Cox, Jr., "Gender Differences in the Upward Mobility of Black Managers: Double Whammy or Double Advantage?" *Sex Roles* 21 (1989): 825–839; Roy L. Austin and Hiroko H. Dodge, "Despair, Distrust, and Dissatisfaction Among Blacks and Women, 1973–1987," *Sociological Quarterly* 33, no. 4 (1992): 579–598; S. M. Crow, L. Y. Fok, and S. J. Hartman, "Who Is at Greater Risk of Work-Related Discrimination – Blacks or Homosexuals?" *Employee Responsibilities and Rights Journal* 11, no. 1 (1998): 15–26; Susan J. Lambert and Karen Hopkins, "Occupational Conditions and Workers Sense of Community: Variations by Gender and Race," *American Journal of Community Psychology* 23, no. 2 (1995): 151–179; Weber and Higginbotham, "Black and White Professional-Managerial Women's Perceptions," 153–175; and Janice D. Yoder and Patricia Aniakudo, "Outsider Within the Firehouse: Subordination and Difference in the Social Interactions of African-American Firefighters," *Gender and Society* 11, no. 8 (1997): 324–341.

5 Other researchers have referred to the everydayness of racism experienced by African-Americans. For example, Philomena Essed, in her book *Understanding Everyday Racism: An Interdisciplinary Theory* (Newbury Park, CA: Sage Publications, 1991), 50, uses the term *everyday racism* to refer to the integration of racism into everyday situations through practices that activate underlying power relations. See also reference to bouts of racism and sexism described by the African-American women studied by Angela Farrar in her unpublished doctoral dissertation, "It's All About Relationships: African-American and European American Women's Hotel Management Careers" (Ph.D. diss., Virginia Polytechnic Institute and State University, 1995).

6 Jane Mills, *Woman Words: A Dictionary of Words About Women* (New York: Free Press, 1989). Mills draws her example from the scholarly work of Casey Miler and Kate Swift, *Words and Women: New Language in New Times* (London: Victor Gollancz, 1977).

7 According to black feminist thinker bell hooks: "White women and men justified the sexual exploitation of black women by arguing that they were the initiators of sexual relationships with men. From such thinking emerged the stereotype of black women as sexual savages, and in sexist terms as sexual savages, a nonhuman, an animal cannot be raped." See bell hooks, *Ain't I a Woman: Black Women and Feminism* (Boston: South End Press, 1981), 52.

8 Karen M. Ruggiero and Donald M. Taylor, "Why Minority Group Members Perceive or Do Not Perceive the Discrimination That Confronts Them: The Role of Self-Esteem and Perceived Control," *Journal of Personality and Social Psychology* 72, no. 2 (1997): 373–389. In their study, women, Asians, and blacks reacted to negative feedback after information about the probability of discrimination. Results of their study suggested that minority group members minimize discrimination because the consequences of doing so are psychologically beneficial.

9 Other researchers have documented this effect. Because of low expectations for blacks and other minority groups, successful performance creates contradictory effects. In one study, researchers found that dominant group participants set lower-minimum-competency standards, but higher ability standards, for female than for male and for black than for white applicants. They concluded that although it may be easier for

low-status group members to meet (low) standards, these same people must work harder to prove that their performance is ability based. See Monica Biernat and Diane Kobrynowicz, "Gender- and Race-Based Standards of Competence: Lower Minimum Standards but Higher Ability Standards for Devalued Groups," *Journal of Personal and Social Psychology* 72, no. 3 (1997): 544–557.

10 See a discussion of these cultural images in K. Sue Jewell, *From Mammy to Miss America and Beyond: Cultural Images and the Shaping of U.S. Policy* (London: Routledge, 1993), 35–75. Also read Barbara Christian, *Black Feminist Criticism: Perspectives on Black Women Writers* (Elmsford, NY: Pergamon Press, 1985).

11 In her study of black women managers in Great Britain, Linda Martin also found it was difficult for the women to be seen beyond their race and gender. Linda Martin, "Power, Continuity, and Change: Decoding Black and White Women Managers' Experience in Local Government," in *Women in Management: A Developing Presence,* ed. Morgan Tanton (London: Routledge, 1994).

12 Sharon Collins, "Black Mobility in White Corporations: Up the Ladder but out on a Limb," *Social Problems* 44 (1997): 59.

13 D. Thomas and J. Gabarro, *Braking Through: The Making of Minority Executives in Corporate America* (Boston, MA: Harvard Business School Press, 1999): 73–75.

14 When Catalyst surveyed 461 women executives (predominantly white), the women cited stereotyping as the number one obstacle to their advancement followed by exclusion from informal networks. Catalyst, *Women in Corporate Leadership Progress and Prospects* (New York: Catalyst, 1996).

15 There are a number of studies on gender stereotyping. For example, see N. Nicholson and M. A. West, *Managerial Job Change: Men and Women in Transition.* (Cambridge: Cambridge University Press, 1988); and Susan T. Fiske, "Controlling Other People: The Impact of Power on Stereotyping," *American Psychologist* 48 (1993): 612–628.

16 See the work of Deborah Tannen, *You Just Don't Understand: Women and Men in Conversation* (New York: Ballantine, 1990); and L. Smith-Lovin and C. Brody, "Interruptions in Group Discussion: The Effects of Gender and Group Composition," *American Sociological Review* 54 (1989): 434–453.

17 C. Cockburn, *In the Way of Women: Men's Resistance to Sex Equality in Organizations* (Ithaca, NY: ILR Press, 1991): 142.

18 As bell hooks notes: "While assimilation is seen as an approach that ensures successful entry of black people into the mainstream, at its very core it is dehumanizing. Embedded in the logic of assimilation is the white supremacist assumption that blackness must be eradicated so that a new self, in this case a 'white' self, can come into being.' See bell hooks, *Talking Back: Thinking Feminist, Thinking Black* (Boston: South End Press, 1989), 67.

19 Judy B. Rosener, *America's Competitive Secret: Utilizing Women As a Management Strategy* (New York: Oxford University Press, 1995).

20 Jeff Hearn and P. Wendy Parkin, "Gender and Organizations: A Selective Review and Critique of a Neglected Area," in *Gendering Organizational Analysis,* ed. Albert J. Mills and Peta Tancred (London: Sage Publications, 1992).

21 Harvard Business School Professor Herminia Ibarra studied informal networks of middle managers in several industries. She reported that minority managers had fewer intimate informal relationships than did white managers of both genders. See Herminia Ibarra, "Race, Opportunity, and Diversity of Social Circles in Managerial Networks," *Academy of Management Journal* 38 (1995): 673–703. Other research reported that black women are the race and gender group least likely to receive mentoring from the highest status managers in the company, white men. See the research reported in David A. Thomas, "The Impact of Race on Managers' Experiences of Developmental Relationships," *Journal of Organizational Behavior* 2, no. 4 (1990): 479–492.

22   In a study of authority hierarchies at work, Gail McGuire and Barbara F. Reskin found
     that black women faced higher authority and earnings penalties than either black men
     or white women. Compared with black men and white women, black women lost more
     authority and earnings because employers failed to reward their credentials in the same
     way as they did white men's. Gail McGuire and Barbara F. Reskin, "Authority Hierar-
     chies at Work: The Impacts of Race and Sex," *Gender and Society* 7, no. 4 (1993): 487–507.

CHAPTER

28

MAKING DIFFERENCES MATTER: A NEW PARADIGM FOR MANAGING DIVERSITY[1]

DAVID A. THOMAS AND ROBIN J. ELY

From Harvard Business Review (1996), September/October: 79–90

Why should companies concern themselves with diversity? Until recently, many managers answered this question with the assertion that discrimination is wrong, both legally and morally. But today managers are voicing a second notion as well. A more diverse workforce, they say, will increase organizational effectiveness. It will lift morale, bring greater access to new segments of the marketplace, and enhance productivity. In short, they claim, diversity will be good for business.

Yet if this is true – and we believe it is – where are the positive impacts of diversity? Numerous and varied initiatives to increase diversity in corporate America have been under way for more than two decades. Rarely, however, have those efforts spurred leaps in organizational effectiveness. Instead, many attempts to increase diversity in the workplace have backfired, sometimes even heightening tensions among employees and hindering a company's performance.

This article offers and explanation for why diversity efforts are not fulfilling their promise and presents a new paradigm for understanding – and leveraging – diversity. It is our belief that there is a distinct way to unleash the powerful benefits of a diverse workforce. Although these benefits include increased profitability, they go beyond financial measures to encompass learning, creativity, flexibility, organizational and individual growth, and the ability of a company to adjust rapidly and successfully to market changes. The desired transformation, however, requires a fundamental change in the attitudes and behaviors of an organization's leadership. And that will come only when senior managers abandon an underlying and flawed assumption about diversity and replace it with a broader understanding.

Most people assume that workplace diversity is about increasing racial, national, gender, or class representation – in other words, recruiting and retaining more people from traditionally underrepresented "identity groups." Taking this commonly held assumption as a starting point, we set out six years ago to investigate its link to organizational effectiveness. We soon found that thinking of diversity simply in terms of identity-group representation inhibited effectiveness.

Organizations usually take one of two paths in managing diversity. In the name of equality and fairness, they encourage (and expect) women and people of color to blend in. Or they set them apart in jobs that relate specifically to their backgrounds, assigning them, for example, to areas that require them to interface with clients or customers of the same identity group. African American M.B.A.'s often find themselves marketing products to inner-city communities; Hispanics frequently market to Hispanics or work for Latin American subsidiaries. In those kinds of cases, companies are operating on the assumption that the main virtue identity groups have to offer is a knowledge of their own people. This assumption is limited – and limiting – and detrimental to diversity efforts.

What we suggest here is that diversity goes beyond increasing the number of different identity-group affiliations on the payroll to recognizing that such an effort is merely the first step in managing a diverse workforce for the organization's utmost benefit. Diversity should be understood as *the varied perspectives and approaches to work* that members of different identity groups bring.

Women, Hispanics, Asian Americans, African Americans, Native Americans – these groups and others outside the mainstream of corporate America don't bring with them just their "insider information." They bring different, important, and competitively relevant knowledge and perspectives about how to actually *do work* – how to design processes, reach goals, frame tasks, create effective teams, communicate ideas, and lead. When allowed to, members of these groups can help companies grow and improve by challenging basic assumptions about an organization's functions, strategies, operations, practices, and procedures. And in doing so, they are able to bring more of their whole selves to the workplace and identify more fully with the work they do, setting in motion a virtuous circle. Certainly, individuals can be expected to contribute to a company their firsthand familiarity with niche markets. But only when companies start thinking about diversity more holistically – as providing fresh and meaningful approaches to work – and stop assuming that diversity relates simply to how a person looks or where he or she comes from, will they be able to reap its full rewards.

Two perspectives have guided most diversity initiatives to date: the *discrimination-and-fairness paradigm* and the *access-and-legitimacy paradigm*. But we have identified a new, emerging approach to this complex management issue. This approach, which we call the *learning-and-effectiveness paradigm*, incorporates aspects of the first two paradigms but goes beyond them by concretely connecting diversity to approaches to work. Our goal is to help business leaders see what their own approach to diversity currently is and how it may already have influenced their companies' diversity efforts. Managers can learn to assess whether they need to change their diversity initiatives and, if so, how to accomplish that change.

The following discussion will also cite several examples of how connecting the new definition of diversity to the actual *doing* of work has led some organizations to markedly better performance. The organizations differ in many ways – none are in the same industry, for instance – but they are united by one similarity: Their leaders realize that increasing demographic variation does not in itself increase organizational effectiveness. They realize that it is *how* a company defines diversity – and *what it does* with the experiences of being a diverse organization – that delivers on the promise.

THE DISCRIMINATION-AND-FAIRNESS PARADIGM

Using the discrimination-and-fairness paradigm is perhaps thus far the dominant way of understanding diversity. Leaders who look at diversity through this lens usually focus on equal opportunity, fair treatment, recruitment, and compliance with federal Equal Employment Opportunity requirements. The paradigm's underlying logic can be expressed as follows:

> Prejudice has kept members of certain demographic groups out of organizations such as ours. As a matter of fairness and to comply with federal mandates, we need to work toward restructuring the makeup of our organization to let it more closely reflect that of society. We need managerial processes that ensure that all our employees are treated equally and with respect and that some are not given unfair advantage over others.

Although it resembles the thinking behind traditional affirmative-action effects, the discrimination-and-fairness paradigm does go beyond a simple concern with numbers. Companies that operate with this philosophical orientation often institute mentoring and career-development programs specifically for the women and people of color in their ranks and train other employees to respect cultural differences. Under this paradigm, nevertheless, progress in diversity is measured by how well the company achieves its recruitment and retention goals rather than by the degree to which conditions in the company allow employees to draw on their personal assets and perspectives to do their work more effectively. The staff, one might say, gets diversified, but the work does not.

What are some of the common characteristics of companies that have used the discrimation-and-fairness paradigm successfully to increase their demographic diversity? Our research indicates that they are usually run by leaders who value due process and equal treatment of all employees and who have the authority to use top-down directives to enforce initiatives based on those attitudes. Such companies are often bureaucratic in structure, with control processes in place for monitoring, measuring, and rewarding individual performance. And finally, they are often organizations with entrenched, easily observable cultures, in which values like fairness are widespread and deeply inculcated and codes of conduct are clear and unambiguous. (Perhaps the most extreme example of an organization in which all these factors are at work is the United States Army.)

Without doubt, there are benefits to this paradigm: it does tend to increase demographic diversity in an organization, and it often succeeds in promoting fair treatment. But it also has significant limitations. The first of these is that its color-blind, gender-blind ideal is to some degree built on the implicit assumption that "we are all the same" or "we aspire to being all the same." Under this paradigm, it is not desirable for diversification of the workforce to influence the organization's work or culture. The company should operate as if every person were of the same race, gender, and nationality. It is unlikely that leaders who manage diversity under this paradigm will explore how people's differences generate a potential diversity of effective ways of working, leading, viewing the market, managing people, and learning.

Not only does the discrimination-and-fairness paradigm insist that everyone is the same, but, with its emphasis on equal treatment, it puts pressure on employees to make sure that important differences among them do not count. Genuine disagreements about work definition, therefore, are sometimes wrongly interpreted through this paradigm's fairness-unfairness lens – especially when honest disagreements are accompanied by tense debate. A female employee who insists, for example, that a company's advertising strategy is not appropriate for all ethnic segments in the marketplace might feel she is violating the code of assimilation upon which the paradigm is built. Moreover, if she were then to defend her opinion by citing, let us say, her personal knowledge of the ethnic group the company wanted to reach, she might risk being perceived as importing inappropriate attitudes into an organization that prides itself on being blind to cultural differences.

Workplace paradigms channel organizational thinking in powerful ways. By limiting the ability of employees to acknowledge openly their work-related but culturally based differences, the paradigm actually undermines the organization's capacity to learn about and improve its own strategies, processes, and practices. And it also keeps people from identifying strongly and personally with their work – a critical source of motivation and self-regulation in any business environment.

As an illustration of the paradigm's weaknesses, consider the case of Iversen Dunham, an international consulting firm that focuses on foreign and domestic economic-development policy. (Like all the examples in this article, the company is real, but its name is disguised.) Not long ago, the firm's managers asked us to help them understand why race relations had become a divisive issue precisely at a time when Iversen was receiving accolades for its diversity efforts. Indeed, other organizations had even begun to use the firm to benchmark their own diversity programs.

Iversen's diversity efforts had begun in the early 1970s, when senior managers decided to pursue greater racial and gender diversity in the firm's higher ranks. (The firm's leaders were strongly committed to the cause of social justice.) Women and people of color were hired and charted on career paths toward becoming project leaders. High performers among those who had left the firm were persuaded to return in senior roles. By 1989, about 50% of Iversen's project leaders and professionals were women, and 30% were people of color. The 13-member management committee, once exclusively white and male, included five women and four people of color. Additionally Iversen had developed a strong contingent of foreign nationals.

It was at about this time, however, that tensions began to surface. Senior managers found it hard to believe that, after all the effort to create a fair and mutually respectful work community, some staff members could still be claiming that Iversen had racial discrimination problems. The management invited us to study the firm and deliver an outsider's assessment of its problem.

We had been inside the firm for only a short time when it became clear that Iversen's leaders viewed the dynamics of diversity through the lends of the discrimination-and-fairness paradigm. But where they saw racial discord, we discerned clashing approaches to the actual work of consulting. Why? Our research showed that tensions were strongest among midlevel project leaders. Surveys and interviews indicated that white project leaders welcomed demographic diversity as a general sign of progress but that they also thought the new employees were somehow changing the company, pulling it away from its original culture and its mission. Common criticisms were that African American and Hispanic staff made problems too complex by linking issues the organization had traditionally regarded as unrelated and that they brought on projects that seemed to require greater cultural sensitivity. White male project leaders also complained that their peers who were women and people of color were undermining one of Iversen's traditional strengths: its hard-core quantitative orientation. For instance, minority project leaders had suggested that Iversen consultants collect information and seek input form others in the client company besides senior managers – that is, from the rank and file and from middle managers. Some had urged Iversen to expand its consulting approach to include the gathering and analysis of qualitative data through interviewing and observation. Indeed, these project leaders had even challenged one of Iversen's long-standing, core assumptions: that the firm's reports were objective. They urged Iversen Dunham to recognize and address the subjective aspect of its analyses; the firm could, for example, include in its reports to clients dissenting Iversen views, if any existed.

For their part, project leaders who were women and people of color felt that they were not accorded the same level of authority to carry out that work as their white male peers. Moreover, they sensed that those peers were skeptical of their opinions, and they resented that doubts were not voiced openly.

Meanwhile, there also was some concern expressed about tension between white managers and nonwhite subordinates, who claimed they were being treated unfairly. But our analysis suggested that the manager–subordinate conflicts were not numerous enough to warrant the attention they were drawing form top management. We believed it was significant that senior managers found it easier to focus on this second type of conflict than on midlevel conflicts about project choice and project definition. Indeed, Iversen Dunham's focus seemed to be a result of the firm's reliance on its particular diversity paradigm and the emphasis on fairness and equality. It was relatively easy to diagnose problems in light of those concepts and to devise a solution: just get managers to treat their subordinates more fairly.

In contrast, it was difficult to diagnose peer-to-peer tensions in the framework of this model. Such conflicts were about the very nature of Iversen's work, not simply unfair treatment. Yes, they were related to identity-group affiliations, but they were not symptomatic of classic racism. It was Iversen's paradigm that led managers to interpret them as such. Remember, we were asked to assess what was supposed to be a racial discrimination problem. Iversen's discrimination-and-fairness paradigm had created a kind of cognitive blind spot; and, as a result, the company's leadership could not frame the problem accurately or solve it effectively. Instead, the company needed a cultural shift – it needed to grasp what to do with its diversity once it has achieved the numbers. If all Iversen Dunham employees were to contribute to the fullest extent, the company would need a paradigm that would encourage open and explicit discussion of what identity-group differences really mean and how they can be used as sources of individual and organizational effectiveness.

Today, mainly because of senior managers' resistance to such a cultural transformation, Iversen continues to struggle with the tensions arising from the diversity of its workforce.

THE ACCESS-AND-LEGITIMACY PARADIGM

In the competitive climate of the 1980s and 1990s, a new rhetoric and rationale for managing diversity emerged. If the discrimination-and-fairness paradigm can be said to have idealized assimilation and color- and gender-blind conformism, the access-and-legitimacy paradigm was predicated on the acceptance and celebration of differences. The underlying motivation of the access-and-legitimacy paradigm can be expressed this way:

> We are living in a increasingly multicultural country, and new ethnic groups are quickly gaining consumer power. Our company needs a demographically more diverse work-force to help us gain access to these differentiated segments. We need employees with multilingual skills in order to understand and serve our customers better and to gain legitimacy with them. Diversity isn't just fair; it makes business sense.

Where this paradigm has taken hold, organizations have pushed for access to – and legitimacy with – a more diverse clientele by matching the demographics of the organization to those of critical consumer or constituent groups. In some cases, the effort has led to substantial increases in organizational diversity. In investment banks, for example, municipal finance departments have long led corporate finance departments in pursuing demographic diversity because of the typical makeup of the administration of city halls and county boards. Many consumer-products companies that have used market segmentation based on gender, racial, and other demographic differences have also frequently created dedicated marketing positions for each segment. The paradigm has therefore led to new professional and managerial opportunities for women and people of color.

What are the common characteristics of organizations that have successfully used the access-and-legitimacy paradigm to increase their demographic diversity? There is but one: such companies almost always operate in a business environment in which there is increased diversity among customers, clients, or the labor pool – and therefore a clear opportunity or an imminent threat to the company.

Again, the paradigm has its strengths. Its market-based motivation and the potential for competitive advantage that it suggests are often qualities an entire company can understand and therefore support. But the paradigm is perhaps more notable for its limitations. In their pursuit of niche markets, access-and-legitimacy organizations tend to emphasize the role of cultural differences in a company without really analyzing those differences to see how they actually affect the work that is done. Whereas discrimination-and-fairness leaders are too quick to subvert differences in the interest of preserving harmony, access-and-legitimacy leaders are too quick to push staff with niche capabilities into differentiated pigeonholes without trying to understand what those capabilities really are and how they could be integrated into the company's mainstream work. To illustrate our point, we present the case of Access Capital.

Access Capital International is a U.S. investment bank that in the early 1980s launched an aggressive plan to expand into Europe. Initially, however, Access encountered serious problems opening offices in international markets; the people from the United States who were installed abroad lacked credibility, were ignorant of local cultural norms and market conditions, and simply couldn't seem to connect with native clients. Access responded by hiring Europeans who had attended North American business schools and by assigning them in teams to the foreign offices. This strategy was a marked success. Before long, the leaders of Access could take enormous pride in the fact that their European operations were highly profitable and staffed by a truly international corps of professionals. They took to calling the company "the best investment bank in the world."

Several years passed. Access's foreign offices continued to thrive, but some leaders were beginning to sense that the company was not fully benefiting from its diversity efforts. Indeed, some even suspected that the bank had made itself vulnerable because of how it had chosen to manage diversity. A senior executive form the United States explains:

> If the French team all resigned tomorrow, what would we do? I'm not sure what we *could* do! We've never attempted to learn what these differences and cultural competencies really are, how they change the process of doing business. What is the German country team actually doing? We don't know. We know they're good, but we don't know the subtleties of how they do what they do. We assumed – and I think correctly – that culture makes a difference, but that's about as far as we went. We hired Europeans with American M.B.A.'s because we didn't know why we couldn't do business in Europe – we just assumed there was something cultural about why we couldn't connect. And ten years later, we still don't know what it is. If we knew, then perhaps we could take it and teach it. Which part of the investment banking process is universal and which part of it draws upon particular cultural competencies? What are the commonalities and differences? I may not be German, but maybe I could do better at understanding what it means to be an American doing business in Germany. Our company's biggest failing is that the department heads in London and the directors of the various country teams have never talked about these cultural identity issues openly. We knew enough to *use* people's cultural strengths, as it were, but we never seemed to learn from them.

Access's story makes an important point about the main limitation of the access-and-legitimacy paradigm: under its influence, the motivation for diversity usually emerges from very immediate and often crisis-oriented needs for access and legitimacy – in this case, the need to broker deals in European markets. However, once the organization appears to be achieving its goal, the leaders seldom go on to identify and analyze the culturally based skills, beliefs, and practices that worked so well. Nor do they consider how the organization can incorporate and learn from those skills, beliefs, or practices in order to capitalize on diversity in the long run.

Under the access-and-legitimacy paradigm, it was as if the bank's country teams had become little spin-off companies in their own right, doing their own exotic, slightly mysterious cultural-diversity thing in a niche market of their own, using competencies that for some reason could not become more fully integrated into the larger organization's understanding of itself. Difference was valued within Access Capital – hence the development of country teams in the first place – but not valued enough that the organization would try to integrate it into the very core of its culture and into its business practices.

Finally, the access-and-legitimacy paradigm can leave some employees feeling exploited. Many organizations using this paradigm have diversified only in those areas in which they interact with particular niche-market segments. In time, many individuals recruited for this function have come to feel devalued and used as they begin to sense that opportunities in other parts of the organization are closed to them. Often the larger organization regards the experience of these employees as more limited or specialized, even though many of them in fact started their careers in the mainstream market before moving to special markets where their cultural backgrounds were a recognized asset. Also, many of these people say that when companies have needed to downsize or narrow their marketing focus, it is the special departments that are often the first to go. That situation creates tenuous and ultimately untenable career paths for employees in the special departments.

THE EMERGING PARADIGM: CONNECTING DIVERSITY TO WORK PERSPECTIVES

Recently, in the course of our research, we have encountered a small number of organizations that, having relied initially on one of the above paradigms to guide their diversity efforts, have come to believe that they are not making the most of their own pluralism. These organizations, like Access Capital, recognize that employees frequently make decisions and choices at work that draw upon their cultural background – choices made because of their identity-group affiliations. The companies have also developed an outlook on diversity that enables them to *incorporate* employees' perspectives into the main work of the organization and to enhance work by rethinking primary tasks and redefining markets, products, strategies, missions, business practices, and even cultures. Such companies are using the learning-and-effectiveness paradigm for managing diversity and, by doing so, are tapping diversity's true benefits.

A case in point is Dewey & Levin, a small public-interest law firm located in a northeastern U.S. city. Although Dewey & Levin had long been a profitable practice, by the mid-1980s its all-white legal staff had become concerned that the women they represented in employment-related disputes were exclusively white. The firm's attorneys viewed that fact as a deficiency in light of their mandate to advocate on behalf of all women. Using the thinking behind the access-and-legitimacy paradigm, they also saw it as bad for business.

Shortly thereafter, the firm hired a Hispanic female attorney. The partners' hope, simply put, was that she would bring in clients from her own community and also demonstrate the firm's commitment to representing all women. But something even bigger than that happened. The new attorney introduced ideas to Dewey & Levin about what kinds of cases it should take on. Senior managers were open to those ideas and pursued them with great success. More women of color were hired, and they, too, brought fresh perspectives. The firm now pursues cases that its previously all-white legal staff would not have thought relevant or appropriate because the link between the firm's mission and the employment issues involved in the cases would not have been obvious to them. For example, the firm has pursued precedent-setting litigation that challenges English-only policies – an area that it once would have ignored because such policies did not fall under the purview of traditional affirmative-action work. Yet it now sees a link between English-only policies and employment issues for a large group of women – primarily recent immigrants – whom it had previously failed to serve adequately. As one of the white principals explains, the demographic composition of Dewey & Levin "has affected the work in terms of expanding notions of what are [relevant] issues and taking on issues and framing them in creative ways that would have never been done [with an all-white staff]. It's really changed the substance – and in that sense enhanced the quality – of our work."

Dewey & Levin's increased business success has reinforced its commitment to diversity. In addition, people of color at the firm uniformly report feeling respected, not simply "brought along as window dressing." Many of the new attorneys say their perspectives are heard with a kind of openness and interest they have never experienced before in a work setting. Not surprisingly, the firm has had little difficulty attracting and retaining a competent and diverse professional staff.

If the discrimination-and-fairness paradigm is organized around the theme of assimilation – in which the aim is to achieve a demographically representative workforce whose members treat one another exactly the same – then the access-and-legitimacy paradigm can be regarded as coalescing around an almost opposite concept: differentiation, in which the objective is to place different people where their demographic characteristics match those of important constituents and markets.

The emerging paradigm, in contrast to both, organizes itself around the overarching theme of integration. Assimilation goes too far in pursuing sameness. Differentiation, as we have shown, overshoots in the other direction. The new model for managing diversity transcends both. Like the fairness paradigm, it promotes equal opportunity for all individuals. And like the access paradigm, it acknowledges cultural differences among people and recognizes the value in those differences. Yet this new model for managing diversity lets the organization internalize differences among employees so that it learns and grows because of them. Indeed, with the model fully in place, members of the organization can say, We are all on the same team, *with* our differences – not *despite* them.

EIGHT PRECONDITIONS FOR MAKING THE PARADIGM SHIFT

Dewey & Levin may be atypical in its eagerness to open itself up to change and engage in a long-term transformation process. We remain convinced, however, that unless organizations that are currently in the grip of the other two paradigms can revise their view of diversity so as to avoid cognitive blind spots, opportunities will be missed, tensions will most likely be misdiagnosed, and companies will continue to find the potential benefits of diversity elusive.

Hence the question arises: What is it about the law firm of Dewey & Levin and other emerging third-paradigm companies that enables them to make the most of their diversity? Our research suggests that there are eight preconditions that help to position organizations to use identity-group differences in the service of organizational learning, growth, and renewal.

1. *The leadership must understand that a diverse workforce will embody different perspectives and approaches to work, and must truly value variety of opinion and insight.* We know of a financial services company that once assumed that the only successful sales model was one that utilized aggressive, rapid-fire cold calls. (Indeed, its incentive system rewarded salespeople in large part for the number of calls made.) An internal review of the company's diversity initiatives, however, showed that the company's first- and third-most-profitable employees were women who were most likely to use a sales technique based on the slow but sure building of relationships. The company's top management has now made the link between different identity groups and different approaches to how work gets done and has come to see that there is more than one right way to get positive results.

2. *The leadership must recognize both the learning opportunities and the challenges that the expression of different perspectives presents for an organization.* In other words, the

second precondition is a leadership that is committed to persevering during the long process of learning and relearning that the new paradigm requires.

3. *The organizational culture must create an expectation of high standards of performance from everyone.* Such a culture isn't one that expects less from some employees than from others. Some organizations expect women and people of color to underperform – a negative assumption that too often becomes a self-fulfilling prophecy. To move to the third paradigm, a company must believe that all its members can and should contribute fully.

4. *The organizational culture must stimulate personal development.* Such a culture brings out people's full range of useful knowledge and skills – usually through the careful design of jobs that allow people to grow and develop but also through training and education programs.

5. *The organizational culture must encourage openness.* Such a culture instills a high tolerance for debate and supports constructive conflict on work-related matters.

6. *The culture must make workers feel valued.* If this precondition is met, workers feel committed to – and empowered within – the organization and therefore feel comfortable taking the initiative to apply their skills and experiences in new ways to enhance their job performance.

7. *The organization must have a well-articulated and widely understood mission.* Such a mission enables people to be clear about what the company is trying to accomplish. It grounds and guides discussions about work-related changes that staff members might suggest. Being clear about the company's mission helps keep discussions about work differences from degenerating into debates about the validity of people's perspectives. A clear mission provides a focal point that keeps the discussion centered on accomplishment of goals.

8. *The organization must have a relatively egalitarian, nonbureaucratic structure.* It's important to have a structure that promotes the exchange of ideas and welcomes constructive challenges to the usual way of doing things – from any employee with valuable experience. Forward-thinking leaders in bureaucratic organizations must retain the organization's efficiency-promoting control systems and chains of command while finding ways to reshape the change-resisting mind-set of the classic bureaucratic model. They need to separate the enabling elements of bureaucracy (the ability to get things done) from the disabling elements of bureaucracy (those that create resistance to experimentation).

FIRST INTERSTATE BANK: A PARADIGM SHIFT IN PROGRESS

All eight preconditions do not have to be in place in order to begin a shift from the first or second diversity orientations toward the learning-and-effectiveness paradigm. But most should be. First Interstate Bank, a midsize bank operating in a midwestern city, illustrates this point.

First Interstate, admittedly, is not a typical bank. Its client base is a minority community, and its mission is expressly to serve that base through "the development of a highly talented workforce." The bank is unique in other ways: its leadership welcomes constructive criticism; its structure is relatively egalitarian and nonbureaucratic; and its culture is open-minded. Nevertheless, First Interstate had long enforced a policy that loan officers had to hold college degrees. Those without were hired only for support-staff jobs and were never promoted beyond or outside support functions.

Two years ago, however, the support staff began to challenge the policy. Many of them had been with First Interstate for many years and, with the company's active support, had improved their skills through training. Others had expanded their skills on the job, again with the bank's encouragement, learning to run credit checks, prepare presentations for clients, and even calculate the algorithms necessary for many loan decisions. As a result, some people on the support staff were doing many of the same tasks as loan officers. Why, then, they wondered, couldn't they receive commensurate rewards in title and compensation?

This questioning led to a series of contentious meetings between the support staff and the bank's senior managers. It soon became clear that the problem called for managing diversity – diversity based not on race or gender but on class. The support personnel were uniformly from lower socioeconomic communities than were the college-educated loan officers. Regardless, the principle was the same as for race- or gender-based diversity problems. The support staff had different ideas about how the work of the bank should be done. They argued that those among them with the requisite skills should be allowed to rise through the ranks to professional positions, and they believed their ideas were not being heard or accepted.

Their beliefs challenged assumptions that the company's leadership had long held about which employees should have the authority to deal with customers and about how much responsibility administrative employees should ultimately receive. In order to take up this challenge, the bank would have to be open to exploring the requirements that a new perspective would impose on it. It would need to consider the possibility of mapping out an educational and career path for people without degrees – a path that could put such workers on the road to becoming loan officers. In other words, the leadership would have to transform itself willingly and embrace fluidity in policies that in times past had been clearly stated and unquestioningly held.

Today the bank's leadership is undergoing just such a transformation. The going, however, is far from easy. The bank's senior managers now must look beyond the tensions and acrimony sparked by the debate over differing work perspectives and consider the bank's new direction an important learning and growth opportunity.

SHIFT COMPLETE: THIRD-PARADIGM COMPANIES IN ACTION

First Interstate is a shift in progress; but, in addition to Dewey & Levin, there are several organizations we know of for which the shift is complete. In these cases, company leaders have played a critical role as facilitators and tone setters. We have observed in particular that in organizations that have adopted the new perspective, leaders and managers – and, following in their tracks, employees in general – are taking four kinds of action.

They are making the mental connection. First, in organizations that have adopted the new perspective, the leaders are actively seeking opportunities to explore how identity-group differences affect relationships among workers and affect the way work gets done. They are investing considerable time and energy in understanding how identity-group memberships take on social meanings in the organization and how those meanings manifest themselves in the way work is defined, assigned, and accomplished. When there is no proactive search to understand, then learning from diversity, if it happens at all, can occur only reactively – that is, in response to diversity-related crises.

The situation at Iversen Dunham illustrates the missed opportunities resulting from that scenario. Rather than seeing differences in the way project leaders defined and approached their work as an opportunity to gain new insights and develop new approaches to achieving its mission, the firm remained entrenched in its traditional ways, able to arbitrate such differences only by thinking about what was fair and what was racist. With this quite limited view of the role race can play in an organization, discussions about the topic become fraught with fear and defensiveness, and everyone misses out on insights about how race might influence work in positive ways.

A second case, however, illustrates how some leaders using the new paradigm have been able to envision – and make – the connection between cultural diversity and the company's work. A vice president of Mastiff, a large national insurance company, received a complaint from one of the managers in her unit, an African American man. The manager wanted to demote an African American woman he had hired for a leadership position from another Mastiff division just three months before. He told the vice president he was profoundly disappointed with the performance of his new hire.

"I hired her because I was pretty certain she had tremendous leadership skill," he said. "I knew she had a management style that was very open and empowering. I was also sure she'd have a great impact on the rest of the management team. But she hasn't done any of that."

Surprised, the vice president tried to find out from him what he thought the problem was, but she was not getting any answers that she felt really defined or illuminated the root of the problem. Privately, it puzzled her that someone would decide to demote a 15-year veteran of the company – and a minority woman at that – so soon after bringing her to his unit.

The vice president probed further. In the course of the conversation, the manager happened to mention that he knew the new employee from church and was familiar with the way she handled leadership there and in other community settings. In those less formal situations, he had seen her perform as an extremely effective, sensitive, and influential leader.

That is when the vice president made an interpretive leap. "If that's what you know about her," the vice president said to the manager, "then the question for us is, why can't she bring those skills to work here?" The vice president decided to arrange a meeting with all three present to ask this very question directly. In the meeting, the African American woman explained, "I didn't think I would last long if I acted that way here. My personal style of leadership – that particular style – works well if you have the permission to do it fully; then you can just do it and not have to look over your shoulder."

Pointing to the manager who had planned to fire her, she added, "He's right. The style of leadership I use outside this company can definitely be effective. But I've been at Mastiff for 15 years. I know this organization, and I know if I brought that piece of myself – if I became that authentic – I just wouldn't survive here."

What this example illustrates is that the vice president's learning-and-effectiveness paradigm led her to explore and then make the link between cultural diversity and work style. What was occurring, she realized, was a mismatch between the cultural background of the recently promoted woman and the cultural environment of her work setting. It had little to do with private attitudes or feelings, or gender issues, or some inherent lack of leadership ability. The source of the underperformance was that the newly promoted woman had a certain style and the organization's culture did not support her in expressing it comfortably. The vice president's paradigm led her to ask new questions and to seek out new information, but, more important, it also led her to interpret existing information differently.

The two senior managers began to realize that part of the African American woman's inability to see herself as a leader at work was that she had for so long been undervalued in the organization. And, in a sense, she had become used to splitting herself off from who she was in her own community. In the 15 years she had been at Mastiff, she had done her job well as an individual contributor, but she had never received any signals that her bosses wanted her to draw on her cultural competencies in order to lead effectively.

They are legitimating open discussion. Leaders and managers who have adopted the new paradigm are taking the initiative to "green light" open discussion about how identity-group memberships inform and influence an employee's experience and the organization's behavior. They are encouraging people to make *explicit* use of background cultural experience and the pools of knowledge gained outside the organization to inform and enhance their work. Individuals often do use their cultural competencies at work, but in a closeted, almost embarrassed, way. The unfortunate result is that the opportunity for collective and organizational learning and improvement is lost.

The case of a Chinese woman who worked as a chemist at Torinno Food Company illustrates this point. Linda was part of a product development group at Torinno when a problem arose with the flavoring of a new soup. After the group had made a number of scientific attempts to correct the problem, Linda came up with the solution by "setting aside my chemistry and drawing on my understanding of Chinese cooking." She did not, however, share with her colleagues – all of them white males – the real source of her inspiration for the solution for fear that it would set her apart or that they might consider her unprofessional. Overlaid on the cultural issue, of course, was a gender issue (women cooking) as well as a work–family issue (women doing *home* cooking in a chemistry lab). All of these themes had erected unspoken boundaries that Linda knew could be career-damaging for her to cross. After solving the problem, she simply went back to the so-called scientific way of doing things.

Senior managers at Torinno Foods in fact had made a substantial commitment to diversifying the workforce through a program designed to teach employees to value the contributions of all its members. Yet Linda's perceptions indicate that, in the actual day-to-day context of work, the program had failed – and in precisely one of those areas where it would have been important for it to have worked. It had failed to affirm someone's identity-group experiences as a legitimate source of insight into her work. It is likely that this organization will miss future opportunities to take full advantage of the talent of employees such as Linda. When people believe that they must suggest and apply their ideas covertly, the organization also misses opportunities to discuss, debate, refine, and build on those ideas fully. In addition, because individuals like Linda will continue to think that they must hide parts of themselves in order to fit in, they will find it difficult to engage fully not only in their work but also in their workplace relationships. That kind of situation can breed resentment and misunderstanding, fueling tensions that can further obstruct productive work relationships.

They actively work against forms of dominance and subordination that inhibit full contribution. Companies in which the third paradigm is emerging have leaders and mangers who take responsibility for removing the barriers that block employees from using the full range of their competencies, cultural or otherwise. Racism, homophobia, sexism, and sexual harassment are the most obvious forms of dominance that decrease individual and organizational effectiveness – and third-paradigm leaders have zero tolerance for them. In addition, the leaders are aware that organizations can create their own unique patterns of dominance and subordination based on the presumed superiority and entitlement of some groups over others. It is not uncommon, for instance, to find organizations in which one functional area considers itself better than another. Members of the presumed inferior group frequently describe the organization in the very terms used by those who experience identity-group discrimination. Regardless of the source of the oppression, the result is diminished performance and commitment from employees.

What can leaders do to prevent those kinds of behaviors beyond explicitly forbidding any forms of dominance? They can and should test their own assumptions about the competencies of all members of the workforce because negative assumptions are often unconsciously communicated in powerful – albeit nonverbal – ways. For example, senior managers at Delta Manufacturing had for years allowed productivity and quality at their inner-city plants to lag well behind the levels of other plants. When the company's chief executive officer began to question why the problem was never addressed, he came to realize that, in his heart, he had believed that inner-city workers, most of whom were African American or Hispanic, were not capable of doing better than subpar. In the end, the CEO and his senior management team were able to reverse their reasoning and take responsibility for improving the situation. The result was a sharp increase in the performance of the inner-city plants and a message to the entire organization about the capabilities of its entire workforce.

At Mastiff, the insurance company discussed earlier, the vice president and her manager decided to work with the recently promoted African American woman rather than demote her. They realized that their unit was really a pocket inside the larger organization: they did not have to wait for the rest of the organization to make a paradigm shift in order for their particular unit to change. So they met again to think about how to create conditions with in their unit that would move the woman toward seeing her leadership position as encompassing all her skills. They assured her that her authentic style of leadership was precisely what they wanted her to bring to the job. They wanted her to be able to use whatever aspects of herself she thought would make her more effective in her work because the whole purpose was to do the job effectively, not to fit some preset traditional formula of how to be have. They let her know that, as a management team, they would try to adjust and change and support her. And they would deal with whatever consequences resulted from her exercising her decision rights in new ways.

Another example of this line of action – working against forms of dominance and subordination to enable full contribution – is the way the CEO of a major chemical company modified the attendance rules for his company's annual strategy conference. In the past, the conference had been attended only by senior executives, a relatively homogeneous group of white men. The company had been working hard on increasing the representation of women and people of color in its ranks, and the CEO could have left it at that. But he reckoned that, unless steps were taken, it would be ten years before the conferences tapped into the insights and perspectives of his newly diverse workforce. So he took the bold step of opening the conference to people from across all levels of the hierarchy, bringing together a diagonal slice of the organization. He also asked the conference organizers to come up with specific interventions, such as small group meetings before the larger session, to ensure that the new attendees would be comfortable enough to enter discussions. The result was that strategy-conference participants heard a much broader, richer, and livelier discussion about future scenarios for the company.

They are making sure that organizational trust stays intact. Few things are faster at killing a shift to a new way of thinking about diversity than feelings of broken trust. Therefore, managers of organizations that are successfully shifting to the learning-and-effectiveness paradigm take one more step: they make sure their organizations remain "safe" places for employees to be themselves. These managers recognize that tensions naturally arise as an organization begins to make room for diversity, starts to experiment with process and product ideas, and learns to reappraise its mission in light of suggestions from newly empowered constituents in the company. But as people put more of themselves out and open up about new feelings and ideas, the dynamics of the learning-and-effectiveness paradigm can produce temporary vulnerabilities. Managers who have helped their organizations make the change successfully have consistently demonstrated their commitment to the process and to all employees by setting a tone of honest discourse, by acknowledging tensions, and by resolving them sensitively and swiftly.

Our research over the past six years indicates that one cardinal limitation is at the root of companies' inability to attain the expected performance benefits of higher levels of diversity: the leadership's vision of the purpose of a diversified workforce. We have described the two most dominant orientations toward diversity and some of their consequences and limitations, together with a new framework for understanding and managing diversity. The learning-and-effectiveness paradigm we have outlined here is, undoubtedly, still in an emergent phase in those few organizations that embody it. We expect that as more organizations take on the challenge of truly engaging their diversity, new and unforeseen dilemmas will arise. Thus, perhaps more than anything else, a shift toward this paradigm requires a high-level commitment to learning more about the environment, structure, and tasks of one's organization, and giving improvement-generating change greater priority than the security of what is familiar. This is not an easy challenge, but we remain convinced that unless organizations take this step, any diversity initiative will fall short of fulfilling its rich promise.

NOTE

1   This article is based on a three-part research effort that began in 1990. Our subject was diversity; but, more specifically, we sought to understand three management challenges under that heading. First, how do organizations successfully achieve and sustain racial and gender diversity in their executive and middle-management ranks? Second, what is the impact of diversity on an organization's practices, processes, and performance? And,

finally, how do leaders influence whether diversity becomes an enhancing or detracting element in the organization?

Over the following six years, we worked particularly closely with three organizations that had attained a high degree of demographic diversity: a small urban law firm, a community bank, and a 200-person consulting firm. In addition, we studied nine other companies in varying stages of diversifying their workforces. The group included two financial-services firms, three *Fortune* 500 manufacturing companies, two midsize high-technology companies, a private foundation, and a university medical center. In each case, we based our analysis on interviews, surveys, archival data, and observation. It is from this work that the third paradigm for managing diversity emerged and with it our belief that old and limiting assumptions about the meaning of diversity must be abandoned before its true potential can be realized as a powerful way to increase organizational effectiveness.

GLOBALIZATION: OVERVIEW

EVANGELINA HOLVINO

More and more, being a manager means being an international manager. Focusing on the domestic consequences of decisions is no longer enough – managers must be attuned to the implications across countries, oceans, and continents. In Part VII, we investigate those implications by subtly shifting our gaze. Instead of focusing only on international management, we look at the dramatic effects of globalization more broadly – effects on work and organizations, managers and workers, women and men, people in the first and third worlds.[1] As with other parts in this book, we use a complex gender lens to explore how race and ethnicity, social class and nation, not only challenge our thinking about women and gender, but illuminate different parts of the global organizational terrain.

Globalization has many meanings, and most would agree it defies simplification. It presents challenges and opportunities, possibilities and dangers. The global flow of goods, services, money, and people is one way of summarizing what is new about globalization. As Adekanye (1999: 17) notes, "globalization involves the development and movement of financial capital, information technology, trade, the activities of multinationals, etc. In general, it gives prominence to market forces and tends to subordinate local and national trade to global trade." Whether the phenomenon is a blessing or a curse depends to a large extent on where one sits in the broad, global map: an individual's nationality, class background, gender, race, and ethnicity can make all the difference. That is why looking through a lens that acknowledges the "simultaneity" of different identities and its accompanying social processes is so richly revealing when exploring globalization.

For some, more often the elite, "globalization will create worldwide opportunities for growth and development by expanding options for both organizations and people across the world," creating new employment opportunities, developing needed entrepreneurial infrastructures and businesses in developing countries, democratizing governments, and addressing global social problems (Parker, 1996: 235). But globalization can also be understood as a newly developed form of capitalist exploitation that brings greater income disparities, the destruction of natural resources, the homogenization of corporate cultures, the loss of cultural and national identities, and enhanced opportunities only to some (Barber, 1995; Lazarus, 1998/9).

Four phenomena that over the last three decades signal the move towards globalization are: (1) an international division of labor and the transnationalization of production; (2) the reduction of trade barriers and government interference, which transforms the role of nation states; (3) the proliferation of the transnational corporation and the emergence of a global capitalist economic order and class; and (4) the cultural fragmentation, homogenization, and multiculturalism that comes with the "global motions of people" that follow global production (Dirlik, 1997). The implications of these global shifts for managers are immense. Most fundamentally, globalization challenges the whole way we think about organizations. The more traditional "international business" approach assumes the study of "individual, autonomous organizations," but organizations are fast evolving into complex global networks, which make "organization" as a unit of analysis a less useful form to study (Parker, 1996: 238). Increasingly, organizations and organizational life occur in the context of a global world fueled by economic, geopolitical, technological, and cultural processes, which affect not just the way business is done, but national cultures, laws, and political and social life (Parker, 1996: 234). For example, the global economy includes the business of corporations, but it also includes the status of newly developing countries, militarization and arms proliferation, and drug cartels. Viewing these aspects of globalization through a gender lens challenges us to take the perspective of women in different locations with different interests. Thus, we focus here on the impact of globalization and its processes, rather than providing tools or prescriptions for global management (Barlett and Ghoshal, 1992; Parker, 1996).

The impact of the globalized world on women is pervasive: as consumers, as workers, as managers, as mothers, and as citizens. Wichterich (2000: 1) argues that in the new export economies, where comparative advantage is achieved through "low pay without secondary wage-costs, plus weak trade unions and a powerful array of fiscal and investment incentives, . . . female labor power is the most important 'natural' resource. In export factories, women accounted for between 70 and 90 per cent of the total workforce." While women may appear to be advantaged by globalization because of increased opportunities for work, they can also pay a high price for their participation in the global economy. The readings in Part VII portray the contradictory effects of globalization on women and men, and on broader gender, race, and class structures and processes around the world.

Different frames on gender illuminate different aspects of global organizations and their impacts on women. The "glass ceiling," a focus of more conventional frames on gender, refers to the status of women managers and the barriers to their advancement in different countries. Adler and Izraeli (1994) exemplify this approach. They have documented the scarcity of women in executive positions across a variety of countries – a mere 3 percent – and identified both opportunities for and constraints on increasing women's leadership in transnational organizations. Their focus is on the executive suite and on the women in developed and developing countries who, while facing the dilemmas particular to their countries, share the same basic problem: "access to the channels from which firms recruit entry-level managers" (Adler & Izraeli, 1994: 92). Consistent with the Frame 2 "celebrate differences" approach, they argue that women managers provide a competitive advantage in the global economy. Adler has expanded on this notion, applauding what she sees as the feminization of global leadership, as evidenced by the increasing numbers of women who are global leaders and the "spread of traits and qualities generally associated with women to the process of leading organizations with worldwide influence" (Adler, 1997: 182). According to her study of global women leaders, these traits and qualities include: a particularistic approach, well suited for the needs of mass customization; a relational communication style; and a focus on vision, rather than hierarchical status. For global organizations to benefit from these strengths they must eliminate false assumptions about women working abroad, as well as make structural changes in organizational policies and practices to attract and support women – Frame 3 concerns (Adler & Izraeli, 1994). This approach reflects the belief that when companies include women managers in their global operations, they reap the benefits of diversity; thus, the only question remaining is how quickly they do so.

In the first reading in Part VII, "Dangerous liaisons: The feminine in management meets globalization," Marta Calás and Linda Smircich challenge the belief that "celebrating differences" augurs well for women. In this critical look at the discourse of women managers and globalization, these authors argue that incorporating the "patriarchally defined 'female' into traditional managerial activities" for instrumental corporate purposes leaves managerial ideologies intact and may even strengthen them (p. 391). They illustrate how the dominant managerial discourse subtly disadvantages women, while appearing gender-neutral. As a result, more exploitation is likely. They propose alternative female images that would disrupt the dominant discourse and its uncritical stance toward globalization. These images, they argue, could provoke new ways of thinking about consumption and production, encouraging organizations to think beyond the bottom line and acknowledge their responsibility to create a healthier society for both women and men.

But the impact of globalization goes far beyond concerns about international women managers. When we explore gender, race and ethnicity, class, and nationality simultaneously, we see another world – a world into which the next reading, "The nanny chain," by Arlie Hochschild, provides a glimpse. Drawing on Parreñas's (2001) comparative study of Filipino women in Rome and Los Angeles, Hochschild describes the lives of these migrant domestic workers – employees who provide elder care, childcare, or housecleaning in private homes and are paid by individuals or families. She notes some striking commonalities: (1) the majority of these workers maintain transnational households, sending money and gifts to their families at home; (2) many perform domestic work in spite of having a college education; and (3) they face the alienation of not belonging to their country of origin, their work country, or even the migrant communities in their new work countries. This shared experience of dislocation flows from the processes of globalization, she argues, which demand low-wage migrant workers in the economic centers of global capitalism and create what Parreñas calls "the global servants of global capitalism" (2000: 3). In this article, Hochschild traces how "global capitalism helps create a third world supply of mothering [and] a first world demand for it," (p. 404) by creating a "chain of care," which starts in the first world and ends with the "globalization of love." This chain of care creates financial inequities not only between those who can pay for care and those forced to provide it, but also in who gets access to the care itself.

The contrast between the lives of women managers and the lives of women workers globally is perhaps most striking in export processing zones (EPZs). These enclaves of production, with the sole purpose of exporting goods, have proliferated

all over the world as a feature of "development" and free trade. National governments ranging from Sri Lanka to Ireland to Guatemala, as well as US state and city
governments, like North Carolina and San Francisco, have sought to attract investment by offering a range of corporate incentives (Fine & Howard, 1995; Fuentes
& Ehrenreich, 1983). The lives of women in these global factories and "runaway
shops," which usually involve electronics and apparel manufacturing, are not easy.
The transnational and multinational companies draw from a pool of young, rural,
and poorly educated women with few work options. In order to meet their production quotas, these women suffer overwork, injuries, sexual harassment, and even
beatings and sterilization. Still, they are not helpless victims; they organize, develop
networks of support and informal systems to find new work, and otherwise resist
management's attempts to control and exploit them (Hossfeld, 1990; Ong, 1987).

In "*Maquiladoras*: The view from the inside," Maria Patricia Fernández Kelly pre-
sents a slice of the lives of women working in the assembly plants located in the
EPZs, or "free trade zones" on the border between the United States and Mexico.
In Mexico, it is estimated that more than one million women and men are
employed in the *maquilas* (Coalition for Justice in the Maquiladoras, 1999). Using
her own experience as a participant observer in the *maquiladoras* of Ciudad Juarez,
Fernández-Kelly explores the impact of globalization on the women working there.
While many have documented the situation of women (and men) in EPZs (see,
e.g., Salinger, 1997; STITCH & MSN, 2000; Zavella, 1991), this research "from the
inside" presents a close-up picture of how local women experience globalization in
their everyday lives and communities. Managers in developed countries can no
longer ignore the travails of these workers as "over there," because they are
integrally bound together in the same global system of production and distribution
(Holvino & Scully, 2001).

The final reading in Part VII explores yet another side of globalization that is
rarely considered but cannot be ignored: US soldiers abroad and the prostitutes
who service them. The US military, which took on a multinational reach after World
War II, was one of the world's first truly global organizations. It established and currently maintains bases around the world, which have an enormous impact on the
local communities that host them, including the growth of prostitution. Cynthia
Enloe articulates the intricate connections between war and militarized peace and
the inequalities they create. She explores how the military constructs not only
certain kinds of masculinities and femininities, but the racial, ethnic, and class
identities that make possible certain kinds of organizational activities as well. For
example, the particular militaristic masculinity of the soldier can only be created
in relation to other social identities – in this case, the woman of color prostitute in
the brothels near the base, the family members she supports, and the local men in
her life. All intertwine to maintain the particular masculine identity that helps
sustain the military organization. From the perspective of this article, we see that
"work organization" often means something beyond the transnational business
enterprise and involves formal and informal organized activities and entities:
churches, nongovernmental organizations, political parties, clubs, criminal networks, and terrorist groups.

To some, these readings may take us far afield. What do domestic workers or sex
workers have to do with business, transnational corporations, and work organizations? They draw our attention to the pervasive and far-flung impact of globalization and international business. When we place management in its broader social

environment, we see farther. If we think of this global world in a more critical and nuanced fashion, other organizations, activities and workers come to the fore, all connected in the "new global (dis)order" (Deng, 1993). By viewing the seemingly neutral processes of organizing work through a lens that focuses our attention on gender, race, class, ethnicity, and nationality simultaneously, we expand the boundaries of "organization" and are able to pay attention to the multiple economic and social issues that link organizations, the lives of their diverse stakeholders, and the global and local environments in which they all operate.[2]

NOTES

1 Though we are aware of the contested nature of these terms, we use first world to refer to people from the United States, Canada, the countries of Western Europe, and other industrialized countries like Japan, Australia, and New Zealand, most of which were colonizers and are geographically located in the Northern hemisphere (De Shazer, 1994). The third world refers to colonized and decolonized countries of Asia, Africa, Latin America, the Middle East, and the Caribbean. For a historical summary of other terms that describe more nuanced worldwide economic divisions see Anderson and Cavanah (2000: 6–11).

2 I would like to thank Prof. Marta Calás of the University of Massachusetts at Amherst for her generosity in providing resources for this Part of the Reader and for insightful discussions over the years that have influenced my approach to globalization and gender.

REFERENCES

Adekanye, T. 1999. Economic significance and impact of women's work on agricultural development and rural economy: Formal and informal sectors. Keynote paper prepared for the Seminar on the Economic Role of Women in Rural and Agricultural Development. Greek Ministry of Agriculture, The Austrian Development Co-operation and CTA. Athens, Greece (October).

Adler, N. 1997. Global leadership: Women leaders. *Management International Review*, 37 (special issue 1): 171–96.

Adler, N. & Izraeli, D. N. 1994. Where in the world are the women executives? *Business Quarterly*, Autumn: 89–94.

Anderson, S. and Cavanah, J. with T. Lee and the Institute for Policy Studies 2000. *Field guide to the global economy*. New York: The New York Press.

Barber, B. 1995. *Jihad vs. McWorld*. New York: Ballantine Books.

Barlett, C. A. and Ghoshal, S. 1992. What is a global manager? *Harvard Business Review*, 70: 124–32.

Coalition for Justice. 1999. Annual report. ⟨Http://www.maquilasolidarity.org.⟩

Deng, F. 1993. Africa and the new world dis-order: Rethinking colonial borders. *Brookings Review*, 11 (2): 32–9.

De Shazer, M. K. (1994). *A poetics of resistance: Women writing in El Salvador, South Africa, and the United States*. Ann Arbor: MI: The University of Michigan Press.

Dirlik, A. 1997. The postcolonial aura: Third world criticism in the age of global capitalism. In A. McClintock, A. Mufti, and E. Shohat (eds.), *Dangerous liaisons: Gender, national, and postcolonial perspectives*: 501–28. Minneapolis: University of Minnesota Press.

Fine, J. and Howard, M. 1995. Women in the free trade zones of Sri Lanka. *Dollars and Sense*, November/December: 26–7, 39–40.

Fuentes, A. and Ehrenreich, B. 1983. *Women in the global factory*. Boston: South End Press.

Holvino, E. and Scully, M. A. 2001. Bodies and shops: Whose sweat and whose equity? Paper presented at the Critical Management Studies conference, Manchester, UK, July 11–13. (Forthcoming in the CGO Working Paper series.)

Hossfeld, K. J. (1990). "Their logic against them": Contradictions in sex, race, and class in Silicon Valley. In K. Ward (ed.), *Women workers and global restructuring*: 149–78. Ithaca, NY: Cornell University Press.

Lazarus, N. 1998/99. Charting globalization. *Race & Class*, 40(2–3): 91–109.

Ong, A. 1987. *Spirits of resistance and capitalist discipline: Factory women in Malaysia*. New York: State University of New York Press.

Parker, B. 1996. Evolution and revolution: From international business to globalization. In S. R. Clegg, C. Hardy, and W. R. Nord (eds.), *Managing Organizations: Current Issues*: 234–56. London: Sage.

Parreñas, R. S. 2001. *Servants of globalization: Women, migration, and domestic work*. Stanford, CA: Stanford University Press.

Salinger, L. 1997. From high heels to swathed bodies: Gendered meanings under production in Mexico's export processing industry. *Feminist Studies*, 23: 549–59.

STITCH & Maquila Solidarity Network. 2000. *Women behind the labels: Worker testimonies from Central America*. Washington, DC: STITCH.

Wichterich, C. 2000. *The globalized woman: Reports from a future of inequality* (translated by Patrick Camiller). London: Zed Book.

Zavella, P. 1991. Mujeres in factories: Race and class perspectives on women, work, and family. In M. Di Leonardo (ed.), *Gender at the crossroads of knowledge*: 312–36. Berkeley: University of California Press.

CHAPTER 20

DANGEROUS LIAISONS: THE "FEMININE-IN-MANAGEMENT" MEETS "GLOBALIZATION"

29

MARTA B. CALÁS AND LINDA SMIRCICH

From *Business Horizons* (1993) 36(2):71–81

HELP WANTED

Seeking transforming manager. Impatient with rituals and symbols of hierarchy. Favors strengthening networks and interrelationships, connecting with coworkers, customers, suppliers. Not afraid to draw on personal, private experience when dealing in the public realm. Not hung up by a "What's in it for me?" attitude. Focuses on the whole, not only the bottom line; shows concern for the wider needs of the community. If "managing by caring and nurturing" is your credo, you may be exactly what we need. Excellent salary and benefits, including child care and parental leaves.

Contact CORPORATE AMERICA
FAX: 1-800-INTRUBL

An Equal Opportunity Employer
We do not discriminate on the basis of sex, race, age,
disabilities, or sexual orientation.

How soon can we expect to see such a want ad? Soon, no doubt, if recent literature is to be believed. Since the mid-1980s, books and articles have appeared that, like our fictitious advertisement, support approaches to management based on traits and orientations traditionally associated with women, the female, and the feminine. A common story runs through these examples: Currently, business firms in the U.S. are suffering countless setbacks. Changes are needed. Therefore, if women *and* women-oriented qualities are brought into organizations and allowed to exert influence, it is likely that changes in the right direction will occur. Tom Peters (1990) best articulated this sentiment:

> It's perfectly obvious that women should be better managers than men in today's topsy-turvy business environment. As we rush into the 90s, there is little disagreement about what business must become: less hierarchical, more flexible and team-oriented, faster and more fluid. In my opinion, one group of people has an enormous advantage in realizing this necessary new vision: women.

In principle, we cannot do other than share the sentiment, as Peters' statement seems to argue for more managerial opportunities for women. But it is important to approach this discussion by cautiously asking the following questions: What is the historical significance of recent discussions about "women's ways of leading" and the "female advantage"? Do they really help create new opportunities for women? Do they mark a new era of openness to difference, signaling the arrival of real receptivity to qualities that were once undervalued? Or do they signal only more of the same, or worse?

Recent research has argued that there are dangers associated with such "feminine-in-management" positions. We have pointed out (Calás et al. 1991) that although these positions are presented as a call for change in organizational thinking, they in fact do little more than restate existing management approaches under a different name. The dangers, we argued, are very real insofar as their apparent valuing of some "essential women's" qualities maintains an illusion of opportunity and equality for women in the managerial world while obstructing critical examination of the pervasive theoretical assumptions sustaining that world.

In this article we further analyze the problems and dangers associated with the feminine-in-management positions. As we point out below, the current appearance of these positions is not arbitrary, nor do they represent a natural progression toward more advanced organizational knowledge. Rather, we see a repetition of a cycle common in both academic and managerial circles when a need for change appears. On those occasions there is a tendency to obscure the need for funda-mental change – which would alter the established balance of power – with a surface change that maintains that same balance while creating the appearance of a radical rethinking of what is. Women have been used for this purpose on more than one occasion. Therefore, if such is the case with the feminine-in-management, what is the "essential female" obscuring? What else is happening that propels managers and management theorists to "cherchez la femme"?

Other writings that call attention to the contemporary economic scene faced by American corporations have been appearing concurrently (Reich 1991; Kuttner 1991; Porter 1990; Ohmae 1990; Thurow 1992). In these writings the corporate actor is discussed within the wider environmental context of a "global reality". Dif-ferent from earlier times, the arguments go, American corporations are no longer competing on familiar grounds. Contemporary managers face a more complicated competitive field where not all actors play by the same rules. Like the feminine-in-management literature, these writings announce changes, both behaviorally and structurally, for America's corporate ways.

But why these parallel discourses now? We argue that there is, in fact, a close relationship between feminine-in-management and "globalization." If approached separately, each of these managerial discourses *appears* to bring about fundamen-tal changes in corporate America. However, when taken together, one – the feminine-in-management – maintains the *domestic* balance of power that allows for the other – globalization – to fight for continuing that same balance in the *inter-national* arena. Together they keep in place America's traditional social, cultural, and economic values, not effecting any transformational changes.

We propose that the lines of thought portrayed by these two parallel discourses might hurt both women and organizations insofar as their "solutions" to manage-rial troubles repeat an old quick-fix way of thinking prevalent in the U.S. There-fore, we will also analyze the more long-term dangers associated with such positions.

As we will show in our conclusions, "thinking feminine" may be the necessary thing to do at this point, but not as it has been so far presented by the feminine-in-management.

A BRIEF HISTORY OF THE FEMININE-IN-MANAGEMENT RHETORIC

For about 20 years, literature on women and management stressed women's abilities as managers as equivalent to those of men. But in the mid-1980s, general discussions about the place of women in management took a turn. Besides talk about how women could perform managerial roles as well as men (the equality discussion), a case was now being made that women's unique "feminine skills" could make important contributions to organizational management (the difference discussion), on which the feminine-in-management rhetoric is based.

The "women's difference" talk finds its support in recent research literature on the psychology of women (Gilligan 1982; Chodorow 1978; Miller 1976). These works show that traditional views of gender differences have not been culturally neutral; rather, qualities associated with males have been prized and those associated with females have been devalued. Yet because value systems are social and cultural constructions, it is possible to reconceptualize female characteristics as positive – even though different – rather than as inferior to male characteristics.

Clearly, the appeal of these ideas stems from their implications for revaluing women and feminine qualities in various kinds of activities, including approaches to management. For instance, Marilyn Loden (1985) was one of the first to argue, under the women's difference umbrella, that women's managerial styles could be what was needed for solving American productivity problems. Similar arguments followed in other periodicals (*Cosmopolitan, Organization Dynamics, Harvard Business Review, Academy of Management Executive*) and books (*Reinventing the Corporation, Megatrends 2000, The Female Advantage*). In these writings, what was once disparaged as female patterns in need of overcoming for success in management were now positioned as special and useful for organizations.

For example, Jan Grant (1988) proposed that "women may indeed be the most radical force available in bringing about organizational change," thanks to qualities gained in experiences with their families and communities. In Grant's view, women's skills at communication and cooperation, their interests in affiliation and attachment, and their orientation toward power as a transforming and liberating force to be used for public purposes rather than for personal ambition and power over others are critically needed human resource skills in contemporary organizations.

More recently, Judy Rosener (1990) described "interactive leadership" as characteristic of some of the executive women she studied. Patterns unique to women's socialization made them comfortable with encouraging participation and facilitating inclusion, sharing power and information, enhancing the self worth of others, and energizing and exciting others about their work.

Perhaps the best representative of these ideas in the popular business literature has been posited by Sally Helgesen (1990) in her close-up study of four female executives, whose images of organizational structure were more similar to a web or circle than a hierarchy or pyramid. From this, Helgesen articulates a notion of authority not at the head of an organization, but at its heart, as "authority comes

from connection *to* the people around rather than distance *from* those below."
Helgesen, like others, argues that the "integration of the feminine principles into
the public realm offers hope for healing" the conditions of modern life, pervaded
by "feelings of pointlessness, sterility and the separation from nature."

The writings about the feminine-in-management have been challenged on
scientific grounds. Serious concerns have been raised about the adequacy of their
research methods and the empirical base of their claims. Our concerns about them
here are more cultural and historical. As these writings are gaining an important
status as new representations of *good* management, they deserve analysis that goes
beyond the question of their scientific adequacy – are they true? – in favor of asking,
"Why are they being spoken?" and "Why are they being spoken now?"

Our argument is this: The appropriation of the "women's difference" discourse
by management writers is merely another episode in a long history of economic
reasoning that ends up valuing women out of instrumental necessity. From the girls
of the Lowell mills in the 1800s to Rosie the Riveter in World War II, we have seen
the ebb and flow of cultural discourses that support the movement of women from
the domestic to the public sphere and back again.

From a historical perspective, the current female advantage rhetoric is part of
another repetition of this cycle – in this case because there are instrumental advantages to feminizing the national economy under conditions of globalization. We
consider that this recent turn toward "women's ways of leadership" is nothing other
than a 1990s version of the "conquest" by women of the American business office
in the 1930s. As analyzed in *Fortune* ("Women in Business . . ." 1935), the business
office was the "new land lying in the wilderness at the frontiers of industrial
advance" that women came to dominate – not because female labor was cheaper,
as the "crass economist" might argue, or because they were "physically better
adapted" to the office, as "the solemn findings of [psychometric] science" might
contend. Instead, *Fortune* asserted:

> The whole point of the whole problem is merely that the modern office necessitates
> a daily, intimate, and continuing relation which is much more possible between a man
> and a number of women than between a man and a number of men. . . . It is, if you
> will, a relation based upon sex. . . . The whole point of the whole problem, in other
> words, is that women occupy the office because the male employer wants them there.

At a time when sexism did not need to be covered up with a veneer of civility,
the *Fortune* writer candidly observed that women make the office "a more pleasant,
peaceful, and homelike place." In a very perceptive analysis, the writer further
stated:

> In the field of the office it was not the *work* of the home which was carried over into
> the industrial setting, but the *setting* of the home which was carried over to the indus-
> trial work. The work was new work but it was done by women not because it was new
> but because they were women. And more importantly, it was the employing male, not
> the eager female applicant, who was responsible for the result. . . . Indeed, and at the
> risk of further roiling the feminist pride, it must be said that woman's greatest indus-
> trial conquest has been made not only through the male but through the institution
> of marriage. It is marriage – or rather its imitation – which, as we have seen, explains
> and justifies the existence of the lady at the secretary's desk.

This writer's commentary is particularly interesting because in its bluntness (or, as some might say today, his incisive structural analysis), it uncovers the powerlessness embodied in the feminine-in-management, which now as then merely contributes to supporting the industrial activities of a patriarchal society.[1] This is clearly seen when the author refers to the achievements of two particular women:

> . . . in spite of their success, in spite of the importance of their positions and the satisfaction of their work, it still remains true that the women of the office have won their places *not by competition with men but by the exercise of qualities with which no competition was possible.* . . . Both of them are there as women. It is a great triumph. But it is a triumph for their womanhood and not for their ambition. [emphasis added]

The current feminine-in-management discourse parallels this earlier discourse. They both incorporate a patriarchally defined "female" into traditional managerial activities and their instrumental orientation. The feminine-in-management rhetoric maintains intact – even strengthens – traditional managerial ideologies, because it is the "female" constructed under patriarchy who is given voice and presence, *extending* the patriarchal family's female role from the private to the public domain. As we shall see, this is the primary role that the feminine-in-management performs in the discourses of globalization – as suggested by the saying, "Behind every successful man there is a woman."

EXTENDING THE HOUSEHOLD UP TO THE NATIONAL BORDER

Consider the following scenario: Some years have passed and most organizations are "globalized." Decisions are no longer made at the national level under national premises. Globalization means a trans- or supranationally coordinated decision-making system that feeds from a network of national organizations, both large and small. Who are the players in this situation, and how are they positioned?

The rhetoric enabled by the feminine "web-and-connection" metaphors plays very well here. Web-and-connection brings to mind dual images: those of good, caring interpersonal communication and, at the same time, closer interorganizational relations. The first image supports change toward "flatter" national organizations, where team-based groups would reduce hierarchy and reduce the "bossing" systems; the second image supports strong network structures and new, more powerful hierarchies at the global level.

In this order of things, non-hierarchical ("feminized") national organizations would be the equivalent of the feminized 1930s offices, because the feminine-in-management would bring the traditional values of the American household up to the national border. That is, the private/public divide (women in the household, men out in the world) will not have disappeared. It will have been displaced and recreated on a larger scale, as the hierarchy and authority system are reenacted beyond the "national household" in the global arena. Said differently, the national organization – as feminine as it might become – would be a powerless pawn in a globalized organizational world.

More than international imperatives drive this turn of events. If we observe the feminine-in-management within the context of current American society, some other very important facts are uncovered that further promote the structural feminization of national organizations. Demographically, it is evident that America's labor force is becoming increasingly diverse. Many have praised these demographic changes as a guarantee that the "diverse," including women, will occupy better organizational positions denied them in the past. It is seldom acknowledged that the trends toward flatter organizations (that is, more team-based and with less middle management layers) may eliminate many of these opportunities.

At the same time, close scrutiny of the discourses of globalization reveals that the issue of diversity is treated by speaking simultaneously from "both sides of the mouth." America's "diversity" is often presented as a complicating factor in its competitive situation. It is easy to find very open claims about Japan's – or even Sweden's – advantages because, as this rhetoric goes, those countries have a homogeneous population. Others consider that Japanese plants in the U.S. have an unfair advantage because they are able to choose "prime" locations where the population is young, non-diverse, and non-unionized. Ironically, these comments are often made by the same people who criticize Japan for not offering equal opportunities to women, for engaging in sexual harassment, or for having hinted that the U.S. is in trouble because of racial problems.

In this situation, the "web-and-connection" metaphor plays a fundamental role. At the domestic level, reducing the organizational hierarchy reduces the number of the "diverse" who will be appointed to managerial positions. Meanwhile, the feminine-in-management would help in converting "diversity" into homogeneous "team-players" under a caring, motherly gaze. Yet whose idea of a "good mother" is portrayed by the feminine-in-management? One cannot fail to observe that the values represented by the feminine-in-management literature are those of white, formally educated, middle- to upper-middle-class American women, and that it is their mothering styles, family values, and relationship to children that are represented in the "authority through connection" metaphors.

We should not be too quick to praise the feminine-in-management arguments insofar as they distract us from observing their dire consequences: the feminine-in-management simply extends the established power structure by moving the values of those who are "second best" into the vacated domestic (national) managerial spaces. By focusing only at the micro-organizational level, the feminine-in-management creates an illusion of opportunity and change. But when placed at the larger macro-societal level, it becomes a major support for the discourses of globalization, which benefit only a selected few. The organizations created by the meeting of these two discourses locate a certain class of feminine values in the "middle manager" position (the home office) while the rank-and-file – embodied in the values of the "diverse" – keep the national (home) fires burning. In the meantime, the strategists (not a feminine or diverse image, to be certain) move to a higher, more valuable international playing field where decisions are made.

Therefore, the second "conquest of the office" by women represents little more than a simple displacement of power from the national to the global economy. This displacement further legitimizes the traditional power-holders as certain "family values" become reenacted in the public domain, and a whole army of "organizational wives" (Huff 1990) play their patriotic roles in sustaining the heroic "boys" who serve abroad.

TO SERVE WITH PRIDE AND DISTINCTION

The discourses of globalization create awareness of another national reality: America is not a high-wage manufacturing economy anymore, and manufacturing's replacement, the service economy, will not bring about high-wage jobs ("The Global Economy . . ." 1992). One of the marks of globalization is the move of labor-intensive operations toward low-wage world regions coupled with the concomitant displacement of national workers from manufacturing jobs. Yet even manufacturing firms maintaining national operations often restructure into workplaces with lower wages (or fewer jobs). In the meantime, most new jobs in the service sector are in lower-paying occupations. Is it accidental that the rank-and-file jobs for "the new labor force" – comprising a higher proportion of women and minorities – are not the same high-paid, "making-things" jobs of a past American economy?

Beyond the rank-and-file level, global competitiveness has also brought about the age of the lean-and-mean organization. Regardless of the causes (takeover events and associated reorganizations, added control capabilities "at a distance" with sophisticated management information systems), the very material consequence of these organizational activities is the elimination of middle management layers, resulting in a large number of mostly white males being "outplaced" by their organizations. Under these conditions, cheaper managers are needed and, from our viewpoint, the feminine-in-management rhetoric provides precisely the low-cost answer for national restructuring toward global competitiveness.

Both Tom Peters and Lester Thurow give us glimpses of the positive economic consequences of "feminizing" national organizations. For Peters (1990), in an abnormal world (topsy-turvy) the "abnormal" (women) must have the advantage by being able to do what no man seems capable of doing: work in a less hierarchical organization. How much are these less hierarchical jobs worth? Obviously not too much, if "outplaced" executives are not rushing to take them. This becomes even more explicit in Thurow's words, which, though not referring to women, clearly articulate a "feminized" workplace (Thurow 1992):

> To use office automation efficiently requires major changes in office sociology. The efficient way to use word processors is to eliminate secretaries or clerks and to require managers to type their own memos and call up their own files. But a personal secretary is a badge of prestige and power. No one wants to give up that badge.

These changes, as Thurow reminds us, would require "a boss to do less bossing," something that he believes American executives are incapable of doing because they covet power too much. His prescribed ideological changes for solving this problem are perfectly matched by Grant's (1988) version of the feminine-in-management, in which women's transforming and liberating force works toward public purposes rather than for personal ambition and power over others. But what Grant does not say and Thurow does is that to obtain more efficient and less hierarchical organizations, bosses should not only boss less and reduce organizational layers, but also "reduce their own salaries and employment opportunities" (Thurow 1992).

Under conditions of globalization, the feminine-in-management rhetoric can contribute several images that eventually naturalize the further exploitation of labor rather than improving managerial opportunities for women. Think, for example, of the following clichés associated with women: "a woman's work is never done," which is equivalent to extended hours for the same pay; "she did it as a labor of love," which is equivalent to unpaid work.

As has been well documented, occupations that become "feminized" – including managerial and professional positions – experience declines in salaries and wages. Whereas explanations for this fact vary, the condition remains. Such a situation, however, provides the ideal context for the globalized firm, which would encounter equally ready and willing "affordable labor" on any side of the border.

Moreover, because the feminine-in-management rhetoric is based on the possibility of abstracting some "essential human traits" that can be observed in many people (and that may even be sex-neutral), "feminized" jobs may end up mostly occupied by men as unemployment, provoked by globalization, soars. For example, Jelinek and Adler (1988) note that women can be role models and coaches for men: "Increasingly, the best of our male managers too will be working to acquire and hone important skills formerly seen as 'female' – those centering on relationships, communication, and social sensitivity."

Uncritical support for the feminine-in-management ignores the way it contributes unintentionally to the formation of a "feminized" work culture (in a patriarchal sense), where all work available, regardless of the job holder's sex, would be "women's work" and women's salaries (Ferguson 1984). The feminine-in-management, as it extends the values of the household to the workplace, would provide the ideal metaphor for carefully done, high-quality, cheap work, performed by docile workers: "housework" (Folbre 1991). Globalization, meanwhile, as it extends the rhetoric of national emergency to the international marketplace, would provide the ideal motto: "To serve with pride and distinction."

TRAINING THE DOER FOR FEELINGS, NOT THINKING

Another aspect of the globalization rhetoric that has acquired prominent coverage refers to education. The typical storyline in this respect emphasizes American student's lack of general education and the cost of such a lack because of competition with better-educated workers from other national (mostly Japan and Germany). The problem is frequently stated as one in which the U.S. is falling behind in technological innovation; the solution is usually stated in terms of more general training in science and mathematics. Behind this story also lies a promise: more and better (high-paying) jobs for better-educated people.

Various elements are problematic in this story. For example, there is no acknowledgement that very well-educated people (people with college degrees) have trouble finding jobs, or that there is a difference between training and education, between being a doer and being a thinker, between technological competence and knowledge. Further, it is seldom acknowledged that the secondary education of Japanese and European students not only contains more math and science, but also spans other socio-humanistic subjects and critical thinking skills.

Unfortunately, in the American context, education for globalization translates into higher education for a few elite thinkers – the "smartest" 25 percent of the population, according to Thurow – while the rest would require no more than a basic "doer" training. In Thurow's view, what is needed is

> ... to set a quality standard for the noncollege bound. Here the high-wage business community in each state should write an achievement test that would cover what they think high-school graduates need to known to work at America's best firms. ... [T]hose that had passed this "business achievement test" would have their diplomas so stamped. ... [L]eading high-wage business firms would commit themselves to hiring only those with stamped diplomas. ... [T]he achievement test ... would be written by employers to insure that Americans clearly understood that this is what their children must learn if they want to have high-wage jobs. It wouldn't be a test written by ivory-tower professors or education bureaucrats.

The turn toward "vocational training" for the majority of the population under the guise of "better education" may be supported by various aspects of the feminine-in-management rhetoric. The imagery of women as "concrete-feelers" in contrast to men as "abstract-thinkers" has been with us for several centuries. Rarely, we observe, has the feminine-in-management rhetoric argued for women's superior intellectual capabilities. Rather, it emphasizes the traditional oppositions of "thinking/feeling" and "abstract/concrete" by focusing on women's better interpersonal relations and trustworthiness, their care-and-connection practices that would humanize the work-place, the healing processes they could contribute for the wellness of an alienated work force, and their concrete, no-nonsense attitude and practical orientation toward everyday problems.

These abilities, we agree, are probably going to be very much in demand for managing the large percentage of "educated" American workers who will not find high-wage jobs, regardless of their stamped diplomas. They would be particularly useful as ways to pacify emotionally the vast majority of these workers (euphemistically, "human capital") who will have to adjust downward their expectations of better pay under globalization. In the meantime, the truly educated few – the abstract thinkers, or "symbolic analysts" as Robert Reich would call them – will reap the fruits of this situation from the distance of their own very well-paid, cosmopolitan global spaces.

HEART-TO-HEART OR HEAD-TO-HEAD?

In the rhetoric of globalization, there is little that is not written in the language of warfare. For example, Thurow's book subtitle is *The Coming Economic Battle Among Japan, Europe, and America*; Ohmae's is *Power and Strategy in the Interlinked Economy*. References are constantly made to "winners and losers" in the global economy, where the world is a battleground, and where the U.S. should be able to outsmart everyone else. Predictably, the imagery also refers to intellectual prowess in which one would strategize a better game than one's opponent ("war games").

It would appear that this discourse offers little space for Helgesen's "female advantage" to reduce – as she urges us to do – the Warrior values of our dominant culture. Yet for all her talk about women's more holistic view of the world and greater social consciousness, at the end the "female advantage' offers no more than the ability to "master the Warrior skills of discipline, will and struggle necessary to achieve success in the public realm" (Helgesen 1990). Furthermore, she suggests incorporating these values with those of another Jungian archetype, the Martyr, to produce an androgynous Magician who – irrespective of Helgesen's praise – is little more than a shrewd trickster and manipulator.

Another way to understand the feminine-in-management rhetoric is as a cover-up for the usual way managerial activities have been portrayed from time immemorial in the U.S.: as a fight and struggle among enemies (labor and management, business and government, local and international competitors). The words "competitive advantage" and "female advantage" seem to be used unself-consciously in the same paragraphs that claim some kind of unique "all heart, all peace" managerial goodness assumed to come from women's qualities. Yet aside from the oxymoronic quality of these juxtapositions, their more problematic material consequence is the way they objectify women managers into convenient weapons for the international fight, as when women are a "powerful resource for sustainable competitive advantage" (Jelinek and Adler 1988), or when "treating women as a business imperative is the equivalent of a unique R&D product for which there is a huge demand" (Schwartz 1992).

Perhaps the feminine-in-management rhetoric simply fuels the current version of the Trojan wars under the guise of globalization. How many rescues of how many Helens of Troy might be used as the occasion for another "war"? Will it be the rescue of "sexually harassed" Japanese women who lack the "real opportunities" given to American women, as *Business Week* claims ("Revenge of the 'Office Ladies'" 1992)? Will the "new-and-improved," restructured, and globalized American corporation serve as the Trojan Horse?

IMPLICATIONS: OTHER IMAGES OF WOMEN FOR RETHINKING GLOBALIZATION

We want to call attention to the relationships that may exist between two currently popular managerial discourses – the feminine-in-management and globalization – both of which claim to be bringing much needed changes to the managerial field. Our primary intention is to argue that, despite their claims, the assumed changes are only a surface rhetoric. Analyzed together, they cancel each other as they maintain existing power relations that benefit only a few. For example, these discourses speak of better opportunities for all but hold onto the established order when facing the reality of an increasingly diverse work force. They speak of growing productivity and wealth while making acceptable the lowered expectations brought about by a service economy. They speak of the importance of education and human capital while fostering little more than technical competencies for narrow thinkers. They bring in an emblematic sign of peace to soften the rough edges of a rhetoric that bespeaks of war.

Though our analysis may appear as merely an exercise in criticism, our intention is to unmask the impossible promises resulting from the contradictions in these discourses once they are placed in their broader institutional and social contexts. We believe analyses that cut through the rhetoric of the latest managerial quick-fix have important implications for management. They help us understand the connections that exist between the activities of any particular organization – when following these popularized prescriptions – and the perhaps unintended consequences those same activities may bring to the greater society to which we all belong.

For example, uncritical support of a "care-and-connection" managerial style could be a very naive way to try to manipulate a labor force that is neither naive nor reacting to any prior managerial style, but is rather concerned about layoffs or poor pay. Uncritical support of what is little more than vocational training in secondary education – as a way of reducing short-term organizational training costs – would merely contribute to reducing underemployment, since in the long run few would be educated enough to merit high wage jobs. Who would be the critical thinkers? Who would innovate and create new and better employment opportunities for a whole society? The feminine-in-management and their counterpart discourses of globalization are short-sighted, elitist palliatives for the realities of the contemporary world. Thus it may be possible that in a few years we will look back and view our business organizations – those "feminine" and "globalized" American corporations – as the main perpetrators of a situation from which there is no return: bringing the capabilities of our nation to its lowest common denominator in the name of doing just the opposite.

In these last paragraphs we offer a different way of thinking "feminine": a way that would bring a different set of images of "women" into a globalized economy. Yet this time, they are images that call for effecting a radical change in the way we think about management and the way we would design our organizations for a better society. These images, which are already around us, are the more critical aspects of "the feminine" discussed in feminist theory and appearing in some management writing. Unfortunately, the more critical inspirations from feminist theories have been absent in the feminine-in-management literature because the latter, as it stands now, is just another form of women pleasing men – of making sure it says what is acceptable to say in management *now*, by maintaining privileges for a few even if the rest of society is worse off.

For example, conventional managerial wisdom considers that, in a global economy, good management creates opportunities to produce and sell an abundance of goods in foreign markets, keep jobs at home, and keep the home population's ability to consume ("the good standard of living") alive and well. This ideal situation is supported by exporting both the goods and the values of a consumer society so the rest of the world will live (consume) as we do while supporting our "democratic values." Yet shouldn't we be wary of managerial strategies that promote consumerism both at home and abroad while pretending this is what we should call "a good standard of living" for the whole world?

The imagery that sustains these strategies is actually a feminine one of "the consumer as impulse shopper" (Fischer 1993) of the "buy now and pay later" variety, scrambling for scarce bargain basement merchandise. It is the imagery of short-term gratification in spite of the impoverishing consequences of these consumption activities in the long run, as we are experiencing now in our own country. This is an imagery that the feminine-in-management promotes as much as any other managerial approach (Helgesen's descriptions of her women's cocktail parties, meeting places, and Hérmès scarves), because what it promotes, regardless of method, are the same old goals: more sales, better market share, and to take away from competitors, particularly those from other nations.[2]

In contrast, we want to offer the imagery of "the frugal housewife," who can do with consuming less and saving for "a rainy day"; who is able to improve what she already has by conserving and preserving; who shares scarce resources with her neighbors (baby clothes) to be able to produce a "common wealth." Such imagery may be able to bring about a form of management that not only avoids exploitation of both people and resources, but that is more likely to effect a true cooperation among nations – a better life for all, yet a better life that doesn't hinge on incremental consumption of disposable "goods."

Perhaps the "world-class standards" we export to other nations could be a concept of the good life in which people would better appreciate their own abilities and endowments; where good health and good education – not training – are the primary goods to be had for everybody in every society; where decent food and living conditions would be basic human rights and the basis for a pact among nations – a pact under the premises of "sustainable growth"; where growth is meaningful insofar as it contributes to sustaining "the global family."

We could play with many more images. What about redefining "innovation" through imagery of "female ingenuity" (being able to do anything with a hairpin)? Such imagery would help us appreciate the talents of many different peoples – particularly those who, because of scarcity, have been able to make do with much less – while helping us learn from them, instead of killing those talents with instrumental education of the "What is it good for?" variety. (Remember that old phrase about necessity being the mother of invention?)

What about using "women's gossiping" as imagery to construct an extended network of real worldwide information for the "global village"? That is certainly not what we have right now, in spite of all our claims about the information age and communication satellites. For example, Headline News's "Around the World in 30 Minutes" repeats the same very selective "news" for 24 hours with a minimum of information about the realities of other nations – especially nations that do not agree with our point of view. Or what about fully embracing "mother nature" as a female who hasn't yet been offered "equal opportunity," or who hasn't been covered by "affirmative action," or who has been blatantly "sexually harassed?" Would it help in giving the environment a better chance?

What about the image of the "hysterical woman"? The hysterical woman releases her emotions to cry and scream in moral indignation for the crimes against humanity that are constantly committed in the name of economic rationality. She would denounce, time and again, the illogic and the irrationality of a world in which millions of people die of hunger while productive lands are kept barren to maintain a reasonable price for food in the market.

Perhaps the day that we, who are in business professions in capitalist societies, allow this image of the "hysterical woman" to overcome us as an inspiration for a management theory will be the day that, paradoxically, we will come back to our senses. That will be the day when we will define "the good economy" as the positive results of having complied with worldwide social imperatives, rather than the other way around. Otherwise, we will have to confess that the logic of democracy and capitalism, of our organizations, and of our governments, would all have failed miserably.

So, perhaps we need to place another advertisement:

> **HELP WANTED**
>
> Seeking hysterical person. Willing to become enraged when observing world-wide exploitation, esp. when done in the name of free market economy. Ready to act in world forums to denounce such conditions. Ready to help others develop their critical voices to create a global network of well-informed peoples, who won't accept being called "less developed" or be undervalued for their own local talents and capabilities. Not afraid to call attention to the travesty of conspicuous consumption in the name of progress and demonstrate the negative long-term consequences of a "First World standard of living." If you are willing to create new forms of business organizations ready to promote sane globalization for a sustainable planet,
>
> Contact THE WORLD
> FAX: 1-800-IS-READY
>
> We are the best in the business of
> Thinking and Acting Globally and Locally. ❒

NOTES

1   While the notion of "patriarchy" varies somewhat in different feminist theories, here we mean sex-gender relations that naturalize and universalize social practices wherein men/masculine values dominate over women/feminine values. This form of domination is particularly pervasive when women uncritically assume stereotypical feminine patterns within traditional structural arrangements.
2   Popularized "managerial wisdom" explains the global economy as one that produces opportunities to sell an abundance of goods in foreign markets, keeping jobs and a high standard of living at home. Seldom is it explained that such is only one side of the story. The true ideal of a globalized free market economy means that no country will import more than it is able to export, and that the end value of such transactions should equal zero at both the individual country and aggregate global level. Otherwise, globalization translates into exploitation of other nations through consumerism.

REFERENCES

M. B. Calás, S. Jacobson, R. Jacques, and L. Smircich, "Is a Woman Centered Theory of Management Dangerous?" paper presented at the National Meetings of the Academy of Management, Miami, August 1991.

N. Chodorow, *The Reproduction of Mothering* (Berkeley: University of California Press, 1978).

K. E. Ferguson, *The Feminist Case Against Bureaucracy* (Philadelphia: Temple University Press, 1984).

E. Fischer, "A Poststructural Feminist Analysis of the Rhetoric of Marketing Relationships," forthcoming in *International Journal of Research in Marketing,* January 1993.

N. Folbre, "The Unproductive Housewife: Her Evolution in Nineteenth-Century Economic Thought," *Signs, 16*, 3 (1991): 463–484.

C. Gilligan, *In a Different Voice: Psychological Theory and Women's Development* (Cambridge, Mass.: Harvard University Press, 1982).

"The Global Economy: Who Gets Hurt?" *Business Week*, August 10, 1992, pp. 48–53.

J. Grant, "Women as Manager: What They Can Offer to Organizations," *Organizational Dynamics*, Spring 1988, pp. 56–63.

S. Helgesen, *The Female Advantage: Women's Ways of Leadership* (New York: Doubleday/Currency, 1990).

A. S. Huff, "Wives – Of the Organization," paper presented at the Women and Work Conference, Arlington, Texas, May 11, 1990.

M. Jelinek and N. J. Adler, "Women: World Class Managers for Global Competition," *Academy of Management Executive*, February 1988, pp. 7–19.

R. Kuttner, *The End of Laissez-Faire: National Purpose and the Global Economy After the Cold War* (New York: Alfred A. Knopf, 1991).

M. Loden, *Feminine Leadership – or – How to Succeed Without Being One of the Boys* (New York: Times Books, 1985).

J. B. Miller, *New Psychology of Women* (Berkeley, Calif.: University of California Press, 1976).

J. Naisbitt and P. Aburdene, *Megatrends 2000* (New York: Avon, 1990).

J. Naisbitt and P. Aburdene, *Re-inventing the Corporation* (New York: Warner, 1985).

K. Ohmae, *The Borderless World: Power and Strategy in the Interlinked Economy* (New York: Harper, 1990).

T. Peters, "The Best New Managers Will Listen, Motivate, Support: Isn't That Just Like a Woman?" *Working Woman*, September 1990, pp. 216–217.

M. E. Porter, *The Competitive Advantage of Nations* (New York: Free Press, 1990).

R. B. Reich, *The Work of Nations* (New York: Knopf, 1991).

"Revenge of the 'Office Ladies,'" *Business Week*, July 13, 1992, pp. 42–43.

J. F. Rosener, "Ways Women Lead," *Harvard Business Review*, November–December 1990, pp. 119–125.

F. N. Schwartz, "Women as a Business Imperative," *Harvard Business Review*, March–April 1992, pp. 105–113.

L. Thurow, *Head to Head: The Coming Economic Battle Among Japan, Europe and America* (New York: Morrow, 1992).

"Women in Business: II . . . being a commentary upon the great American office and the distinction between the girl who works to marry and the girl who marries to work." *Fortune*, August 1935, pp. 50–86.

THE NANNY CHAIN

ARLIE RUSSELL HOCHSCHILD

From The American Prospect (2000) January: 32–6

Vicky Diaz, a 34-year-old mother of five, was a college-educated schoolteacher and travel agent in the Philippines before migrating to the United States to work as a housekeeper for a wealthy Beverly Hills family and as a nanny for their two-year-old son. Her children, Vicky explained to Rhacel Parreñas, were saddened by my departure. Even until now my children are trying to convince me to go home. The children were not angry when I left because they were still very young when I left them. My husband could not get angry either because he knew that was the only way I could seriously help him raise our children, so that our children could be sent to school. I send them money every month.[1]

In her forthcoming book *Servants of Globalization*,[2] Parreñas, an affiliate of the Center for Working Families at the University of California, Berkeley, tells an important and disquieting story of what she calls the "globalization of mothering." The Beverly Hills family pays "Vicky" (which is the pseudonym Parreñas gave her) $400 a week, and Vicky, in turn, pays her own family's live-in domestic worker back in the Philippines $40 a week. Living like this is not easy on Vicky and her family. "Even though it's paid well, you are sinking in the amount of your work. Even while you are ironing the clothes, they can still call you to the kitchen to wash the plates. It . . . [is] also very depressing. The only thing you can do is give all your love to [the two-year-old American child]. In my absence from my children, the most I could do with my situation is give all my love to that child."

Vicky is part of what we could call a global care chain: a series of personal links between people across the globe based on the paid or unpaid work of caring. A typical global care chain might work something like this: An older daughter from a poor family in a third world country cares for her siblings (the first link in the chain) while her mother works as a nanny caring for the children of a nanny migrating to a first world country (the second line) who, in turn, cares for the child of a family in a rich country (the final link). Each kind of chain expresses an invisible human ecology of care, one care worker depending on another and so on. A global care chain might start in a poor country and end in a rich one, or it might link rural and urban areas within the same poor country. More complex versions start in one poor country and extend to another slightly less poor country and then link to a rich country.

Global care chains may be proliferating. According to 1994 estimates by the International Organization for Migration, 120 million people migrated – legally or illegally – from one country to another. That's 2 percent of the world's population. How many migrants leave loved ones behind to care for other people's children or elderly parents, we don't know. But we do know that more than half of legal migrants to the United States are women, mostly between ages 25 and 34. And migration experts tell us that the proportion of women among migrants is likely to rise. All of this suggests that the trend toward global care chains will continue.

How are we to understand the impact of globalization on care? If, as globalization continues, more global care chains form, will they be "good" care chains or "bad" ones? Given the entrenched problem of third world poverty – which is one of the starting points for care chains – this is by no means a simple question. But we have yet to fully address it, I believe, because the world is globalizing faster than our minds or hearts are. We live global but still think and feel local.

FREUD IN A GLOBAL ECONOMY

Most writing on globalization focuses on money, markets, and labor flows, while giving scant attention to women, children, and the care of one for the other. Most research on women and development, meanwhile, draws a connection between, say, World Bank loan conditions and the scarcity of food for women and children in the third world, without saying much about resources expended on caregiving. Much of the research on women in the United States and Europe focuses on a chainless, two-person picture of "work–family balance" without considering the child care worker and the emotional ecology of which he or she is a part. Fortunately, in recent years, scholars such as Ernestine Avila, Evelyn Nakano Glenn, Pierette Hondageneu-Sotelo, Mary Romero, and Rhacel Parreñas have produced some fascinating research on domestic workers. Building on this work, we can begin to focus on the first world end of the care chain and begin spelling out some of the implications of the globalization of love.

One difficulty in understanding these implications is that the language of economics does not translate easily into the language of psychology. How are we to understand a "transfer" of feeling from one link in a chain to another? Feeling is not a "resource" that can be crassly taken from one person and given to another. And surely one person can love quite a few people; love is not a resource limited the same way oil or currency supply is. Or is it?

Consider Sigmund Freud's theory of displacement, the idea that emotion can be redirected from one person or object to another. Freud believed that if, for example, Jane loves Dick but Dick is emotionally or literally unavailable, Jane will find a new object (say, John, Dick and Jane's son) onto which to project her original feeling for Dick. While Freud applied the idea of displacement mainly to relations within the nuclear family, the concept can also be applied to relations extending far outside it. For example, immigrant nannies and au pairs often divert feelings originally directed toward their own children toward their young charges in this country. As Sau-ling C. Wong, a researcher at the University of California,

Berkeley, has put it, "Time and energy available for mothers are diverted from those who, by kinship or communal ties, are their more rightful recipients."

If it is true that attention, solicitude, and love itself can be "displaced" from one child (let's say Vicky Diaz's son Alfredo, back in the Philippines) onto another child (let's say Tommy, the son of her employers in Beverly Hills), then the important observation to make here is that this displacement is often upward in wealth and power. This, in turn, raises the question of the equitable distribution of care. It makes us wonder, is there – in the realm of love – an analogue to what Marx calls "surplus value," something skimmed off from the poor for the benefit of the rich?

Seen as a thing in itself, Vicky's love for the Beverly Hills toddler is unique, individual, private. But might there not be elements in this love that are borrowed, so to speak, from somewhere and someone else? Is time spent with the first world child in some sense "taken" from a child further down the care chain? Is the Beverly Hills child getting "surplus" love, the way immigrant farm workers give us surplus labor? Are first world countries such as the United States importing maternal love as they have imported copper, zinc, gold, and other ores from third world countries in the past?

This is a startling idea and an unwelcome one, both for Vicky Diaz, who needs the money from a first world job, and for her well-meaning employers, who want someone to give loving care to their child. Each link in the chain feels she is doing the right thing for good reasons – and who is to say she is not?

But there are clearly hidden costs here, costs that tend to get passed down along the chain. One nanny reported such a cost when she described (to Rhacel Parreñas) a return visit to the Philippines: "When I saw my children, I thought, 'Oh children do grow up even without their mother.' I left my youngest when she was only five years old. She was already nine when I saw her again but she still wanted for me to carry her [weeps]. That hurt me because it showed me that my children missed out on a lot."

Sometimes the toll it takes on the domestic worker is overwhelming and suggests that the nanny has not displaced her love onto an employer's child but rather has continued to long intensely for her own child. As one women told Parreñas, "The first two years I felt like I was going crazy. . . . I would catch myself gazing at nothing, thinking about my child. Every moment, every second of the day, I felt like I was thinking about my baby. My youngest, you have to understand, I left when he was only two months old. . . . You know, whenever I receive a letter from my children, I cannot sleep. I cry. It's good that my job is more demanding at night."

Despite the anguish these separations clearly cause, Filipina women continue to leave for jobs abroad. Since the early 1990s, 55 percent of migrants out of the Philippines have been women; next to electronic manufacturing, their remittances make up the major source of foreign currency in the Philippines. The rate of female emigration has continued to increase and includes college-educated teachers, businesswomen, and secretaries. In Parrenas's study, more than half of the nannies she interviewed had college degrees and most were married mothers in their 30s.

Where are men in this picture? For the most part, men – especially men at the top of the class ladder – leave child-rearing to women. Many of the husbands and fathers of Parreñas's domestic workers had migrated to the Arabian peninsula and other places in search of better wages, relieving other men of "male work" as construction workers and tradesmen, while being replaced themselves at home. Others remained at home, responsible fathers caring or helping to care for their children. But some of the men tyrannized their wives. Indeed, many of the women migrants Parreñas interviewed didn't just leave; they fled. As one migrant maid explained:

> You have to understand that my problems were very heavy before I left the Philippines. My husband was abusive. I couldn't even think about my children, the only thing I could think about was the opportunity to escape my situation. If my husband was not going to kill me, I was probably going to kill him. . . . He always beat me up and my parents wanted me to leave him for a long time. I left my children with my sister. . . . In the plane . . . I felt like a bird whose cage had been locked for many years. . . . I felt free. . . . Deep inside, I felt homesick for my children but I also felt free for being able to escape the most dire problem that was slowly killing me.

Other men abandoned their wives. A former public school teacher back in the Philippines confided to Parreñas: "After three years of marriage, my husband left me for another woman. My husband supported us for just a little over a year. Then the support was stopped. . . . The letters stopped. I have not seen him since." In the absence of government aid, then, migration becomes a way of coping with abandonment.

Sometimes the husband of a female migrant worker is himself a migrant worker who takes turns with his wife migrating. One Filipino man worked in Saudi Arabia for 10 years, coming home for a month each year. When he finally returned home for good, his wife set off to work as a maid in America while he took care of the children. As she explained to Parreñas, "My children were very sad when I left them. My husband told me that when they came back home from the airport, my children could not touch their food and they wanted to cry. My son, whenever he writes me, always draws the head of Fido the dog with tears on the eyes. Whenever he goes to Mass on Sundays, he tells me that he misses me more because he sees his friends with their mothers. Then he comes home and cries."

THE END OF THE CHAIN

Just as global capitalism helps create a third world supply of mothering, it creates a first world demand for it. The past half-century has witnessed a huge rise in the number of women in paid work – from 15 percent of mothers of children aged 6 and under in 1950 to 65 percent today. Indeed, American women now make up 45 percent of the American labor force. Three-quarters of mothers of children 18 and under now work, as do 65 percent of mothers of children 6 and under. In addition, a recent report by the International Labor Organization reveals that the average number of hours of work per week has been rising in this country.

Earlier generations of American working women would rely on grandmothers and other female kin to help look after their children; now the grandmothers and aunts are themselves busy doing paid work outside the home. Statistics show that over the past 30 years a decreasing number of families have relied on relatives to care for their children – and hence are compelled to look for nonfamily care. At the first world end of care chains, working parents are grateful to find a good nanny or child care provider, and they are generally able to pay far more than the nanny could earn in her native country. This is not just a child care problem. Many

American families are now relying on immigrant or out-of-home care for their *elderly* relatives. As a Los Angeles elder-care worker, an immigrant, told Parreñas, "Domestics here are able to make a living from the elderly that families abandon." But this often means that nannies cannot take care of their own ailing parents and therefore produce an elder-care version of a child care chain – caring for first world elderly persons while a paid worker cares for their aged mother back in the Philippines.

My own research for two books, *The Second Shift* and *The Time Bind*, sheds some light on the first world end of the chain. Many women have joined the law, academia, medicine, business – but such professions are still organized for men who are free of family responsibilities. The successful career, at least for those who are broadly middle class or above, is still largely built on some key traditional components: doing professional work, competing with fellow professionals, getting credit for work, building a reputation while you're young, hoarding scarce time, and minimizing family obligations by finding someone else to deal with domestic chores. In the past, the professional was a man and the "someone else to deal with [chores]" was a wife. The wife oversaw the family, which – in pre-industrial times, anyway – was supposed to absorb the human vicissitudes of birth, sickness, and death that the workplace discarded. Today, men take on much more of the child care and housework at home, but they still base their identity on demanding careers in the context of which children are beloved impediments; hence, men resist sharing care equally at home. So when parents don't have enough "caring time" between them, they feel forced to look for that care further down the global chain.

The ultimate beneficiaries of these various care changes might actually be large multinational companies, usually based in the United States. In my research on a Fortune 500 manufacturing company I call Amerco, I discovered a disproportionate number of women employed in the human side of the company: public relations, marketing, human resources. In all sectors of the company, women often helped others sort out problems – both personal and professional – at work. It was often the welcoming voice and "soft touch" of women workers that made Amerco seem like a family to other workers. In other words, it appears that these working mothers displace some of their emotional labor from their children to their employer, which holds itself out to the worker as a "family." So, the care in the chain may begin with that which a rural third world mother gives (as a nanny) the urban child she cares for, and it may end with the care a working mother gives her employees as the vice president of publicity at your company.

HOW MUCH IS CARE WORTH?

How are we to respond to the growing number of global care chains? Through what perspective should we view them?

I can think of three vantage points from which to see care chains: that of the primordialist, the sunshine modernist, and (my own) the critical modernist. The primordialist believes that our primary responsibility is to our own family, our own community, our own country. According to this view, if we all tend our own primordial plots, everybody will be fine. There is some logic to this point of view. After all, Freud's concept of displacement rests on the premise that some original first object of love has a primary "right" to that love, and second and third comers don't fully share that right. (For the primordialist – as for most all of us – those first objects are members of one's most immediate family.) But the primordialist is an isolationist, an antiglobalist. To such a person, care chains seem wrong – not because they're unfair to the least-cared-for children at the bottom of the chain, but because they are global. Also, because family care has historically been provided by women, primordialists often believe that women should stay home to provide this care.

The sunshine modernist, on the other hand, believes care chains are just fine, an inevitable part of globalization, which is itself uncritically accepted as good. The idea of displacement is hard for the sunshine modernists to grasp because in their equation – seen mainly in economic terms – the global market will sort out who has proper claims on a nanny's love. As long as the global supply of labor meets the global demand for it, the sunshine modernist believes, everything will be okay. If the primordialist thinks care chains care bad because they're global, the sunshine modernist thinks they're good for the very same reason. In either case, the issue of inequality of access to care disappears.

The critical modernist embraces modernity but with a global sense of ethics. When the critical modernist goes out to buy a pair of Nike shoes, she is concerned to learn how low the wage was and how long the hours were for the third world factory worker making the shoes. The critical modernist applies the same moral concern to care chains: The welfare of the Filipino child back home must be seen as some part, however small, of the total picture. The critical modernist sees globalization as a very mixed blessing, bringing with it new opportunities – such as the nanny's access to good wages – but also new problems, including emotional and psychological costs we have hardly begun to understand.

From the critical modernist perspective, globalization may be increasing inequities not simply in access to money – and those inequities are important enough – but in access to care. The poor maid's child may be getting less motherly care than the first world child. (And for that matter, because of longer hours of work, the first world child may not be getting the ideal quantity of parenting attention for healthy development because too much of it is now displaced onto the employees of Fortune 500 companies.) We needn't lapse into primordialism to sense that something may be amiss in this.

I see no easy solutions to the human costs of global care chains. But here are some initial thoughts. We might, for example, reduce the incentive to migrate by addressing the causes of the migrant's economic desperation and fostering economic growth in the third world. Thus one obvious goal would be to develop the Filipino economy.

But it's not so simple. Immigration scholars have demonstrated that development itself can *encourage* migration because development gives rise to new economic uncertainties that families try to mitigate by seeking employment in the first world. If members of a family are laid off at home, a migrant's monthly remittance can see them through, often by making a capital outlay in a small business or paying for a child's education.

Other solutions might focus on individual links in the care chain. Because some women migrate to flee abusive husbands, a partial solution would be to create local refuges from such husbands. Another would be to alter immigration policy so as to encourage nannies to bring their children with them. Alternatively, employers or even government subsidies could help nannies make regular visits home.

The most fundamental approach to the problem is to raise the value of caring work and to ensure that whoever does it gets more credit and money for it. Otherwise, caring work will be what's left over, the work that's continually passed on down the chain. Sadly, the value ascribed to the labor of raising a child has always been low relative to the value of other kinds of labor, and under the impact of globalization, it has sunk lower still. The low value placed on caring work is due neither to an absence of demand for it (which is always high) nor to the simplicity of the work (successful caregiving is not easy) but rather to the cultural politics underlying this global exchange.

The declining value of child care anywhere in the world can be compared to the declining value of basic food crops relative to manufactured goods on the international market. Though clearly more essential to life, crops such as wheat, rice, or cocoa fetch low and declining prices while the prices of manufactured goods (relative to primary goods) continue to soar in the world market. And just as the low market price of primary produce keeps the third world low in the community of nations, the low market value of care keeps low the status of the women who do it.

One way to solve this problem is to get fathers to contribute more child care. If fathers worldwide shared child care labor more equitably, care would spread laterally instead of being passed down a social-class ladder, diminishing in value along the way. Culturally, Americans have begun to embrace this idea – but they've yet to put it into practice on a truly large scale (see Richard Weissbourd, "Redefining Dad," *TAP*, December 6, 1999). This is where norms and policies established in the first world can have perhaps the greatest influence on reducing costs along global care chains.

According to the International Labor Organization, half of the world's women between ages 15 and 64 are working in paid jobs. Between 1960 and 1980, 69 out of 88 countries for which data are available showed a growing proportion of women in paid work (and the rate of increase has skyrocketed since the 1950s in the United States, Scandinavia, and the United Kingdom). If we want developed societies with women doctors, political leaders, teachers, bus drivers, and computer programmers, we will need qualified people to help care for children. And there is no reason why every society cannot enjoy such loving paid child care. It may even remain the case that Vicky Diaz is the best person to provide it. But we would be wise to adopt the perspective of the critical modernist and extend our concern to the potential hidden losers in the care chain. These days, the personal is global.

NOTES

1   Special thanks to: *Rhacel Parreñas for permission to draw from her dissertation "The Global Servants: (Im)Migrant Filipina Domestic Workers in Rome and Los Angeles," Department of Ethnic Studies, University of California, Berkeley.*

2   [Published 2001 as *"Servants of Globalization: Women, Migration, and Domestic work.* Stanford, CA: Stanford University Press.]

CHAPTER

31

MAQUILADORAS: THE VIEW FROM THE INSIDE

MARIA PATRICIA FERNÁNDEZ KELLY

From K. B. Sacks and D. Remy (eds.) (1984) *My Troubles are Going to Have Trouble with Me*, New Brunswick, NJ: Rutgers University Press

Since the end of World War II, and particularly during the last two decades, there has been an increasing trend for the large monopolies of the highly industrialized nations to transfer more parts of their manufacturing operations to underdeveloped areas of the world (Palloix, 1975: 57–63). The industrial countries have thus become administrative and financial headquarters for the international management of refined manufacturing activities (Fröbel, Heinrichs, and Kreye, 1976). Large numbers of working people throughout the underdeveloped world are experiencing directly the impact of multinational investment.

There is a somewhat mechanical tendency to interpret social events in underdeveloped areas as an automatic effect of the requirements of capital accumulation at a global level, without regard for local diversity or independent activity, particularly among working classes and class fractions (O'Brien, 1975). Participant observation contributes to understanding the effects of, and workers' responses to, the international political and economic system at the level of the factory and the household. It shows workers as more than the cheap labor they appear to be when viewed from a global demands-of-capital viewpoint. Yet insights derived from political economic theory can inform ethnographic data collection and illuminate the details often missed in broader analytical efforts.

Along the Mexican side of the United States–Mexico border, there has been a huge expansion of manufacturing activities by multinational corporations. This has incorporated large numbers of women into direct production in the last fifteen years. As a result of implementation of the Border Industrialization Program since 1965, more than one hundred assembly plants, or *maquiladoras*, have sprung up in Ciudad Juarez, across the border from El Paso, Texas. This set of programs has made it possible for multinational firms to collaborate with Mexican state and private enterprise to foster the emergence of a booming export industry along the border. More than half of the plants are electric or electronic firms. Most of the rest are apparel assembly plants (see Newton and Balli, 1979).

The importance of the program in recent years may be appreciated by noting that *maquiladoras* account for about half of U.S. imports from underdeveloped countries under assembly industry tariff provisions, as compared with only 10 percent in 1970. In 1978 they provided the Mexican economy with more than ninety-five thousand jobs and $713 million in value added in this class of production in all of Latin America (Newton and Balli, 1979: 8). They rank third, behind tourism and petroleum sales, as a contributor to Mexican foreign exchange. The objective circumstances that have determined the growth of the *maquiladora* industry are the availability of what appears to be an inexhaustible supply of unskilled and semiskilled labor, and extremely high levels of productivity.

The plants themselves are small, and most subcontract from corporations with their headquarters in the United States. Although nationally recognized brands are represented in Ciudad Juarez, the vast majority of these industries are associated with corporations that have regional rather than national visibility. The low level of capital investment in the physical plant often results in inadequate equipment and unpleasant working conditions.

While all *maquiladoras* employ an overwhelming majority (85 percent) of women, the apparel industry hires women whose position in the city makes them especially vulnerable to exploitative labor practices. They tend to be in their midtwenties, poorly educated, and recent migrants to Ciudad Juarez. About one-third of the women head households and are the sole supports of their children.

LOOKING FOR A JOB: A PERSONAL ACCOUNT

What is it like to be female, single, and eager to find work at a *maquiladora*? Shortly after arriving in Ciudad Juarez, and after finding stable lodging, I began looking through the pages of newspapers, hoping to find a want ad. My intent was to merge with the clearly visible mass of women who roam the streets and industrial parks of the city searching for jobs. They are, beyond doubt, a distinctive feature of the city, an effervescent expression of the conditions that prevail in the local labor market.

My objectives were straightforward. I wanted to spend four to six weeks applying for jobs and obtaining direct experience about the employment policies, recruitment strategies, and screening mechanisms used by companies to hire assembly workers. I was especially interested in how much time and money an individual worker spent trying to get a job. I also wanted to spend an equal amount of time working at a plant, preferable one that manufactured apparel. This way, I expected to learn more about working conditions, production quotas, and wages at a particular factory. I felt this would help me develop questions from a workers' perspective.

In retrospect, it seems odd that it never entered my head that I might not find a job. Finding a job at a *maquiladora* is easier said than done, especially for a woman over twenty-five. This is due primarily to the large number of women competing for jobs. At every step of their constant peregrination, women are confronted by a familiar sign at the plants – "no applications available" – or by the negative responses of a guard or a secretary at the entrance to the factories. But such is the arrogance of the uninformed researcher. I went about the business of looking for a job as if the social milieu had to conform to my research needs.

By using newspapers as a source of information for jobs, I was departing from the common strategy of potential workers in that environment. Most women are part of informal networks which include relatives, friends, and an occasional acquaintance in the personnel management sector. They hear of jobs by word of mouth.

Most job seekers believe that a personal recommendation from someone already employed at a *maquiladora* can ease the difficult path. This belief is well founded. At many plants, managers prefer to hire applicants by direct recommendation of employees who have proven to be dependable and hard working. For example, the Mexican subsidiary of a major U.S. corporation, one of the most stable *maquiladoras* in Juarez, has an established policy not to hire "outsiders." Only those who are introduced personally to the manager are considered for openings. By resorting to the personal link, managers decrease the dangers of having their factories infiltrated by unreliable workers, independent organizers, and "troublemakers."

While appearing to take a personal interest in the individual worker at the moment of hiring, management can establish a paternalistic claim on the worker. Workers complain that superintendents and managers are prone to demand "special services," like overtime, in exchange for granting personal "favors" such as a loan or time off from work to care for children. Yet workers acknowledge a personal debt to the person who hired them. A woman's commitment to the firm is fused with commitment to the particular personnel manger or superintendent who granted her the "personal favor" of hiring her. Anita expressed the typical sentiment, "If the group leader demands more production [without additional pay], I will generally resist because I owe her nothing. But if the *ingeniero* asks me to increase my quota on occasion, I comply. He gave me the job in the first place! Besides, it makes me feel good to know that I can return the favor, at least in part."

Only those who are not part of the tightly woven informal networks rely on impersonal ways to find a job. Recently arrived migrants and older women with children looking for paid employment for the first time find it especially difficult. As a "migrant" to Ciudad Juarez, I too lacked the contacts needed for relatively stable and well-paid jobs in the electronics industry. Instead, I too entered the apparel industry.

This was not a random occurrence. Ciudad Juarez electronics *maquiladoras* tend to employ very young, single women, a preferred category of potential workers from management's point of view. Workers also prefer electronics because it has large, stable plants, regular wages, and certain additional benefits. In contrast, the apparel-manufacturing sector is characterized by smaller, less stable shops where working conditions are particularly strenuous. Many hire workers on a more or less temporary basis, lack any commitment to their employees, and in the face of a fluctuating international market, observe crude and often ruthless personnel recruitment policies.

One such firm advertised for direct production workers in the two main Juarez newspapers throughout the year, an indication of its high rate of turnover. Despite a grand-sounding name, this small plant is located in the central area of the city rather than in one of the modern industrial parks, hires only about one hundred workers, and is surrounded by unpaved streets and difficult to reach by public transportation. The shoddy, one-story plant, with its old-fashioned sewing machines and crowded work stations, reflects the low level of capital investment made in it.

I went into its tiny office in the middle of summer to apply for a job. As I entered, I wondered whether my appearance or accent would make the personnel manager suspicious. He looked me over sternly and told me to fill out a form now and to return the following morning at seven o'clock to take a dexterity test. Most of the items were straightforward: name, age, marital status, place of birth, length of residence in Ciudad Juarez, property assets, previous jobs and income, number of pregnancies, and general state of health. One, however, was unexpected: what is your major aspiration in life? All my doubts surfaced – would years of penmanship practice at a private school in Mexico City and flawless spelling give me away?

I assumed the on-the-job test would consist of a short evaluation of my skills as a seamstress. I was wrong. The next morning I knocked at the door of the personnel office where I filled out the application, but no one was there. In some confusion, I peeked into the entrance of the factory. The supervisor, Margarita, a dark-haired woman wearing false eyelashes, ordered me in and led me to my place at an industrial sewing machine. That it was old was plain to see; how it worked was difficult to judge. I listened intently to Margarita's instructions. I was expected to sew patch pockets on what were to become blue jeans from the assortment of diversely cut denim parts on my left. Obediently I started to sew.

The particulars of "unskilled" labor unfolded before my eyes. The procedure demanded perfect coordination of hands, eyes, and legs. I was to use my left hand to select the larger part of material from the batch next to me and my right to grab the pocket. There were no markers to show me where to place the pocket. Experienced workers did it on a purely visual basis. Once the patch pocket was in place, I was to guide the two parts under a double needle while applying pressure on the machine's pedal with my right foot.

Because the pockets were sewed on with thread of a contrasting color, the edge of the pocket had to be perfectly aligned with the needles to produce a regular seam and an attractive design. Because the pocket was diamond shaped, I also had to rotate the materials slightly three times while adjusting pressure on the pedal. Too much pressure inevitably broke the thread or produced seams longer than the edge of the pocket. The slightest deviation produced lopsided designs, which then had to be unsewed and gone over as many times as it took to do an acceptable pocket. The supervisor told me that, once trained, I would be expected to sew a pocket every nine to ten seconds. That meant 360 to 396 pockets every hour, or 2,800 to 3,168 every day!

As at the vast majority of apparel-manufacturing *maquiladoras*, I would be paid through a combination of the minimum wage and piecework. In 1978 this was 125 pesos a day, or U.S. $5.00. I would, however, get a slight bonus if I sustained a calculated production quota through the week. Workers are not allowed to produce less than 80 percent of their assigned quota without being admonished, and a worker seriously endangers her job when unable to improve her level of output. Margarita showed me a small blackboard showing the weekly bonus received by those able to produce certain percentages of the quota. They fluctuated between 50 pesos (U.S. $2.20) for those who completed 80 percent of the quota, to 100 pesos for those who completed 100 percent. Managers call this combination of steep production quotas, minimum wages, and modest bonuses an "incentive program."

I started my test at 7:30 A.M. with a sense of embarrassment about my limited skills and disbelief at the speed with which the women in the factory worked. As I continued sewing, the bundle of material on my left was renewed and slowly grew in size. I had to repeat the operation many times before the product was considered acceptable. I soon realized I was being treated as a new worker while presumably being tested. I had not been issued a contract and therefore was not yet incorporated into the Instituto Mexicano del Seguro Social (the national social security system). Nor had I been told about working hours, benefits, or system of payment.

I explained to the supervisor that I had recently arrived in the city, alone, and with very little money. Would I be hired? When would I be given a contract? Margarita listened patiently while helping me unsew one of many defective pockets and then said, "You are too curious. Don't worry about it. Do your job and things will be all right." I continued to sew, aware of the fact that every pocket attached during the "test" was becoming part of the plant's total production.

At 12:30, during the thirty-minute lunch break, I had a better chance to see the factory. Its improvised quality was underscored by the metal folding chairs at the sewing machines. I had been sitting on one of them during the whole morning, but until then I had not noticed that most of them had the Coca Cola label painted on their backs. I had seen this kind of chair many times in casual parties both in Mexico and in the United States. Had they been bought, or were they being rented? In any event, they were not designed to meet the strenuous requirements of sewing all day. Women brought their own colorful pillows to ease the stress on their buttocks and spines. Later on, I was to discover that chronic lumbago is a frequent condition among factory seamstresses (Fernández, 1978).

My questions were still unanswered at 5 P.M. when a bell rang to signal the end of the shift. I went to the personnel office intending to get more information. Despite my overly shy approach to the personnel manager, his reaction was hostile. Even before he was able to turn the disapproving expression on his face into words, Margarita intervened. She was angry. To the manager she said, "This woman had too many questions: Will she be hired? Is she going to be insured?" And then to me, "I told you already, we do piecework here; if you do your job, you get a wage; otherwise you don't. That's clear isn't it? What else do you want? You should be grateful! This plant is giving you a chance to work! What else do you want? Come back tomorrow and be punctual."

This was my initiation into applying for a job. Most women do not job-hunt alone. Rather, they go with friends or relatives and are commonly seen in groups of two or three around most factories. Walking about the industrial parks while following other job seekers was especially informative. Very young women, between sixteen and seventeen, often go with their mothers. One mother told me she sold burritos at the stadium every weekend and that her husband worked as a janitor but that their combined income was inadequate for the six children. Her daughter Elsa was sixteen. "I can't let her go alone into the parks," the mother explained. "She's only a girl and it wouldn't be right. Sometimes girls working in the plants are molested. It's a pity they have to work, but I want to be sure she'll be working in a good place."

At shift changes, thousands of women arrive at and leave the industrial parks in buses, taxis, and *ruteras* (jitney cabs). During working hours only those seeking jobs wander about. Many, though not the majority of these, are "older women." They face special difficulties because of their age and because they often support their children alone. Most of them enter the labor force after many years dedicated to domestic chores and child care. Frequently, desertion by their male companions forces their entry into the paid labor force. A thirty-one year old mother of six children explained, "I have been looking for work since my husband left me two months ago. But I haven't had any luck. It must be my age and the fact that I have so many children. Maybe I should lie and say I've only one. But then the rest wouldn't be entitled to medical care once I got the job." Women need jobs to support their children, but they are often turned down because they are mothers.

I finally got a job at a new *maquiladora* that was adding an evening shift. I saw its advertisement in the daily newspapers and went early the following morning to apply at the factory, which is located in the modern Parque Industrial Bermudez. Thirty-seven women preceded me. Some had arrived as early as 6 A.M. At 10, the door that separated the front lawn from the entrance to the factory had not yet been opened, although a guard appeared once in a while to peek at the growing contingent of applicants. At 10:30 he finally opened the door to tell us that only those having personal recommendation letters would be permitted inside. This was the first in a series of formal and informal screening procedures used to reduce the number of potential workers. Thirteen women left immediately. Others tried to convince the guard that, although they had no personal recommendation, they knew someone already employed at the factory.

Xochitl had neither a written nor a verbal recommendation, but she insisted that her diploma from a sewing academy gave her claim to a particular skill. "It is better to have proof that you are qualified to do the job than to have a letter of recommendation, right?" I wondered whether the personnel manager would agree. The numerous academies in Ciudad Juarez offer technical and vocational courses for a relatively small sum of money. The training does not guarantee a job because many *maquiladora* managers prefer to hire women with direct experience on the job, or as one manager put it to me, "We prefer to hire women who are unspoiled, that is, those who come to us without preconceptions about what industrial work is. Women such as these are easier to shape to our own requirements."

Xochitl's diploma was a glossy document dominated by an imposing eagle clutching a terrestrial globe. An undulating ribbon with the words "labor, omnia, vincit" complemented the design. Beneath it was certification of Xochitl's skills. A preoccupied expression clouded Xochitl's face while she looked at her certificate again. The picture on its left margin, of a young girl with shiny eyes, barely resembled the prematurely aged woman in line with me. At thirty-two, Xochitl was the mother of four children. She took up sewing at home to supplement the money her husband made peddling homemade refreshments. When there was work available (which was not always), she sewed from 6 A.M. until 3 P.M. She could complete three beach dresses, for which she received 22 pesos (U.S. $0.80) a day. The dresses were then sold in the market for approximately 150 pesos. She resented her contractor's high profit but felt she had no other choice. Most of her income was spent on food, clothing, and in attempts to furnish her two-room adobe house. She had already been standing outside the factory for over 3½ hours. All this time she could have been sewing at home and minding the children. Her husband might not approve of her looking for work in the factory, either. He felt it was one thing to sew at home, another to work in a factory.

The young, uniformed guard seemed unperturbed by the fluctuating number of women standing by the door. To many of us, he was the main obstacle lying between unemployment and getting a job from someone inside. To the women, he appeared arrogant and insensitive. "Why must these miserable guards always act this way?" nineteen-year-old Teresa asked. "It would seem that they've never had to look for a job. Maybe this one thinks he's more important than the owner of the factory. What a bastard!"

Teresa turned to me to ask if I had any sewing experience. "Not much," I told her, "but I used to sew for a lady in my hometown."

"Well then, you're very lucky," she said, "because they aren't hiring anyone without experience." She told me that she and her sister worked with about seventy other women for three years in a small shop in downtown Juarez. They sewed pants for the minimum wage but had no insurance. When the boss could not get precut fabric from the Unite States for them to sew, he laid them off without pay. For the last three months they had been living on the little their father earned from construction work, painting houses, selling toys at the stadium, or doing other odd jobs. "We are two of nine brothers and sisters (there were twelve of us in total but three died when they were young)."

"I am single, thanks be to God, and I do not want to get married," she informed me. "There are enough problems in my life as it is!" But her sister Beatriz, who was standing in line with us, had married an engineer when she was only fifteen. Now she is divorced and has three children to support. "They live with us too. Beatriz and I are the oldest in the family, you see; that's why we really have to find a job."

"I also used to work as a maid in El Paso. I don't have a passport, so I had to cross illegally as a wetback, a little wetback who cleaned houses. The money wasn't bad. I used to earn up to thirty-five dollars a week, but I hated being locked up all day. So I came back and here I am."

I asked Beatriz if her husband helped support her children.

"No," she said emphatically, "and I don't want him to give me anything, not a cent, because I don't want him to have any claim or rights over my babies. As long as I can support them, he won't have to interfere."

I asked if there were better jobs outside of *maquiladoras*. "I understand you can make more money working at a *cantina*; is that true?"

Both of them looked at me suspiciously. *Cantinas* are an ever-present reminder of overt or concealed prostitution. Teresa acknowledged that she could earn more there but asked:

> What would our parents think? You can't stop people from gossiping, and many of those "*cantinas*" are whorehouses. Of course, when you have great need you can't be choosey, right? For some time I worked there as a waitress, but that didn't last. The supervisor was always chasing me. First he wanted to see me after work. I told him I had a boyfriend, but he insisted. He said I was too young to have a steady boyfriend. Then, when he learned I had some typing skills, he wanted me to be his secretary. I'm not stupid! I knew what he really wanted; he was always staring at my legs. So I had to leave that job too. I told him I had been rehired at the shop, although it wasn't true. He wasn't bad looking, but he was married and had children. . . . Why must men fool around?

The guard's summons to experienced workers to fill out applications interrupted our conversation. Twenty women went into the narrow lobby of Camisas de Juarez, while the rest left in small, quite groups. For those of us who stayed, a second waiting period began. One by one we were shown into the office of the personnel manager, where we were to take a manual dexterity test, fitting fifty variously colored pegs into fifty similarly colored perforations on a wooden board in the shortest possible time. Clock in hand, the personnel manager told each woman when to begin and when to stop. Some were asked to adjust the pegs by hand; others were given small pliers to do so. Most were unable to complete the test in the allotted time. One by one they came out of the office looking weary and expressing their conviction that they would not be hired.

Later on, we were given the familiar application form. Again, I had to ponder what my greatest aspiration in life was. But this time I was curious to know what Xochitl had answered.

"Well," she said, "I don't know if my answer is right. Maybe it is wrong. But I tried to be truthful. My greatest aspiration in life is to improve myself and to progress."

Demonstrating sewing skills on an industrial machine followed. Many women expressed their doubts and concern when they rejoined the waiting women in the lobby. Over the hours, the sense had increased that all of us were united by the common experience of job seeking and by the gnawing anxiety that potential failure entails. Women compared notes and exchanged opinions about the nature and difficulty of their respective tests. They did not offer each other overt reassurance or support, but they made sympathetic comments and hoped that there would be work for all.

At 3:30 P.M., seven hours after we arrived at the plant, we were dismissed with no indication that any of us would be hired. They told us a telegram would be sent to each address as soon as a decision was made. Most women left disappointed and certain that they would not be hired. Two weeks later, when I had almost given up all hope, the telegram arrived. I was to come to the plant as soon as possible to receive further instructions.

Upon my arrival I was given the address of a small clinic in down town Ciudad Juarez. I was to bring two pictures to the clinic and take a medical examination. Its explicit purpose was to evaluate the physical fitness of potential workers. In reality, it was a pregnancy test. *Maquiladoras* do not hire pregnant women in spite of their greater need for employment. During the first years of its existence, many pregnant women sought employment in the *maquiladora* program knowing they would be entitled to an eighty-two day pregnancy leave with full pay. Some women circumvented the restrictions on employing pregnant women by bringing urine specimens of friends or relatives to the clinic. Plant managers now insist on more careful examinations, but undetected pregnant women sometimes get hired. The larger and more stable plants generally comply with the law and give maternity leave, but in small subcontracted firms, women are often fired as soon as the manager discovers they are pregnant.

After my exam at the clinic, I returned to the factory with a sealed envelope containing certification of my physical capacity to work. I was then told to return the following Monday at 3:30 P.M. to start work. After what seemed like an unduly long and complicated procedure, I was finally hired as an assembly worker. For the next six weeks I shared the experience of approximately eighty women who had also been recruited to work the evening shift. Xochitl, Beatriz, and Teresa had been hired too.

WORKING AT THE *MAQUILADORA*

The weekday evening shift began at 3:45 and ended at 11:30 P.M. A bell rang at 7:30 to signal the beginning of a half-hour dinner break. Some women brought sandwiches from home, but most bought a dish of *flautas* or *tostadas* and a carbonated drink at the factory. On Saturdays the shift started at 11:30 A.M. and ended at 9:30 P.M., with a half hour break. We worked, in total, forty-eight hours every week for the minimum wage, an hourly rate of about U.S. $0.60.

Although wages are low in comparison to those of the United States for similar jobs, migrants flock to zone 09, which includes Ciudad Juarez, because it has nearly the highest minimum wage in the country (only zone 01, where Baja California is located, has a higher rate). Legally, *maquiladoras* are also required to enroll their workers in the social security system and in the national housing program (Instituto Nacional a la Vivienda). As a result, investment per work hour reached U.S. $1.22 in 1978. For women who have children, the medical insurance is often as important as the wage.

Newcomers receive the minimum wage but are expected to fulfill production quotas. My new job was to sew a narrow bias around the cuff openings of men's shirts. My quota of 162 pairs of sleeves every hour meant one every 2.7 seconds. After six weeks as a direct production operator, I still fell short of this goal by almost 50 percent.

Sandra, who sat next to me during this period, assured me that it could be done. She had worked at various *maquiladoras* for the last seven years. Every time she got too tired, she left the job, rested for a while, then sought another. She was a speedy seamstress who acted with the self-assurance of one who is well-acquainted with factory work. It was difficult not to admire her skill and aloofness, especially when I was being continuously vexed by my own incompetence.

One evening Sandra told me she thought my complaints and manner of speech were funny and, at the end of what turned out to be a lively conversation, admitted to liking me. I was flattered. Then she stared at my old jeans and ripped blouse with an appraising look and said, "Listen Patricia, as soon as we get our wage, I want to take you to buy some decent clothes. You look awful! And you need a haircut." So much for the arrogance of the researcher who wondered whether her class background would be detected. Sandra became my most important link with the experience of *maquiladora* work.

Sandra lived with her parents in "las lomas" in the outskirts of the city. The area was rugged and distant, but the house itself indicated modest prosperity. There were four ample rooms, one of which was carpeted. The living room walls were covered with family photographs. There were an American television and comfortable chairs in the room. There were two sinks in the kitchen as well as a refrigerator, blender, beater, and new American-made washing machine (waiting until the area got its hoped-for running water). Sandra's father was a butcher who had held his job at a popular market for many years. Although in the past, when his three daughters were small, it had been difficult to stay out of debt, better times were at hand. He had only two regrets: his failing health and Sandra's divorce. He felt both matters were beyond his control. He considered Sandra a good daughter because she never failed to contribute to household expenses and because she was also saving so she could support her two children, who were currently living with her former husband. Sandra had left him after he beat her for taking a job outside the home.

Even with Sandra's help, I found the demands of the factory overwhelming. Young supervisors walked about the aisles calling for higher productivity and greater speed. Periodically, their voices could be heard throughout the workplace: "Faster! Faster! Come on girls, let's hear the sound of those machines!"

My supervisor, Esther, quit her job as a nurse for the higher wages as a factory worker because she had to support an ill and aging father after her mother's death three years earlier. Although her home was nice and fully owned, she was solely responsible for the remaining family debts. She earned almost one thousand pesos a week in the factory, roughly twice her income as a nurse.

The supervisor's role is a difficult one. Esther, like the other supervisors, often stayed at the plant after the workers left, sometimes until one in the morning. She would verify quotas and inspect all garments for defects, some of which she restitched. She would also prepare shipments and select materials for the following day's production. Management held supervisors directly responsible for productivity levels as well as for workers' punctuality and attendance, putting the supervisors between the devil and the deep blue sea. Workers frequently believed that supervisors were the ones responsible for their plight at the workplace and regarded abuse, unfair treatment, and excessive demands from them as whims. But while workers saw supervisors as close allies of the firm, management directed its dissatisfaction with workers at the supervisors. Many line supervisors agreed that the complications they faced on their jobs were hardly worth the extra pay.

One young woman at another factory told me, "Since I was promoted to a supervisory capacity I feel that my workmates hate me. We used to get along fine. I would even go so far as to say that we shared in a genuine sense of camaraderie. Now, they resent having to take orders from me, a former assembly worker like themselves. They talk behind my back and ask each other why it was I and not one of them who was promoted" (Fernández, 1978).

For some months this woman labored under considerable stress. Her problems were compounded when she had to decide who among her subordinates would have to be laid off as a result of plant adjustments. Caught between the exigencies of management and the resentful attempts of workers to manipulate her, she came close to a nervous breakdown. A short time afterward she asked to be transferred to her old job. From her point of view it was not worth being "a sandwich person."

Although my supervisor, Esther, was considerate and encouraging, she still asked me to repair my defective work. I began to skip dinner breaks to continue sewing in a feeble attempt to improve my productivity level. I was not alone. Some workers, fearful of permanent dismissal, also stayed at their sewing machines during the break while the rest went outside to eat and relax.

I could understand their behavior; their jobs were at stake. But presumably my situation was different. I had nothing to lose by inefficiency, and yet I felt compelled to do my best. I started pondering upon the subtle mechanisms that dominate will at the workplace, and about the shame that overwhelms those who fall short of the goals assigned to them. As the days passed, it became increasingly difficult for me to think of factory work as a stage in a research project. My identity became that of a worker; my immediate objectives, those determined by the organization of labor at the plant. I became one link in a rigidly structured chain. My failure to produce speedily had consequences for others operating in the same line. For example, Lucha, my nineteen-year-old companion, cut remnant thread and separated the sleeves that five other seamstresses and I sewed. Since she could only meet her quota if we met ours. Lucha was extremely interested in seeing improvements in my level of productivity and in the quality of my work. Sometimes her attitude and exhortations verged on the hostile. As far as I was concerned, the accusatory expression on her face was the best work incentive yet devised by the factory. I was not surprised to find out during the weeks I spent there that the germ of enmity had bloomed between some seamstresses and their respective thread cutters over matters of work.

Although the relationship between seamstresses and thread cutters was especially delicate, all workers were affected by each other's level of efficiency. Cuffless sleeves could not be attached to shirts, nor could sleeves be sewed to shirts without collars or pockets. Holes and buttons had to be fixed at the end. Unfinished garments could not be cleaned of lint or labeled. In sum, each minute step required a series of preceding operations effectively completed. Delay of one stage inevitably slowed up the whole process.

From the perspective of the workers, the work appeared as interconnected individual activities rather than as an imposed structure. Managers were nearly invisible, but the flaws of fellow workers were always present. Bonuses became personal rewards made inaccessible by a neighbor's laziness or incompetence. One consequence of these perceptions was that workers frequently directed complaints against other workers and supervisors. In short, the organization of labor at any particular plant does not automatically lead to feelings of solidarity.

On the other hand, the tensions did not inhibit talk, and the women's shared experiences, especially about longings for relief from the tediousness of industrial work, gave rise to an ongoing humorous dialogue. Sandra often reflected in a witty and self-deprecatory manner on the possibility of marriage to a rich man. She thought that if she could only find a nice man who would be willing to support her, everything in her life would be all right. She did not mind if he was not young or good looking, as long as he had plenty of money. Were there men like that left in the world? Of course, with the children it was difficult, not to say impossible, to find such a godsend. Then again, no one kept you from trying. But not at the *maquiladora*. Everyone was female. One could die of boredom there.

Sandra knew many women who had been seduced and then deserted by engineers and technicians. Other women felt they had to comply with the sexual demands of fellow workers because they believed otherwise they would lose their jobs. Some were just plain stupid. Things were especially difficult for very young women at large electronics plants. They needed guidance and information to stay out of trouble, but there was no one to advise them. During the first years of the *maquiladora* program, sexual harassment was especially blatant. There were *ingenieros* who insisted on having only the prettiest workers under their command. They developed a sort of factory "harem." Sandra knew of a man – "Would you believe this?" – who wanted as much female diversity as possible. All of the women on his crew, at his request, had eyes and hair of a different color. Another man boasted that every woman on his line had borne him a child. She told me about the scandals, widely covered by the city tabloids, about the spread of venereal disease in certain *maquiladoras*. Although Sandra felt she knew how to take care of herself, she still thought it better to have only female fellow workers. The factory was not a good place to meet men.

Fortunately, there were the bars and the discotheques. Did I like to go out dancing? She did not think I looked like the type who would. But it was great fun. Eventually Sandra and I went to a popular disco, the Cosmos, which even attracted people from "the other side" (the United States), who came to Juarez just to visit this disco. It had an outer-space decor, full of color and movement, and played the best American disco music. If you were lucky, you could meet a U.S. citizen. Maybe he would even want to get married, and you could go and live in El Paso. Things like that happen at discotheques. Once a Jordanian soldier in service at Fort Bliss had asked Sandra to marry him the first time they met at Cosmos. But he wanted to return to his country, and she had said no. Cosmos was definitely the best discotheque in Juarez, and Sandra could be found dancing there amidst the deafening sound of music every Saturday evening.

The inexhaustible level of energy of women working at the *maquiladoras* never ceased to impress me. How could anyone be in the mood for all-night dancing on Saturdays after forty-eight weekly hours of industrial work? I had seen many of these women stretching their muscles late at night trying to soothe the pain they felt at the waist. After the incessant noise of the sewing machines, how could anyone long for even higher levels of sound? But as Sandra explained to me, life is too short. If you don't go out and have fun, you will come to the end of your days having done nothing but sleep, eat, and work. And she didn't call that living. Besides, where else would you be able to meet a man?

Ah men! They were often unreliable, mean, or just plain lazy ("wasn't that obvious from the enormous number of women who had to do factory work in Ciudad Juarez?"), but no one wanted to live alone. There must be someone out there worth living for – at least someone who did not try to put you down or slap you. Sandra could not understand why life had become so difficult. Her mother and father had stayed married for thirty years and they still liked each other. There had been some difficult times in the past, but they had always had each other. She knew a lot of older folks who were in the same situation. But it was different for modern couples.

At 11:15, Sandra's talks about men stopped, and we prepared to go home. We cleaned up our work area and made sure we took the two spools and a pair of scissors we were responsible for home with us to prevent their being stolen by workers the following morning. As soon as the bell range at 11:30, we began a disorderly race to be the first to check out our time cards. Then we had to stand in line with our purses wide open so the guard could check our belongings. Women vehemently resented management's suspicion that workers would steal material or the finished products. The nightly search was an unnecessary humiliation of being treated as thieves until proven innocent by the guard.

Once outside the factory, we walked in a group across the park to catch our bus. There was a lot of laughing and screaming, as well as teasing and exchanging of vulgarities. Most of the time we could board an almost-empty bus as soon as we reached the main avenue. Sometimes, when we had to wait, we became impatient. In jest, a woman would push another worker toward the street, suggesting provocative poses for her to use to attract a passerby to offer a ride. When a car did stop, however, they quickly moved away. To joke was one thing, but to accept a ride from a man, especially late at night, was to look for trouble.

Individually, the factory women appeared vulnerable, even shy, but as a group, they could be a formidable sight. One night a man boarded the bus when we were already in it. His presence gave focus to the high spirits. Women immediately subjected him to verbal attacks similar to those they often received from men. Feeling protected by anonymity and by their numerical strength, they chided and teased him; they offered kisses and asked for a smile. They exchanged laughing comments about his physical attributes and suggested a raffle to see who would keep him. The man remained silent through it all. He adopted the outraged and embarrassed expression that women often wear when they feel victimized by men. The stares of whistling women followed him as he left the bus.

Although I only saw one such incident, I was told that it was not uncommon. "It is pitiful," a male acquaintance told me; "those girls have no idea of what proper feminine behavior is." He told me he had seen women even paw or pinch men while traveling in buses and *ruteras*. According to him, factory work was to blame: "Since women started working at the *maquiladoras* they have lost all sense of decorum." The women see it as a harmless game fostered by the temporary sense of membership in a group. As Sandra liked to remind me, "Factory work is harder than most people know. As long as you don't harm anybody, what's wrong with having a little fun?"

CONCLUSIONS

In telling of my experience, I have tried to acquaint the reader with a new form of industrial employment from a personal viewpoint. Textile and garment manufacturing are, of course, as old as factories themselves, but *maquiladoras* epitomize the most distinctive traits of the modern system of production. They are part of a centralized global arrangement in which central economies such as the United States have become the locus of technological expertise and major financial outflows, while Third World countries increase their participation in the international market via the manufacture of exportable goods.

This global system of production has had unprecedented political and economic consequences. For example, the fragmentation of labor processes has reduced the level of skill required to perform the majority of assembly operations required to manufacture even the most complex and sophisticated electronics products. In turn, the geographical dispersion of production has curtailed the bargaining ability of workers of many nationalities vis-à-vis large corporations. At times, workers in Asia, Latin America, and the Caribbean seem to be thrust into competition against one another for access to low-paying, monotonous jobs. Labor unions and strikes have limited potential in a world where factories can be transferred at ease to still another country where incentives are more favorable and wages cheaper.

More than two million workers are presently employed in export-processing zones located in less developed countries. Perhaps most significant is the fact that between 85 percent and 90 percent of them are women. Under the Border Industrialization and *Maquiladora* Programs, Mexico is participating in this global arrangement by offering attractive stimuli and customs leeway to multinational corporations mainly involved in electronics and garment manufacturing. More than 156,000 women are employed in *maquiladoras*. In spite, or perhaps because, of Mexico's increasing economic difficulties, the number of such plants will increase in the next years. Several devaluations of the Mexican currency have placed the country in a competitive position with respect to Taiwan and Hong Kong as a source of cheap labor.

From the point of view of business, *maquiladoras* are a great success. But as the preceding narration suggests, the experiences of working women employed at the plants give reason for concern. Low wages, strenuous work paces, the absence of promotions, the temporary nature of employment, and unsatisfactory working conditions combine to make *maquiladoras* a precarious alternative. Such factories thrive only in labor markets characterized by very few occupational choices.

It is evident from the testimony of workers that women seek *maquiladora* jobs compelled by their need to support families whether they be formed by parents and siblings or by their own children. Male unemployment and underemployment play an important part in this. Multinationals tend to relocate assembly operations to areas of the world where jobless people automatically provide an abundant supply of cheap labor. Sandra's longing for male economic support and regrets over the irresponsibility of men represent a personal counterpoint to a structural reality where men are unable to find remunerative jobs while women are forced, out of need, to join the ranks of the industrial labor force.

The same testimony demonstrates that *maquila* women would prefer to withdraw from the exhausting jobs available to them and give full attention to home and children. Husbands and fathers frequently press women to leave their jobs to adjust to a conventional understanding of what gender roles should be. Nevertheless, when women retire from wage labor to become housewives and mothers, they often face dire alternatives. Later, they may have to seek new forms of employment because of the inability of their men to provide adequately for their families. Older and with children to provide for, they then face special constraints in a labor market that favors very young, single, childless women. The life profile of *maquiladora* women is, then, a saga of downward mobility, a fate contrary to the optimistic expectations of industrial promoters.

The segregation of the labor market on the basis of sex tends to weaken the bargaining position of both men and women as wage earners. But perhaps more important is the observation that the same segregation produces a clash between ideological notions about the role of women and their actual transformation into primary wage earners. This has given rise to tensions perceived both at the household and community levels. *Maquiladora* workers have become notorious in that they challenge conventional mores and values regarding femininity. Concerns about young women's morality, virtue, and sexual purity are, in part, reflections of widespread anxiety and fear that, as a result of wage earning, women may end up subverting the established order. *Maquiladora* workers may see their riotous behavior toward a man in a bus as an innocuous diversion. Others, however, see it as a clear sign that women are losing respect for patriarchy.

Maquiladoras are hardly a mechanism for upward mobility, hardly the bold entrance to middle-class respectability, hardly the key to individual economic autonomy. All these are issues that should be of concern to government officials and social planners. Yet, while *maquiladoras* have taken advantage of women's vulnerability in the job market, they have also provided a forum where new forms of consciousness and new challenges are present. For younger *maquila* workers who are living with parents and siblings and have few or no children of their own, wage labor offers the cherished possibility of retaining at least part of their income for discretionary purposes.

REFERENCES

Fernández Kelly, M. P. 1978. "Notes from the Field." Ciudad Juarez, Mexico. Mimeo.

Fröbel, J. R., J. H. Heinrichs, and O. Kreye. 1976. "Tendency Towards A New International

Division of Labor Force for World Markets Oriented Manufacturing." *Economic and Political Weekly* 11: 71–83.

Newton, J. R., and F. Balli. 1979. "Mexican In-Bond Industry." Paper presented to the seminar on North-South Complementary Intra-Industry Trade. UNCTAD United Nations Conference, Mexico, D.F.

O'Brien, Philip. 1975. "A Critique of Latin American Theories of Dependency." In I. Oxaal, T. Barnett, and D. Booth, eds., *Beyond the Sociology of Development.* London: Routledge and Kegan Paul.

Palloix, C. 1975. "The Internationalization of Capital and the Circuit of Social Capital." In H. Radice, ed., *The International Firms and Modern Imperialism.* New York: Penguin.

CHAPTER

32

IT TAKES TWO

CYNTHIA ENLOE

From S. P. Sturdevant and B. Stolzfus (eds.) (1992) *Let the Good Times Roll: Prostitution and the U. S. Military in Asia*, New York: The New Press

Since U. S. occupation troops in Japan are unalterably determined to fraternize, the military authorities began helping them out last week by issuing a phrase book. Sample utility phrases: "You're very pretty" . . . "How about a date?" . . . "Where will I meet you?" And since the sweet sorrow of parting always comes, the book lists no less than 14 ways to say goodbye. – Time, 15 July 1946[1]

On a recent visit to London, I persuaded a friend to play hooky from work to go with me to Britain's famous Imperial War Museum. Actually, I was quite embarrassed. In all my trips to London, I had never gone to the Imperial War Museum. Now, in the wake of the Gulf War, the time seemed ripe. Maybe the museum would help me put this most recent military conflict in perspective, see its continuities with other wars, clarify its special human, doctrinal, and technological features. I was in for a disappointment.

It was only the British experiences of the "great" wars that were deemed worthy of display. Malaya, Aden, Kenya, the Falklands – those British twentieth-century war sites didn't rate display cases. In fact, Asia, Africa, and the Caribbean didn't seem much on the curators' minds at all. There were two formal portraits of Indian soldiers who had won military honors for their deeds, but there were no displays to make visible to today's visitors how much the British military had relied on men and women from its colonies to fight both world wars. I made a vow to go to the Gurkha Museum on my next trip. The only civilians who received much attention in the Imperial War Museum were British. Most celebrated were the "plucky" Cockney Londoners who coped with the German blitz by singing in the Underground. Women were allocated one glass case showing posters calling on housewives to practice domestic frugality for the cause. There was no evidence of the political furor set off when white British women began to date – and have children with – black American GIs.

Still my friend's and my disappointment with the museum's portrayal of Britain's wars did serve to make us wonder what a realistic curatorial approach would be. What would we put on display besides front-line trenches (at least they showed the rats), Cockney blitz-coping lyrics, and unannotated portraits of Sikh heroes?

Brothels. In my war museum there would be the reconstruction of a military brothel. It would show rooms for officers and rooms for rank-and-file soldiers. It would display separate doors for white soldiers and black soldiers. A manikin of the owner of the business (it might be a disco rather than a formal brothel) would be sitting watchfully in the corner – it might be a man or a woman, she or he might be a local citizen or a foreigner. The women might be white European, Berber, Namibian, or Puerto Rican; they might be Korean, Filipina, Japanese, Vietnamese, African-American, or Indian. Depending on the era and locale, they might be dressed in sarongs or miniskirts topped with T-shirts memorializing resort beaches, soft drinks, and aircraft carriers.

In this realistic war museum, visitors would be invited to press a button to hear the voices of the women chart the routes by which they came to work in this brothel or disco and describe the children, siblings, and parents whom they were trying to support with their earnings. Several of the women might compare the sexual behavior and outlooks of these foreign men with those of the local men with whom they had been involved. Some of the women probably would add their own analyses of how the British, American, French, or United Nations troops came to be in their countries.

Museum goers could step over to a neighboring tape recorder to hear the voices of soldiers who have patronized brothels and discos while on duty abroad. The men might describe how they imagined these women as being different or similar to women from their own countries. The more brazen might flaunt their sexual prowess. Some of the soldiers, however, probably would talk about their feelings of loneliness abroad, their sense of what it means to be a man when you're a soldier, the possible anxieties about meeting the expectations of one's officers and buddies as far as sexual performance is concerned.

War – and militarized peace – are times when sexual relations take on particular meanings. A museum curator – or journalist, novelist, or political commentator – who edits out sexuality, who leaves it "on the cutting-room floor," gives the audience a skewed and ultimately unhelpful account of just what kinds of myths, anxieties, and inequalities are involved fighting a war or sustaining a militarized form of peace.

It is for this reason that the oral histories and photographs contained here are so vital. They help us to make sense of the dependence of the military on particular presumptions about masculinity in order to sustain soldiers' morale and discipline. Without a sexualized "rest and recreation" (R & R) period, would the U.S. military command be able to send young men off on long, often tedious sea voyages and ground maneuvers? Without myths of Asian women's compliant sexuality would many American men be able to sustain their own identities of themselves as manly enough to act as soldiers? Women who have come to work as prostitutes around American bases in Asia tell us how a militarized masculinity is constructed and reconstructed in smoky bars and in sparsely furnished boardinghouses. If we look only at boot camps and the battlefield – the focus of most investigations into the formation of militarized masculinity – we will not be able adequately to explain just how masculinity is created and sustained in the peculiar wars necessary to sustain a military organization.

The women who have been generous enough to tell their stories here reveal how sexuality is as central to the complex web of relationships between civil and military cultures as the more talked about security doctrines and economic quid pro quos. Women also remind us of how difficult it is sometimes to map the boundaries between sexual relations and economics. This doesn't mean that all sexual relations, even those commercialized by a prostitution industry next to a military base, can be reduced simply to economics. The women who tell their stories to Saundra Sturdevant and Brenda Stoltzfus are less concerned with parsing analytical categories than with giving us an authentic account of the pressures, hopes, fears, and shortages that they must juggle every day in order to ensure their physical safety, hold on to some shred of self-respect, and make ends meet for themselves and their children.

These stories also underscore something that is consistently overlooked in discussions of the impact of military bases on local communities: the fact that local women working in brothels and discos mediate between two sets of men, foreign soldiers and local men. These two are rarely talked about simultaneously, but the women who have taken part in this project know that they must be. These women detail how their relationships with local male lovers and husbands created the conditions that make them vulnerable to the appeals of the labor-needy disco owners. Unfaithfulness, violent tempers, misuse of already low earnings, neglectful fathering – any combination of these forms of behavior by the local men with whom they were involved became the major launching pad for work as a prostitute. This means, too, that children have to be talked about. Most of the women who speak here have children – some fathered by local men, others by foreign soldiers. Prostitution and fathering: the two are intimately connected in these women's lives.

This is not, of course, to argue that local men are the root of the commercialized and militarized sex that has become so rife in countries allied to the United States. Without local governments willing to pay the price for the lucrative R & R business, without the U.S. military's strategies for keeping male soldiers content, without local and foreign business entrepreneurs willing to make their profits from the sexuality of poor women – without each of these conditions, even an abusive, economically irresponsible husband would not drive his wife into work as an Olongapo bar woman. Nonetheless, local men must be inserted into the political equation; the women here make that clear. In fact, we need to widen our lens considerably to fully understand militarized prostitution. Here is a list – probably an incomplete one – of the men whose actions may contribute to the construction and maintenance of prostitution around any government's military base:

husbands and lovers
bar owners, local and foreign
local public-health officials
local government zoning-board members
local police officials
local mayors
national treasury or finance-ministry officials
national-defense officials
male soldiers in the national forces
local male prostitution customers
foreign male soldier-customers
foreign male soldiers' buddies

foreign base commanders
foreign military medical officers
foreign national-defense planners
foreign national legislators

Among these different men there may be diverse masculinities. Women in Okinawa, Korea, and the Philippines describe how they had to learn what made American men feel that they were manly during sex; it was not always what they had learned made their Korean, Japanese, or Filipino sexual partners feel manly. Sexual practice is one of the sites of masculinity's – and femininity's – daily construction, but that construction is international. Tourists, colonial officials, international technocrats and businessmen, and soldiers have long been the internationalizers of sexualized masculinity. Yet the entire R & R policy and its dependent industry only work if thousands of Asian women are willing and able to learn what American military men rely on to bolster their sense of masculinity: bar owners, military commanders, and local finance-ministry bureaucrats depend on Asian women to be alert to the differences among masculinities.

Each of these groups of men, therefore, is connected to one another by the women working in the base-town bars. But they also may be connected to one another quite directly. For example, Australian researcher Anne-Marie Cass has found that at least some Filipino male soldiers are adopting what they see to be an American form of militarized masculinity. The men most prone to this practice are those in the Scout Rangers, the elite fighting force of the Philippine Constabulary. They act as though the American film character Rambo epitomizes the sort of attributes that make for an effective combat soldier: "a soldier in khaki or camouflage, sunglasses or headbands, open shirt, bare head, and well armed, lounging in a roofless jeep travelling down a Davao City street, gun held casually, barrel waving in the air."[2] One consequence of this form of borrowed, intimidating masculinity, according to Cass, was that local prostitutes servicing Filipino soldiers performed sexual acts with customers that they otherwise would have refused to engage in.

A woman who goes to work in a foreign military brothel or disco finds herself negotiating among all these mainly male actors. She has direct contact, however, with only some of them. She never hears what advice the foreign base commander passes on to his troops regarding the alleged unhealthiness or deviousness of local women. She never hears what financial arrangements have been made between local and foreign medical officials to guarantee the well-being of her soldier-customers. She rarely learns what a soldier who wants to marry her and support her children is told by his military chaplain or superior officer. She does not have access to the discussions among foreign legislators when they decide not to hold hearings on their government's military prostitution policies. Consequently, she makes her assessments using what information she has.

Much of it comes from the women with whom she works. As these interviews reveal, the relationships among women working in the bars are not always supportive or sisterly. The environment does not encourage solidarity. There has been collective action – for example, protests among bar workers in Olongapo against being forced to engage in boxing matches for the entertainment of male customers. But, despite growing efforts by local feminists to provide spaces for such solidarity, collective action remains the exception. Most women rely on a small circle of friends to accumulate the information necessary to walk the minefield laid by the intricate relationships among the several groups of men who define the military prostitution industry. They teach one another how to fake orgasms, how to persuade men to use condoms, how to avoid deductions from their pay, how to meet soldier-customers outside of their employers' supervision, how to remain appealing to paying customers when they are older – their valued status as a virgin, a "cherry girl," long gone.

Readers will be listening to these women tell their stories at a time when the end of the Cold War and the frailty of industrialized economies are combining to pressure governments in North America and Europe to "downsize" their military establishments. The U.S. Department of Defense has announced the closing of military bases at home and abroad. One of the apparent lessons of the Gulf War in the eyes of many American strategists is that the United States now has the administrative capacity rapidly to deploy large numbers of troops overseas without maintaining a costly and often politically risky base in the region. Simultaneously, Mount Pinatubo in the Philippines has spewed its deadly ash so thickly over Clark Air Force Base that even this facility, which until recently the Bush administration had wanted to keep, now appears to be too uneconomical. All this points to a rollback in the numbers and size of American bases overseas. It might be tempting, consequently, to listen to Asian women's stories as if they were tales of a bygone era.

That would, I think, be a mistake. Large bases still exist in Okinawa, southern Korea, and the Philippines. Even with some cutbacks, the number of American men going through those bases on long tours and on shorter-term maneuvers is in the thousands. Governments in Seoul, Tokyo, and Manila have made no moves to cancel the rest-and-recreation agreements that exist with Washington – agreements that spell out the conditions for permitting and controlling the sort of prostitution deemed most useful for the American military. Nor has the no-prostitution formula in Saudi Arabia adopted to fight the Gulf War – a formula imposed on the United States by a Saudi regime nervous about its own Islamic legitimacy – been adopted anywhere else.

Listening to women working as prostitutes is as important as ever. For political analysts, it will provide information for creating a more realistic picture of how fathering, child rearing, man-to-man borrowing, poverty, private enterprise, and sexual practice each play vital roles in the construction of militarized femininity and masculinity. For antibase campaigners, it will shake confidence in relying only on economic approaches to base conversion. Marriage, parenting, and male violence all will have to be accepted as serious items on a political agenda if the women now living on wages from prostitution are to become actors, not mere symbols, in movements to transform foreign military bases into productive civilian institutions. Listening is a political act.

NOTES

1 Quoted by Anne Farrer Scott, "Women and War," *Hungry Mind Review* (Summer 1991): 23.
2 Anne-Marie Cass, "Sexuality, Gender and Violence in the Militarized Society of the Philippines," unpublished paper prepared for the Australian Sociological Association Conference, Brisbane, 12–16 December 1990, 6.

I INDEX

Note: the abbreviation AAWEs stands for African-American women executives.